ISBN 978-1-304-35050-3

The World War Deception

Hamad Subani

Version 2.0

How the two World Wars were staged for the Creation and Expansion of the Soviet Union.

For the thugs at Dalhousie University. Without their incessant persecution and attempts at suppression, I would have never realized the value of this line of research.

Contents

Introduction

Why write this book?

This book originated as a term paper for a class I took at Dalhousie University. The essay in question winded up in the hands of The Powers That Be. Since then, I was forced to live in a state of siege, dealing with repeated attempts at entrapment by government intelligence agencies. I decided that if this essay could reduce me to a persona non-grata, I really had to share its contents with those concerned. Readers are recommended to visit my website for more information on this book and me.

- www.cabaltimes.com

This book, and its predecessor, the aforementioned term paper, evolved out of my extensive research into The Powers That Be. This research gradually crystallized over several years, spanning several libraries, dozens of maps, hundreds of websites and all relevant conspiracy literature.

I do not appreciate this books being used as a critique of Socialists, Leftists, Marxists or even Communists. The focus of this book is the geographical entity known as the former Soviet Union, its benefactors and its operators.

What this book is trying to accomplish - A brief summary of The World War Deception

The World Wars as a whole have not usually been dealt with from a conspiracy angle. And doing so becomes all the more imperative when old catchalls such as “Pearl Harbour” and “Clash of Civilizations”are being recycled and thrust upon us. Roughly speaking, this book attempts to explain the two World Wars combining the insightfulness of Fritz Springmeier with the accuracy and thoroughness of Antony C. Sutton.

This book is not about the history of the two World Wars. It is about the role of the Powers that Be in the two World Wars. Therefore, general history, narrative, timelines, and discussion of important events will not be duplicated. It is assumed that the reader has basic familiarity concerning the two World Wars. If not, a side-by-side read of introductory literature, such as the Wikipedia articles on the two World Wars should suffice.[1]

Apart from a revision of the World Wars from the perspective of Soviet expansion, this book provides original insight into the following topics

- Russia's "Manifest Destiny"
- The role of the Kemalists in the destruction of the Ottoman Caliphate
- The Gallipoli debacle of World War I
- The Armenian Genocide
- The motivation behind Stalin's purges
- The efforts to ensnare Japan into a war with the Allies
- How Hitler engineered Nazi defeat
- How the creation of India and Pakistan relate to the World War Deception
- How many postwar developments tie into the World War Deception

The Powers that Be are referred interchangeably as The Criminal Elite, Cabal Operatives, Internationalists or the Illuminati. In November 1998, Fritz Springmeier, a researcher from Portland Oregon, published a book[2] which isolated thirteen families closely associated with major developments in modern and medieval history. Springmeier referred to them as The Illuminati. Before the book could be critically evaluated, Springmeier became a living proof of his claims. In March 2001, he was framed for robbery and was sent to prison, where he resided for ten years. I followed up the case in great detail and I am convinced that a successful researcher like him, being under surveillance, was unlikely to involve himself in activity that could result in his imprisonment and defamation. It is unlikely that the charges made against him hold ground. And the labels attached to him are mere slander. I suggest those who suppose otherwise to read Springmeier's books and judge for themselves. And this would not be the first time those exposing the Powers That Be have faced danger. Milton William Cooper, another author, ended up being

---

[1] "World War I." Wikipedia, The Free Encyclopedia. 5 Dec 2006, 13:27 UTC. Wikimedia Foundation, Inc. 6 Dec 2006 <http://en.wikipedia.org/w/index.php?title=World_War_I&oldid=92216708>.

[2] Fritz Springmeier, Bloodlines of the Illuminati (Spring Arbor distributors, 1998). Several web versions are available online.

killed in a 2001 'altercation' with Arizona police.[3] Whether you agree with Springmeier and his version of the 'Illuminati' or not, the facts laid out by Springmeier in his books have cost him his freedom. And therefore, his writings deserve more critical attention.

A further discussion of "The Illuminati" is beyond the scope of this book. Except for the fact that the group in question appears to be very ancient, is international in its operations, has access to banking capital, propagates itself through exclusive bloodlines, usually operates from the Western world and is behind key developments in global history. A commonly agreed theme is that Adam Weishaupt of Bavaria formally reorganized the external arms of this group as "The Illuminati" on 1st May 1776.[4] This book will refer to the Powers That Be interchangeably as the Criminal Elite, Cabal operatives, Internationalists or The Illuminati. The author does not endorse any other definition or attribution to "The Illuminati" other than that of Fritz Springmeier. Springmeier does not delve into esoteric diversions, and sticks to identifying specific families and bloodlines. Again, this book only covers the involvement of the aforementioned group in the World Wars, and not their general history.

It should be noted that a concurrent development related to the two World Wars is the rise of usury-banker dynasties such as the Rothschilds and the Rockerfellers. And the increasing separation of church and state in the Western world, which enabled the Criminal Elite to openly prescribe a wide variety of formulae for reorganizing the nation state on their terms. Another important phenomenon is colonialism. This was preceded by conquest/acquiescence of the West to the The Powers That Be. At this point, the aims and objectives of the Criminal Elite, started masquerading as "national interests." A good example of this phenomenon is the British East India Company, a private joint-stock company that flew the banner of Britain. With a firm base established in

---

[3] Milton William Cooper, Behold a Pale Horse (Light Technology Publications, 1991).
[4] Secret documents penned by Weishaupt were leaked, which resulted in the Elector of Bavaria cracking down on the Illuminati and Freemasonry in the region. The order was assumed to be extinct, but that is what scientists have said regarding the Coelacanth, a fish deemed extinct only to be found alive again. There are many esoteric references pointing towards the Order. An interesting seal appeared on American issued one-dollar bills in 1778. This seal is assumed to be similar to the seal the Illuminati adopted in 1776. Further, the date May 1st was adopted as Labour Day and also approved as Law Day by the American Bar Association. And 1776 was also the year of declaration of American Independence. The new tower to be built at the site of the former World Trade Center is also 1776 feet tall.

Europe, The Powers That Be turned their attention to other parts of the world. But the same 'rule by deception' practiced at home could not be established overseas due to a variety of reasons. And therefore the relationship with these overseas territories was "colonial" (short term and predatory).

In other words, the Criminal Elite now harnessed all major forces in the West, military, religious and ideological. Colonization of the rest of the world resulted in local subordinates being propped up by the Criminal Elite.

However, there were limits to the degree of subordination, which could be achieved through the existing political structures in Western countries and in colonization abroad. Therefore, new religion-free solutions were invented as a solution to all the woes and disasters the Criminal Elite had accomplished through existing political structures. While Communism portrayed in great detail the inequalities of the then systems, the extreme form of monopolistic state capitalism it offered in disguise was a far stronger form of control for the Criminal Elite. The basic trick was as simple as the old joke, "Money is the root of all evil; therefore give me your money." The power structure proposed was the most absolutist, which resulted in the creation of the largest land-grab enterprise in contemporary human history, the Soviet Union.

Colonization had brought up to eighty five percent of the world under the Criminal Elite. Through it, the Criminal Elite groomed local subordinates. Power was then delegated to these local subordinates. The colonists would soon depart on schedule, but only after making arrangements that ensured the colonies still remained under indirect control of the Criminal Elite. It was planned that all the colonial possessions (and maybe more) would be transferred back to the Criminal Elite via Revolution and direct Soviet conquest, with the World Wars being the smokescreen for these operations. Every effort was made and every opportunity for bloodshed was invoked. But even the best-laid plans can go wrong.

Things did go to a great extent according to plan in the Western World. Revolution was sold to the idealistic, the confused, the Godless, romantics, opportunists. But from the onset, there were some problems. It was realized that a Communist Revolution on its own was of insignificant value. It would only bring forth local leaders and local interests. What was needed was a direct hegemony of the Soviet Union, which was firmly under control of the Criminal Elite. The Soviet Union did not have the military resources for such a global endeavor. The Criminal Elite in the Western world would arrange for direct and indirect aid to the Soviets.

The Soviet Union would be bitterly opposed by large blocs of people. Direct Soviet aggression against these people would become a war of epical proportions, and would make the Soviets a public enemy. Therefore it was necessary to create villians who would represent opposition to the Soviet Union.

It was devised to bundle up opposition to the Soviets and destroy it by hurling it against the Soviet Union in a controlled manner. Nothing was left to chance. The leadership of these opposing blocs comprised of Cabal operatives themselves. Even if these oppositional blocs received popular support, it was unlikely they could ever win against the masters of deception and intrigue. These opposing blocs would go down in history as the aggressors and the Soviets would emerge as the victors and the liberators. These opposing blocs were fascism/extreme nationalism such as that of Adolf Hitler, Franco, Mussolini and Chiang Kai-Shek. And narrow communal/identity movements such as Pan-Slavism, Pan-Islamism and Pan-Turkism, to name a few. In addition, existing blocs such as the Ottoman Empire and the Japanese Empire were also conned into serving as oppositional blocs and were later destroyed. As Friedrich Engels would say in 1849,

> [...] The coming world war will cause not only reactionary classes and dynasties to disappear from the face of the earth, but entire reactionary peoples, too. And that will also be progress.[5]

In almost every theatre of the two World Wars (pun intended), confrontations (or lack thereof) and the ensuing outcomes were more or less staged.

---

[5] Engel's NRZ articles of January 13th and February 14th and 15th 1849. These articles can be found in Nachlass Volume III, page 233-64. An English translation can be found in Blackstock and Hoselitz, p. 56-84. Quoted in Bertram D. Wolfe, "Nationalism and Internationalism in Marx and Engels," American Slavic and East European Review 17.4 (1958) 414.

How the Identification Crisis blurs our vision

In more civilized times, the King and his paid minions would go to war. The dangers of warfare would extend to those personally willing to take the gamble, whatever their motives. Then came the bewildering concepts of self-identification, ranging from ideological preference to affiliation with geographic localities. The idea was to create ideologies that large sections of population could identify with. By then, the Powers that Be had consolidated their position as intellectuals, who churned out and even operated such ideologies. Now, large sections of population could be summoned and controlled by the operators of such ideologies.

When the Powers That Be arrange for a state to go to war, it is assumed that all individuals in it also go to war. If they win, all the murder and barbarism they accomplish are considered justified. If they lose, all the murder and barbarism they accomplish are treated as evidence of their being on the wrong side. As far as right and wrong is concerned, thinkers produced by the Powers That Be have gradually reduced this to a matter of opinion. In other words, the performance of the Criminal Elite is no longer to be evaluated in moral terms. To quote one of my elitist Professors, "Do not try to appeal to my moral instincts…I may not hold those values." What the Powers That Be won't tell you is that their "values" are not on a different point of the moral scale. Rather, they free from morality itself, and operate outside it. Except for the Powers That Be, who decide when, where and over what issue, a war must be fought, the rest of us are expected to fulfill our role as "human resources" and gun fodder.

Individualism becomes non-existent in war. In the case of the ideological or national state, the individual and his own priorities merge into the flags, anthems, resources, technology, geography and cheerleaders of the nation state. Taking advantage of this dysfunctional "identification crisis," The Powers That Be have long used the concept of the ideological or national state to use, subjugate and destroy the very "citizens" of the state itself. Not surprisingly, The Powers That Be propped and promoted ideological nation states in the non-Western world as well, in the aftermath of colonialism. These nation states, whether based on race, language or culture, became effective managerial units of The Powers That Be, in the absence of direct colonialism.

When war is not on the table, the "identification crisis" surfaces in different forms, such as modern sport. Where people feel the necessity to watch, cheerlead and engage in aggressive behaviour in the name of teams whose activity, achievements or exercise are of no beneficial use to them.

Not all the individuals who fall in line are seduced by those purporting to represent their geographic locale. Just as working for the Coke® Company does not mean you are a Coke® fan, many individuals join armies out of opportunism. Many are pushed into war. People do take risks and chances to secure the personal inducements promised to them by the nation state. Usually, such mass mobilization is characterized by an absence of options, such as economic downturn or depression. At least until the odds of returning alive are good, the war is considered lucrative. Though murder should be the last thing to cross a sane person's mind, and should be worthy of extreme personal consideration, war brings the mercenaries to the forefront. Western thinkers such as Adam Smith's and Ayn Rand have aptly characterized their subject populations as economically motivated animals, and therefore moral qualms are never an issue for those who fall in line. And those who pretend to advance the interests of the flock are considered as heroes.

The two aforementioned factors, the "identification crisis" and the mercenary response to inducements, exist in a culture in varying degrees. In this book, we will see how the prevalence of these factors in Russian culture made many of its people, a vanguard for the agenda of The Powers That Be.

The Approach

Most critical minded people are receptive to the existence of conspiracy. But what matters is the ability to identify the physical manifestations of conspiracy, and their impact on our individual and collective lives. Again, even in such cases, any discussion of conspiracy is irrelevant without proper reconstruction of motives and the determination of the identity of the characters involved.

In other words, I intend to apply a forensic reconstructionist approach to what can be considered as a crime scene. While such approach has become a staple of television entertainment, it is almost non-existent (in the Western context) when it comes to mass murder, or war. Though conspiracy constitutes a major part of modern history, the very notion of conspiracy is anathema in academic circles. To quote James Fetzer, a retired philosophy professor at the University of Wisconsin Duluth,

> [...] The President himself has acknowledged that 9/11 was a pivotal event of the 21st century. Colleges and universities are the pivotal institutions that are entrusted with the responsibility of studying significant historical events. Therefore it is completely appropriate that university and college faculty should be studying the events of 9/11. Second of all, according to the government itself, 9/11 was an event that involved the activities of a group acting in concert with nineteen Islamic fundamentalists allegedly hijacking foreign aircraft, outfoxing the most sophisticated air defense system in the world, perpetrating these atrocities under the control of a man in a cave in Afghanistan. What that means is, according to the government, 9/11 involved a conspiracy. Third point, therefore if colleges and universities are to fulfill their academic obligations by studying the most significant event of the 21st century, the pivotal event that changed everything, they must necessarily embrace the study of conspiracy theories. There is no alternative.[6]

But here's how a popular text for an American history class I took at Dalhousie University deals with 9/11

> The attacks on the World Trade Center and the Pentagon, government intelligence indicated, had been planned and orchestrated by Middle Eastern agents of a powerful terrorist network known as Al Qaeda.[7]

Establishment Universities are thus a focal point for covering up information and disseminating misleading information.

How this Approach differs

The approach and argumentation of this book is unconventional, as far as academic history is concerned. Academic history incorporates an elitist conception. This consists of establishing precedent with supportive arguments of a small number of "scholars." These supportive arguments are reincarnated as muppets to advance one's thesis. The writer is expected to feign "objective and scholarly disinterestedness," advancing his thesis by having the muppets doing the heavy lifting. In

---

[6] James Fetzer speaking at the University of Wisconsin (Madison) about the political assaults taking place against academics that are studying the events of 9/11. 1/11/06. <http://www.youtube.com/watch?v=_967jIpFVfo> Accessed 6/12/06.

[7] Alan Brinkley, The Unfinished Nation – A Concise History of the American People Volume II: From 1865. 4th ed. (New York: McGraw Hill 2004) 944.

other words, the shadow of The Powers That Be and their institutions never leave you. If you rebel, you are labeled as a "revisionist." This implies that an all-true standard version of events was revealed to establishment historians in a flash from the heavens. And anything contrary is a "revision" of the same! We are expected to entrust them to do all the scholarly thinking for humankind (while we tune back into CNN). Since the presence of organized conspiracy is never even considered in Western academic circles, most research resembles the quest of blind men trying to understand the dimensions of an elephant. Worse, the Powers that Be monitor all discourse that takes place in the academic arena. They plug any gaps with flimflam, disinformation, or even distracting revelations, as the situation warrants. You may find tonnes of relevant information in scholarly journals. But nothing pointing in the direction of The Powers That Be gets beyond the editor's desk of major publications.

History consists of the actions taken by people (including The Powers That Be, of course). And therefore, these actions can easily be understood, related to, or reconstructed by other people as well. Who in turn, do not necessarily have to be historians who graduated from educational institutions. All that matters is the extent to which one can devote oneself to reconstruction, relation and understanding. As well as the level of relevant factual information one is exposed to. I don't feel any compulsion to establish precedent with elitist historians or give consideration to what they have to say. Factual information can be used as raw material to reconstruct a scenario. In the same way the trajectory of a bullet or bloodstains can be used to independently reconstruct a crime scene.

What they will say

Any discourse on an important topic is bound to generate agreement, disagreement, criticism and further discussion. This book is a compilation of what makes obvious sense to me concerning the two World Wars. And I suppose those who are trying to make sense of the same will find it very beneficial. But depending upon the reader's background, personal beliefs, prejudices and exposure, the same response cannot be guaranteed for everyone. Nevertheless, I welcome and encourage debate and criticism.

For The Powers That Be, it all makes perfect sense. But for public consumption, they will feign incomprehension and incredulity to lead away their flock. As my experience with the essay that formed the draft for this book shows, The Powers That Be may cloak their animosity to my conclusions, in attacks on the integrity of the work. Since I have been through this drill before, following the submission of the draft essay in Dalhousie University, I will bring to attention some of the usual tactics as well as my counter arguments. Thanks to Dalhousie University for acquainting me with this skullduggery.

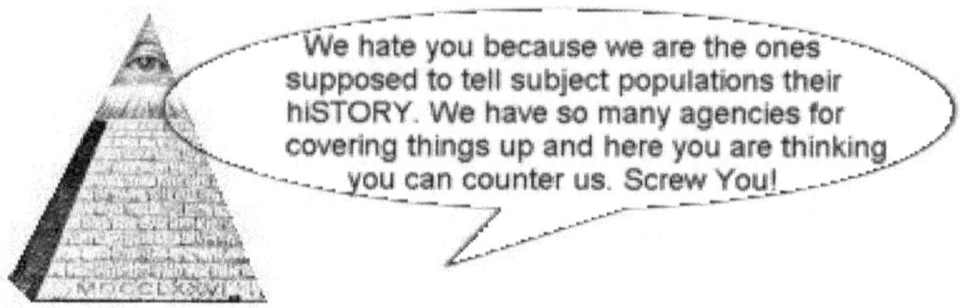

The World Wars spanned the efforts and resources of thousands of people. Similarly, covering up the World Wars through official history is a large-scale operation that involves thousands of people. But as rude as the above interjection may sound, such objection is rarely heard from The Powers That Be. Instead, The Powers That Be use all sorts of devious and circuitous routes to make their arguments sound like scientific-rational objections, purportedly made from a disinterested scholarly and objective perspective. This allows them to attract many dupes from the subject population into their camp.

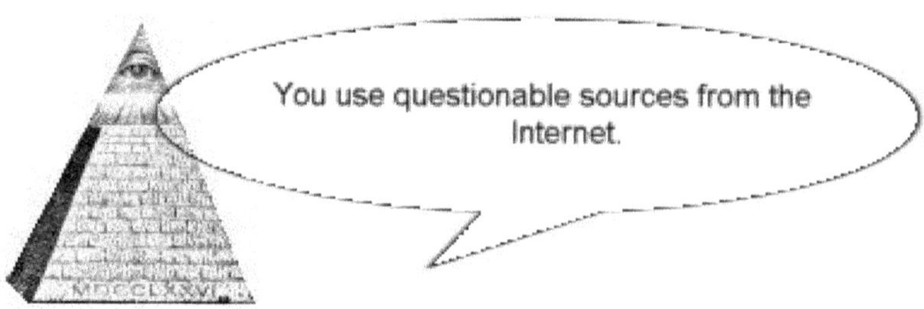

A URL in a footnote need not imply that a statement is sourced from the electronic nether land of UFO cultists, doomsayers or bloggers. Most of the web addresses I link to are electronic versions, reviews, extracts and excerpts of actual speeches, television documentaries and printed media. For example,

- ❖ A reference to a print book now available online.[8]

[8] There are some issues when quoting from a book available online. Page numbers cannot be accurately referenced, since the electronic document may not have page numbers corresponding to the actual print version. And in some cases, the electronic document

- ❖ A news item archived on a web server. The Powers that Be raised a furor about a website I had used in the essay version of this book. That web address contained an archived version of an old New York Times article!

Though inclusion of the web address is not even necessary in the above cases, since a reference to the actual printed media suffices, I do so for the sake of those interested in further research. But if the Cabal wants to find fault, so be it. Pure web references, which cannot be found in print media, represent less than five per cent of all references in this book.

There are a few things I would like to make clear on the use of web sources. First, I believe that many people have relevant opinions, even if the Oxford University Press does not publish them. Therefore, when I encounter opinion, which makes sense and has quality, I prefer to use it. That such opinion is on a web server as opposed to print media does not in any way compromise the quality of the opinion. The Powers that may be rant on how anyone can put anything on the web these days. But the same applies to official print and television media as well. Except that information in the mainstream media cannot be just inserted by anyone; it is largely the exclusive preserve of the Criminal Elite. The problem with the Internet is that the Powers that Be cannot monitor and control it completely. Therefore everything on it is presumed to be guilty until the establishment gives it a clean bill of health. Information in the much-vaunted academic printings can also be inaccurate, biased and stupefying. How many forged manuscripts and fake diaries have we heard of? In addition, academic writing is getting more politicized than the stuff you find on right-wing blogs. To quote the author of a University level textbook published by Cambridge and used in a Dalhousie University history course that I attended, "But in many ways the history of American foreign policy has confirmed his [President Wilson's] essential genius (and the convictions of Henry Luce as well) – his understanding that the expansion of American Power worldwide might indeed be of benefit not only to this country but to the cause of humanity in general so long as it was dedicated to the promotion of

---

may have no page numbers at all. I have thus made reference to the chapter and the exact web address in such cases. One can find the exact quote or reference by going to the Website, clicking Edit>Find in Microsoft Internet Explorer®, and typing a sesrch term into the field.

democratic government worldwide."[9] Another author in the same text says. "What is also interesting is the extent to which the developed world has come to resemble the United States, for better and for worse. All the rich countries appear to be quite stable. [...]"[10] Is stability a patented American attribute? Yet another author in the same text states, [...] today there appears to be one dominant global civilization, the American, and several atavisms masquerading as civilizational challenges [...]."[11] You can find similar statements on reactionary and racist blogs, but notice how the same statements polished by the officious credentials of University heavyweights are made to appear more credible and scholarly.

Secondly, I believe that the key to better understanding is insight. Insight is not proprietary to print media. We are more likely to find more creative expressions of insight in an atmosphere of less censorship, such as the Internet. The most profound insights can be found in the most unlikely places. But since quoting directly from the Internet is engendered to be unprofessional, the establishment media resorts to plagiarizing from the Internet. Let me illustrate by two examples.

- **The AMERICAblog Case:** Aravosis of AMERICAblog bought the cell phone records of General Wesley Clark from an online data broker for $89.95. An edited version of these records was published[12] on his Website for the sake of demonstrating the threat to privacy, and how law enforcement agencies were keeping silent on the issue. In the controversy that followed, major print and television outlets gave coverage to the breach in privacy. Data brokers were summoned before the US Congress. But very few gave credit, or even made reference to AMERICAblog.

---

[9] Tony Smith, "Making the World Safe for Democracy in the American Century,'" Michael J. Hogan ed., The Ambiguous Legacy - U.S. Foreign Relations in the "American Century." (Cambridge: Cambridge University Press, 1999) 50-51.
[10] Robert Jervis, "America and the Twentieth Century: Continuity and Change," Michael J. Hogan ed., The Ambiguous Legacy - U.S. Foreign Relations in the "American Century." (Cambridge: Cambridge University Press, 1999) 119.
[11] Bruce Cumings, "The American Century and the Third World," Michael J. Hogan ed., The Ambiguous Legacy - U.S. Foreign Relations in the "American Century." (Cambridge: Cambridge University Press, 1999) 300.
[12] John Aravosis, AMERICAblog, "AMERICAblog just bought General Wesley Clark's cell phone records for $89.95," 12/01/06, < http://americablog.blogspot.com/2006/01/americablog-just-bought-general-wesley.html> Accessed 06/12/06.

- **The Aztlan.net Anthrax case:** On October 9th 2001, Aztlan.net, a Hispanic anti-Zionist Website published an interesting theory[13] on whom they thought was the culprit behind the fatal Anthrax letters. The Website in question has a big presence on the Internet but mainstream media and academics pretend to ignore it and never directly link to it. Aztlan.net outlined that the alleged perpetrators were involved in an attempt to frame an Arab scientist for the Anthrax scare. With the cat out of the bag, the establishment media moved in for a cover-up. I recall that major search engines blocked the Aztlan.net article during those months. The Powers that Be, finally found another patsy. An American scientist working for the US Army involved in the development of biological weapons started being treated like a suspect. Though not convicted, he was portrayed as guilty in court of public opinion by almost all major television and print media. Then another American scientist, Dr. Bruce Ivings was framed as a suspect. No charges were filed because Dr. Ivings conveniently committed suicide under strange circumstances. There was no reference in mainstream media to Aztlan.net in the sequence of events ending with the suicide of Dr. Bruce Ivings.

As cases such as these demonstrate, the Internet has started the shape the discourse of television and print media. But any disclosure emanating from the Internet is treated like an anonymous tip, never to be credited. But this book will give due credit to all web sources, no matter how obscure or controversial they are. If the best insight into the World Wars surfaces on a Yahoo Geocities® homepage, by an author using a pseudonym for protecting his identity, am I to wait until some establishment historian plagiarizes it for his 'peer reviewed journal article' or should I give due credit and reference him directly? Expecting academics to realize the validity of web sources is like expecting Microsoft® to sell open source operating systems.

Apart from opinion, I see no issue in sourcing factual information from appropriate sites on the Internet. The perception engendered among people is that if the major league newspapers and TV networks didn't cover it, it never happened. Things either happen or they don't. And the Internet cannot be generalized as representative of everything that doesn't happen. When factual information is quoted from the Internet,

---

[13] Hector Carreon, Aztlan.net "FBI closes in on Anthrax suspect," 2/26/02, < http://www.aztlan.net/zack.htm> Accessed 06/12/06. This article contains a good overview as well as a link to the original 9/10/06 article.

care has been taken to ensure that the source is a reachable person with a real name. Though I personally do not see the logic of such a practice. Many great works of literature and history are of anonymous origin. Secondly, the persecution I have endured following the events at Dalhousie University have convinced me why many talented people prefer to remain anonymous.

It is theoretically possible to accurately substitute each and every web reference in this book with references from print publications. But even doing that (without a grant) may not convince some.

That being said, I also refer to books, academic journals and mainstream media whenever I find relevant information and insights. Simply put, I do not agree with present day norms on the "zoning" of insights and information.

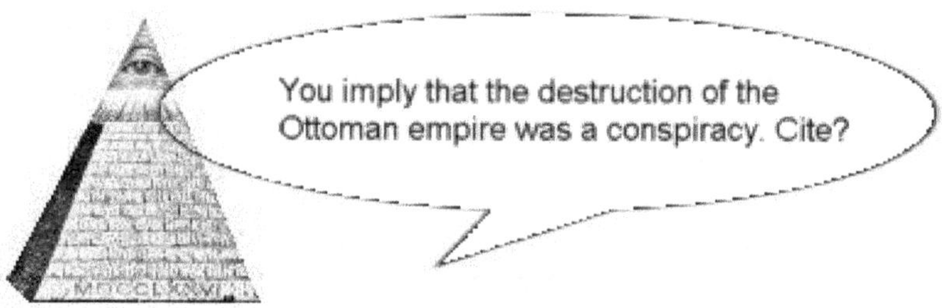

The Criminal Elite expects me to furnish signed affidavits in which the conspirators claim they indulged in conspiracy. Or I must cite some previous published source in this regard, even if I am the first to stumble upon the existence of conspiracy. This book alludes to obvious cases and hints of Criminal Elite activity. A witness, who stands by his personal observation, that the World Trade Center was brought down by controlled demolition, cannot be expected to furnish absolute mathematical and scientific evidence in this regard. In fact, even the conspirators probably couldn't. I believe this book will lead to a better understanding of the World Wars for those who seek answers.

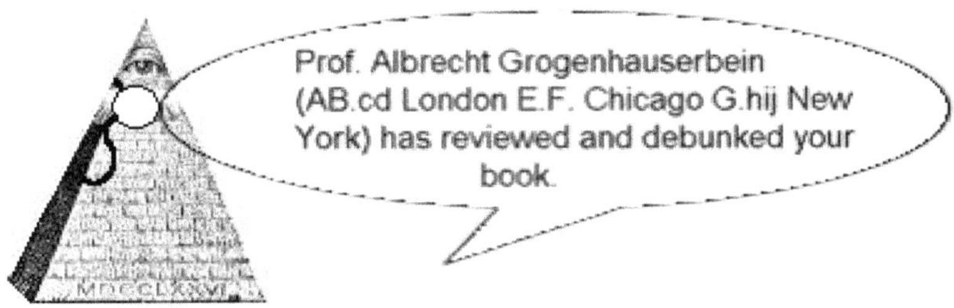

How exactly do you "debunk" an entire book? Do you imply that all the facts and footnotes contained within are also negated, and are now exiled from the literary world? The reality is that even the "debunkers" are not very keen on debunking. All they are trying to do is attach a warning sign, in case members of the subject population wander off Oprah's reading list and stumble upon the book.

As for the credentials of Prof. Albrecht Grogenhauserbein, it is important to note that bloodlined Cabal operatives seem to have no difficulty acquiring them in Western society. As a University student, I am privy to this. On the other hand, I the Professor who agreed to be my thesis mentor was chased out of University.

I expect establishment historians, along with their "peer reviewed journals" to comfortably keep us blind about the reality of the two World Wars for another fifty years, as they have done in the past fifty years. It is not surprising that those who have produced revolution in the field of applied history are not the historians, but individuals like Edward Said, who was a Professor of English and Comparative Literature.[14] Truth seekers on the other hand, will not be accepted by academic history, due to their claims not being "well-researched." The problem is that such material will never be "well-researched," because there are no grants or promotions involved in the production of such literature.

[14] Zachary Lockman, Contending Visions of the Middle East – The History and Politics of Orientalism (Cambridge: Cambridge University Press 2004) 182. According to Lockman, many regard Said's book Orientalism as "[...] the most influential scholarly books published in English in the humanities in the last quarter of the twentieth century (190)." Lockman further contends that the same book was responsible for the explosive development of "postcolonial studies" from the 1980s onwards (210).

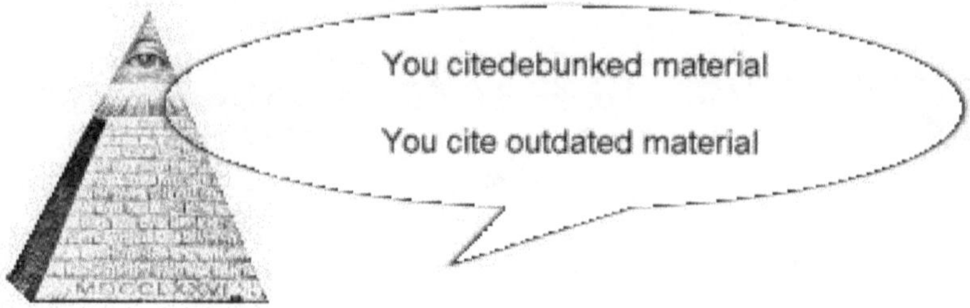

For my stance on 'debunked' literature, please see the previous section.

Establishment historians have a peculiar attitude towards material they consider being out of date. While it is true that material a few decades old will not represent current historiographical developments, facts cannot become out of date. As in the case of archives and historical manuscripts. For example, a present day leading researcher Fritz Springmeier, may be shunned as out of date twenty years from now. But if suppose there has not been any new research at par with his, would it be wise to dismiss him as outdated?

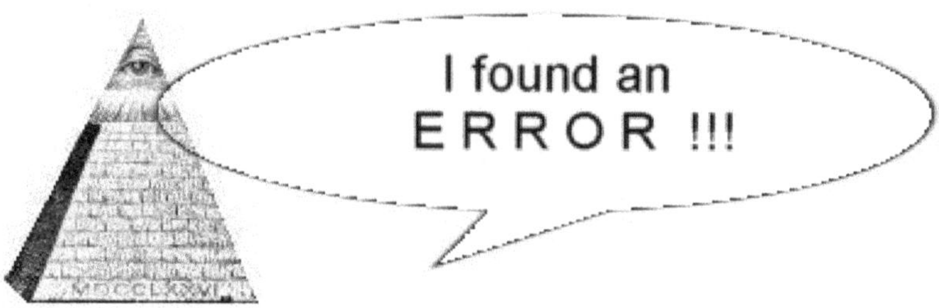

This book builds solely upon human knowledge. With the little known aspects of a vast topic to cover, errata are expected to creep in. But it should be noted that The Powers That Be try to portray one instance of error as representative of the entire book. Though not a sincere exercise in error finding, such maneuvers help The Powers That Be to herd away large sections of the subject population from the material. Sadly, the Western subject population has a short attention span. This is best illustrated by the John F. Kennedy assasination. The Western subject population finally tuned en masse to the notion of conspiracy when presented with the excellent movie of JFK, directed by Oliver Stone. In other words, if it's not on DVD/VHS, it will have issues being accepted as politically correct. It is impossible to compete with the shills using more impressionable media to tell the subject population otherwise. As the writers of 'The Holy Blood and the Holy Grail' would discover,

> We found ourselves subjected to a veritable blitz. Broad generalities and pedantic trivialities were launched against us like a Luftwaffe of flies. We could have swatted most of them. We did, in fact, swat a great many. But it takes only a moment for a voice, arrogating the resonance of authority, to stigmatize a book – to label it irresponsible, implausible, poorly researched or simply bad. It takes rather longer to refute such charges. One must do so point by point, citing specific examples. One must become embroiled in minutiae and academic quibbles that do not make for good television.[15]

I usually get this response from individuals (non-Elite) who unwillingly stumble upon my work but regard it as a nuisance because it threatens their worldview. Its not a case of confusion or misinformation. They happen to be stingy on devoting time for doing their own research and figuring things out. For them, it's not a conspiracy until it directly and adversely affects their personal well-being. Some of them are found in highly professional fields as well. And they can be recognized by an attitude of kowtowing, and like tumbleweed, going along with the drift. They resonate their lazy disinterestedness in the form of such objections.

A physics Professor from the Brigham Young University, Prof. Steven Jones, wrote a scholarly paper on how the World Trade Center may have been brought down in a controlled demolition.[16] In September 2006, the University where he had worked since 1985 placed him on paid leave. This may have been part of an effort to cut his access to sophisticated laboratory equipment, which he was using (with success[17]) to find traces

---

[15] Michael Baigent, Richard Leigh and Henry Lincoln, The Holy Blood and the Holy Grail (London: Arrow Books, 1996), 2.
[16] Dr. Steven E Jones, "Why Indeed did the WTC Buildings Completely Collapsed," Journal of 911 Studies September 2006 Vol. 3. An archived copy can be found at <http://www.scholarsfor911truth.org/WhyIndeedDidtheWorldTradeCenterBuildingsCompletelyCollapse.pdf> Accessed 06/12/06.
[17] Lab analysis revealed chemicals such as iron, manganese and fluorine. Dr. Steven E. Jones on C-Span. An archive copy can be found at <http://www.youtube.com/watch?v=F5kBkOX-qgg&NR> Accessed 06/12/06.

of explosives in the World Trade Center rubble. The University where I studied also had a huge engineering department and a lab with all kinds of equipment. Yet serious analysis of such a significant event, which was witnessed by all, never seemed to be an option for faculty, staff or students. It seems they simply don't look beyond their immediate prospects, and anything controversial is considered to be a bad career move. Their research happens to be strictly in line with profits and grants. Are these the "objective scholars" we are to entrust interpretation of history with? Wouldn't it be erroneous to mistake their silence as a lack of scholarly support for conspiracy theory?

Fair Dealing Notice

Every effort has been made in adhering to the Copyright Act of Canada, which also satisfies the requirements for the protection of copyrighted work under the Berne convention.

Copyrighted material reproduced in this book, whether text or pictures, has been thoroughly and meticulously scrutinized to make sure it falls within the "Fair Dealing" clause of the Copyright Act of Canada.

The following consideration has been made when reproducing copyrighted texts.

- All relevant attribution and source information has been provided.
- Theories and intellectual effort of other individuals has been credited to them.
- The purpose of reproduction is in accordance with the author's right to conduct scholarly research.
- The purpose of reproduction is in accordance with the author's right to freedom of expression.
- Reproduction of copyrighted material has been undertaken only when it was necessary for the production of this book and the execution of its thesis. And non-copyrighted material could not be found as a substitute.
- The topic of the scholarly research is an issue of immediate and monumental importance.
- The amount of copyrighted text quoted is fairly moderate or even miniscule, when compared to the whole work.
- The quoting of the text does not adversely impact the prospects of the copyright holder and his or her authorized publisher.
- Those seeking to reproduce this book were informed of the presence of copyrighted material, and were asked to reproduce the copyrighted material (if they chose to) within the legal Copyright provisions of their respective jurisdiction.
- Some of the copyrighted material quoted in the book is obscure. And its usage in this book will result in wider public dissemination of the copyrighted work; a goal of the Copyright Act of Canada.

The following considerations have been made when reproducing copyrighted images and illustrations.

- All relevant attribution and source information has been provided. When the original source/author and copyright information is not available, the source and copyright have been designated as NA (Not Available). This in no way abrogates the rights or ownership of the copyright holders. If the copyright holder informs us, we will certainly update the information in the next edition of this book.
- Reproduction of copyrighted material has been undertaken only when it was necessary for the production of this book and the execution of its thesis. And non-copyrighted material could not be found as a substitute.
- The purpose of reproduction is in accordance with the author's right to conduct scholarly research.
- The purpose of reproduction is in accordance with the author's right to freedom of expression.
- The topic of the scholarly research is an issue of immediate and monumental importance.
- The purpose of using the image was solely to illustrate the object in question. And not in any way, to infringe upon the rights of the photographer. And in such cases, non-copyright or public domain images were not readily available.

- The images displayed have in most cases been thumbnailed. They have been reduced in size and resolution quality. This will ensure that those seeking further reproduction of a particular image for purposes beyond 'Fair Dealing' will have to consult the author of the image, and this book will thus not serve as a conduit for piracy.
- When public domain images are used, the term 'Copyright may not be applicable' is displayed. Since different jurisdictions have different conditions for a work to be public domain.
- The image in some cases may be a historically significant photo or the photo of a famous individual.
- Almost all images are reproduced for informational purposes.
- The usage of the image does not adversely impact the prospects of the copyright holder and his or her authorized publisher.
- Those seeking to reproduce this book were informed of the presence of copyrighted material, and were asked to reproduce the copyrighted material (if they chose to) within the legal Copyright provisions of their jurisdiction.
- Some of the copyrighted material referenced in the book is obscure. And its usage in this book will result in wider public dissemination of the copyrighted work; a goal of the Copyright Act of Canada.

It is to be made clear that none of the authors of the copyrighted material quoted in this book claim to concur with the conclusions of the author of this book. And it should not be assumed as such, unless the author(s) of the copyrighted material express a statement of concurrence. And neither should the author of this book be seen as concurring with the views of authors quoted. It is impossible for me to determine the views, activities and affiliations of authors quoted for the sake of factual reference.

Disclaimer

Cabal Times provides the materials comprising the "The World War Fraud" on an **as-is** and as-available basis for **informational purposes** only. Hamad Subani or Cabal Times assumes no responsibility for any errors or omissions in the material. Neither do Hamad Subani or Cabal Times make any commitment to update the information contained herein. Further, Hamad Subani or Cabal Times cannot screen for truth, defamation or accuracy any content contained herein. This book is provided as an attempt to grapple the real facts concerning the two World Wars. Taking into consideration the magnitude of these two disastrous events, not all facts can be covered; neither can all errors be omitted. Hamad Subani or Cabal Times cannot promptly remove any defamatory, obscene, inappropriate, unlawful or inaccurate content after transmission. If something genuinely objectionable is brought to our notice, we may look into the matter. If you disagree, you must not waste your time any further by reading this book.

Hamad Subani or Cabal Times makes no, and expressly disclaims any, representations or warranties, express or implied, regarding this book including, without limitation, any implied warranties of merchantability or fitness for a particular purpose. Hamad Subani or Cabal Times makes no, and expressly disclaims any, warranties, express or implied, regarding the correctness, accuracy, completeness, timeliness, and reliability of the text, the references to other books, journals and periodicals, graphics, links to other sites and any other items accessed from or via this book or the Internet, or any other material. Or that the services will be uninterrupted, error-free or free of viruses or other harmful components. Under no circumstances shall Hamad Subani or Cabal Times, its owner, or any of their respective partners, officers, directors, employees, agents, associates or representatives be liable for any damages, whether direct, indirect, special or consequential damages for lost revenues, lost profits, defamation, or otherwise, arising from reading this book, using this book, selling this book, printing this book or accessing this book.

The terms of this Disclaimer are subject to change without prior notice. Please consult the latest edition of the book for the latest disclaimer.

Licensing

Changelog

New to Version 2.0

- Finally, A changelog!
- A massive rewrite of the section on the Romanovs, including a lot of new material on Ivan the Terrible and Peter the Great.
- Inclusion of all the known Secret Treaties pertaining to World War I in Chapter Two, which have long been forgotten by contemporary authors.
- More new material on Rakovsky and proper context and referencing for the Red Symphony.
- Information on the sinking of a Japanese super submarine headed to bomb the Panama Canal.
- New information on the role of Canadian mining companies.
- Minor corrections, additions and changes.

A note on the "World War Quotes" attributed to Albert Pike

In his official imprimatur, Cardinal Caro Rodriguez made reference to certain letters attributed to Albert Pike and addressed to Mazzini. To quote,

> In 'The Cause of World Unrest,'[18] I read a letter attributed by Le Diable AUXIX Siecle to Albert Pike, in which the author exposes to Mazzini the plan of attack upon Catholicism in Italy, to make it seek its last refuge in Russia. At the end of the letter he says: "Therefore when the autocratic empire of Russia will have become the citadel of Papal Christianity (Papist Adonaism), we shall unchain the Nihilist and Atheistic revolutionaries, and we shall provoke a formidable cataclysm, which will show clearly to the nations, in all its horror, the effect of absolute heresy, mother of savagery, and the most bloody disorder. Then citizens everywhere obliged to defend themselves against an enraged minority of revolutionaries, will exterminate those destroyers of civilization, and the multitude- disillusioned with Christianity whose deistic spirit will be from that moment on without direction and anxious for an ideal- without knowing where to put their worship will receive the true Light, by means of the Universal manifestation of the pure Luciferian doctrine finally made public; a manifestation which will raise a general movement of reaction, which will follow the destruction of Atheism and Christianity, both conquered and exterminated at the same time." If this letter is not authentic, it is in part at least a prophecy which has prevailed since 1896, twenty years before the Revolution of the anarchists and atheists were unloosed on Russia, not in any way proposed by the Grand Sovereign Mason because the Papacy is not so easily moved as kings or revolutionaries have imagined.[19]

At another place, the Cardinal is quoted as follows,

---

[18] Nesta Webster, The Cause of World Unrest (London: Richards Limited, 1920) 77-78.

[19] Jose Maria Cardinal Caro Y. Rodriguez, The Mystery of Freemasonry Unveiled – With a reprint of Pope Leo XIIIth Encyclical Humanum Genus 2nd edition (Imprimatur, Jose Maria Cardinal Caro Y. Rodriguez, Cardinal Archbishop of Santiago, Chile, 1920s). 86.

> The other indication of the participation of Masonry in the Revolution and the present upheaval in Russia is a letter in "LE DIABLE AU XIX SIECLE" (1896), Attributed to Albert Pike "Sovereign Pontiff of Universal Masonry," assisted by ten Ancients of the Grand Lodge of the Supreme Orient of Charleston to the very illustrious Joseph Mazzini, dated August 15th 1871 [....] It's publication is catalogued in the British Museum of London and the plan attributed to Pike is also in part in 'LE PALLADISME' OF MARGIOTTA," p. 186 published in 1895.[20] It is a plan to destroy Catholicism, to throw the Pope out of Italy and force him to seek refuge in Russia; and then, when the autocratic empire has become the citadel of Papal Christianity, "we," continues the author of the letter, "shall unleash the Nihilists and Atheists, and we shall provoke a formidable social cataclysm which in all its horror will show clearly to the nations the effects of absolute atheism, origin of savagery and of the most bloody turmoil. Then everywhere, the citizens obliged to defend themselves against the world minority of revolutionaries, will exterminate those destroyers of civilization, and the multitude, disillusioned with Christianity, whose deistic spirits will be from that moment without compass, anxious for an ideal, but without knowing where to render its adoration, will receive the TRUE LIGHT through the universal manifestation of the pure doctrine of Lucifer, brought finally out in public view, a manifestation which will result from the general reactionary movement which will follow the destruction of Christianity and Atheism, both conquered and exterminated at the same time."[21] Pike was a Luciferian. The part of the plan relative to the Papacy has failed, as on many other historic occasions, the plans and intentions of human power against the Pope have failed. As to the sad realization of the second part, namely, the "FORMIDABLE SOCIAL CATACLYSM," no one in our time can ignore it.[22]

Cardinal Rodriguez obviously mistook the First World War, unfolding during his time, as the social cataclysm. But Pike's quote alludes to the Second World War, the Third World War and it's aftermath as well.

---

[20] Domenico Margiotta, Culte de Satan-Lucifer -Palladism: Cult of Satan-Lucifer (Grenoble, 1895), p. 186.

[21] Quoting Nesta Webster, The Cause of World Unrest (London: Richards Limited, 1920) 77.

[22] Jose Maria Cardinal Caro Y. Rodriguez, The Mystery of Freemasonry Unveiled – With a reprint of Pope Leo XIIIth Encyclical Humanum Genus 2nd edition. (Imprimatur, Jose Maria Cardinal Caro Y. Rodriguez, Cardinal Archbishop of Santiago, Chile, 1920s) 119.

One of the sources Cardinal Rodriguez referred to was Nesta Webster. I have obtained the exact quote from Nesta Webster's book, The Cause of World Unrest,

> In the year 1896, there appeared in Paris a curious publication called *Le Diable au XIX Siecle*. It was an attack upon Freemasonry and came out in parts, illustrated with grotesque and repulsive engravings. The name on the title page is Dr. Bataille, but it is stated in the British Museum Catalogue that the real authors were Gabriel Jogand-Pages and Charles Hacks [This is the same British Museum which would later deny the very existence of this letter to William Guy Carr]. The book with evident knowledge and a show of authority, set out to trace the connection between Freemasonry and revolutions, but its sensationalism and the extremely doubtful character of some of the documents produced brought it into disrepute. It is now forgotten, and yet it contains a good deal that can be verified from other sources, and some things also which seem to be verified by recent events. In particular, there is a letter –or an alleged letter –said to have been written by Albert Pike, the "Sovereign Pontiff of Universal Freemasonry," assisted by ten ancients of the Grand Lodge of the Supreme Orient at Charleston, to "the very illustrious brother" Giuseppe Mazzini. This letter is dated (in Masonic style) August 15th 1871, and sets forth an anti-clerical policy which Mazzini is to follow in Italy. The measures proposed, including secular education, the expulsion of the religious orders, and so forth, need not detain us. What is our purpose occurs towards the end of the letter, on page 605 (Vol.II). The writer explains that owing to the working out of this policy the Pope may be driven at some future time out of Italy, and that established religion will then find its last refuge in Russia. And the letter proceeds:
>
> "That is why when the autocratic Empire of Russia will have become the citadel of Papal Christianity (adonaisme papiste), we shall unchain the revolutionary Nihilists and Athiests, and we shall provoke a formidable social cataclysm, which will demonstrate clearly to the nations, in all its horror, the effect of absolute unbelief, mother of savagery and the most bloody disorder. Then everywhere, the citizens, obliged to defend themselves against the mad minority of revolutionaries, will exterminate these destroyers of civilization, and the multitude, disillusioned of Christianity, whose deist soul will up to that moment be without compass, thirsting for an ideal, but not knowing where to bestow their worship, will receive the True Light by the universal manifestation of the pure Luciferian doctrine, at last made public, a manifestation which will arise from the general movement of reaction following the destruction of Atheism and Christianity, both at the same time, vanquished and exterminated."

> Now this letter is at least as old as 1896 (if it is a forgery); If it is genuine, it is as old as 1871. It must therefore be considered remarkable, whether as a forgery or as a genuine document. For it predicts what has happened in Russia, and it claims for its authors that they were preparing to bring about what has happened.[23]

The content of the letter in question pertaining to the World Wars ran as follows:

> The First World War must be brought about in order to permit the Illuminati to overthrow the power of the Czars in Russia and of making that country a fortress of atheistic Communism. The divergences caused by the "agentur" (agents) of the Illuminati between the British and Germanic Empires will be used to foment this war. At the end of the war, Communism will be built and used in order to destroy the other governments and in order to weaken the religions.
>
> The Second World War must be fomented by taking advantage of the differences between the Fascists and the political Zionists. This war must be brought about so that Nazism is destroyed and that the political Zionism be strong enough to institute a sovereign state of Israel in Palestine. During the Second World War, International Communism must become strong enough in order to balance Christendom, which would be then restrained and held in check until the time when we would need it for the final social cataclysm.
>
> The Third World War must be fomented by taking advantage of the differences caused by the "agentur" of the "Illuminati" between the political Zionists and the leaders of Islamic World. The war must be conducted in such a way that Islam (the Moslem Arabic World) and political Zionism (the State of Israel) mutually destroy each other. Meanwhile the other nations, once more divided on this issue will be constrained to fight to the point of complete physical, moral, spiritual and economical exhaustion...We shall unleash the Nihilists and the atheists, and we shall provoke a formidable social cataclysm which in all its horror will show clearly to the nations the effect of absolute atheism, origin of savagery and of the most bloody turmoil. Then everywhere, the citizens, obliged to defend themselves against the world minority of revolutionaries, will exterminate those destroyers of civilization, and the multitude, disillusioned with Christianity, whose deistic spirits will from that moment be without compass or direction, anxious for an ideal, but without knowing where to render its adoration,

---

[23] Nesta H. Webster, The Cause of World Unrest – With an Introduction by the Editor of The Morning Post (London: Grant Richards Ltd., 1920) 76-78.

will receive the true light through the universal manifestation of the pure doctrine of Lucifer, brought finally out in the public view. This manifestation will result from the general reactionary movement, which will follow the destruction of Christianity and atheism, both conquered and exterminated at the same time.

Carr's source for these quotes was either the imprimatur of Cardinal Rodriguez or some other material the Cardinal directed him to. He was not able to ascertain the source said to be in the British Museum. To quote a footnote from the same book,

> The Keeper of Manuscripts recently informed the author that this letter is NOT catalogued in the British Museum Library. It seems strange that a man of Cardinal Rodriguez's knowledge should have said that it WAS in 1925.[24]

Carr included his own commentary on the letter in question. To quote,

> After three global wars and two major revolutions, the United States would remain the only world power, but, during the third revolution which Pike said would be the greatest social cataclysm the world has ever known, the United States was to be disintegrated by internal treachery, and fall into the hands of the Luciferian conspirators "Like over-ripe fruit." Pike set forth quite clearly that World War One was to enable the directors of the W.R.M. [World Revolutionary Movement] to subjugate Russia and turn that Empire into the stronghold of atheistic-communism. This was accomplished with the first major revolution in 1917. Communism and Nazism were to be used, together with anti-Semitism, to enable the directors of the W.R.M. to foment World War Two. This was to end with the destruction of Nazism as a world power, because it would, by then, have served its purpose. The Sovereign State of Israel was to result from World War Two, as was also the United Nations. Political Zionism was to be used to enable the directors of the W.R.M. to foment World War Three, by playing up the real and supposed differences between Israel and the Arab states.[25]

Juri Lina drew upon another source in a 2004 book. This source was mentioned by Cardinal Rodriguez and refers to the historian Domenico Margiotta. To quote:

> Pike wrote a letter to Giuseppe Mazzini (whose alias was Emunach Memed), dated 15 August 1871 (or as he wrote it 0871). The historian

[24] William Guy Carr, Satan, Prince of This World (Omni Publications, 1997) 22 note 9.
[25] William Guy Carr, Satan, Prince of This World (Omni Publications, 1997) 84.

Domenico Margiotta published the letter in his book "Le Palladisme: Culte de Satan-Lucifer" ("Palladism: Cult of Satan-Lucifer", Grenoble, 1895, p. 186).

The inherent antagonism between different ideologies was to be stirred up and made to explode in three world wars and three revolutions. The First World War was to destroy the three European empires, at that time being the last remaining bulwarks against illuminism. One of these (Russia) was to be made a centre of atheist totalitarianism (communism). The Second World War was to erupt from heightened tensions between the Jewish race (and its spiteful Zionism) and extreme European nationalism (nazism and fascism). This war would weaken Europe economically and politically and communism would expand and become as strong as all Christianity, but not stronger, until the time was ripe for the final destruction of all society. A third reason for the Second World War was to create a Jewish state in Palestine. Gradually, it would be possible thereby to heighten the tensions between Judaism and Islam until it broke out in a war, which would involve all of the world powers. The three revolutions, which would aid this carefully planned dissolution of all human civilization, were the Russian, the Chinese and the Indo-Chinese.

Someone seems to have implemented most of this evil scheme, despite the fact that it was announced as early as 1895. Concerning the last stage, General Pike wrote the following: "We shall unleash the Nihilists and Atheists and provoke a formidable social cataclysm which in all its horror will show clearly to the nations the effect of absolute atheism, origin of savagery and of the most bloody turmoil. Then everywhere, the citizens, obliged to defend themselves against the world minority of revolutionaries, will exterminate those destroyers of civilization, and the multitude, disillusioned with Christianity, whose deistic spirits will from that moment on be without compass (direction), anxious for an ideal, but without knowing where to render its adoration, will receive the true light through the universal manifestation of the pure doctrine of Lucifer, brought finally out in the public view, a manifestation which will result from the general reactionary movement which will follow the destruction of Christianity and atheism, both conquered and exterminated at the same time."

Atheist communism was suddenly abolished in the Soviet Union in 1991 as part of the effort to expand the European Union - the most sinister of masonic projects, which will lead to the forming of the United States of Europe, the dream of Giuseppe Mazzini.[26]

---

[26] Juri Lina, Architects of Deception (Stockholm: Referent Publications, 2004) 197-198.

The attribution to Albert Pike cannot be verified, until new evidence emerges. Nevertheless, the sources of Cardinal Rodriguez (leaving aside the British Museum) pre-date World War II. Nesta Webster's 'The Cause of World Unrest' was published in 1920, after World War I. Domenico Margiotta's 'Palladism: Cult of Satan-Lucifer,' was published in 1895, long before World War I. To quote Cardinal Rodriguez, "[...] Authentic or not, the letter had been published [or written] long enough before the events, not to be an invention accommodated POST FACTUM."[27]

Some text from the "letter" has been used in this book because it aptly summarizes the creation, unfolding and outcome of the World Wars.

---

[27] Jose Maria Cardinal Caro Y. Rodriguez, The Mystery of Freemasonry Unveiled – With a reprint of Pope Leo XIIIth Encyclical Humanum Genus 2nd edition. (Imprimatur, Jose Maria Cardinal Caro Y. Rodriguez, Cardinal Archbishop of Santiago, Chile, 1920s) 118.

Chapter 1
The "Special Mission" of Russian Tyranny

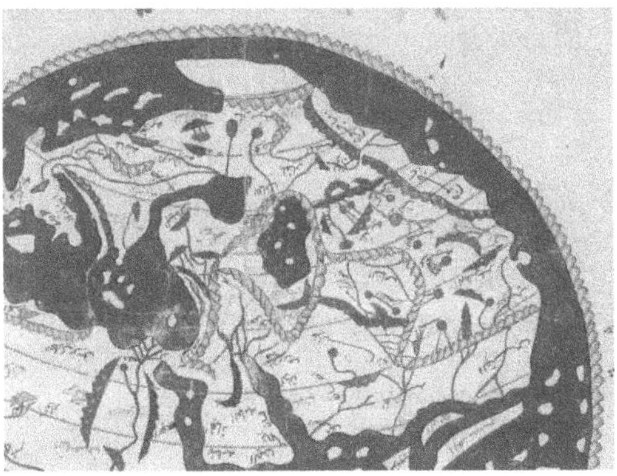

Section of a map of the world by Muslim philosopher Al-Idrisi (Dated CE 1154). Even then, Russia had acquired a menacing reputation. The area of North East Russia is being identified as the realms of the mythical Gog and Magog (Ard Yajuj and Ard Majuj).

#1. The Russian nation must be constantly on a war footing to keep the soldiers warlike and in good condition. No rest must be allowed, except for the purpose of relieving the state finances, recruiting the Army, or biding the Favourable moment for attack. By this means peace is made subservient to war, and war to peace, in the interest of aggrandisement and increasing prosperity of Russia.

#9.We must progress as much as possible in the direction of Constantinople and India. He who can once get the possession of these points is the real ruler of the world. With this in view we must provoke constant quarrels at the one time with Turkey, at another with Persia. We must establish wharves and docks in the Euxine and by degrees make ourselves master of that sea, as well as the Baltic, which is a doubly important element in the success of our plan. We must hasten the downfall of Persia, push on to the Persian Gulf, if possible re-establish the ancient commerciality with the Levant through Syria, and force our way into the Indies, which are the storehouses of the world. Once there, we can dispense with English gold.

-The Alleged Testament of Peter the Great, ~1700

The position of Russia in Central Asia is that of all civilized states which are brought into contact with half-savage nomad populations possessing no fixed social organization [...] the tribes on the frontier

> must be reduced to a state of submission [...] It is the peculiarity of Asiatics to respect nothing but visible and palpable force. The moral force of reasoning has no hold on them [...] Very frequently of late years the civilization of these countries, which are her neighbors on the Continent of Asia, has been assigned to Russia as her special mission.
>
> *-The Gorchakov Circular on Russia's Mission in Central Asia, 1864*[28]

> An agreement which we concluded in 1915 with Great Britain and France, and to which Italy has adhered, established in the most definite fashion the right of Russia to the Straits and Constantinople.... I repeat that absolute agreement on this point is firmly established among the Allies.
>
> *- Prime Minister of Russia, M. Trepoff, making a statement in the Duma on December 2nd 1917.*[29]

For a better understanding of the World Wars, it is necessary to carefully study the nation which was the centerpiece of these two World Wars. It is important to understand its history, its people and all the factors, which made this locale pivotal to the two World Wars.

Origins of the Romanovs

Even before the Muscovite state was formed, the Romanovs were considered an elite family. The last Rurik Tsar Basil Shiusky commented on the origins of the Romanovs as an "[...] early branch of the princely houses of Suzdal and Kiev [...]" predating the Muscovite rulers themselves.[30] But other evidence suggests they were of purely Germanic origin. Their earliest common ancestor was a boyar named Andrei Kobyla. He was the son of a Prussian prince named Glanda Kambila, who came to Russia in the second half of the 13th century. Apparently, Glanda Kambila was one of the leaders of the Old Prussian rebellion of 1260-1274 against the Christian Teutonic Order. In other words, the Romanov arrival in Russia was a rather inauspicious consequence of their anti-Christian activities. Andrei Kobyla quietly assimilated among the boyar families that represented the Rurik dynasty, which was then in control of Moscow. It would be much later, during the reign of Rurik

[28] Major Problems in the History of Imperial Russia Ed. by James Cracraft (D.C Heath and Co, 1994) 410-411.
[29] Frederick Seymour Cocks, The Secret Treaties and Understandings: Text of the Available Documents (London: Union of Democratic Control, 1918)17.
[30] Nicholas V. Riasanovsky, A History of Russia (Oxford University Press, 1963) 190.

Tsar Ivan the Terrible that Roman Zakharin-Yurievone, a branch of descendants of Andrei Kobyla, emerged to prominence.

The Byzantine Connection

The entire Mongol invasion and destruction of the Islamic world was a multiphase program to reverse the threat of the Seljuk Turks to the Byzantine Empire and Constantinople, the gateway to Western Europe. The Illuminati royalty of the Byzantine Empire were covertly involved in this venture from the very beginning through Nestorean Christian missions among the Mongols, and they had even intermarried among the Mongols[31] to ensure the program continued as per their specifications. But even before the Seljuk threat been extinguished, a new one arose in its place. This was the Ottoman Empire, and Amir Timur's venture was primarily directed against it. While Timur's focus was the Middle East, where he killed five percent of the world's then population, a side-project was the destruction of the Mongol Golden Horde, which had become too Islamized, and which held control over Russia. The Romanovs emerged after the destruction of the Mongol Golden Horde, and filled the power vacuum. This was not a coincidence. Had Amir Timur not destroyed the Golden Horde, Russia would have probably been more Asiatic, as opposed to the superficially Christianized realm it became.

Amir Timur assumed he had put an end to the Ottoman threat to the Byzantine Empire by taking the Sultan prisoner. But after him, the Ottomans made a miraculous comeback, and captured Constantinople, putting an end to the Byzantine Empire for good. In 1472, Zoe/Sophia, the niece of the last Byzantine Emperor Constantine XI Palaiologos was married to the Rurik Grand Prince of Moscow Ivan III.[32] This was arranged by Pope Paul II. While being an important event in the history of Christianity (as the Orthodox Church of Byzantine became the official Church in Imperial Russia), it was also the beginning of Russia's misfortunes. Subsequent rulers represented a predatory cabal, foreign to Russia, a historical enemy of free people that specialized in the preying on the unlucky ones who inadvertently became their subjects, perpetually tightening the noose on them as far as they could. And the boundaries of their aggression were not just restricted to their unlucky

[31] This Mongol-Byzantine royalty are referred to as crypto-Byzantines in conspiracy literature, and they later established the Safavid Empire in Iran.

[32] The Byzantine Empire had employed a similar ploy with the Kievan Rus State (882-1283), which posed a serious military threat to them. After Christianization didn't work out, their king Vladimir the Great was wedded to Princess Anna, the sister of Byzantine emperor Basil II. But this marriage was not as consequential as the marriage of Ivan III.

subjects. They were meant to be perpetually increased, as far as they possibly could, by endless wars. Autocracy, excessive taxation, serfdom, and large standing armies to act as a personal guard of the ruler became a part of the Russian equation only after this marriage. It is important to distinguish such rule from that of the earlier Rurik Princes, who in contrast, gave judicious consideration to all shareholders of the enterprise of the State. This was the transformation of the Muscovy State into an instrument of perpetual aggression, both on its subjects and on the free people outside its borders.

The emblem of the Byzantine Empire became the emblem of the Rurik and Romanov dynasties.

Queen Sophia was considered to be a shrewd and conspiratorial character, who soon started dictating her husband's policies. Soon enough, her husband went to war with remnants of the Golden Horde. It is no coincidence that both crypto-Byzantines like Amir Timur and newly created allies of the Byzantine Empire like the Ruriks would find common enemies. Ivan III also began a conflict with Sweden which controlled present-day Finland (and Russia's access to the Baltic Sea). This conflict was started by Ivan III in alliance with Denmark, and it would last through several centuries. Ivan III is also credited with kickstarting Russia's conflict with the Polish people, the animosity of which has not ceased to the present day. Queen Sophia is believed to have introduced Byzantine ceremonies and court etiquette to the Kremlin, as well as the idea of Moscow as a "Third Rome" succeeding Constantinople. Artists and masters were invited from Western Europe to beautify Moscow, which was now being seen as the new Constantinople. This may explain the later Rurik enmity with the Ottomans, and the obsession with capturing the real Constantinople from them. These became a distinctive hallmark of subsequent Russian rulers. After the marriage, the Rurik dynasty (and subsequently the Romanovs) adopted the emblem of the extinct Byzantine Empire. This emblem represents the double-headed eagle of Lagash, an artifact of mystery Babylon that has been repeatedly used in Freemasonry.

Ivan the Terrible and the Destruction of Asiatic Russia

Queen Sophia Palaiologina ensured that her own son became the next Rurik Grand Prince of Moscow, rather than a grandson from a previous marriage (who was a more legitimate candidate). This son ruled as Vasili III, and he continued the policies initiated by his mother of pushing the Golden Horde further south and making the Crimean Khanate a vassal. The powers of the boyars and the nobility started being curbed. Vasili III also captured Smolensk, the great eastern fortress of Lithuania, chiefly through the aid of a traitor, Prince Mikhail Glinski. He married the niece of Mikhail Glinski, and from her, he had a son that succeeded him as Ivan IV (Ivan the Terrible). A few months after his coronation, Moscow was nearly destroyed by a fire which was blamed on Mikhail Glinski and his mother. Ivan IV continued the Byzantine policy of consolidating all power at the expense of the boyars and the nobility. As a substitute, he created a standing army and a prototype parliament to undermine the power of the nobility. He also bureaucratized the Church so that it could be better controlled and introduced Russia's first printing press so that religious scripture could be used for proselytizing among Asiatic populations. He was the first Grand Prince of Moscow to crown himself as the Tsar, which made him a demigod like his ancestral Byzantine royals. He introduced the first laws restricting the mobility of the peasants, which led to the later development of serfdom.

Ivan IV instituted a new political system called *Oprichnina* to override the traditional system of boyars by virtue of which boyars with a longer history of service and loyalty got access to higher posts. The *Oprichnina* was a separate territory under direct control of the Tsar and free from the influence of the nobles and the boyars. This territory which existed north of Moscow was used to raise a strong personal guard for the Tsar, and in return, the personal guard was allowed to administer the *Oprichnina* as their estates. But unlike previous landlords, they could not be held accountable. And their oppression of peasants soon led to a dangerous shortfall in the production of grains.The personal guard of the Tsar was used to persecute and destroy the influential families of Suzdal and Kiev, who represented Russia's old aristocracy prior to the takeover of the Rurik dynasty by the Byzantines. Up to 10,000 nobles were expelled. Ivan also destroyed the city of Novgorod which once rivalled Moscow because of his dislike of the powerful boyars of the Novgorod Republic which bordered the Arctic. Up to 27,000 of its citizenry were killed by the *Oprichniki*, who also burnt and pillaged neighbouring villages and even churches. The city of Novgorod and the Novgorod Republic would never recover, and slowly faded away. Ivan IV encouraged the *Oprichniki* to participate in drunken revelry. And this was facilitated by opening taverns. The revenue from selling vodka was considerable, but also led to the impoverishment of peasants.

Ivan IV developed exceedingly good relations with British royalty, and the British Muscovy Company was given trading privileges in Russia. This was the beginning of a historical relationship between the two predatory powers.[33] When Ivan IV moved against the powerful Tatar Khanate of Kazan in east (another remnant of the Golden Horde), the city's walls were reportedly blown up by a British sapper. This was followed by a large massacre of Kazan Tatars (estimates are upwards of 65,000) and all their buildings, libraries and mosques were razed. On the other hand, Ivan IV had the famous St. Basil's Cathedral built in Moscow to honour the victory. The destruction of the Kazan Khanate opened up Siberia for Ivan IV. Soon, the Khanate of Sibir was conquered with the aid of Cossacks. When Ivan IV advanced south into the Astrakhan Khanate, he ended up provoking the first Russo-Turkish War. This led to the Ottomans backing the Crimeans in their raids into Muscovy. One such raid resulted in Moscow being gutted so badly that Ivan IV avoided it for several years because of the lack of shelter for his entourage. The burning of Moscow, coupled with grain shortage from excessive taxation (which was used to finance these new conflicts by the *Oprichniki*) made Ivan IV realize how dangerously ineffective the monstrous *Oprichnina* he had created had become. It was dismantled, and replaced with a

Qolsharif and his students defend their madrassa and the Cathedral Mosque during the Siege of Kazan (1552). By Firinat Xalikov

St. Basil's Cathedral was built by Ivan the Terrible to honor the destruction of Kazan.

[33] It can be argued that this historical relationship secretly continued even later in the Soviet era through highly placed British spy rings, such as the Cambridge spy ring in British Intelligence.

"reformed" boyar council. Apparently it was too early to get rid of the nobility, and this would have to be done slowly over the course of the next few centuries.

The reign of Ivan IV was marked by a new wave of hostility towards Islam. Throughout areas that he controlled, mosques were ordered to be demolished. It was as if the Byzantines had succeeded in transplanting not just themselves into the Muscovy State but also their hatred of the religion of the Ottomans.

With the Illuminati in charge of Rurik dynasty, the Romanovs coexisted peacefully on the sidelines. But Ivan IV's marriage to Anastasia Romanovna catapulted them to centrestage. Anastasia was the first wife of Ivan IV and she was meant to bear his successor. In addition to her, Ivan IV had seven more wives throughout his life. The Eastern Orthodox Church restricted marrying the fourth time. Ivan IV got around this each and every time by having a wife either poisoned, brutally murdered or banished, and claiming that he did not consummate the marriage. And the occasion of a wife being murdered was used to arrest and kill powerful nobles whom he had marked for elimination. Only Anastasia didn't go through this because of her bloodline (the rest of the wives were from the subject population). Anastasia's son Ivan Ivanovich was meant to be the next Tsar, but Ivan IV accidentally killed him when he struck him on the head with his scepter. Anastasia's other son, the simple-minded Feodor I became the next Tsar.

Trouble? Or a Time to Break Free?

The period between the Rurik Tsar Ivan IV and the Romanovs has been characterized by establishment historians as a "Time of Troubles." Indeed, the Illuminati was in trouble because the Rurik dynasty and the boyars had a window of opportunity to rescue Russia from the disastrous program she had been put on.

The simple-minded Feodor I didn't seem to have the appetite for continuing the program Russia had been put on by the Powers That Be. Neither was he enthusiastic about continuing the alliance with Britain. He married the daughter of his father's powerful minister Boris Godunov. Godunov was a member of Ivan's personal guard and secret police. When Ivan IV accidentally murdered his own son, Godunov was present and tried to intervene, only to receive blows from the Tsar. The Tsar had appointed him and Anastasia's brother Nikita Romanovich as regents for Feodor I. After Nikita died, Godunov became the real kingmaker in Moscow. When Feodor I died childless, Godunov became the next Tsar. His reign was characterized by prudency. Godunov was succeeded by his sixteen year old son Feodor II.

The Powers That Be had no intention to allow the Godunovs to continue any further. Boris Godunov was an Asiatic Tatar by ethnicity, and obviously did not have the bloodline credentials that the Ruric Byzantines or the Romanovs had. What they needed was another suitable candidate. Ivan IV did have another son by his eighth marriage to a non-bloodlined commoner but this son, Dmitri Ivanovich, had been killed in suspicious circumstances after the death of Ivan IV. Therefore, another Dmitri (who became known as False Dmitriy I) was resurrected in Poland. He was helped by a number of nobles and even the Jesuits, who seemed to have been suspiciously close to him. Soon enough, he marched to Moscow (while being guarded by Western European mercenaries) and a number of boyars and Cossacks were arranged to join him. A coup was conducted and both Feodor II and his mother were murdered. Staying true to the historical agenda of the Powers That Be, False Dmitriy I began preparation for a massive war with the Ottomans, and ordered the mass production of firearms. He brought back the noble families exiled by Boris Godunov such as the Shuiskys, the Golitsins and the Romanovs, and made Fyodor Nikitich Romanov (son of Nikita Romanovich) the metropolitan archbishop of Rostov. But when he started allowing Catholic and Protestant soldiers whom he had brought along to pray in Eastern Orthodox Churches, public opinion turned against him because they were regarded as heretics. An important boyar Prince Vasily Ivanovich Shuisky turned against him. After ten months of his reign, a group of boyars and commoners stormed the Kremlin and False Dmitriy I was killed. Vasily Shuisky became the next Tsar. Another bogus Dmitriy (False Dmitriy II) was pulled out to bring down Vasily. In an eerie premonition of socialism, False Dmitriy II drew large crowds of peasanats by promising to abolish the estates of the boyars. Although Fyodor Nikitich Romanov (the son of Anastasia's brother Nikita Romanovich) is described by establishment historians as a "captive" of False Dmitriy II, he contributed to the popular support of False Dmitriy II, and in return, was promoted to the title of *Patriarch of all Russia*. Tsar Vasily Shuisky made the ingenious move of cultivating an alliance with Sweden to strengthen his support base. In response, the King of Poland and Lithuania Sigismund III Vasa went to war with Muscovy. Given the fact that both the false Dmitrys had been supported by magnates of the Polish-Lithuanian Commonwealth, it is clear whose side Polish royalty was on. Russo–Swedish forces were destroyed and the childless Tsar Vasily Shuisky was forced to abdicate in July 1610. Soon after, Polish-Lithuanian troops entered Moscow facing little resistance. Instead of False Dmitriy II, a Polish commander proposed a rival candidate for Tsar: Sigismund's son, Władysław. It is clear that Polish royalty were reluctant to become Tsars, as this would be a great boon to the Catholics of Poland, whom the Powers That Be have always detested. They were merely acting as placeholders until the Powers That Be sorted things out in Moscow. This was necessary because they did not want any of the remaining boyars to lay claim to the title of Tsar. And this became all the more necessary when the candidate of The Powers That Be, False Dmitriy II, was killed in December 1610. Polish leadership soon discredited themselves by showing intolerance towards members of the Orthodox Church. Władysław never entered Moscow, and by 1612, Polish-Lithuanian troops faced an uprising and had to leave. A Grand National Assembly elected as Tsar Michael Romanov, the son Fyodor Nikitich Romanov[34] in 1613. And maybe, the British Secret Service was involved behind the scenes, along with many other conspirators.

Romanov Connections

The Romanov family was connected by descent to the royal ruling elites of Britain and Germany. Just like the Germanic House of Saxe-Coburg and Gotha changed its name to the House of Windsor before World War I, the Romanovs too, quickly discarded their Germanic image for a Russian one. Later, we see heavy Romanov intermarriage among all the major European royalty, such as the British House of Orange and the German Kaiser. Intermarriage, characteristic of elite bloodlines, was so heavily pronounced that the Romanovs even produced genetic anomalies such as hemophiliacs. This suggests the preservation of a particular bloodline common to European royalty. The most interesting connections are those to British royalty. To quote,

> In 1586, Tsar Boris Godunov offered the huge salary of 2000 English pounds a year, with a house and all provisions free, to John Dee, the English magus and spy master, to enter his service. Dee's son Dr. Arthur Dee, who like his father was an alchemist and Rosicrucian, went to Moscow to work as a physician. Mikhail Romanov, the first Tsar of the Romanov dynasty, allegedly ascended the throne with the help of Dr. Arthur Dee and the British Secret Service. Before their rise to

[34] Fyodor Nikitich Romanov had been taken prisoner by the supporters of the King of Poland and Lithuania Sigismund III Vasa, for not acknowledging him as Tsar of Muscovy. He was quietly released after his son became Tsar.

power the Romanovs were accused by their enemies of practicing magic and possessing occult powers.[35]

Indeed, we see that later Romanovs had a tendency to entertain occult celebrities like music composer Debussy and Monsieur Philippe.

In addition, The Romanov family is interspersed with Bohemian royals by intermarriage. Bohemia occupies special importance to the Illuminati. It is believed that its American counterpart is the "Bohemian Grove," a redwood forest in Sonoma County (California), where the Western ruling elite, including American Presidents have been sighted. Anti-Bohemian Grove activist Alex Jones managed to infiltrate the Bohemian Grove and photographed bizarre rituals taking place before a huge stone owl.[36]

Researcher Fritz Springmeier who was the first to associate the Romanovs with the thirteen families that constitute the "Illuminati" also claims that there was also a Prussian branch of the Romanov family, and that Grand Prince Alexis Romanov came to America where his granddaughter Mary Teissier became a lover of billionaire J. Paul Getty.[37]

Secret Societies and Occultists

The Romanovs were host to secret societies and the occult. They had an unusually strong relationship with secret societies such as Freemasonry. Noted Russian historian Marc Raeff comments on the officially passive attitude towards these groups as "[...] one of the many mysteries that still surround Alexander's [I] personality and reign."[38] One such society, *The Southern Society* was modeled after the German *Tugenbund.* According to Fritz Springmeier, to original German *Tugenbund* was created to counter Napoleon, who had kidnapped the French Revolution

---

[35] Mehmet Sabeheddin, "The Secret of Eurasia – The key to Hidden History and World Events," New Dawn No. 68 (September-October 2001), <http://www.newdawnmagazine.com> An archive is available at <http://www.geocities.com/integral_tradition/key.html> Accessed 12th May 2003.

[36] Alex Jones, "Dark Secrets Inside the Bohemian Grove," Infowars.com <http://www.infowars.com/bg1.html> Web page as of 16/03/04

[37] Fritz Springmeier, Bloodlines of the Illuminati (Spring Arbor distributors, 1998) 257. GlobalGrey PDF edition 2013 <http://www.globalgrey.co.uk/Pages/Books-Conspiracies/Bloodlines-Of-The-Illuminati.html> Web page as of 03/07/13.

[38] Marc Raeff, The Decembrist Movement (Prentice Hall Inc.-New Jersey, 1966) 6.

from the Illuminati.[39] Apart from involvement in secret societies, there are clear instances of Tsarist involvement in ancient orders linked to The Powers That Be, namely the Order of St. John /Knights of Malta[40] which spawned the Order of Russian Knights. Tsar Paul I, despite being a follower of the Russian Orthodox Church, became grandmaster of this Catholic order. Even Rasputin had a rich esoteric background. He was a member of a Siberian sect known as Khleisty. This sect advocated immersion in debauchery as a prerequisite to redemption, a phenomenon which bears similarity with Sabbatean Judaism.

Prominent elitist figure and occultist, Helena Petrovna Blavatsky, was among the elite of Russian nobility. She was the cousin of Tsarist Prime Minister Count Witte. The Russian government would offer her consular assistance whenever she would run out of money in the course of her travels. To quote, "As early as 1887 H.P. Blavatsky had become a topic of debate in "mystic Petersburg" and received the prestigious support of Ukhtomsky's friend the mysterious Tibetan Dr. Badmaev, soon to become notorious for the favor he received at the Russian imperial court and his relationship with Rasputin."[41] In 1891, the future Tsar, Nicholas II visited Blavatsky at her Indian headquarters in Adyar.[42]

For those acquainted with the esoteric context of symbols used by The Powers That Be, a study of Romanov symbolism will be highly entertaining. None of these symbols bear elements local to Russia or even ancient Russia. Rather, they represent an extension of a secret heritage common to Bohemian-European royalty.

---

[39] Fritz Springmeier, Bloodlines of the Illuminati (Spring Arbor distributors, 1998) 181. GlobalGrey PDF edition 2013 <http://www.globalgrey.co.uk/Pages/Books-Conspiracies/Bloodlines-Of-The-Illuminati.html> Web page as of 03/07/13.

[40] Order of St. John/Knights of Malta/ Hospitallers are derived from the Templar Knights, who have a strange history. (Not related to Teutonic Knights) The Merovingians passed on the myth that Christ had never died but married and had progeny; and they were the progeny. Those recruited into the Templar Knights would put their lives on the line for defending what they thought was the bloodline of Jesus. The Merovingians later resurfaced as Cathars, who would conduct a major Gnostic heresy against the Catholic Church. When they were uprooted, it is believed the Templars camouflaged themselves as Catholic orders while the Catholic Church itself was infiltrated.

[41] Mehmet Sabeheddin, "The Secret of Eurasia – The key to Hidden History and World Events," New Dawn No. 68 (September-October 2001), <http://www.newdawnmagazine.com> An archive is available at <http://www.geocities.com/integral_tradition/key.html> Accessed 12th May 2003.

[42] Sabeheddin

Imperial Russian Coat of Arms

Symbol associated with Freemasonry

An ancient Hittite Eagle of Lagash

The Dragon on the coat of arms of Nikita Romanovitch
Right: Another Royal Russian coat of arms reads like an almanac of the occult

The Worst of European Royalty?

As far as Western ruling families go, the Romanovs were undoubtedly among the worse the Illuminati had to offer. The Illuminati is known to mould and carve society as per its terms, But in Imperial Russia, there was little need for that because the subject population already had their Asiatic culture vandalized and decimated by early Tsars. They were exceptionally docile towards authority. The Tsar occupied a demigod status, which ensured centuries of unwavering loyalty and command over a vast expanse of territory. This arrangement crippled social, intellectual and industrial development to a large extent, and substitute models of development were hastily imported from Western Europe towards the end of the 18th century.

Occasionally, such rulers revert back to their humanity, and when they do, assassinations become obligatory. For example, Tsar Alexander II almost stole the thunder of the revolutionaries through drastic reforms. He was finally killed, after a record nine assassination attempts were made on him. It is interesting to note that Tsar Alexander II developed a close relationship with another renegade, Abraham Lincoln (who was also assassinated). The basis of this alliance (which at one point involved the Russian Navy steaming in to American ports) was a common loathing of Britain as a troublemaker. It is suspected that the death of Tsar Paul I, as well as his son, Alexander I, involved members of Freemasonry.[43]

Unlike the Catholic Church, Russian Orthodox Church was like a toothless cat, failing to protect both itself and its subjects. It would never rival or dictate state power. The Romanovs usurped all important prerogatives of the church, and Tsars such as Peter the Great openly lampooned the church.

Tsar Peter I and the Obliteration of Asiatic Russian Culture

Previously, we have covered the Byzantine-Rurik Tsar Ivan IV, who was rightly deemed by his population as the "Terrible." The Romanovs also produced their own version of such a character in the form of Peter I. But by then, the Russian population was too enfeebled to call him "Terrible," and stuck to the moniker "Great," which had been created by establishment historians. He is credited with bringing Russia back on track with the original Illuminati program, and making it more amenable to the program by Westernization and the removal of Asiatic aspects of Russian culture.

Peter I began vandalizing all Asiatic elements of Russia's culture and heritage, and began forcibly substituting them with Western elements. Boyars were required to shave their beards and adopt Western clothing. Even a tax was introduced for long beards and traditional robes. The boyars were further deprived of the status and privileges they held because of their lineage by a new order of precedence which favoured merit in service to the Tsar. This made them more disposable. While

---

[43] Quoting 'Great Crimes of Masonry,' by Trod. Jose Maria Cardinal Caro Y. Rodriguez, The Mystery of Freemasonry Unveiled – With a reprint of Pope Leo XIIIth Encyclical Humanum Genus 2nd edition (Imprimatur, Jose Maria Cardinal Caro Y. Rodriguez, Cardinal Archbishop of Santiago, Chile, 1920s) 158.

Peter I was usurping the hereditary prerogatives of the boyars, he was also strengthening and consecrating his own hereditary rights. Among the earlier Ruriks, the position of Grand Duke was not hereditary but appointed. The most honourable and capable of the candidates was chosen by the boyars. Slowly, this system was being transformed into an autocratic monarchy since the Rurik Prince Ivan III. Peter I represented the second biggest phase of this transformation after Ivan IV.

Realizing that the Ottomans could not be destroyed singlehandedly, he travelled to Western Europe hoping to create an anti-Ottoman alliance. While such an alliance never came to fruition, his return saw an ever-increasing role of Western European mercenaries and Western European technology in the Russian army. Such extreme were the changes after his return that some have tried to reason by proposing that the Peter I who had returned was a West European imposter.[44] Russia's subsequent development as a Maritime power was modelled roughly on the British Empire. Russians started being sent to Western Europe for training. Consistent with the original Byzantine venture to recapture Constantinople, Peter I sent a delegation to Malta to scout the possibility of a future Russian Naval Base, and to observe the training of the Knights of Malta and their fleet. As a result, the Russian army became more Westernized, more machine-like and more amenable to control. On the other hand, Asiatic elements of the Russian army, such as the Cossack regiments, began being purged.

When Peter I returned from Europe, he is also said to have introduced Western Freemasonry into Russian politics. In fact some sources conclude that he went to Western Europe to obtain knowledge of Freemasonry, and that his mentor was an English Freemason and architect Sir Christopher Wren. Soon after him, assasinations and conspiracies became more and more commonplace in court politics.[45] On the other hand, the Russian Orthodox Church started being deprived of its adherents because of a new law of Peter I, according to which Russian men could no longer become monks before the age of 50. As a substitute to Scripture, secular education was encouraged for the first time ever, and was even made mandatory for some officials. Books, plays and literature from Western Europe started being translated into Russian to supplant traditional Russian culture. Ivan IV had earlier established the

---

[44] Those who believe such theories point out to the fact that he immediately sent his wife to a convent upon returning, among many other inconsistencies.

[45] Officially, the first Russian Masonic lodge would open much later in 1756 in St. Petersburg.

first printing press. Peter I used it to further supplant Russia's Asiatic literary culture with a West European one. For example, he issued very strict orders for old books to be brought from monasteries, villages and cities to Moscow for making copies through a printing press. Skeptics believed that he was secretly purging literature that was representative of Russia's Asiatic culture. As in the case of Ivan IV's *Oprichnina,* a huge government bureaucracy filled with officials appointed solely by the Tsar began to emerge, and boyars who revolted were brutally suppressed. New taxes were levied to finance wars. Peter I cracked down on home-brewed vodka by creating liquor licenses for those selling vodka. Drinking was completely legalized, and propaganda was produced to encourage it. This monopoly on vodka brought revenues for the Treasury, which in turn were used to finance the Tsar's grandiose schemes. But the Russian peasants became more impoverished, and started being characterized by drunkenness and escapism. The calendar of Russia was changed to a Western one starting with the birth of Christ. And this was probably to obscure Russia's pre-Romanov history. The Romanovs may have fabricated the notion of Mongol Russia being a period of darkness, which helped the Romanovs appear as enlightened. This was done through hstorians of German origin. Russia's oriental style coins called Kopeks were replaced with new ones, and paper money was introduced which better served the Treasury by allowing for inflation.

Equally mysterious is Peter I's close friendship with a black Falasha Jew named Abram. Abram was a slave of the Ottoman court, presumably because his family had rebelled against the Ottomans. In 1704, Abram was ransomed and brought to Moscow by the deputy of the Russian ambassador, on orders of his superiors (one of whom was Pyotr Andreyevich Tolstoy, great-grandfather of the celebrated writer Leo Tolstoy). Abram was immediately taken into the home of Tsar Peter I, and thereafter accompanied him in military campaigns. The Tsar became his official godfather. Abram soon became known as Abram Petrovich Gannibal, and he studied in France as a military engineer (presumably to aid the Tsar's war on the Ottomans). In France, he was friends with intellectuals such as Denis Diderot, the Baron de Montesquieu and Voltaire. Abram married into European royalty, and many British aristocrats descend from him. Even Alexander Pushkin, one of the greatest Russian poets and the founder of modern Russian literature was a descendant of Abram.

Unable to have much of a decisive success against the Ottomans, Peter I turned his attention to the Baltic Sea, going to war with the Swedes, and founding the city of Saint Petersburg (Germanically named after Saint Peter the Apostle) on the coast of the Baltic (in captured Swedish territory). This city was constructed along Westernized lines, as opposed to the Asiatic architecture of Moscow. But of course, this did not mean that Peter I preferred a less corrupt administration or a less autocratic rule (as in the case of Western Europe). He was only interested in making his war machine more efficient, and in using Western culture to supplant Russia's vibrant Asiatic culture. For example, in 1718, Peter I investigated why the ex-Swedish province of Livonia was so orderly. It was discovered that the Swedes spent as much administering Livonia (approximately 300 times smaller than his empire) as he spent on the entire Russian bureaucracy.[46] He quickly dismantled Livonia's Swedish government, and a more autocratic Russianized government was installed.

While establishment historians have continued to portray Peter I as a great "reformer," a thorough study of the effects of his wars and "reforms" on the serfs and subject population is warranted. For example, there is indication that the population on the whole, decreased by millions. And his war with the Swedes may have been genocidal in intent.

Successors to Western European Colonialism

It is no surprise that Russia was thus selected as the ideal successor to European colonialism. The Russian subject population could be used for this purpose. And unlike the populations of Western Europe, they would not demand a large personal share from the spoils of colonialism. The World Wars would be the smokescreen through which this Russian advance would be made.

As early as 1700, a document called the Testament of Peter the Great had surfaced in Europe. It outlined plans for Russian world domination in explicit terms. It called for Russia to always be on a war footing. And for Russian direct intervention in the affairs of Germany, Poland, Sweden and Austria. Britain was to be retained as a secret ally until Russia took Contanstinople, India and Syria. Then Russia would would counter

[46] Richard Pipes, Russia under the old regime (New York: Scribner, 1974) 281.

Britian too and even take the East Indies. Greeks were to be used against Turks, and Turks were to be expelled from Europe. The last point of the document (#14) ends with "Thus Europe can and must be subjugated." Establishment historians dismissed the Testament of Peter the Great as a hoax, and attributed it to Napoleon (who was also blamed for the Protocols of Zion at one point).

The so-called "Great Game" between Imperial Russia and the then dominant colonial force, Britain, was engineered to the advantage of Russia. In the name of thwarting Russian influence, the British would advance and conquer local principalities, create modern nation states and install local rulers connected by blood to the Illuminati. A case in point is that of British Afghanistan. It was intended that these client rulers would later further Russian influence during the World Wars. The nation states that succeeded British-European colonies allowed a few select people to extend dominion over vast stretches of territory. These nation states would act as managerial units of the land and people they encompassed. Their leaders, though local, were clients of the the Powers that Be, and in some cases, connected by blood to the European ruling elite. In essence, modern day nation-states that succeeded European colonies were intended to be a stepping-stone for the future establishment of the New World Order.

Gerard Encausse (Papus), an occultist, seemed to have foreknowledge of the dialectical World Wars being engineered for the future Soviet Union by "[...] sinister forces in Berlin."[47] Dr. Badmaev, an occultist connected to Blavatsky, would reiterate that Russia had far greater goals in the East. He had connections with the Tibetan Llamas and he used his connections to secure the support of Mongolian tribes during the Russo-Japanese war. George Gurdjieff was a British spy in Central Asia. Dr. Badmaev may have been referring to Gurdjieff when he would write to Tsar Nicholas II that he was training two disciples for future activities in Peking and Petersburg.[48] In this twilight era preceding the World Wars, shadowy efforts were underfoot for the creation of a Greater Russia, or the Soviet Union.

---

[47] Sabeheddin, Mehmet. The Secret of Eurasia – The key to Hidden History and World Events. The article appeared in New Dawn No. 68 (September-October 2001), http://www.newdawnmagazine.com <http://www.geocities.com/integral_tradition/key.html> Accessed 12th May 2003.

[48] Sabeheddin, Mehmet. The Secret of Eurasia – The key to Hidden History and World Events. The article appeared in New Dawn No. 68 (September-October 2001), http://www.newdawnmagazine.com <http://www.geocities.com/integral_tradition/key.html> Accessed 12th May 2003.

It is no coincidence that Helena Blavatsky's Theosophical Society would be headquartered in India and would play a major role in overcoming British influence (in favor of future Russian influence). When Lenin was awaiting transfer to Russia in a sealed train, he outlined some terms and conditions for the German Foreign Ministry, which arranged his transfer. The German government wanted to use Lenin to displace the existing power structure in Russia, while Lenin wanted to establish Communism. To quote Sutton,

> A subsequent document outlined the terms demanded by Lenin, of which the most interesting was point number seven, which allowed "Russian troops to move into India"; this suggested that Lenin intended to continue the tsarist expansionist program.[49]

As such, the emergence of the Soviet Union was more akin to the revitalization and facelift of a medieval Illuminati mission, rather than the emergence of a New Order.

Collusion with Revolutionaries

The Tsarist regime was deliberately lenient of revolutionary activity. The assassination of Tsar Alexander II by nihilists could not have been conducted without official collusion. Many members of the Russian nobility were working directly and indirectly with the Powers that Be in preparation for revolution. The future course of events in this region was predetermined. Examples of some nobles who worked openly for revolution were the likes of Prince Peter Krotompkin, a Russian noble. At a time when revolutionary sentiment was brewing, the regime forced expensive urban industrialization, creating the essential ingredients for revolution: industrial workers, conditions of economic disparity and urban ghettoes. This was a necessary step, since Russian peasants and their agrarian economy were incapable of fomenting revolution. During conditions of turmoil, a priest named Father Gapon, lead Russian people into massive protest march to the Tsar's palace, where they were fired on. The entire incident was staged to foment disaffection, and was carried out with the cooperation of the Russian nobility.

---

[49] Z. A. B. Zeman, Germany and the Revolution in Russia, 1915-1918. Documents from the Archives of the German Foreign Ministry (London: Oxford University Press, 1958) 6, doc. 6, reporting a conversation with the Estonian intermediary Keskula and p.92 no.3. Quoted in Antony C Sutton, Wall Street and the Bolshevik Revolution (Buccaneer Books, 1993). Chapter Three of the Online edition. <http://reformed-theology.org/html/books/bolshevik_revolution/chapter_03.htm> Accessed 25/10/06.

A Farewell Farce

The actions of the last Tsar Nicholas II can be interpreted as collusion with the Powers that Be in fomenting the revolution. Did Nicholas II collaborate in fomenting the revolution as a part of his commitment to the larger aims of the powers his family represented? He was assured of safe exit for his family and wealth. The Tsar was a relatively small player in this conspiracy. And it is not unusual for small players of the Powers that Be to step aside and abandon their prerogatives during such important undertakings. Instead of staying in the capital where the clouds of revolution were gathering, Nicholas II headed to the border to command his army. Even when it became clear that the revolutionaries had gained the upper hand, Nicholas was pathetically reluctant to give the *Duma* a progressive increase in power. Diplomat Nicholas De Basily prepared the abdication script in favor of Prince Aleksei whose medical condition (hemophilia) had made him an adored figure among loyalists. But De Basily was shocked when he found the script altered in favor of Nicholas's brother Michael.[50] When Michael ascended, he surrendered all power to the *Duma*. De Basily further recounts how Nicholas II "[...] accepted fate without the least revolt, the least show of anger or ill humor."[51] Or had the Tsar colluded? Did Nicholas II transfer a large quantity of his wealth to Chase Bank of New York[52] in foreknowledge of turbulent times?

After Nicholas II abdicated to the advantage of the revolutionaries, a Provisional Government was set up to enable Bolshevik transition. It derived its name from the very fact that it was meant to function temporarily, until the Bolsheviks arrived and consolidated. As Antony Sutton notes, "Provisional" was the very name this government went by

---

[50] "Nicholas De Basily recounts the abdication of Nicholas 2,1917," Major Problems in the History of Imperial Russia. Edited by James Cracraft (D.C Heath and Co, 1994) 655.

[51] Major Problems, 658

[52] Sherman H. Skolnick, The Overthrow of the American Republic Part 54. Archive available at <http://www.rense.com/general52/over54.htm> Accessed May 12th 2003.

when it started operating.[53] It consisted of many of the former Elite and Freemasons.

Historian Edgar Lucille[54] is of the opinion that the Romanov family was never assassinated and quotes a 1920 newspaper article, which stated that out of the 10,000 inhabitants of Ekaterinburg, no one saw the murder or burial of the royal family. He further describes the room where the murder allegedly took place and points out that it could hardly accommodate 6 people; yet by official accounts, 34 people including the Romanovs were present. Researcher Sherman Skolnick managed to obtain a 1970 Chicago Tribune article[55] claiming that Emperor William II of Germany (cousin of the Romanovs) had included a secret clause in the Brest-Litovsk treaty that no harm was to come to the Romanov family, and that they were taken to Odessa where they boarded an Allied ship.[56] Recent DNA analysis conducted by Alec Knight, a senior researcher at Stanford debunks the earlier DNA analysis which the Russian government used to validate the official story. According to his team, the bones found were too badly decomposed to obtain DNA and "The handling of the samples throughout the investigation has been characterized as 'rude violations of archaeological and forensic norms [...]"[57]. Knight's team also managed to obtain real Romanov DNA from a finger of Grand Duchess Elisabeth (sister of Empress Alexandra), which had been preserved by a monk. They discovered that it did not genetically tally with the DNA obtained by the earlier researchers.[58]

The conclusion of the abstract of their report is as follows:

---

53 Antony C Sutton, Wall Street and the Bolshevik Revolution (Buccaneer Books, 1993). Chapter Two of Online edition. <http://reformed-theology.org/html/books/bolshevik_revolution/chapter_02.htm > Accessed 25/10/06.

54 In a TV interview with researcher Sherman Skolnick on his TV program 'Broadsides,' a segment of which has been put online. It must be noted that Mr. Edgar is only limited to correcting a fallacy of history. <http://www.skolnickstv.com/video/russian.ram> Web page as of 16/03/04. The program "Broadsides" aired on Chicago Public Access Cable TV on Channel 21. I have not been able to ascertain the episode number.

55 UPI, "US Aided Rescue of Czar Nicholas, British hint," The Chicago Tribune December 14th 1970. An archive copy can be found here: <http://www.shout.net/~bigred/Tsar.htm> Accessed 12th may 2003

56 Sherman Skolnick, Great Secrets of the 20th Century Part 1. Web page as of 16/03/04 <http://www.skolnicksreport.com/great_secrets.html>

57 A. Knight, L.A Zhivotovsky, ,D.H. Kass, D.E. Litwin, L.D. Green, P.S. White, J.L Mountain, "Molecular, forensic and haplotypic inconsistencies regarding the Ekaterinburg remains," Annals of Human Biology 31.2 (2004) 130.

58 A. Knight et all, 129.

> Considering molecular and forensic inconsistencies, the identity of the Ekaterinburg remains has not been established. Our mtDNA haplotype results for Elisabeth provide yet another line of conflicting evidence regarding the identity of the Ekaterinburg remains.[59]

The report also gives a very brief history of the remains at Ekaterinburg. One can reasonably judge that the circumstances of the last days of the Romanovs were indeed contrary to official accounts:

> In 1918 the Family of Nicholas II, last Emperor of Russia, disappeared, presumably murdered by the Urals Reds. Shortly thereafter the White government appointed investigator, Judge N. Sokolov, concluded that The Family had been shot in Ekaterinburg, Russia, and that their bodies had been chopped into pieces, burned to shards of bone, and destroyed by soaking in sulphuric acid (Sokolov 1925, O'Conor 1971). There are many remains buried in shallow, unmarked mass graves near Ekaterinburg, victims of the Russian Civil War (Summers and Mangold 1976).One such grave, assumed to contain remains of The Family, was claimed to be discovered and opened in 1991 (Gill et al. 1994). The case has been characterized by extreme irregularities at every level (e.g. Massie 1995, Zhivotovsky 1999,McNeal 2001). Activities at the burial site and with the remains are no exception. Crucial evidence has been proven fraudulent. There is evidence that the 'Yurovsky Note', detailing the location of the grave and thereby providing the means for the 'discovery', was forged (Buranov 1994). The grave was of unknown age and had been opened several times prior to its official 'discovery' (Zhivotovsky 1999). The two 'discoverers' of the grave were described in Gill et al. (1994) as 'amateur historians' when in fact at least one was an agent of the Internal Minister of the USSR. They had opened the site in 1979 and removed several skulls and other bones and then added skulls and bones about a year later (Zhivotovsky 1999). There are also indications that the grave had been opened by the State Security services in 1946 (Koltypin-Wallovskoy et al. 1998). The purported site of the murder, the Ipatiev house in Ekaterinburg, was levelled and entirely destroyed in 1977 on the insistence of KGB Chairman Yuri Andropov and under the direction of Boris Yeltsin, at that time the First Secretary of the Sveldlovsk (Ekaterinburg) district branch of the USSR Communist Party (Massie 1995, McNeal 2001).[60]
>
> [Please obtain the original article for references within this quote]

[59] A. Knight et all, 129.

[60] A. Knight et all, 129-130.

Another recent book by Shay McNeal has reached similar conclusions.[61] The Romanovs and the Illuminati component of Russian nobility were secretly relocated to America and Western Europe. Great effort has been made by the mainstream media to "debunk" any such claims. For example movies were made on the establishment version of the last days of the Romanovs to silence rumors of their escape.

The "White Russians"

A flag of the White Army's armored train bears an Ancient Egyptian winged disc, a symbol used by the Powers that Be in many present day corporate logos. This flag can be presently found in the Moscow Red Army Museum.

After the Romanovs abdicated, White Russians, or loyalist troops lead by the likes of Anton Denikin fought against the revolutionaries. But as one can suppose, such movements were also compromised by Cabal operatives, who systematically betrayed them. In effect, the White Russian movement was nothing more than a dialectical process for larger goals of the Powers that Be. Later, the Nazis used Croats and Belorussians to carry out some of their genocide policies. White Russians were also reorganised in Yugoslavia during World War II. The idea was to use such movements as dialectical adversaries to the Soviet Union. They would be able to round up all armed opposition to the Soviet Union and betray them. Later, the leadership of the White Russians was evacuated when the movement collapsed. To quote, "Essentially every White Russian War Criminal from W.W. II that survived the war was placed on one NATO payroll or another by the Illuminati. The White Russian Nazis were settled in the NY-NJ area, especially in South River, NJ. One of the worst was Stankievich who ended up living in Richmond Hills and working for the CIA. He got a job working for Radio Liberty in NY."[62] Another was made head of a New York County Medical Society![63] This clearly proves entire sections

---

[61] Shay McNeal, The Secret Plot to Save the Tsar: The Truth Behind the Romanov Mystery (William Morrow, 2002). Also see Robert K. Massie, The Romanovs – The Final Chapter (Random House, 1995)

[62] Fritz Springmeier, The Illuminati formula used to create an undetectable total mind controlled slave (Web edition) p.411. There are several editions available online.

[63] Fritz Springmeier, The Illuminati formula used to create an undetectable total mind controlled slave (Web edition) . p.411

of the White troops were working for the Powers that Be, as was the former Russian nobility. Between 1948 and 1950 over 200 Byelorussian Nazis and their families were brought into New Jersey.[64]

The Subject Population

The preceding sections discussed Russian rulers. This section is devoted to the Russian subject population at the time of the later Romanovs. It is important to note that their original Asiatic culture and heritage had been mangled, vandalized and decimated by the early Tsars. But they were still responsible for allowing such a catatstrophe to happen. Russians are often portrayed as victims of the Revolution. This cannot be further from the truth. It is true that the Powers that Be, following the Bolshevik Revolution, systematically destroyed certain sections of Russian society, such as the Orthodox Christians. Other Russian groups such as the kulaks were also destroyed because they were obstacles to Sovietization. But the mainstream Russian population was more or less apathetic; as they were to the various tyrants the Romanovs had produced. And they were not the chief victims of Communism as often portrayed. Large sections of the population were collaborators, and it was largely non-Russians who suffered the wrath of the Soviet Union.

Going back to earlier times, Russia was ruled by the worst of European Royalty. Russians were supposedly Christian. But their Tsar, Peter the Great, openly ridiculed their Church and tried to supplant German culture as opposed to Russian culture. His "reforms" set aside large communities of unmarried men (soldiers, sailors, officials) without their family moorings. This lead to the emergence of full-scale prostitution.[65] Yet, there was rarely a whimper of dissent. Later we see the same public indifference towards Catherine the Great (of horse sex fame) and her "Potemkin villages." These were prosperous appearing facades of towns, which were propped up along the route of the Empress by one of her ministers named Potemkin. Not surprisingly, Soviet Russia could be characterized as a giant Potemkin village.

---

[64] Mae Brussells, "The Nazi Connection to the Dallas JFK murder," The Rebel January 1984: ?? An archived copy is available at: <http://www.maebrussell.com/Mae Brussell Articles/Nazi Connection to JFK Assass.html> Web page as of 16/03/04

[65] Pravda.ru, "Three Centuries of Russian Prostitution," Pravda 30th April 2002 <http://english.pravda.ru/fun/2002/04/30/28157.html> Accessed 14/12/06.

This indifference is not the product of servile loyalty. It is a tendency to exchange personal freedom, personal authority and firearms for any promise of inducements and personal security; regardless of which bully offers the same. For example, the only major rebellion the Tsars ever faced was the Pugachev revolt. Pugachev was of Cossack Asiatic origin, rather than Russian. Variants of this particular Turkic stock formed great dynasties in the Islamic world. But those that became part of Christian Russia degenerated into bands of Tsarist mercenaries. And when Pugachev did revolt, he did not do so in the name of the people or some ideal, but in the name of the king. In other words, the greatest instance of social unrest in eighteenth century Russia was a case of people following a loyalist to the monarchy (rather than opposing the monarchy). Again, Pugachev was not in favor of a "people's republic" or an alternate King. He instead advocated freedom from the oppressive nobility, rather than the monarchy which spawned such "nobility." Not surprisingly, Pugachev's failure was the result of him being betrayed to the Imperial police by Russian peasants.

Prerogatives of the politically toothless Orthodox Church were mercilessly attacked and usurped. Yet the Christian masses never seemed to convey any notable indignation. In the Russian context, religion, ethnicity and culture are rarely invoked in struggles against tyranny. Instead we see culture, religion, ethnicity, racism and xenophobia being used to justify how Russians were more deserving for access to the state's pig trough. Such parasitism would later become the foundation of the Soviet state.

Serfdom, a vestige of the feudal age, was rampant in Russia. It would be late in 1861 when it would be abolished on an official level, long after Western Europe.

English historian Donald Mackenzie Wallace[66] saw the Tsarist agricultural peasant commune (the *Mir*) as an economic oligarchy rather than being at the suffering end of Tsarist despotism. He pointed out how collectors of oppressive taxes from the *Mir* were never attacked or avoided. Even though the geographical vastness of Russia had the potential of a Wild West for freebooters and frontiersmen. Yet, we see the near absence of separatism among the Russian people.

---

[66] "Donald Mackenzie Wallace Explains the Mir and the Zemstvo, 1877". Major Problems in the History of Imperial Russia Edited by James Cracraft. (D.C Heath and Co, 1994) 346, 351.

Realizing that the Russian people were too rudimentary, even for a farcical Soviet revolution, the Powers that Be decided that it was necessary to change the social structure. They tried to "reform" the communes, creating a more class-oriented structure as a precursor to Marxist revolution. But it was clear that Russian peasants were not interested in activity which threatened their immediate prospects and exposed them to personal risk.

Therefore, the Romanovs forced industrialization from the top. This created displaced populations, urban ghettoes and starving workers necessary as prerequisites for a Marxist revolution. But even after the revolution, Russian people remained just as accommodating to tyranny as they were under the Romanovs. Populations that are accommodating to tyranny become assets for the Powers That Be, and can be used for extending tyranny into other regions. The Criminal Elite had long before assessed Russia as an ideal location to stage wars and revolutions to advance their New World Order.

The Russian masses also identified with the state's efforts to promote the dysfunctional and parasitic socio-political structure among neighboring free populations. For example, a document by Tsarist Prime Minister Gorchakov refers to the nomadic non-Russian people as "[...] half-savage nomad populations possessing no fixed social organization [...]" who had to be reduced to submission.[67] Even though unlike most Russians, Asiatic populations resisted attempts at Tsarist tampering with their social structure.

Once the revolution was staged and the Soviet Union was established, the Criminal Elite expected the Russian people to revert back to their role as their agents of influence, now headquartered in Moscow instead of St. Petersburg. Therefore, long before the revolution, railroads were built into Eastern and Central Asia. And Russian populations were transplanted among the locals. These populations were expected to govern the locals as Cabal operatives on behalf of Moscow (after the revolution). To strengthen their position, the Tsars and later the Communists would forcibly Russify the local populations. Local populations who succumbed to Russification (such as the Ukrainians) would end up being devastated by the Russian ruling Elite transplanted among them. But local populations such as the Central Asians, who stuck

---

67 "The Gorchakov Circular on Russia's Mission in Central Asia, 1864". Major Problems in the History of Imperial Russia Edited by James Cracraft.(D.C Heath and Co, 1994) 410.

to their culture and resisted Russification managed to retain a degree of their independence.

Dysfunction

There are some very visible signs of dysfunction and parasitism in this region, owing to heavy and sustained control of the Criminal Elite. The Illuminati displays a tendency to mould and carve subject societies on its own terms. The Illuminati Safavids of Iran managed to permanently contort Iranian society and tampered with the Islamic religion within a few centuries. Russia has been subjected to Illuminati rule right from its earliest origins. And this has fostered the creation of social malaises beneficial to higher powers. These unique dysfunctions were further developed under Soviet rule. And since Soviet rule extended over many non-Russian people, these dysfunctions are clearly visible among non-Russian populations as well, such as Uzbeks, Latvians etc.

Domestic Spying and Surveillance

Domestic spying was not a creation of the Soviet regime, though it reached its crescendo under the Soviets. It was a part and parcel of Russian urban culture long before the revolution. To quote Congressman Henry J. Hyde,

> Russia's notoriety for eavesdropping and espionage stretches back even to the czars. James Buchanan, U.S. minister in St. Petersburg during 1832-33 and later U.S. President, recounted that 'we are continually surrounded by spies both of high and low degree. You can scarcely hire a servant who is not a secret agent of the police.'
>
> An 1850-53 successor, Neill S. Brown, reconfirmed that 'the opinion prevails that ministers are constantly subjected to a system of espionage, and that even their servants are made to disclose what passed in their households, their conversations, associations, etc.' Otto von Bismarck, who represented Prussia from 1859 to 1862, stated 'it was especially difficult to keep a cypher secure at St. Petersburg, because all the embassies were of necessity obliged to employ Russian servants and subordinates in their households, and it was easy for Russian police to procure agents among these.' The tradition intensified and became more sophisticated under the Bolsheviks and their successors. The wife of the Italian ambassador in Moscow during 1927-30 said: 'Spying on the part of the authorities was so common as not even to be thought of as spying.'[68]

---

[68] Henry J. Hyde, "A Brief History of Russian Spying," Spybusters.com <http://www.spybusters.com/Great_Seal_Bug.html> Accessed June 4th 2006.

Outrageous restrictions on the movement of people and goods within domestic borders

The outrageous internal passport system in Russia was originally introduced by the Romanovs around 1910. Joseph Stalin reinstated it in 1932. This system helped chain subject populations to their designated areas. Peasants were prevented from migration.

In present day Russia, such outrageous restrictions are still in place, keeping people chained to their administrative areas like cattle. Internal passports are required and free movement of goods is still a rarity. Such measures result in the flourishing of illegal activity, but nevertheless allow the continued maintenance of official control over all affairs. Though prostitution is officially outlawed, the internal passport system prevents migrant females from obtaining legitimate work. And instead, criminal gangs with "valid documentation" smuggle in female recruits for the underground prostitution market. According to an official source, 130,000-150,000 women and children were in prostitution in Moscow alone.[69] According to the Angel Coalition, more than 500,000 women from the former Soviet Union have been trafficked to more than 50 countries in the past 10 years.[70]

The restrictions through which certain people and groups are chained like cattle bear parallels with the caste system of 19th century India. But any such parallels with Asiatic people are considered seriously offensive.

Escapism

Excessive drinking as a form of self-indulgent escapism is a distinguishing character of the former Soviet Union. The average person drinks between 6 and 12 gallons of vodka a year, more spirits than any other nation.[71] More fatal forms of escapism, such as suicide, are also common.

Ringing in the old

---

[69] Donna M. Hughes, "Nyet to Trafficking- Russians show political will to fight prostitution," June 18th 2003 National Review Online <http://www.nationalreview.com/comment/comment-hughes061803.asp> Accessed 12/12/06.

[70] Kester Kenn Klomegah, "Poverty Drives Russian Women into Prostitution Abroad," The Dawn Internet edition August 31st 2005 <http://www.dawn.com/2005/08/31/int10.htm> Accessed 12/12/06.

[71] History Channel, Organized Crime-Russia. Aired Oct. 20th 2006.

The continuity of old corruption, such as a parasitic bureaucracy remains a defining legacy of the Soviet Union. And the Powers that Be retain their hold over Russia through it. Many people are still completely devoid of skills of industry related to free enterprise, such as the ability to negotiate and sign contracts. Despite the "opening up" of Russia for global investors, many foreign investors are recoiling. For example, Paul Tatum, a US hotel developer refused to pay "protection money" and was gunned down in front of his two bodyguards. Business texts advise foreign investors to prefer the eastern Pacific Coast of Russia instead of European Russia.[72] The criminal legacy of traditional Russian centers of power in European Russia is clearly reflected in this advice. Around 2000, the economy of the entire of Russia was smaller than South Korea.[73]

Mafias and high-tech fraud

The flourishing success of mafias and organized crime throughout the former Soviet Union is by the deliberate design of The Powers That Be. In some cases, the Mafiosi have literally replaced the Communist party. Russian crime syndicates populate the high end of the criminal spectrum, such as organized ATM fraud, launching extortionist denial of service attacks on corporate websites, engineering of computer viruses, email spamming and phishing. Organized Crime from these areas has also extended into North America and Western Europe with the fall of the iron curtain. Brighton Beach, the Southern tip of Brooklyn, has become a nerve center for Russian organized crime. This area started being flocked by Russians since the late 1970s when Russian Jews were allowed to leave the Soviet Union.[74]

In addition to crime, regular business happens to be equally seedy in Russia. An estimated 80 per cent of businesses pay protection money, and the mob controls most of the banks.[75] In a survey, more than 800 business experts were asked to identify countries where the practice of giving "gifts" in exchange for getting business from suppliers and customers, was most flagrant. Russia along with China emerged at the

---

[72] Helen Deresky, International Management –Managing Across Borders and Cultures 5th ed. (New Jersey: Pearson-Prentice Hall, 2004), 265.
[73] Bruce Cumings, "The American Century and the Third World," Michael J. Hogan ed., The Ambiguous Legacy - U.S. Foreign Relations in the "American Century." (Cambridge: Cambridge University Press, 1999) 297.
[74] History Channel, Organized Crime-Russia. Aired Oct. 20th 2006.
[75] History Channel, Organized Crime-Russia. Aired Oct. 20th 2006.

top of the list.[76] Gangland murders and bombings are described as business disputes by the Russian press, and are ignored by citizens.[77]

Everyone is a party man

The unquestioning support of state sponsored military intervention, military build-up, development of weapons of mass destruction, military testing on civilian population, combined with an antiwar culture of negligible influence, ensures that Russia remains a menace to all of its unlucky neighbors. The Russian army is notorious for a culture of parasitism and ragging of new recruits. Non-Russian recruits are subjected to racial abuse. The result of this institutionalized parasitism is that the Criminal Elite in the World Wars, and later in Afghanistan, and still later in Yeltsin's Chechnya, mercilessly used Russian troops as gun fodder. In the Second World War, more than 11,285,000 Soviets were sacrificed on the Eastern front.

Were these alarming casualties a result of faith in the Soviet cause or a lack of options on behalf of the participants? The following points can be gleaned from the Russian past:

- The rulers of Russia have little regard for human life, including the lives of their subject population.
- The rulers of Russia have engaged in mammoth undertakings, such as the Russo-Turkish wars, compensating for tactical effectiveness by herding huge numbers of soldiers into war.
- Soviet casualties in the Second World War appear more logical when viewed as a continuum of this phenomenon.

As we are aware, the people of these regions were conditioned to being blindly herded by those who ran the State, since the time of the Tsars. Questioning orders or rebellion is almost unheard of. Russians herded into World War II would rather take a chance at risking their life killing enemy soldiers rather than consider the consequences of refusal. Their motivation was not usually the noble sentiments of fighting the Nazis or establishing the rule of the Proletariat, as often portrayed. Soviet leadership and Soviet ideology was as totalitarian as Nazism, and probably even worse, when we consider the body count. By the beginning of World War II, Stalin's regime had murdered at least 30

---

[76] Barbara Crosette, "Russia and China Called Top Business Bribers," New York Times on the Web (May 17th 2002). Also see transparency.org.
[77] History Channel, Organized Crime-Russia. Aired Oct. 20th 2006.

million people.[78] Overall, he had murdered three times more people than Hitler.[79]

Losses in the Second World War

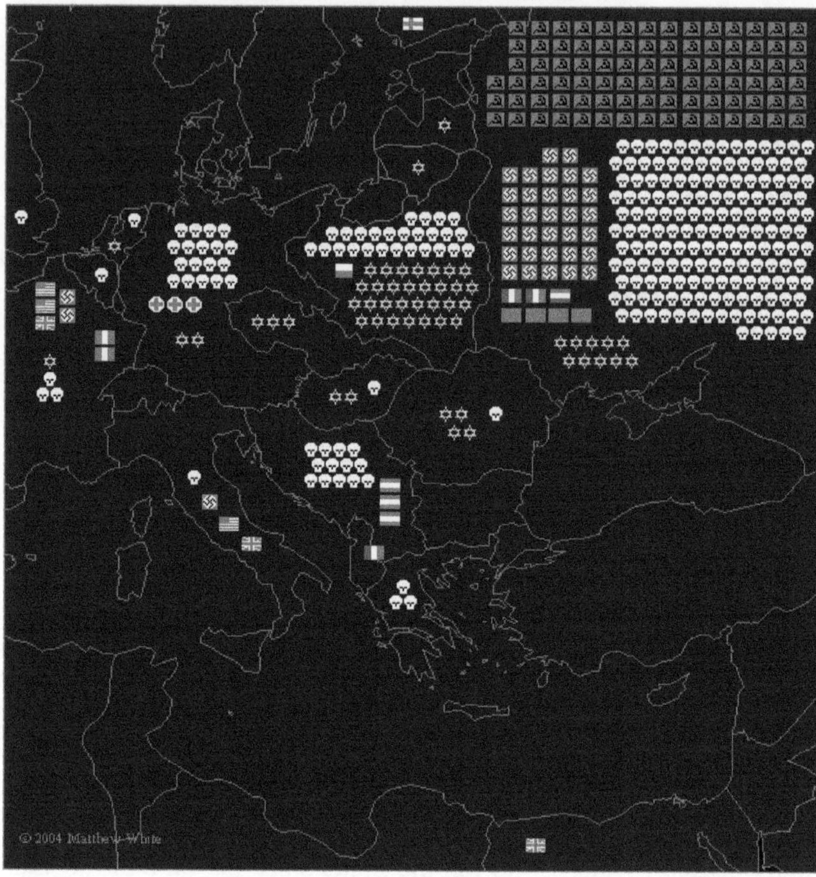

Each symbol indicates 100,000 dead in the respective theatre of operation. The skulls represent civilian casualties; the Stars of David represent Jewish Holocaust victims, while the flags represent military casualties.

Note that the author of this map disavows any affiliation or concurrence with the author of this book or the views taken in this book or on this page. However, the author granted permission for reproduction with the above caveat.

---

[78] Eric Margolis, "The 20th Century's Worst Crime Goes Unpunished," The Toronto Sun November 16th 2003. Also published on ericmargolis.com <http://www.ericmargolis.com/archives/2003/11/the_20th_centur.php> Accessed 13/12/06

[79] Eric Margolis, "The 20th Century's Worst Crime."

When the Soviets finally flew their banner over the Reichstag, their role as victorious liberators was propagandized by The Powers That Be. As multitudes of present day neo-Nazi groups in Russia demonstrate, the subject population would have been equally willing to play the role of fascists if they had been ordered to do so.

It is clear that the enormous Soviet war casualties were the result of unmotivated, ill-equipped and inexperienced youth being herded into the war. But since there was no culture of questioning orders, the troops exhausted themselves as gun fodder. These very people, who would demonstrate "sacrifice" when herded against the Nazis, would later display extreme docility versus the Soviet state. During the German invasion of the Second World War, Soviet forces used inhumane tactics such as the scorched earth policy of decimating towns and cities rather than losing them to the enemy. There are previous parallels to this event. When Napoleon stole the French Revolution from the Illuminati, all European states ganged up against him. Russia was the most prominent among these states. Napoleon was lured into Russia where the Tsar would devastate cities and towns rather than surrender them. In this war too, Russian conscripts trudged along, only to be used as gun fodder. They never considered what could be comparatively so worse about French occupation.

Restrictions on private gun ownership

Highly regulated public gun ownership symbolizes the plight of a citizenry who have failed to defend themselves. Firearms and weapons are concentrated exclusively in the hands of the state and crime syndicates. These are exactly the conditions that made the genocides of the Soviet era possible. After the fall of the iron curtain, firearms have proliferated through illegal channels. But on an official level, gun ownership is still discouraged.

More Weapons for the Elite

Russia continues the development of biological weapons for the Criminal Elite. Novosibirsk, the scientific capital of Siberia has 50 research facilities and 13 full universities, while its population is only 2.5 million.[80] The Soviet State Center of Virology and Biotechnology,

---

[80] Michael Davidson and Michael Ruppert, "A Career in microbiology can be harmful to your health," Fromthewildreness.com <http://www.fromthewilderness.com/free/ww3/02_14_02_microbio.html> Accessed August 31st 2006.

known as Vector, is now a leading recipient of aid in an American program.[81] A controversial scientist who was linked to the initial outbreak of AIDS in the Congo worked and experimented in the Soviet Union.[82] One can imagine how the entire Soviet Union and its population could have served as a giant laboratory for the Criminal Elite. Even if human introduced contagions became epidemics, everything could be covered up.

The subject population has been adequately brainwashed into viewing technology as a redeeming factor, even if it is developed for destructive ends and has no public utility. This is especially true in the case of the Russian Space program

Time to move on!

The dearth of attempts to seek reconciliation with the horrors of the past only reflects a past which is still alive. Many Russian buildings still sport Soviet emblems. Soviet trinkets and cornucopia is even sold at former gulags. Compare that to the prospect of Nazi memorabilia being sold at Auschwitz. For many Russians who had no issues with genocides, the past was even supposed to be good, since they got their food coupons and daily rations on an uninterrupted basis.

The very fact that people can be made to take ownership, and even be defensive of all the wars, atrocities and genocides conducted in their name is disturbing, and is a psychological phenomenon that requires more detailed study.

Back off, that's *our* porridge!

Periodic and organized outbursts of racism and street riots are still witnessed against the luckless non-Russians who live in Russian metropolises. These race riots are meant to be a statement of ethnic Russian privilege to the State's pig trough. It is important to note that confrontations with state authority, on the other hand, are sparse and even non-existent. In some newly "independent" former Soviet republics, Russians still enjoy special parasite privileges over the locals. Uzbekistan can be considered a case point. Russian forces stationed in Uzbekistan follow directions from Moscow and reserve the right to

---

[81] Free Press International 24/01/05, "Author Theorizes Forty biologists killed before unleashing ultimate epidemic," Free Press International <http://freepress2005.blogspot.com/2005/01/author-theorizes-40-microbiologists.html> Accessed August 31st 2006.

[82] See the CBC documentary 'Eyewitness: Origin of AIDS.'

intervene militarily when its interests, such as its Russian minorities are threatened (1995).[83] Uzbeks constitute only 10% of their national army while the Uzbek air-force is exclusively manned by Russians (1995).[84]

A note on present day Russia

The Soviet Union was imploded when it was time to reorganize the area on the basis of nation states for the upcoming "Clash of Civilizations." Russia was meant to play the role of a nationalist nation state with a reactionary ideology. Present Russian leaders are moving their country in that direction. Russia, along with China and Iran is expected to play a role antagonistic to the West in the upcoming clash of civilizations. And their conquered citizenry are expected to trudge along without complaint.

---

[83] Shaheen Ayubi. "Uzbekistan's Long Road to Democracy and Political Stability." Journal of South Asian and Middle Eastern Studies 18.3 (1995) 13.
[84] Ayubi, "Long Road to Democracy," 13.

Chapter Two
World War One

The First World War must be brought about in order to permit the Illuminati to overthrow the power of the Czars in Russia and of making that country a fortress of atheistic Communism. The divergences caused by the "agentur" (agents) of the Illuminati between the British and Germanic Empires will be used to foment this war. At the end of the war, Communism will be built and used in order to destroy the other governments and in order to weaken the religions.

-A quote attributed to Albert Pike, August 15th 1871[85]

Adolph Strakhov, "1870-1924 V. Ulianov (Lenin)," 1924.

[85] For a detailed discussion on this quote, see the introductory section "A note on the World War Quotes attributed to Albert Pike."

In order to create the preconditions for global revolution spearheaded by Russia, it was necessary to destroy and discredit existing systems. Though the Powers that Be were in a position to establish Bolshevism in Russia without a World War, such a sudden change would look like an obvious conspiracy rather than the 'natural course of history,' which the Powers that Be seek to imitate. The destruction of the then empires would pave the way for the creation of nation-states, which would play a dialectical role in advancing Soviet influence.

"Revolution" in Russia

World War I

World War I created the catastrophe necessary to break down existing institutions and the existing order in Russia.

Nicholas II plays his part

The Chapter on the Romanovs covers events in Russia up to the eve of the Revolution. Even when it became clear that the revolutionaries had gained the upper hand, Tsar Nicholas II was pathetically reluctant to give the *Duma* a progressive increase in power. Diplomat Nicholas De Basily prepared the abdication script in favor of Prince Aleksei whose medical condition had made him adorable among the masses. But De Basily was shocked when he found the script altered in favor of Nicholas's brother Michael, who completely surrendered all power to the *Duma*.[86] He further recounts how Nicholas II "[...] accepted fate without the least revolt, the least show of anger or ill humor."[87]

The Rakovsky Document

Outside intervention in the revolution can be detected by reading between the lines of history texts. However, a single document, which has been of the most critical importance to researchers in this area, is the complete transcript of the interrogation of captured Illuminati operative Christian Rakovsky alias Chaim Rakover (a Trotskyite, an early Bolshevik, and the former Soviet ambassador to France) by the Stalinist

---

[86] "Nicholas De Basily recounts the abdication of Nicholas 2,1917," Major Problems in the History of Imperial Russia Edited by James Cracraft.(D.C Heath and Co, 1994) 655

[87] Major Problems 658.

police.[88] Since Rakovsky knew he would be executed, he made a desperate attempt to save his life by spilling the beans on who were behind the Trotskyites and the revolution itself. At one point, he refers by name to the Illuminati but for the rest of the interview refers to them as 'they'. It is clear that Rakovsky was highly placed among 'them' Ambassador Davies was present at the trial of Rakovsky and flashed him a secret Masonic signal. A few days prior to the trial, the forces of Stalin received a radio message from a powerful station, which read "Amnesty or the Nazi danger will increase." It was encrypted in the cipher of Stalin's own embassy in London.

Rakovsky

The trial of the group that Raokovsky belonged to stretched from March 2nd to13th 1938. Rakovsky was tried along with many others suspected of being involved in a Trotskyite plot against Stalin (Stalin had fled to Norway by then). Rakovsky did testify before the Military Collegium of the Supreme Court of the U.S.S.R. To quote the proceedings,

> The trial is of Nikolai Ivanovich BUKARIN, Alexei Ivanovich RYKOV, Genrikh Grigorievich YAGODA, Nikolai Nikolayevich KRESTINSKY, **Khristian Georgievich RAKOVSKY**, Arkady Pavlovich ROSENGOLTZ, Vladimir Ivanovich IVANOV, Mikhail Alexandrovich CHERNOV, Grirori Fedorovich GRINKO, Isaac Abramovich ZELENSY, Sergei Alexeyevich BESSONOV, Akmal IKRAMOV, Faizulla HODJAYEV, Vasily Fomich SHARANGOVICH, Prokopy Timofeyevich ZUBAREV, Pavel Petrovich BULANOV, Lev Grigorievich LEVIN, Dmitrv Dmitrievich PLETNEV, Ignaty Nikolayevich AZAOV, Venvamin Adamovich MAXIMOV, and Pyotr Petrovich KRYUCHOV on charges of treason to the country, espionage, committing acts of diversion, terrorism, wrecking, undermining the military power of the U.S.S.R. and of provoking a military attack of foreign states upon the U.S.S.R., i.e., of crimes covered by Articles 581a, 587, 588, 588, 589 and 5811 of the Criminal Code of the R.S.F.S.R.

[88] The questioning of the accused Christian Georgievitch Rakovsky by Gavriil Gavriilovitch Kus'min on the 26th January, 1938. An archive of the interrogation can be found online < https://archive.org/details/RedSymphony> Web page as of 22/01/14

As in the interrogation, Rakovsky completely confessed his guilt in court, and made some even more astounding claims in a plea presented on March 2nd. To quote Rakovsky in page 759 of the proceedings

> I was an active member of the "block of Rights and Trotskyites." I committed the gravest crimes against the state. I am doubly a spy. In 1924 I established criminal connections with the British Intellience Service, and in 1934 I established criminal connections with the Japanese intelligence service. In 1927 I carried on negotiations with some of the Right capitalist circles in France, the object of these negotiations being in the long run also directed against the Soviet Union. In 1935 I took advantage of the fact that the French Minister Laval was on a visit in Moscow, accompanied by French journalists, in order to attempt in a conversation with one of them (I mentioned his name) to hinder, to disrupt, the Franco-Soviet rapprochement. Citizens Judges, I informed you about Trotsky's letter of July 1934, in which he wrote of the necessity of isolating Stalin internationally, that is to say, of strengthening, consolidating the capitalist encirclement around the Soviet Union. I belonged to the so-called "Fifth Column" of which the Procurator spoke yesterday, and I have deserved all those maledictions which are now sweeping from all corners of the Soviet land against us sitting here in the dock, maledictions of which the speech for the prosecution delivered by the Procurator, however severe and trenchant it was with regard to us, was perhaps but a weak reflection.

Rakovsky also made this claim:

> We were the vanguard of foreign aggression, of international fascism, and not only in the USSR but also in Spain, China, throughout the world." The summation of the "court" contains the statement, "There is not a single man in the world who brought so much sorrow and misfortune to people as Trotsky. He is the vilest agent of fascism....[89]

The trial of Rakovsky began on 12th March and at 5:30 the very day, Hitler ordered his armored divisions to enter Austria. Unlike most of his co-defendants, who were immediately executed, Rakovsky was sentenced to twenty years of hard labor. In 1941, he was at Oryol prison, southwest of Moscow. When the Nazis started moving towards Oryol,

---

89 Report of Court Proceedings in the Case of the Anti-Soviet "Bloc of Rightists and Trotskyites" Heard Before the Military Collegium of the Supreme Court of the USSR (Moscow: People's Commissariat of Justice of the USSR, 1938), p. 293. Antony C Sutton, Wall Street and the Bolshevik Revolution (Buccaneer Books, 1993). Chapter Two of Online edition.
<http://reformed-theology.org/html/books/bolshevik_revolution/chapter_02.htm > Accessed 25/10/06.

Rakovsky was reportedly shot outside the prison along with 150 political prisoners in what became known as the Medvedev Forest massacre. But according to another theory, Rakovsky escaped to France. Arthur Koestler's 1940 novel *Darkness at Noon* was inspired by victims of the Moscow Trials. According to George Orwell, his main character, the disillusioned Rubashov, may have been based on Rakovsky, or some of the other Old Bolsheviks on trial.[90]

The Rakovsky interrogation was done in 1938 by Stalin's seasoned interrogator Gavriil Kus'min (alias René Duval) in the presence of a sound technician and Dr. Landowsky. The interrogation was done in French, and was recorded by the technician. Dr. Landowsky had slipped drug pills into the glass of Rakovsky, and he was later tasked with translating the interrogation for Stalin (He secretly saved a carbon copy for himself). Dr. Landowsky was a Russianized Pole who had studied in France, and spoke fluent French. Given his knowledge of the effects of chemicals on the human body, he was forced to work at the chemical laboratory of the NKVD near Moscow. He kept notes of what he had seen and heard during prisoner interrogations inside hollow legs of his table. How he came to Petrograd or how he was killed is unknown. But several copybooks were found on his dead body in hut in Petrograd by a Spanish Communist volunteer in Russia during World War II. He returned with them to Spain and they were published by Editorial E.R.S.A. under the well-known publisher Senor Don Mauricio Carlavilla as the 40th Chapter of a book which appeared in Madrid in Spanish as *Sinfonia en Rojo Mayor*. This chapter was translated into English by historian George Knupffer in 1968.[91] Historian George Knupffer refers to it as "[…] one of the most important political documents of the 21st century […]"[92] The revelations in the document stand for themselves and do not require commentary. Neither will they be summarized or incorporated in this book. But they will be used to justify the independent conclusions reached by the author.[93]

---

90 George Orwell, "Arthur Koestler," 1946. <http://www.george-orwell.org/Arthur_Koestler/0.html> Retrieved 22/01/14.

91 Dr. J. Landowsky, RED SYMPHONY trans. George Knupffer (Palmdale: Christian Book Club of America, 2002).

92 The questioning of the accused Christian Georgievitch Rakovsky by Gavriil Gavriilovitch Kus'min on the 26th January, 1938. An archive of the interrogation can be found online < https://archive.org/details/RedSymphony> Web page as of 22/01/14

93 The author will indicate whenever a conclusion is borrowed from the Rakovsky document.

Soviet Communism

It is fair to assume that the Powers That Be were seeking neither socialism nor a parliamentary democracy, but only a complete Communist revolution in Russia. This can be ascertained from the process of historical development initiated by the Illuminati. From the split in the church, which legalized usury to Adam Smith's publication of "The Wealth of Nations" that summarized, that economies were best left to the "invisible hand" of the market forces.[94] By then, the "market forces" happened to be the bankers who had managed to gain control over private capital and industry. This was taken to a whole new level by Mayer Amschel who created the richest and most powerful banking dynasty in history, the house of Rothschild. Mayer Amschel Rothschild[95] was able to pull the purse strings of sovereign nations, pushing them into wars of his choice. For example, the various nations that ganged up against Napoleon were having their purse strings pulled by the House Rothschild.[96] Napoleon had betrayed the Illuminati by appropriating their secular revolution for himself, and he turned it into a religious-nationalist movement. Mayer Rothschild profited from this war by using his advance knowledge of Napoleon's defeat to manipulate the London Stock exchange.[97] This was also the era where European nations would embark upon colonization to increase the prospects of the forces behind private capital. By the time of his death in 1812, Mayer Rothschild instructed his five sons to set up camp in major European countries, and one son headed for America.

The logical sequel of such degree of financial oligarchy would be Soviet Communism, which would completely abolish competing private capital and enterprise in favor of monopoly capitalism by an omniscient agency known as the "state." Though there would be no opportunity for usury banking, the Soviet state gave the bankers what they craved most: unlimited control over the lives of individuals and their property. Instead of generating prosperity, the Soviet system specialized in confiscating

---

[94] The Date of Publication of "The Wealth of Nations" is 1776, which has significance to the Illuminati. The multi volume "Fall of the Roman Empire" was also published the same year.

[95] He later created the title Rothschild for himself (meaning Red Shield). No relation to the Red banner of the Communists has been proven.

[96] Fritz Springmeier, Bloodlines of the Illuminati (Spring Arbor distributors, 1998) 181. GlobalGrey PDF edition 2013 <http://www.globalgrey.co.uk/Pages/Books-Conspiracies/Bloodlines-Of-The-Illuminati.html> Web page as of 03/07/13.

[97] Fritz Springmeier, Bloodlines of the Illuminati (Spring Arbor distributors, 1998) 183. GlobalGrey PDF edition 2013 <http://www.globalgrey.co.uk/Pages/Books-Conspiracies/Bloodlines-Of-The-Illuminati.html> Web page as of 03/07/13.

prosperity. The connection between early Communist ideologues and the banker oligarchy are shadowy at best, such as statements made by Rakovsky. Further documentation is needed. But there were clear connections between the Bolsheviks and the Western industrial-banking elite located at 120 Broadway. For example, an American pro-Soviet journalist, John Reed, contributed regularly to the Metropolitan magazine. At that time, Harry Payne Whitney, a director of Guaranty Trust, owned this magazine.[98] In 1915, Tsarist authorities in Russia arrested Reed. Yet Reed managed to secure his release using his connections. When he arrived back in America, some of the literature he had brought back with him was seized. Upon this, he wrote a letter to William Franklin Sands, executive secretary of American International Corporation[99], requesting him to secure his release.[100] Sands wrote from his 120 Broadway office to Frank Polk, acting US Secretary of State, urging restraint towards Reed![101] On March 19th 1920, Reed was about to be executed in Finland due to his involvement with the Bolsheviks. Once again, Sands intervened to secure his release.[102]

Rakovsky describes with contentedness, how various spin-offs of Communism, be it Hitler's National Socialism or Stalin's National Communism were still materialist philosophies, and would eventually result in the synthesis of Communism. Which in turn, would be ultimately be inherited by the powers running the Soviet Union. In fact, Fascism was created with the sole purpose of being clashed against Communism for the triumph of the latter.

Alexander Kerensky

Another Internationalist operative within the Provisional Government itself was Alexander Kerensky, who being Prime minister of the Provisional Government and a 'Socialist Revolutionary,' allowed the

---

[98] Antony C Sutton, Wall Street and the Bolshevik Revolution (Buccaneer Books, 1993). Chapter Eight of Online edition. <http://reformed-theology.org/html/books/bolshevik_revolution/chapter_08.htm > Accessed 25/10/06.
[99] AIC was an investor in the United Fruit Company, which played a controversial role in several revolutions in South America.
[100] Antony C Sutton, Wall Street and the Bolshevik Revolution (Buccaneer Books, 1993). Chapter Eight of Online edition. <http://reformed-theology.org/html/books/bolshevik_revolution/chapter_08.htm > Accessed 25/10/06.
[101] U.S. State Dept. Decimal File, 360. D. II21.R/20/221/2, /R25 (John Reed). The letter was transferred by Mr. Polk to the State Department archives on May 2, 1935. Quoted in Sutton, Bolshevik Revolution Chapter Eight.
[102] U.S. State Dept. Decimal File, 360d.1121 R 25/72. Quoted in Sutton, Bolshevik Revolution Chapter Eight.

Bolshevik takeover[103]. It is interesting to note that even the socialist Kerensky would later launch an offensive on Ottoman Turkey, which was also the nemesis of the Internationalists. The new proto-socialist Kemalist Turkey was first recognized by Bolshevik Russia. The Bolsheviks even ceded territory to it in a 1921 treaty. Kemalist Turkey would collaborate with the Bolsheviks to devour the Armenian state. As Lenin would later reveal, Kerensky did deliberately conceal the secret Sykes-Picot agreement, in which the Ottoman Middle East was to be allocated to European powers, in particular, Russia.

The Bolsheviks

The Bolsheviks were the vanguard of European banking interests. The case of Leon Trotsky is most relevant. Leon Trotsky was in possession of an American passport, granted to him by Woodrow Wilson.[104] Trotsky left New York for a rendezvous with Lenin in Switzerland. He left New York aboard the S.S. *Kristianiafjord* on March 26, 1917.[105] On 3rd April 1917, the ship carrying him and his fellow Bolshevik recruits was grounded when it docked at Halifax.[106] Trotsky and his associates were detained at a camp for political prisoners in Amherst (Nova Scotia), because they were suspected of seeking to foment disturbance in Russia, as German agents. In fact, it was known that Trotsky was in possession of $10,000 sourced from Germany.[107] But Canadian authorities were pressed into letting the Trotsky party leave. According to Canadian Lieutenant Colonel John Bayne MacLean, Washington pressed for the release of Trotsky on account of his American passport.[108] Sutton comments on the two influential individuals who sought Trotsky's release, "There was little in the career of either Deputy Postmaster

---

[103] Confirmed by the Rakovsky interrogation. Kerensky played a part in the initial Bolshevik takeover. Historians Melgunov and Daniels believe the October Revolution was not inevitable. Ronald Grigor Suny, Towards a Social history of the October Revolution. The structure of Soviet History - essays and documents (Oxford University Press, 2003) 12.

[104] Antony C Sutton, Wall Street and the Bolshevik Revolution (Buccaneer Books, 1993). Chapter Two of Online edition. <http://reformed-theology.org/html/books/bolshevik_revolution/chapter_02.htm > Accessed 25/10/06.

[105] Sutton, Bolshevik Revolution Chapter Two

[106] Sutton, Bolshevik Revolution Chapter Two

[107] Sutton, Bolshevik Revolution Chapter Two. Also see Michael Futrell, *Northern Underground* (London: Faber and Faber, 1963); Stefan Possony, Lenin: The Compulsive Revolutionary (London: George Allen & Unwin, 1966); and George Katkov, "German Foreign Office Documents on Financial Support to the Bolsheviks in 1917," International Affairs 32 (Royal Institute of International Affairs, 1956).

[108] Quoting Macleans, June 1919, pp. 66a-666. Sutton, Bolshevik Revolution Chapter Two

General Coulter or Major General Gwatkin that would explain an urge to release the Menshevik Leon Trotsky."[109] Later when the Bolshevik revolution erupted, the Menshevik Iuli Martov would write, "[...] the Bolsheviks rely on a hired gendarmerie."[110] Who were Trotsky's German benefactors?

Wall Street joins the Revolution

Vladimir Lenin did not have an Elite bloodline. He was merely a member of a Masonic lodge in Switzerland, which was secretly working for world revolution.[111] However, he was allowed to cheerlead the revolution after his Illuminati friend, Kaiser Wilhelm recognised his abilities. But real authority was to be held by Trotsky.

Lenin's 'friends' in the German government organised his transit to Russia in the famed sealed train. Chancellor Theobald von Bethmann-Hollweg approved this support. He was a descendant of the Frankfurt based Bethmann banking family.[112] Lenin was neither stopped at the Russian border.

In August 1917, the American Red Cross made a curious mission to Russia. Unlike normal Red Cross missions, this mission consisted of a disproportionately large number of American bankers and corporate directors.[113] One member of this mission, William Boyce Thompson, director of the Federal Reserve Bank of New York, gave the Kerensky government $2 million, for propaganda to be used for continued war against Germany.[114] Later, he would give the Bolsheviks $1 million to combat pan-German propaganda.[115] Thompson would be in London on

---

[109] Sutton, Bolshevik Revolution Chapter Two

[110] Iuli Martov. "Iuli Martov's letter to A.N Stein June 16th 1918," The Structure of Soviet History - essays and documents (Oxford University Press, 2003)77.

[111] Jose Maria Cardinal Caro Y. Rodriguez, The Mystery of Freemasonry Unveiled – With a reprint of Pope Leo XIIIth Encyclical Humanum Genus 2nd edition (Imprimatur, Jose Maria Cardinal Caro Y. Rodriguez, Cardinal Archbishop of Santiago, Chile, 1920s) 87.

[112] Antony C Sutton, Wall Street and the Bolshevik Revolution (Buccaneer Books, 1993). Chapter Three of Online edition. <http://reformed-theology.org/html/books/bolshevik_revolution/chapter_03.htm > Accessed 25/10/06.

[113] Antony C Sutton, Wall Street and the Bolshevik Revolution (Buccaneer Books, 1993). Chapter Five of Online edition. <http://reformed-theology.org/html/books/bolshevik_revolution/chapter_05.htm > Accessed 25/10/06.

[114] Sutton, Bolshevik Revolution Chapter Five

[115] Quoting The Washington Post of February 2, 1918. He also cites Hermann Hagedorn's biography The Magnate: William Boyce Thompson and His Time (1869-1930). Sutton, Bolshevik Revolution Chapter Five

December 10th 1917 and request Prime Minister Lloyd George to recognize the Bolsheviks.[116] Another member of this mission, the socialist oriented mining magnate Raymond Robins, would lobby for American recognition of the Bolsheviks in 1918.[117] Robins is also associated with an attempt to send subversive Bolshevik revolutionaries to Germany, which culminated in the abortive Spartacist revolt of 1918.[118] Yet another member of this mission, a Wall Street lawyer named Thomas D. Thacher wrote on April 13, 1918 to Lord Northcliffe, the director of British propaganda, "[…] fullest assistance should be given to the Soviet Government in its efforts to organize a volunteer revolutionary army."[119] If these individuals were merely opportunist prospectors looking for gain, why would they consider the Bolshevik state, which was anti-capitalist and at that time, very turbulent? Its geographical boundaries at that time extended only from Moscow to Petrograd. Unofficial ambassadors such as Raymond Robins (American), Bruce Lockhart (British) and Jacques Sadoul (French) were used to sway the governments of their respective countries towards accepting the Bolsheviks, even though official consulate staff suggested otherwise.[120]

Other Western elites bypassed all formalities and directly went to work for Bolshevik propaganda. Robert Minor, a San Antonio judge and cartoonist, with ancestral ties to George Washington as well as associates of Thomas Jefferson and General Sam Houston (First President of Republic of Texas), was arrested in Paris on June 8th 1919 for disseminating Bolshevik propaganda among German and Allied troops.[121] But all charges were dropped.

---

[116] Quoting British War Cabinet papers, no. 302, sec. 2 (Public Records Office, London). Sutton, Bolshevik Revolution Chapter Five.

[117] Sutton, Bolshevik Revolution Chapter Five

[118] Quoting John Bradley, *Allied Intervention in Russia* (London: Weidenfeld and Nicolson, 1968.). Sutton, Bolshevik Revolution Chapter Five.

[119] Sutton notes: "Letter reproduced in full in Appendix 3. It should be noted that we have identified Thomas Lamont, Dwight Morrow, and H. P. Davison as being closely involved in developing policy towards the Bolsheviks. All were partners in the J.P. Morgan firm. Thacher was with the law firm Simpson, Thacher & Bartlett and was a close friend of Felix Frankfurter." Sutton, Bolshevik Revolution Chapter Five

[120] Antony C. Sutton, Wall Street and the Bolshevik Revolution. Chapter Six of Online edition.
<http://reformed-theology.org/html/books/bolshevik_revolution/chapter_06.htm>
Accessed 25/10/06.

[121] According to Sutton, a Scotland Yard Secret Special Report, No. 4, entitled, "The Case of Philip Price and Robert Minor," implicates Minor. In addition to the U.S. Start' Dept. Decimal File, 316-23-1184 9. Antony C Sutton, Wall Street and the Bolshevik

The October Revolution and Lenin' s Betrayal

Once the October revolution took place, Lenin emerged as a highly popular leader. He decided to keep the revolution for himself. The point at which he deviates is most likely to be his October 24th 1917 letter to committee members in which he orders seizing power from Kerensky and the Provisional Government. The Trotskyites were instead seeking to await the opening of Congress to confer legitimacy to the Bolshevik Government. Zinoviev and Kaminev (then Trotskyites) sought to thwart Lenin's move by leaking his plan to the press.[122] Lenin's claim that the opposition he faced was part of a foreign conspiracy obviously has some merit. For example, Lenin later alleged that Menshevik leaflets were found at the site of the Kronstadt naval mutiny.[123] To thwart the Trotskyites, he attacked all the deviations from the original Communist doctrine his enemies were indulging in. His exposure of Kerensky and the Sykes-Picot agreement clearly indicate he was now at odds with the Powers That Be. And it seems that it took time for them to realise the success of his rebellion. By the time they did, Lenin had established himself as an icon of Communism. The chief elitist operative, Trotsky, was now forced to be subordinate to Lenin, or risk losing his position among the Bolsheviks. Lenin would later carry out his own mini-purges through Stalin, although he allowed many Illuminati operatives to co-exist as long as they did not sabotage him.

A second case of Lenin being at odds with the Illuminati occurs when he refuses to continue the 'bourgeoisie' World War I. One may argue that he didn't have a better option, but it is more plausible that unlike Trotsky, he didn't have the support of the Illuminati for continuing the war. The Russian Army had been devastated in World War I, and were it not for Allied intervention on the Western front, Russia would have surrendered to Germany. But nevertheless, the Illuminati were in a position to re-equip Russia and subvert German military success on the Eastern front from within. And it can be said that Trotsky's Red army was created just for that purpose. The humiliating terms of Brest-Litovsk were never

---

Revolution (Buccaneer Books, 1993). Chapter Six of Online edition. <http://reformed-theology.org/html/books/bolshevik_revolution/chapter_06.htm> Accessed 25/10/06.

[122] V. I. Lenin, "Letter to Central Committee members -October 24 (Nov. 6) 1917," The Structure of Soviet History - essays and documents (Oxford University Press, 2003) 45.

[123] V.I Lenin, "Resolutions of the Tenth Congress of the Russian communist party, "On Party Unity" and "Syndicalist and Anarchist deviation in our party" March 1929," The Structure of Soviet History - essays and documents (Oxford University Press, 2003) 113.

meant to be signed, and were instead meant to force Lenin to reconsider his rebellion. But Lenin surprised everyone by signing the treaty. Trotsky's antics at Brest-Litovsk, in which he showed contempt, rather than bargain for favourable concessions from the Germans, made treaty a disaster for the Soviets.[124] This further proves that the Illuminati, through Trotsky, sought to discourage signing of the Treaty.

In going against them, Lenin clearly opened himself to a war with them. We see a stepped up increase in the number of attempts to assassinate Lenin, including one in which (according to Rakovsky) Trotsky was involved. Another involved an assassin linked to British Intelligence.[125] Rakovsky goes to the extent of saying that the last doctor who treated Lenin (Dr. Levin) was a Trotskyite! However, the pyramidal power structure created by Soviet Communism guaranteed that Lenin could successfully start his own cabal, while turning his back on his masters.

Continued Outside Financial Support for the Revolution

Despite such unprecedented developments, the Powers That Be realised that it was in their best interests to fully support the newly established Soviet state. Lenin represented a leadership problem, which could be dealt with at leisure.

Ludwig Martens, a German citizen, ran the Soviet Bureau in the United States.[126] Representatives of the Lusk Committee raided the Bureau offices on June 12th 1919. A.A. Heller, a commercial attaché to the Soviet Bureau claimed,

> Among the people helping us to get recognition from the State Department are the big Chicago packers, Armour, Swift, Nelson Morris and Cudahy ..... Among the other firms are . . . the American Steel Export Company, the Leigh Machine Company, the Adrian Knitting Company, the International Harvester Company, the Aluminum Goods Manufacturing Company, the Aluminum Company

---

[124] The Rakovsky interrogation supports this conclusion.

[125] A Lithuanian Jew Rosenblum who went by the name O'Reilly. He was considered to be the best spy of British intelligence.

[126] Antony C Sutton, Wall Street and the Bolshevik Revolution (Buccaneer Books, 1993). Chapter Seven of Online edition. <http://reformed-theology.org/html/books/bolshevik_revolution/chapter_07.htm > Accessed 25/10/06.

of America, the American Car and Foundry Export Company, M.C.D. Borden & Sons.[127]

The New York Times followed up these claims. The corporate directors tended to be evasive, but documents seized by the Lusk Committee did corroborate Heller's account on many instances.

There were also Russian bankers who assisted the Bolsheviks. Such as newly formed Bolshevik bankers like Abram Givatovzo, the brother-in-law of Trotsky and Kaminev.[128] Exiled Tsarist bankers were also prominent in this activity, which hints at obvious collusion of Russian Royalty.

Lenin's Betrayal not Forgiven

At the same time, the Illuminati realized that it was necessary to keep Lenin in a less powerful bargaining position. This was accomplished by shipping out Soviet gold, in exchange for the extremely urgent foreign purchases made by the Soviet Union. The shipments were made to Guaranty Trust in New York, and their Soviet origin was obfuscated.[129] These shipments were roughly worth the then equivalent of $20 million.[130]

In January 1922, Guaranty Trust, with support of secretary of Commerce Herbert Hoover, participated in the formation of the first Soviet International Bank (Ruskombank).[131] And Max May of Guaranty Trust would become head of its foreign department.[132]

Similarly, in 1919, a loan of $5 million and an additional loan of £10 million sterling were made to the White Russian Aleksandr Kolchak.[133] Gold was taken in exchange and was shipped to the United States. Thus,

---

[127] Quoting *New York Times,* November 17, 1919. Sutton, Bolshevik Revolution Chapter Seven.
[128] Sutton, Bolshevik Revolution Chapter Seven.
[129] Antony C Sutton, Wall Street and the Bolshevik Revolution (Buccaneer Books, 1993). Chapter Nine of Online edition. <http://reformed-theology.org/html/books/bolshevik_revolution/chapter_09.htm> Accessed 25/10/06.
[130] Sutton, Bolshevik Revolution Chapter Nine.
[131] Sutton, Bolshevik Revolution Chapter Nine.
[132] Sutton, Bolshevik Revolution Chapter Nine.
[133] Quoting U.S. State Dept. Decimal File, 861.51/649. Antony C Sutton, Wall Street and the Bolshevik Revolution (Buccaneer Books, 1993). Chapter Ten of Online edition. <http://reformed-theology.org/html/books/bolshevik_revolution/chapter_10.htm > Accessed 25/10/06.

the Illuminati were able to prop Kolchak against Lenin, and control Kolchak at the same time.

Jewish Revolution?

Some have taken the presence of Jews in the October Revolution as a sign of "Jewish Conspiracy." Henry Ford in his *Dearborn Independent* popularized this outlook. But my analysis has found it to be superficial. It is true that many Jews partook in Revolution. But they were not given any option by the White Russians, who engaged in many atrocities against Jewish communities. Again, most would be killed or deported to the gulags following the purges of Stalin. Those that remained did not live as Commissars with dachas in Crimea. They were goaded into migrating en masse, to populate Israel.

The Powers that Be are certainly not organized on loosely knit religious-communal associations. Instead, Jewish leadership and the Zionist state appear to be subverted into playing a role, like every other major entity, as pawns in a game.

Stalin

Some have suggested the Stalin, like Hitler, was also the son of an Illuminati banker. Clifford Shack[134] has put up a convincing claim in this regard, by creating a permutation out of new revelations in the book *Stalin: The First In-depth Biography based on Explosive New Documents from Russia's Secret Archives* by Edvard Radzinsky. Though further corroboration is warranted, there are a few details, which do fit the picture. For example, Stalin went to great lengths to cozy up with Lenin, to the extent of establishing a homosexual relationship. The Illuminati was targeting Lenin at that time. And Stalin's desperate attempts to infiltrate the Lenin camp are not at odds with this strategy. However, as we shall read, Stalin later developed ideas of his own, as demonstrated by his crackdown on Freemasonry, Theosophy and Secret Societies he believed were working against him in concert with his elitist enemies.

---

[134]Shack's claim that Stalin was the illegitimate offspring of a Georgian woman and a Rothschild banker who was visiting the region, makes some sense, when we consider extensive Rothschild involvement in the Georgian Baku oil fields. Clifford Shack, "Was Stalin a Rothschild?" Cliff Shack <http://www.geocities.com/cliff_shack/stalinrothschild.html> Accessed 23/10/06.

According to Rakovsky, Lenin's death was to pave way for Trotsky, but a stroke of ill fortune resulted in Trotsky becoming ill and unable to take part in the power struggle. Instead, Stalin emerged. Once in power, Stalin instead began showing independence. He imitated Lenin by attacking another Illuminati proposition: Permanent Revolution. This was the idea of continuing the Revolution until all countries adopted Soviet hegemony. Instead, Stalin gave the Revolution a Nationalist character. He thus threw water on the very fire the Illuminati sought to inflame through the Great Depression. Though the prospect of 'Permanent Revolution' may sound insane from today's perspective, the euphoria of 1917, in an age of minimal communication can be best understood by analysing the activities of internationalist Communists in other countries. For example, in Canada, Communism was not popular with the locals, so an influx of socialist leaning Scandinavians was created around this period. And various Soviet operatives moved in to lay the groundwork by sabotaging localized Socialism, which was seen as a threat to Permanent Revolution.

The rebellion of Lenin, followed by the unpredictable nature of Stalin, cost the conspirators heavily. The Powers That Be could not coordinate revolutions elsewhere. Therefore, the Second World War had to be hastily arranged. It would also allow deliverance of a resource and expertise rich Germany, a possible coup against Stalin and what Rakovsky considered most important, the dialectics, or the victory of International Soviet based Communism over German National Socialism.

The Allied strategy of securing Gallipoli was meant to establish a supply line for the Bolsheviks, so that the Red Army could further pursue the war as well as advance into the Mediterranean. This strategy was laid waste by the bravery of the Ottoman forces, who successfully resisted the waves of Allied soldiers. Were it not for the bravery of these Ottoman soldiers, the Red Army could have advanced up to its World War II boundaries during World War I. The Second World War was meant to enable the territories lost by Russia during World War I to be recovered and expanded. Before its onset, Gallipoli would be secured under a Bolshevik friendly Kemalist Turkey. Turkey would be neutral during World War II, and Gallipoli would finally function as a conduit of supplies for the Red Army. This conduit was critical to Soviet advances and victory in World War II. Fascism would emerge in Italy and Spain, and extend into North Africa. The idea was to give the Soviets dialectical opposition (similar to the Nazis) to retry advancing into the

Mediterranean. But again, logistical factors and the infighting between Lenin, and later Stalin and the Illuminati laid waste to this opportunity as well.

The Destruction of the Austro-Hungarian Empire

The Austro-Hungarian Empire was a hodgepodge of several disparate nationalities and ethnic groups bundled together. It was formed when the Illuminati Hapsburgs (Merovingian bloodline) reached an agreement with the Hungarians.

The Hapsburgs were also known as the House of Lorraine. A secret society founded around 1873, the Hieron d Val d'Or, called for an Empire in Europe, under the Hapsburgs and the Pope.[135] The term used was "Holy Roman Empire" and this would later be used as a rallying cry for the Nazis. Surprisingly, the "Holy Roman Empire" advocated by Hieron d Val d'Or was a secular one, where nations were like provinces, ruled by a special elite.[136] There are obvious similarities with the Soviet Union. The choice of using Archduke Franz Ferdinand as a sacrificial lamb to kick-start World War I, was probably because the House of Lorraine had drifted away from the long term goals of the Powers that Be.

The biggest tensions within this empire were between the Slavs (mainly Serbs supported by Russia) and the Austrians (supported by Germany). Since the Austro-Hungarian Empire was impotent, it was chosen as an ideal staging ground for war between Germany and Russia. Given the Austro-Hungarian Empire's centrality to Europe and the Ottomans, it was guaranteed to create conflagration between all major powers as well.

Pan-Slavism

Pan-Slavism emerged as a movement in 1848, and was characterized by opposition of the Slavic people to both Germans and Bolsheviks. After Soviet rule was established, Pan-Slavism was recycled to justify Russian hegemony.

---

[135] Michael Baigent, Richard Leigh and Henry Lincoln, The Holy Blood and the Holy Grail (London: Arrow Books, 1996) 207.
[136] Baigent et all Holy Grail 201.

It is important to note why the Illuminati would partake in the creation and leadership of such movements. In order to create pre-conditions for the success of Soviet based International Communism, various exclusive and reactionary ideologies had to be nurtured, which would encompass a large swathe of people and by default, their territories. It was intended that blocs such as these (with their compromised leadership) would be crashed against the Soviet Union. The Soviets would then get due cause to crush all people associated with such oppositional blocs, and annex their territory. However, this is not exactly how things later unfolded.

Symbol of the Black Hand

The Black Hand, an organization, which spawned from the Pan-Slavist national movement, played a major role in triggering World War I. The Black Hand bears convincing similarity with other Secret Societies such as the Skull and Bones. In fact, the symbol of the Black Hand was identical to the Nazi SS 'Death heads' flag and the insignia of the Skull and Bones Secret Society. The Black Hand also had connections to other mainstream secret societies such as Freemasonry. Gavrilo Princip, the assassin of Archduke Franz Ferdinand was a member of the Black Hand. He also had a close associate who was a Freemason.[137] Others have attributed Freemasonry with more direct involvement. To quote Cardinal Caro Rodriguez, the Archbishop of Santiago Chile,

> In Austria, the famous crime of Sarajevo, cause of the Great War was decreed, announced with anticipation, and executed in time by Masonry. "A high Masonic dignitary of Switzerland, expressed himself in the year 1912, on this matter in the following way: 'The heir is a person of great talent, a pity that he is condemned; he will die on the way to the throne.' Madame Thebes announced his death two years before it took place. The principal culprits were all Masons. "All this," says Wichtl,[138] "is not a supposition, but judiciously proved facts which are intentionally silenced." The murder of Emperor Franz Josef was attempted but failed. The instigator was the brother of William

[137]Gavrilo Princep testified that his colleague, Ciganovich, "told me he was a Freemason." Mary E. Durham, The Sarajevo Crime (London: George Allyn and Unwinn, Ltd, 1925) 85 – 86.

[138] Weltfreimaurerei (World Masonry) (Witchl), Reference by Cardinal Rodriguez.

> Oberdank, in whose honor the Masons Udine and Trieste have formed a new lodge bearing his name.[139]

Serbia is still a playground of the Powers that Be. The Serbian 'nationalism' of Slobodan Milosevic was their creation. To fuel the present agenda of 'Clash of Civilizations,' Milosevic and his cohorts were carving a religious-cultural bloc out of Yugoslavia. Since the Muslims of the Balkans are westernized, they proved incapable of defending themselves. But when *mujahideen* from all over the world began converging in the Balkans, the Powers that Be realized that they were creating an Afghanistan in Europe's backyard. NATO engaged in a bombing campaign against the Serbs. The idea was to discourage the further influx of *mujahideen* by providing an emergency 'shotgun resolution' to the Balkan crisis. Most supporters of Milosevic were clueless about what had happened and many fled to other Western countries. Some took to blaming the Jews. Milosevic himself committed "suicide" rather than face further punitive action. Conspiracy theorists have doubts about the termination of his life. It could have been an exit strategy. The successor who ousted Milosevic was assassinated, typical of the intrigues that characterize this region.

Destruction of the German Empire

The Illuminati links of German Royalty will be touched upon in the next chapter.

Apart from such links, American capital was secretly diverted towards Germany, and some of it would be used in German covert activities prior to the outbreak of World War I. Some of these covert activities would involve assistance to the Bolsheviks. One such example is that of Joseph Caillaux, who became premier of France in 1911, and John Louis Malvy, who became his undersecretary. Their political careers were cut short by scandal. But they went on to form a radical socialist party and conduct an abortive Bolshevik style revolution, using "German" funds.[140] According to the French interrogation, there were links, in particular, to

---

[139] Jose Maria Cardinal Caro Y. Rodriguez, The Mystery of Freemasonry Unveiled – With a reprint of Pope Leo XIIIth Encyclical Humanum Genus 2nd edition (Imprimatur, Jose Maria Cardinal Caro Y. Rodriguez, Cardinal Archbishop of Santiago, Chile, 1920s) 158.

[140] Antony C Sutton, Wall Street and the Bolshevik Revolution (Buccaneer Books, 1993). Chapter Four of Online edition. <http://reformed-theology.org/html/books/bolshevik_revolution/chapter_04.htm> Accessed 25/10/06.

Guaranty Trust.[141] In 1919, the U.S. Senate Overman Committee established that the U.S. based Guaranty Trust Company (J.P. Morgan interests) was funding the German war effort.[142]

Germany also needed Nickel to make stainless steel. At that time, 80% of the world's nickel was controlled by Inco, which mined the rich copper deposits of Sudbury in Canada (Nickel is found in the process of extracting copper). This company represented J.P. Morgan interests, which had absorbed the Canadian Copper Company in 1902. This could not have been possible without the corruption of major Canadian officials. Almost all of Inco's nickel was now earmarked for the Allied war effort. But Inco's New Jersey refinery secretly sold 40% of its production to Germany.[143] To quote,

> And that's how during the battle at Vimy, soldiers from Sudbury were shot at with bullets plated with nickel from their own mines.[144]

And,

> In August 1916, the public also learned that the German submarine *Deutschland* left the port of Baltimore loaded with 340 tonnes of nickel from Sudbury.[145]

When Germany would go to war in August 1914, The Illuminati rulers, leaders and military commanders of the German Empire arranged for Germany to invade Belgium and France, rather than focus on the Eastern front, where there were more opportunities (at Bolshevik expense). This move also arranged for Britain to get involved, since Britain had a treaty with Germany and France over Belgian neutrality. During this campaign, German military commanders would not allow the use of railroads, further slowing German advances into France. The German advance east of Paris was halted at the First Battle of Marne. Some historians blame the Chief of German General Staff, Helmut Von Moltke for the failure of this offensive. The huge battles on the Western front and on the seas were of significance in the outcome of the war. They helped truncate German forces that would otherwise be successfully deployed against

---

141 Sutton, Bolshevik Revolution Chapter Four.

142 Quoting U.S., Senate, Overman Committee, 2:2009. Sutton, Bolshevik Revolution Chapter Four.

143 The Hole Story, prod. Richard Desjardins and Robert Monderie, National Film Board of Canada, 2011.

144 The Hole Story, Desjardins and Monderie.

145 The Hole Story, Desjardins and Monderie.

the Bolsheviks on the Eastern front. These battles also helped distract the soldiers and civilians of the nations involved from the real hidden goals of the war.

On May 7th 1915, a German torpedo sank the British Ocean Liner Lusitania. Though it was later found that munitions aboard the Lusitania were likely to have caused the fatal secondary explosions, the death of 128 Americans was used as a propaganda coup for American involvement in the war. According to Springmeier, the Lusitania was sent without its escort into a naval war zone.[146] Springmeier also claims that an elitist was sent a telegram not to sail aboard the Lusitania, but failed to receive it, and sailed to his death.

Above: A celebration of the end of World War I in 1918 in New York. The pyramid in front of the Grand Central Railway Terminal was made of the helmets of dead or captured German soldiers! There were two such pyramids, each consisting of up to 12,000 helmets, on either end of "Victory Way," which was also adorned with captured German war equipment, ribbons, bells, American flags and eagles.

---

[146] Fritz Springmeier, Bloodlines of the Illuminati (Spring Arbor distributors, 1998) 210. GlobalGrey PDF edition 2013 <http://www.globalgrey.co.uk/Pages/Books-Conspiracies/Bloodlines-Of-The-Illuminati.html> Web page as of 03/07/13.

As if Germany had not made enough enemies, Deputy chief of staff Erich Ludendorff proposed a policy of unrestricted submarine warfare in 1917. The Powers That Be were keen on involving America into the war. Only American resources could be used to bring the war to a conclusion advantageous to the newly formed Soviet Union. The argument that Germany made such a fatal gamble to merely strangle one of the many Allied supply lines is rather illogical. We are told that the U-boats somehow did not sink the two million American soldiers who were transported to Europe because of the use of depth charges and armed escorts. But it is more likely that these boats carrying American soldiers were deliberately avoided. Similarly, the exposure of the Zimmerman telegram, in which Germans propose Mexico to join the war on their side, can only be an outrageous provocation by Cabal operatives within German ranks.

Another secret treaty was signed with the Ottoman Empire in August 1914. This allowed the Ottomans to enter into the war and gamble their entire centuries old empire in the rigged sweepstake.

Similarly, Austria would concentrate most of its forces against Serbia, such that little consideration was given to fight Russia.

Towards the end of World War I, he Bolsheviks were saved by the Treaty of Brest-Litovsk. But this Treaty was modified to the disadvantage of the Bolsheviks due to certain developments in Bolshevik leadership, which have been discussed earlier.

The German Empire collapsed at the end of World War I. This lead to the creation of the Weimar Republic, which was more on the lines of a nation state, suitable for the future rise of fascists. Even among the victorious Allied nations, governments acquired new powers, created new ministries and imposed completely new taxes. All of these developments would persist to this very day

---

Destruction of the Ottoman Empire

> The Turkish Revolution was the death knell of the Turkish Empire. The example of Turkey, in a word, seems to remind us that a revolution may not be a drastic though healthful process but a scourge.-*Nesta H. Webster*[147]

[147] Nesta H. Webster, The Cause of World Unrest – With an Introduction by the Editor of The Morning Post (London: Grant Richards Ltd., 1920) 143.

Infiltration

Realizing that the Ottomans were difficult to contain militarily, infiltration of the Royal Ottoman household became an important prerogative of the European Illuminati. The Ottomans had a practice of not marrying among local nobles, who could use their newly acquired status to dilute the Sultan's power. Instead, the Sultan would maintain a harem of captured "slaves" from areas they had conquered. These "slaves" were preferred for breeding the next generation of Sultans, since they possessed no local roots, and therefore could not establish a local power base to engage in intrigues against the Sultan.

All that changed with the arrival of Hurrem Sultana, a concubine of Ukrainian origin who was also known as Roxelana. The Sultan of course, was oblivious to the motives of such scornful and deceptive people. Once Hurrem managed to infiltrate the harem of Suleiman I, she used all sorts of charms on the Sultan to become his favorite. She then upgraded her status by leaving the harem and moving into the Sultan's palace itself, breaking an Ottoman tradition followed since Mehmed II. She used a variety of tricks and sedition to eliminate her rivals and pave the way for her son to become the next Sultan. Prior to her, no concubine could play a decisive role in deciding who would be the future Sultan. She even moved into the political arena, arranging the assassination of Greek convert Ibrahim Pasha, who was successfully inflicting defeat on both the European Illuminati Royals and the Safavids of Iran. Hurrem also insisted that the Sultan write her letters from the campaign front, presumably for espionage on behalf of the European Illuminati. Hurrem maintained communication and correspondence with the son of Sigismund II, the Polish king and the Safavid Shah Tahmasp's sister.[148] She had a rival concubine's son killed, to ensure that her own son became Sultan.

Like a virus attacking a cell, Hurrem opened the palace door for similar female operatives of dubious European origin, such as the illegitimate children of Venetian Royals. For example, Nurbanu, the wife of the next Sultan, Selim II, was born Cecilia Vonier-Baffo, the illegitimate daughter of two Venetian noble families.[149] These new concubines would become unofficial diplomats for their European countries of origin, creating a channel for active espionage. For example, Nurbanu

[148] Leslie P. Pierce, The Imperial Harem – Women and Sovereignty in the Ottoman Empire (NY: Oxford University Press, 1993) 221.
[149] Pierce, The Imperial Harem 92.

was in active correspondence with the Medici family of Italy.[150] Springmeier has identified the Medici family with the Merovingians. The intrigues and conspiracies of these women would make the harem the real power in Ottoman politics. This influence translated into fundamental changes during the reign of Suleiman I, such as the lapse of the *ghazi* (jihad prerogatives of the Sultan) and the physical relocation of the harem into the Sultan's political area. There was also a lapse of the grooming of princes as warriors and a lapse of their public lives as a result of their being confined to the harem, for use as chess pieces by the harem women during power struggles. Power was concentrated in the palaces of Istanbul, and there were an alarming number of depositions[151] instead of the traditional open contests for Kingship. The unique military nature of the Ottoman state was compromised and would gradually move towards the separation of military, administration and religion in the 19th century, not unlike a European nation state. These developments were reflected on the frontlines in the form of major reversals and failures. It is no wonder classical Ottoman history traces the decline of the Ottoman Empire to the rise of the harem during the reign of Suleiman I.

However, infiltrating the Sultan's harem wasn't enough. The Sultan's most loyal followers were the janissaries. These fighters were motivated by religion and were thus difficult to control, unlike modern armies, which bear a mercenary nature. They would only fight when they found just cause. The janissaries formed an effective balance against the power of the Sultan and the harem. Gradually, the janissary ranks were corrupted by intrigues directed from within the harem.

In 1826, Mahmud II massacred the janissaries. They were first instigated to revolt and then wiped out by the new "modern" troops. This incident is reminiscent of the conspiratorial workings of European secret societies. In fact, Muhammad Ali, the Freemason who ruled Egypt, destroyed the great Mamluks of Egypt in a similar treacherous fashion (1811). Highly motivated troops such as the janissaries were difficult to control by political powers; and were unlikely to fight as mercenaries. As their history demonstrated, they, on many occasions, forced the hand of the Sultan to alter his decisions. Nevertheless, the new 'modern' troops continued to be highly motivated by notions of jihad. It was only after the wiping out of the Caliphate that the Turkish army would have secular mercenary-like troops, similar to their European counterparts.

---

[150] Pierce, The Imperial Harem 226.

[151] Out of the 27 Sultans following Suleiman I, 13 were forcibly deposed

Ottoman administrative ranks slowly began to be infiltrated by the Illuminati. But despite this control over the Sultan and the administration, the Powers that Be had limited room for maneuver. The official agenda of the Ottoman state continued to be jihad and Islam. And the Powers that Be couldn't change this reality from within, since they would risk exposing themselves. Therefore an external opposing force, the CUP, was created to destroy the Caliphate.

The extent to which the Sultans and the Ottoman administrative machinery was compromised manifested in the staged Ottoman defeat in World War I, the conduction of the Armenian Holocaust and the dissolution of the Caliphate.

An obstacle for Zionism

Throughout contemporary history, the Illuminati used various external enemies to destabilize the Ottoman Empire. The most prominent of these enemies would be the Russian Empire. During the reign of Tsar Alexander I, the Southern Society, a secret society closely connected with imperial circles emerged. The Southern Society drafted a proposal on the Jewish question, a prototype of Zionism long before Herzl, which suggested Russian troops give support to Jews who "[...] after traversing European Turkey they could cross over into Asiatic Turkey where, upon seizing sufficient territory, they could establish a separate Jewish state [...]"[152] If this proposal reflects official Russian policy, it may help explain their perpetual state of border conflict with the Ottomans. This conflict claimed the lives of millions of Russians. Rather than Arabs, the Ottomans with their self-proclaimed status as custodians of Jerusalem, represented the only real obstacle to Zionism.

However, European powers such as the Romanovs should not be mistaken as sincere supporters of the Jewish faith and its practitioners. Unlike the Ottomans who gave Jews a favorable status and special minority privileges, Jews in all European states were confined to ghettoes. It was only after the French Revolution and Napoleon (non-Illuminati) that emancipation was considered. And when Jews were finally freed from the ghettoes, it is not surprising that the Illuminati came up with the idea of Israel, to re-ghetto all European Jews. To quote Edwin Montagu in a response to British PM Lloyd George's support for the creation of Israel, "All my life I have been trying to get out of the

[152] Marc Raeff, The Decembrist Movement (Prentice Hall Inc.-New Jersey, 1966) 146.

ghetto. You want to force me back there."[153] Montagu was the only Jewish member of the British cabinet during the 1917 Balfour Declaration, and vociferously objected to the creation of Israel.

The Crimean War

Background

Christian minorities were very well protected in the Ottoman Empire. In 1690, the Roman Catholic Church was even granted authority over all churches in the Holy places. Around 1850, Louis Napoleon of France took up the cause of Roman Catholicism. He requested the Ottomans to recognize France as a "sovereign authority" in the Holy Land.[154]

It is important to note that Napoleon and his successors did not represent an Illuminati bloodline. They had in essence, kidnapped the French revolution from the Illuminati and turned it into a French religious-nationalist movement. It is not surprising that Louis Napoleon would later be targeted by Freemasonry. To quote,

> On January 14, 1858, at the entrance of the Opera de Paris three deadly bombs were exploded, killing eight persons and wounding 176. It was the execution of the plan to kill Napoleon II, a plan instigated by Mazzini and Ledru-Rollin and agreed upon in London in 1857.[155]

The most prominent opposition Louis Napoleon would face would be from the Romanovs. Tsar Nicholas I responded by putting a counterclaim to Louis Napoleon on behalf of the Russian Orthodox Church. A French proposal to share authority with the Russian Orthodox Church was rejected by Russia.[156]

In 1853, Russia invaded Moldovia and Wallachia, autonomous regions within the Turkish Empire. Turkey declared war on Russia. In the same

---

[153] Henry Makow, "British Jewry tried to stop Zionism," Savethemales.ca 11/03/06. <http://www.savethemales.ca/001458.html> Web page as of 02/10/06

[154] Trevor Royle, Crimea: The Great Crimean War, 1854-1856 (Palgrave Macmillan, 2000) 19.

[155] Jose Maria Cardinal Caro Y. Rodriguez, The Mystery of Freemasonry Unveiled – With a reprint of Pope Leo XIIIth Encyclical Humanum Genus 2nd edition (Imprimatur, Jose Maria Cardinal Caro Y. Rodriguez, Cardinal Archbishop of Santiago, Chile, 1920s) 161-162.

[156] Marjie Bloy, "The Crimean War: Immediate Causes," The Victorian Web < http://www.victorianweb.org/history/crimea/immcauses.html> Accessed 1st Oct. 2006.

year, the Russian Black Sea Fleet destroyed and sank the Turkish fleet. Britain invited itself into the conflict under the pretext of protecting the Ottoman Empire from Russian expansion. Britain even made the rare gesture of cooperating with France for this purpose.

It is commonly accepted that Ottoman Turkey was by then, the sick man of Europe. And depended solely upon British assistance. This can't be further from the truth. The Ottomans managed to successfully defeat the Russians at the border of Romania and Bulgaria, as well as in Armenia. Russian losses would be so heavy that the Tsar seriously began contemplating the abolition of serfdom, which was hindering Russia's chances at modern warfare. Russian intellectual Leo Tolstoy gave a graphic description of Russian losses in *The Sebastopol Sketches.*

The Russian Empire had annexed Crimea in 1783. But most of its population comprised of Crimean Muslim Tatars. When the British and French brought their naval fleets to Dardenelles and the Black Sea, the Russians saw the war as a pretext to destroy the local Muslim inhabitants. They began confiscating the land of the Tatars, forcing them to migrate en masse to Turkey. This migration hurt the Crimean economy so badly that the Russians had to halt the process because agricultural production had been crippled. These atrocities were committed under Tsar Nicholas I, the same Tsar who had hypocritically struck a quarrel with the Ottomans over the protection of Russian Orthodox Christians from alleged Ottoman mistreatment.

Enter Britain

Though Louis Napoleon was undoubtedly sincere in his opposition to Russia and support for the Ottoman Empire, the Illuminati quickly made Britain a counterpart in this venture. The motives were multifold.

1. British presence in this venture could be used to hinder the French naval campaign against Russia, as well as provide first-hand information on French moves. It is important to note that the European Illuminati were still recovering from the actions of Napoleon Bonaparte. They saw considerable danger in his nephew achieving any sort of success.
2. The British would prevent the Ottomans from fighting directly in the Crimean campaign, and prevent a possible French-Ottoman alliance. Despite internal intrigues, degradation and corruption, the Ottoman Empire was still very robust. The British could instead be used as pseudo-opposition for the

Russians, and thus prevent the Ottomans from gaining any real victory.

The commander of British troops in Crimea was Lord Raglan, who distinguished himself in the anti-Napoleon campaigns of the Duke of Wellington. Once in Crimea, he earned notoriety for creating logistical nightmares and military debacles for British forces in Crimea. Lord Raglan was so averse to the idea of military cooperation with the Ottomans that he refused to purchase supplies of wood from them, which were necessary for protection from the winter and for lighting fires.

One such famous debacle was the 'Charge of the Light Brigade' (1854), in which Lord Raglan confused a British cavalry of more than 600 to march into the mouth of Russian canons. Raglan, of course was safely behind.[157] Later, Lord Alfred Tennyson would write (emphasis mine):

> 'Forward, the Light Brigade!'
> Was there a man dismay'd?
> Not tho' the soldiers knew
>   Some one had blunder'd:
> *Theirs not to make reply,*
> *Theirs not to reason why,*
> *Theirs but to do & die,*
> Into the valley of Death
>   Rode the six hundred.

These sentiments aptly sum up how the British are expendable for the secret goals of the Powers That Be.

The Baltic Theatre

Similarly, the concurrent British Baltic campaign against the Russians was punctuated with the same sloppy half-heartedness. Finland was a Grand Duchy of Russian Empire and important to Russian trade.

To quote, "It was felt that early and decisive action in the Baltic may have led to an earlier conclusion to hostilities, and many of [British Admiral Sir Charles] Napier's Captains expressed frustration at the Vice

---

[157] See map made by Stephen Luscombe, "The Crimean War: Charge of the Light Brigade," 25th October 1854. Britishempire.co.uk <http://www.britishempire.co.uk/forces/armycampaigns/europeancampaigns/crimeanwar/crimeanwar.htm> Web page accessed 1st Oct. 2006.

Admiral's timidity."[158] The fortress of Bomarsund off Southern Finland received minimal damage from the British navy, according to Russian historian Major-General Borodkin.[159] A quote on the landings at Bomarsund is as follows:

> It appears that many British captains were exasperated at Napier's restraint in holding back the main bulk of the British fleet whilst the smaller ships and mainly French troops engaged the fortress. It was largely felt that Napier failed to grasp the advantages offered by the technological merits of the steam engine.[160]

Instead of trying to win the Finnish population and enticing them to rebel against the Russians, the British Navy engaged in bombardment of the shores, with little regard for the impact on local Finnish population.

Balkan changes after the Crimean War (Ottoman losses in yellow).
From Literary and Historical Atlas of Europe, by J.G. Bartholomew, 1912

The Aftermath

When the Crimean War was finally concluded in the 1856 Treaty of Paris,[161] the Powers that Be had the Treaty provisioned to maximum Ottoman disadvantage. Since the Ottomans would never agree to Russian conquest of the Danubian Principalities, these Principalities were instead transferred to the European dominated "Great Powers" instead of Russia alone. Since Russians were unpopular in these areas, it was unlikely that

---

158 British Embassy Helsinki, "News: Special Feature: The Baltic Campaign of the Crimean War: Introduction," British Embassy Helsinki <http://www.britishembassy.gov.uk/servlet/Front?pagename=OpenMarket/Xcelerate/ShowPage&c=Page&cid=1065719062885> Accessed 1st Oct. 2006.

159 British Embassy, Helsinki, "News: Special Feature: The Baltic Campaign of the Crimean War: Bomersund," British Embassy Helsinki <http://www.britishembassy.gov.uk/servlet/Front?pagename=OpenMarket/Xcelerate/ShowPage&c=Page&cid=1077042157317> Accessed 1st Oct. 2006.

160 British Embassy, "Crimean War: Bomersund."

161 The complete articles of the Treaty can be found on Amit Mendelsohn's Website. <http://www.amitm.com/thecon/lesson5.html> Accessed 1st Oct. 2006.

direct transfer to Russia was a feasible option. It is interesting to note how a little paperwork turned Ottoman victories in the region into a catastrophic loss. The Ottomans officially lost all claims for further expansion in the Balkans. The Powers that Be would then carve new nation-states in these regions, which would never return to the Ottoman realm. The Treaty also provisioned that the Ottoman Empire speed up its decay by pursuing more aggressive "Westernization."

The treaty with its neutralization of the Black Sea appeared to be of disadvantage to Russia. But as soon as Louis Napoleon was toppled by conspiracy, France assumed neutrality towards Russia. Bismarck would encourage Russia to denounce the Black Sea clauses of the 1856 treaty. And Russia once again established a fleet in the Black Sea. But of course, this violation of the treaty did not mean that the Danubian principalities were to be consequentially returned to the Ottomans.

As part of a reward for "British support," Britain was allowed to open a bank in Turkey. Such banks would later play a major role in the bankrupting of the Ottoman Empire. When the Ottoman government would not be able to pay back, British creditors would move in, consolidating their monopoly over various goods and the collection of various taxes.

Russo-Turkish war 1877-1878

The purpose of this war was to expand Russian influence in the Balkans. Intriguers on the Ottoman side ensured that the Ottoman army was used only in small fractions of its actual capacity. Since Russian domination was still unpalatable to the people of the Balkans, nation states were created, which were to be gradually transferred to Russian domination. Romania, Serbia, Montenegro and Bulgaria were carved out of the former Ottoman Balkans. The Muslim population of Bulgaria was decimated, and Bulgaria would be Christianized. According to some sources, up to 200,000 Muslims perished. In addition, the Black Sea port of Batum, the key to newly discovered oil in the Baku region (1873) was incorporated into the Russian Empire. The Rothschilds, who already had strong banking connections in the region, may have influenced Russia's decision to go to war.[162] This port would fall back to the Ottomans during World War I. But Mustafa Kemal would promptly return it to the Soviets later on.

---

[162] Clifford Shack, "Oil and the Holocaust," Cliff Shack <http://www.geocities.com/cliff_shack/oil_chrono.html> Accessed 01/11/06.

Mustafa Kemal

Mustafa Kemal was born in the Greek city (then Ottoman) of Salonica in 1881. His family was outwardly Muslim but was very likely to have been Sabbatean.

An undated postcard from Salonica

The city of Salonica bears special significance to the Sabbateans, who are also known as Frankists and Donmeh (also doenme or doenmeh). The Sabbateans may be Jewish[163] but are not recognized as such by mainstream Jewish communities.[164] They are accused of following Sabbetai Zevi, who was considered to be a heretic. Zevi declared himself Messiah in 1666, and was taken to the Sultan. To avoid punishment, he outwardly embraced Islam and his followers did likewise.[165] Rabbi Barry Chamish even suggests that the Sabbateans are engaged in covert opposition to Jews and mainstream Judaism.[166] There were probably 70,000 Sabbateans in Salonica, out of a total population of 100,000 at that time.[167] They spoke a dialect of Spanish,[168] and they trace their ancestry to a group of Spanish Jews who were forced to leave Spain due to Christian persecution (the Inquisition). Ironically, some of them were active in the intrigues that brought down Moorish Spain, paving way for the Inquisition.

Salonica was identified as a source of the alien strains of intellectualism, such as secularism and nationalism, which were supplanted in the

---

[163] They are considered by some to be descendants of the Sephardim who were expelled from Spain following Christian takeover of the Islamic kingdoms. Avigdor Levy, The Jews of the Ottoman Empire (Princeton, 1994) 203-212, 215-273.

[164] Joseph Hantman, "The Turkish Israeli Connection and its Jewish Roots," Kulanu quarterly newsletter summer 1999, Volume 6 Number 2, page 3.

[165] Joachim Prinz, The Secret Jews (Random House, 1973) 111-122.

[166] Barry Chamish, "Kerry, Gaza and the New Sabbatean Holocaust," barrychamish.com Published 09/02/04. An archived copy is available at: <http://www.redmoonrising.com/chamish/Feb04.htm#February%209> Accessed 09/10/06.

[167] Quoting Vicomte Leon de Poncins in The Secret Powers behind the Revolution page 66, David M. Pidcock, Satanic Voices – Ancient and Modern Internet edition (Oldbrook, Milton Keynes: Mustaqim, 2002) 50.

[168] Pidcock, Satanic Voices 51.

Ottoman Empire. For example, Tekin Alp, one of the main figures in the Pan-Turanian (Pan-Turkic) movement was a Salonican Sabbatean.[169]

A lot of insight into Mustafa Kemal's Sabbatean background can be obtained from an article by journalist Hillel Halkin, which was published in a progressive New York based Jewish newspaper.[170] The following are some statements culled from the same source.

- ❖ Very little is known about Kemal's father, Ali Riza. Lord Kinross, in his 1964 book "Ataturk" even refers to Ali Riza as a "shadowy personality."
- ❖ Itamar Ben Avi, the son of Eliezer Ben-Yehuda (a pioneer of Hebrew revival) recalls an incident during his years as a journalist. He walked into a hotel in Jerusalem and came across Mustafa Kemal engaged in drinking. To quote " 'I'd like to meet him,' I said, because the minute I looked at him I was startled by his piercing green eyes." During this meeting, Kemal disclosed that he was a descendant of Sabbetai Zevi, and he was even able to recall a secret prayer of the Sabbateans. The prayer verse in question has been proved to be an authentic Sabbatean one.
- ❖ According to Israel's second President Yitzchak Ben-Zvi in his book on lost Jewish communities "*The Exiled and the Redeemed* (1950)," the Sabbateans engaged in wife swapping. Ben-Zvi writes, "There is reason to believe that this ceremony has not been entirely abandoned and continues to this day."

Halkin makes no reference to Kemal's private life, which was fairly controversial as well. To quote Irfan and Margarete Orga's account on Kemal's early years (around 1903),

> He tried to be a gay dog, and made the rounds of the brothels, followed respectable women in the streets, and showed a taste for homosexuals. But he formed no attachments. His body burned, for a woman or a boy, but his heart remained like an icicle. [...] He felt at home with the prostitutes and the homosexuals because they were so much worse off than he. The underlying sadism of his nature came out. He never credited people with feelings since he had none himself – save the fundamental urge to conquer, and to see others submit to his will.[171]

---

[169] Quoting The Times History of the War (Vol. III, 1914-18), The Times Printing House, London, page 80. [169] Pidcock, Satanic Voices 52.
[170] Hillel Halkin, "WHEN KEMAL ATATURK RECITED SHEMA YISRAEL - "It's My Secret Prayer, Too," He Confessed," Forward January 28th 1994. Several archived versions are available on the internet.
[171] Irfan Orga & Margarete Orga, Ataturk (London: Michael Joseph, 1962) 20.

Around 1913, Kemal was sent to Sophia as a Military Attache by Enver. Here he led a scandalous private life. To quote,

> As once before, he found himself more at home with pimps and prostitutes, and lesser men whom he could wholeheartedly despise. With little work of importance at the Embassy he had plenty of time for gambling and womanizing. He drank to excess with the deferential pimps and homosexuals. He bedded with the town tarts, and then flew into passionate, brutal rages because he was wasting his time and his life. He contracted venereal disease and turned against women. For a time he contented himself with the young and fair of his own sex, while in the background Ali Fethi murmured awful warnings and tried, unsuccessfully, to bring him to his senses.[172]

On Kemal's failure to develop relationships with women, the authors comment,

> He had never loved a woman. He knew men, and was accustomed to command. He was used to the rough camaraderie of the Mess, the craze for a handsome young man, fleeting contacts with prostitutes. But the softer emotions had passed him by.[173]
>
> As often as before, Mustafa Kemal took to drink, and was seen in the Pera nightclubs insulting all German officers within earshot, and ogling the light women. Drink brought out his brutality and his sensualism, and he avenged himself on chaperoned Fikriye with the prostitutes and pretty young boys who hung about the gambling dens. Soon he found himself mixed up with disgruntled misfits who spent their time plotting against the government. Less able than he to alter anything they were infinitely more dangerous, for whereas he fought for an ideal they fought for personal glory; or were in the pay of another country.[174]

During the war against the Greek invasion, Kemal indulged in scandalous conduct. To quote,

> He lived alone at Can Kaya for a time, and took his pleasures where he found them. He often drank half the night with Osman or some handsome wild youth who had taken his fancy. He was frequently bored. He was always restless. He longed for an audience who would accept his self-eulogising and recognise his greatness. Despite his

---

[172] Orga, Ataturk 52.
[173] Orga, Ataturk 92.
[174] Orga, Ataturk 95.

> orgies he controlled the life of the Grand National Assembly with an eagle eye [...].[175]

At the end of his career, he engaged in more scandalous conduct. To quote,

> He gave strange parties to alleviate loneliness, where prostitutes acted as hostesses and copulation took place between courses. He seduced the wives of his opposers and his enemies. [...] His targets were the rich and the safe and the highly respected.[176]

Mustafa Kemal's first serious relationship was with his Sabbatean cousin Fikriye. Since she had an unimportant background, his mother prevented marriage. But Fikriye lived with Kemal like a wife, until she was struck by tuberculosis. Since she was no longer attractive as well, Kemal had her dispatched to a sanatorium in Germany. When Fikriye learnt of Kemal's marriage to Latife later on, she returned to Can Kaya to meet Kemal, but was refused entry by Kemal's adjutant, Rusuhi. The next morning, she was found dead near the gates of Can Kaya, with a bullet in her heart.[177] The incident was hushed up.[178]

When Kemal was 41, he came across the 24 year old sophisticated and foreign educated Latife Usakligil, who offered him her home in Smyrna. He tried making a mistress out of her but Latife insisted on marriage.[179] Realising that he could use Latife as a trophy wife to further his agenda on the "liberation" on Turkish women, Kemal married her. But his drinking habits and his visits to prostitutes soon shocked Latife.[180] And unlike Kemal, Latife was not anti-Islamic.[181] Mustafa Kemal also turned out to be a hypocrite on his claims to "liberate" Turkish women. To quote,

> Mustafa Kemal was a morose, moody, and essentially earthy creature. His ideas for the country were firmly based on Western policy, but in his own home he was a despot, and remarkably old fashioned about a woman's place. If there was to be any talking, he was to do it and Latife was expected to give him unqualified admiration.[182]

---

[175] Orga, Ataturk 165.
[176] Orga, Ataturk 252.
[177] Orga, Ataturk 249.
[178] Orga, Ataturk 249.
[179] Orga, Ataturk 211.
[180] Orga, Ataturk 226.
[181] Orga, Ataturk 246.
[182] Orga, Ataturk 247.

In 1980, a Turkish court banned publication of the letters and diaries of Latife Usakligil, Kemal's wife of two years.[183] The publication ban was meant to come to an end in 2005 but was renewed by Turkish authorities. Some have speculated that Kemal's affairs with men were a factor in their separation. Despite failure in his personal life, Kemal took it upon himself to transfer a number of young orphan girls from villages and small towns to Can Kaya, "to be taught the modern way of life."[184] There were questions about his motives, and rumors grew that the girls were being used sexually.

In addition to Halkin, several other sources corroborate Kemal's Sabbatean background.

- Dr. Joachim Prinz refers to Mustafa Kemal and Djavid Bey as "ardent 'doenmehs.'"[185]
- A reference to Kemal being of Spanish-Jewish descent can be found in an American magazine.[186]

From the very beginning, Mustafa Kemal showed strains of manipulativeness, accompanied with cynicism towards everyone other than himself. It is a peculiar trait of the secretive and the intriguers, to be cynical towards the rest of humanity. He had a tendency of looking down his nose at people whom he suspected of being more learned than him.[187] His eyes were cold, and his malicious smile even irritated his friends.[188] He was generally lonesome[189] and sought to maintain superiority over others by achieving academic distinction, rather than making friends. While he would later learn to conceal his cynicism in his public speeches, some aspects of this cynicism, such as his permanent smirk, became his hallmark.

Kemal's first expression of political thought was badly written poetry with pantheistic undertones.[190] Despite being an ardent supporter of any anti-Sultan activity, Kemal was initially shunned from secret societies since he was seen as pushy and domineering, always trying to run the

---

[183] BBC News, "Ataturk Diaries to remain secret," BBC.com Published 04/02/05. <http://news.bbc.co.uk/2/hi/europe/4235691.stm> Accessed 16/10/06.
[184] Orga, Ataturk 273.
[185] Joachim Prinz, The Secret Jews (Random House, 1973) 111-122.
[186] The Literary Digest, October 14th 1922, page 50.
[187] Irfan Orga & Margarete Orga, Ataturk (London: Michael Joseph, 1962) 14.
[188] Orga, Ataturk 14.
[189] Orga, Ataturk 18.
[190] Orga, Ataturk 19.

show himself.[191] He eventually joined a secret society called *Vatan ve Hurriyat* (Motherland and Liberty). *Vatan ve Hurriyat* may have been an offshoot of Masonry, since its members greeted each other with special handclasps, secret passwords and signs.[192] It is interesting to note the similarity of the name of this secret society with those that propped up elsewhere in Europe. Liberty is an abstract notion, used and reused by the Powers that Be to the present day. And the call for "Motherland" is bound to elicit support from racists, chauvinists and the parochial. In the *Vatan ve Hurriyat*, Kemal distinguished himself with his anti-Islamic credentials.[193]

Interestingly, Kemal always feigned hostility towards the Germans. He advocated that they be kicked out, and their assets be frozen and confiscated.[194] This was in 1903, long before the alliance with Germans began to do more harm than good. His anti-German views would loudly echo throughout the rest of his career. But in practice, Kemal would display inconsistency. And on occasions, he would work with certain German officers without the slightest show of disapproval. For example, Kemal happily went to work for Von Sanders at Gallipoli, and never questioned his controversial leadership. It was as if Kemal only sought to create public spectacles of his anti-German views. If Kemal was highly placed in the echelons of the Powers that Be, he would have been privy to the intended outcome of the German alliance. And he would therefore try to secure his political future by being remembered for his foresight rather than step into a sinking ship. When the German Military Mission arrived in 1913, Kemal made the loudest protests and made sure all his protests were documented. When he became the hero of Gallipoli, he tried to become Minister of War by raising a storm of protest against Enver and the Germans. His protests against Falkenhayn amounted to insurrection. During Crown Prince Vahdettin's visit to Germany, even the Kaiser[195] and Marshall von Hindenburg[196] were not spared from Kemal's anti-German sentiment. Similarly, he appeared to be privy to the disastrous plan of the Turkish Army running the nation in World War I, and made a point of creating spectacles that would identify himself with the peasants rather than the Army. To quote, "We shall bring the Turkish peasant to the same level. The peasant shall be the master of

---

[191] Orga, Ataturk 20.
[192] Orga, Ataturk 20.
[193] Orga, Ataturk 21.
[194] Orga, Ataturk 20.
[195] Orga, Ataturk 116.
[196] Orga, Ataturk 116.

Turkey."[197] As in the case of Russia, where the confused and bewildered masses were used to destroy the existing order and supplant the domination of the Illuminati, the Turkish "peasants" were later on expected to play an analogous role. Unlike other groups, they certainly would not acquire the means to threaten Kemal. And Kemal was keen to maintain his access to the emerging political vehicle of peasant populism, rather than Enver's Army, which would go down in infamy. Around the same time, the Committee of Union and Progress (CUP; also known as "Young Turks.") was gaining ground in Turkey. Kemal was quick to join the CUP. But he discovered that he could never rival the powerful personalities that dominated the CUP. He resigned claiming that military and politics should not mix.[198] He refused a toast by German Colonel von Andertin to the success of the Army in crushing the Albanian revolt, claiming that the Ottoman Army was not representative of the Turkish people.[199] In an eerie prediction of the destruction of the Ottoman Army and the emergence of a nationalist Turkish nation state amidst the Greek invasion, Kemal claimed in 1909, "...the day will come when the Turkish Army, not the Ottomans, will proclaim the independence of the *Turkish* nation, a day when all of us are soldiers in the field, fighting for a common cause: our own survival..."[200] He sneered at the distinct individualism of the Ottoman-Turkish culture, which contrasted with the servile domesticated culture of European countries. To quote, "How can I hope to make a nation out of them? They are as full of jealousy and hatred as a pampered woman surveying her rival. We shall never have peace."[201]

As ringleader of *Vatan ve Hurriyat*, Kemal was arrested and detained. His military career would have been over, were it not for the generous second chance extended to him by Ismail Hakki Pasha, the Director General of Military Training.[202] Hakki Pasha appointed Kemal to a Cavalry Division in Syria, which was fighting a Druze insurrection.[203] But once in Syria, Kemal once again organized a branch of *Vatan ve Hurriyat*,[204] and spent most of his time stirring new intrigues. But Kemal realized that his intrigues would be of no avail in an outpost such as

---

197 Orga, Ataturk 54.
198 Orga, Ataturk 34.
199 Orga, Ataturk 35.
200 Orga, Ataturk 35.
201 Orga, Ataturk 189.
202 Orga, Ataturk 22.
203 Orga, Ataturk 23.
204 Orga, Ataturk 24.

Syria, and he secretly returned to Salonica on a leave of absence.[205] In Salonica, he turned his family home into a secret meeting center for anti-Sultan activity, and was eventually reported to the government by spies. When he learnt of an order for his arrest, he fled back to Syria. Ahmet Bey, an officer at the port of Jaffa posted him to a unit in Gaza and hindered Istanbul's request for an arrest.[206] Kemal busied himself in his duties so that the affair would be forgotten, and was made a first-captain in July 1907. The same year, he managed to secure a transfer back to Salonica and was appointed to the staff of the Third Army Headquarters in Salonica. At Salonica, he sought to revive the *Vatan ve Hurriyat.* But when he discovered the Committee of Union and Progress (CUP; also known as "Young Turks.") rising meteorically, he chose to join it again. It was at the CUP that Kemal first ran into Enver Pasha. Enver made it clear that Kemal could not waltz into the Central Committee of the CUP solely on account of his ambitions, and that he had to follow the same routine as everybody else.[207] This was the beginning of Kemal's antipathy towards Enver. In response, Kemal began to make his presence felt, shouting down Enver and criticizing the Central Committee of the CUP.[208] He was allowed to become a member of the Central Committee in order to keep him from disrupting the affairs of the CUP.

When the Young Turks snatched power from Sultan Abdul Hamid II, Mustafa Kemal's position catapulted. But he was still a background figure with no share of the glory, since unlike Enver, he took no personal risks in the coup. Enver had him posted in Libya to keep him away. But he returned to Salonica, and took part in putting down the anti-CUP revolt in Istanbul. But he was forced to return back to Salonica, while Enver soaked the limelight in Istanbul. At the 1909 annual meeting of the CUP at Salonica, Kemal tried to rid the CUP of its leading officers such as Enver, claiming (once again) that soldiering and politics should not mix, and insisting that officers who wanted to continue in the Party resign from the Army and vice versa.[209] Since he realized that he had no future in the Party in the presence of a dominant Enver, he offered his token resignation from the Party. But not many followed suit as he had expected. Since it was clear that he was directing more intrigues from Salonica, in 1911 Enver sent him to crush the Albanian revolt. The revolt was brutally crushed, but the Minister of War, Mahmut Shevket Pasha

[205] Orga, Ataturk 25.
[206] Orga, Ataturk 25.
[207] Orga, Ataturk 26.
[208] Orga, Ataturk 27.
[209] Orga, Ataturk 34.

recalled him on charges that he was inciting his officers to revolt.[210] He had incited them on nationalist lines, and they cried the slogan "Turkey for Turks."[211] To prevent a future recurrence of such behaviour, he was installed in the War Office, where he could be watched.[212] He grew jealous of Enver,[213] and tried to stir intrigues against him, but without success. For this purpose, he tried cultivating friendship with Djemal Pasha, a move that also failed. To quote, "He hated everyone and everything. He was very proud, and casual patronage and indifference of Cemal and his associates stung him."[214] With the Italian invasion of North Africa, Mustafa Kemal set off to North Africa in October 1911. Enver had volunteered to fight on that front, and Kemal did not want Enver to steal all the glory.[215] The Minister of War did not endorse his trip to North Africa, and refused to provide transport.[216] Yet, Kemal made a circuitous journey across British occupied Egypt on his own. The Khedive of Egypt (whose bloodline had been compromised by the Powers that Be) personally assisted Kemal on this journey.[217] Even the British, who would normally arrest any Turkish officers heading to Tripoli, appeared to be incredibly lax, allowing Kemal to slip through.[218] With the outbreak of the Balkan war in October 1912, Mustafa Kemal was appointed to a key position in the defense of Gallipoli. He was promoted to lieutenant colonel, but was not allowed to take part in Enver's heroic reconquest of Adrianople.[219] To prevent his further intriguing in Istanbul, Enver sent him to Sofia as a Military Attache. When Enver left Istanbul for the Sarikamis campaign, Hakki Pasha was put in command of the War Office. Hakki Pasha recalled Kemal in 1914 and put him in command of the newly formed 19th Division. This division was based at Maidos, on the Southern shore of the Gallipoli Peninsula.

Kemal's role in the defense of Gallipoli will be discussed in the section on Gallipoli. After Gallipoli, Kemal became Brigadier-General (Pasha). And he became even more intriguing and self-righteous, to quote, he

---

[210] Orga, Ataturk 38.
[211] Orga, Ataturk 38.
[212] Orga, Ataturk 38.
[213] Orga, Ataturk 39, 42.
[214] Orga, Ataturk 39.
[215] Orga, Ataturk 40.
[216] Orga, Ataturk 40.
[217] Orga, Ataturk 41.
[218] Orga, Ataturk 41.
[219] Orga, Ataturk 48.

"[…] accepted greatness as his due."[220] He tried to win the anti-German foreign minister Nasimi Bey for bringing down Enver. But Nasimi Bey reported suspicions about him to the Military Command.[221] Similarly, the anti-German Djemal Pasha avoided him as well. Mustafa Kemal attempted to topple the then CUP leadership through a conspiracy instigated by Major Yakup Cemal.[222] The conspirators were executed. Major Yakup Cemal confessed to a plot of assassinating Enver and installing Mustafa Kemal as the Minister of War.[223] Enver transferred Kemal to the Russian front, making him commander of the 16th Army Corps (consisting of two divisions) in February 1916. One of the conspirators in the plot, Dr. Hilmi Beik escaped and joined Kemal. Kemal refused to return him to stand trial.[224] In the Caucasus, Kemal regrouped what had remained of the Turkish Army after the Sarikamis disaster, and took back Bitlis and Mush from the Russians. Once again, Mustafa Kemal threw in all Turkish reserves, resulting in appalling casualties for the Turks.[225] Was Kemal planning another disaster on this critical front? If he was, he had got himself covered, by keeping copies of letters he sent to Istanbul meticulously filed.[226] The letters to Istanbul were addressed to Enver, in which Kemal pleaded for supplies and ammunition,[227] claiming that the shortages could create disaster for the Turkish Army, and Enver could be thus blamed. With the Russian Revolution of 1917, the Russians pulled back, and Van and Batum fell to the Turks as well. Kemal was made General, and commanded the 2nd Army based in Diyarbekir. His Chief of Staff, Colonel Ismet, would become his lifelong protégé.

Mustafa Kemal's role in Ottoman campaigns in the Middle East and his subsequent role after the fall of Enver will be discussed in the next sections.

About the CUP

The CUP had its roots in the secret lodges and fraternities of Salonica. It was founded in 1894. Some of its early leaders were openly non-Muslim. For example, Abdullah Cevdet, an early leader, was a Bahai. Similarly, Mehmed Djavid Bey, the Ottoman minister of finance, represented the

---

220 Orga, Ataturk 91.
221 Zallum, Khilafah 82.
222 Zallum, Khilafah 84-85.
223 Orga, Ataturk 95.
224 Zallum, Khilafah 84-85.
225 Orga, Ataturk 97.
226 Orga, Ataturk 97.
227 Orga, Ataturk 97.

Sabbateans of Salonica in the CUP.[228] Not surprisingly, the CUP initially advocated materialism, nationalism and racism. Many of the original Salonican operatives of the CUP maintained a staunch anti-Islamic attitude. For example, Ahmed Riza Bey, the President of the Chamber refused to take an oath in the name of Allah to abide by the constitution, claiming that he was a Positivist like the revolutionary Senhor Machado of Portugal.[229] Later, the Salonicans began concealing their anti-Islamic attitudes to dupe sincere Muslims into joining their cause. Some of the organizations associated with the origins of the CUP are listed below:

- Italian Freemasonry: Masonic lodges existed in Turkey as early as 1738.[230] But the movement was suppressed by Abdul Hamid II (1976-1909). However, the suppression could never be extended to lodges of foreign countries, such as those of Italian Freemasonry. It is clear that the CUP flourished under the protection of an Italian Masonic lodge.[231]
- The Balkan Committee: An early occult organization connected to the CUP.[232]
- The Acacia: A secret Young Turk Council formed in 1908 and directed out of Salonica.[233]
- The Macedonia Risorta, a Masonic lodge established by a Salonican Jew named Emmanuele Carasso.[234] He later played a role in the formation of the Commission that deposed Sultan Abul Hamid.[235]
- The Labor et Lux, another Masonic lodge. Refik Bey referred to this lodge along with the Macedonia Risorta, as playing a major role in the CUP takeover.[236]

---

[228] Quoting The Times History of the War (Vol. III, 1914-18), The Times Printing House, London, page 308. David M. Pidcock, Satanic Voices – Ancient and Modern Internet edition (Oldbrook, Milton Keynes: Mustaqim, 2002) 51.
[229] Nesta H. Webster, The Cause of World Unrest – With an Introduction by the Editor of The Morning Post (London: Grant Richards Ltd., 1920) 146.
[230] Pidcock, Satanic Voices 132.
[231] Irfan Orga & Margarete Orga, Ataturk (London: Michael Joseph, 1962) 26.
[232] Confidential telegram from Sir Gerard Lowther to Sir Charles Harding, Constantinople, May 29th 1910. Quoted in Pidcock, Satanic Voices 48.
[233] Quoting Vicomte Leon de Poncins in The Secret Powers behind the Revolution page 66, Pidcock, Satanic Voices 50.
[234] Nesta H. Webster, The Cause of World Unrest – With an Introduction by the Editor of The Morning Post (London: Grant Richards Ltd., 1920) 144.
[235] Webster, World Unrest 144.
[236] Webster, World Unrest 145.

- The Grand Orient Ottoman: Created on 1st May 1909 by the unification of 45 Turkish lodges. Mahmoud Orphi Pasha was made the Grand Master.[237]
- The CUP may have covertly received funding from "German agents" abroad. For example, Nesta Webster claims that Liam Mellows, who brought together the Irish Sinn Fein and the Bolsheviks and attempted a revolution in Ireland, went on to found a mysterious Turkish organization in America in 1918, which forwarded money to Turks.[238]

Realizing that the real strength of the Ottoman state lay in its military officers and commanders, the CUP opened its doors to all officers. However, once the CUP seized power, only ethnic Turkish officers were allowed.[239] The CUP thus became a vehicle of promoting chauvinism, racism and bigotry, symptomatic of the emergence of fascism in the Western world. Many other groups, who comprised the polyglot structure of the Ottoman state, were alienated. These groups went on to form their own committees on nationalistic lines. The CUP thus deliberately created a schism between Arabs and Turks by pursuing a policy of discrimination against Arabs.[240] As a result, the Ottoman Administration began distancing itself from Arabic, and by default, Islam as well. To further relieve the Islamic duty of the Ottoman State as custodians of Mecca and Medina, European Powers conspired to severe the Arabian Peninsula from the Ottomans.[241] This move also helped secure the largest oil reserves in the world, which have been kept at the exclusive disposal of Western countries ever since. The CUP's discriminatory policy fuelled the revolts in Yemen, Kurdistan, Albania, Arabia and Syria.[242] Economically, the CUP's Revolution improved nothing, with the exception of German interests in Turkey.[243]

Though the CUP's covert mandate was always the dissolution of the Caliphate and the dismantling of the Ottoman Empire as a jihad state, it attracted many sincere Muslims who were disillusioned with the then state of affairs. These people, such as Enver Pasha, and Djemal Pasha gained entry into the helm of the CUP. And because of their military

---

[237] Quoting Vicomte Leon de Poncins in The Secret Powers behind the Revolution page 66, Pidcock, Satanic Voices, 50. Also referred to in Webster, World Unrest 146.
[238] Webster, World Unrest 209.
[239] Zallum, Khilafah 19.
[240] Zallum, Khilafah 20.
[241] Zallum, Khilafah 75.
[242] Irfan Orga & Margarete Orga, Ataturk (London: Michael Joseph, 1962) 31.
[243] Orga, Ataturk 37.

strengths and abilities, became difficult for the Powers that Be to dislodge. However, there were others, such as Minister of Interior, Talat Pasha, who had Salonican connections to Freemasonry, and was usually at odds with Enver and Djemal, though he himself had no military credentials.[244] In effect, the CUP was less compromised than the Sultan and the administration. This is why the CUP was forcibly disbanded after World War I. The "powerless" Sultan Wahid-ud-Deen undertook the disbandment. And it also helped rid the opponents of Kemal, as well as those opposed to dissolution of the Caliphate. The pretext used was that the CUP was behind the Armenian Holocaust.

The CUP rebelled against the Sultan in 1908. The revolution commenced in Macedonia and spread to Rumelia, with Turkish officers refusing to take orders from Istanbul. Enver proclaimed the Revolution and was clearly the mastermind behind it. His intensive planning waylaid any efforts by Istanbul to counter the Revolution. When Istanbul marched in troops, they joined Enver's cause. Mustafa Kemal was also present. But since Kemal undertook no personal risk, he was not given credit, and sulked in the background while Enver reaped the glory. The CUP declared a constitution on 21st July in Salonica, forcing the Sultan to accept it. Then they marched on Istanbul to put down an anti-CUP revolt and occupied Istanbul on April 24th 1909. Sultan Abdul Hamid was deposed and Mehmet V was installed.

However, once in power, the CUP ruled more or less like a secret society. During World War I, they would meet in a secret, closed, windowless room in an unnamed villa in Istanbul, and their entire leadership never assembled as a Congress.[245] The CUP seemed to have an inside cabinet consisting of 90 members of Masonic lodges, who voted as directed by Talat Pasha.[246] The CUP ideologues were intent on removing Islamic aspects of the Ottoman state under the name of modernization. They paid little regard to the unpopularity of such measures by their Ottoman subjects. There were many demonstrations demanding the ouster of the CUP.[247] In Anatolia and Libya, religious groups made demonstrations,

---

[244] Talat, as Minister of Interior, may have played a role in the Armenian Genocide. Altay Atli "Cemal Pasa," turkeyswar.com < http://www.turkeyswar.com/whoswho/cemal/who-talat.htm> Accessed 01/11/06.

[245] G. Stefanovics, Enver Pasha and his Times <http://www.geocities.com/enver1908/> Accessed 22/10/06

[246] Webster, World Unrest 148.

[247] Abdul Qadeem Zallum, How the Khilafah was Destroyed (Gloucester: Al-Khilafah Publications, 2000) 37. Several copies are archived online.

shouting death to the revolutionaries.[248] The CUP's Revolution was hardly a reflection of the sentiments of the masses. And it succeeded only because the Army backed it. The reaction to the CUP Revolution in Istanbul portrays a rather grim reception. To quote,

> In the capital, notably at Taksim Barracks, the soldiers reacted with violence. They killed or locked up their officers. They marched from their barracks shouting religious slogans and death to the infidel. They were the defenders of the faith, the warriors of Islam. They and their fathers before them had borne poverty and ill treatment for their holy Sultan; they wanted nothing of the new Government but to be allowed to keep their God and their Faith.
>
> They caused chaos and terror in the streets of Contantinople. They looted the shops, and set fire to the Christian churches. They raided the Military Schools and whenever they caught an officer they killed him. They had been told that education was their enemy, and the enemy of Islam, so they raided newspaper offices, smashed the presses and murdered the editors. They shot dead the minister of Justice outside his office, and forced the Prime Minister to resign.
>
> The one newspaper they had not time to raid, *Volkan*, fanned the flames of their righteous anger and saved itself. *Volkan* ranted against the new government and called them 'men of no honour who blindly imitate the West,' and 'ignoramuses who are so puffed-up with their few days'education that they think they can look down on the students of the Sacred Law…' […][249]

The CUP used the Army to crush the aforementioned revolt in Istanbul.

The Ottoman Empire in World War I

This book emphasizes the fall of the Ottoman Empire for two reasons. Firstly, the fall of the Ottoman Empire eliminated the only real adversary the Soviets would face in their expansion into Eastern Europe and Asia. The elimination of this 'jihad state', which officially engaged in jihad in the region, also meant that the Middle East would be secured for Illuminati activity. This will play a crucial role in World War III. The second major adversary of the Soviet Union, the Japanese Empire, was taken out in the Second World War. Secondly, the fall of the Ottoman Empire, and with it, the straits of Istanbul, was crucial for the planned Soviet expansion into the Mediterranean, North Africa, and the Middle

[248] Irfan Orga & Margarete Orga, Ataturk (London: Michael Joseph, 1962) 30.
[249] Orga, Ataturk 32.

East. Although this plan never came to fruition, it was an important hidden component of the World Wars.

The Ottoman Empire was dragged into World War I in October 1914 on grounds of a secret alliance with Germany. Ottoman leadership and Ottoman royalty were compromised by the Illuminati, but not as badly as German leadership. Compromised elements within the Ottomans wholeheartedly acquiesced to gestures of friendship from Germany. The result was an influx of Germans, and German influence over the Ottoman military machine. The Powers that Be now had a direct foothold in the heart of the Ottoman Empire, and could engineer Ottoman defeat from their centers in Europe. The two Empires had been earmarked for doom, and the smokescreen of a World War was all that was needed to send them to their graves.

The exact machinations, which lead to the Ottomans agreeing to gamble their entire centuries old empire in this rigged sweepstake, require further investigation. Nesta Webster credits the CUP for delivering the Ottoman state into this alliance of doom.[250] She pointedly refers to Djavid Bey and Talat Pasha as the architects of this alliance.[251] From what can be discerned, the Ottoman Sultan Abdul Hamid had first instigated the alliance by responding to the friendly overtures of the Kaiser in 1898. Prior to this alliance, various efforts were made by the Illuminati rulers of Germany to seek friendship. For example, Kaiser Wilhelm indulged in theatrics, such as wearing a fez on official visits and circulating rumors that he had embraced Islam during a pilgrimage to Mecca![252] The Germans went further than just making friendly gestures. They were suspected in the assassination of Shevket Pasha,[253] Enver's Minister of War who was persuading Enver that an alliance with Germany was not in the best interests of the Ottoman Empire.

---

[250] Nesta H. Webster, The Cause of World Unrest – With an Introduction by the Editor of The Morning Post (London: Grant Richards Ltd., 1920) 143.

[251] Webster, World Unrest 146. Webster saw the German "alliance" as predatory and part of the CUP revolution conspiracy. She claimed that after a similar revolution overthrew Portuguese Royalty, their overseas colonies were absorbed by Germany. To quote, "[…] we see an alien movement seizing authority and overthrowing the established forms of Government and religion and the predatory German coming in to seize the spoils (154-155)."

[252] Channel4.com, "The First World War," Channel 4 < http://www.channel4.com/history/microsites/F/firstworldwar/cont_jihad_1.html> Accessed 23/10/06.

[253] Irfan Orga & Margarete Orga, Ataturk (London: Michael Joseph, 1962) 49.

As mentioned before, many sincere and capable Muslims had joined the CUP, and risen in its ranks to leave behind the actual Illuminati operatives in obscurity. If the Powers that Be would deny them leadership, it would expose the fledgling CUP as a conspiratorial organization. For example, the activities of Minister of War Enver Pasha were critical to the early success of the CUP. Therefore he rose within the CUP, despite his non-Illuminati credentials. He may have been allowed his major role so that he could be used as a scapegoat to transfer the burden of defeat from the conspirators. Of all officials, only Enver Pasha is credited as the architect of the German alliance by establishment historians. Some modern Turkish historians have gone to considerable lengths to defame him, accusing him of everything from military failures to the Armenian genocide. There is indeed, a certain degree of culpability on behalf of Enver, for making the German alliance a success. But this does not justify his scapegoating. German military methods affected the impressionable Enver.[254] And when he returned from Berlin, he brought with him a German Military Mission to reorganize the Ottoman Army. The key figures in this mission were:

a. Colonel Otto Liman von Sanders, who was made Inspector General of the Turkish Army, only one degree lower than Enver.[255]
b. General Baron von der Goltz, who took over command of the Black Sea Army Corps.
c. General Bronsart von Schellendorf, who became a technical advisor to Enver.[256]
d. General Kress von Kressenstein, who was made Chief of Staff of Djemal Pasha.[257]

Such major German presence did not guarantee that the Ottoman Empire was to ally with Germany when World War I broke out. Britain was still a possible ally. But when an Ottoman Mission was sent to London, it was given a cold shoulder.[258] Obviously, the Powers that Be sought no last minute alterations to their plans. To further alienate the Ottoman Empire, the British deliberately infuriated Turkish public opinion. The Turkish public had contributed for two battleships to be built by Britain for Turkey, at a cost of four million pounds. Collection boxes had been set

---

[254] Orga, Ataturk 49.
[255] Orga, Ataturk 50.
[256] Orga, Ataturk 50.
[257] Orga, Ataturk 50.
[258] Orga, Ataturk 56.

up outside mosques, coffee houses and railway stations.[259] The last installment had been paid, and the battleships were to be handed over on 2nd August 1914. Turkish crew was already in Britain waiting to take command, and special celebrations had been planned in Istanbul. On August 3rd, Winston Churchill declared that the battleships had been embargoed, and a day later, the Royal Navy acquired them.

This move was meant to prod the Ottoman leadership into an alliance with Germany. The Germans simultaneously presented two battleships as a gesture of friendship. Since the whole drama was being orchestrated by the Powers that Be, these German battleships were already in the Western Mediterranean at that time, and had strangely evaded British warships. Despite the fact that Britain had declared war with Germany on August 4th, and its Navy had been on high alert in the Mediterranean, where the British traditionally held supremacy. The two German battleships showed up at Dardenelles, and requested permission to be let through the Straits. Enver realized that allowing them through would be an act of formalizing an Ottoman-German alliance. He countered Allied protests with the argument that the ships were now part of the Turkish Navy,[260] and thus averted being trapped into entangling the Ottoman Empire into a confrontation with the Allies. These ships were later used to bombard the Russian Black Sea ports.

But by October 31st 1914, the Ottoman Empire was eventually dragged into the war.

Ismail Enver

Enver Pasha's Caucasian Campaign and Subsequent Engagements

"War until Final Victory" – Enver Pasha[261]

Prior to the Caucasian Campaign, Enver Pasha had distinguished himself on several fronts. Around

[259] Orga, Ataturk 57.
[260] Orga, Ataturk 58.
[261] Altay Atli, "Enver Pasa," Turkeyswar.com < http://turkeyswar.com/whoswho/enver/who-enver.htm > Accessed 01/11/06.

1911, the Italians had backed Christian rebels in Albania as well as the uprising of the Imam of Sanaa in Yemen. At the same time, Italy invaded Libya. But Enver managed to successfully counter them in Yemen and Tripoli. In the case of Tripoli, Enver volunteered to personally fight on the front, and commanded the whole front from a tent.[262] The Italian advance was thrown back to Tripoli, and the Italians agreed with Enver to avoid any further advances. Enver had to conclude peace with them only because of the outbreak of the Balkan wars. But Enver made the decision of allowing Ottoman troops to remain in Libya.[263] Later, these troops along with the Sanussi tribals would wage a successful rebellion against the Italians in May 1915 (World War I). During the Balkan Wars, the Serbs, Greeks and Bulgarians made sweeping advances, shoving the Turks off the European mainland. When Enver returned from Tripoli, a new government had taken office, and the CUP cabinet had been forced to resign amidst allegations of official interference in elections.[264] The new government was pursuing peace negotiations with the Balkan powers. Enver gathered the disaffected young officers who were against surrender and staged a coup. He broke into the Cabinet meeting where the peace terms were being discussed and shot dead the Minister of War, Nazim Pasha.[265] When the various Balkan states began fighting over their shares, Enver made a swift advance and recaptured Adrianople in 1913. The Bulgarians had abandoned the city and the city was thus captured without battle.[266] Following his success at Adrianople, he married the Sultan's daughter, Princess Naciye. He made public his plans to bring all Muslims together under a revived Ottoman Empire.[267] Enver also made a concerted attempt to crush the rebellion of Al-Saud and his Wahhabi followers, but had to abandon this quest due to the outbreak of World War I.[268] Later, Al-Saud would consolidate the oil rich Arabian Peninsula for Western interests.

Although World War I was primarily meant to create the conditions of revolution in Russia, the Powers that Be had decided that the Central Powers were not expected to make gains at the expense of an instable Russia. Instead, they were to divert their energies elsewhere, fighting all of the other Allies except Russia. The losses Russia inevitably made

---

[262] Irfan Orga & Margarete Orga, Ataturk (London: Michael Joseph, 1962) 40.
[263] G. Stefanovics, Enver Pasha and his Times <http://www.geocities.com/enver1908/> Accessed 22/10/06
[264] Orga, Ataturk 48.
[265] Orga, Ataturk 48.
[266] Stefanovics, Enver Pasha
[267] Orga, Ataturk 49.
[268] Stefanovics, Enver Pasha

were to be recuperated through "permanent revolution," along with huge additional gains to be made in World War II.

Although it was obvious that Enver Pasha could not see through this diabolical plot, he intelligently discerned that the greater enemy was towards the East. In the last months of 1914, Enver Pasha set off for the Caucasus, with a huge army numbering 100-200,000.[269] This campaign presented the biggest threat to Illuminati aspirations in both the World Wars. Unlike other Ottoman commanders who would coordinate offensives from long distance, Enver personally led this campaign.

The Powers that Be and their operatives among both Ottoman and German commanders tried their best to dissuade Enver Pasha. When the campaign commenced, literally all powers in the region ganged up to oppose him. The Russian Tsar left his turbulent capital for the Caucasian front, to inspire morale. The Armenians engaged in active sabotage of the Ottoman supply lines. Even the British would try to intervene. One can only imagine the extent of conspiracy to thwart Enver's campaign.

The British were engaging the Ottomans on other fronts. And Enver's campaign against the Russians has been seen by some as diversionary. But Enver's Caucasian campaign had potential to seriously disturb British India. The Afghan people and the Pathans of the North-West Frontier Province on the Eastern border of British India, were likely to become hostile to the Raj at the first appearance of Enver's army. Likewise, the British immediately mobilized forces to prevent Enver from advancing into Persia.

Enver planned for his army to fight along different routes, with all units converging upon Sarakamis together for a unified ambush. The plan initially worked and the speed of Turkish advance made the Russians initially retreat. But the Ottoman army was defeated, and retreated with heavy losses.

Apart from the abrasive effect of winter, it is not clear what exactly lead to Enver Pasha's abandonment of the campaign. Everything, from the strength of the Ottoman and Russian armies to the number of casualties on both sides, and the acquisitions made, is disputed. In addition, official Kemalist history has gone to great lengths to discredit Enver.

---

[269] Facts and figures related to this campaign are subject to controversy. We do know that the army was sizably large.

But what is clearly discernable is Enver's outrage at German commanders. Enver had rightly begun to see the alliance with Germans as 'incompatible,' though of course he couldn't obviously notice the conspiracy and sabotage that was taking place. He had begun to have second thoughts about the alliance with Germany itself. He would later create his own German-free 'Army of Islam' in the Caucasus (after the treaty of Brest-Litovsk was concluded by the Germans). To quote Enver,

> "Why should we feel any obligation to the Germans?" Enver would say [to Ambassador Morgenthau]. "What have they done for us which compares with what we have done for them? They have lent us some money and sent us a few officers, it is true, but see what we have done! We have defeated the British fleet---something which neither the Germans nor any other nation could do. We have stationed armies on the Caucasian front, and so have kept busy large bodies of Russian troops that would have been used on the western front. Similarly we have compelled England to keep large armies in Egypt, in Mesopotamia, and in that way we have weakened the Allied armies in France. No, the Germans could never have achieved their military successes without us; the shoe of obligation is entirely on their foot."[270]

By then, the Ottomans had already captured Trebizond, Erzurum, Kars, Van and Batumi. And they had defeated Armenian rebels. In order to prevent Enver Pasha from taking Georgia, the Powers that Be had the German "allies" of the Ottomans intervene. A German military force secured Georgia to prevent Ottoman expansion. Strangely, the German high command was worried about Ottoman influence in a far distant land, among all other immediate threats it faced. Despite that Enver had lent some of his best fighters to the Germans, who saw action in the trenches of Ukraine and Poland.[271] The commander of this German force was none other than General Kress von Kressenstein, who had played in important role in Ottoman defeats throughout World War I. This sudden interest in securing Georgia from the Ottomans may be related to the presence of Rothschild oil interests in the region.

The Army of Islam, under Enver's command, avoided Georgia and instead marched through Azerbaijan, reaching Baku in August 1918. The Azerbaijanis, the Kashkais, the Lurs, the Turkomans and the Kurds of Northern Persia welcomed Enver's army.[272] By then, Enver had also begun fomenting unrest in British occupied Persia through Salat-ed-

---

[270] Stefanovics, Enver Pasha

[271] Stefanovics, Enver Pasha

[272] Stefanovics, Enver Pasha

daulah, leader of the Kashkais. This was done with the aid of Enver's special German agent, Wasmuss.[273] The Bolshevik revolution had disintegrated Russian forces in these areas. But the British came to the rescue of Bolshevik interests, dispatching Colonel Lionel Dunsterville from Persia. He was at the head of a small but well-armed Allied force, complete with armored cars. He was forced to retreat. But the war had ended by then, and Ottomans would lose Baku and many Caucasian territories after the armistice. The Army of Islam collapsed, along with the fall of Enver after Ottoman defeat in World War I. Enver had originally planned to rally all that was left of the Ottoman army and fight a guerilla war against the occupying Allies.[274] But he was forced by the conspirators in the CUP to sign a truce with the Allies. Once the Allies signed the truce, they refused to further negotiate with Enver, paving way for the rise of Mustafa Kemal.

Enver Pasha had also begun to uncover the hidden agenda of the Kemalists, who were preparing for a takeover of Turkey. In 1920, Enver tried to overthrow Mustafa Kemal but failed. When the Allied forces put Turkey under occupation, they further demanded the extradition of those whom they saw as responsible for the war. This was done to further eliminate all possible rivals of the Kemalists. As a result, Enver had to flee to Germany. Upon instigation of Germany, Enver was deceived into considering friendly terms with the Bolsheviks.[275] The Powers That Be were estranged with Lenin, and therefore decided to use Enver as a neutral go-between to secure a German truce with the Soviet Union. They still saw Enver as a potentially useful pawn for the creation of reactionary ideologies opposed to the Soviet Union, such as Pan-Islamism and Pan-Turanism. In Germany, he would meet Orientalists propounding pan-Islamist and pan-Turanian theories.[276] On behalf of the German Chief of Staff (of the South Eastern front) Von Seeckt, Enver proposed a military-economic alliance between Germany and the Soviet Union.[277] This was finalized as the Treaty of Rapallo in 1922.[278] The Internationalist operative Christian Rakovsky would later reveal his Stalinist interrogators that this treaty was the sole doing of the Illuminati. The treaty in question allowed the Soviet Union to rebuild and refurbish

---

[273] Stefanovics, Enver Pasha

[274] Abdul Qadeem Zallum, How the Khilafah was Destroyed (Gloucester: Al-Khilafah Publications, 2000) 94.

[275] Quoting H.B. Paksoy. Stefanovics, Enver Pasha

[276] Quoting H.B. Paksoy. Stefanovics, Enver Pasha

[277] Stefanovics, Enver Pasha

[278] Stefanovics, Enver Pasha

itself for World War II using German resources! It also allowed the existence of secret German military installations on Soviet soil, for the purpose of offering training for the Soviets.[279] These would be used to coordinate Soviet rebuilding as well as for spying on the Lenin regime, which had run afoul of the Powers That Be.

On 16th August 1920, Enver finally arrived in Russia. He had evidently mistaken Bolshevik propaganda as a sincere desire to fight British colonialism. Bolshevik leader Karl Radek had convinced him towards the same end.[280] Once in Russia, he was kept as a virtual prisoner, to be used as a pawn when circumstances favored the Soviets. In April 1921, he was dispatched to Batumi. With the Greek offensive almost succeeding in dislodging the Kemalists and the popularity of Kemal waning, it was expected that Enver would enter Anatolia, leading a Soviet backed revolutionary force. Unbeknown to Enver, these supposed liberators would later transfer Anatolia to Soviet hegemony and would also uproot Islam from Anatolia. However, this exercise was cancelled after the Powers that Be secured Anatolia under Mustafa Kemal. Enver was more pan-Islamist than Bolshevik. Enver expected the Bolsheviks to be sympathetic to his idea of an "Army of Islam" in Central Asia, which would coordinate the liberation of the Indian subcontinent from British rule. It is obvious that Ottoman loyalists like Enver were seething with revenge at the activities of the British against the Ottoman Empire in World War I. Djemal Pasha joined Enver for this purpose and contributed by modernizing the Afghan army. He and Enver had sent Ottoman officers in advance, to train this future army in Afghanistan, with the aim of establishing in Islamic state in the Punjab.[281] Djemal sought to use the Turks of the "Basmachi" movement against British India. And for this purpose, he spent nearly one year traveling between Russia and Germany, trying to obtain weapons for the Afghans.[282] But an Armenian assassinated Djemal in Tblisi on July 21st 1922. The ARF's (Armenian Revolutionary Federation) account hints at likely collaboration between the Bolsheviks and the ARF.[283] According to

---

[279] Stefanovics, Enver Pasha

[280] Stefanovics, Enver Pasha

[281] H.B. Paksoy, "Basmachi Movement from within: Account of Zeki Velidi Togan," Nationalities Papers 23.2, June 1995, 373-399. An archived copy of this article can also be found at
<http://www.angelfire.com/on/paksoy/togan.html> Accessed 09/10/06.

[282] Altay Atli, "Cemal Pasa," turkeyswar.com <
http://www.turkeyswar.com/whoswho/cemal/who-cemal.htm> Accessed 01/11/06.

[283] According to the ARF version, the assassination was carried out at the Cheka headquarters, where coincidentally, Lavrenti Beria was also present. And he is said to

another account by an Azerbaijani Professor named Musa Kasimov (as narrated by Atli Altay),

> [...] the assassin was Sergo Lobadze, who was working for the secret police in Georgia. Lobadze himself was murdered seven months after the incident and the motivation behind Moscow's decision to eliminate Cemal Paşa was to prevent him from entering Turkey again, because, after spending time in Moscow, Central Asia and Caucasus, he was in possession of vital information and documents that could turn the public opinion in Turkey against the Soviet Union."[284]

Talat Pasha, who had also fled Turkey, sought to join Enver and Djemal. But an Armenian assassinated him in Berlin on March 1921. Unlike the later assassinations of Enver and Djemal, only Talat's assassination was confirmed to have been conducted by a genuine Armenian (Soghomon Tehlirian of the ARF).

When Enver Pasha began to recognize the Bolsheviks as the real enemy, he turned against them. Before he could gather a following, it was decided to pre-empt him. The Bolsheviks of the Tashkent Soviet consisting of Russian soldiers and non-Muslim Slav railway workers launched an attack on Kokand (near Dushanbe) killing 14,000. Enver headed a platoon-sized force, sword in hand, and was killed while assaulting a machine-gun position on 4th August 1922. He died at the age of 42.

Symbol of the Armenian Revolutionary Federation

Even with the defeat and dismemberment of Ottoman Turkey, the triumvirate of the three Pashas, Enver, Talat and Djemal, emerged as a new threat to the Powers that Be. These three Pashas had effectively ruled Ottoman Turkey since 1913, as the most powerful people in the Committee of Union and Progress (CUP). When Turkey was placed under Allied occupation, they were forced to flee. But as we discuss later, some CUP members such as Mustafa Kemal stayed behind in Turkey, and would not be harassed by the British, since

---

have commented on the possible role of Dashnak. Bolshevik collusion is obvious. Armenian Youth Federation, Greece. "Declaration: The Punishment – of those responsible for the Armenian Genocide," AYF Greece <http://www.hyeetch.nareg.com.au/genocide/punish_p1.html> Accessed 09/10/06.

[284] Altay Atli, "Cemal Pasa," turkeyswar.com < http://www.turkeyswar.com/whoswho/cemal/who-cemal.htm> Accessed 01/11/06.

they were meant to play an important role in the planned dissolution of the Caliphate.

Even in exile, Enver and Djemal were still seen as a grave threat to Kemalism, as well as Illuminati plans for the Indian subcontinent and Central Asia. Armenians insist that their assassinations were part of a conspiracy (Operation Nemesis) carried out by the Armenian Revolutionary Federation (Dashnak), seeking revenge for the Armenian Genocide[285]. However, it is more likely that this organization had been compromised, and was being used by the Powers that Be to eliminate all the CUP leaders who posed a threat to Kemalist Turkey. The British who had occupied Turkey would not arrest Kemalist operatives. Remaining CUP members were forced to flee and live as fugitives, and some were eliminated. For example, many prominent non-Kemalists, such as those that formed the Ittehad Committee in Berlin became targets of the Armenian Dashnak. Enver, who was considering marching into Turkey already had 29 branches of his organization working in Istanbul, and in each division of Anatolia.[286] He thus constituted the most serious threat to Kemal. Actual blame for the Armenian Genocide was in this stage, little more than finger-pointing (and still is). Not surprisingly, the Dashnak never targetted Mustafa Kemal or his supporters.

Gallipoli

Gallipoli was meant to be a focal point of World War I. However, the outcome was totally different from what had been planned. The idea was to snatch the straits of Gallipoli, and later Constantinople, from the Ottomans and secure the most important supply route for the newly created Soviet Union. At the same time, the fall of Constantinople, the seat of the Ottomans, would deal a devastating blow to the Caliphate. And perhaps even result in dissolution of the Caliphate.

There were indications that while British Empire was willing to carry out the sacrifices required for the conquest of Gallipoli, they were to be ultimately awarded to Russia. On December 2nd 1917, the Prime Minister of Russia, M. Trepoff, made the following statement in the Duma:

---

285 Armenian Youth Federation, Greece. "Declaration: The Punishment – of those responsible for the Armenian Genocide," AYF Greece < http://www.hyeetch.nareg.com.au/genocide/punish_p1.html> Accessed 09/10/06.

286 Irfan Orga & Margarete Orga, Ataturk (London: Michael Joseph, 1962) 191.

> An agreement which we concluded in 1915 with Great Britain and France, and to which Italy has adhered, established in the most definite fashion the right of Russia to the Straits and Constantinople.... I repeat that absolute agreement on this point is firmly established among the Allies.[287]

This secret pact was known as the Constantinople Agreement of March 18th 1915. It was later exposed and is discussed in detail in the next section. As per the secret pact, Russia would control Istanbul, the Western parts of the Bosphorus, the Marmara Sea and the Dardenelles, part of Thrace, the northwestern area of Asia Minor, the islands of Imbros and Bozcaada, and the four islands in the Marmara.[288] As per the treaty, Arabia was to be given independence, ensuring that Ottomans no longer controlled important centers of Islam and that oil resources were consolidated by American corporations. Lenin later exposed the treaty when he fell out with the Illuminati. The treaty would also allow the Soviets reciprocally, to advance into the Mediterranean, North Africa, the Middle East and South West Europe under the guise of fighting Fascism. The importance of Gallipoli to Russia is best illustrated by the following quote:

> General Nikolai Golovin wrote in his book "The Russian Army in the World War" that when the Ottoman Empire declared war on Russia and closed the Straits to Russian shipping in October 1914, suddenly Russia lost access to 98 percent of its imports! And that meant, all of those critical munitions and materiel that Russia depended upon could not be made up in Russia's few factories. Nor could they be shipped into blockaded Petrograd, nor into hardly used Archangel, nor Vladivostok in the Far East--not with a single line of track stretching 5,000 miles. Russia depended on the Black Sea trade in the 19th and 20th centuries. And that is why the British climbed down and allowed Russia to stake a claim for Constantinople after a victorious conclusion to the war. Russia absolutely needed the Straits, and the Russians dreamed of the day they could claim "Tsargrad" as their southern gateway.[289]

To quote Nicolai Bukharin around 1917,

---

[287] Cocks, Secret Treaties 17.

[288] Irfan Orga & Margarete Orga, Ataturk (London: Michael Joseph, 1962) 129.

[289] G. Stefanovics, Enver Pasha and his Times <http://www.geocities.com/enver1908/> Accessed 22/10/06

> [...] the Bolsheviks are aiming at the reconstruction of a great and powerful Socialist Russia, which cannot exist if she does not hold the straits of Constantinople.[290]

Gallipoli had acquired a Suez Canal like significance after the discovery of oil in Baku (See Russo Turkish War of 1877-1878). Russian engineer F.N. Semyonov drilled the world's first modern oil well in Baku in 1848. While Rothschild interests had consolidated this region[291] and the Black Sea port of Batum, moving the oil out through Gallipoli on a regular basis would be unfeasible until Gallipoli itself was consolidated. World War I presented the only opportunity to accomplish the same. The Rothschilds had entered the Russian oil business in 1885. In 1892, Marcus Samuel, the founder of Shell Oil which later became synonymous with the Rothschilds, had his Murex oil tanker sail from London to Batum and then through the Suez Canal. With the emergence of oil fuelled naval ships and automobiles, control over oil markets was decisive for the war. In addition, the newly formed Soviet Union would require capital. And exporting oil presented the most lucrative venture for the Soviet Union.

The failure of the Allied attempt to secure Gallipoli lead to the Powers That Be backing of Mustafa Kemal and the wars of Turkish "independence," which resulted in the creation of Kemalist Turkey. The straits would finally be consolidated under a new Bolshevik-friendly Kemalist regime. Kemalist Turkey remained neutral in World War II. This allowed the straits to be used as a supply route to the Soviets, and the Axis powers were surprisingly nonchalant. But Soviet plans to use the straits for expansion into the Mediterranean never materialized, due to a number of unexpected obstacles, which will be discussed in the chapter on World War II.

As early as November 1914, Churchill had presented a plan for the invasion of Gallipoli. Secretary of State for War, Lord Kitchener, appointed General Sir Ian Hamilton to carry out the Allied mission. This was an operation of critical importance. Therefore we find key figures in the British elite taking serious interest in the affair.

---

[290] Quoting a London edition of the Pravda that contained a report of a meeting held in the Great Hall of the Moscow Polytechnic Museum, during which Bukharin spoke on behalf of the Soviet of People's Commissars. Nesta H. Webster, The Cause of World Unrest – With an Introduction by the Editor of The Morning Post (London: Grant Richards Ltd., 1920) 151.

[291] Clifford Shack, "Oil and the Holocaust," Cliff Shack <http://www.geocities.com/cliff_shack/oil_chrono.html> Accessed 01/11/06.

The German Marshall Otto Liman Von Sanders supervised the defense of Gallipoli from the Ottoman side. Von Sanders hailed from a royal Prussian family in Pomerania. The relationship of German aristocracy with the Illuminati will be discussed in the next chapter. Typical of German elites, he became a Lieutenant General without having commanded troops in a battle. The Minister of War Enver Pasha handed over command of the Ottoman army to Von Sanders, who was only one notch below Enver in terms of authority. Enver had returned from the Caucasus and had entrusted Von Sanders with the Gallipoli command. Enver's plan for the defense of Gallipoli was two Armies, one defending the Asian side and the other defending the European side.[292] Von Sanders protested against this plan, since he wanted all command in his hands. And Von Sanders was subsequently granted full command. Von Sanders arrived at Gallipoli on March 26th 1915. The Turkish Army at Gallipoli was called the Fifth Army and consisted of six divisions totaling 60,000 men.[293]

Otto Liman Von Sanders

"GEN. LIMAN VON SANDERS PASHA, Commander in Chief of the Turkish Army. (Photo © by American Press Assn.)" from The Project Gutenberg eBook, The New York Times Current History: the European War, February, 1915. URL http://www.gutenberg.org/files/18880.

Even though Mustafa Kemal was well known for his prickly attitude towards Germans, Von Sanders quickly established a rapport with him and wanted to put his 19th division to the strategic Cape Helles command.[294] But Enver personally intervened to prevent Mustafa Kemal's appointment to this strategic area, since he personally mistrusted Kemal. As we shall see, the successful outcome of the Gallipoli campaign was not exactly the genius of von Sanders and Kemal. Kemal's role was retroactively exaggerated. Von Sanders preferential attitude for Kemal, among the six division commanders is strange, and may reflect the mutual camaraderie between elements of the

292 Altay Atli, "Gallipoli:Part II," turkeyswar.com <http://www.turkeyswar.com/campaigns/gallipoli_cont.htm> Accessed 01/11/06.

293 Irfan Orga & Margarete Orga, Ataturk (London: Michael Joseph, 1962) 62.

294 Orga, Ataturk 63.

Illuminati. The roles and bravery of other division commanders are slighted, and in many cases, information and data is outright missing.

On March 1915, 16 Allied battleships tried to enter the straits but Turkish mines damaged many of them, and three of them sank. The British Royal Navy suffered the most serious loss of its time.

This paved the way for large-scale involvement of Allied ground armies. The disastrous Allied landings would be the biggest sea-borne landings of World War I, which demonstrates the importance of this campaign to the Powers that Be.

Of the six divisions, Von Sanders stationed two of them in the North near Bulagir, two in the Asiatic coast and one at the strategic Cape Helles area. Mustafa Kemal's division was kept in the vicinity of Maidos as a reserve. Von Sanders believed that the attack would take place at the Asiatic shore. But the Allies landed on April 25th 1915 at Ari Burnu on the European shore, and Von Sanders had left this entire region exposed. The Allies had intended to land at Gaba Tepe but a current drifted them north to Ari Burnu. The inhospitable terrain of Ari Burnu slowed the progress of the 8000 men who had landed. But they straggled towards Chunuk Bair. The peaks of Chunuk Bair gave a vantage point to view the whole peninsula and the capture of Chunuk Bair was critical to Allied success. It is suspicious why Von Sanders did not keep this area better defended. His reasoning went against the very basic logic of Turkish defense, which emphasized on holding the heights to wear the enemy down.[295] Even as the Allies began moving towards Chunuk Bair, Von Sanders still believed that the main Allied assault was to happen elsewhere.[296]

Mustafa Kemal headed towards Chunuk Bair with one of his four regiments and started engaging the advancing Allies. Soon, he threw in all remaining three regiments, even though he had no authority to do so as a division commander.[297] These were the only reserves of the entire 5th Army, and there would have been serious repercussions for the Turks if there was a heavy attack elsewhere.[298] Mustafa Kemal had these regiments slaughtered in a kamikaze-like frenzy. To quote one of his orders, "I am not ordering you to attack, I am ordering you to die. There

---

[295] Orga, Ataturk 65.
[296] Orga, Ataturk 65.
[297] Orga, Ataturk 66.
[298] Orga, Ataturk 66.

is no going back. Every centimeter of ground is sacred fatherland. Some time will pass before we are all dead, and during that time other forces and other commanders will take our places…"[299] The following day, he was given another two regiments, but the enemy continued landing men, supplies and equipment. The Allies had captured some of the peaks of Sari Bair and had no intention to leave. Some commanders were growing pessimistic with Mustafa Kemal's plans, but Mustafa Kemal insisted on his wisdom and told them "You see only your own battle, you know…"[300] He also tried to astound them into believing he had a grand plan and was in possession of knowledge about the enemy strategy.[301] But the Allied advance could not be halted.

Turkish counterattacks were launched without preliminary firing, and the Turks were ordered to swarm enemy positions on foot. The success of these attacks relied on the element of surprise, and the Allies always appeared to be notified in advance. Such attacks lead to heavy casualties and entire Turkish regiments were wiped out. As the war turned to a stalemate, rotting bodies on both sides threatened what was left of the remaining armies with infection.[302] On May 22nd 1915, Von Sanders had Mustafa Kemal conduct negotiations for an armistice with the British Commander Sir Ian Hamilton.

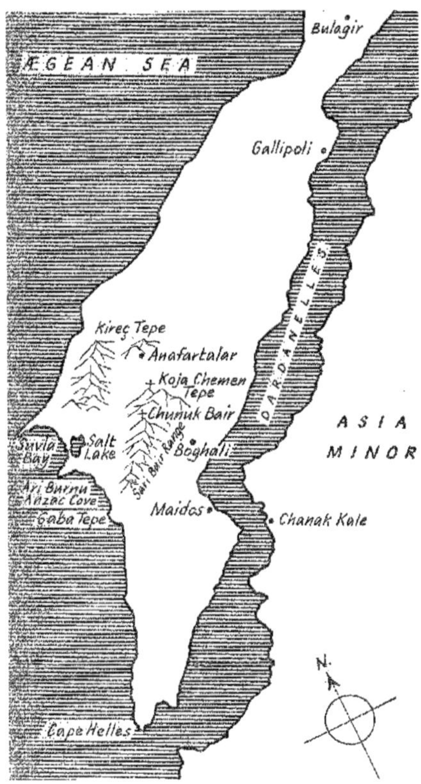

At the beginning of June 1915, Enver arrived from the capital for an inspection of Turkish forces at Gallipoli. He forbade Mustafa Kemal's plan for attacking Ari Burnu, rightly pointing out that

[299] Orga, Ataturk 67.
[300] Orga, Ataturk 70.
[301] Orga, Ataturk 70.
[302] Orga, Ataturk 76.

Kemal had a tendency to sacrifice his troops.[303] It was obvious that Enver was too naïve to suspect sabotage on Kemal's part. Feigning indignation, Kemal resigned, only to be brought back by Von Sanders. Kemal launched the attack, and ended up sacrificing his troops in another failure. But he blamed Enver's interference for the failure.[304] He resigned again, only to be brought back by Von Sanders. Von Sanders was beginning to be regarded as dangerously optimistic, and his promised German aid and ammunition never materialized,[305] forcing many Turks to fight with their bayonets. Sensing the incompetence of Von Sanders and its implications for the German-Turkish alliance, the German high command installed Colonel von Lossow in his staff, and Von Sanders was to give him voice in all future plans.[306]

On August 6th 1915, 25,000 British troops landed at Suvla Bay, and proceeded towards the Sazli Dere valley. This valley lead to the highest peaks of the Sari Bair range, Chunuk Bair and Koja Chemen, which would give the enemy a vantage point over the entire Gallipoli peninsula. Mustafa Kemal appeared to have either a premonition or outright foreknowledge of the attack. In May, he had taken his Corps Commander Esad Pasha to Sazli Dere, and told him of an attack coming from Suvla Bay and proceeding from Sazli Dere to the peaks of Sari Bair.[307] Kemal made every attempt to document his premonition/foreknowledge in numerous letters to Esad Pasha, presumably for later credit.

Von Sanders responded to the landing at Suvla Bay by having Major Willmer send a battalion to confront the enemy. This small battalion never returned. Yet, Major Willmer sent back the confusing message that "No big attack by the enemy has taken place."[308] But when it became obvious that a major offensive was underway, only Mustafa Kemal's division was in the vicinity for countering the offensive. By August 8th, the enemy Navy was shelling Chunuk Bair and Turkish regiments that had tried taking it back had been destroyed. The two divisions at the North end of the peninsula had to be finally recalled. Their Corps commander, Fevzi Bey were expected to relieve Willmer. But since these divisions made it on foot across the Gallipoli peninsula, Fevzi Bey

[303] Orga, Ataturk 79.
[304] Orga, Ataturk 80.
[305] Orga, Ataturk 80. Quoting Admiral von Usedom, commander of the Dardenelles defences, who wrote to the Kaiser that ammunition was critically short and had to be delivered from Germany.
[306] Orga, Ataturk 80.
[307] Orga, Ataturk 78-79.
[308] Orga, Ataturk 82.

refused to attack Suvla Bay immediately, as Von Sanders had ordered. Fevzi claimed that his division commanders were against an attack, as the soldiers were exhausted, and pushing them into the battlefield would massacre them.[309] Fevzi insisted that he instead attack next morning (August 9th). If Von Sanders had his way, he probably would have destroyed these two divisions as well by having them swarm enemy positions in such a fatigued state.

Von Sanders had Fevzi Bey removed from his command the very day, and instead gave Mustafa Kemal command over all the troops engaged against the Suvla Bay invasion (Anafartalar section). Mustafa Kemal had long been clamoring that all remaining troops should be united under his sole command. Numerous divisions were merged with his division, along with Fevzi Bey's two divisions, which had just arrived from Bulagir. The dawn attack on Suvla Bay took place on the 9th, but with Kemal commanding the divisions rather than Fevzi. The Turks streamed downhill on the British wearily moving upwards. Within a few hours, the British were wiped out. But news came that the British had taken Chunuk Bair, which seems to have been left undefended by design. Chunuk Bair gave the Allies a vantage point over the entire peninsula.

Mustafa Kemal gathered all the remaining troops and threw them on Chunuk Bair the next morning. The commander of the 8th division, Ali Reza Beg protested that the attack would not be effective since the men had no sleep for three nights.[310] But just as Von Sanders had tried to override the now vindicated wisdom of Fevzi Bey, Kemal insisted the attack take place the very next morning. Despite the Allies being obviously aware of the position and intention of the Turkish force, Kemal once gain insisted on using an element of surprise, and commenced the attack without the use of gunfire to soften up the enemy position.[311] The Turks rushed forward in a suicidal rampage and suffered heavy casualties, but after a few hours, no enemy soldiers remained on either Suvla Bay or Ari Burnu. The British attacked two more times before giving up, and each time, Mustafa Kemal threw in all remaining forces in a similar suicidal manner.

---

[309] Orga, Ataturk 84.
[310] Orga, Ataturk 89.
[311] Orga, Ataturk 90.

The British evacuation was conducted in complete secrecy.[312] Throughout this campaign, which lasted until the retreat and evacuation of the Allies around December 1916, up to 141,000 Allies were killed or wounded. An equal amount may have perished from illnesses contracted during the campaign. On the Turkish side, up to 251,000 were killed or wounded. The Turks claimed that the Allies used poison gas on Turkish trenches, created human barricades out of the bodies of Turkish soldiers and attacked makeshift hospitals. But these were not the only sources of Turkish losses. To what extent did Von Sanders and Mustafa Kemal contribute to the Turkish victory (if they did)? Was the Turkish victory intentional? Or was it the result of the exceptional heroism of Turkish soldiers? Was Von Sander's disastrous planning, Mustafa Kemal's presence in the vicinity of the Allied assaults and his possible foreknowledge of them all coincidences? Who was the hero of Gallipoli? Mustafa Kemal or the Turks he had sacrificed? The Turks were chanting Allah! Allah![313] as they leapt to their deaths, rather than any slogans of Kemal's nationalist jingoism. Did Von Sanders and Mustafa Kemal make secret arrangements to prevent the British withdrawal from becoming a far more catastrophic rout for the British? After World War I, Mustafa Kemal would address the families of the ANZAC soldiers who had died, consoling them, claiming that there was no difference between the Allies and the Turks who had fought and died at Gallipoli. A comprehensive evaluation of the leadership of these commanders at Gallipoli may yield a few answers to these mysteries, but is beyond the scope of this book.

Unlike other Ottoman fronts such as those in the Caucasus and the Middle East, Gallipoli was unique. It was the home turf of the Ottomans for centuries. All necessary fortifications were already present. The role of the Turkish army was largely defensive, and as such, saved them from the debacles engineered for them in other parts of the Ottoman Empire. And the repercussions of defeat were clearly visible for all Turks. Apart from political repercussions, the loss of the Caliphate held an ominous portent among all Muslims, and such a failure was seen as blight on their religious conviction. Secondly, the then Turkish army was still radically different from its European counterparts. Contemporary European

---

[312] Abdul Qadeem Zallum, How the Khilafah was Destroyed (Gloucester: Al-Khilafah Publications, 2000) 86.
[313] Orga, Ataturk 90.

armies were organized for efficient command and control by the higher echelons. The soldiers could be herded into dangerous situations, if destruction of the army was what the Powers that Be desired.[314] The troops were not expected to question or act independently, and were to blindly trust their chain of command. The relationship of the European troops to their commanders was very contractual. In their then military literature, soldiers were referred to as "human resources" and "human material." In other words, they were putty in the hands of the Powers that Be. Again, personal conviction did not play the same strong role as it played in the Ottoman forces, who saw themselves as mujahideen. Though highly motivated and independent regiments such as the janissaries had been disbanded long ago, religious motivation continued to be a prime source of inspiration for Ottoman troops, until the emergence of Mustafa Kemal's new "Westernized" generation of Turks. Such unique attributes of Ottoman command structure are ironically described in Western literature as Oriental vices. A motivated Ottoman soldier had little sanctity for higher authority and chain of command. He only followed them for enabling his personal pursuit of jihad. Therefore, regardless of how much the Ottoman military command had been compromised by the Powers that Be, the effectiveness of the compromise was limited by the nature of Ottoman troops.

The Ottoman Empire in 1914, before World War I.

Credit for Gallipoli thus swings towards the Ottoman forces that fought with everything they had. The relationship between Gallipoli and the Bolsheviks has been discussed earlier in this chapter, under the section "Revolution in Russia: Stalin."

[314] This may have happened to the German Army during World War I, particularly on the Western front.

The Secret Treaties - The Smoking Gun of the World War Deception

The Allies had entered into several Secret Treaties with the Russian Empire, which were never meant to be seen or scrutinized by the public eye. When Lenin fell apart with the Illuminati, he made these agreements public, which caused great consternation among the Powers That Be.

The Sykes Picot Agreement

The Sykes Picot Agreement of May 16th 1916 can be considered as irrevocable proof of World War I being rigged. This agreement was a secret arrangement between Britain and France over how they would divide up the remains of the Ottoman Empire among themselves. The Russian Empire was also party to the negotiations. Though a Zionist state is not specifically outlined, Palestine is earmarked for "International Administration." But on November 9th 1917, a letter was published from Mr. Balfour in which he stated that "His Majesty's Government view with favour the establishment of a national home for the Jewish people."

Sykes-Picot Agreement, 1916

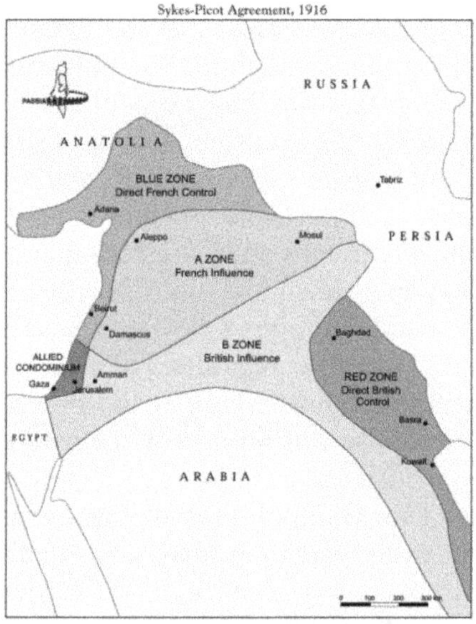

Palestinian Academic Society for the Study of International Affairs (PASSIA)

The Sykes Picot Agreement helped lay the foundation for the future State of Israel. Extending colonial rule was not the immediate motive of the Sykes Picot agreement. The long-term aim was to create the present day nation-states out of the former Caliphate. These puppet nation-states will play an important role in the future dialectical struggle against Zionism (World War III). Note that the German Empire, which was also defeated in World War I, was not carved into similar nation-states. In fact, carving out nation-states from the Caliphate, without due consultation of the defeated party went against all international norms.

The Bolsheviks printed the full texts of the Sykes-Picot Agreement in the *Izvestia* and *Pravda* on November 23rd 1917. The *Manchester Guardian* followed by reprinting the texts on November 26th 1917.

Unless the entire Middle Eastern theatre of World War I (October 24th 1914-August 10th 1920) was rigged by both sides, how could the drafters of the Sykes Picot agreement been so certain about the future map of the Middle East, which was contingent upon the following series of major future events?

1. The defeat of Kressenstein's August 3rd 1916 expedition at Roumani. This expedition could have closed the Suez Canal and reversed the fortunes of the British. If the Germans considered aerial bombardment the Suez Canal, the British supply route from India would have been cut off, creating serious implications for the British.
2. The breaking of the Turkish defensive line in Southern Palestine on 31st October 1917.
3. The success of General Allenby's main attack on Ottoman positions on September 19th 1918. This attack could have gone wrong at several different points, and could have spiraled into another Gallipoli.
4. The defeat of Mustafa Kemal's Seventh Army in Syria (1918), his retreat to Aleppo, and his consecutive abandonment of Aleppo as well. Note that Mustafa Kemal would later negotiate for peace with the Allies, agreeing to the boundaries outlined in the Sykes Picot agreement.[315]

The Secret Treaty between France and Russia

The Bolsheviks also released a series of telegrams that outlined a Secret Treaty between France and Russia. The first telegram is dated March 9th 1916, and the last one is dated March 11th 1917. The Bolshevik Revolution took place the next day, and therefore we can assume that the Treaty was still in the process of being finalized. The telegrams were printed by the *Manchester Guardian* on December 12th 1917. The following are the key points of the telegrams.

1. The Russian Empire seemed keenly intent on keeping indirect control over Poland, and requested that the question of Poland

[315] Zallum, Khilafah 99.

be excluded from international discussion, and that Poland not be placed under Allied control.

2. France wanted the Rhine River to serve as their boundary with Germany, and also wanted certain German areas, such as the iron district of Alsace-Lorraine, and the coal mine district of the Saar Valley. The Russian Empire was content with France's demands, provided the Allies let Russia set its own boundaries on the Eastern front.
3. France alluded to another Secret Treaty with Russia in 1916, and confirmed that the "question of Constantinople and the Straits" would be settled "in accordance with Russia's aspirations."

Why was the Russian Empire being leniently given a free hand over Poland and the redrawing of its Eastern boundaries?

This also sheds an interesting light on the Gallipoli campaign. The Allies were forced to evacuate Gallipoli by December 1917. But France was so confident of its own claim in Gallipoli in March 1917 that it was negotiating the transfer of its claim to the Russian Empire. It is clear that the defeat at Gallipoli was an unwelcome surprise. Nevertheless, why was France abdicating its own claim to Gallipoli in favour of the Russian Empire?

The later Soviet Union was the ultimate beneficiary of these concessions intended for the Russian Empire (with the exception of Gallipoli).

The Secret Treaty between Italy and the Allies

Italy had been allied with the German and Austro-Hungarian Empires since 1882 as part of the Triple Alliance. But having Italy enter the war as an Axis country would seal off the entire Mediterranean to the Allies, who were seeking to capture the Straits of Dardenelles, Istanbul, and the Ottoman Empire in the Middle East. Therefore Italy had to be goaded into entering the war with the Allies, even if it clearly wasn't in its best interests. And this could not have been accomplished without the complicity of Italian leaders. A secret pact, known as the Treaty of London was concluded between Britain, France, Russia and Italy, and signed on April 26, 1915. It was designed to have Italy enter the war with the Allies in return for portions of the Adriatic coastline of the neighbouring Austro-Hungarian Empire (its former ally), islands in the Mediteranean, portions of Asiatic Turkey, a share of German colonies in Africa and a loan of £50,000,000 from Britain. The terms of the pact remained a secret until they appeared in the *Isvestia* on November 28th 1917. A translation was printed in the *Manchester Guardian* on January 18th 1918, and, in *The New Europe* on January 17th 1918.

While Italy had been promised much, the Powers That Be never intended to deliver, as a strong Italian presence in the Adriatic and the Mediterranean would upset future Soviet presence in the region. The Treaty of London was subsequently nullified as a secret contract and was overridden by the Treaty of Versailles. Even President Woodrow Wilson was keen on Italy being cheated of her gains, and in his January 1981 *Fourteen Points* statement, he insisted that Italy be awarded territory only on recognizable lines of nationality and ethnicity. The Powers That Be tried to console Italy by allowing an occupation of Anatolia, but the Italians were forced to evacuate.

In World War II, Italy would be resurrected as a fascist Axis state, serving as dialectical opposition to the Soviet Union. It was intended that Italian advancement into North Africa would serve as a pretext for a Soviet push into the region, but this failed due to a variety of reasons.

The Secret Treaty between Russia and Britain

Rumours of a secret treaty between Russia and Britain, which awarded the Russian Empire Istanbul and the Straits of Dardenelles had been brewing in Britain for quite some time. The British Foreign Secretary was quizzed about it in the House of Commons. To quote,[316]

> May 30, 1916.
> "Mr. Outhwaite asked the Secretary of State for Foreign Affairs whether his attention had been called to an interview in England with Professor Paul Miliukoff, leader of the Constitutional Democrats in the Russian Duma, in which he stated our supreme aim in this war is to get possession of Constantinople, which must belong to Russia entirely, and without reserve; and can he say whether this statement represents the views of the Russian Government as regards its supreme aim in the war?"
>
> Sir Edward Grey: "Professor Miliukoff is a distinguished member of the Duma, but it is not necessary or desirable to make official comments on unofficial statements."

---

[316] Frederick Seymour Cocks, The Secret Treaties and Understandings: Text of the Available Documents (London: Union of Democratic Control, 1918) 16-17.

> Mr. Outhwaite: "Did Professor Miliukoff correctly interpret the views of the Russian Government; does it follow under the pact of London that this country cannot consider terms of peace until Russia has secured Constantinople?"
>
> Sir Edward Grey: "The honourable member is asking for a statement which I do not think it desirable to make."

On December 2nd 1917, the Prime Minister of Russia, M. Trepoff, made the following statement in the Duma:

> An agreement which we concluded in 1915 with Great Britain and France, and to which Italy has adhered, established in the most definite fashion the right of Russia to the Straits and Constantinople.... I repeat that absolute agreement on this point is firmly established among the Allies.[317]

Confirmation of this secret pact finally came when the Bolsheviks printed out a telegram from the Tsarist archives. A translation appeared in the *Manchester Guardian* December 12th 1917. The telegram was dated March 18th 1915, and was from the Russian Minister of Foreign Affairs (M. Sazonoff) to the Russian Ambassador at Paris. To quote the telegram,

> Now the British Government has given its complete consent in writing to the annexation by Russia of the Straits and Constantinople within the limits indicated by us, and only demanded security for its economic interests and a similar benevolent attitude on our part towards the political aspirations of England in other parts.[318]

The Bolsheviks printed out another secret document in the *Pravda*, and subsequently, a translation which appeared in *The New Europe* of December 20th 1917, and in the *Manchester Guardian* of February 22nd 1918.

The document is in the form of a memo issued to the Russian Foreign Office, supposedly prepared for the information of a minister. It claims that on March 4th 1915, the Russian Minister of Foreign Affairs sent a memo to the French and British ambassadors. To quote

---

317 Cocks, Secret Treaties 17.

318 Cocks, Secret Treaties 17-18.

> [.......][The memorandum] set forth the desire to add the following territories to Russia as the result of the present war:
>
> The town of Constantinople, the western coast of the Bosphorus, the Sea of Marmora, and the Dardanelles; Southern Thrace, as far as the Enos-Media line; the coast of Asia Minor between the Bosphorus and the River Sakaria, and a point on the Gulf of Ismid to be defined later; the islands in the Sea of Marmora, and the Islands of Imbros and Tenedos. The special rights of France and England in the above territories were to remain inviolate.
>
> Both the French and British Governments express their readiness to our wishes, provided the war is won, and provided a number of claims made by France and England, both in the Ottomon Empire, and in other places, are satisfied.[319]

Commenting on this demand of the Russians, Frederick Cocks writes

> This arrangement would give to Russia the whole of Turkey in Europe, with the exception of a small piece of territory in the north around Adrianople and Kirk Kilisse, which was apparently reserved as a bait to induce Bulgaria to join the Allies [.......] It would also give to Russia the Asiatic shores of the Bosphorus, the peninsula of Scutari, and about 80 miles of the Black Sea coast of Asia Minor. Tenedos and Imbros are islands in the Aegean, lying off the entrance of the Dardanelles. The Asiatic shores of the Sea of Marmara and the Dardanelles do not appear to have been included.[320]

In addition, the memo claimed that the Russians were developing an understanding with the British and French on a number of issues.

1. Istanbul was to be a free port of transit.
2. Recognition of the Sykes-Picot agreement (which was later formalized on May 16th 1916).
3. Reaffirmation (along with some modification) of the Anglo-Russian Agreement 1907, in which Persia was divided into a northern Russian sphere and a southern British sphere.
4. The question of the future of the Islamic holy cities of Mecca and Medina.
5. Confirmation that Italy was in agreement with these Russian demands.

---

319 Cocks, Secret Treaties 19.

320 Cocks, Secret Treaties 19: Note#1.

The next document printed by the *Manchester Guardian* was a confidential telegram dated March 20th 1915, from the Russian Minister of Foreign Affairs (M. Sazonoff) to the Russian Ambassador at London. Given the importance of this telegram to the thesis of this book, I found it necessary to quote it in its entirety.[321]

> No.1265
>
> Referring to the Memorandum of the British Government (? Embassy) here of March 12, will you please express to Grey the profound gratitude of the Imperial Government for the complete and final assent of Great Britain to the solution of the question of the Straits and Constantinople, in accordance with Russia's desires. The Imperial Government fully appreciates the sentiments of the British Government and feels certain that a sincere recognition of mutual interests will secure for ever the firm friendship between Russia and Great Britain.
>
> Having already given its promise respecting the conditions of trade in the Straits and Constantinople, the Imperial Government sees no objection to confirming its assent to the establishment (1) of free transit through Constantinople for all goods not proceeding from or proceeding to Russia, and (2) free passage through the Straits for merchant vessels.
>
> In order to facilitate the breaking through of the Dardanelles undertaken by the Allies, the Imperial Government is prepared to co-operate in inducing those States whose help is considered useful by Great Britain and France to join in the undertaking on reasonable terms.[322]
>
> The Imperial Government completely shares the view of the British Government that the holy Moslem places must also in future remain under an independent Moslem rule. It is desirable to elucidate at once whether it is contemplated to leave those places under the rule of Turkey, the Sultan retaining the title of Caliph, or to create new independent States, since the Imperial Government would only be able to formulate its desires in accordance with one or other of these assumptions. On its part the Imperial Government would regard the separation of the Caliphate from Turkey as very desirable. Of course the freedom of pilgrimage must be completely secured.

---

321 Cocks, Secret Treaties 22-24.

322 According to Cox, Russia failed to nudge other States into participating in the Gallipoli debacle.

The Imperial Government confirms its assent to the inclusion of the neutral zone of Persia in the British sphere of influence. At the same time, however, it regards it as just to stipulate that the districts adjoining the cities of Ispahan and Yezd, forming with them one inseparable whole, should be secured for Russia in view of the Russian interests which have arisen there. The neutral zone now forms a wedge between the Russian and Afghan frontiers, and comes up to the very frontier line of Russia at Zulfagar. Hence a portion of this wedge will have to be annexed to the Russian sphere of influence. Of essential importance to the Imperial Government is the question of railway construction in the neutral zone, which will require further amicable discussion.

The Imperial Government expects that in future its full liberty of action will be recognised in the sphere of influence allotted to it, coupled in particular with the right of preferentially developing in that sphere its financial and economic policies.

Lastly, the Imperial Government considers it desirable simultaneously to solve also the problems in Northern Afghanistan adjoining Russia in the sense of the wishes expressed on the subject by the Imperial Ministry in the course of the negotiations last year.[323]

(Signed) "SAZONOFF"

This document is the single most important confirmation of the thesis of this book, that there was collaborative conspiracy of Western nations to to expand Russian influence on every possible front, and particularly into Mediterranean And had the Allied campaign at Gallipoli succeeded, Britian would have quietly abdicated its gains to Russia, opening up the Middle East, Europe and Africa to the future Soviet Union. The 141,000 Allies killed or wounded at Gallipoli were a sacrifice for the future Soviet Union. But this is not the only conspiracy the document alludes to.

According to the document, the Russian Empire was instrumental in finalizing the abolition of the Caliphate, and in the creation of Saudi Arabia as an "Islamic" power, which was meant to substitute the role the Ottomans had played the region for centuries as protectors of the Islamic Holy Cities. Having a traditional enemy of the Islamic World assent to its creation wasn't exactly an auspicious beginning for Saudi Arabia.

---

[323] What this statement alludes to remains a subject of speculation. It can be assumed that Britain was secretly arranging further Russian expansion into Afghanistan.

When reading the document carefully, we find allusions to another "Islamic" power, the Islamic Republic of Iran. Strangely enough, Britain and Russia are agreeing to cooperate in playing a "developmental" role in Iran, rather than trying to push each other out and establish European supremacy. This confirms the notion that Iran was being carefully nurtured for a future role as another independent "Islamic" power. Do the roots of the Islamic Republic of Iran go this far?

The Secret Treaty between Britain, France and Russia

On November 24th 1917, the Isvestia published a Memorandum dated March 6th 1917 that was found in the secret papers of the Russian Foreign Office. An English translation appeared in the *Manchester Guardian* on January 19th 1918.

This was a Treaty between Britain, France and Russia outlining their "zones of influence and territorial asquisitions" in Asiatic Turkey. Britain was to obtain Southern Mesopotamia, with Baghdad, and two ports in Syria. France was to obtain Syria, the Adana Vilayet, and Western Kurdistan. Russia was to obtain the important Black Sea port of Trebizond, Erzerum, Bitlis, Van, and territory in Southern Kurdistan. An Arab State or confederation of States was also proposed. Reaffirming the Sykes Picot agreement, Palestine was to be subject to a special regime.

The Mesopotamian Campaign

As outlined in what would later become known as the Sykes Picot agreement, the Powers that Be pursued their plan of creating nation states in the territories of the Ottoman Empire. In April 1915, British forces advanced towards Baghdad after occupying Basra with their Indian troops. War minister Enver Pasha wisely chose to send the German general, Baron von der Goltz. There are many reasons to believe Goltz did not have a compromised background. Unlike other German generals, he rose by his expertise, rather than family connections. There were attempts to derail his career as a German military historian after he wrote books rightly critical of German military leadership. And despite his brilliant efforts in reorganizing the Ottoman army for which he was honorably titled Pasha, German Marshall Otto Liman Von Sanders was on bad terms with Goltz. In fact, the German military mission in Istanbul always sought to snub him.

Goltz assumed command of the Ottoman Fifth Army at the Battle of Ctesiphon. The British under General Charles Townsend proceeded to march along the Tigris to take Baghdad. Townsend had up to 10,000 Indian troops as well as naval support. When Townsend decided to retreat, Goltz started pursuing the British. Townsend garrisoned his forces in the fortress of Kut, which was in the middle of the Tigris River. On December 7th 1915, Goltz laid siege to Kut and built fortifications facing it. He also built defensive positions to take on British reinforcements arriving from the South.

Generalfeldmarschall Wilhelm, Freiherr von der Goltz.

British reinforcements were consecutively defeated, and up to 23,000 Allied soldiers were killed or wounded. Up to 8000 Allied soldiers were taken prisoner.

This Ottoman victory caused great consternation among the Powers That Be. In order to prevent any such victory in the future, the Powers that Be had Goltz poisoned. Those involved in his murder were obviously the same Ottomans who would later partake in the anti-Caliphate plot.

With Goltz out of the way, the British then marched onto victory, taking Baghdad and Mosul.

The British conquest of Sinai and Palestine

The commander of the Ottoman army in the Middle East was Djemal Pasha. Based on his background, there is reason that Djemal Pasha did not have a Sabbatean background. Even though he was a close associate of Mustafa Kemal. It is true that the Allies had started secretly negotiating with him, enticing him to rebel at the time when Gallipoli was about to fall to the Ottomans. He agreed to rebel, on condition that the unity of all parts of the Ottoman Empire (except Gallipoli) be preserved, and the institution of Caliphate not be abolished (Though he insisted that the Sultanate be abolished in favor of a new one centered on Djemal's bloodline).[324] Djemal's foresightedness can be discerned in his demand to abolish the Sultanate, yet preserve the institution of the

[324] Zallum, Khilafah 78.

Caliphate. Though he could not have known, he was able to discern the extent to which the Ottoman royalty had been compromised. Since these demands ran counter to Illuminati agenda, the negotiations were called off.

Like Enver, Djemal started becoming highly critical of German officers, whom he later believed had hijacked the Ottoman Sultan.[325] Though it may never be known to what extent he was knowledgeable about the Armenian Genocide, it is clear that he didn't approve of what was happening. He is quoted as telling a German officer upon seeing the deportations in Mamure, "I am ashamed of my nation."[326]

Djemal Pasha
Project Gutenberg eText 10338

The Germans encouraged the Ottomans to attack Suez. The commander chosen was Kress von Kressenstein, who was part of Von Sanders millitary mission to Turkey. But instead of Von Sanders, Kressenstein answered to Erich von Falkenhayn, who will be discussed later.

Kressenstein's attack on Suez (January 28th 1915) was conducted without any element of surprise. Kressenstein implemented the dangerously impractical idea of using inflatable pontoon boats to cross the Suez, but these could not be deployed due to machine gun fire from the other side. His attack was a defeat for the Ottomans and gave the British the justification they needed to advance into the Middle East from Egypt.

Kress von Kressenstein

Image source: firstworldwar.com. Copyright: Unknown

---

[325] Zallum, Khilafah 77.

[326] Armeniapedia, "Armenian Genocide Quotes." 16/12/06 Armeniapedia <http://www.armeniapedia.org/index.php?title=Armenian_Genocide_Quotes#Cemal_Pasha> Accessed 16/12/06.

On August 3rd 1916, Kressenstein attacked Roumani, east of the Suez Canal. Allied forces in Egypt, commanded by Sir Archibald Murray had already fortified and strengthened Roumani, obviously using their foreknowledge of Kressenstein's moves. The Turks were encircled and defeated. Despite having the resources, Germans never conducted an aerial bombardment of the Suez Canal. Even a temporary blockage of the Suez Canal would have serious repercussion for the British Empire in India.

Ottoman troops muster on the Plain of Esdraelon, in preparation for the attack on the Suez Canal.

With the commencement of the Arab revolt, Enver reluctantly ordered Mustafa Kemal to command the Turkish forces in Arabia. Kemal reached Damascus on February 23rd 1917 but refused to take command.[327] Enver came on March 15th, quarrelling violently with Kemal over his refusal to take command. On the other hand, Fahreddin Pasha, commander of the Turkish Army in Medina refused Enver's orders to evacuate Medina to provide reinforcements at the Sinai front, where the British were massing for an invasion. When Djemal Pasha clarified Enver's order for the evacuation of Medina, Damascus was hit by an electrical blackout, which Djemal Pasha saw as an omen.[328]

On 26th March 1917, the British began to inch towards Palestine. But were forced to retreat at Gaza. On 19th April 1917, the British re-attacked

---

[327] Irfan Orga & Margarete Orga, Ataturk (London: Michael Joseph, 1962) 102.
[328] Orga, Ataturk 102.

the Ottoman fortress of Gaza. Considering the importance of securing Jerusalem, resources from the European theatre were diverted to the British in Egypt, such as tanks and poison gas. The attack failed miserably. With Gaza failing to be captured, the British would instead capture the Beersheba oasis. Beersheba was an important point in the Turkish defense line.

The British army was supplemented and organized under General Edmund Allenby, who previously played in important role in the Boer war. Allenby was an acquaintance of the racist British colonialist Cecil Rhodes. He was also on good terms with Lord Kitchener. The Boer War took place after European banking families picked up the scent of gold and diamond reserves in the area. The first task was to remove the rather independent minded Boers squatting all over these precious reserves, and supplant them with British farmers. In the Boer war, the first prototype versions of concentration camps were created. Ironically, the Powers That Be would use the legacy of the Boer farmers to later bring apartheid to South Africa.

Erich von Falkenhayn
from a WWI postcard,

The Turkish army was still under Kressenstein. But was greatly disadvantaged because the new Chief of General Staff Erich von Falkenhayn had concentrated Turkish forces on the Mesopotamian front in an attempt to take back Baghdad. Falkenhayn was not part of the German Millitary Mission of Von Sanders. Instead he represented the German High Command in Berlin. With the German Millitary Mission failing to counter Ottoman losses in the Middle East, Falkenhayn sold Enver a grandiose plan of assembling the Ottoman troops on the Caucasian front. Though these troops were no longer an effective fighting force, the Russian Revolution had freed them from engagement. And the Powers that Be did not want Ottomans to take advantage of the confusion in Russia and make gains at the expense of the Bolsheviks. These troops were to be assembled into a highly mobile strike force (known as Thunderbolt) for use in the Middle East. But Falkenhayn neither consulted the German Military Mission[329] nor local Turkish officers. And his planning was bound to fail. Falkenhayn was

329 Orga, Ataturk 103.

instrumental in pushing Germany into World War I. He also played an important role in the questionable strategy of avoiding large German operations in the Eastern front, which prevented Germany from fully subjugating Russia (which would have also finished Bolshevism). He was known as "the Blood Miller of Verdun" for his role in making Verdun a catastrophe for both Germans and the Allies, and thus contributing to making the West, rather than the East the focal point of World War I. When he commanded Ottoman forces, he avoided deportation measures against rebellious Jews in Palestine. But were such measures of the "Blood Miller" taken out humanitarianism or were they part of a larger hidden strategy?

Falkenhayn's plan consisted of retaking Baghdad by ground and attacking the Suez Canal by air.[330] The Suez Canal linked Britain with its Indian colony, which was supplying troops for the Baghdad offensive. But since the Ottoman Army had no adequate air force, they would have to rely on the German air force for the Suez offensive. The plan was shaky and there was not much chance that the German air force could succeed in making the Suez Canal inoperable, given the limited number of aircraft the Germans had deployed on this front. On the other hand, Ottoman ground troops could have had a reasonable success. It is strange why Falkenhayn would stress so much importance on Baghdad whereas the single biggest British offensive was coming from Sinai, and the capture of the Suez Canal would also have been a setback for British troops in Baghdad and British India. When Falkenhayn earlier supervised Kressenstein's attack on Suez, it ended in a disaster.

Mustafa Kemal was presumably aware of the intended failure-by-design of Falkenhayn's plans. He started a campaign of attrition against Falkenhayn to create publicity for his own future career in Turkey. Djemal Pasha who had always been skeptical of Germans joined him. Kemal wrote to Enver that Islamic countries should have an Islamic commander rather than the likes of Falkenhayn.[331] When Mustafa Kemal was ordered to merge his 7th Army with Thunderbolt, he resigned. But he still retained informal command, refusing to carry out Falkenhayn's orders. Enver ordered him back to Diyarbekir, but he refused. Finally, Enver had to recall him to Istanbul on indefinite sick leave and Ahmet Fevzi Pasha took over command of the 7th Army. In Istanbul, Mustafa Kemal continued to stir intrigues against Enver. To quote, "By attacking Von Falkenhayn publicly, and unsettling the 7th Army, it would seem he

---

[330] Zallum, Khilafah 87.
[331] Orga, Ataturk 106.

was heading for insurrection."[332] But did Kemal have a better plan than Falkenhayn for the Ottoman front in the Middle East? Or was he seeking to supplant himself in the aftermath of Falkenhayn's planned failures and engineer further defeat for the Ottomans? It is clear that Kemal, as in the case of Gallipoli, would probably destroy all his allotted reserves and then retreat. The Ottoman Empire and protection of the Holy lands meant nothing for him. As he would write to Enver during this period, "Our aim must be to defend, *not* attack. We must defend *Turkey.* Not a single soldier must be sacrificed for the Empire but saved for Turkey..."[333] The British would have been overjoyed at such parochial nationalist sentiments. They had successfully managed to instill similar sentiments among the Arabs. And now Mustafa Kemal was doing the same for the Turks.

Southern Palestine was again attacked on 31st October and this time, the Allies managed to break through Turkish defenses. But they failed to encircle and destroy the Turkish army.

The flag of the Arab Revolt bears an esoteric triangle.

By this time, the British had managed to create significant unrest in Ottoman Arabia through their agent Lawrence of Arabia (T.E. Lawrence). The British had managed to dupe Hussein bin Ali, the Ottoman governor of Mecca, that he would be made king of the Middle East if he betrayed the Ottomans. Later, it was Hussein who would be betrayed by the Allies. Nevertheless, Hussein managed to stir significant unrest throughout Arabia, at a critical time, when Ottoman forces were concentrated elsewhere. This uprising of Hussein became known as the Arab Revolt. This "revolt" commenced in 1908. T.E. Lawrence managed to convince operatives of the Arab Revolt to attack the newly finished Hejaz railway line. The Ottomans had put significant effort in the completion of the Hejaz railway line, which was to link Damascus to Mecca. Apart from being of immense assistance to pilgrims, the railway line would offer logistical support for Ottoman forces. In addition, the railway line, along with the Baghdad-Berlin railway, was bound to change the face of the Middle East. The enormous potential for cultural exchange, interaction and trade would have transformed the Middle East as we know it.

[332] Orga, Ataturk 107.
[333] Orga, Ataturk 106.

Not surprisingly, this railway line was seen as one of the biggest threats to the future "New World Order" of divisive and quibbling nation-states in the same region. Lawrence would have the railway line repeatedly attacked.

An abandoned locomotive of the Hejaz Railway at Hadiya. Arabia and the Middle East lack a coordinated railway system to this day. Hajj pilgrims are instead shuttled in buses.

Meanwhile Mustafa Kemal was approached by Hakki Pasha to accompany Crown Prince Vahdettin on a tour of Germany. Enver appointed him officially and awarded him a medal to placate him. During this tour of Germany, Kemal tried his best to persuade the Crown Prince to start moving against Enver and the Germans, and to bring Kemal forward as a replacement. He made several public spectacles of his opposition to the Germans and their war plans.[334] He requested that when they return to Istanbul, the Sultan request command of the 5th Army based in Istanbul, and make Kemal Chief of Staff.[335] Vahdettin did not budge, as he feared rousing the wrath of Enver. And Kemal, fearing that his plot may have been discovered, used his illness as an excuse to leave Istanbul for Carlsbad. The Sultan started planning his moves cautiously. He made Izzet Pasha, an enemy of Enver, his *aide-de-camp*, and Enver was divested of his title as Vice-Generalissimo of the Army.[336] Kemal then crept back to Istanbul, and tried to persuade Vahdettin to override Enver, taking personal leadership of the country, and making a separate peace with the Allies.[337] Apparently, Kemal felt no qualms in using the Sultan's Islamic mantle to cloak his own dark ambitions. But the Sultan once again backtracked out of fear for Enver. Since Enver had got wind of the affair, the Sultan arranged an exit for Kemal's presence in royal circles by personally asking Kemal to command the 7th Army on the Syrian front. The future of the Ottoman Empire now rested on the outcome of this front. And the Powers that Be could not risk an Ottoman success on this front. Enver had to be kept away from this front at all costs.

On September 19th 1918, General Allenby mounted a full scale attack on Ottoman Palestine. For this critical phase, the Ottoman army was now

---

334 Orga, Ataturk 115-118.
335 Orga, Ataturk 118-119.
336 Orga, Ataturk 121.
337 Orga, Ataturk 122.

commanded by Otto Liman Von Sanders (Falkenhayn was recalled back to Berlin after his monumental failures). As mentioned before, Mustafa Kemal commanded the Seventh Army (based in Judea and the valley of Jordan).

Allenby's final assault on Palestine began with an Arab attack on a Hejaz railway station in southeast Syria. This was meant to be a diversion, fooling the Ottomans into concentrating their forces away from Palestine. But on September 17th 1918, a devout Indian Muslim in the British army deserted and notified the Ottomans of the attack along the Mediterranean coast being prepared for September 19th. Colonel Rafet, who held up the line on the shore, notified Mustafa Kemal. Kemal was not actively taking his command, feigning illness. Even though he could have taken a leave of absence and entrusted command to some capable officer. Instead of taking action on information received from the defector, he passed the matter over to Von Sanders.[338] Von Sanders moved his best troops away from the coast and towards the East, believing that the Indian had been sent to trick them.[339] Had Von Sanders been intent on Ottoman victory, he could have easily verified the information of the Indian through spies. Allied air force disabled Ottoman communications by bombing their Telephone Exchange. Nazareth, the headquarters Von Sanders soon fell. Yet, Von Sanders managed to escape. Mustafa Kemal was bedridden in Nablus, claiming he had kidney problems.[340] When the British attack commenced, his Seventh Army was the first to bear the brunt of British assault. He had his Seventh Army retreat along the railway line, all the way to Damascus.[341] The rearguard was decimated by British machine gun fire. At one point, his Seventh Army passed through a canyon. At the same time, Allied air force "coincidentally" spotted The Seventh Army and destroyed most of its equipment. The railway line proved to be a helpful visible marker for the Allied air force, and Kemal's insistence that Ottoman troops follow it all the way back to Turkey is suspicious. At Damascus, Kemal convinced Von Sanders to retreat another 100 miles towards Aleppo, abandoning Syria to the Allies.[342] Even Von Sanders became uncomfortable with such outright betrayal and had Kemal take full responsibility of giving up Syria without a shot being fired.[343] From

[338] Orga, Ataturk 125.
[339] Orga, Ataturk 125.
[340] Zallum, Khilafah 91.
[341] Zallum, Khilafah 91.
[342] Zallum, Khilafah 91.
[343] Zallum, Khilafah 91.

Aleppo, Kemal sent the Sultan a telegram, suggesting that Izzet Pasha be made the head of government, and requesting the dismissal of Enver.[344] No reply was received due to the confusion following the end of World War I and the fall of the Enver, Talat and Djemal triumvirate. The next government starred Izzet Pasha as its head, as Kemal had wished. Suspiciously, the Allies also pressed demands on the Sultan identical to those of Kemal.[345] Kemal then abandoned Aleppo as well, rather than create a final line of defense.[346] It is also said that he was in contact with T.E. Lawrence.[347] The significance of the Arab Revolt has been grossly exaggerated. The Arab Revolt was still in no position to face disciplined Ottoman troops, and would not have been successful without internal intrigues among the Ottomans.

Djemal Pasha, who was still in Syria, had used his military powers to discontent the Arab population with his policy of executions. The basis of his anger were seized documents found in the French consulate in Damascus, which indicated that the Arabs were coordinating their uprisings with the Allies. As despicable as they may be, Djemal Pasha's executions pale in comparison to the ruthlessness of present day "Arab leaders."

Turkish forces were regrouping, and could have driven out the British from Northern Syria, were it not for the signing of the Anglo-Turkish Armistice of Mudros on October 31st 1918.[348] The German officers were recalled, and Von Sanders gave command of all soldiers in Southern Turkey to Mustafa Kemal.[349]

This final conflict culminated in the end of up to 600 years of Ottoman rule in the Middle East. Did both sides stage it? The most decisive phase in Ottoman defeat was at Megiddo (Armageddon) in Palestine. This place has some kind of symbolic significance for the Illuminati. The Allies were willing to sacrifice up to 550,000 of their forces in the Middle Eastern campaign, despite the Middle East not being as important as the European front. This resulted in a brief stalemate on the European front. America was thus involved in World War I to bring the war to a quick end.

---

[344] Zallum, Khilafah 92.
[345] Zallum, Khilafah 101.
[346] Zallum, Khilafah 92.
[347] Zallum, Khilafah 92.
[348] Orga, Ataturk 128.
[349] Orga, Ataturk 128.

The Armenian Holocaust[350]

> Everywhere people are awaiting a *new world order.* We intend to introduce a great resettlement policy…remember the extermination of the Armenians.
>
> \- *Adolf Hitler, 1931*[351]
>
> *(emphasis mine)*

The Armenian Holocaust started around April 1915 and lasted till 1918. Up to 800,000 Armenians were killed, out of the estimated two million Armenians in the Ottoman Empire. It is important to note that these victims were mainly the Armenians in Anatolia, rather than Armenia proper. This was done while the Ottomans, under War Minister Enver Pasha, were fighting the Middle East Campaign against Allied forces.

The Armenians enjoyed favored status in the Ottoman Empire as protected minorities. This position was a regal application of Islamic law concerning minorities by the then Ottoman Sultans. Armenians established themselves as key players in business and many of them acquired positions of influence and wealth. That the Armenians would face such deplorable circumstances in an Empire known for its multiculturalism casts a sad legacy for the Ottoman Empire.

Armenian Genocide, 1915

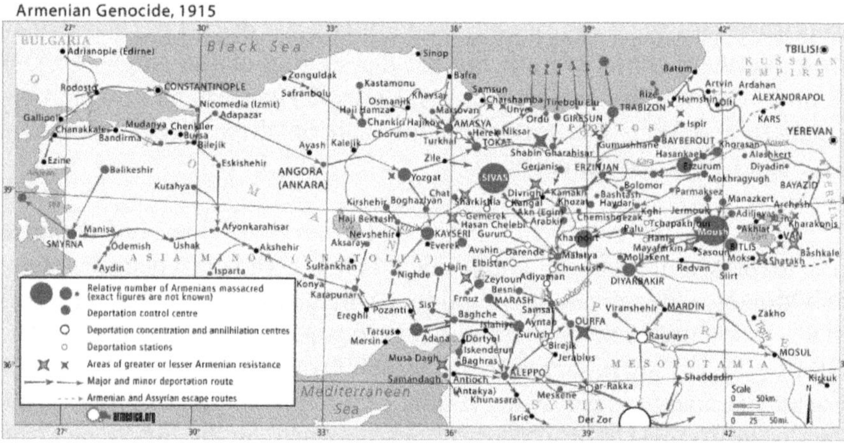

Why?

Increased outside infiltration into the Ottoman leadership corresponds to change in official Ottoman attitudes towards the Armenians in Anatolia.

---

[350]I am following Fisk's reasoning that the term Holocaust can be justifiably used for the Armenian genocide. Fisk, Great War 419.

[351] Robert Fisk, The Great War for Civilisation: the Conquest of the Middle East (London: Fourth Estate, 2005) 405.

First there were the massacres of Sultan Abdul Hamid in 1894 and 1897. In 1909, shortly after the CUP seized power, there were massacres in Cicilia (Southern Turkey). These were traced to the Sultan, who was subsequently deposed. There are many reasons why the Powers that Be sought to reverse the traditional Ottoman policy as well as the demographics of the polyglot Ottoman state.

The Sultan, members of the Ottoman administration and the CUP were engaged in a conspiracy to replace Islam with a jingoism based on Turkish nationalism, the secular republic that Mustafa Kemal would later create. And the Powers that Be would have exclusive monopoly over this new phenomenon of "Turkish nationalism." It would be their contrivance for claiming control over all Turkish people. Islam would be portrayed as outdated, and replaced with Turkish nationalist jingoism. Present day Turkey subjects the practitioners of the Islamic religion to surveillance and persecution.

However, powerful and sizable religious minorities could not be brought into similar direct control by making them repudiate their beliefs for this jingoism. Further, they weren't Turks. So forcing them subscribe to the prescribed Turkish nationalist jingoism would be all the more problematic. These religious minorities, Armenians, Greeks, Assyrians, would develop an autonomous status, preventing uniform imposition of Turkish nationalism, and by default, control of the Powers that Be. It is important to note that the Armenian Church, one of the oldest in the world, did not promulgate separation of the Church and State. Like the Irish, the Armenians had a Buddhist-like spirituality that was not institutionalized by the Church, as in the case of British or West European Christianity. If Armenians were to be given exclusive status in Kemalist Turkey, the few Muslims who refuted Turkish nationalism would demand a similar status for their religious observance, throwing Turkish nationalism in jeopardy. Therefore, the destruction of these minorities was imperative to the creation of the power structure that would later inherit Anatolia. The fact that genocides can be committed in the name of the Turkish people, and the Turkish people can be made defensive about such atrocities, testifies to the extent to which modern day Turkish society has been controlled and compromised by the Powers that Be.

In addition, the Illuminati sought to maintain their own stranglehold over all business in the Ottoman Empire and the later state of Turkey. And the Armenians would always prove to be serious competition. Since Islamic commercial law (in the Ottoman Empire) could not be radically modified to the detriment of the Armenians, the Powers that Be resorted to violence against those they saw as making their pie smaller. The argument that Armenians were extortionist economic parasites is self-defeating. The Armenian Holocaust continued to deeply hurt the Turkish economy even after World War I, since the Turks could not create a substitute merchant class overnight. And this economic breakdown resulted in inadequate food supplies for the desperate Ottoman Army,[352] turning potential victories into defeats. Therefore the motives behind the Armenian Holocaust go beyond the immediate ends of the Turkish military commanders in World War I.

The Armenians represented a peculiar brand of Christianity that flourished in the shadow of the Islamic world. Similar to the manner in which Coptic Christianity continued to thrive in Islamic Egypt (until the Arab Spring). Such variations of Christianity were free from the religious bureaucracy of European institutionalized Christianity, as in Papal Christianity and Protestantism. Going by this logic, it would seem rational that Armenians were liquidated once traditional strongholds of the Illuminati (such as Germany) began to make inroads into the Ottoman Empire.

Another interesting perspective is the Soviet one. Armenia had been earmarked for Soviet occupation, due to its strategic location with respect to the Baku oilfields. While the Soviets would have been able to suppress and snuff out religious and political dissent in Armenia, the Soviets could never accomplish the same in Anatolia. If left on their own, Anatolian Armenians would create a huge outcry over their compatriot's fate in the Soviet Union. They would clamor for an independent homeland. In this case, the Soviets managed to outsource the Armenian Holocaust to the Ottoman Empire.

Before the successes of Kemalism, there were even plans to turn Anatolia into a Soviet proxy (see previous section on Enver Pasha). Since the Ottoman Empire was also earmarked for destruction, it could be used as a proxy for activities that would bring grave discredit to any other power. The confusion following the abolition of the Caliphate and defeat in World War I provided ample opportunity for the real masterminds to cover their tracks and arrange for scapegoats. This also enabled the Russians to obtain a favorable "protector" status in Armenia,

---

[352] Orga, Ataturk 98.

which continues to this day. Even though the Soviets used World War II to "resettle" large number of Armenians elsewhere.[353] Although the Armenian Holocaust did not extend into Armenia proper, significant portions of Eastern Anatolia would be purged of Armenians. These areas would later fall to the Soviets. To quote:

> The worst atrocities happened in 1915, which coincided with big advances by the Russians into Turkish Armenian territory. The Russians entered a barren, empty land, and part of their post-war plans drawn up in early 1916 was to annex this area and turn it into a Cossack territory suitable for colonization. The Russians reasoned that, since there were almost no people, there were no further claims to the land.[354]

Today, most of the Armenians live as a Diaspora. Only three million remain in Armenia, which is indirectly controlled by Russia. Armenia completely succumbs to Russian control due to Turkish backing of Azerbaijan. This arrangement also works vice versa, allowing Azerbaijan to be controlled by Turkey.

Who did it?

Enver Pasha and Djemal Pasha do not bear consistency as characters associated with the conduction of the Armenian genocide. In the section titled "Infiltration," I have discussed how the administration and the Sultan were more compromised by the Powers that Be than the CUP.

Enver Pasha is often blamed as a mastermind behind this Holocaust. But there is strong reason to believe that it was not the *top* CUP *military* leadership (Enver and Djemal), but the CUP civilian leadership such as that of Talat Pasha,[355] the Germans, the Sultan and his administrative officers and mercenaries (as opposed to regular Ottoman forces) were the real masterminds and executioners of this secret Holocaust. It is important to note that the Sultan, despite being theoretically powerless, had a lot of sanctity attached to his orders. A governor of a vilayet would most likely cower upon receiving orders or personal requests from the Sultan. Enver and Djemal, who seemed to have been oblivious to the

---

[353] A top-secret report by Beria to Stalin (Dated July 4th 1944) refers to the 'resettlement' of 9621 Armenians to Central Asia. Report from Beria to Stalin, July 4th 1944. Quoted in Suny, Ronald Grigor Suny, The structure of Soviet History - essays and documents (Oxford University Press, 2003) 314.

[354] G. Stefanovics, Enver Pasha and his Times <http://www.geocities.com/enver1908/> Accessed 22/10/06

[355] See section on origins of CUP.

machinations that had compromised the Sultan, could have been silenced on this issue only by the personal request of the Sultan.

Consistent with the theory that the Holocaust was organized by the Ottoman State rather than the Armies commanded by the CUP, we find governors of vilayets playing an important role, using Kurdish mercenaries and criminal gangs. More disciplined and efficient Ottoman forces, such as those of the Major Armies were not used, at least in the more gruesome executions. This is because the Ottoman Armies responded only to directives from CUP military leadership, namely Enver and Djemal, who were unwilling to divert forces from the battlefront. The existence of a so-called "Special Organization" attributed to the CUP and its alleged role as the planners of the Holocaust is debatable.

However, lower level CUP members such as Mustafa Kemal may have used Ottoman Army units under their charge for the Holocaust. In 1918, Kemal would abandon Syria to the Allies, after the British air force bombed the Ottoman Seventh Army. Kemal managed to escape any blame and was not scrutinized. If such was the nature of Enver's "authority" over his command, there is no telling what else Kemal could have been accomplished unbeknownst to Enver.

Mustafa Kemal was not associated with CUP leadership at the commencement of Armenian Holocaust. However, he was in charge of Ottoman forces in Eastern Anatolia after Enver's failed Sarakamis campaign of 1914. In January 1915, Kemal used the pretext that Armenians were rebelling with Russian support to move into Van on the borders of Armenia. Up to 50,000 Armenians were forced to abandon their homes and ended up being dispersed throughout Russia.[356] Elsewhere in his career, Kemal had been quoted for making racist slogans, such as "Turkey for Turks!"[357] While accompanying Crown Prince Vahdettin on the 1918 visit to Germany, Mustafa Kemal launched into a vituperative tirade with the governor of Alsace-Lorraine,

> What do you know about the Armenian problem? [...] how dare you discuss something of which you have no knowledge? We have sacrificed our own interests to ally ourselves with your country, but we will not sacrifice our nation to the machinations of the Armenians who have plotted to destroy us. What right have you to take sides with the

---

[356] Stefanovics, Enver Pasha

[357] Irfan Orga & Margarete Orga, Ataturk (London: Michael Joseph, 1962) 92.

> Armenians against us? Have you heard both sides? Have you studied the question properly? [...] We came here to study the German situation, not to discuss the rights and wrongs of the Armenian problem.[358]

In August 1916, Kemal captured Van, Mush and Bitlis, which would be subsequently recaptured by the Russians after Kemal had rid these areas of Armenians. Later, Kemal managed to recapture most of Turkish Armenia throughout 1919. During the Turkish War of Independence, Kemalists may have burnt down Smyrna, which was home to Greek and Armenian communities. In the 1923 Treaty of Lausanne, Kemal and the Bolsheviks conspired to thwart the creation of an Armenian state, which could have been a useful buffer for Turkey against the Soviets. Clearly, Kemal had displayed a bigger antipathy towards the Armenians than Enver and Djemal are credited with.

The Armenian Holocaust was recycled to further pave the way for Kemal and the dissolution of the Caliphate. Sultan Mehmed held court-martials on November 25th 1918. These were used to discredit and punish Kemal's remaining rivals at the CUP. The CUP itself was disbanded. It is important to note that the CUP had, at that point, become an effective opposition to the abolishment of the Caliphate. The people singled out as "executers of the Armenian genocide" by the Armenian Revolutionary Federation had two things in common; first, they were and still remained powerful rivals to Kemal. Secondly, they continued to influence popular opposition to the dissolution of the Caliphate. It can never be known whether these accused were responsible for the Armenian Holocaust or not. All of them were killed by the ARF before they ever stood trial. The Armenian people were thus provided closure by the sacrifice of scapegoats. The murder of these scapegoats was necessary because dragging them to trial would open a larger can of worms on who was responsible, and would shed light on the conspiracies against the Ottoman Empire. Later, Western Orientalists would further feed disinformation on the whole issue. It is important to note that fabricating evidence, be it telegrams, diaries or messages, are standard fare for establishment historians. One will be familiar with the prevalence of such methods when studying the Third Reich.

Enver's attitude towards Armenians does not appear to be consistent with that of the executioner of genocide. In 1918, The Army of Islam reached Baku under Enver's leadership. This march was accomplished

---

[358] Orga, Ataturk 118.

across Armenian territory. Although there was sporadic fighting with the Armenians, there were no massacres or deportations, as those that occurred in Ottoman controlled Anatolia. This was despite that Russia had evacuated the region by then, leaving the Armenians with no support base. Enver even allowed the Dashnaktiun party to run a government at Yerivan.[359] Does Enver sound like the sinister mastermind of the Armenian Holocaust?

Apart from the obvious implication of Talat Pasha and figures in the Ottoman administration, very little is known about the real "masterminds." The orders for the conduction of the Holocaust were highly secretive. The orders were deliberately vague, ranging from deportation, to relocation and resettlement, obfuscating the grisly details. This required enlistment and cooperation of local authorities. It should be noted that residents of the Ottoman Empire were completely oblivious to such sophisticated deceptions. Nevertheless, there were many instances when Muslims of the Ottoman Empire defied orders and took risks to save Armenians when they could.

The Armenian Holocaust was a learning experience for the Powers that Be, as the later Jewish Holocaust would prove. The Jewish Holocaust seems to have been based on the Armenian Holocaust.

1. Effective use of **death marches** (later seen elsewhere as well, such as Stalin's Ukraine)
2. Years, probably a decade of **meticulous planning**. A cursory look at the map at the beginning of this chapter will dispel all doubts that the Armenian Holocaust was the result of a tantrum of Enver Pasha.
3. The effective use of **railways**. This may have been a hidden agenda of German railroad interests in the Ottoman Empire. Pursuers would drive Armenians like cattle towards the railway stations.[360] Armenians were then packed into cattle trucks, up to ninety per wagon, which would be the same average used during the Jewish Holocaust.[361] Germans working on the development of Ottoman railroads were indirectly being used for this purpose. In addition, there were numerous "Germans" who would later resurface as Nazis. Their presence in Turkey may have been to

---

[359] Stefanovics, Enver Pasha

[360] Robert Fisk, The Great War for Civilisation: the Conquest of the Middle East (London: Fourth Estate, 2005) 403.

[361] Fisk, Great War 400.

observe, and possibly, offer their expertise on this project. Among those who "gleaned at first hand"[362] were:

a. Franz von Papen,[363] chief of staff of the Fourth Turkish Army. Later played a major role in facilitating the rise of Hitler. He became Hitler's Vice-Chancellor and President of Prussia. He later became special ambassador to Austria, and assisted in the Nazi annexation of Austria.
b. Lieutenant General Hans von Seeckt,[364] chief of Ottoman General Staff. He would later engineer the Illuminati treaty of Rapallo (see section on Enver). He later played a role in the rise of Hitler. From 1934-1935, he served as an advisor to Chiang Kai-Shek.
c. Rudolf Hess[365] would go on to later play a major role in the Jewish Holocaust.
d. Max Erwin von Scheubner-Richter,[366] who witnessed the Armenian Holocaust first hand and sent detailed reports on the methodology used back to Berlin. He would become Hitler's closest advisors and would compose racist editorials in a Munich newspaper.
e. General Bronsart von Schellendorf, a senior member of the Turkish military mission, who issued deportation orders for Armenians, calling for harsh measures to be used. He would later author an article in a German newspaper denying the Armenian Holocaust.[367]
f. Kanstantin Freiherr von Neurath had an important position in the German Embassy in Istanbul (1915-1916) and was instructed by Chancellor Hollweg to monitor operations against Armenians.[368] He later became a foreign minister in Papen's cabinet.
g. Vahakn N. Dadrian has noted many other Germans who served in Turkey and were likely to have been complicit in the Armenian genocide, and later served the Nazis.

---

[362] Fisk, Great War 403.
[363] Fisk, Great War 404.
[364] Fisk, Great War 403.
[365] Fisk, Great War 404.
[366] Fisk, Great War 404.
[367] General Lieutenant Bronsart von Schellendorf, "A Witness for Talaat Pasha," Deutsche Allgemeine Zeitung July 24, 1921.
[368] Vahakn N. Dadrian, German Responsibility in the Armenian Genocide: A Review of the Historical Evidence of German Complicity (Watertown MA: Blue Crane Books, 1996) 199.

Among those in his list are Count F. W. Von der Schulenburg, Frederic Hans von Rosenberg, Wilhelm Solf, Albert Ballin, Major General Otto von Lossow and Major General Kress von Kressenstein.

h. Many other German officers, who preferred to remain silent.[369]

Armenia and the Powers that Be

As if Armenians did not have enough, they are also host to ancient Cabal bloodlines. These bloodlines generally inhabit an elitist position among them. And as one may suspect, such bloodlined elite didn't become casualties of the Armenian Holocaust.

The region of Armenia in the Caucasus has a very ancient history. It was and still is a hotbed of Cabal activity. For example, the "Christian" Armenian kingdoms in this region bear seals identical to their Illuminati counterparts in Western Europe. Esotericists may be able to make some interesting connections in this regard. The Illuminati Safavids, who ruled Persia in medieval times and subjected the religion of Islam to shameful manipulations and permutations, originated in Armenia. Prior to morphing into the descendants of the Prophet of Islam, the early Safavids had ancestors among the Christian royals based in Trebizond,[370] linked to Byzantine Royalty. The Safavids were noted for preventing Ottoman expansion into Europe. Whenever the Ottomans would campaign against Europe, the Safavids would create a diversion in the Middle East. Similarly, Safavid infiltration and intermarriage with the Mughals led to the crash of the Mughal Empire in India.

During my studies at Dalhousie University, one of the cabal operatives who tried entrapping me on numerous occasions would pass off as an "Armenian" in his public life. One can only wonder what role such "Armenians" may have played in the Armenian Holocaust.

Armenian assassins were used to eliminate enemies of Kemal and those opposed to the dissolution of the Caliphate. In addition, Armenian assassins were used to cover up murders originating from the Bolsheviks and other parties.

---

[369] Fisk, Great War 406.

[370] V. Minorsky, "The Poetry of Shah Isma'il I," Bulletin of the School of Oriental and African Studies University of London 10.4 (1942), 1053a.

Opponents of the Armenian Holocaust claim that Armenians were used by the Powers that Be to depopulate indigenous Muslims during the Soviet rule of the Caucasus. Such indigenous Muslim groups, such as the Tartars, were neutral during the Armenian Holocaust. Armenia is still ruled by the Powers that Be (via Russia). Armenia is used to pressure Azerbaijan to remain a proxy of Kemalist Turkey (and vice versa).

Denial

The Armenian Holocaust is denied for two main reasons

Firstly, the investigation into this atrocity will throw light on the last days of the Ottoman Empire and the machinations responsible for its downfall. Many Western Orientalists are involved in the cover-up. In fact, my initial suspicions were ticked off by the fact that Western academics seemed soft towards an "Islamic" atrocity, rather than propagandizing it. Imagine if that happened in Darfur. Many Western countries preferred to remain silent when the Armenian Holocaust was unfolding. For example, the British Foreign Office, which closely monitored the Ottoman State and sought anything that could be converted into war propaganda, seems to have deliberately excluded the Armenian Holocaust.

Secondly, recognition of this atrocity will create claims for an Armenian homeland. The Powers that Be are in no mood to fragment their authority in the region, and instead rule through larger blocs such as Turkey and Russia.

The Rise of Mustafa Kemal

When studying the dissolution of the Ottoman Caliphate, it is pertinent to understand the importance of the Caliphate to the then Muslim people. This will explain why Mustafa Kemal had to take such a convoluted path to accomplish its dissolution.

The Ottomans saw themselves as religious people, as upholders of the Islamic faith. They did not confine religion to a "Papal style" autonomy of religious heads in Mecca, and instead saw all the lands before them as proving grounds for their commitment to Islam. Even when their leadership was compromised, Cabal operatives within the Ottoman state machinery had limited room for mischief, as opposed to "secular" and "modern" states. Therefore, the sabotage and dissolution of the Ottoman Caliphate was critical to the goals of the Powers that Be. The Ottomans were the self-proclaimed protectors of the Islamic World, and the custodians of the three Holy Mosques of Islam. Therefore, any opposition to the Caliphate was seen as a disloyalty towards Islam. And it is unlikely that such an endeavor would acquire popular Muslim support. Not surprisingly, the earliest calls for dissolution of the Caliphate came from urban "modernists," non-Muslim minorities and similar Westernized dupes and their backers. However, in mainland Turkey, neither modernism nor westernization held sway. As always, the sentiment of jihad and establishment of the Islamic faith solely moved the Turkic masses, as was demonstrated at Gallipoli. Kemalists tapped into this support base in initial stages by pretending to be Islamically motivated. The Muslims who joined them would be betrayed later. Mustafa Kemal was chosen for the project to abolish the Caliphate because only he and a handful of officers were willing to abolish the Caliphate and seek the severance of Arabic speaking lands[371] in the name of Turkish nationalism. Other Turkish Army officials were reluctant to go that far.

The two faces of Mustafa Kemal

This composite picture was created from two images. The image on the left represents Kemal in 1912, wearing a turban, traditional Ottoman clothes and trousers. In addition, he is clutching the sword of Jihad, and minarets can be seen in the studio background (HU042303| RM| © Hulton-Deutsch Collection/CORBIS). All Rights Reserved. Partially and Minimally Reproduced under Fair Dealing.

The Kemal on the right is the new modern and secular 1926 Kemal, who is even executing people for following the traditional Ottoman dress code. (U103662P-A| RM| © Bettmann/CORBIS). All Rights Reserved. Partially and Minimally Reproduced Under Fair Dealing

After World War I, all significant portions of the Ottoman Empire were earmarked for division, as was planned in advance by the Allies. At this time, Mustafa Kemal's only credential was the Ottoman success at Gallipoli. Modern Turkish historians have exaggerated this attribute. The loss of Syria at his hands overshadowed his "success" at Gallipoli. He had no chance of

[371] Abdul Qadeem Zallum, How the Khilafah was Destroyed (Gloucester: Al-Khilafah Publications, 2000) 120.

becoming commander in chief of the Armed Forces.[372] There were far more capable and battle seasoned Ottomans available for this job. Despite a feather in his cap like Gallipoli, he was treated as a pariah in Istanbul. And were it not for Von Sanders allowing Kemal to step into his shoes, Kemal would probably never have become a leader.

All of Turkey was intended to be under Allied occupation at the close of World War I. Allied occupation was most prominent in the Bosporus. Had the British managed to achieve victory at Gallipoli, they would have definitely awarded the Straits to Russia's successor, the Soviet Union, in accordance with the Secret Treaty which was discussed earlier. But in the absence of a clear-cut victory, their support of the Soviets in this strategic area had to be less overt. As soon as the truce was declared, British warships rushed to secure this area, which was vital for material support to the newly formed Soviet Union. Up to 60 Allied vessels arrived.[373] This was done before any negotiations took place. The Sultan remained in Istanbul, but was powerless. However, the Allies had little control over Northern Anatolia and the Ottoman administrative machinery continued to frustrate the efforts of the Allies.

Uproar in Istanbul after Ottoman defeat in World War I.

The British did however, get to work in fulfilling the part of the Secret Treaty which alluded to the abolition of the Caliphate. They fully committed themselves to the rise of Mustafa Kemal. They refused to deal with Enver, paving the way for the rise of the Kemalists. To eliminate all possible rivals of the Kemalists, the British further stipulated that those responsible for the war were to be handed over.[374] As a result, Enver and hundreds of highly capable Ottoman officials had to flee or live as fugitives. Note that there were no such demands for extraditing the officials of Germany responsible for her entry in the war. Then, the British requested a new government, headed by Izzet Pasha. Kemal had also made a similar demand to the Sultan at the end of the war. The British would then abandon Izzet Pasha in favor of another government by Tawfiq Pasha. Tawfiq Pasha was a former Ottoman ambassador to Britain, and was suspected of having

[372] Zallum, Khilafah 112.
[373] Irfan Orga & Margarete Orga, Ataturk (London: Michael Joseph, 1962) 130.
[374] Zallum, Khilafah 102.

close ties with the British.[375] Even at this point, the parliament known as *Al-Mabutan*, consisted of many Enver loyalists.[376] As well as many non-Turks, who disagreed to the abolition of the Caliphate. Mustafa Kemal tried to dissolve this parliament through constitutional means.[377] When this failed, the Sultan issued a decree to dissolve the parliament. This decree was finalized on the same day Mustafa Kemal held an emergency secret meeting with Sultan Wahid-ud-Deen.[378] This incident hints at the extent to which Ottoman Royalty had been compromised. The Sultan then installed a new government headed by his relative, Damad Farid. This new government was a puppet of the British High Commissioner in Istanbul, and thus further estranged itself from its subjects. The British worked towards discrediting the Ottoman State by concluding the armistice of Mudros on October 30th 1918. As per this treaty, the Ottomans were recognized as a State entitled only to Anatolia. Even the heroically defended area of Bosporus and Gallipoli was awarded to Allied control. The British further discredited the Ottoman parliament by ensuring that any law passed required the signature of the British army. The stage was set for Kemal to save the day, who on the other hand, had kept a low profile and feigned retirement from political activity until then.[379]

In order to further facilitate the rise of Mustafa Kemal, the Powers that Be arranged for the British to arrest his rivals at the CUP. In January 1919, at least 30 former members of the CUP were arrested. At the same time, the British publicly avoided Kemal to dispel any notion of collaboration. Though he was now a notable CUP member.

To promote Mustafa Kemal indirectly, the British insisted that the Ottoman Sultan dispatch a strongman to quell alleged disturbances and unrest in Eastern Turkey.[380] The idea was to give Mustafa Kemal a position with sweeping powers. Consequently, Kemal was made Inspector General of the Third Army based in Samsun. Kemal left Istanbul for Samsun on 15th May 1919. Around the same date, the British fleet was seen on the coast of Izmir.[381] Damad Farid Pasha and the British had notified the Wali of Izmir in advance, that as per the conditions of

---

[375] Zallum, Khilafah 103.
[376] Zallum, Khilafah 104.
[377] Zallum, Khilafah 104.
[378] Zallum, Khilafah 106.
[379] Zallum, Khilafah 106.
[380] Zallum, Khilafah 114.
[381] Zallum, Khilafah 115.

the truce, the Allies were to occupy Izmir. The Wali was expected prevent protests and keep the Ottoman army inside the barracks.[382] But the commander of the British fleet, Admiral Colthorpe, surprised the Wali upon disembarkation when he announced that the Greeks would be carrying out the occupation of Izmir! When the Greeks consolidated Izmir, they provoked Muslims locals by engaging in violence. On 19th May 1919, Mustafa Kemal showed up in Izmir, though his original destination was supposed to be Samsun. He gathered the humiliated Muslim population of Izmir and called for peaceful demonstrations. At the same time, he organized telegrams to be dispatched, and Turkish nationalist messages were sent all over Turkey.[383] For the first time, he refused orders of Istanbul to return immediately. The Western press gave undue publicity to this "rebellion." Gradually, Kemal began attracting followers and sympathizers. He organized militias around Izmir. But when he called for a parallel government of his own based in Ankara, many of his followers expressed disgust at his attempt to sabotage the Caliphate. And Kemal temporarily backed down from challenging Istanbul.

The British high Commissioner, Admiral Colthorpe was warned by Captain Hurst of the British Army in Samsun about Kemal and the threat he posed to Allied occupation of Anatolia. The Powers that Be responded, and had Hurst's unit replaced in its entirety. George Kidson, head of the Eastern Department of the British Foreign Office downplayed any such concerns.

The British devised a plan to dismantle existing Ottoman administration, from Istanbul and into Anatolia. Kemal's biggest rival, the Sultan and his loyalists, would thus be isolated and made more powerless. The British further polarized the Sultan in Istanbul by pressuring him into avoiding any form of agreement with Kemal. Greeks, Armenians and other minorities were encouraged to reject all of the Sultan's moves to establish a parliamentary government. Kemal's movement on the other hand, was still in its infancy, and wasn't influential enough to be considered an alternative to the Ottoman State. But it was being carefully nurtured.

Around 1918, Kemal met a Bolshevik delegation lead by Colonel Semyon Budyonny and secured their support. The Soviets were seeking to annex parts of the Caucasus. Strangely, Kemal was accommodating

---

[382] Zallum, Khilafah 115.
[383] Zallum, Khilafah 118.

despite his "nationalism." In fact, the Bolsheviks exclusively supplied weapons to Kemal's Army. During the later war with the Greeks, the Soviet envoy S. Aralov wrote back to Moscow, "In the absence of our material and moral assistance, it [Turkish Government] may not be able to resist and may retreat."[384] The Soviet government would pour material assistance into Kemalist Turkey during the Greek War of Independence. Mustafa Kemal was provided with 10,000,000 gold rubles and enough armaments to equip three Turkish divisions.[385] With Russian money, Kemal purchased guns and ammunition from America.[386] It can be assumed that at this stage, the Bolsheviks not only saw Kemal as an ally, but also as the key to the prospect of delivering Anatolia and Gallipoli to direct Bolshevik control. In accordance, Mustafa Kemal issued a proclamation from Angora, dated July 8th 1920 that was addressed to "Brothers of Islam and Communist Comrades."[387] To quote from it,

> Communist Comrades, an abominable crime is about to be perpetrated. The Great Powers have decided to exterminate a fresh victim, whose blood will be sucked by the capitalists of Europe. Our peasants are dying, weapon in hand. They can be sure that the days are near at hand when Islam, the ally of Communism, will avenge them.

On July 20th 1920, Mustafa Kemal issued another curious proclamation,

> We [Bolsheviks?] have armies ready to march from Persia to Anatolia. After the Bolshevik victory in Poland the Bolsheviks will enter Roumania. The Roumanians will answer the call to arms by a general strike. The Bulgars too, are ready to unite with the Bolsheviks. The aim of our armies is to guard our independence and deliver the capital from the British.[388]

When direct Bolshevik takeover of Eastern Europe and Persia failed to materialize, Kemal suddenly dropped the Communist rhetoric altogether.

Conquests were arranged for the Kemalists by the Powers that Be. The British poured into Samsun, pretending to secure it. Mustafa Kemal sent

---

384 Harish Kapur, Soviet Russia and Asia 1917-1927 (NY: The Humanities Press, 1967) 114.
385 Kapur, Soviet Russia 114.
386 Irfan Orga & Margarete Orga, Ataturk (London: Michael Joseph, 1962) 188.
387 Quoting the Daily Express. Nesta H. Webster, The Cause of World Unrest – With an Introduction by the Editor of The Morning Post (London: Grant Richards Ltd., 1920) 151.
388 Quoting Morning Post, July 20th 1920. Webster, World Unrest 152.

a small band of followers. And instead of confronting them, the British departed using their naval vessels.[389] The Illuminati within the occupying Greeks made the foolhardy decision to occupy rural areas around Izmir as well. When they proceeded to do this, they were attacked. This resulted in more communal violence between the Greeks and Turks. And more Turks began rallying around Kemal.

In June 1919, Mustafa Kemal declared an independent national government based in Ankara. This was a direct challenge to the Sultan based in Istanbul. Kemal offered the rationale that the Sultan's government had surrendered to the Allies. Mustafa Kemal then installed himself as "President," in the true fashion of a dictator.

On 23rd July 1919, the Ardh-Rum conference was held to discuss the situation the Caliphate was facing. The creation of an "Executive Parliamentary Committee" was decided upon, and Kemal was made the chairman.[390] Istanbul saw this as an open rebellion, and created an army of volunteer Muslims for putting down the Kemalists for good. The British prevented the deployment of this army, citing conditions in the truce. At the same time, they refused to take any measure against the Kemalists. Damad Farid Pasha contributed to Kemal's undue publicity by trying to arrest him. Not surprisingly, Kemal eluded arrest. This conference was followed by another conference at Sivas, where Kemal made himself chairman without a ballot.[391] Many members of the conference objected to the "Executive Parliamentary Committee" claiming itself to be the government, since it neither had the resources for such an undertaking, and neither could it combat the full blown Allied occupation of Anatolia.[392] Kasim Kara Bakir Pasha, the only military commander who retained his status after the War and did not surrender his equipment and army to the Allies, insisted that Kemal try not to monopolize the debate.[393] The Sultan's decision to have members of this conference arrested by Kurdish mercenaries came as a godsend to Kemal's waning popularity and his agenda for parallel government. The Kemalists gave a deadline to Istanbul for establishing communication between Kemal and the palace. This deadline of 12th August 1919 was unheeded, and the Kemalists then severed all links with Istanbul. During

---

389 Abdul Qadeem Zallum, How the Khilafah was Destroyed (Gloucester: Al-Khilafah Publications, 2000) 125.
390 Zallum, Khilafah 128.
391 Zallum, Khilafah 130.
392 Zallum, Khilafah 130.
393 Zallum, Khilafah 131.

this conference, Turkish intellectual Halide Edib proposed an American Mandate, which would preserve the country's old and new frontiers. Halide Edibe questioned Kemal's idea of Turkish "independence," which centered on liberating two or three provinces of Anatolia.[394] But this proposal was shot down by Mustafa Kemal, who realized that the territories of the Ottoman Empire under an American mandate was contrary to the Illuminati agenda of fragmenting the Middle East. In addition, an American mandate could also prevent the creation of a secular Caliphate-free Turkey based on regional nationalism, because the then America was unlikely to push for the abolition of the Caliphate.

Other parties arranged mediation between Istanbul and Kemal. He agreed to come to terms, provided the government of Damad Farid Pasha was dismissed in favor of a new government headed by Ali Ridha Pasha, the War Minister.[395] This was done on 2nd November 1919. In accordance with this, Kemal was expected to disband the "Executive Parliamentary Committee." But Kemal stalled the dissolution, making all sorts of excuses.[396] Some of his own supporters, such as Izzet Pasha, opposed him on this. Kemal then moved to Ankara and took residence there. Kemal claimed that his rationale for the "Executive Parliamentary Committee" continuing to operate in Ankara was that a move to Istanbul would subject them to British influence. But upon insistence of many members, this committee was finally moved to Istanbul. This parliament convened on 28th January 1920. But instead of Mustafa Kemal, Rauf Beik was elected as the Speaker.

Failing to accomplish his objective through parliamentary "reform," Kemal once again resorted to rebellion. This time, he had weapons and resources flowing towards him from many unknown parties, while the British turned a blind eye. For example, Kemalists were seen gathering trucks full of explosives and ammunition in Gallipoli, an area heavily guarded by the British.

With the Sultan's parliament gaining greater legitimacy and the cause of Mustafa Kemal waning, the British moved in to once again jeopardize and humiliate the Ottoman Sultan's parliament. On 7th March 1920, Saleh Pasha replaced Ali Ridha, upon insistence of the British. On 10th March 1920, Lord Curzon complained of harassment of Europeans and

---

[394] Irfan Orga & Margarete Orga, Ataturk (London: Michael Joseph, 1962) 147.
[395] Zallum, Khilafah 133.
[396] Zallum, Khilafah 134.

the slaughter of Christians in Istanbul.[397] Using this pretext, British warships arrived at Istanbul. British control over Istanbul was consolidated. But at the same time, British staff evacuated Ankara, Kemal's center of operation. Kemal would later arrest the small number of Britons who had stayed behind,[398] in order to prevent them from spreading news that the British were turning a blind eye to Kemal's activities. The British then arrested many followers of Kemal, who were known for their personal disagreement and rivalry with Kemal. The parliament was dissolved on 5th April 1920 and Damad Farid Pasha returned, ruling the country on behalf of the British. The Sultan further alienated the masses with his complete capitulation. The Powers that Be within the Ottoman royalty arranged for an official fatwa against Kemal and a demand for his execution. This only made Kemal more popular. Kemal resurrected the "Executive Parliamentary Committee." But this time, it was based in Ankara and was meant to be a Turk-only institution, which gave more sweeping powers to Kemal and his band of militant nationalists.[399] Hypocritically, he still tried to appeal to Muslim sentiments. The inaugural session was held on 23rd April 1920, after Friday prayer.[400]

Shadowy intrigues within the Ottomans destroyed all attempts at reconciliation between the Sultan and Kemal, and the Ottoman parliament was further discredited when it was dissolved once again. While I have earlier mentioned how the Illuminati had compromised Ottoman royalty since medieval times, the full extent of their machinations within Istanbul remains unclear.

Even at this point, Kemal concealed his nationalism and called for jihad. He even claimed his support for the Sultan, claiming that he sought to save the Sultan by organizing an independent government in Ankara and having the Sultan ratify it. Muslim mujahideen left Istanbul and flocked towards Kemal's movement. Ismet Inonu, the elected President of the last Ottoman parliament also defected. And this gave further legitimacy to Kemal. Many other members of the Ottoman parliament followed suit. Kemal's "Executive Parliamentary Committee" was turned into a National Assembly. Even at this stage, the first article of its constitution stipulated that the Sultan and the Caliphate were to be recognized.

---

397 Zallum, Khilafah 143.
398 Zallum, Khilafah 145.
399 Zallum, Khilafah 146.
400 Zallum, Khilafah 146.

In order to create further conflagration between the Ottoman State and Kemal, intrigues within the Ottoman parliament, as well as British intervention prevented the possibility of making Kemal President of the Ottoman parliament. Doing so would strengthen Kemal, but would not dislodge the Sultan. It would not disband the Ottoman administration and neither would it abolish the Caliphate, as was planned. The Powers That Be wanted the Ottoman Caliphate was to play an unpopular, isolated and oppositional role to Kemal. The British allied with local Ottoman Lords and administrative elites as well, isolating them from their popular support base.

In preparation for war with the Ottoman State and the Sultan, Kemal organized nationalist militias under a unified command. This was essential to ensure that his authority would not be diluted when he would later establish a dictatorship. Kemal's main source of weapons was from the theft of arms from Allied depots.[401] Were these depots deliberately left unguarded? A raid at a French depot at Akbas yielded 8000 rifles, 40 machine guns and 20,000 boxes of ammunition for the nationalists.[402] The British, on the other hand, deliberately avoided using their air force and larger forces against Kemal. The British disbanded the Kuvâ-i İnzibâtiyye, which was formed in April 1920 to fight the Nationalists. Instead, the British suggested using Greeks to fight the Kemalists, who were disliked by Turks. The Nationalists used very trick in the book to woo supporters of the Sultan. For example, the Nationalists sent Rafet Pasha by train to Konya, to negotiate with the Sultan loyalist, Colonel Fahreddin. He and his officials were asked to board the train for talks. Once on board, the train sped full speed to Ankara, while Rafet Pasha held them at gunpoint.[403]

Nevertheless, Ottoman loyalists joined together to fight the Kemalists. By May 1920, all provinces except Ankara had joined en masse to fight the Kemalists.[404] Volunteers rushed to join the cause of the Caliphate. Exactly when the doom of the Kemalists became imminent, The Allies announced the conditions of the Treaty of Sevres (August 1920).[405] Till then, these conditions had been kept secret.[406] These conditions were designed to be outrageously humiliating and unacceptable to the Turkish

---

401 Orga, Ataturk 153.
402 Orga, Ataturk 154.
403 Orga, Ataturk 157.
404 Zallum, Khilafah 149.
405 Zallum, Khilafah 149.
406 Zallum, Khilafah 149.

people. And their acceptance by the Ottomans would thus completely discredit the Sultan-Caliph. For example, the treaty proposed that portions of Southern Anatolia be passed to the Italians, portions of Western Anatolia including Smyrna be passed to the Greeks, and the Bosphorus, Dardenelles and the Sea of Marmara be internationalized. At the same time, British Prime Minister Lloyd George announced that the Allies sought to liberate non-Turkish nations. This announcement was widely circulated throughout the Western press, causing immense outrage in Turkey against the Sultan-Caliph.[407]

Mustafa Kemal's mysterious friends

Harold Courtenay Armstrong

As far as the official story goes, Captain Harold Courtenay Armstrong was a British military attaché in Istanbul prior to World War I. He was taken prisoner by Enver Pasha when his division was captured. During his imprisonment, he requested a meeting with Enver Pasha, the most powerful man in the Ottoman Empire (Zallum, 171). It is not known what took place during the lengthy meeting, but Enver became very angry and ordered that Armstrong be kept incommunicado in solitary confinement (Zallum, 171). Was Armstrong trying to seduce Enver with an offer of a kingdom in postwar Middle East similar to the one offered to Djemal Pasha? If so, how could a "soldier" of his rank have the authority to do so? Whom, or what force did he actually represent? Or had Armstrong made revelations to Enver to win him over, similar to those the mysterious Christian Rakovsky would later make to Stalin. It was believed Armstrong had "friends" among the Ottomans. These friends may have helped him escape. (Zallum, 171). After the war, he was assigned back to Istanbul and given numerous official duties. He was in direct contact with Mustafa Kemal during the Turkish War of Independence. Armstrong would write a book on Kemal, entitled *Grey Wolf, Mustafa Kemal: An Intimate Study of a Dictator*. (Beaufort Books, ISBN 0836969626, 1972) He also wrote another book, *Lord of Arabia: Ibn Saud: An intimate study of a King*. (Simon Publications, ISBN: 1931541280, 2001) While both these books go by the standard storyline, they did reveal the author's "intimate" knowledge of the subjects.

Sir Charles Harrington

Sir Charles Harrington was the British Commander-in-Chief in Turkey during Allied occupation after World War I. He was obviously the most powerful Briton in Turkey. During the Greco-Turkish wars, Harrington covertly helped the Kemalists. While not allowing the Greeks to cross the neutral zone (Dardenelles) into Turkey, Harrington allowed the Kemalists to freely cross across this zone into Greece (Zallum, 166).

When Harrington died on 24th March 1940, The Times carried an obituary, which mentioned that "In the wake of the Greek defeat by the Turks in 1921, the Allied forces Commander in Chief Sir Harrington was given wide powers to cooperate with Mustafa Kemal" (Zallum, 172).

[407] Zallum, Khilafah 149.

In February 1921, the London Conference was held by the British, who sought to revise the terms of the Treaty of Sevres, to their own detriment. This only proves that the Treaty of Sevres was merely a temporary tool for resurrecting Kemal, and was not intended for serious implementation. At this conference, the British sent two invitations to Turkey. One was for the Ottoman delegation and the other was for the Kemalists. Only the Kemalists would predominate the talks. Though nothing came out of the talks, the Kemalists of Ankara began to achieve recognition in international circles as the legitimate authority in Turkey.

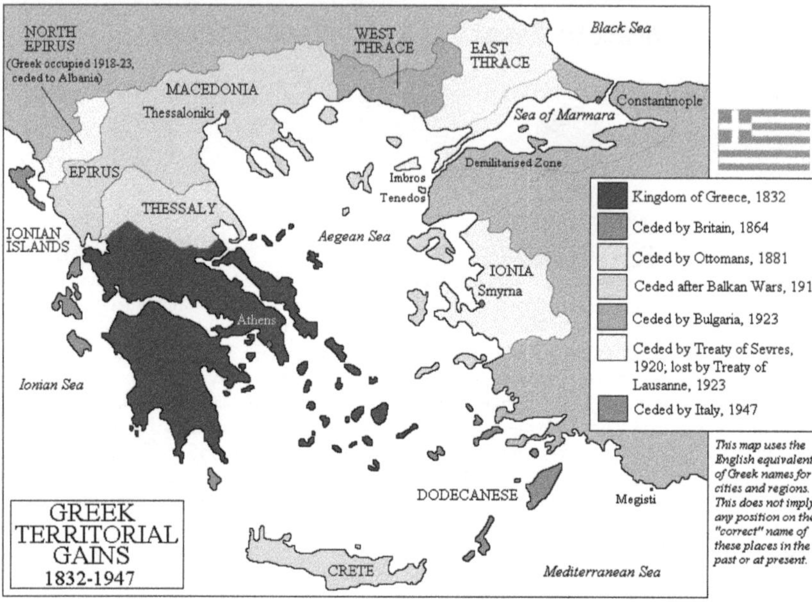

The Greeks had first landed on May 15th 1919. In March 1921, more Greeks were landed in Western Anatolia. Britain pretended that its backing of the Greeks was out of fears of Italian expansion in Southern Anatolia. Around this time, the Illuminati operating on the Greek side had fed the Greeks with delusions of grandeur, such as the re-conquest of Constantinople. The idea behind this Greek invasion was to force all disparate groups of Turkey and former members of the Ottoman administrative elite to rally around Kemal. He could thus effectively fill in the vacuum left behind by the Ottoman state, taking advantage of the threat of foreign invasion. Once duped into invading Anatolia by the British, the Greek invasion was abandoned by the British, and received very little outside support compared to the Kemalists. The Greeks would later blame British Prime Minister Lloyd for the abandonment.[408] In fact, Britain later declared neutrality in the conflict, even though the conflict took place on territory occupied by Allies.[409] On many occasions, the British covertly supported the Kemalists. For example, General Harrington had his forces in the neutral zone prevent Greek occupation of Istanbul.[410] Mustafa Kemal, on his part, made the Greek invasion a rallying point for his leadership. He would go around with a Quran in his hand, urging Turks for jihad. Mustafa Kemal created his initial support base by manipulating genuine religious sentiments of the Turks, who at that point were totally unaware of Kemal's concealed animosity to Islam and the Caliphate. He also used outlaws such as the Circassian Ethem and Demirci Mehmet Efe, whom he disposed later. Tribunals were formed to deal with those who resisted the Nationalists, and they were permitted to carry out death sentences.[411] Nationalist commanders who became too popular had their command taken away. For example, Ali Fuat Pasha, who had become popular in Anatolia was sent off to Moscow as an ambassador.[412] Mustafa Kemal issued a decree confiscating forty per cent of all food, clothing, bedding, oil, petrol, motor spares and accessories to support his war effort.[413] The Greeks managed several decisive victories, pushing deeper into Anatolia. Mustafa Kemal's leadership began to be questioned by his followers, and it was likely that he and his loyalists would be ousted in a coup. Mustafa Kemal mustered his forces for an advance on the Greeks. On 7th September 1922, the Greek army began retreating.[414] Prior to their retreat, the hopelessly incompetent General Hacianestes had become their new Commander-in-Chief through internal intrigue,[415] replacing the bright General Papulos. General Hacianestes represented the unpopular Royalist faction among the Army.[416] General Hacianestes ignored local conditions and terrain, while conducting all his battles from the safety of Smyrna![417] This indicates that Greek leadership was internally compromised, and was playing its part in the resurrection of Mustafa Kemal.[418] On 9th

---

[408] Orga, Ataturk 205.
[409] Zallum, Khilafah 161.
[410] Zallum, Khilafah 162.
[411] Orga, Ataturk 171.
[412] Orga, Ataturk 172.
[413] Orga, Ataturk 181.
[414] Zallum, Khilafah 164.
[415] Orga, Ataturk 198.
[416] Orga, Ataturk 202.
[417] Orga, Ataturk 203.
[418] See the section on Onassis in Chapter Five for details.

September 1922, Kemalists entered Izmir without firing a single shot.[419] By September 11th 1922 (significant date for the Illuminati), a truce was declared. By the evening of the 30th, the Greek Army had been destroyed. While the Greeks engaged in atrocities, the Kemalists also became notorious for their butchery. The forces of Mustafa Kemal burnt Smyrna. Despite Turkish victory not being a complete testament of Kemal's capability, the Western press gave him huge publicity throughout the battles with the Greeks. Kemal proceeded northwards into European Turkey to reclaim more land from Greece. This time, General Harrington and the heavily armed British in the neutral zone allowed the Kemalists to pass through, without a shot being fired.[420]

In March 1921, the Kemalists signed a "Treaty of Friendship and Brotherhood" with the Bolsheviks. Batumi, a port that was the key to exporting oil from Baku, was given to the Bolsheviks. The Bolsheviks and Kemalists would collaborate to strangle remnants of the Armenian independence movement. In October 1921, Mustafa Kemal signed the Treaty of Kars with the Soviet Union. He established peaceful and cooperative relations with the Soviets. The support of the Soviets was critical to Kemalist success in the Greco-Turkish war. No genuine Muslim leader of the Turks would ever consider cozying up with the atheist Bolsheviks. The Bolsheviks presented the gravest danger to the welfare and security of all Muslim and Turkic people in the Caucasus and Central Asia. On the other hand, real Muslim leaders like the Ottoman War Minister Enver Pasha rightly saw the Russians as the biggest enemy in the World War. Enver died fighting the Bolsheviks in Tajikistan.

It was expected that the Kemalist government in Ankara would merge with the Caliphate in Istanbul, with Kemal becoming Prime Minister and the Sultan becoming a constitutional monarch. But Kemal advocated separation of the Caliphate and the Sultanate. Deprived of its moral authority without the Caliphate, the Sultanate would gradually be abolished. Numerous councils were held and most people rejected the idea. Then Kemal held a haphazard ballot involving a show of hands.[421] Despite the disputed ballot, Kemal proceeded to separate the Caliphate from the Sultanate. Five days later, Rifat Pasha held a coup in Istanbul, which was still under the control of General Harrington. The Sultan left on a British steamer on November 17th 1922. The next Sultan, Abdul

---

[419] Zallum, Khilafah 164.
[420] Zallum, Khilafah 166.
[421] Zallum, Khilafah 175.

Majid, was unofficially appointed as Caliph and many Muslims pledged allegiance to him.

In 1922, the Conference of Lausanne officially recognized the Kemalists. But the conference was wound up on 4th February 1923, after talks with Turkey started failing. Abdul Qadeem Zallum makes it explicit that the Allies were actively seeking the dissolution of the Caliphate and secularization of Turkey as a prerequisite for further talks.[422] While there are no such explicit statements in the text of the treaty, there may have been secret clauses (as there were in the Treaty of Brest-Litovsk).[423] The return of Ismet after an abrupt stalling of the talks was followed by Kemal's increasing attacks on the Caliphate. Kemal's choice of sending Ismet Inonu to the conference was opposed in the National Assembly. Kemal responded by dissolving the Assembly. But the new Assembly also turned against him. Rauf Pasha began emerging as a serious threat to Kemal. Faced with imminent downfall, Kemal engineered confusion and chaos in the Assembly, which helped discredit the Assembly.[424] The Assembly was forced to admit its failure and requests were made to Kemal to form a new government. On 29th October 1923, Kemal announced the necessity of abolishing the Assembly itself in favor of a Republic, with him as the "elected" President. This would give far more authoritarian power than was possible under an Assembly. He then announced the secularization of the state. At the height of this crisis, Agha Khan, leader of the Ismaili sect in India sent a letter of protest in favor of the Caliphate.[425] Agha Khan and his followers were considered controversial, due to their favorable relations with the British in India. And Mustafa Kemal used this to give the impression that the British were behind the prolongation of the Caliphate! Supporters of Caliphate were threatened with death.[426] By 3rd March 1924, the Caliphate was abolished. Four days later, Ismet Pasha requested resumption of the Conference of Lausanne. The treaty of Lausanne was signed on 24th July 1924. In this treaty, apart from the secret clauses on the dissolution of the Caliphate, Britain and Kemalist Turkey conspired to deny the Kurds statehood. The Kurds consist of nomadic tribes, which are difficult to control. Therefore, denying the Kurds nationhood figures prominently in Cabal agenda to this day. Following the terms of the treaty, the British would finally evacuate the prized straits of Istanbul to a new Bolshevik-

---

[422] Zallum, Khilafah 177.
[423] See section "A Farewell Farce" in Chapter One.
[424] Zallum, Khilafah 180-181.
[425] Zallum, Khilafah 183.
[426] Zallum, Khilafah 185.

friendly Turkey, which was unlikely to ever threaten the supply line to the Soviets in the upcoming World War II. Neither was this new Turkey ever to establish itself as a major power in the region. Nor would it ever consider taking back the Middle Eastern territories snatched from it in World War I.

In November 1918, the "powerless" Ottoman Sultan, Wahid-ud-Deen, suddenly acquired the power to move against his otherwise perpetual rival, the CUP. By 1926, the CUP was disbanded. Many of its members faced military trials over the Armenian genocide. Mustafa Kemal was in no way put to disadvantage. It is important to note that the CUP ironically represented the last vestige of opposition against Kemal and the dissolution of the Caliphate.

In conclusion, it can be said that the Sultans of this period were completely compromised, and represented European bloodlines. They would thus play a collaborative role with those opposed to the Caliphate and the Ottoman Empire, similar to the role the Romanovs played during the Bolshevik Revolution. There were many instances where the Sultans were presented with the opportunity to save both the Caliphate and the Ottoman Empire. But they chose not to, and instead focused on dissolving Assembly after Assembly, lending more credence to the Kemalists, and undertaking covert Illuminati projects such as the Armenian Holocaust. No wonder the Sultans escaped all due prosecution and went off to live in France and Switzerland. Djemal Pasha was prescient when he considered that the Ottoman Empire and the Caliphate could be saved if the Sultan and his family were arrested, and Djemal and his successors were instead installed as Sultans.[427]

The Powers that Be were expecting that with the removal of Islam from official offices, they could rule indefinitely through standard methods of deception as employed in the West. But when this didn't work, they came out in full force, engaging in open thuggery and terrorism. Throughout his tenure, Mustafa Kemal never democratized the system. And he would disband opposition parties without any qualms. He even resorted to more controversial methods. For example, when Sukru Bey, the outspoken deputy of Trabzon attacked Kemal's personal extravagance in 1922, he disappeared. His dismembered body was found near Can Kaya, and a henchman of Kemal was a prime suspect.[428] Despite his populist image,

---

[427] Zallum, Khilafah 78.
[428] Irfan Orga & Margarete Orga, Ataturk (London: Michael Joseph, 1962) 227.

there had been two serious attempts on his life.[429] And using such attempts on his life as an excuse to destroy opposition, Kemal hanged every prominent man in the country opposed to his policies.[430] The majority of the people were worse off than before.[431] In 1931, it was decided that people should be "educated" on what the Revolution had done for the country.[432] And a massive program of brainwashing and historical revisionism was undertaken to alienate the new Turkish generation from its past.

The Powers that Be had originally planned Turkey to be a major theatre of World War II as well. Turkey was to develop a fascist government, sympathetic to the Axis. Or was to become a playground of the Axis itself, as the 1936 threat of Italian aggression manifested. This was comparatively easy, considering all that remained was the beaten up husk of a country. Turkey would then be invaded and conquered by the Soviet Union. When we recall that Djemal Pasha had come across detailed Soviet plans for a future invasion of Turkey, the plot makes perfect sense. But like the Allied debacle at Gallipoli, the plan never materialized due to a number of reasons.

But Mustafa Kemal may have been diligently preparing the groundwork in anticipation. If that was the case, the following are his achievements in this regard:

a. The establishment of a dictatorial regime. In 1928, Mustafa Kemal took up residence in the former Sultan's Dolmabahce Palace.[433]
b. The destruction of Islam in every possible way. The Soviets saw religions as rival ideologies, and the ground was being cleared in Turkey.
c. The destruction of the family unit by the fostering of feminism and immorality. The Soviets preferred citizens without any anchor of their own, since such citizens could have their beliefs dictated and controlled by the state.
d. The governmental imposition of industrialization at the expense of agriculture. This would have eased the transition of the Turkish economy to the Soviet Union in the future.

---

429 Orgas Ataturk 245.
430 Orgas Ataturk 272.
431 Orgas Ataturk 252.
432 Orgas Ataturk 283.
433 Orgas Ataturk 275.

The Soviets rigorously applied the same concept in Russia, despite its detriment to the peasants. Since industries gave less autonomy to subject populations than farms (with the exception of collective farms). The very peasant whom Kemal espoused soon became crushed under industrialization, monopolies and taxation.

e. The substitution of religion with an exclusive and reactionary ideology based on ethnicity and race. This would have been particularly helpful if Turkey was to play a dialectical role as a Fascist adversary of the Soviets.
f. The uprooting of all remnants of the sophisticated Ottoman culture, from dress to names of towns and cities.
g. The severing of links to the past, by changing the script of the Turkish language.
h. The destruction of the highly evolved Ottoman system of administration and jurisprudence (European civil and penal codes were substituted).
i. The destruction of the strong private enterprise of Armenians and Greeks. This was necessary for a future Soviet state controlled economy.

The all-knowing Mustafa Kemal appeared to be in the know as usual. On his deathbed in October 1938, he told Celal Bayar and his adopted daughter Afet,

> Listen! You have only a short while before you accomplish these things. There will be a war soon, and you must mobilize all the resources to help you succeed in your task.[434]

Present day Turkey is a very different place than the Turkey of the Ottomans. Massive propaganda, irreligiousness and hero worship have taken a toll on the psyche of the people. Most Turkish people regard Mustafa Kemal with a sense of endearment bordering on the metaphysical. The Ataturk is supposed to be always looking over them, through the massive statues and posters on every street corner. Turkey has degenerated from a World power into a nation state infamous for its corruption, and is far more illiberal and intolerant than any of the European states it seeks to emulate. In fact, Western countries use Turkey as an outsourcing hub for the torture of "terrorist" detainees. And despite its attempts at emulating the West, Turkey is yet to gain entry into the European Union. For every new generation of brainwashed

---

[434] Orgas Ataturk 295.

Turks, official Turkish historians pretend to forget the Ottoman period; or refer to the Ottoman Empire as a spoof of Byzantium.

Chapter Three
The Roots of Nazism

> Follow Hitler! He will dance, but it will be to my tune. We have given him the means to maintain contact with them (meaning the "masters"). Don't grieve for me for I have influenced history more than any other German.[435]
>
> *-Dietrich Eckart on his deathbed, 1923*

[435] Wulf Schwarzweller, The Unknown Hitler: His Private Life and Fortune (National Press Inc. and Star Agency, 1989) 69. Quoted in Scott Lively and Kevin Abrams, The Pink Swastika-Homosexuality in the Nazi Party 4th ed. (Sacramento: Veritas Aeterna Press, 2002) 122.

One of the most bizarre chapters in human history, the Nazis, is still wrapped in an enigma. What was the Illuminati connection to the Nazis? Were they enemies of the Illuminati, it's bye-products or its offshoots? This chapter will attempt to answer some of these questions. The author is convinced that the Nazis were indeed lock, stock and barrel Illuminati, and they performed exactly as was planned. Penetrating such levels of cover-ups in actions and motives to arrive at the pristine truth is impossible. An investigator is only left with a fraction of the scrambled bits and pieces, which point to a rather incomplete picture. The complete picture may never be known. But in its absence, we can discern several obvious and subtle clues, which point towards the Powers that Be and their agenda. This chapter offers no final verdict. It is rather a collection of peculiar facts which all point in the direction of the Powers that Be. There is room for digression and disagreement.

While examining the Nazis, it is necessary to bear in mind the limitations of the Illuminati and the human tendency to play favorites when presented with different players in a scenario. Even if there is a heavy element of the Illuminati involved with the Nazis, it is necessary to note that the Nazis were successful only because they tapped into huge local reservoirs of nationalism, prejudice, godlessness, regionalism, self-righteousness and racism. Evidence of this can be found in the fact that even today, some identity movements flaunt the Illuminati swastika as "their" symbol. The success of Nazism in Germany testifies to the complete stranglehold the Illuminati possess over German society. It is no surprise that the German people have still failed to come to terms with this bizarre chapter of their history. They would rather believe Hitler to be a patriotic madman, than see him as a decepticon, as a pawn of mysterious interests.

Although it is unlikely that we will witness another Great War centered on Germany, the Powers that Be are still as strong in Germany as they were in 1912. One only has to look at the symbols on present day German city squares and government buildings to gauge their strong presence. While it may be true that the German-centeredness of the two World Wars was a decision the Powers that Be made, there are certain aspects of German culture (as opposed to say, French culture), which made this possible. According to management textbooks, German personal and organizational lifestyle is heavily compartmentalized, and a strict regimen is followed, as evidenced by the strong presence of public signs dictating what is allowed and what is forbidden.[436] Therefore, the managerial "compartment" exercises final authority and centralized control over all other "compartments." Though the presence of consensus may appear to compensate for this concentration of power, one can only imagine the degree of manipulation possible by the Criminal Elite. The fact that the German people largely stood by Hitler until he brought the Soviets and the Allies all the way to Berlin is indicative of a bigger issue. The way in which Hitler and the Nazi leadership was given a blank check to not only commit atrocities, but to also engineer German defeat, indicates the subject population's blind trust in those laying claim to nationalism.

One of the biggest obstacles to fully understanding the Nazis are some "revisionists" dedicated preserving the cardboard-cut image of Hitler as a savior gone bad. They do not tolerate any other interpretation of Hitler. Some of these confused revisionists are often made into sacrificial lambs by the Powers that Be, so that their erroneous perspectives can be popularized for disinformation. And many other such "revisionists" are disinformation specialists themselves! (usually the ones who don't go to jail). Tens of thousands of people were involved in coordinating the World War conspiracy. How many more could be engaged in covering it up in government archives, in Universities and on online websites? Apart from specializing in Holocaust denial, we also find some of these "revisionists" rushing to protect Hitler from any blemishes, be it the Reichstag fire, homosexuality, connections to major bankers or even occultism. In other words, they are upholding the image of Hitler as the Powers that Be contrived for us to see. It is true that Hitler superficially appears as the lone non-Cabal player in World War Two. But this image drastically fades upon closer inspection. Even if Hitler had a populist cause such as rebuilding Germany, far too many of his actions defy rational explanation.

The following discourse pertains to secret societies associated with the rise of Nazism. As one may imagine, secret societies are found operating only where there is a need for covertness, intrigue and conspiracy. But establishment history denies these connections and puts a populist spin on Nazism. And when they admit the role of secret societies, they see these connections as having only peripheral importance.

---

[436] Excerpt from a letter by Dr. Jin K. Kim, State University of New York 2001. Quoted in Helen Deresky, International Management –Managing Across Borders and Cultures 5th ed. (New Jersey: Pearson-Prentice Hall, 2004) 105.

The List Society

In Germany, some aspects of the Theosophical movement combined with local nationalism, occultism and anti-Semitism. This brand of Theosophy became known as **Ariosophy**. The leading figures of Ariosophy were two Austrian occultists and homosexuals,[437] **Guido von List** and Lanz von Liebenfels. The former founded the List Society in 1903. The following are some conclusions drawn from an article by Jackson Spielvogel and David Redles.[438]

- Franz Hartmann, a prominent Theosophist, derived List's teachings, racial doctrine and swastika symbolism from Helena Blavatsky.[439]
- The kinship between List's Ariosophy and Theosophy is also especially noticeable in *Prana*, a German occult monthly for applied spiritualism. It was published by the Theosophical publishing house at Leipzig and edited by Johannes Baltzli, a Theosophist who was secretary of the List Society and biographer of Guido von List.[440]
- Contributors to the *Prana* included the Theosophists Franz Hartmann, C.W. Leadbeater, and Guido von List.
- A companion of Guido von List was Harald Gravelle, an occultist and leading theosophist in Germany. [441]
- Strong parallels emerged between List's ideas and Nazism, such as:
  - List worshipped Wotan, the Norse storm god. Hitler would see himself as an incarnation of Wotan.[442]
  - List fancied the double lightning bolt, which would later be adopted by the SS.

---

437 Scott Lively and Kevin Abrams, The Pink Swastika-Homosexuality in the Nazi Party 4th ed. (Sacramento: Veritas Aeterna Press, 2002) 108, 111.

438 Jackson Spielvogel and David Redles, "Hitler's Racial Ideology: Content and Occult Sources," Simon Wiesenthal Center – Museum of Tolerance Online > Multimedia Learning Center > Annual 3. 1997 < http://motlc.wiesenthal.com/site/pp.asp?c=gvKVLcMVIuG&b=395043>

439 Johannes Baltzli, Guido von List (Leipzig 1917) 45-46. See also George Mosse, "The Mystical Origins of National Socialism," Journal of the History of Ideas 22.1(1961): 85-87. As quoted in Spielvogel and Redles, "Hitler's Racial Ideology."

440 Spielvogel and Redles, "Hitler's Racial Ideology."

441 Lively and Abrams, Pink Swastika 108

442 Hannah Newman, The Rainbow Swastika- A Report to the Jewish People About New Age Anti-Semitism: Nazism and the New age <http://philologos.org/__eb-trs/naF.htm> Web page as of 11/07/2004

- List made proposals for a Germanic state based on Aryanism, occultism and anti-Semitism. All of these propositions were incorporated into the Nazi state.
- List promoted the swastika popularized by Blavatsky. Nazis would adopt the swastika.
- List's racist and occult magazine *Prana* would advocate vegetarianism and alcohol abstention.[443] Both of these attributes characterized Hitler.
- List proposed an order of militant occultist males. Ernst Rohm would later lead the brown shirts, which was mainly composed of homosexual militarists. Ernst Roehm was a notorious molester of boys. Hitler executed Roehm after his sexual excesses became widely known.[444] It is important to note that the Nazis would usually send the more effeminate homosexuals to the concentration camps, and such exercises would also help cover their own homosexuality.

Caption: In 1937 at the House of German Art Museum, Nazi Führer Hitler and Italian dictator Mussolini enjoy a homoerotic exhibit—an immense statue of two naked muscular men holding hands. (For decency's sake, *Power of Prophecy* has blackened out the genital area of one of the naked men pictured)

Texe Marrs, "Unmasking the sexual perversions of the Illuminati: Two on a saddle Part 1," Power of the Prophecy <http://www.texemarrs.com/012002/two_on_a_saddle.htm> Web page as of 11/07/2004. Copyright: Unknown

---

[443] George Mosse, "The Mystical Origins of National Socialism," Journal of the History of Ideas 22.1 (1961): 87-88. Quoted in Spielvogel and Redles, "Hitler's Racial Ideology."

[444] Texe Marrs, "Unmasking the sexual perversions of the Illuminati: Two on a saddle Part 1," Power of the Prophecy <http://www.texemarrs.com/012002/two_on_a_saddle.htm> Web page as of 11/07/2004

Order of New Templars

The second major ariosophist, **Lanz von Liebenfels** founded the Order of New Templars. He established the first New Templar castle in the Burg Werfenstein in 1907, and had a swastika flag flown over it.[445] Such castles would later become Hitler's "Order Castles" for special training. The following are some conclusions drawn from Spielvogel and Redles.

- The name "Order of New Templars" was a strange choice considering the fact that the Templar knights were products of a heresy and were bitter opponents of the Christian Teutonic Knights native to Germany.
- Liebenfels served on the board of directors of the proto-Nazi List Society that has been linked to Theosophy.
- A friend of Lanz claimed that he had direct contact with Blavatsky and her successor, Annie Besant.[446]
- Harald Gravelle, an occultist and a leading theosophist in Germany was a companion of Lanz von Liebenfels.[447]
- Liebenfels claimed he had personal contact with Hitler and Hitler visited him in 1909 to obtain some back issues of *Ostara* (a racist occult monthly published by Liebenfels).[448]
- Liebenfels is credited with the famous quote written to a friend among the New Templars: "**Do you know that Hitler is one of our pupils? You will still live to see that he, and thereby we, also will triumph and kindle a movement that will make the world tremble.**"[449] Hitler would later ban Liebenfel's writings in 1933 to cover his connection to Liebenfels.
- Almost all historians accept the direct impact of Lanz von Liebenfels on Hitler.[450] In addition, there are striking parallels between Theosophy, the Ariosophy of List and Liebenfels and Hitler's own ideas. Furthermore, Hitler did emphasize in Mein Kampf that in

---

[445] Jackson Spielvogel and David Redles, "Hitler's Racial Ideology: Content and Occult Sources," Simon Wiesenthal Center – Museum of Tolerance Online > Multimedia Learning Center > Annual 3. 1997 < http://motlc.wiesenthal.com/site/pp.asp?c=gvKVLcMVIuG&b=395043>

[446] Wilfried Daim, Der Mann, der Hitler die Ideen gab (Munich, 1958) 120-21. Quoted in Spielvogel and Redles, "Hitler's Racial Ideology."

[447] Lively and Abrams, Pink Swastika 108

[448] Wilfried Daim, Der Mann, der Hitler die Ideen gab (Munich, 1958) 20- 21. Quoted in Spielvogel and Redles, "Hitler's Racial Ideology."

[449] Wilfried Daim, Der Mann, der Hitler die Ideen gab (Munich, 1958) 12. Quoted in Spielvogel and Redles, "Hitler's Racial Ideology." The authors give additional information in their reference as well.

[450] Spielvogel and Redles, "Hitler's Racial Ideology."

Vienna he established “a world picture and a philosophy which became the granite foundation”[451] of all his actions. The List Society and Liebenfels were based in Vienna in the same timeframe as that of Hitler.

- Hitler in a conversation with Hermann Rauschning asked, “How can we arrest racial decay? Shall we form a select company of the really initiated? An Order, the brotherhood of Templars around the holy grail of pure blood?”[452] Hitler’s taste for Templarism and the Holy Grail is totally out of sync with Christianity. Germany and even Nazism. It reflects deeper esoteric undercurrents.

Nazi Esoterics

Leibstandarte SS Panzer Division

Key on a United States seal.

The Nazi Eagle. This may be a refrence to the phoenix, a mythical bird which rises from the dust and is reduced to ashes, not unlike the planned short term lifecycle of the Nazi state.

Waffen Mountain Division of the SS based in Albanische Nr 1 – Skanderberg. What’s the eagle of Lagash doing here? The significance of this emblem has been discussed in chapter one.

SS Volunteer Grenadier Division, based in Böhmen-Mahren. The Beast and a hermetic cross of Lorraine, which was used by the Templar Knights.

Waffen Grenadier Division of the Italianische Nr I incorporates a well-known symbol of Fascism.

---

[451] Adolf Hitler, Mein Kampf, trans. Ralph Manheim (Boston, 1943) 22. Quoted in Spielvogel and Redles, “Hitler’s Racial Ideology.”

[452] Anonymous, New World order-The movie: Nazis and Aryans. <http://www.geocities.com/newworldorder_themovie/nazisandaryans.html> Web page as of 11/07/2004

Waffen Grenadier Division of the SS based in Charlemagne. A Phoenix and a Fleur de lis. The Fleur de lis represents the baptismal lily used to crown King Clovis I, an ally of the Merovingians.

Panzer SS Grenadier division of the Reichsführer. The oats surrounding an icon is a common element to several emblems, including the UN and the Soviet seal.

Panzer SS Grenadier division, Götz von Berlichingen. The raised fist is common to many revolutionary ideologies, such as Communism.

Waffen SS Grenadier division of the Lettische Nr II. Note the similarity of the symbol with the Communist sickle and hammer, as well as the present day Euro currency symbol.

A cross associated with the Rosicrucian Society, a secret society with mysterious beliefs. Note the circle overlaid on the cross.

Left: A Nazi Iron Cross Second Class. The Cross depicted was also used by Germany in World war I.

Below: Two Fasces can be found in the US House of Representatives

Battle flag of the Nazi armed forces (Wehrmacht). Note similarity to Rosicrucian cross (left).

Right: The British Victoria Cross, one of the highest military awards. Note similarity to Nazi Iron Cross.

Higher Armanen Order

In 1911, Guido von List formed an elite occult organization called The Higher Armanen Order. After the fall of the Third Reich, a book written by Guido von List was found in Hitler's private library. On the inside cover was written the inscription: “To Adolph Hitler, my dear brother in Armenen”.[453]

Order Novi Templi

The Order Novi Templi was founded by Lanz von Liebenfels after he was thrown out of a Cistercian order for his alleged homosexuality. This organization practiced Tantric sex rituals. Ordo Novi Templi was based on Satanist Aleister Crowley’s Ordo Templi Orientalis (still in existence). Hitler would later condemn Crowley to hide his own Satanist connections. According to Lively and Abrams, Eckart was involved in Tantric occult sex rituals and may have initiated Hitler into them as well.[454] To quote Ravenscroft, Eckart initiated Hitler into “a monstrous sadistic magic ritual [...] after which he was sexually impotent.”[455] Another report alleges Eckart organized rituals involving “gifted” Russian peasant women.[456] In another instance, an unidentified associate disclosed to Springmeier that his father who was highly placed among the Powers that Be described witnessing Hitler kill a man by pulling out his heart while he was alive.[457]

Anthroposophical Society

Rudolf Steiner, a member of the German Theosophical society broke away from Theosophy to form the Anthroposophical Society, which is a blend of Theosophy, Gnosticism, holistic earth-worship, and racism.[458] One of its prominent members was Rudolf Hess. Steiner’s group would later face a crackdown from Hitler who was apparently trying to hide his Theosophist roots. The influence of Anthroposophical society can be found today in 600 Waldorf schools in 32 different countries including Israel!

---

453 Lively and Abrams, Pink Swastika 111

454 Lively and Abrams, Pink Swastika 122.

455 Trevor Ravenscroft, The Spear Of Destiny (Weiser books 1982) 155, 173.

456 Anonymous, New World Order- The Movie: Nazis and Aryans <http://www.geocities.com/newworldorder_themovie/nazisandaryans.html> Web page as of 11/07/2004

457 Fritz Springmeier, The Illuminati formula used to create an undetectable total mind controlled slave (Web Edition) 410

458 Hannah Newman, The Rainbow Swastika- A Report to the Jewish People About New Age Anti-Semitism; Human history according to the new age < http://philologos.org/__eb-trs/naG.htm> Web page as of 11/07/2004

Germanen Order

This Masonry-based order was formed in 1912 by various followers of List and Liebenfels. Under the cover of "German studies," this order specialized in the dissemination of anti-Semitic material and the conduction of political assassinations. Some 354 enemies of the nationalists were killed over several years.[459] Rudolf von Sebottendorf was made the head of the order's Bavarian branch.

The assassination of Communists, socialists and Jewish idealists such as Kurt Eisner, who proclaimed a socialist republic in 1918, is mistakenly taken as proof that the Nazis and proto-Nazi organizations such as the Germanen Order were fighting foreign influence. But such activity was consistent with bigger goals of the Powers That Be. They were merely wiping out all opposition, including indigenous Communism. These were prerequisites for delivering a defeated Fascist Germany to the Soviet Union.

Sebottendorf (real name: Adam Rudolf Glauber) was associated with Turkish Freemasonry and even wrote a book about its history. During the Balkan war of 1912-13, Sebottendorf directed the Turkish Red Crescent and was named Master of the Order of Rosé Garland (RosenKranz).[460] Was he also a Rosicrucian? Interestingly, Sebottendorf wrote an autobiographical novel entitled *The Rosicrucian Talisman*.
Sebottendorf's association with Bavaria has its own significance, Bavaria was the home of Adam Weishaupt, considered to be the founder of the modern Illuminati, and has always been a hotbed of conspiracy and intrigue.

Thule Society

In order to avoid association with terrorism, the Bavarian chapter of the Germanen Order changed its name to the Thule Society in 1917, with Sebottendorf remaining as its head. Thule was a mythical island called Hyperborea, similar to Atlantis, which was the legendary Nordic homeland.[461] This was the center of a lost civilization. But not all was purportedly lost. The remaining secrets were supposedly being guarded by ancient beings that later took refuge in Tibet. Those "initiated" were

---

[459] Lively and Abrams, Pink Swastika 119.

[460] Servando Gonzalez, The Swastika and the Nazis: The Hess Connection Note# 1 (1998)
<http://www.intelinet.org/swastika/swasti04.htm> Accessed 17/12/06.

[461] Spielvogel and Redles, "Hitler's Racial Ideology." Note# 37

to establish contact with them to create a new race of supermen who would wipe out inferior races.[462] Blavatsky had reached similar conclusions in her writings. To quote, "The Aryan Race was born and developed in the far North, though after the sinking of the Continent of Atlantis its tribes migrated further south into Asia."[463]

Thule Society emblem

In 1919, Thulists assassinated Kurt Eisner, a Jewish intellectual who had formed a Socialist government. After the assassination, there was a raid on the Thule's headquarters and six Thulists were shot. This event appears to be staged, with some non-bloodlined Thulists being used as sacrificial lambs to draw public apathy against the Communists. This event happened on Walpurgisnacht,[464] a high day in witchcraft. In response, Sebottendorf organized 20,000 demobilized soldiers, who would become known as the Freikorps and were later referred to as the storm troopers. It is not clear how Sebottendorf attained the resources for such activity. These soldiers would join the street riots against the Communists while flying the swastika. When the Communists were finally vanquished, the Thule society organized a political arm, the NSDAP, which would become the Nazi party. The Powers that Be would use different means to get the Nazis elected. Despite their efforts, the Nazis never acquired more than 37% of the vote. But that was enough to legitimize the Nazis.

National Socialism was adopted for dialectical reasons, as confessed by Illuminati operative Christian Rakovsky in an interrogation with Stalin's secret police (1938)[465] As Rakovsky said, International Communism would triumph over National Socialism and Fascism. Like Communism, National Socialism was another materialist philosophy meant to rally

---

[462] Wulf Schwarzweller, The Unknown Hitler: His Private Life and Fortune (National Press Inc. and Star Agency, 1989) 66f. Quoted in Lively and Abrams, Pink Swastika 121.

[463] Helena P. Blavatsky, The Secret Doctrine Vol. 2. page 812. Quoted in Spielvogel and Redles, "Hitler's Racial Ideology."

[464] Wiccans identify this day as a Druid feast in honour of Bel (Baal), whom Helena Blavatsky identifies as part of an astrological trinity.

[465] The questioning of the accused Christian Georgievitch Rakovsky by Gavriil Gavriilovitch Kus'min on the 26th January, 1938. An archive of the interrogation can be found online < https://archive.org/details/RedSymphony> Web page as of 22/01/14

Germans. But it was earmarked for destruction via the Soviet Union and International Communism. It is thus obvious why Communism was not alloted to Hitler. Communism had been pre-assigned to the Soviets, the future victors of the War.

One would expect Hitler to distance himself from anything remotely socialist due to his issue with Jewish influence. Yet, Hitler openly sympathised with Socialism and Communism. To quote Hitler, "I have learnt a great deal from Marxism, as I do not hesitate to admit." And further, "I have always made allowance for this circumstance, and given orders that former Communists are to be admitted to the party at once."[466] And elsewhere ""We are socialists, we are enemies of today's capitalistic economic system for the exploitation of the economically weak [...]"[467] The plan was fostering Fascism (In Italy and Spain too) and crashing it against the Soviets while ensuring the triumph of the latter. Fascism was a transitory construct to ensure gains for Soviet Communism. Not surprisingly, prominent elitists like Time magazine's Henry Luce were vigorously peddling Fascism at this time[468] In short, Fascism whether in Germany, Italy or Spain, was created as a makeshift construct, destined to fall before Soviet Communism in an ignoble fashion. And the Soviets would appear as the natural and victorious alternative. According to Springmeier, "Controlled opposition gives people a chance to vent their anger without threatening their [Illuminati] control. It also gives them dialectic conflicts which they can control to their advantage."[469] According to the Hegelian dialectic, conflict produces change, and controlled conflict produces controlled change.

Sebottendorf later attacked Anthroposophists and Freemasons, presumably to obfuscate the Thule's link to them. When the Thule would later become obscure, Sebottendorf sought to revive it in 1933. The Nazi party responded by ejecting him. He responded by writing a book *Before Hitler Came*, which exposed the Nazi Thule link. He was subsequently expelled from Germany. The Nazis had all copies confiscated.

---

466 Hermann Rauschning, published conversations with Hitler in Hitler Speaks (1939). Full quote at Roots of evil by George <http://www.interlog.com/~girbe/roots.html> Web page as of 16/03/04

467 Hitler on 1st May 1927. < http://willysutton.blogspot.com/2004/03/ssalistinn-adolf-hitler.html> Web page as of 16/03/04

468 Steven P. Meyer and Jeffrey Steinberg, "Henry Luce's Empire of Fascism," Executive Intelligence Review. June 25th, 2004. < http://www.larouchepub.com/other/2004/site_packages/3125ccf_luce.html > Accessed 05/11/06.

469 Fritz Springmeier, Deeper Insights into the Illuminati Formula (Web Edition) 58

Sebottendorf died or disappeared in 1945. Prominent Thulists who later became high ranking Nazis are:[470]

- Max Amann, Editor of Nazi Party publications. Hitler also made him head of the Nazi Eher Verlag, the most lucrative position in the Nazi hierarchy.[471] Hitler enlisted as a volunteer in a Bavarian regiment at the outbreak of World War I. He would later wear an Iron Cross First Class, which he claimed was awarded for capturing 12 Frenchmen. The entire story is controversial and there was no mention of the feat in the regiment's history.[472] However, Hitler's regimental sergeant major at that time was Max Amman.[473] And this connection may help explain how Hitler obtained the military decoration. In addition to Amman, the regimental adjutant, a Jewish man named Hugo Gutman, made persistent efforts to allow Hitler to receive this decoration.[474]
- Baron von Sebottendorf, highly placed in Turkish Freemasonry and head of the Thule. Sebottendorf's newspaper, the *Munchener Beobachter* became the official Nazi propaganda sheet a year later, and it was renamed the *Volkishcer Beobachter* (Under Alfred Rosenberg).
- Hans Frank, governor of Occupied Poland.
- Anton Drexler, founder of the German Workers' Party.
- Gottfried Feder, co-founder of the Nazi Party.
- Karl Harrer, first chairman of the NSDAP, alleged to have founded the German Workers Party within the Thule society.[475]
- Hans George Grassinger, founder of NSDAP.
- Rudolf Hess, Hitler's Minister of State.
- Dr. Heinz Kurz, SS leader.
- Freidrich Krohn, designer of Nazi insignia.

---

[470] The list was supplied by Baron Von Sebottendorf, Before Hitler Came And Quoted in Jean-Michel Angebert, The Occult and the Third Reich (Macmillan, 1974) 169. Quoted from Hannah Newman, The Rainbow Swastika- A Report to the Jewish People About New Age Anti-Semitism; Nazism and the new age <http://philologos.org/__eb-trs/naF.htm> Web page as of 11/07/2004. Note that all the individuals after Eckart are not on Newman's list and have been later added (after confirmation) by the author of this book.

[471] Walter C. Langer, The Mind of Hitler – The Secret Wartime Report (NY & London: Basic books Inc., 1972) 123.

[472] Langer, The Mind of Hitler 122.

[473] Langer, The Mind of Hitler 123.

[474] Langer, The Mind of Hitler 234.

[475] Baron Von Sebottendorf "Before Hitler came," (Munich: 1933) Dedication page. Quoted in Spielvogel and Redles, "Hitler's Racial Ideology."

- Ernst Roehm, leader of the Storm Troopers.
- Alfred Rosenberg, Foreign Services chief, propagandist, author of *The Myth of the Twentieth Century*, which propounded Blavatsky's ideas.
- Julius Streicher, (*Gauleiter* of Franconia)
- Adolf Hitler (as a "visiting brother").
- Dietrich Eckart, a leading Thulist and founding member of the German Workers Party. He "took credit for initiating Hitler into Blavatsky's *Secret Doctrine* and for putting him in contact with 'the powers.' Hitler later dedicated *Mein Kampf* to Eckart."[476] He also became editor for Editor-in-Chief of the *Völkischer Beobachter*.
- Hans Kahnert, who founded Germany's largest "gay rights" organization, which counted SA Chief Ernst Roehm among its members.[477]
- Heinrich Himmler, leader of the SS and occultist. He claimed to believe he was the reincarnation of King Heinrich I the Fowler![478] He was even nicknamed the black Jesuit.[479] What could be the connection to Jesuits?
- Grafin Hella von Westarp, Thule secretary.
- **Gustav Franz Maria Prinz von Thurn und Taxis**, a German royal aristocrat with relations to the Bohemian European aristocracy.[480] The presence of this aristocrat in the Thule society hints at a larger role the German aristocracy played in Nazism.
- Putzi Hanfstaengl? A close friend of Roosevelt who helped finance the official Nazi propaganda sheet, the *Völkishcer Beobachter*. A year prior, this paper was Sebottendorf's *Munchener Beobachter*, and was published by the Thule Society. There is no evidence to indicate he was a member of the Thule, but he could have been connected indirectly.

---

476 Hannah Newman, The Rainbow Swastika- A Report to the Jewish People About New Age Anti-Semitism; Nazism and the new age <http://philologos.org/__eb-trs/naF.htm> Web page as of 11/07/2004.

477 Jonathan Katz, Gay American History (NY: Thomas Y. Crowell Company, 1976) 632 n94. Quoted in Lively and Abrams, Pink Swastika 119.

478 Dusty Sklar, The Nazis and the Occult (1989) 85. Quoted in Hannah Newman, The Rainbow Swastika- A Report to the Jewish People About New Age Anti-Semitism; Nazism and the new age <http://philologos.org/__eb-trs/naF.htm> Web page as of 11/07/2004.

479 Dusty Sklar, The Nazis and the Occult (1989) 86-87. Citing Nuremberg Trials witness Walter Schellenberg. Quoted in Hannah Newman, The Rainbow Swastika- A Report to the Jewish People About New Age Anti-Semitism; Nazism and the new age <http://philologos.org/__eb-trs/naF.htm> Web page as of 11/07/2004

480 Peter Levenda, Unholy Alliance (Avon Books, 1995) ??

Vril Society

The Vril Society or Luminous lodge was an occult secret society in Pre-Nazi Berlin. It has been described as an inner circle of the Thule society.[481] Vril referred to divine energy, attributed to supernatural beings in the entrails of the earth. The term Vril made its way into Western literature through an obscure French writer, Louis Jacolliot.[482] Jacolliot maintained the company of Theosophists and produced writings in the typical Theosophist genre of Aryanism.

- The term Vril was revitalized by Theosophist_Bulwer Lytton in his novels.
- Jacolliot's teachings reached England through S.L. Mathews, Grand Master of the Golden Dawn society and the Vril society was also in close contact with the English Order known as the Hermetic Order of the Golden Dawn,[483] which specialized in the learning of Eastern occult. This organization had close ties with Helena Blavatsky.
- Vril or light force is also a reference to "the light bearer" or Lucifer.

Ahnenerbe

The Society for the Study of Ancestral Heritages, the Ahnenerbe, was an organization founded in 1935 privately by Frederick Hielscher. Hielscher was a mystic, a spiritual teacher of Wolfram Sievers, and a friend of the Swedish explorer Sven Hedin.[484] SS soldiers received a crash course on the meaning of the Germanic runes and other "Aryan symbols" from Hielscher. Under Himmler, the Ahnenerbe emerged as the official SS branch in charge of the research on ancient symbols and other esoteric subjects. Outwardly, the Ahnenerbe claimed its mission as finding the "Vril." The Ahnenerbe's task was to search for evidence of the roots of the Aryan race in South East Asia, apart from "scientific experiments" and research into occult practices.

In other words, the Ahnenerbe was entrusted with searching for more pseudo-historical rationales the German people should support Hitler's suicidal march towards the South East, which would eventually

---

[481] Servando Gonzalez, Origins of the Swastika: The Hausofer Connection. <http://www.intelinet.org/swastika/swasti02.htm> Web page as of 11/07/2004
[482] González, Swastika: Hausofer
[483] González, Swastika: Hausofer
[484] González, Swastika: Hausofer

culminate in the destruction and subjugation of Germany by the Soviet Union. In a similar fashion, Blavatsky had dug up the swastika from India to prove that Germans had mystical reasons for advancing towards the South East. Secondly, the Ahnenerbe would also engage in pillage on behalf of Nazi elite in conquered territories. To quote Gonzalez, "[...] it seems that Germany spent more money and devoted more resources on the Ahnenerbe than America did on the atomic bomb. More than fifty departments in this branch of the SS succeeded in spending over a million marks on such "scientific" research."[485]

Some of its research appears to be subjects that would be of significant appeal to the Powers that Be, such as gathering information on the origins of Rosicrucianism and conducting a thorough search for the lost relics and treasures of the Merovingians and Cathars. Very little is known about the details of the research undertaken. The archives of the Ahnenerbe mysteriously disappeared after the war.[486] Angebert notes that the documents dealing with the Ahnenerbe are listed in the U.S. National Archives but are not available to researchers.[487]

Freemasonry

Since Freemasonry was too important for the Powers that Be for their projects, it is no surprise that Freemasonry was secretly allowed to coexist by the Nazis. The three main Prussian Grand lodges refused to accept Jews. And they were allowed to operate after their Grand Master sent formal written oaths of allegiance to Hitler and changed their organization name to Frederick the Great Association. Frederick the Great was a key patron of Freemasonry in Germany.[488] These three lodges were populated with high-ranking Nazi officials. Since Hitler pretended to outlaw Masonry and its "Jewish influence," most of us are

---

[485] González, Swastika: Hausofer
[486] González, Swastika: Hausofer
[487] Jean-Michel Angebert, The Occult and the Third Reich (Macmillan, 1974) 259-260. Quoted in Hannah Newman, The Rainbow Swastika- A Report to the Jewish People About New Age Anti-Semitism; Nazism and the new age <http://philologos.org/__eb-trs/naF.htm> Web page as of 11/07/2004
[488] Alain Bernbeim MPS, "German Freemasonry and Its Attitudes Toward The Nazi Regime," The Philaltethes Magazine February 1997. As archived at <http://www.freemasonrywatch.org/attitude.html> Web page as of 11/07/2004

Top Left: A Scottish rite lapel pin (no longer used).
Courtesy "Tyler" Copyright: Unknown; Source: <http://www.freemasonrywatch.org/2index.html> Accessed 01/12/06

Top Right: A Hitler Youth Flag. The number 33 is on the top.

ready to believe Hitler and the Nazis were free of Masonic influence. But records show that these three Nazi approved lodges were also recognized as "regular" Freemasonry by American and British lodges![489] Other lodges that accepted Jews were considered clandestine. The Nazis shut down these "clandestine" lodges to cover up their own ties to Freemasonry. Though Freemasonry plays dumb when presented with unsavory characters, there is evidence, such as the Masonic trinket pictured above (no longer in use) and the following statement of Hitler quoted by Hermann Rauschning, the Nazi President of the Danzig Senate who defected to the Allies in 1939 and wrote the book, *Hitler Speaks* which contained statements of Hitler:[490]

> All the supposed abominations, the skeletons and death's head, the coffins and the mysteries, are mere bogeys for children. But there is one dangerous element and that is the element I have copied from them. They form a sort of priestly nobility. They have developed an esoteric doctrine more merely formulated, but imparted through the symbols and mysteries in degrees of initiation. The hierarchical organization and the initiation through symbolic rites, that is to say, without bothering the brain by working on the imagination through magic and the symbols of a cult, all this has a dangerous element, and the element I have taken over. Don't you see that our party must be of this character...? An Order, the hierarchical Order of a secular priesthood.

---

[489] Alain Bernbeim MPS, "German Freemasonry and Its Attitudes Toward The Nazi Regime," The Philaltethes Magazine February 1997. As archived at <http://www.freemasonrywatch.org/attitude.html> Web page as of 11/07/2004

[490] As reproduced on the Freemasonrywatch Website, which is critical of Freemasonry. <http://www.freemasonrywatch.org/P2.html> Web page as of 11/07/2004

-Adolf Hitler praising Freemasonry

To quote Ralf Melzer on Freemasonry in Nazi Germany,

> Not a single declaration of belief in the Weimar Republic can be found in the Masonic journals Am rauhen Stein (On the Rough Stone) of the Grand Lodge of Friendship and the Bundesblatt (Federal Paper), of the Grand National Mother Lodge. Instead, the Fatherland was mysticized in contrast to the political reality, and the journals postulated a "national self-contemplation." Most members of the Old- Prussian lodges and even some members of the few dogmatic Humanitarian lodges did not find the central elements of the Nazi Party's ideology to be contradictory to their Masonic beliefs. Instead, they found the ideology to be rather complementary to their own understanding of Freemasonry. Before the Nazis came to power, the president of the Verein deutscher Freimaurer (German Freemason Association), Diedrich Bischoff, even suggested an inspiration of the "Third Reich" based on or through Masonic idealism.[491]

In addition, there are several credible links between the Nazis and Freemasonry. For further research, one should make the following considerations.

- Why didn't Hitler shut down all Masonic lodges instead of making exceptions to his anti-Semitism?
- The Old Prussian Lodges were also known as the Bavarian Illuminati![492] They also shared Hitler's disdain for Jews.[493] Was Hitler refusing to bark at his master's voice?
- Why was Freemasonry adorning some Nazi insignia at that time, such as the ring pictured earlier? And how does the number 33,

---

491 Ralf Melzer PhD, "In the Eye of a Hurricane: German Freemasonry in the Weimar Republic and the Third Reich," Totalitarian Movements & Political Religions 4.2 (2003): 113-132 Exact page number of the quote unavailable. Also published in Heredom Research Journal Scottish Rite of Freemasonry, Southern Jurisdiction U.S.A Vol.10 (2002)

492 Jean-Michel Angebert, The Occult and the Third Reich (Macmillan, 1974) 157. Quoted in Hannah Newman, The Rainbow Swastika- A Report to the Jewish People About New Age Anti-Semitism; Nazism and the new age <http://philologos.org/__eb-trs/naF.htm> Web page as of 11/07/2004

493 Jean-Michel Angebert, The Occult and the Third Reich (Macmillan, 1974) 157. Quoted in Hannah Newman, The Rainbow Swastika- A Report to the Jewish People About New Age Anti-Semitism; Nazism and the new age <http://philologos.org/__eb-trs/naF.htm> Web page as of 11/07/2004

important to Freemasonry, appear on the Hitler Youth flag pictured above?

- ❖ Since International Freemasonry recognized the Prussian lodges as "regular," what was the relationship between International Freemasonry and Nazism?
- ❖ Why did Hitler idolize Frederick the Great, who was a great patron of Freemasonry in Germany? It was Frederick, who along with the Rothschild financial interests and other Royals of Europe lead the campaign to quash Napoleon, who had stolen the French revolution from the Powers that Be. Given Hitler's purported anti-Semitism, this was a strange choice of heroes. Strangely enough, the memorial stamp released in 1933 to mark the opening of the first Nazi Reichstag featured Frederick the Great. In addition, Hitler ordered the three Prussian lodges to change their name to Frederick the Great Association to cover up their association with Freemasonry.
- ❖ The Vril society discussed earlier is connected to Freemasonry through the Hermetic Order of the Golden Dawn[494], which was linked to the Theosophical Society of Blavatsky. The Hermetic Society of the Golden Dawn was formed in England in 1887. Its three founding members were prominent Rosicrucians and at the same time, early members of the first Masonic lodge of research Quatuor Coronati Lodge No. 2076.[495] This society consisted of occultists devoted to the study of magic. Among its early members were the poet W. B. Yeats, the actress Florence Farr, the writer Arthur Machen, and the Satanist Aleister Crowley, who in 1905 broke away to found his own Order, the Argenteum Astrum. The Golden Dawn was also popular among members of the British aristocracy. Among its affiliates were the Duke of Bedford, the Duke of Hamilton, and Sir Ivone Kirkpatrick. S. L. Matthews, the Grand Master of the Golden Dawn Society, introduced the ideas of Vril society founder Jacolliot to England.[496] Before the war, Nazi party philosopher Karl Hausofer maintained close contacts with British members of the Golden Dawn. Hausofer later urged Hess to make direct contact with the Duke of Hamilton, a Scottish member of the Golden Dawn.[497]

---

[494] Servando González, Origins of the Swastika: The Hausofer Connection. <http://www.intelinet.org/swastika/swasti02.htm> Web page as of 11/07/2004

[495] González, Swastika: Hausofer

[496] González, Swastika: Hausofer

[497] González, Swastika: Hausofer

- To quote a Mason watcher "Tyler," "The previous Duke of Kent - George Edward Alexander Edmund was installed as Grand Master by King George VI in 1939. He died three years later in 1942 in a mysterious plane crash in Scotland, six months after it was alleged he and the Duke of Hamilton had kept a moonlight appointment with Rudolf Hess on the Caledonian Moor. Historians tell us that the late Grand Master was Pro-Nazi and traveled the Fatherland in order to better educate the King about National Socialism, so as to allow the Empire to 'come to an understanding' with The New World Order."[498] A new book has emerged which places Rudolf Hess on the same ill-fated plane![499] While we are told that these activities were peace negotiations, they appear as collusion towards the ultimate goal of Soviet subjugation of Germany.
- Around 1946 leading German Masons secretly agreed never to mention Masonic events from the 1920-1935 period.[500]
- In 1934, the Nazis would launch a severe crackdown on the non-Prussian Freemasonry lodges. Instead of the square and compass, an inconspicuous little blue flower, the forget-me-not, was used as a lapel pin by Masons, to avoid persecution.[501] In March 1938, the Nazis launched a fund-raising drive selling badges and lapel pins at minimum price. The badge used by the Nazis for the fund-raising turned out to be the same forget-me-not pin chosen by the Freemasons in 1926. In fact, both were made in the same factory in Selb![502] Were the Nazis infiltrated by the Masons? Was it coincidence? Or was the common source of the both the trinkets reflective of something darker?
- As seen in the case of Hitler's bogus anti-occultism and bogus anti-homosexuality, Hitler would launch purges of Freemasons who weren't of the three Prussian lodges to cover up the Nazi connections to Freemasonry.

---

[498] "Tyler," The Dukes of Kent Freemasonrywatch <http://www.freemasonrywatch.org/P2.html> Web page as of 11/07/2004

[499] Lynn Picknet, Clive Prince and Stephen Prior, Double Standards – The Rudolf Hess Coverup (Time Warner Paperbacks, 2002)

[500] W.Bro. Alain Bernheim 33°, " 'The Blue Forget-me-not,' Another Side of the Story," Masonic Papers <http://www.freemasons-freemasonry.com/bernheim3.html> Web page as of 11/07/2004

[501] Bernheim, "The Blue Forget-me-not,' Another Side of the Story."

[502] Bernheim, "The Blue Forget-me-not,' Another Side of the Story,"

The Significance of Germany to the Criminal Elite

Nazism was a product of the Illuminati. This inference can be made by virtue of its location; Germany. This country has always been a hub of Criminal Cabal activity. It would be very improbable that a non-Illuminati movement would take root in the very playground of the Illuminati. Consider the following:

- The Kaiser of Germany is related by bloodline to Romanov and British royalty, a common bloodline that may be traced to the earlier predecessors of the Illuminati such as the Merovingians.
- The Merovingians had a foothold in Germany through the Frankish Clovis, who made Germanic tribes subject of the Merovingian dynasty around 500 A.D.
- Berlin has always been an important center of Freemasonry in the world.
- The Astors, important old world Illuminati originated in Germany.
- Frederick the Great was a major patron of Freemasonry in Germany, and is said to have started the original Prussian lodges. His life was filled with secret society intrigues. Frederick the Great was also Hitler's personal hero.
- Kaiser Wilhelm was a friend of the German ruling elite Krupp family. The police commissioner would conduct damage control for the activities of Friedrich Alfred Krupp who was a pedophile. His wife was thrown into a mental asylum when she notified the authorities.
- The modern Illuminati was formalized in 1776 by Adam Weishaupt, a professor of Canonic law at the University of Ingolstadt in Bavaria. Secret documents penned by Weishaupt were leaked, which resulted in the Elector of Bavaria cracking down on Freemasonry in the region. The order was assumed to be extinct, but that is what scientists have said regarding the Coelacanth, a fish deemed extinct only to be found alive again. There are many esoteric references pointing towards the Order. An interesting seal appeared on American issued one-dollar bills in 1778. This seal is similar to the seal the Illuminati adopted in 1776. Further, the date May 1st was adopted as Labor Day and also approved as Law Day by the American Bar Association. And 1776 was also the year of declaration of American

Independence. The new tower to be built at the site of the former World Trade Center is also 1776 feet tall.

- The German province of Bohemia has always been a hotbed of Illuminati intrigue. British, German and Romanov royalty would frequently intermarry among "Bohemians," which indicates a common bloodstock. For some reason, the name "Leopold" keeps recurring among the Bohemian elite.
- Bohemia is of central importance to the Illuminati. It is believed that its American counterpart is the "Bohemian Grove," a redwood forest in Sonoma County (California), where many operatives of Western ruling elite, including American Presidents have been sighted. Anti-Bohemian Grove activist Alex Jones managed to infiltrate the Bohemian Grove and photographed bizarre rituals taking place before a huge stone owl.[503]
- Lenin was considered a friend/spy of the Kaiser. The Kaiser's head of Secret Police was Max Warburg, who is associated with the Rothschilds. Max Warburg arranged Lenin's journey to Russia in a sealed train. It is fair enough to believe the Kaiser fled to Belgium[504] in World War I to allow larger powers to use Germany as a staging ground for World War II.
- The Rothschild banking dynasty of Mayer Amschel rose from the ghettoes of Frankfurt. Though his five sons would spread out, one of them (Amschel) would remain in Frankfurt and another, Salomon would settle in Vienna.
- Amschel Rothschild of Frankfurt was the son of the founder of the Rothschild dynasty. Springmeier claims that Mayer Amschel adopted Bismarck as a son.[505] Bismarck would later emerge as the dictator of Prussia, who unified many regions into a single powerful entity. After Amschel died, Bismarck remained close to the Rothschilds. In fact Bismarck's main banker was Bleichroder, who had links to the Rothschilds and was probably the richest man in Berlin. Bleichroder was also an important Satanist and a high-ranking Mason. Amschel's brother, James Rothschild of France had a son named Alphonse, who is believed to have been pulling the strings of Bismarck, along with

---

[503] Alex Jones, "Dark Secrets Inside the Bohemian Grove," Infowars.com <http://www.infowars.com/bg1.html> Web page as of 16/03/04

[504] Another Illuminati stronghold infamous for organized pedophilia.

[505] Fritz Springmeier, Bloodlines of the Illuminati (Spring Arbor distributors, 1998) 201. GlobalGrey PDF edition 2013 <http://www.globalgrey.co.uk/Pages/Books-Conspiracies/Bloodlines-Of-The-Illuminati.html> Web page as of 03/07/13.

those of Bleichroder.[506] Bismarck may have been used by the Rothschilds to declare war on France and to crush Napoleon III. Alphonse Rothschild even sent his family from France to England,[507] probably with foreknowledge of the fall of France to anti-Napoleon forces. Alphonse had completely infiltrated the finances and personal life of Napoleon III, and the two even shared a mistress![508] Bismarck is credited with starting the socialization of Germany in 19th century, which allowed the Powers that Be to create powerful state institutions which still control the people of Germany to this day.

- According to information acquired from an 1876 break-in at the "tomb," the name given to the Skull and Bones meeting hall on Yale University campus, "Bones is a chapter of a corps in a German University.... General Russell, its founder, was in Germany before his Senior Year and formed a warm friendship with a leading member of a German Society. He brought back with him to college, authority to found a chapter here."[509] This American chapter became known as "The Order of Skull and Bones." This order plays an important role in American politics. In one American election, both the Republican and Democratic Presidential candidates, George Bush and John Kerry, were Bonesmen.
- A certain German "King," Adolphus Busch, acquired Ulysses Grant's St. Louis property and built a magnificent castle on it called Grant's Farm.[510] Ulysses Grant is often associated with America's most powerful ruling elite.
- Present day Germany is among the most powerful voting members of the World Bank. The German economy is the backbone of the Globalist Banking Oligarchy. Fritz Springmeier, an expert on mind control reports of mind control programming as well as bizarre rituals in German castles. There are also growing sightings of German "special forces" at the creepy new Denver airport. The FBI has verified a German

---

[506] Springmeier, Bloodlines 201.
[507] Springmeier, Bloodlines 202.
[508] Springmeier, Bloodlines 201.
[509] Kris Millegan, "The Order of the Skull and Bones-Everything you wanted to know but were afraid to ask," July 1997 CTRL.org An archived copy is available at <http://www.mega.nu:8080/ampp/skull.html> Web page as of 11/07/2004
[510] Springmeier, Bloodlines 391.

connection to Mohammed Ata and the 911 conspiracy, upon insistence of independent investigators.[511]

The Origins of the term "Nazi."

Just like the symbolism of the Nazis, the origin and meaning of the term 'Nazi' are multifold. It may be a mischievous play on the Aramaic and Hebrew term "Nassi." "Nassi" has several similar meanings ranging from Prince, Chief, head of a community, head of the multitudes of Israel etc.[512] For example, the leader of the Marrano community in Istanbul during the reign of Selim II was a certain Don Joseph Nassi.[513] In Modern Hebrew it is refers to the President of Israel. According to a Hebrew Website "Why is the *Nassi* equivalent to *Moshiach*? First of all the simple meaning of the term Moshiach is "anointed one," which personifies the *Nassi*, who was chosen and anointed to be the *Nassi* and Shepherd of Israel."[514] And further "the Nassi of the generation is the redeemer of the generation. The role of every generational Nassi and Shepherd of the Jewish People is to be the "Moshe Rabbeinu" of that generation. As the Zohar teaches, an emanation from Moshe is present in every generation."[515]

Torah Judaism sees the *Nassi* as chosen by God. It is not surprising that a movement directed against Orthodox Judaism would mock the term *Nassi*.

Hitler's staged rise to power

Though we are told that Hitler started his career as a failed artist turned anti-Semite, it is more likely that he had been selected by the Powers that Be and was playing along a previously scripted plan. The following seldom mentioned predictions come from occultists, who credited these predictions to their "occult powers." Their real source of knowledge was more likely their connections to the people behind Hitler. The occultist mentor of Hitler, Lanz Von Liebenfels wrote to one of his Templar brothers,

---

[511] Daniel Hopsicker, "FBI Terror Alert in South Pacific," Mad Cow Morning News <http://www.madcowprod.com/11162006.html> Accessed 14/12/06

[512] . In Arabic, it refers to someone who persuades for a good cause.

[513] Andrew C. Hess, "The Battle of Lepanto and its Place in Mediterranean History," Past and Present (57) Nov. 1972, 64.

[514] Sichos in English. Vol. 28 < http://www.sichosinenglish.org/books/sichos-in-english/28/12.htm> Web page as of 11/07/2004

[515] Sichos in English. Vol. 28 < http://www.sichosinenglish.org/books/sichos-in-english/28/12.htm> Web page as of 11/07/2004

> Do you know that Hitler is one of our pupils? You will still live to see that he, and thereby we, also will triumph and kindle a movement that will make the world tremble.[516]

Hitler would later ban Liebenfel's writings in 1933 to cover his connection to Liebenfels. Joseph Goebbels is quoted as telling his aide-de-camp, Prince Schaumburg-Lippe,

> You'll think I'm crazy, but listen to me: Hitler will bring us to a catastrophe. But his ideas, once they have been transformed, will acquire a new strength.[517]

Dietrich Eckart was a leading Thulist who died in 1923 and who possibly initiated Hitler into Tantric occult sex rituals.[518] Among his last words was this proclamation:

> Follow Hitler! He will dance, but it will be to my tune. We have given him the means to maintain contact with them (meaning the "masters"). Don't grieve for me for I have influenced history more than any other German.[519]

Further, Eckart is quoted as introducing Hitler into Munich occult circles as "the long awaited savior."[520] Eckart was following his own mission revealed to him in a séance, according to which "Lord Maitreya" (a telepathy superstar among Theosophists) would soon make his appearance as a German messiah to "lead the Aryan race to final victory

---

[516] Wilfried Daim, Der Mann, der Hitler die Ideen gab (Munich, 1958) 12. Quoted in Jackson Spielvogel and David Redles, "Hitler's Racial Ideology: Content and Occult Sources," Simon Wiesenthal Center – Museum of Tolerance Online > Multimedia Learning Center > Annual 3. 1997
< http://motlc.wiesenthal.com/site/pp.asp?c=gvKVLcMVIuG&b=395043>

[517] Jean-Michel Angebert, The Occult and the Third Reich (Macmillan, 1974) 234. Quoted in Hannah Newman, The Rainbow Swastika- A Report to the Jewish People About New Age Anti-Semitism: Nazism and the New age <http://philologos.org/__eb-trs/naF.htm> Web page as of 11/07/2004

[518] See previous section on Ordo Novi Templi.

[519] Wulf Schwarzweller, The Unknown Hitler: His Private Life and Fortune (National Press Inc. and Star Agency, 1989) 69. Quoted in Scott Lively and Kevin Abrams, The Pink Swastika-Homosexuality in the Nazi Party 4th ed. (Sacramento: Veritas Aeterna Press, 2002) 122.

[520] Hannah Newman, The Rainbow Swastika- A Report to the Jewish People About New Age Anti-Semitism: Nazism and the New age <http://philologos.org/__eb-trs/naF.htm> Web page as of 11/07/2004

over the Jews."[521] Eckart claimed he was charged with the responsibility of "nurturing"[522] this messiah. To Alfred Rosenberg he said:

> I believe in Hitler; above him there hovers a star.[523]

Was this star the Satanic pentagram found on corporate logos? Hanussen, Hitler's favorite astrologer also predicted that Hitler was going through tough times that would continue until Hanussen performed an occult ceremony in Hitler's native hometown. He returned, informing Hitler that his rise to power would begin on January 30th 1933[524] and said to him,

> I see victory for you, It cannot be stopped.[525]

Erik Jan Hanussen's *Berliner Wochenschau* printed the startling prophecy that within one year's time the future Führer would become Chancellor.[526] He would later predict the Reichstag fire.

Madame Blavatsky's Theosophy movement had also predicted the coming of a "new messiah to usher in a New Age." The Nazis would wholeheartedly adopt her views on racial evolution theories and her Atlantean myths.

Hitler's Elitist Origins

Fritz Springmeier recently re-introduced readers in his book to the idea that Hitler's father may have been the product of a Rothschild breeding program instituted to create operatives in different places, among different people and in various sectors of society. The origins of these operatives were meant to be secret and untraceable. To quote

---

521 Joseph Carr, The Twisted Cross (Vital Issues Press, 1985) 110. Quoted in Newman, Swastika: Nazism and the New Age.
522 Joseph Carr, The Twisted Cross (Vital Issues Press, 1985) 110. Quoted in Newman, Swastika: Nazism and the New Age.
523 Dusty Sklar, The Nazis and the Occult (1989) 53. Quoted in Newman, Swastika: Nazism and the New Age.
524 Stephen Lemons, Hitler's Clairvoyant Salon.com <http://www.salon.com/people/feature/2002/02/27/hanussen/> Web page as of 11/07/2004
525 Peter Levenda, Unholy Alliance (Avon Books, 1995) ??
526 Stephen Lemons, Hitler's Clairvoyant Salon.com <http://www.salon.com/people/feature/2002/02/27/hanussen/> Web page as of 11/07/2004

Springmeier (as is, including formatting errors) from his bloodlines text,[527]

> According to Walter Langer, a psychoanalyst who wrote the book The Mind of Adolf Hitler-the Secret Wartime Report (Basic books, 1972), the demonic German leader was a grandson of a Rothschild. Adolf's father, Alois Hitler, was the illegitimate son of Maria Anna Schicklgruber. It was generally supposed that the father of Alois Hitler was Johann Georg Hiedler. "There are some people who seriously doubt that Johann Georg Hiedler was the father of Alois.... [an Austrian document] was supposedly prepared that proved Maria Anna Schicklgruber was living in Vienna at the time she conceived. "At that time she was employed as a servant in the home of [a] Baron Rothschild. As soon as the family discovered her pregnancy she was sent back to her home ... where Alois was born." It is believed that Hitler (who was totally created by Satan's Empire) attacked Austria first, in order to destroy the Austrian records that proved his Jewish ancestry.

Walter Langer was a psychoanalyst whose book *Psychology and the Human Living* is still in print. He was commissioned to write *The Mind of Adolf Hitler* as a secret wartime report in 1943 for "Wild Bill" Donovan of the OSS. The report was classified as top-secret for over a quarter of a century, until Langer's colleagues convinced him to release the report for the benefit of everybody. The OSS had quietly declassified the report by then, and a colleague of Langer made the discovery when he stumbled upon a copy in the National Archives. It was then printed for the first time in 1972. Langer got the impression that Lord Halifax (the British Ambassador to the US) was passed a copy of the then top-secret report well in advance of it being made public.[528] Langer was also asked to make a German translation of the report for unknown parties.[529]

Alois Hitler was born in 1837 when Salomon Mayer Rothschild (one of the five sons of the first Mayer Amschel Rothschild) lived in a Vienna

---

[527] Fritz Springmeier, Bloodlines of the Illuminati (Spring Arbor distributors, 1998) 193. GlobalGrey PDF edition 2013 <http://www.globalgrey.co.uk/Pages/Books-Conspiracies/Bloodlines-Of-The-Illuminati.html> Web page as of 03/07/13.

[528] Langer's brother William attended a reception of Halifax in Washington during which Lord Halifax said: "Langer? Langer? You must be the author of the interesting study of Hitler that I read some time back." Halifax could not have obtained the original copies printed by the OSS through official channels, with the exception of the President and the Secretary of State. Walter C. Langer, The Mind of Adolf Hitler – The Secret Wartime Report (Basic Books Inc. 1972) 21-22.

[529] Walter C. Langer, The Mind of Adolf Hitler – The Secret Wartime Report (Basic Books Inc. 1972) 22.

mansion. Salomon had an unhappy marriage and his wife mainly stayed in Frankfurt and Vienna, while his son Anselm Salomon worked in Paris. Hitler's grandmother Maria Anna Schicklgruber was a girl working in the Rothschild household, who got pregnant and moved back to her village home in Spital.[530] The father of the child was generally assumed to be Johann Georg Hiedler, a miller's assistant.[531]

Schicklgruber died when the child, Alois Hitler, was five years of age. It was only 35 years after Schicklgruber's death that Hiedler would claim Alois as his own son (Alois bore his mother's name until he was forty years of age).[532] It is supposed that Hiedler on his deathbed left his name to Alois.[533] But there is no explanation how and why Alois changed it to Hitler. The villagers claimed Alois changed the name for a "legacy" of his own,[534] but such pursuits of legacy were uncommon among Austrian peasants of that backward region. Both Alois and his later sons exhibited traits uncharacteristic of Austrian peasant families.[535]

Alois left his home village at an early age to seek his fortune in Vienna where his mother had worked. The next twenty-three years of his life are largely unaccounted for.[536] He eventually became a domineering customs officer. He was known for his abusive relationship with members of his household.[537] The effects of the peculiar household relationships would manifest throughout Hitler's life. In his 12th year of schooling, Hitler barely escaped being expelled for "sexual indiscretion."[538] According to Rauschning, Hitler would wake up at night shrieking "He! He! He's been here!"[539] During such episodes, he would gasp for breath and act as if choking.[540] Such episodes may have been nightmares reminiscent of his father's abuse.

Alois' ambitiousness was noticeably not at par with the backward Austrian peasants of Waldviertel. In addition, he fathered many children (7-8) from three marriages, which was more typical of elite families.

---

530 Citing Hansjurgen Koehler and Fritz Thyssen. Langer, The Mind of Hitler 101.
531 Langer, The Mind of Hitler 101.
532 Langer, The Mind of Hitler 101.
533 Langer, The Mind of Hitler 101.
534 Langer, The Mind of Hitler 101.
535 Langer, The Mind of Hitler 102.
536 Langer, The Mind of Hitler 103.
537 Langer, The Mind of Hitler 104.
538 Langer, The Mind of Hitler 132.
539 Langer, The Mind of Hitler 104.
540 Langer, The Mind of Hitler 188.

Salomon Mayer von Rothschild

Alois Heidler

Hitler's mother, Klara Hitler (Poelzl)

Adolf Hitler, age 12

Adolf Hitler's mother, Klara Poelzl, was the third wife of Alois. Klara was Alois's second cousin, who was reared as a foster daughter during his first marriage.[541] Four years after the birth of Adolf Hitler, Alois retired from civil service at the age of 56 and rapidly moved across several different villages. While Alois was working in Branau, a Jewish man named Prinz acted as Hitler's godfather.[542] Hitler too, would leave for Vienna after his mother died in 1907. In Vienna, he seemed to drop out of sight for ten months.[543] Hanisch, a friend of Hitler indicates that when he and Hitler were destitute, he went with Hitler to seek help from a well-to-do Jew whom Hitler said was his father (or godfather).[544] In Vienna, Hitler was on good terms with Jews.[545] He sent two postcards to Dr. Bloch, who was his Jewish family doctor in Linz.[546] His companion in Vienna, Reinhold Hanisch, often joked with Hitler that he may be Jewish.[547]

It is extremely likely that Hitler was involved in perversions. According to Texe Marrs, "As Chancellor, he carried on sexually with his 15-year-old niece, Gelli, who killed herself rather than continue giving in to his bizarre and beastly sexual fetishes."[548] These activities were of a

---

[541] Langer, The Mind of Hitler 102.
[542] Langer, The Mind of Hitler 102.
[543] Langer, The Mind of Hitler 181.
[544] Langer, The Mind of Hitler 181.
[545] Langer, The Mind of Hitler 119.
[546] Langer, The Mind of Hitler 119. In addition to Dr. Bloch, Hitler got along with several other Jews in these formative years, such as his landlady in Vienna, his Jewish cook Fraulein Kunde, Jewish art dealers of Vienna and Hugo Gutmann, who assisted him in obtaining the Iron Cross. Robert G. L. Waite in Langer, The Mind of Hitler 233-234.
[547] Reinhold Hanisch, "I was Hitler's Buddy," The New Republic April 5th 1939, page 272 [73]. Quoted by Langer, The Mind of Hitler 119.
[548] Texe Marrs, "Unmasking the sexual perversions of the Illuminati: Two on a saddle Part1," Power of the Prophecy <http://www.texemarrs.com/012002/two_on_a_saddle.htm> Web page as of

degrading and masochist nature, which Langer has discussed in detail.[549] According to other versions of the story, Gelli was killed. Another lover, Rene Mueller, committed suicide.[550] Yet another lover, Unity Mitford, attempted suicide.[551] His last lover, Eva Braun attempted suicide twice. Apart from such bizarre episodes, one of his hidden hobbies was his love for pornography.[552] According to Ernst Hanfstaengl, the Vienna flophouse where Hitler lived in had a reputation of being a meeting point for homosexuals.[553] One source claims that at that time that Hitler was listed as a sexual deviant in Viennese police records.[554] Rauschning indicates that Hitler had a homosexual relationship with Foerster, the Danzig gauleiter.[555] According to Gregor Strasser, the personal bodyguard of Hitler was 100 percent homosexual.[556] As Rauschning would further claim,

> Most loathsome of all is the reeking miasma of furtive, unnatural sexuality that fills and fouls the whole atmosphere around him, like an evil emanation. Nothing in this environment is straightforward. Surreptitious relationships, substitutes and symbols, false sentiments and secret lusts- nothing in this man's surroundings is natural and genuine, nothing has the openness of a natural instinct.[557]

At the outbreak of World War I, Hitler enlisted in a Bavarian regiment as a volunteer.[558] Hitler would wear an Iron Cross First Class, which he claims he was awarded for capturing twelve Frenchmen single-handedly.[559] This medal is never awarded unless the recipient had already been awarded the Second Class decoration.[560] And there is no mention of the award in the history of the regiment.[561] For some reason, he spent four years in the same regiment but was never advanced beyond the rank of First Class Private or Lance Corporal. Rauschning claims that

---

11/07/2004. Gelli's brother Leo Raubal accused Hitler of causing Gelli's death. Langer, The Mind of Hitler 110.

[549] Langer, The Mind of Hitler 134.

[550] Langer, The Mind of Hitler 171.

[551] Langer, The Mind of Hitler 171.

[552] Langer, The Mind of Hitler 92.

[553] Langer, The Mind of Hitler 119.

[554] Langer, The Mind of Hitler 119-120.

[555] Langer, The Mind of Hitler 174.

[556] Langer, The Mind of Hitler 174.

[557] Herman Rauschning, The Voice of Destruction 263. Quoted in Langer, The Mind of Hitler 92.

[558] Langer, The Mind of Hitler 121.

[559] Langer, The Mind of Hitler 122.

[560] Langer, The Mind of Hitler 122.

[561] Langer, The Mind of Hitler 122.

a high-ranking Nazi confided to him that Hitler could not be promoted in this period, because he was court marshaled after being found guilty for pederasty with an officer.[562] Rauschning also claims that in Munich, Hitler was found guilty of being in violation of paragraph 175, which deals with pederasty.[563] No further corroboration of these accounts has been discovered. After World War I, Hitler appeared before an inquiry with a "charge list" against some of his war comrades, alleging their Communist sympathies, which resulted in their execution.[564] Was this a measure to eliminate those who would have been privy to his less meritorious record?

When Hitler gained power in Germany, The Austrian Chancellor Dolfuss conducted an investigation into the origins of Hitler. It was found that a servant girl came to Vienna and worked as a domestic servant for rich families. She ended up being seduced and went to her village to bear the child. Dolfuss checked the police registration records of workers working in Vienna and managed to dig out her registration card, which showed she had been working at the Rothschild mansion. Hitler assassinated Dolfuss and Hitler would first annex Austria, to destroy the records Dolfuss had in his possession. Later, Hitler had the village in question razed to the ground by Nazi forces. According to a newspaper report, Hitler's brother Alois Jr. was sent to a concentration camp in 1942 because he talked too much.[565] The only relative whom Hitler maintained open contact with was his elder half-sister Angela. She married an official named Raubal in Linz.[566] Her daughter Gelli's relationship with Hitler has been discussed earlier.

Later, a high level Gestapo officer, Hansjurgen Koehler actually viewed a copy of the Dolfuss documents, which were given to him by Heydrich, the overlord of the Nazi Secret Service. He wrote a book, Inside the Gestapo, which revealed that the file in question caused huge consternation. It was Koehler's recollection, which became a source for Walter Langer's research in this regard. Prior to Koehler, German industrialist Fritz Thyssen had come up with a similar account when he defected from Germany. After Langer's research, Robert G. L. Waite

---

[562] Langer, The Mind of Hitler 124.
[563] Langer, The Mind of Hitler 124.
[564] Langer, The Mind of Hitler 125.
[565] Langer, The Mind of Hitler 108.
[566] Langer also notes that in Vienna, Angela was the manager of Mensa Academica Judaica, and during riots, she defended Jewish students from attack, beating the Aryan students with a club. Langer, The Mind of Hitler 109.

confirmed that Hitler had inquiries made through the Gestapo in 1935, 1938, 1941, 1942, 1943 and 1944,[567] presumably to find out what was known about his origins and which details required attention for the purpose of covering up. These reports have now been made available. Similarly, Hitler had asked his private lawyer Hans Frank to investigate his paternal lineage.[568]

There are other accounts independent of Walter Langer as well. For example, Henry Makow has brought to attention another account,[569]which is quoted verbatim as follows:

> From *Blood and Banquets: A Berlin Social Diary* (Garden City, 1942) p.178 **by Bella Fromm**, Diplomatic Columnist for the *Vossiche Zeitung*, a leading Berlin newspaper in the 1930's. Bela Fromm belonged to a prominent Jewish family. The Jewish banker mentioned is rumored to be a Rothschild.
>
> > **August 15, 1934**
> > Richard came to see me all hot and flustered. "Bellachen Hitler has Jewish blood in his veins. Paul Wiegler, our fiction editor, found out through Viennese friends!
> >
> > "Hitler had a very beautiful grandmother. She was vain, ambitious, and money-greedy. She had a job as a lady's maid in Vienna, at a wealthy, non-Aryan banker's house. It is known that she brought an illegitimate child into her marriage with Schicklgruber. Well, that offspring of her romance with a Jewish banker was Adolph Hitler's father.
> >
> > I became very indignant! "That would be the most disgraceful blow of all to the Jews ---if it were true! Haven't we enough to bear, without adding a Jewish Hitler to our burden?"

The powers that Be have responded by spreading disinformation that Hitler only became aware of his secret lineage through an attempt to blackmail him, for which he ordered an investigation by his lawyer Hans Frank. Whereas it is more likely that both Alois and Adolph Hitler were batting for the Powers that Be all along.

---

567 Langer, The Mind of Hitler 231.

568 Hans Frank told Hitler that his grandmother had become pregnant while working as a domestic servant in a Jewish household in Graz. Langer, The Mind of Hitler 234.

569 Henry Makow, Note on homepage on January 8th 2006 Savethemales.ca <http://www.savethemales.ca/>

Hitler's Political Career

To quote Walter Langer,

> [...] this apparently insignificant and incompetent ne'er-do-well was later able, in the course of a relatively few years, to talk his way into the highest political offices, hoodwink the experienced leaders of major powers, turn millions of highly civilized people into barbarians, order the extermination of a large segment of the population, build and control the mightiest war machine ever known, and plunge the world into history's most devastating war.[...][570]

To quote Dorothy Thompson,

> He is formless, almost faceless, a man whose countenance is a caricature, a man whose framework seems cartilaginous, without bones. He is inconsequent and voluble, ill poised and insecure. He is the very prototype of the little man.[571]

Was Hitler indeed a one-man-show as he is portrayed to be? To compensate for Hitler's shortcomings, the Powers that Be portrayed him as more presentable for the German masses, through the use of thousands of posters and custom photographs. He would be portrayed in newsreels as the only one who did not wear a steel helmet, even though there would be huge security precautions whenever he appeared in public.[572] Hitler compensated for the "rasping quality"[573] of his voice by using it to rouse the emotions of the audience. He would start slowly, trying to assess the mood of the audience. And once when he was able to gauge it, he would talk concurrently, while slowly building a tempo towards a climax. Hitler stressed his use on emotional trappings by saying "We must distrust the intelligence and the conscience and must place our faith in our instincts."[574] To Hanfstaengl, he said, "The masses are like a woman."[575] Why did Hitler seek such a high use of emotion? Was he trying to stampede his listeners towards objectives that could not otherwise hold water?

---

[570] Walter C. Langer, The Mind of Hitler – The Secret Wartime Report (NY & London: Basic books Inc., 1972) 11.

[571] Dorothy Thompson, "Good Bye to Germany," Harper's Magazine December 1934 pp 12-14 [307]. Quoted in Langer, The Mind of Hitler 44.

[572] Langer, The Mind of Hitler 95.

[573] Langer, The Mind of Hitler 45.

[574] Langer, The Mind of Hitler 190.

[575] Langer, The Mind of Hitler 203.

Apart from Hitler's oratory and objectification, many other measures were undertaken to pacify the subject population into accepting him. Unemployment disappeared and roads and buildings that could never have been conceived in postwar Germany sprung up.[576] The Volkswagen Beetle was developed with the aim of providing a car for every German household. Were all these desperate appeasing measures undertaken for winning the trust of the German people for allowing Germany to be sacrificed for larger goals of the Powers that Be?

A 1930 tourist poster depicting the new German highway system. Available online courtesy Randall Bytwerk, the German Propaganda Archive at Calvin College <http://www.calvin.edu/academic/cas/gpa> Accessed 10/12/06. © Copyright German Federal Archives in Koblenz. Minimized Reproduction under Fair Dealing

Among his close associates, Hitler would go through well-timed fits of rages to drive them into confusion.[577] He often ran away from unpleasant, unexpected and difficult situations.[578] He would also withdraw from situations claiming he was depressed.[579] Even his close associates could never connect with him, and they noted an ever-present aloofness in him.[580] He was very secretive when it came to his real dealings. To quote, "His mind is full of compartments, Hanfstaengl says, and his dealings with every individual are carefully pigeonholed."[581] There are indications of a double personality in Hitler, one being a soft, sentimental and indecisive individual and the other being the Hitler the world knew.[582] Close associates noted sudden alternations between these two personalities.[583] Why would Hitler undertake such strenuous mental gymnastics? Or is this complex personality indicative of hidden goals and hidden agendas? How is it that an individual with such personal afflictions, such controversial origins and such chequered past, literally walked into the highest corridors of power?

---

[576] Langer, The Mind of Hitler 55.
[577] Quoting Rauschning. Langer, The Mind of Hitler 76.
[578] Langer, The Mind of Hitler 77.
[579] Langer, The Mind of Hitler 80.
[580] Langer, The Mind of Hitler 83.
[581] Langer, The Mind of Hitler 99.
[582] Langer, The Mind of Hitler 127.
[583] Langer, The Mind of Hitler 128.

German Elitist Families, the Nazis, and the Rothschilds

Coat of arms

The palace of Thurn und Taxis at Regensburg © br-online.de All Rights Reserved. Minimized Reproduction Under Fair Dealing.

Those who read the section on Thule society will remember that a powerful member of that society was Gustav Franz Maria Prinz von **Thurn und Taxis**, a powerful aristocrat with a bloodline common to many European royals. Gustav Franz was allegedly "murdered," by Communists, in the incident that precipitated the mobilization of the Freikorps. His murder saved the House of Thurn und Taxis from being identified with the later Nazis. Fritz Springmeier discovered that "[...] The House of Thurn and Taxis was of the Black Nobility. In 1516 Holy Roman Emperor Maximilan I (of the Merovingian bloodline and husband of a member of the Black Nobility) commissioned the House to create a mounted postal service between Vienna and Brussels."[584] This service spread to central Europe and its head office became Frankfurt. In fact the word "taxi" may have been derived from this service. Instrumental to the early success of Mayer Amschel Rothschild was his infiltration of the Thurn und Taxis Postal system. The house of Thurn und Taxis was on so good terms with Mayer Amschel that they allowed him to spy on mail being passed through their system. This surveillance activity helped the house of Rothschild to keep abreast of developments and became so crucial to their success that the Rothschilds set up their own private postal system, making them the best and fastest informed individuals in Europe. To quote Springmeier, "The business with Thurn und Taxis helped Mayer receive the title 'Imperial Crown Agent' in 1800. This title served as a passport that allowed him to travel throughout the Holy Roman Empire. It also provided the right to bear arms, and it freed him from having to pay the taxes and obligations upon the Jews of that period."[585]

---

[584] Fritz Springmeier, Bloodlines of the Illuminati (Spring Arbor distributors, 1998) 179. GlobalGrey PDF edition 2013 <http://www.globalgrey.co.uk/Pages/Books-Conspiracies/Bloodlines-Of-The-Illuminati.html> Web page as of 03/07/13.
[585] Springmeier, Bloodlines 179.

More German Elitist Families

According to the research of Fritz Springmeier[586], Mayer Amschel Rothschild (the first main Rothschild) made the acquaintance of General von Estorff in Hanover. Estorff was a numismatist who was impressed by Mayer's knowledge of the subject. In 1763 General Estorff left Hanover and joined the Court of Prince William IX of Hesse-Hanau who was a Freemason. The house of Hesse-Hanau's income came from the loaning of Hessian soldiers to other countries. Hessian troops were used by England against the American Revolution, in fact the colonial armies fought with more Hessian soldiers than Englishmen. The House of Hesse-Cassel is said to have made a lot of money off the American Revolution. In 1801 the Rothschilds became crown agents of the Landgrave William of Hesse-Cassel. When Napoleon invaded the province of Hesse, Mayer Amschel Rothschild was instrumental in saving the wealth of Landgrave from being plundered by Napoleon. The Hesse Dynasty has lasted up to the 20th century, and had strong connections with the British Royal family. Prince Philip of Hesse-Kassel (not to be confused with Prince Phillip, Duke of Edinburgh) was a messenger between Hitler and Mussolini. The Nazis would later pretend to distance themselves from German aristocracy, in order to avoid damaging the postwar prospects of these families. The House of Hesse is still a powerful force in Germany.

Coat of arms of Hesse

The town of Kassel bears 13 clover leafs

Hessian Mercenaries

Kassel Industrial area.

Anti-Semitism, with Exceptions

In the previous section, we discussed Hitler's bogus anti-occultism and bogus anti-homosexuality. Nazi anti-Semitism was for real. But exceptions were made for some individuals of obvious Jewish origin, who were major players in this venture. Note that such participation in

586 Springmeier, Bloodlines 176.

Nazism was definitely not open to all. The following represent a tiny minority of visible Jews who became associated with Nazism solely on account of their connections to the Powers that Be. This proves that the inherent goals of Nazism went far beyond mere anti-Semitism.

- **Alfred Rosenberg** was a Jewish-German émigré from Russia who became a member of the Thule society and is credited with introducing the Protocols of Zion among Nazi circles.[587] He also wrote a prominent piece of Nazi literature, *The Myth of the Twentieth Century*, in which he recycled the Aryan-evolution ideas of Blavatsky. Interestingly, Rosenberg's mentor was Houston Stewart Chamberlain who wrote *Foundations of the nineteenth century*, a favorite reading of Hitler. He was the nephew of Field Marshal Neville Chamberlain, who became the Prime minister of Britain and extended the Nazis a wide window for rearmament. Rosenberg is quoted in his writings as: "The earth-centered Jew lacks a soul" and elsewhere, "[the continuing existence of the Jew] would lead to a void, to the destruction not only of the illusory earthly world but also of the truly existent, the spiritual."[588] Rosenberg is considered to be among the major anti-Semitic thinkers within the Nazi party.

Alfred Rosenburg

- **Eric Jan Hanussen** was a famous astrologer and a master of the occult (considered to be among the ranks of Houdini) who taught Hitler body language and public speaking. Hanussen claimed to be a Danish baron (and dyed his hair blond), but his real name was Herman Steinschneider, the son of a rich Jewish family from Prossnitz, Bohemia. Hanussen was the friend whom Hitler turned to during his early political frustrations in 1926. He also groomed Hitler in staging dramatic public meetings.[589] Hitler invited him to

Hanussen

[587] Servando González, Origins of the Swastika: The Hausofer Connection <http://www.intelinet.org/swastika/swasti07.htm> Web page as of 11/07/2004
[588] Dusty Sklar, The Nazis and the Occult (1989) 147-148. Quoted in Hannah Newman, The Rainbow Swastika- A Report to the Jewish People About New Age Anti-Semitism; Nazism and the new age <http://philologos.org/__eb-trs/naF.htm> Web page as of 11/07/2004.
[589] Walter C. Langer, The Mind of Hitler – The Secret Wartime Report (NY & London: Basic books Inc., 1972) 32.

his headquarters at the Hotel Kaiserhof in Berlin for a private session.[590] He predicted that Hitler was going through tough times, which would continue until he performed an occult ceremony, in Hitler's native hometown. He returned informing Hitler that his rise to power would begin on January 30th 1933[591] and said to him, "I see victory for you. It cannot be stopped."[592] Erik Jan Hanussen's *Berliner Wochenschau*, printed the prophecy that within one year's time the future Fuehrer would become Chancellor.[593] Hitler and Hanussen would further meet about a dozen times between 1932 and 1933.[594] He also predicted the Reichstag fire (a staged event) and some even believe he was involved in this incident.[595] It seems more likely that Hanussen was using his occult knowledge as a cover for his connections to the real source of knowledge, the Powers That Be behind Hitler. Hitler reportedly killed Hanussen in 1933 for knowing too much.

- **Reinhardt Heydrich:** The real name of his father Bruno Heydrich was Suss. Reinhardt was appointed Protector of Bohemia. Israeli Historian Bryan Mark Rigg supports this claim in his book *Hitler's Jewish Soldiers* along with providing analysis that certain Jewish Nazis were extended special privilege by Hitler.

Reinhardt Heydrich

- **The Rothschilds:** Hitler's origins have been discussed earlier. The Rothschild connection to I.G. Farben, the Nazi military industrial complex, will be discussed in chapter four. In addition, Hitler did not embark upon freezing of Rothschild assets in Germany, apart from a few cosmetic closures of banks. Neither did any Rothschilds end up in in the concentration camps.

---

590 Stephen Lemons, Hitler's Clairvoyant Salon.com <http://www.salon.com/people/feature/2002/02/27/hanussen/> Web page as of 11/07/2004

591 Lemons, "Clairvoyant."

592 Peter Levenda, Unholy Alliance (Avon Books, 1995) ??

593 Lemons, "Clairvoyant."

594 Lemons, "Clairvoyant."

595 Lemons, "Clairvoyant."

❖ **Kanaris:** Kanaris was an important spy of Hitler who played a role in destroying the Weimar republic preceding the Nazi regime. He later became head of the Abwehr, or German military intelligence. He may have been of Jewish-Greek origin. He is now portrayed as a courageous hero resisting Hitler. Regardless of his ethnic background, he was privy to the deepest intrigues of the Reich. One of his associates, Mata Hari, was equally mysterious. Henry Makow made Kanaris the center of one of his writings. To quote:

Kanaris

> Prince Michel Sturdza's aptly titled book *The Suicide of Europe* (1968) reveals some secrets of Kanaris. Sturdza was Romanian Foreign Minister from Sept.-Dec. 1940. He was a leader in the pro-Nazi, anti-Communist, nationalist Christian "Legionary" movement. Before assuming his post in 1940, Sturdza was visiting Berlin. No one wanted to speak to him with the exception of Admiral Wilhelm Canaris, the wily chief of the Abwehr, German Army Intelligence. Canaris had a request that both surprised and shocked Sturdza. He asked him to cooperate with Canaris' counterpart in Bucharest, a certain Moruzov who Sturdza suspected was a Communist agent. Pressed on this, Canaris said Moruzov was providing the "best information concerning Soviet Russia's military preparations." Before leaving Berlin, Sturdza received a visit from Canaris' deputy, a Captain Muller, "bearer once more of his chief's insistences, which left my wife and me perplexed. Captain Muller informed us that Great Britain had never been and would never be defeated. He added: "What I am about to tell you, coming from a Prussian officer, might perhaps be considered as an act of high treason. Pay attention however. Don't under any circumstances take the responsibility as Minister of Foreign Affairs in your country, of pushing it into a war where you have Great Britain as an adversary. You will be crushed. Great Britain is always victorious." This was a peculiar thing for a German Army Intelligence official to say especially since Germany appeared invincible in August 1940. It had just conquered France in June and sent the British packing.[596]

---

[596] Henry Makow, "Are World Wars orchestrated?" Savethemales.ca <http://www.savethemales.ca/> Web Page as of 20/05/05

Nazis and Cathars…what' s the Connection?

When the Nazis associate themselves with long forgotten esoteric beliefs, such those of the Cathars, they hint at their secret heritage. Such associations should not be dismissed lightly. Nazism provided an opportunity to divert the resources of the German state towards research on long forgotten movements started by predecessors of the Illuminati.

A Cathar coin shows a peculiar cross, used by secret societies. A derivative of this cross can be found on the Nazi battle flag.

The Ahnenerbe was the SS branch in charge of the research on ancient symbols and other esoteric subjects. This SS division would conduct treasure hunts for long lost Cathar relics, which are believed to be of extreme value and importance to the Powers That Be. Anthony Sutton quotes *Hitler et la Tradition Cathare* by Jean-Michel Angebert which sheds light on the 1933 crusade of *Schutzstaffel* member Otto Rahn in search of the Holy Grail. Something of importance was found in the Cathar stronghold in Southern France.[597] By September 1935 Rahn was writing excitedly to the chief of the Ahnenerbe about the places he visited in his investigation into the Grail traditions of Germany, requesting complete confidence in the matter with the exception of Himmler.[598] Rahn did find something of relevance, which the Powers that Be sought. The Nazis immediately dispatched Knight of Malta Otto Skorzeny.[599] According to Col. Howard Buechner who wrote *Emerald Cup - Ark of Gold: The Quest of S.S. Lt. Otto Rahn of the Third Reich*, Rahn died in mysterious circumstances in the Tyrolean mountains on a day sacred to the Cathars. It can be inferred that Skorzeny and the Powers that Be had some role in the death of Rahn. Buechner relates a story according to which the local descendants of the Cathars [Actual Merovingian descendants have been located in the region] happened to be on top of the mountain celebrating some mystical rite when an S.S.

[597] Antony C. Sutton, Wall Street and the Rise of Hitler (GSG & Associates, 1976). Ebook edition. <http://reformed-theology.org/html/books/wall_street/introduction.htm> Web page as of 16/03/04

[598] Anonymous, "Otto Rahn and the Quest for the Holy Grail," <http://www.geocities.com/CapitolHill/6824/otto.htm> Web page as of 16/03/04

[599] Anonymous, "New World Order-The movie: Knights of Malta," <http://www.geocities.com/newworldorder_themovie/knightsofmalta.html> Web page as of 11/07/2004

helicopter came down to scoop up Otto Skorzeny and his treasure. "At exactly high noon on March 16, 1944, a small German aircraft appeared. It flew over Montsegur several times, dipping its wings in salute. Then it used skywriting equipment and formed a huge Celtic cross in the sky. The Celtic Cross was a sacred emblem of the Cathars."[600] There are actual Merovingian descendants in the area where the Nazi plane made a Cathar cross in the sky. Why were the Nazis sending greetings to them in the valley below? In addition, it is widely believed that Himmler hid the artifacts obtained in his Wewelsburg castle, from where they vanished after the war. Why would the chief of the SS seek to preserve and protect artifacts that were of no significant value for German heritage or Nazi ideology? Neither the movements dating to medieval Southern France nor the Cathar relics could be of any use to the Nazi-Aryan dogma. The Cathars were responsible for a major anti-Christian Gnostic heresy. As we have discussed earlier, the Cathars and the Merovingians preceding them were early predecessors of the Illuminati. Since the Nazis were earmarked for destruction, they were being used as a clearinghouse for research that required state backing and which could never have been accomplished otherwise. The Ahnenerbe had over 50 departments and wasted over a million marks in such "research." At the end of the war, its entire libraries vanished.

Influences on Hitler's Peculiar Brand of Christianity

One would expect Hitler, purporting to be a champion of everything German, to revitalize Christianity. Indeed, there is a commonly spread misinformation that Hitler was a devout Catholic (With no explanation why he ordered the persecution of Catholics). Hitler talks of his own peculiar faith as "The old beliefs will be brought back to honor again. The whole secret knowledge of nature, of the divine, of the demonic. We will wash off the Christian veneer. [...] I want to see in the eyes of youth the gleam of the beast."[601] Hitler even saw himself replacing God. He would hang a gigantic poster of himself at one huge Nuremberg rally, with the caption lifted from the Christian gospel of John, "In the

---

[600] Quoting Buechner. Tracy Twyman, "The Real Tomb of God: The Grail, The Ark, the Emerald Tablet, and the Forgotten Father of Mankind," 21st Century Radio <http://www.21stcenturyradio.com/realtomb-twyman.htm> Web page as of 16/03/04

[601] This quote may have come from Rauschning or Bormann. "Nazis: The Occult Conspiracy," BMG Distribution, narr. Malcolm McDowell, dir. Tracy Atkinson and Joan Barron, Discovery Channel, 22nd February 1998.

beginning was the Word"[602] and indoctrinating German youth to pray to him![603] To quote Hitler "If Jehovah has lost all meaning for us Germans, the same must be said of Jesus Christ, his son.... He certainly lacks those characteristics, which he would require to be a true German. Indeed, he is as disappointing, if we read the record carefully, as is his father [...]."[604] And elsewhere, Hitler said, "Conscience is a Jewish invention. It is a blemish, like circumcision.... There is no such thing as truth, either in the moral or in the scientific sense. The new man would be the antithesis of the Jew."[605] In Hitler's words, Christianity "only added the seeds of decadence such as forgiveness, self-abnegation, weakness, false humility and the very denial of the evolutionary laws of survival of the fittest."[606] However, there was still a necessity to hypocritically appease the large number of German Christians. Nazi-approved sermons in German churches proclaimed, "Adolf Hitler is the voice of Jesus Christ."[607] As Reichsminister for Church affairs Hans Kerrl would say, "There has arisen a new authority as to what Christ and Christianity really are- that is Adolf Hitler. Adolf Hitler...is the true Holy Ghost."[608] It is important to note that before launching his "Final Solution," Hitler tried purging all churches and pastors who showed any resistance to existing Nazi policies. Refusal by a church to sponsor a Hitler Youth chapter was considered sufficient grounds to close it down.[609] There was a certain religious atmosphere to Hitler's large rallies. To quote, "All the stagings were designed to create a supernatural and religious atmosphere, and Hitler's entry was more befitting a god than a man."[610]

As Hannah Newman comments on the work of French writer Jean-Michel Angebert, author of *The Occult and the Third Reich*, "Their far-ranging documentation allows them to conclusively show that Nazism

---

[602] Hannah Newman, The Rainbow Swastika- A Report to the Jewish People About New Age Anti-Semitism; Nazism and the New age < http://philologos.org/__eb-trs/naF.htm> Web page as of 11/07/2004
[603] Dusty Sklar, The Nazis and the Occult (1989) 56. Newman, Rainbow Swastika; Nazism and the New Age.
[604] Hitler in "What the Christian Does Not Know About Christianity," As quoted in Dusty Sklar, The Nazis and the Occult (1989) 56. From Newman, Rainbow Swastika; Nazism and the New Age.
[605] Dusty Sklar, The Nazis and the Occult (1989) 57-58. Quoted in Newman, Rainbow Swastika; Nazism and the New Age.
[606] Newman, Rainbow Swastika; Nazism and the New Age.
[607] Newman, Rainbow Swastika; Nazism and the New Age.
[608] Walter C. Langer, The Mind of Hitler – The Secret Wartime Report (NY & London: Basic books Inc., 1972) 56.
[609] Newman, Rainbow Swastika; Nazism and the New Age.
[610] Langer, The Mind of Hitler 56.

was/is an initiation into the classical Gnostic 'path of enlightenment.'"[611] Why would the Nazis and Hitler choose anti-Christian Gnostism as opposed to all the other different flavors of Christianity? This particular creed traces itself to the Jewish Merovingians of Southern France. This can only be explained when we consider Nazis a complete extension of Illuminati agenda. As Newman quotes Angeberts' English translator, Lewis A.M. Sumberg, "nearly all historians missed the 'militant neo-Paganism' and 'Gnostic racism' in Nazism 'because they have brought conventional outlooks and methodologies to their examination of an unconventional phenomenon.'"[612] To quote Rudolf Olden who was a witness to this Nazi phenomenon "The innermost circle was privy to the hard-core Gnostic teaching on the Grail, immortality and godhood."[613] The climax of this indoctrination would be the SS training, and it corresponded to the Nazi view of "pure" Gnostic, Hindu and Buddhist philosophy, which was convoluted to emphasize Aryan duty and honor in place of gentleness and compassion[614] Newman points out that advancing Russian troops found the bodies of hundreds of Tibetans in Berlin. The presence of Tibetans indicates the use of Buddhist discipline for the purpose of indoctrination at an anti-human level. The subsequent murder of the Tibetans points to attempts to hide the Gnostic-Buddhist connection to Nazism.[615]

Contrary to popular belief of Hitler being a champion of the Christian world against "Jews,"

> Nazism attempted to wean the masses from standard Christianity by removing the Jewish-influenced 'negative' parts, that is the Old Testament and most of the New Testament, imposing Gnostic meanings on key passages, adding colorful pagan legend, and repackaging it in their 1920 platform as 'positive Christianity.'[616]

---

[611] Hannah Newman, The Rainbow Swastika- A Report to the Jewish People About New Age Anti-Semitism; Nazism and the New age < http://philologos.org/__eb-trs/naF.htm> Web page as of 11/07/2004

[612] Jean-Michel Angebert, The Occult and the Third Reich (Macmillan, 1974) x. Quoted from Newman, Rainbow Swastika; Nazism and the New Age.

[613] Jean-Michel Angebert, The Occult and the Third Reich (Macmillan, 1974) 178, quoting Rudolf Olden, Hitler the Pawn (1936) 233. Quoted from Newman, Rainbow Swastika; Nazism and the New Age.

[614] Jean-Michel Angebert, The Occult and the Third Reich (Macmillan, 1974) 220-221. Quoted from Newman, Rainbow Swastika; Nazism and the New Age.

[615] Newman, Rainbow Swastika; Nazism and the New Age.

[616] Newman, Rainbow Swastika; Nazism and the New Age. Quoting Jean-Michel Angebert, The Occult and the Third Reich (Macmillan, 1974) 202-203.

Newman points out an interesting case of a German youth who explained the Nazi triumph of will, not in militaristic but in Gnostic terms to a French writer in 1937. To quote, "I am studying the conception of the world.... We refuse to think and to be; we refuse to stand by helplessly under the determinism of the so-called laws of matter. What we want is inside, an inner structure.... We shall not let anyone stop us from building before God and before men that which must be built!" The French writer remarked on the similarity of this Nazi sentiment to the extinct (as he thought) French Templar philosophy.[617] Hitler in a conversation with Hermann Rauschning asked, "How can we arrest racial decay? Shall we form a select company of the really initiated? An Order, the brotherhood of Templars around the holy grail of pure blood?"[618] Hitler's taste for Templarism is asynchronous with both Nazism and Germany. It only serves to reflect his Illuminati background.

Otto Rahn who was sent Grail hunting in the Cathar region of Southern France proposed a "New Order" in which the states of Europe, and perhaps all other nations, would adopt the Cathar beliefs in the interest of world peace."[619] It is rumoured that Rahn even formed a neo-Catharist circle within the SS.[620] There are a number of different interpretations of the Holy Grail. But the real interpretation is the quest for the pure bloodline; a reference to the original Merovingian Jews descended from the tribe of Benjamin. They landed in France around 70 A.D after their temple was destroyed in Jerusalem. They may have started the legend of the Holy Grail, projecting themselves as the progeny of Christ to induce local Christians into protecting them and fighting for them against the Catholic Church. The Cathars would extend this myth, claiming that the material world was faulty (and must be therefore left to Satan) and real union with God can be obtained through "Gnosis." It is obvious that the Powers that Be recycled this highly successful dogma for Nazis, carefully editing out the "Jewish Merovingian bloodline" from it.

---

[617] Alphonse de Chateaubriand quoted in Jean-Michel Angebert, The Occult and the Third Reich (Macmillan, 1974) 175. Quoted in Newman, Rainbow Swastika: Nazism and the New Age.

[618] I suppose this is another of Rauschning's quotes. Anonymous, New World order- The movie: Nazis and Aryans. <http://www.geocities.com/newworldorder_themovie/nazisandaryans.html> Web page as of 11/07/2004

[619] Anonymous, "Otto Rahn and the Quest for the Holy Grail," <http://www.geocities.com/CapitolHill/6824/otto.htm> Web page as of 16/03/04

[620] Anonymous, "Otto Rahn and the Quest for the Holy Grail," <http://www.geocities.com/CapitolHill/6824/otto.htm> Web page as of 16/03/04

According to Hanna Newman, the concept of an inherited god-consciousness appears in Gnostic teaching which describe Christ, not as Jewish but as a Gnostic initiate. And who didn't actually die on the cross, but achieved a singular level of Aryan racial purity and corresponding god-consciousness (his Jewish identity was dismissed by Gnostics as an Oriental fiction). For Gnostics, the God of Jesus Christ was not the Most High and only God, but a "demiurge,"[621] aspiring to be as such, as every Gnostic initiate would. In search of this holy blood which contains the coveted god-knowledge, every member of the SS was screened for purity of Aryan lineage, and was taught his duty to father as many racially pure children as possible. Himmler claimed that if conception took place in an Aryan cemetery, the resulting child would receive the spirit of "all the dead heroes" buried there! And accordingly, lists of Nordic cemeteries were published in the SS periodical Das Schwarze Korps.[622] Alternately, the Grail was defined in Gnostic symbolism as the "philosopher's stone," the "third eye"[623] and the spiritual "crown" of Lucifer.[624] Newman defines the relevance of the Illuminati "all seeing eye" as the Knowledge of self-as-god which Lucifer (Satan) exhibited, and which he offered to mankind in the Garden of Eden.[625]

Helena Blavatsky of the Theosophical Society agreed with the Gnostics that the Jewish God belonged to a class of the lower and material.[626] We thus see the Merovingian bloodline heresy, Cathar Gnosticism and Blavatsky's Aryan race evolution blended together to form a potent concoction.

Blavatsky referred to the "moral wretchedness" of Jews who partake and lead in worldly materialism and sex. According to Blavatsky, This God of Jews who is credited as the creator of heaven and earth is no other than Cain, a son of Satan and a lower angel unlike Blavatsky's hip "ascended masters." Simply put, her position is that since this world is

---

[621] Hannah Newman, The Rainbow Swastika- A Report to the Jewish People About New Age Anti-Semitism; Nazism and the New age < http://philologos.org/__eb-trs/naF.htm> Web page as of 11/07/2004

[622] Dusty Sklar, The Nazis and the Occult (1989) 144. Quoted in Newman, Rainbow Swastika; Nazism and the New Age.

[623] Currently used in visual motifs of the Powers that may be, such as the strange seal on the US one dollar bill.

[624] Jean-Michel Angebert, The Occult and the Third Reich (Macmillan, 1974) 264. Quoted in Newman, Rainbow Swastika; Nazism and the New Age.

[625] Newman, Rainbow Swastika; Nazism and the New Age.

[626] Dusty Sklar, The Nazis and the Occult (1989) 114. Quoted in Newman, Rainbow Swastika; Nazism and the New Age.

evil, the God who created it must also be evil; in fact he must be Satan! As such, Gnosticism was rewired by Blavatsky to undermine Judaism, upon which Christianity is based. Nazi party philosopher and Thule Society member, Alfred Rosenberg would echo Blavatsky's sentiments. Rosenberg is quoted in his writings as: "The earth-centered Jew lacks a soul" and elsewhere, "[the continuing existence of the Jew] would lead to a void, to the destruction not only of the illusory earthly world but also of the truly existent, the spiritual."[627] Rosenberg's other writings hint at a profound understanding of Gnosticism and Theosophy.

Hitler would be later quoted in a similar vein as, "The Jew is the anti-man, the creature of another god. He must have come from another root of the human race."[628] Hitler also pretended to adhere to a strict regimen, to set an example for his adherents. He would be depicted as shunning material pleasures and physical appetites. He was said to stick to a vegetarian diet - all classic Gnostic elements of "purification from the world." Such exercises were mere performances for his loyal followers. For example, Hitler was not as committed to Gnostic notions of purity when it came to sex, as his sexual perversions demonstrate.

Since the Powers that Be had decided that the suicide of Fascist Germany had to be brought out by a suicidal advance eastwards, Himmler pointed out that the ultimate Nazi goal was to secure a perimeter across the Urals. He would use the same Gnostic terms for Asians, which were applied to Jews by Rosenberg accusing them of being the "... end of beauty, and culture, of the creative power of this earth."[629] Hitler, Hausofer and

---

[627] Dusty Sklar, The Nazis and the Occult (1989) 147-148. Quoted in Hannah Newman, The Rainbow Swastika- A Report to the Jewish People About New Age Anti-Semitism; Nazism and the new age <http://philologos.org/__eb-trs/naF.htm> Web page as of 11/07/2004.

[628] Dusty Sklar, The Nazis and the Occult (1989) 146. Quoted in Newman, Rainbow Swastika; Nazism and the New Age.

[629] These remarks were made in the 1943 Posen Speech to SS elite. The full quote goes as follows: "This will enable us to create the preconditions for the entire Germanic people, and for all of Europe, led, ordered, and trained by us, the Germanic people, over generations, to resist the fateful struggle with an Asia certain to break forth once again. We don't know when that will be. When the 'mass man' arises on the other side with 1 - 1.5 billion people, then the Germanic people with its, I hope, 250 - 300 million people, together with the other European peoples, for a total of 600 - 700 million people, on a perimeter extending the Urals, or, in 100 years extending over the Urals, will carry on its battle for life against Asia. Woe, if the Germanic people should fail to resist in this struggle. That would be the end of beauty, and culture, of the creative power of this earth. That is the distant future, that is what we are fighting for."

Bormann later pretended to kill themselves in ceremonial fashion along with their wives. This has parallels with the Gnostic-Cathartic rite of "Endura," an honorable suicide that was always to be done by pairs of intimate friends.[630]

Another Gnostic theme, which would later be found in Nazism, is dualism. Just as the Gnostics divided the world into spirit and matter (so that the matter would be left to the Powers that Be while the masses were left to quibble over the spiritual), this theme was extended to darkness and light, fire and ice, good and evil. All these forces would collide with each other to achieve balance and jump to a "higher state." Similarly humans would also follow a path of evolution leading to better races and the former World Order had to be destroyed to move onto the New World Order. To quote Hitler himself,

> Creation is not finished. Man is clearly approaching a phase of metamorphosis. The earlier human species has already reached the stage of dying out.... All of the force of creation will be concentrated in a new species... [which] will surpass infinitely modern man.... Do you understand now the profound meaning of our National Socialist movement?"[631]

These sentiments are clearly echoed in Blavatsky's Theosophy!

Gnosticism has been recycled for the present day in the form of the New Age Movement. It can be observed in sci-fi movies such as The Matrix. During the shootout at Columbine, the perpetrators wore trenchcoats identical to characters in The Matrix. It can only be imagined how hardcore indoctrination of these teachings may have impacted members of the Nazi military. Extermination Camp commandants who executed thousands of Jews would make bizarre Gnostic statements such as "This is where Heaven and Earth meet. A crossing point to the other world. But don't worry, you won't be left behind."[632] Note the reference to the

---

As quoted in Anonymous, New World Order-The Movie: Nazism and Aryans <http://www.geocities.com/newworldorder_themovie/nazisandaryans.html> Web page as of 11/07/2004.

[630] Jean-Michel Angebert, The Occult and the Third Reich (Macmillan, 1974) 275 Note # 11. Quoted in Newman, Rainbow Swastika: Nazism and the New Age.

[631] Adolf Hitler, quoted by Hermann Rauschning, Hitler Speaks 147, as translated in Jean-Michel Angebert, The Occult and the Third Reich (Macmillan, 1974) 178. Quoted in Newman, Rainbow Swastika: Nazism and the New Age.

[632] Anonymous, New World Order-The Movie: The Occult <http://www.geocities.com/newworldorder_themovie/occult.html> Web page as of 11/07/2004.

New World, which according to Gnostic Theosophy can only be reached by the most evolved race by destroying the existing order.

Hegel and Nietzsche

Apparently, the Gnostics and Blavatsky were not the only ones laying the groundwork for anti-Christian ideas before Hitler came. Hegel and Nietzsche had created philosophical underpinnings for an anti-Christian anti-Semitic World Order. Nietzsche's final work The Antichrist started with the phrase "Let us see ourselves for what we are. We are Hyperboreans."[633] One of Hitler's friends, Bernhard Forster, was Nietzsche's brother-in-law.[634] The proto-Nazi Thule Society derived its name from Thule, the island of Hyperborea where "godmen" lived. Hegel and Nietzsche are also associated with the early theorizing of dialectics, or how phenomena such as conflicts could be manipulated to produce a desired outcome. Nazism/Fascism would serve as a dialectical casualty in the emergence of the Soviet Union.

Richard Wagner and Pan-Germanism

Richard Wagner (1813-1883) was a gifted German composer associated with producing musical operas, which carried some of the earliest imprints of German nationalism. These productions were organized long before the actual emergence of Nazism, in order to prepare the necessary groundwork.

Among Wagner's well known works are Gnostic themes such as the Holy Grail and the struggle between Light and Darkness. From what can be derived from accounts on Wagner, he composed his operas, but many of the esoteric themes and ideas expressed in them came from his employers at the opera company where he worked. Though oblivious to their motives in kindling German nationalism, Wagner sensed something suspicious and sounded the alarm by directing his rage against "Jews." If only Wagner had been more definite and instead brought to our attention the names of individuals and secret societies involved, his warning would have probably been heeded.

Hitler was an avid fan of Parsifal, a Wagner opera which carried the Gnostic theme of "[...] pure, noble blood, in [whose] protection and

---

633 Jean-Michel Angebert, The Occult and the Third Reich (Macmillan, 1974) 124. Quoted in Newman, Rainbow Swastika; Nazism and the New Age.
634 Newman, Rainbow Swastika; Nazism and the New Age.

glorification the brotherhood of the initiated have come together."[635] Nazis appropriated many of Wagner's works for the purpose of propaganda. But Hitler never forgave Wagner for attempting to sound the alarm on the Illuminati. To quote Time Magazine,[636]

> Hitler is noted as a fanatical fan of Wagnerian operas. Less known is the fact that before he rose to become the Fuhrer, in the 1920s, Hitler sexually abused Richard Wagner's grandson, Wieland Wagner.

The Protocols of the Learned Elders of Zion

In order to set the temperament for the rise of the Nazis, a number of events were staged throughout previous decades, where Jews were blamed for everything gone wrong.[637] Since mainstream Western thought denies the existence of secret societies and secret bloodlines as the basis of their civilization, it is not surprising that visible minorities are regularly made into scapegoats. Present day TV shows like *24* carry similar inflammatory hatred directed towards Muslims, the new scapegoats.

The Protocols of the Learned Elders of Zion was a document detailing world domination by a secret society. It emerged around 1884, and was attributed to "Jews." This allegation proved to be contradictory. To quote Baigent, Leigh and Lincoln,

> They [The Protocols] contain, for example, a number of enigmatic references-references that are clearly not Judaic. But these references are so clearly not Judaic that they cannot plausibly have been fabricated by a forger either.[638]

Baigent et all draw attention towards references in the Protocols of an International Church, a Masonic Kingdom and a statement at the end of the document, "Signed by the representatives of Sion of the 33rd Degree." While the "Priory of Zion" is a fictional secret society to which the Protocols are sometimes attributed, the "Priory of Sion" is not. This

---

[635] D. Sklar, The Nazis and the Occult p. 146. Quoted in THE RAINBOW SWASTIKA
[636] Quoting Time magazine, August 15, 1994, p. 56. Texe Marrs, Power of the Prophecy. Unmasking the sexual perversions of the Illuminati: Two on a saddle Part 1. <http://www.texemarrs.com/012002/two_on_a_saddle.htm> Web page as of 11/07/2004
[637] In the case of the Dreyfuss affair, it is noticeable that Western media suddenly became very prominent in spreading the story of the scandal.
[638] Michael Baigent, Richard Leigh and Henry Lincoln, The Holy Blood and the Holy Grail (London: Arrow Books, 1996), 201.

"Priory of Sion" is not Jewish or Zionist. It is based in France and is well connected with other European secret societies. It seems that those who sought to attribute the document to "Jews" didn't do a very thorough editing of the original document on which it was based.

In 1923, Nazi party propagandist, Alfred Rosenberg made a German translation of the Protocols. They would be used to rouse the German public's support for Nazi anti-Semitism. Around the same time, White Russians used the Protocols to justify acts of violence against the Jews, scaring well-established Russian Jews into considering Zionism. The timing of the emergence of the Protocols and their subsequent translations are indeed suspicious, and appear to be synchronous with a larger plan associated with the World Wars.

From what can be discerned about the origins of the Protocols, it is clear that mystics and secret societies associated with the Romanovs played a major role in the origins of the Protocols. One such Russian royal was Yuiliana Glinka. She was a personal companion of the Russian mystic Helena Blavatsky. She was also a devoted Theosophist. A rare early edition of the Protocols of the Learned Elders of Zion credits her with originally finding the document![639]

One too many Chamberlains

British occultist Houston Stewart Chamberlain, wrote his epic *Foundations of the Nineteenth Century* in 1900 based on the ideas of Blavatsky. He tried to integrate the ideas of Nietzsche and Wagner, all the time being a non-Aryan Englishman! He was the nephew of Neville Chamberlain, who extended the Nazis a generous window for rearmament. Chamberlain was the mentor of Nazi party philosopher Alfred Rosenberg who wrote his own version of Chamberlain's book, *The Myth of the Twentieth Century*.

Nazi Preference for Occult Dates

It is no secret that the Powers that Be arrange major activities on days corresponding to little known occult festivals. Even in the absence of formal communication, the Powers that Be use events on such dates to signal each other across the globe, that everything was going as per plan. The recurrence of major events in Hitler's rise occurring on such dates only point to the events being planned earlier. If Hitler was a "one man

[639] Newman, Rainbow Swastika; Nazism and the New Age.

show" it was very unlikely that he could coincidentally choose such dates. Take the following instances:

- German Communists shot six Thulists in 1919 on the date of *Walpurgisnacht,* which Wiccans identify as a Druid feast in honor of Bel, a derivative of the Canaanite calf-god Baal. Helena Blavatsky identified Bel as part of an astrological trinity in *The Secret Doctrine volume 2*. After the murder of these Thulists, the Thule society took to the streets and organized the Freikorps.
- On the Halloween night of 1932, the pagan Sabbat of Samhain, Hitler's mistress Eva Braun attempted suicide but survived. This event would later be used by biographers (without reference to the significance of the date) to show how Hitler had become "hopeless," in this period. Such depictions contribute to the "one man show" interpretation of Hitler.
- Hitler's chief astrologer Hanussen predicted that Hitler's return to power would begin on January 30th, a date roughly equivalent to the pagan Sabbat of Oimelc; one of the four "cross-quarter" days of the witches' calendar. This was printed in his paper *Berliner Wochenschau* well in advance.[640]
- Walpurgisnacht was again chosen for the day Hitler would purportedly kill himself.

The Nazis as New World Order me-tooers

Hitler has been quoted in his own words speaking of a New World Order,[641] a favorite catch phrase of the Cabal. In another 1931 interview with a Leipzig newspaper editor, Adolph Hitler made a declaration of the true significance of his National Socialist movement, "The Frenchman Gobineau and the Englishman Chamberlain were inspired by our concept of a new order-a new order, I tell you, or if you prefer, an ideological glimpse into history in accordance with the basic principle of the blood […]."[642] In the Nazi case, the "New Order" referred to the rise of the Soviet Union. On September 11th 1990, President George Bush

[640] Stephen Lemons, Hitler's Clairvoyant Salon.com <http://www.salon.com/people/feature/2002/02/27/hanussen/> Web page as of 11/07/2004

[641] Jean-Michel Angebert, The Occult and the Third Reich (Macmillan, 1974) 155. Newman, Rainbow Swastika; Nazism and the New Age.

[642] Jackson Spielvogel and David Redles, "Hitler's Racial Ideology: Content and Occult Sources," Simon Wiesenthal Center – Museum of Tolerance Online > Multimedia Learning Center > Annual 3. 1997 < http://motlc.wiesenthal.com/site/pp.asp?c=gvKVLcMVIuG&b=395043>

(senior) announced that "Out of these troubled times, our-objective-a new world order-can emerge-Today, that new world is struggling to be born, a world quite different from the one we have known." Note the date, September 11th 1990.

Nazi links to British Elite

The overt cooperation of some British royals with the Nazis is usually dismissed as an extension of their blood ties to Germany. But there may be more to the nature of these ties. British royals are interspersed with Bohemians, Bohemia being a medieval stronghold of the Illuminati. When the World Wars were started, it is obvious that these ties would be revived again in order to coordinate Allied advances and Nazi retreat/treachery such that the Soviet Union would get the lion's share of territory. While it is true that the entire British administration, especially their Intelligence was involved, some royal families became extremely notorious for their overt cooperation with the Nazis.

- Rudolf Hess had close contacts with the Duke of Hamilton, a Scottish member of the Golden Dawn. He met him at the Berlin Olympics. Events such as the Olympics are used by the Criminal Elite to discuss their upcoming plans under the pretext of watching sports. They serve as a cover for Cabal operatives of different countries to gather together without raising suspicion, and such gatherings were critical at a time of limited means of communication. It was on the Duke of Hamilton's estate where Hess would later land his plane. The Golden Dawn had close contacts with Blavatsky's Theosophical society in its early stages. Nazi party ideologue Karl Hausofer also had close contacts with British members of the Golden Dawn. Among other British Golden Dawn affiliates were the Duke of Bedford and Sir Ivone Kirkpatrick. Another Briton, S. L. Matthews, the Grand Master of the Golden Dawn Society, introduced Vril society founder Jacolliot's ideas in England.[643] To quote a Mason watcher "Tyler," "The previous Duke of Kent - George Edward Alexander Edmund was installed as Grand Master by King George VI in 1939. He died three years later in 1942 in a mysterious plane crash in Scotland, six months after it was alleged he and the Duke of Hamilton had kept a moonlight appointment with Rudolf Hess on the Caledonian Moor. Historians tell us that the late Grand Master was Pro-Nazi and traveled to the

---

643 Servando González, Origins of the Swastika: The Hausofer Connection. <http://www.intelinet.org/swastika/swasti02.htm> Web page as of 11/07/2004

Fatherland in order to better educate the King about National Socialism, so as to allow the Empire to 'come to an understanding' with The New World Order."[644] A new book has emerged which places Rudolf Hess on the same ill-fated plane![645] We are told that these activities were peace negotiations, though they may be collusion towards the ultimate goal of Soviet subjugation of Germany.

- At the end of the war, the American forces in Germany seized records of communication between the Nazi government and British royals, which revealed King Edward III being supportive of the Nazis on not just annexing Czechoslovakia but in the persecution of Jews as well![646] MI5 agent Anthony Blunt was assigned to bring these American records to London, even though Blunt was considered to be a Nazi traitor! Blunt would later resurface as a Soviet double agent and a member of the original Philby cell.[647] Kim Philby at that time was also spying for the Nazis. This proves that the ultimate loyalty of these people lay with the Soviet Union. Blunt was never tried for treason and instead put in charge of royal paintings at Buckingham palace.[648]
- There were also wiretaps between King George and the German ambassador to England, Von Ribbentrop.[649]
- The Duke of Windsor (King Edward VIII) also had ties to the Germans and later went to live in a Rothschild castle in Austria.[650] The scandal may have caused him to abdicate.
- Colonel Charles "Dickie" Ellis was a Fascist senior agent who later admitted he was a double agent paid by the Nazis, though he was never dismissed by the Queen or charged with treason.[651]

---

[644] "Tyler," The Dukes of Kent Freemasonrywatch < http://www.freemasonrywatch.org/P2.html> Web page as of 11/07/2004

[645] Lynn Picknet, Clive Prince and Stephen Prior, Double Standards – The Rudolf Hess Coverup (Time Warner Paperbacks, 2002)

[646] Loftus, John & Aarons, Mark. The Secret War Against The Jews (N.Y. St. Martin's Griffen, 1997) Quoted in A.C. Ross, Fascist Treachery <http://www.bigelowconsulting.com/CRAweb/essay13.htm> Web page as of 11/07/2004. Note: an archived version is available at <http://web.archive.org/web/20041205024342/http://www.bigelowconsulting.com/CRAweb/essay13.htm>

[647] Ross, Fascist Treachery

[648] Ross, Fascist Treachery

[649] Ross, Fascist Treachery

[650] Louis Kilzer, Churchill's Deception (Simon & Schuster, 1994). Quoted by Henry Makow, "Hitler didn't want world war," Savethemales.ca <http://www.savethemales.ca/000369.html> Web page as of 11/07/2004

[651] Ross, Fascist Treachery

- During this period, Kim Philby was spying for the Soviets and the Nazis. He became editor for the magazine of the Anglo-German Fellowship organization, run by a group of rich and powerful British pro-Nazis[652] who were also known as the Cliveden set.[653] He began openly courting German Nazis.[654] British Intelligence operatives like Philby managed to function as efficient coordinators and mediators between the Nazi and Soviet Illuminati.
- Philby was admitted into the Anglo-German Fellowship organization through senior British agent, Robert Bruce Lockhart who was active in Moscow during the 1918 Bolshevik Revolution. Lockhart, along with Sidney Reilly conspired in an attempt to assassinate Lenin, which failed, and Lockhart was sentenced to death in absentia.[655] This may appear as British anti-Bolshevik activity. But Lenin had gone rogue with the Illuminati and they tried their best to dispose him (finally poisoning him) to return to power to Trotsky. With Stalin, an understanding was reached regarding the war, though Stalin had to be disposed later. Reilly was actually a Lithuanian Jew by the name of Rosenblum who was considered to be the best spy/assassin of British intelligence, according to Rakovsky.[656] Reilly returned for a second attempt at Lenin, which also failed.
- The fifth man of the Cambridge spy ring provided Stalin with exclusive intelligence on Churchill and Roosevelt's conversations on the Soviet Union. The spy in question also seemed to have access to American Intelligence.[657] Author Roland Perry wrote The Fifth Man in 1994 in which he deduced that the infamous Cambridge Soviet spy ring of Kim Philby, Donald MacLean, Guy Burgess and Anthony Blunt had a fifth spy, Victor Rothschild, the head of the British arm of the Rothschild dynasty. After serving the Nazis, the Cambridge spy ring would serve the Soviet Union by transferring every piece of technology they could lay their hands on, to the Soviet Union. Roland considered Rothschild to be far more effective than

---

[652] Ross, Fascist Treachery

[653] Henry Makow, "Hitler didn't want world war," Savethemales.ca <http://www.savethemales.ca/000369.html> Web page as of 11/07/2004

[654] John Costello, & Oleg Tsarev, Deadly Illusions (N.Y. Crown Publishers, 1993) Quoted in Ross, Fascist Treachery

[655] Anthony Cave Brown, Treason In The Blood (N.Y. Houghton Mifflen, 1994) Quoted in Ross, Fascist Treachery

[656] The questioning of the accused Christian Georgievitch Rakovsky by Gavriil Gavriilovitch Kus'min on the 26th January, 1938. An archive of the interrogation can be found online < https://archive.org/details/RedSymphony> Web page as of 22/01/14

[657] Roland Perry, The Fifth Man (London: Pan Books, 1994) xx.

any of the rest. He would become an MI5 security inspector, which gave him exclusive access to all classified projects. Soviet scientists seemed to have obtained the basics of every classified British project, from biological warfare and radar to nuclear weaponry.

❖ One of Hitler's top intelligence officers, Horst Kopkow, ordered the deaths of more than a 100 captured British secret agents in concentration camps. After the war, the MI6 snatched Kopkow from war crimes investigators and faked his death.[658] He went to work for the MI6 and may have died in 1996.[659]

A discussion of the roots of Nazism would be incomplete without a thorough evaluation of the ideas of the Theosophical Society of Helena Blavatsky. The next chapter is devoted to the same.

---

658 Sarah Helm, "MI6 protected Nazi who killed 100 British agents," The Times May 14th 2005 <http://www.timesonline.co.uk/article/0,,2-1611185,00.html> Accessed 13/12/06.

659 Sarah Helm, "MI6 protected Nazi who killed 100 British agents," The Times May 14th 2005 <http://www.timesonline.co.uk/article/0,,2-1611185,00.html> Accessed 13/12/06.

Chapter Four
Helena Blavatsky and the Theosophical Society

Satan and his rebellious host would thus prove, when the meaning of the allegory is explained, to have refused to create physical man, only to become the direct Saviors and the Creators of "*divine* Man."

-H.P. Blavatsky, The Secret Doctrine, p. 193 note c, Volume I

A brief history of HPB and the Theosophical Society

The Theosophical Society and the movement known as Theosophy is credited solely to Helena Petrovna (1831-1891) who became Helena Blavatsky or Madame Blavatsky/HPB after her first marriage, though she would be married three more times after she divorced General Nicephore Blavatsky. She was born in what is present day Ukraine among highly placed Imperial Russian nobility. Imperial Russia's Minister of Finance, Sergei Witte was among her cousins. Since Russian nobility is generally sympathized as victims of the Bolsheviks, their Illuminati connections are often overlooked. Chapter one of this book sheds light on these little known connections.

Helena Petrovna Blavatsky

HPB had a rather strange and haunted childhood, which was characterized with an obsession with the occult.[660] Her social life has some reflections of lesbianism.[661] Her particular area of interest were séances, or spiritual communication with the dead. In New York, she met Henry Steele Olcott, a lawyer turned spiritualist who was also interpreting séances. During these séances, HPB would act as a "medium" and souls, which had "ascended," would spiritually communicate "higher consciousness" to her once she tuned into their "frequency." HPB would offer vivid recollections of

---

[660] Ellie Crystal, "Helena Petrovna Blavatsky," Crystalinks <http://www.crystalinks.com/blavatsky.html> Web page as of 11/07/2004

[661] "Mrs. Besant's extraordinary transformations from Anglican minister's wife through birth control propagandist and labour leader to Theosophist…are…well known… Arthur Nethercot, her biographer, suggests an element of the lesbian in the rapid domination of Mrs. Besant by H. P. Blavatsky. James Webb, The Occult Underground (LaSalle Illinois: Open Court Publishing Co. 1974) 94. "She addressed Annie in suspiciously fulsome and endearing terms," writes Nethercot, "'Dearest,' 'My Dearest,' 'Dearly Beloved One,' and signing herself 'Very adoring.'" Nethercot also reports that "she dispatched missives to Annie...and addressed them to 'My Darling Penelope' from 'Your...female Ulysses'" Arthur H. Nethercot, The First Five Lives of Annie Besant (Chicago: University of Chicago Press, 1960) 306. Both these quotes are from Scott Lively and Kevin Abrams, The Pink Swastika-Homosexuality in the Nazi Party 4th ed. (Sacramento: Veritas Aeterna Press, 2002) 106.

their description and the message they conveyed. However, A New York neuropathologist, Dr. George Beard claimed in an interview that Olcott had probably been misled and HPB became Beard's instant opponent.[662] Through a later interview with the Daily Graphic, HPB became famous throughout New York as a spiritualist.[663]

In 1875, William Olcott, HPB and William Q. judge formed the Theosophical Society.[664] It is interesting to note that the name "Theosophical" was furnished by Charles Sotheran, a high-ranking mason and Rosicrucian![665]

Can it be considered that HPB herself was a honorary Freemason? Freemasonry is generally off limits to females and instead, a curious semi-official substitute is available for females, known as Co-Masonry. A popular Website[666] critical of Freemasonry dug up the following (Emphasis on Rosicrucian order added):

> Masonic Diversion: But Blavatsky wasn't a Freemason!
>
> Fact: Blavatsky was a Freemason. There is considerable literature relating to Blavatsky's Masonic connections. In her Scrapbook, vol. III, p.256, on January 1878, she recorded that she received a diploma of the 32nd Degree in the Ancient and Primitive Rite of England and Wales. In the following month the issue was raised in the Franklin Register and Norfolk County Journal, the material of which has been published in H.P. Blavatsky. Collected Writings. Volume One. 1874-1868. On p.309, we learn that the Ancient and Primitive Rite was originally chartered in America, on 9 November 1856, with David McClellan as Grand Master, and that it submitted entirely in 1862 to the Grand Orient of France.
>
> *-The Secret Zodiacs of Washington DC, David Ovason*
> *Preface by C. Fred Kleinknecht, 33°, Sovereign Grand Commander,*
> *The Supreme Council, 33° (Mother Council of the World), Southern Jurisdiction, USA, Washington DC*

---

662 Ellie Crystal, "Helena Petrovna Blavatsky," Crystalinks <http://www.crystalinks.com/blavatsky.html> Web page as of 11/07/2004
663 Crystal, Blavatsky
664 Crystal, Blavatsky
665 Crystal, Blavatsky
666 Freemasonrywatch.org, <http://freemasonrywatch.org/luciferquotes.html> Web page as of 13/09/2006

We, the Thrice-Illustrious Sovereign Grand Master General, and we, the Sovereign Grand Conservators, thirty-third and Last degree of the Sovereign Sanctuary of England, Wales, etc., decorated the Grand Star of Sirius, etc., Grand Commanders of the Three Legions of the Knights of Masonry, by virtue of the high authority with which we are invested, have declared and proclaimed and by these presents do declare and proclaim our illustrious and enlightened Brother, H. P. Blavatsky, to be an Apprentice, Companion, Perfect Mistress, Sublime Elect Scotch Lady, Grand Elect, **Chevaliere de Rose Croix**, Adoniramite Mistress, Perfect Venerable Mistress, and a crowned Princess of Rite of Adoption.

Given under our hands and the seals of the Sovereign Sanctuary for England and Wales, sitting in the Valley of London, this 24th day of November 1877, year of true light 000,000,000.

John Yarker, 33° Sovereign Grand Master
M. Caspari, 33° Grand Secretary
A. D. Loewenstark, 33° Grand Secretary

To quote Cardinal Caro Rodriguez,

> Madame Blavatsky, the promoter and founder of Theosophy in Europe, was also a member of the Masonic Lodges; her successor, Annie Besant, President of the Theosophical Society in 1911 was Vice President and great Teacher of the Supreme Council of the International Order of co-Masonry...the theosophical doctrines on the nature of God and the soul and the relations between God and the soul, are the same doctrines as taught in masonry.[667]

Theosophist Annie Besant in Masonic Regalia

This photo is from a Masonic Hall. The original caption read:

The V. Ills. Bro. Annie Besant 33°.
First M.P.G.C., of British Federation and leader of Co-Freemasonry in the British Empire

According to one source,[668] HPB even joined Garibaldi's national revolutionary

[667] Jose Maria Cardinal Caro Y. Rodriguez, The Mystery of Freemasonry Unveiled – With a reprint of Pope Leo XIIIth Encyclical Humanum Genus 2nd edition (Imprimatur, Jose Maria Cardinal Caro Y. Rodriguez, Cardinal Archbishop of Santiago, Chile, 1920s) 226.
[668] Mehmet Sabeheddin, "The Secret of Eurasia – The key to Hidden History and World Events," New Dawn No. 68 (September-October 2001),

militia, and fought in the battle of Mentana, where she was severely wounded. Garibaldi's movement attempted to forcibly unify Italy as a prelude to Fascism. At that time, there were also plans set in motion to displace the Vatican Papacy and relocate it to Imperial Russia, where it could be later dismantled for good by the Soviets.

The official activities of the Theosophical Society are summed up as follows,

> After its establishment the Theosophical Society expounded the esoteric tradition of Buddhism aiming to form an universal brotherhood of man, studying and making known the ancient religions, philosophies and sciences, and investigating the laws of nature and divine powers latent in man. The direction of the society was claimed to be directed by the secret Mahatmas or Masters of Wisdom.[669]

HPB pictures herself[670] with three "ascendant masters" who apart from dictating spiritual consciousness from the undead don't seem to mind posing for a photo op. The masters in the background are supposed to be Kuthumi, El Myora, and Saint Germain. One "ascended master" of Blavatsky was referred to as Moriah; a term used interchangeably with the term "Illuminati" and roughly meaning "the winds of change."

To quote Secret Society critic Nesta Webster on the esoteric teachings of the Theosophical Society,

> That the teachings of the Eastern School would not be taken seriously by any real Orientalist and that they could learn far more by studying the works of recognized authorities on these subjects at a University or at the British Museum does not occur to them [harmless enthusiasts who comprise the outer ranks of the Theosophical Society] for a moment. Nor would this fulfill the purpose of the leaders. For

---

<http://www.newdawnmagazine.com> An archive is available at <http://www.geocities.com/integral_tradition/key.html> Accessed 12th May 2003.

669 Ellie Crystal, "Helena Petrovna Blavatsky," Crystalinks <http://www.crystalinks.com/blavatsky.html> Web page as of 11/07/2004

670 Crystal, Blavatsky

> Theosophical Society is not a study group, but essentially a propagandist society which aims at substituting for the pure and simple teachings of Christianity the amazing compound of Eastern superstition, Cabalism, and Eighteenth century charlatanism which Mrs. Besant and her coadjutors have devised.[671]

Shortly after the establishment of the Theosophical Society, a scandal erupted in which some followers of Theosophy alleged the letters attributed to the "Mahatmas" were forgeries of either HPB or her friends. A book *Who wrote the Mahatma's letters* by the Hare brothers was fairly critical of the authenticity of the letters.

Such scandals did not discourage Blavatsky from the publication of her first book, *Isis Unveiled* (1877). Since large scale industrialization compounded with atheist influence had created a spiritual vacuum in the West, people flocked to buy her book expecting answers. HPB claimed in her book that the Ascended Masters/ Mahatmas had revealed to her "…the basic precepts and the secret knowledge which they protected".[672] This book launched Blavatsky as "a pioneer esotericist of our age".[673]

To escape the tremors of the scandal, HPB and Olcott headed to India for studies in Buddhism and Hinduism. The spiritual background of India appealed to Blavatsky and her associates. And Blavatsky claimed to have received correspondence from several other major Masters/Mahatmas. In 1882, the headquarters of the Theosophical Society became Adyar (Madras) and HPB constructed a shrine room for the special séances.[674] A scandal erupted when one of the former manager of the shrine, Emma Cutting Coulomb, published letters that she claimed were from HPB containing instructions on how the séance correspondence was to be done through certain secret panels in the shrine.[675] In 1884, Richard Hodgson of the London based Psychical Research Society (PRS) paid a visit to Adyar and issued a scathing report alleging HPB and her associates, especially one Indian named Damodar, were conducting

---

[671] Quoting Nesta Webster in Secret Societies and Subversive Movements page 306. Jose Maria Cardinal Caro Y. Rodriguez, The Mystery of Freemasonry Unveiled – With a reprint of Pope Leo XIIIth Encyclical Humanum Genus. 2nd edition. (Imprimatur, Jose Maria Cardinal Caro Y. Rodriguez, Cardinal Archbishop of Santiago, Chile, 1920s). 228.

[672] Crystal, Blavatsky

[673] Website dedicated to Blavatsky Blavatsky.net <http://www.blavatsky.net/blavatsky/madame-blavatsky.htm> Web page as of 11/07/2004

[674] Crystal, Blavatsky

[675] Crystal, Blavatsky

fraud and trickery.[676] In India, spiritualism is a lucrative business and protégés like Damodar are available dime a dozen. And HPB had adopted quite a few. HPB had to relocate back to Europe as a result of this scandal.

The Theosophist position has always been that Coulomb not only doctored the letters herself but also constructed the secret panels to defame HPB! And that Hodgson's report was "biased." In 1986, The Psychical research Society published an article agreeing with the Theosophist position and "vindicating" HPB. Since the original Coulomb letters are said to have been "lost," very little can be reconstructed. In addition to documented controversies, the arbitrary nature of telepathy with the "disembodied masters" allowed HPB to exercise her dictum in an arbitrary fashion. For example, any scandal undesirable to her would be swept under the rug as a product of the forces of Kali Yuga! Cardinal Caro Rodriguez quotes Nesta Webster on the scandals of the Theosophical Society,

> Suffice it to say here that its course, like that of most secret societies, have been marked by violent dissensions amongst the members- the Blavatsky-ites proclaiming the divine infallibility of their leader- whilst at a same time, scandals of a peculiarly unsavory kind have been brought to light. This fact has indeed, created a serious schism in the ranks of the Theosophists, which shows that a number of perfectly harmless people are to be found amongst them. Yet the peculiar recurrence of such scandals in the history of secret societies leads one inevitably to wonder how far these are to be regarded as merely deplorable accidents or as the results of secret society methods and teachings. That the men against whom charges of sexual perversion were brought were not isolated examples of those tendencies is shown by a curious admission on the part of one of Blavatsky's 'chelas' or disciples.[677]

Among those who publicly opposed this new spiritualism of "mediums" was escape artist Harry Houdini, who mocked and satirized the phenomenon. In October 1926, Houdini was viciously punched in the stomach on two separate occasions, rupturing his appendix and leading

---

[676] Helena Petrovna Blavatsky <http://www.crystalinks.com/blavatsky2.html> Web page as of 11/07/2004

[677] Quoting Nesta Webster in <u>Secret Societies and Subversive Movements</u> page 306. Jose Maria Cardinal Caro Y. Rodriguez, <u>The Mystery of Freemasonry Unveiled – With a reprint of Pope Leo XIIIth Encyclical Humanum Genus</u> 2nd edition (Imprimatur, Jose Maria Cardinal Caro Y. Rodriguez, Cardinal Archbishop of Santiago, Chile, 1920s) 227.

to his death. His opponents among the spiritualists were suspected to be involved.[678] A 2006 biography of Houdini has again suggested that Houdini may have been murdered.[679]

Before settling in India, HPB became the first Russian to acquire American citizenship.[680] Maybe she didn't want to be looked upon as a Russian spy in India. Though the Hodgson expose of the Theosophical Society was one of the reasons HPB left for Europe, another reason was a hushed up scandal involving "Russian spies." In her letter on why she left India, Blavatsky makes only a sly hint to it.[681] In chapter one, I have alluded to the future role of Russia (the Soviet Union) in the Indian subcontinent, as had been prescribed by the Powers that Be.

But there is reason to believe Blavatsky was receiving correspondence, albeit not from the Great White Brotherhood residing in the Himalayas, but from a Rosicrucian brotherhood that backed her. The link to Rosicrucianism is not usually acknowledged, even though HPB declared herself to be one[682] and in one of her letters to Prof. Corson, she judges a symbol in "[…] my own Rosicrucian way […].[683] Let us not forget that the name Theosophical Society was the brainchild of a Rosicrucian. As we shall further see, the current symbol of the Theosophical society bears similar elements with a Rosicrucian symbol. In a similar vein, a Rosicrucian associated with Freemasonry confided to Nesta Webster that,

---

678 Larry McShane, "Book Paints Escape Artist Houdini as Spy," Saturday October 28th 2006. Associated Press <http://sfgate.com/cgi-bin/article.cgi?f=/n/a/2006/10/28/entertainment/e100630D77.DTL> Accessed 30/10/06.

679 William Kalush & Larry Sloman, The Secret Life of Houdini, the making of America's first superhero (Atria Books, 2006).

680 Crystal, Blavatsky

681 H.P. Blavatsky, letter by HPB to brothers of Aryavarta, April 1890, "Why I do not return to India," This letter was published in the Theosophist of January 1922. Blavatsky.net < http://www.blavatsky.net/blavatsky/arts/WhyIDoNotReturnToIndia.htm> Web page as of 11/07/2004

682 Citing H.P. Blavatsky, Collected Writings Vol. I (Wheaton: TPH 1977) 100. Maria Cissor Sisson, "Helena Blavatsky and the Enigma of John King," Blavatsky Archives Online <http://www.blavatskyarchives.com/sisson1.htm> Accessed 23/12/06.

683 H.P. Blavatsky, letter to Prof. H. Corson, date not available. "Some Unpublished letters of H. P. Blavatsky, compiled by E.R. Corson. Theosophical University Press Online Edition <http://www.theosociety.org/pasadena/corson/cors-lt1.htm> Accessed 23/12/06.

> [...] "Theosophy is not the hierarchy," implying that it was only part of a world organization, and darkly hinting that if it does not carry out the work allotted to it, another body of adepts would take control. [...][684]

In 1887, HPB started a monthly magazine from London named Lucifer.[685]

In 1888, Blavatsky came out with her magnum opus, *The Secret Doctrine*.[686] In this work, Lucifer (a pseudonym for Satan) suddenly rises to prominence, as seen in the following quotes:

> It is not only one of the most hidden secrets of Nature -- that of generation, over whose solution the Embryologists have vainly put their heads together -- but likewise a divine function that involves that other religious, or rather dogmatic, mystery, the "Fall" of the Angels, as it is called. Satan and his rebellious host would thus prove, when the meaning of the allegory is explained, to have refused to create physical man, only to become the direct Saviours and the Creators of "*divine* Man."
>
> *-Page 193 Vol I*
>
> Thus "SATAN," once he ceases to be viewed in the superstitious, dogmatic, unphilosophical spirit of the Churches, grows into the grandiose image of one who made of terrestrial a divine MAN; who gave him, throughout the long cycle of Maha-kalpa the law of the Spirit of Life, and made him free from the Sin of Ignorance, hence of death.
>
> *-Page 198 Vol I*
>
> It is "Satan who is the god of our planet and *the only* god," and this without any allusive metaphor to its wickedness and depravity.
>
> *-234 Vol 2*

---

684 Quoting Nesta Webster in Secret Societies and Subversive Movements page 306. Jose Maria Cardinal Caro Y. Rodriguez, The Mystery of Freemasonry Unveiled – With a reprint of Pope Leo XIIIth Encyclical Humanum Genus 2nd edition (Imprimatur, Jose Maria Cardinal Caro Y. Rodriguez, Cardinal Archbishop of Santiago, Chile, 1920s) 227.

685 Blavatsky.net < http://www.blavatsky.net/blavatsky/madame-blavatsky.htm> Web page as of 11/07/2004

686 Available online at <http://www.theosociety.org/pasadena/sd/sd-hp.htm> Web page as of 11/07/2004.

"Satan, or Lucifer, represents the *active,* or, as M. Jules Baissac calls it, the 'Centrifugal Energy of the Universe' in a cosmic sense. He is Fire, Light, Life, Struggle, Effort, Thought, Consciousness, Progress, Civilization, Liberty, Independence.

-245 Vol 2

[…] the greatest of modern Kabalists, namely Eliphas Levi, describes Satan in the following glowing terms: -- "It is that Angel who was proud enough to believe himself God; brave enough to buy his independence at the price of eternal suffering and torture; beautiful enough to have adored himself in full divine light; strong enough to reign in darkness amidst agony, and to have built himself a throne on his inextinguishable pyre. It is the Satan of the Republican and heretical Milton […]."

506-507 Vol 2

LUCIFER -- the spirit of Intellectual Enlightenment and Freedom of Thought -- is metaphorically the guiding beacon, which helps man to find his way through the rocks and sandbanks of Life, for Lucifer is the **L**OGOS in his highest,

162 Vol 2

But in antiquity and *reality*, Lucifer, or *Luciferus*, is the name of the angelic Entity presiding over the *light of truth* as over the light of the day.

512 Vol 2

Lucifer is divine and terrestrial light, the "Holy Ghost" and "Satan," at one and the same time

513 Vol.2

In the footsteps of the Aryans

The feature attraction of *The Secret Doctrine* was a race-based theory of evolution in which progress depended upon reincarnation, karma, human eugenics, and balance with the Earth.[687] According to Jackson Spielvogel and David Redles,

---

[687] Hannah Newman, The Rainbow Swastika- A Report to the Jewish People About New Age Anti-Semitism; Human history according to the new age < http://philologos.org/__eb-trs/naB.htm> Web page as of 11/07/2004.

> Blavatsky emphasized the concept of races as paramount in the development of human history. According to Blavatsky, there are seven root races of mankind, with each root race containing seven sub-races. The present root race is the fifth, the Aryan, and was preceded by the fourth or Atlantean race. The Aryans evolved from the fifth sub-race of the Atlanteans. According to Blavatsky, "The Aryan Race was born and developed in the far North, though after the sinking of the Continent of Atlantis its tribes emigrated further south into Asia."[688] The Aryans, following a migratory pattern that went south and west from Asia, ultimately created the great Hindu, Persian, Greco-Roman, and later European cultures. Hitler, like his party ideologist, Alfred Rosenberg, also claimed Aryan origins for all of these cultures [689]

Blavatsky's experience in India contributed to developing the "Aryans in the Himalayas" theory. Prior to the Aryan invasion, the Indus valley was home to a relatively sophisticated civilization. The Aryans overran the local Indian Indus Valley civilization[690] around 1600-1800 BC. The theory of the movement of Aryans into India has become controversial due to partisan politics in India. But recently, genetic evidence has been presented to vindicate the theory of a large scale Aryan migration. To quote,

> [...] 20%–30% of Indian mtDNA haplotypes belong to West Eurasian haplogroups, and the frequency of these haplotypes is proportional to caste rank, the highest frequency of West Eurasian haplotypes being found in the upper castes. [...] Moreover, the affinity to Europeans is proportionate to caste rank, the upper castes being most similar to Europeans, particularly East Europeans.[691]

---

688 H.P. Blavatsky, The Secret Doctrine vol. 2 (London, 1928) 812, as quoted by Spielvogel and Redles.

689 H.P. Blavatsky, The Secret Doctrine vol. 2 (London, 1928) 111, 278, 411, 527; Adolf Hitler, Mein Kampf trans. Ralph Manheim (Boston, 1943) 264-65, 294, 393, 423; Alfred Rosenberg, Der Mythus des 20. Jahrhunderts (Munich, 1934) 21-35. Rosenberg begins with the Atlantis legend. As quoted in Jackson Spielvogel and David Redles, "Hitler's Racial Ideology: Content and Occult Sources," Simon Wiesenthal Center – Museum of Tolerance Online > Multimedia Learning Center > Annual 3. 1997
< http://motlc.wiesenthal.com/site/pp.asp?c=gvKVLcMVIuG&b=395043>

690 Robert Heine-Geldern, "The Coming of the Aryans and the end of the Harappa Civilization," Man 56 (Oct. 1956) 139.

691 Michael Bamshad, Toomas Kivisild,W. Scott Watkins, Mary E. Dixon, Chris E. Ricker, Baskara B. Rao, J. Mastan Naidu, B.V. Ravi Prasad, P. Govinda Reddy, Arani Rasanayagam, Surinder S. Papiha, Richard Villems, Alan J. Redd, Michael F. Hammer, Son V. Nguyen, Marion L. Carroll, Mark A. Batzer and Lynn B. Jorde, "Genetic

The Aryans were herded into India by a religious elite, which propagated itself through exclusive bloodlines, not unlike the Sumerians and ancient Egyptians. This clique had complete control over the group since the clique was firmly rooted as a priestly caste. Violent efforts were made to preserve these bloodlines and their privileges by the creation of a pyramidal society, where groups of people were frozen in their respective castes, all subordinate to this highest bloodline. However, in a place as vast and complex as the Indian subcontinent, the bloodlines did not survive. And the contrivances created to secure them remain only as a legacy. This Aryan elite class, known as the "high caste," still holds influence in India, though it certainly bears no connections to the secret ruling elite of the West, and even its bloodline appears to have been considerably diluted.

Most surprisingly, the leaders of the Aryans had connections with the ancient and forgotten mystery religions of Egypt and Babylon, which the Illuminati also draw upon. In 1935, Dr. Pran Nath published an article in the Times of India[692] in which he proposed his well-researched claim that ancient literature pertaining to the Aryan period contains numerous commonalities with Babylon and ancient Egypt. Dr. Nath had even found a copper scroll of Babylonian king Nebuchadnezzar I in Prabhaspatan (Gujarat).

One of the many legacies of the Aryans was the swastika, which adorns Vishnu temples and is seen on Hindu religious gear. In *The Secret Doctrine*, Blavatsky wrote about the occult significance of the swastika, characterizing it as the most sacred symbol in India. To quote, "The *Svastica* is the most philosophically scientific of all symbols, as also the most comprehensible. It is the summary in a few lines of the whole work of *creation,* or evolution [...]"[693] The swastika was nothing more than an arcane figment of history in the Western world before Blavatsky. But by 1884, a Theosophical lodge had been established in Germany and the race-based mysticism of Theosophy became combined with local anti-Semitic and nationalist movements. In 1892, a periodical entitled *Lotus Blossoms* featuring the writings of HPB became the first German

---

Evidence on the Origins of Indian Caste Population," Genome Research 11 (2001): 994.

[692] Dated 19th March 1935

[693] H.P. Blavatsky, The Secret Doctrine Vol.2 (Theosophical University Press Online Edition) 98.

publication to sport the theosophical swastika upon its cover.[694] According to Hannah Newman, Theosophy acted as a conduit for the Aryan caste system to be sublimated into Nazi racial purity laws.[695]

The swastika counts among the greatest mysteries in symbolism. Even the insightful research of Servando Gonzalez on this topic ends on an inconclusive note.[696] However, there is evidence that early predecessors of the Illuminati used the swastika. Gonzalez points a monastery in Loudum (dated 1334) where the names of several Carmelite brothers are engraved in the staircase.[697] Brother Guyot has a rose overlaid with a swastika beside his signature. The rose symbolizes the Rosicrucians, who rescued and preserved the mystical teachings of Babylon. Egyptian civilization, another derivative of Babylon, acted as a shelter for these teachings.[698] Present day Western ruling elite heavily use Egyptian symbolism such as the eye of Horus, Pyramids and obelisks. Again, we find the swastika on a mummy-like (Egyptian connection again) gravestone called the Ogham stone, which was unearthed in Aglish, Ireland and dates to the fifth century. Celtic Christianity and Druid civilization found in the same region bear similar symbolism and the shape of the stone represents the casket used in Masonic rituals. The interesting symbolism on the Ogham stone is the Splayed cross/Templar cross/Maltese cross which was introduced in Europe by the Merovingians, descendants of the Israeli tribe of Benjamin. Even before Merovingians, we find the splayed cross in Babylon. Boyd Rice makes a note of it above the head of the first Sumerian King in a 2000 BC rendering.[699] Was the crucifixion of Christ on a four armed cross meant

---

[694] Nicholas Goodrick-Clarke, The Occult Roots of Nazism: Secret Aryan Cults and their Influence on Nazi Ideology (New York: New York University Press, 1992) 25. Scott Lively and Kevin Abrams, The Pink Swastika-Homosexuality in the Nazi Party 4th ed. (Sacramento: Veritas Aeterna Press, 2002) 108.

[695] Hannah Newman, The Rainbow Swastika- A Report to the Jewish People About New Age Anti-Semitism; Human history according to the new age < http://philologos.org/__eb-trs/naB.htm> Web page as of 11/07/2004.

[696] Servando González, Origins of the Swastika: Epilogue. < http://www.intelinet.org/swastika/swasepil.htm> Web page as of 11/07/2004

[697] Quoting Louis Charbonnay, Lassay. L'Esoterisme de quelques symboles géométriques chrétiens (Paris: Editions traditionnelles, 1960). Servando González, Origins of the Swastika: The Hausofer Connection. Note # 5. <http://www.intelinet.org/swastika/swasti02.htm> Web page as of 11/07/2004

[698] To complicate things, L.A Waddell has written a book *Egyptian Civilization: It's Sumerian Origin and Real Chronology.* Is this is why the Illuminati uses symbolism such as the pyramids and the eye of Isiris?

[699] Boyd Rice, "The Sumerian Origins of the Iconography of the Templars, Masons & Merovingians," Dagoberts Revenge

to symbolize the identity of the perpetrators? The splayed cross alongside the swastika on the Ogham stone clearly indicates a link between the two. It can also be said that the splayed cross may be a derivative of the swastika. But if that is the case, what does the swastika/splayed cross/cross symbolize? Fritz Springmeier made an expose of 13 Illuminati "bloodlines" existing and operating to this day. According to many, these 13 bloodlines are nothing but heretic variants of the twelve tribes of Israel plus an Oriental family added lately to the consortium (And therefore the number 13 symbolism). According to a Hebrew Website:

> "Beyond the Levite circle, the twelve tribes camped in four groups of three tribes each. To the east were Judah (pop. 74,600), Issachar (54,400) and Zebulun (57,400); to the south, Reuben (46,500), Simeon (59,300) and Gad (45,650); to the west, Ephraim (40,500), Menasseh (32,200) and Benjamin (35,400); and to the north, Dan (62,700), Asher (41,500) and Naphtali (53,400). This formation was kept also while traveling. Each tribe had its own *nassi* (prince or leader), and its own flag with its tribal color and emblem."[700]

Following on this, some have drawn the conclusion that the four arms of the splayed cross/swastika/cross thus represent the heretic variants of the twelve tribes and the geographic directions (North, South, East and West) these heretic variants took. Note that the reference is to heretic variants of the twelve tribes of Israel, rather than the original twelve tribes of Israel itself. These heretic variants remained completely unknown to the Jewish community. And given their commitment to anti-Semitism and their historic opposition to Judeo-Christian values, they should be regarded as a secret counter-movement to original Judaic ideals, operating well beyond the confines of the Jewish community.

<
http://web.archive.org/web/20040607071402/http://dagobertsrevenge.com/articles/rlc/icon.shtml> Web page as of 24/12/2006.

[700] The Parsha in a nutshell- Bamidar Numbers 1:1-4:20, Chabad Online Media Center, Bamidbar magazine, #5761, May 25th 2001.
< http://www.chabad.org/parshah/article.asp?AID=2121> Web page as of 11/07/2004

A Swastika on a present-day Indian temple.

The Ogham Stone
Copyright:Unknown

The 1334 swastika overlaid on a (Rosicrucian?) Rose.

See Louis Charbonnay-Lassay. L'Esoterisme de quelques symboles géométriques chrétiens. Paris: Editions traditionnelles, 1960. © Servando González, Origins of the Swastika: The Hausofer Connection. Note # 5. <http://www.intelinet.org/swastika/swasti02.htm> Web page as of 11/07/2004. Minimized Reproduction Under Fair Dealing.

The splayed cross in a Sumerian rendering from 2000 BC.

©Boyd Rice. "The Sumerian Origins of the Iconography of the Templars, Masons & Merovingians." Dagoberts Revenge<http://www.dagobertsrevenge.com/articles/rlc/icon.shtml> Web page as of 11/07/2004. Minimized Reproduction Under Fair Dealing.

But how did the swastika end up in India? The swastika was brought to India by the Aryans (1600-1800 BC) who introduced a sophisticated pyramidal caste system, which would dominate India for centuries. Was the enigmatic priestly class guiding the Aryans one of the aforementioned tribes, who while moving east found their way across the Indus?

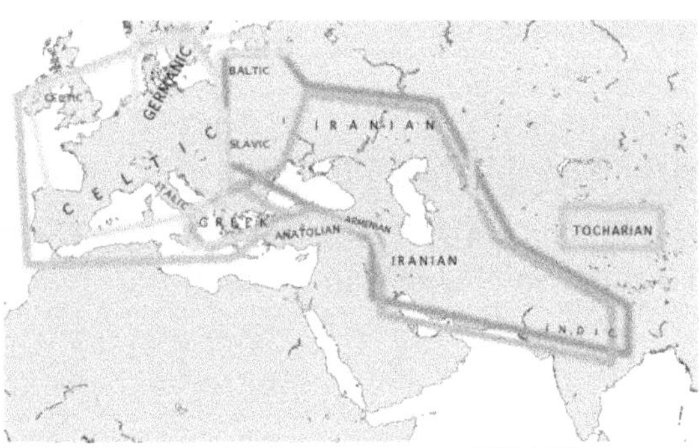

Indo European language groups, 500 BC

German Indologist Friedrich Max Muller, a contemporary of Blavatsky was a pioneer in studying the Aryan origins of India's Vedic culture. Max Muller was also a proponent of the then nascent Aryan Invasion theory, which has credibly solved many riddles of India's past. The timing of propounding the Aryan Invasion theory happened to be synchronous with Germany's emergence. The groundwork for Nazism was being laid and the Aryan Invasion theory would be later used as ideological fodder for Hitler's suicidal advance eastwards. Muller happens to be associated with key Elitists of his time. Such as Felix Mendelssohn, grandson of Jewish philosopher Moses Mendelssohn (who was said to be the mentor of Adam Weishaupt, founder of the Illuminati of Bavaria). This is not meant to imply that the Aryan Invasion theory was a concoction. Rather, the Powers that Be were deliberately unveiling little known areas of human history to further their ongoing venture.

Muller advocated Theosophy. According to Monsignor Munro, the Roman Catholic bishop of St. Andrews Cathedral in Glasgow, "the [Muller] lectures were nothing less than 'a crusade against divine revelation, against Jesus Christ and Christianity'. The pantheism taught by Muller made 'divine revelation simply impossible, because it reduced God to mere nature, and did away with the body and soul as we know them".[701] Muller's conception of God was similar to that of Nietzsche. According to it, God(s) was simply a form of expression for a thought or idea that had become ossified over time. Hypocritically, Muller also advocated Christianizing of the non-Christian world, in order to popularize the Illuminati's colonial stranglehold of India. European Colonialism was necessary for the development of a more Westernized, classless and atheistic-oriented society as a precursor to Soviet domination. It is obvious that Muller, in his correspondences, would refer to such goals in couched and inconspicuous terms such as "Christianizing." He is also associated with "reformist" Hindu movements in India, such as Brahmo Samaj. A similar movement, the Arya Samaj, was an offshoot of the Theosophical Society. Critics of such movements claim that they were efforts to standardize Hinduism, so that its scattered locus of control could be concentrated in the hands of a few intellectual elite.

Anti-Judaism and Anti-Semitism

HPB's *The Secret Doctrine* gave anti-Judaism and anti-Semitism a pseudo-scientific polish. To quote Spielvogel and Redles,

---

[701] Lourens Peter van den Bosch, "Theosophy or Pantheism? Friedrich Max Muller's Gifford Lectures on Natural Religion." Here-Now4U Online Magazine < http://www.here-now4u.de/eng/theosophy_or_pantheism__friedr.htm> Web page as of 11/07/2004

> [...] Blavatsky had helped to foster anti-Semitism, which is perhaps one of the reasons her esoteric work was so rapidly accepted in German circles. She sharply differentiated Aryan and Jewish religion. The Aryans were the most spiritual people on earth. For them, religion was an "everlasting lodestar." For the Jews, religion was grounded on "mere calculation." They had a "religion of hate and malice toward everyone and everything outside itself."[702] Jewish materialism and selfishness contrasted strongly with Aryan spirituality and selflessness.[703]

Other ways in which HPB's works contributed to anti-Semitism have been discussed in the section "Influences on Hitler's peculiar brand of Christianity" in the previous chapter.

Symbolism

The Theosophical Society's symbol, known as HPB's brooch had a swastika on top. What is interesting is the presence of the Star of David below![704] It is important to note that prior to the advent of Zionism, the Star of David was not largely identified with Judaism or Jews.[705] Rather, it was an esoteric symbol associated with alchemy and secret societies. Did such esoteric groups seize control of Zionism? The serpent in the symbol can also be noticed in the earlier seal of the French revolution.

---

[702] H.P. Blavatsky, The Secret Doctrine vol. 2 (London, 1928) 339-94. As quoted in Spielvogel and Redles.

[703] Jackson Spielvogel and David Redles, "Hitler's Racial Ideology: Content and Occult Sources," Simon Wiesenthal Center – Museum of Tolerance Online > Multimedia Learning Center > Annual 3. 1997 < http://motlc.wiesenthal.com/site/pp.asp?c=gvKVLcMVIuG&b=395043>

[704] Such combinations have been noted elsewhere as well. For example, police in Paris stumbled upon an underground tunnel, which lead to a 400sq.m cave, 18m underground. The cave had an amphitheatre with a cinema, complete with electricity and phones. Swastikas, Stars of David and Celtic Crosses were painted on the ceiling. When the police returned to check who was supplying the electricity, they found that it had been cut, and a note was left saying, "do not try to find us." John Henley, "In a Secret Paris Cavern, the Real Underground Cinema," The Guardian, September 8th 2004. <http://film.guardian.co.uk/News_Story/Guardian/0,,1299449,00.html> Accessed 13/12/06

[705] For a detailed discussion, see O.J. Graham, The Six Pointed Star: Its Origin and Usage (New Puritan Library, 1984).

A brooch worn by Blavatsky, also known as her personal seal. It was also associated with the Theosophical Society. Note the presence of a glyph resembling a Soviet sickle and hammer on the bottom left.

The Star of David started being associated with Judaism around the emergence of Zionism. Prior to that, it was a symbol associated with alchemy (see far right). This may indicate control of Zionism by non-Judaic occult oriented groups.

A symbol associated with the French Revolution. Note the pyramid with the all seeing eye wearing a Jacobin cap. The bottom portion shows a Masonic handshake with the word 'Fraternity' below.

A seal associated with the Rosicrucian movement. See the theosophical seal on the top right.

Another seal associated with the Theosophical Society. The swastika has been minimized. The center bears a Rosicrucian cross. Variants of this peculiar cross can be found on the Nazi battle flag as well as the symbols of several hate groups.

An early symbol associated with alchemy. Variations of the two snakes at each other's tails can be found in modern corporate logos as well.

Compared to the brooch worn by HPB, the present Theosophical Society symbol retains the serpent, but the swastika has been diminished. But with the unique Rosicrucian cross, this symbol only gives confirmation of the Rosicrucian origins of the Theosophical Society. It is interesting to note that the Nazi battle flag would also sport a Rosicrucian cross. At a time when secret communication, let alone regular communication was stifled by physical barriers, these symbols had extreme importance. Operatives from diverse regions would be able to identify which movements and organizations represented what.

The "all-seeing eye" occurs in the text of HPB's *Secret Doctrine*. To quote, "while the "Cyclopean" eye was, and still *is,* in man the organ of *spiritual* sight."[706] Regarding the one eye, even the Prophet of Islam warned his followers as, "[...] If you have any doubt regarding Antichrist, remember that your Sustainer is not one eyed."[707]

The followers of Blavatsky

By the time Blavatsky had died in 1891, she had released several other books through telepathy from the "masters." She was influential in developing the Hermetic Order of the Golden Dawn, which has been identified with Freemasonry. She would be surrounded by the Who's Who of the occult world and famous individuals alike. Only some of her companions, followers and future disciples are listed as follows:

- A.P. Sinnet
- French-born Swedish Countess Constance Wachrmeister
- Horace Greeley
- John L. O'Sullivan, US ex-Ambassador to Portugal
- P. B. Randolph, leading American **Rosicrucian**
- Prince Wittgenstein
- W. B. Yeats, the Irish poet. Yeats' poetry consisted of Masonic imagery such as the lion, the beast, and the rose, and possible Rosicrucian themes. Some of his poetry may be used in mind control. According to Fritz Springmeier,[708] W.B Yeats was a leader of the Golden Dawn and wrote Satanic Masonic rituals for it.
- "AE" (George W. Russell). George William Russell was a leading member of the Dublin Theosophist lodge, and wrote for the Theosophical periodical *The Irish Theosophist*. He was initiated into the Lodge of Isis.
- Barbara Hubbard, widow of Max Hubbard, founder of Scientology, Democratic nominee for US Vice President.
- Johannes Baltzli, secretary of the proto-Nazi List Society and biographer of Guido von List.
- Jiddu Krishnamurti, an Indian Hindu who became a séance medium for Maitreya but later fell into disfavor with the Theosophists.

---

[706] H.P. Blavatsky, The Secret Doctrine Vol.2 (Theosophical University Press Online Edition) 299.

[707] Ubaidah Bin Saamit, a companion of the Prophet quoted him as saying such. Hadith Ahmed.

[708] Fritz Springmeier, Bloodlines of the Illuminati (Spring Arbor distributors, 1998) 225. GlobalGrey PDF edition 2013 <http://www.globalgrey.co.uk/Pages/Books-Conspiracies/Bloodlines-Of-The-Illuminati.html> Web page as of 03/07/13.

- C.W. Leadbeater, English Masonist and contributor to the proto-Nazi List society's *Prana* Digest. Leadbeater was a confirmed English imperialist and connected to Anglican Freemasonry.
- Charles Sotheran, a high Mason, a **Rosicrucian**, and a student of the Kabbala
- Margaret Sanger, Eugenics and birth control advocate (to be confirmed)
- Karl Hausofer, a Blavatsky disciple who shuffled key concepts of *The Secret Doctrine* to form the philosophy of Nazism.[709] Hausofer was also the guru of Rudolf Hess and Anton LaVey, founder of the Church of Satan. LaVey would dedicate his *Satanic Bible* in part to Hausofer.[710] Did Hausofer influence Henry Kissinger's "geopolitics"?
- David Spangler, a Findhorn leader (a New Age community in Scotland where the goat-god Pan is worshiped).[711]
- Baron Rudolf von Sebottendorf was a fan of Blavatsky. Founded the Thule society, which formed the Nazi party.
- Rudolf Steiner, who formed Anthroposophy, considered being a link between Theosophy and Nazism.
- Annie Besant and A.O Hume, influential coordinators of Indian independence, which led to the creation of the nation states of American-backed Pakistan and Soviet-backed India.
- Yuiliana Glinka, personal companion of HPB and devoted Theosophist. A rare early edition of the *Protocols of the Learned Elders of Zion* credits her with originally finding the document![712] For more information, see section on the Protocols in Chapter two.
- Carl Jung, psychoanalyst who advocated Aryan supremacy and separation of "Jewish psychology."[713]
- Jorge Agel Livraga, founder of "New Acropolis," a global forum now in 40 countries, combines Theosophy and Fascism under the guise of the revival of classical Greek/Roman philosophy.

---

709 Joseph J Carr, The Twisted Cross (Vital Issues Press, 1985) 93.

710 Dusty Sklar, The Nazis and the Occult (1989) 63.

711 Hannah Newman, The Rainbow Swastika- A Report to the Jewish People About New Age Anti-Semitism; Nazism and the new age <http://philologos.org/__eb-trs/naF.htm> Web page as of 11/07/2004.

712 Hannah Newman, The Rainbow Swastika- A Report to the Jewish People About New Age Anti-Semitism; Transformation of Society <http://philologos.org/__eb-trs/naG.htm> Web page as of 11/07/2004.

713 See the book by Harvard Professor Richard Noll, The Aryan Christ: The Secret Life of Carl Jung (Random House 1997).

Dutch researcher Michiel Louter alleges this movement seeks to undermine democracy by fostering a return of rule by elitist supermen.[714]

- Baron Bulwer-Lytton, English writer and occultist who wrote *The Coming Race* and *The Last days of Pompeii.*
- Franz Hartmann: Member of the proto-Nazi List society.
- Lanz Von Liebenfels? Founder of the proto-Nazi Order of the New Templars. Likely influence on Hitler.
- Harald Gravelle, homosexual occultist and leading Theosophist in Germany. Also contributed to the pederast journal, *Der Eigene*. Companion of proto-Nazis Liebenfels and List.[715]
- Dr. Gerard Encausse, aka Papus (1865-1916), a leading occultist of his time who was connected to the Russian imperial court. He even had foreknowledge about the upcoming war with Germany.[716]
- A mysterious Mongolian-Tibetan who went by the name of Dr. Badmaev and was closely attached to the Russian imperial court. He believed that Russia had a far greater role to play in the east. He was connected to the Tibetan Llamas.
- Sir Arthur Conan Doyle, the creator of Sherlock Holmes. Doyle's view of crime was domestic violence and theft. He viewed the British Empire and the wars it raged beyond the reproach of Sherlock Holme's deductive crime solving abilities. Doyle decided to put his abilities to a grander use. He reasoned that he could use clues in the world to arrive at some spiritual truth (analogical to clues in a crime scene). All the while, a much bigger crime scene (the activities of the British Empire and the emergence of the New World Order) was unfolding before his very eyes.
- Alexander Russell Webb (1846-1916), one of the earliest American converts to Islam. But was Russell Web sincere in his conversion? Even after converting to Islam, Russell Web

---

[714] Michiel Louter, "Disreputable forces at work among the sect researchers at CESNUR," August 13th 1997, De Groene Amsterdammer. An archived copy is available at
<http://www.rickross.com/reference/apologist/apologist16.html>

[715] Lively and Abrams, Pink Swastika 108

[716] Mehmet Sabeheddin, "The Secret of Eurasia – The key to Hidden History and World Events," New Dawn No. 68 (September-October 2001),
<http://www.newdawnmagazine.com> An archive is available at
<http://www.geocities.com/integral_tradition/key.html> Accessed 12th May 2003.

maintained connections to the Theosophical Society.[717] Webb seemed to have scant interest in mainstream Islam. He exchanged letters with the controversial Ahmadiyya movement, Mirza Ghulam Ahmad Qadian.[718]

Theosophy and the New Age Movement

There is nothing "new" about the New Age Movement. It is simply a revival of antiquated and doomed mystery religions of Babylon and Egypt. The secretive Rosicrucians had managed to save occult aspects of these cultures from extinction and later revived them through the European renaissance. It is not surprising that the same forces would resurface again in the groundwork for the World Wars.

To quote Newman "The organization founded by Helena Blavatsky successively broke into four competing religious groups: (1) The Theosophical Society (headed by Annie Besant); (2) Anthroposophy (Rudolf Steiner and David Spangler) (3) The Arcane School, the 'School of Ageless Wisdom,' and Lucis Trust (Alice Bailey, Benjamin Crème, Robert Muller); (4) 'I AM,' 'The Church Universal and Triumphant' (Guy & Edna Ballard, Elizabeth Clare Prophet)."[719]

The roots of New Age thought and philosophy ultimately lead to Helena Blavatsky and Alice Bailey. In 1922, Alice Bailey established the Lucis trust (named after Lucifer?) to print and disseminate the New Age books of HPB and Bailey. This is clear proof that the UN is not secular as portrayed but clearly has a darker agenda. HPB's 1889 book, *The Key to Theosophy* contains another correspondence between HPB and the "Masters." We are told that humanity would be ready for the New Age sometime at the end of the 20th century.[720] By that time,

> [...] besides a large and accessible literature ready to men's hands, the next impulse will find a numerous and *united* body of people ready to welcome the new torch-bearer of Truth. He will find the minds of men

[717] Umar F. Abd-Allah, A Muslim in Victorian America: The Life of Alexander Russell Webb (Oxford University Press, 2006) 294: note 76.
[718] Abd-Allah A Muslim 124.
[719] Hannah Newman, The Rainbow Swastika- A Report to the Jewish People About New Age Anti-Semitism; Transformation of Society <http://philologos.org/__eb-trs/naG.htm> Web page as of 11/07/2004.
[720] Newman, Rainbow Swastika: Transformation

> prepared for his message, a language ready for him in which to clothe the new truths he brings, an organization awaiting his arrival.[721]

Today, Alice Bailey's teachings are incorporated into public schools throughout the world through the Goals 2000 program.[722]

Hannah Newman jokes that she wouldn't even trust her bank account to the disembodied spirits from whom HPB received correspondence. What entitles them to be trusted with the destiny of the world?

The Rainbow Swastika - A Report to the Jewish People About New Age Anti-Semitism by Hannah Newman is a detailed expose of the plan to dissolve Judaism (upon which Christianity is based) and replace it with a bewildering array of new beliefs. The work also hints at the plan of the Powers that Be to revisit the Nazi experiment. Despite being a serious and legitimate inquiry into the dangers facing Jews and Judaism, this report has largely been ignored. High profile Jewish Protection syndicates don't appear to be concerned. Jewish conspiracy theorist Mae Brussells was also greeted with the same stony indifference when she sought the help of the Israeli state when trying to find the whereabouts of escaped Nazi war criminals.

Theosophy and the Nazi doctrine

The course of race based human evolution charted out in *The Secret Doctrine* became the basis of Nazism. Blavatsky's mythology of Aryan roots in the South East would be used by Hitler in his lebensraum, which also gave the pre-emptive attack on the Soviet Union a pseudo-philosophical underpinning. Hitler adopted the swastika popularized by the Theosophical Society but had it reversed for some bizarre reason. The Thule society, which borrowed heavily from Theosophy, formed the Nazi party. According to Gerard Schuster's *Adolf Hitler-The Occult Messiah*, Hitler was devoted to Theosophy and kept a copy of Blavatsky's *The Secret Doctrine* by his bedside.[723] According to Joseph

---

721 The Key to Theosophy, p.306, italics in original. Quoted by Newman in Rainbow Swastika: Transformation.

722 Hannah Newman, The Rainbow Swastika- A Report to the Jewish People About New Age Anti-Semitism; How Big a Conspiracy <http://philologos.org/__eb-trs/naA.htm> Web page as of 11/07/2004.

723 Hannah Newman, The Rainbow Swastika- A Report to the Jewish People About New Age Anti-Semitism; Nazism and the new age <http://philologos.org/__eb-trs/naF.htm> Web page as of 11/07/2004.

Carr, Hausofer schooled Hitler in *The Secret Doctrine*.[724] The Theosophical Society would later applaud Hitler for his "faith."[725] Blavatsky's sentiments would be echoed, almost verbatim, by Thule Society member and Nazi party philosopher Alfred Rosenberg, when he claimed that "The earth-centered Jew lacks a soul" and elsewhere, "[the continuing existence of the Jew] would lead to a void, to the destruction not only of the illusory earthly world but also of the truly existent, the spiritual."[726] Hitler would be later quoted, as "The Jew is the anti-man, the creature of another god. He must have come from another root of the human race."[727] Hitler would later crack down on Theosophists to cover up Nazi links to them.

---

[724] Joseph J Carr, The Twisted Cross (Vital Issues Press, 1985) 93. Quoted in Newman, Rainbow Swastika; Nazism and the New Age.

[725] The Theosophist, December 1938, p.239. Quoted in Hannah Newman, The Rainbow Swastika- A Report to the Jewish People About New Age Anti-Semitism; Transformation of Society <http://philologos.org/__eb-trs/naG.htm> Web page as of 11/07/2004.

[726] Dusty Sklar, The Nazis and the Occult (1989) 147-148. Quoted in Hannah Newman, The Rainbow Swastika- A Report to the Jewish People About New Age Anti-Semitism; Nazism and the new age <http://philologos.org/__eb-trs/naF.htm> Web page as of 11/07/2004.

[727] Dusty Sklar, The Nazis and the Occult (1989) 146. Quoted in Newman, Rainbow Swastika; Nazism and the New Age.

Chapter Five
World War Two in Europe

The Second World War must be fomented by taking advantage of the differences between the Fascists and the political Zionists. This war must be brought about so that Nazism is destroyed and that the political Zionism be strong enough to institute a sovereign state of Israel in Palestine. During the Second World War, International Communism must become strong enough in order to balance Christendom, which would be then restrained and held in check until the time when we would need it for the final social cataclysm.

-A quote attributed to Albert Pike, August 15th 1871[728]

> […] For not only the fields of death did I have to see with my own eyes, the battlefields where life itself died, I saw much worse. I saw how, by a few words, through a single, abrupt order of one individual, whom the regime empowered, fields of annihilation were created. I saw the eeriness of the death machinery; wheel turning on wheel, like the mechanisms of a watch. And I saw those who maintained the machinery, who kept it going. I saw them, as they rewound the mechanism; and I watched the second hand, as it rushed through the seconds; rushing like lives towards death. The greatest and most monumental dance of death of all time.
>
> *-Adolf Eichmann, September 6th 1961*[729]

---

[728] For a detailed discussion on this quote, see the introductory chapter "A Note on the World War Quotes attributed to Albert Pike."

[729] Guardian.co.uk, "A monumental dance of death," Guardian Online 1/03/00 < http://www.guardian.co.uk/irving/article/0,,191821,00.html> Accessed 11/12/06

The Soviet Union

One must ask why the Soviet Union didn't qualify as an aggressor when it began annexing surrounding territory, and when it was extending its borders far beyond what Russia proper after World War I. When Germany would move its forces into Western Poland, Britain and France would declare war on it. However when Stalin would move his forces into Eastern Poland, the Allies would not see it as an aggression. As Illuminati operative Christian Rakovsky would say, the Allies will attack but not attack the aggressor. And again, it is hard to understand what made the Soviets more appealing to the Allies than the Nazis. Going strictly by body count, The Soviets were the worse of the two evils.

The Ukrainian Genocide

Ukraine is referred to as the granary of Europe. Therefore, complete control over this region was a top Soviet priority. Up to 300,000 well to do Ukrainian peasants (termed as kulaks) were deported to the Urals and Central Asia. In addition, Bolsheviks were dispatched from Russia to assist in forced collectivization of farms. When grain production fell as a result of collectivization, the Bolsheviks forced the Ukrainian peasants to cooperate by introducing repressive measures. Raids were conducted to confiscate grain, regardless of whether it was stored for sowing during the next harvest or for daily consumption. Restrictions were imposed on the movement of people and grains, turning Ukraine into a a giant gulag. Within months, a famine occurred. More than seven million Ukrainians may have perished between 1932-1933, and two million ended up in concentration camps.[730] The Soviets targeted Ukrainian intelligentsia and the Ukrainian Orthodox Church at the same time.

The Stalinist Purges make room for Globalist operatives

Writing of Stalin, Ronald Grigor Suny says "Stalin remains the central mystery within the Soviet enigma and the Great Terror the most opaque episode during his reign."[731] He further states, "There is no consensus

---

[730] Eric Margolis, "The 20th Century's Worst Crime Goes Unpunished," The Toronto Sun November 16th 2003. Also published on ericmargolis.com <http://www.ericmargolis.com/archives/2003/11/the_20th_centur.php> Accessed 13/12/06

[731] Ronald Grigor Suny, The structure of Soviet History - essays and documents (Oxford University Press, 2003) 160.

among the scholars as to the motivation behind the purges".[732] This happens to be one aspect of Soviet history where the role of the Illuminati is at its most obvious. If Stalin knew of the coming of the Second World War and the potential gains the Illuminati had engineered for the Soviet Union, it was fairly plausible that they would allow Stalin to partake in these gains only if he accepted their conditions. Their chief condition would logically be the instalment of *their* operatives in key influential positions, and especially in the military (where the largest number of purges took place). If Stalin baulked, they could use Nazi Germany to create unfavourable circumstances for him, which would most likely result in his overthrow. Therefore, it is highly plausible that a secret deal was reached, in which Stalin would continue as leader of a victorious postwar Soviet Union with new extended borders, provided he return power from the Leninists to the remnants of the Trotskyites, the original engineers of the revolution. Stalin may have caved in after he saw the power of the interests he was dealing with. And indeed, just prior to the war, the tempo of the purges increased dramatically. Revolutionary Nikolai Bukharin who winded up in the purges and got shot, caught wind that there was something bigger than Stalin's insanity involved in the purges. In his plea for his life to Stalin, he states, "There is some kind of *big and bold political idea* of a general purge (a) in connection with preparation for war [...]"[733](emphasis his) and further "I understand that *big* plans, *big* ideas, and *big* interests trump everything [...]"[734](emphasis his). In the interpretation of the purges, if the distraction of Stalin's monstrous persona is set aside, we notice that what is being purged are not the personal enemies of Stalin, but the Leninist usurpers. Given the scale of the purges, it is important to note that not all the replacements (especially in lower levels) were bloodlined Cabal operatives. Many of the replacements were simply a new generation of operatives, free from any connections to the Leninists. Extensive purges of capable military officers shows that only new officers connected to the Powers that Be were to coordinate and lead the Red Army to victory. Prominent Leninists were being removed to make room for operatives loyal to the Globalists in London and New York.[735] All members of Lenin's first

---

[732] Suny, Soviet History 160.

[733] "Nikolai Bukharin's Letter to Stalin-December 10 1937," Quoted in Suny, Soviet History 247.

[734] "Nikolai Bukharin's Letter to Stalin-December 10 1937," Quoted in Suny, Soviet History 247.

[735] There are other theories as well; including a popular opinion that the Nazis had fed spoof intelligence to Stalin that certain members were plotting against him which resulted in the purges. Even if that was the case, it raises another question: Why would the Nazis feed spoof intelligence restricting its implications only to Leninists?

government were disposed and it would be whimsical to assume that all of these were enemies of Stalin. Another factor in favour of the purges being related to the upcoming war is that they ceased by the year 1938.

Stalin in World War II

As far as the role Stalin played in World War II, what we do know is that Stalin acted upon captured Illuminati operative Christian Rakovsky's suggestion for a pact with Hitler and a talk with US ambassador Davies, whom Rakovsky suggests was also an agent of "them." Rakovsky is of the opinion that Stalin didn't have a clue about "them" and therefore the details of the Rakovsky interrogation reaching Stalin was Stalin's first point of contact with "them." But if Stalin was indeed the illegitimate son of a major banker, it is obvious that he did have contact with his backers from the beginning. What is inexplicable is the estrangement and mistrust between him and his backers. It appears that instead of turning over the Lenin camp to his backers, he couldn't resist placing himself in the shoes of Lenin.

It is hard to believe that someone as shrewd as Stalin would be ignorant of the involvement of Illuminati with the Trotskyites. Stalin fully understood their threat, which is illustrated by his initial persecution of Trotskyites to the extent of having Trotsky murdered in Mexico.[736] This Rtook place almost two years after the interrogation of Christian Rakovsky by Stalin's secret police, and Rakovsky had alluded to the fact that the Powers That Be wanted to restore Trotsky. There is reason to believe Stalin was fully informed of Hitler's upcoming aggression considering his aggressive industrialisation and rebuilding of nationalism as opposed to toying with the relatively weak concept of "Proletariat of the world." Stalin dismantled war related industries, and relocated them to the East of the Urals during the German invasion, a move which would literally save the Soviet war machine. This was done well in advance of the war. During the ceremony of the signing of the 1939 Molotov-Ribbentrop agreement, Stalin remarked, "Of course we are not forgetting that your ultimate aim is to attack us."[737] There is indication that he may have had foreknowledge of future Allied involvement, resulting in the future diversion of the Nazis and the outcome of the war itself. Admiral N.G Kuznetsov recollects that when

---

[736] For those who deny conspiracy, the question to be asked is, what force did a "lone intellectual" like Trotsky represent, that Stalin was so keen to have him eliminated?
[737] Dmitri Vokogonov, Stalin, Triumph and Tragedy Ed. and Trans. by Harold Shuckman. (Weidenfield and Nicholson, 1991) 385.

Germany attacked the Soviet Union, all Soviet forces were made combat ready only 10 to 11 hours prior to the attack[738] and Stalin failed to make "[...] the simplest precautionary measures."[739]

Lend-Lease: How Roosevelt built the Red Army

> "Major Jordan," he began, "we know all about you, and why you are here. You might as well understand that officers who get too officious are likely to find themselves on an island somewhere in the South Seas."
>
> A Lend-Lease liaison officer to Major Jordan, January 1944[740]

The Lend-Lease program began in March 1941, nine months before Pearl Harbor. A total of $50.1 billion of supplies were passed over to the Allies by a neutral United States. The Soviets received $11.3 billion, apart from receiving additional aid from Canada. 1,981 American locomotives were supplied to the USSR. The Soviet airforce exclusively used American fuel. A major part of all Red Army trucks were American made. 375,883 American trucks were supplied, along with 14,795 aircraft and 7056 tanks. In addition, $1,674,586,000 worth of "Agricultural Products" was received by the Soviets, which caused shortages and dislocations in the American economy.[741] So much copper was sent to the Soviet Union that bus bars of metal on circuit boards were replaced with conductors of silver, borrowed from the American Treasury's vaults at West Point.[742] By the end of 1941, the Red Army was the largest in the world. In tanks it outnumbered and in airplanes it equaled the rest of the World's armies put together. Unbeknowst to the American public, many items were intended for development of the *postwar* Soviet economy. Crates of telephone wire were shipped to the Soviet Union at a time when the war was ending.[743] In addition, entire factories were delivered. One tire plant, one aluminum rolling mill, several pipe fabricating works, two food factories, three gas generating

---

738 Admiral N.G Kuznetsov, "At The Naval Headquarters," Quoted in Suny, Soviet History 310.
739 Admiral N.G Kuznetsov, "At The Naval Headquarters," Quoted in Suny, Soviet History 313.
740 George Racey Jordan, Richard L. Stokes, From Major Jordan's Diaries (NY: Harcourt, Brace and Company, 1952) 193. An archived copy is available at <http://www.sweetliberty.org/issues/wars/jordan/01.html>
741 Jordan & Stokes, Diaries 127.
742 Jordan & Stokes, Diaries 130-131.
743 Jordan & Stokes, Diaries 132.

units, one petroleum refinery, seventeen steam plants, three hydroelectric plants, five plants for synthetic rubber and two neoprene rubber factories were all billed to the American taxpayer under the Lend-Lease program.[744] In other words, Lend-Lease was also building the postwar Soviet Empire, as well as its future internal Red Army, which would police the conquered subject populations of the Soviet Union.

In addition, the US government provided the Soviets with duplicates of the plates the Americans used to print the currency of Allied occupied Germany. The plane carrying the plates and other printing equipment crashed in Siberia (according to the Soviets) and a duplicate shipment of the same was sent again. The Soviets were not made accountable to the amount of currency they could print. This Soviet printed Allied currency was redeemed for American dollars in Germany. After a deficit of $250,000,000 was charged to the American treasury, the Allied currency could no longer be used to pay Allied personnel in Germany.[745]

Lend-Lease and the Soviet Atomic Bomb

Major George Racey Jordan was a liasion officer for Lend-Lease aid to the Soviets. He later testified before the US Congress that material earmarked for the Soviets also included supplies for rebuilding Soviet industry after the war, as well as the Soviet Atomic bomb.

Among the material ferreted to the Soviets under the Lend-Lease program in 1942 was graphite, over $13 million worth of aluminium tubes, cadmium and thorium.[746]

Jordan came across tonnes of material being airfreighted to the Soviet Union in black suitcases. These suitcases were given the same status of diplomatic pouches and were exempt from inspection. They were always guarded by Russian soldiers. On one occasion Jordan forcibly inpected some of these suitcases to find detailed technical blueprints, maps of sensitive American installations, reports of American foreign attaches to their superiors in Washington, and other sensitive information. Jordan came across a State Department folder with the name of Alger Hiss on it, which contained hundreds of photostats of millitary reports.[747] Another suitcase contained a note on White House letterhead and signed

[744] Jordan & Stokes, Diaries 134-135, 139.
[745] Jordan & Stokes, Diaries 230.
[746] Jordan & Stokes, Diaries 33.
[747] Jordan & Stokes, Diaries 78.

H.H, possibly Harry Hopkins, who was in charge of Roosevelt's Lend-Lease.[748] An exhibit was attached which bore the legend of Oak Ridge, Manhattan Engineering District.[749] The exhibit was about the ongoing development of the atomic bomb, and contained references to uranium, cyclotrons, protons, heavy water etc. At this time, only 200 people were supposed to be privy to this extremely well guarded project The Soviets may have been privy to the Manhattan Project as early as October 1942.[750] Corroborating Jordan was Royall Edward Norton, a navyman who served in Kodiak, Alaska. He recalled inspecting a box on a Soviet bound plane, which contained a blueprint for the atomic structure of uranium.[751]

Jordan claims that Harry Hopkins personally phoned him in April 1943, asking him to arrange a shipment of uranium to the Soviets, and requested that this shipment be off the books.[752] Hopkins was not ignorant of the Manhattan project. He was in fact, chosen as an intermediary to present Roosevelt with the idea of the atomic bomb.[753] The authors of *The Venona Secrets: Exposing Soviet Espionage and America's Traitors* have built a case against Hopkins that he was a Soviet agent.[754] The uranium was sourced from Canada.[755] Lend-Lease administrators issued a certificate of release, without which the consignment could not have moved.[756] A total of 15 boxes were dispatched on June 9th 1943 to the Soviet Union.[757] This was however, the tip of the iceberg. In 1949, it would be proved that three consignments of uranium chemicals had been sent to Russia, totalling 1465 pounds, along with 2.2 pounds of uranium metal, at a time when the American total stock was 4.5 pounds.[758]

Reciprocally, the Lend-Lease conduit also became a venue for active Soviet espionage. To quote Jordan,

---

[748] Jordan & Stokes, Diaries 80.
[749] Jordan & Stokes, Diaries 81.
[750] Jordan & Stokes, Diaries 86.
[751] Jordan & Stokes, Diaries 245.
[752] Jordan & Stokes, Diaries 86.
[753] Jordan & Stokes, Diaries 122.
[754] Herbert Romerstein and Eric Breindel, The Venona Secrets: Exposing Soviet Espionage and America's Traitors (Regnery Publishing Inc, 2001).
[755] Jordan & Stokes, Diaries 95.
[756] Jordan & Stokes, Diaries 98.
[757] Jordan & Stokes, Diaries 99.
[758] Jordan & Stokes, Diaries 95.

> [...] the entry of Soviet personnel into the United States was completely uncontrolled. Planes were arriving regularly from Moscow with unidentified Russians aboard. I would see them jump off planes, hop over fences, and run for taxicabs. They seemed to know in advance exactly where they were headed, and how to get there. It was an ideal set-up for planting spies in this country, with false identities, for use during and after the war.[759]

The Deportation of Crimean Tatars

When the Nazis captured Crimea, up to 8000-20,000 Crimean Tatars were formed into village defence brigades, and served under the Nazis.[760] But when the Nazis retreated, these collaborators were allowed to evacuate with them.[761] When the Red Army returned, an organised deportation of Crimean Tatars was conducted. On the night of 18th may 1944, NKVD motorized infantry units surrounded all Crimean villages, and took all residents at gunpoint to the nearest railway stations.[762] Able-bodied men were separated from women, children and seniors.[763] The trains took them to Tashkent, from where they were scattered throughout the less fertile areas of Uzbekistan, Kazakhstan and Kyrgyzstan.[764] Crimean Tatar males who had been forced into fighting the Red Army on the front (and thus avoided deportation) were demobilized and along with other males from Crimea, were organised into labour brigades in Siberia.[765]

This atrocious event was completely covered up by the Western media. Crimean sources claim that up to 46 per cent of Crimean Tatars were killed in mass executions prior to deportation.[766] Ann Sheehy and Bogdan Nahylo claim that between 200,000-250,000 Crimean Tatars were involved in the deportations, and Crimean sources claim that 110,000 died in the process.[767] The Kremlin "[...] in vivid testimony to the viciousness of the times, claims in its defence that 'only' 22 per cent of this nation died in the deportations."[768] A top-secret report from the

---

759 Jordan & Stokes, Diaries 66.
760 Brian Glyn Williams, "The Crimean Tatar Exile in Central Asia: A Case Study in Group Destruction and Survival," Central Asian Survey 17.2 (1998): 293.
761 Williams, "The Crimean Tatar Exile," 293.
762 Williams, "The Crimean Tatar Exile,"294.
763 Williams, "The Crimean Tatar Exile,"294.
764 Williams, "The Crimean Tatar Exile," 295.
765 Williams, "The Crimean Tatar Exile," 295.
766 Williams, "The Crimean Tatar Exile," 300.
767 Williams, "The Crimean Tatar Exile," 300.
768 Williams, "The Crimean Tatar Exile," 300.

NKVD chief Lavrenty Beria to Stalin, dated July 4th 1944, claims that 183,155 Tatars had been "resettled."[769] A more accurate estimate can be obtained from the work of R.J. Rummel. To quote,

> In his work on genocide in the Soviet Union, R.J. Rummel estimates that out of the 1,600,000 members of the eight Soviet nations deported during the war, almost one in three (approximately 530,000) died, vividly demonstrating that the wartime deportation of Soviet nationalities was one of the best kept examples of genocide in the twentieth century.[770]

The Crimean Tatars, the Volga Germans and the Meshketian Turks were forced to remain in exile throughout the existence of the Soviet Union.[771] Similar to the Crimean Tatars, the Volga Germans were deported for agricultural development of the Kazakhstan steppe. Up to two million Muslims of various nationalities were killed in genocides.[772]

In other words, World War II was used as a smokescreen to disperse and destroy ethnic, religious and national groups. In the case of the Tatars, the Soviets needed able-bodied slaves for the development of the Eastern wastelands. The same top-secret NKVD report quoted earlier makes reference to "able-bodied Tatar special settlers." Many Crimean Tatars have sought to return to Crimea, only to find themselves subjected to racism of the transplanted Slav settlers.

Stalin in Postwar Soviet Union: Koba grows up

After the war, Stalin acquired a monolithic prominence as a war hero. It is clear that he was unwilling to return power to his backers. And neither was he enthusiastic about continuing to be their pawn. What inspired this change of heart may never be known. Either way, his backers figured this out as well, and responded by trying to eliminate Stalin. Stalin was quick to judge the situation and either concocted the "Doctor's plot" or made use of a plot against him to round up enemies. Despite wholehearted assistance to the Soviet Union for the transfer of the

---

[769] Lavrenty Beria, "Report from Beria to Stalin," July 4th 1944. Quoted in Ronald Grigor Suny, The structure of Soviet History - essays and documents (Oxford University Press, 2003) 314.

[770] Williams, "The Crimean Tatar Exile," 300.

[771] Williams, "The Crimean Tatar Exile," 286.

[772] Eric Margolis, "The 20th Century's Worst Crime Goes Unpunished," The Toronto Sun November 16th 2003. Also published on ericmargolis.com <http://www.ericmargolis.com/archives/2003/11/the_20th_centur.php> Accessed 13/12/06

ingredients of the atomic bomb, the Powers that Be were unwilling to transfer technology crucial for assembling the device. This is because it became clear that Stalin had other motives. He wanted to rid the Soviet Union of the Illuminati operatives he had earlier replaced the Leninists with. The large number of Soviet spies caught in the United States hints at Stalin's attempts to desperately obtain this last bit of crucial technology independently, through his own operatives. For example, why were the Rosenbergs executed in a manner as if to send a warning to all Stalin operatives? Why were those seeking to help Stalin easily caught and arrested, unlike those who helped him during the war?[773] With atomic power in his hand, Stalin would be in a position to throttle external pressure. According to new revelations in the book *Stalin: The First In-depth Biography Based on Explosive New Documents from Russia's Secret Archives* by Edvard Radzinsky, Stalin may have been contemplating serious use of these weapons on his globalist enemies in London and New York.

Afterwards, there was clearly some struggle between Stalin and the Powers that Be, and by then, he had "[…] spun it into a vast conspiracy, led by Jews under the United States direction to kill him […]"[774] New research into his last days has shown that he had ordered the construction of four giant prison camps in Siberia, the Arctic circle and Kazakhstan.[775] On 5th March 1953, buses were seen parked all around Moscow to shuttle political prisoners to these camps[776]. It is very likely that all Globalist operatives who had replaced the Leninists prior to the War were earmarked for annihilation. The BBC report further reveals that KGB chief Lavrenty Beria had knowledge of the plan and concludes that it is highly likely that Beria administered poison to Stalin. Concurrently, there was a move on all of Stalin's most trusted henchmen. To quote, "[…] some of the dictator's entourage especially close to him disappeared at the same time."[777]

---

[773] Klaus Fuchs, Jonathan Pollard, Julius & Ethel Rosenberg, Morton Sobell, Elizabeth Terrill Bentley, Aleksandr Semyonovich Feklisov, David Greenglass, Ruth Greenglass, Theodore Hall, William Perl, Harry Gold and Max Elitcher.

[774] Michael Wines, "New Study supports idea Stalin was poisoned," New York Times March 5th 2003. late ed.: A3.

[775] Michael Wines, "New Study supports idea Stalin was poisoned," New York Times March 5th 2003. late ed.: A3.

[776]Leonida Krushelnycky, "The mystery of Stalin's death," BBC News World Edition 24/02/03. <http://newswww.bbc.net.uk/2/hi/europe/2793501.stm> Web page as of 16/03/04.

[777] Nicholas V. Riasanovsky, A History of Russia (Oxford University Press, 1963) 596.

After Stalin, the Soviet Union was transferred to defacto Globalist control, and was managed remotely from centres of the banking elite in the Western world. Only puppets and vain minded weaklings were entrusted with the official high command of the Soviet Union.

Nazi Germany

A Collaborative Effort

Only Germany possessed the location advantage, numbers and resources for a staged aggression against the Soviet Union. The Nazi state was built and run not just by Hitler and "Germans," but by a cosmopolitan group working intricately together. To quote Springmeier,

> As previously mentioned one of the Illuminati survivors I have worked with was alive during W.W.II and has memories of how the Russians, Germans, and Americans in the Illuminati kept working together even during W.W. II. A very close examination of what really went on behind the scenes, especially at the top shows that the parts of the Illuminati have continued to collaborate together even during wars.[778]

Rearming of Germany

The Powers that Be diverted American capital towards the rebuilding of Germany (and therefore Hitler) immediately after the conclusion of World War I. The largest chemical conglomerate in history, I.G Farben, was created by Wall Street capital. This conglomerate became the heart of the Nazi war machine. Synthetic rubber was developed to continue rubber production during blockades. A process of manufacturing ammonia through air was invented to avoid dependence on Chilean nitrates. I.G Farben would produce more than 80% of the rubber the Nazis required, along with the Zyklon B gas used in the Jewish Holocaust. The Rockerfeller owned Standard Oil developed a process of manufacturing synthetic gasoline from coal, so that Germany could participate in the war for the long term. Even the anti-Semitic Henry Ford was called upon to render industrial assistance to the Nazis. The German Steel trust was set up by the Harriman family and Prescott Bush. Interestingly, many of the plants of these Wall Street backed companies

[778] Fritz Springmeier, Bloodlines of the Illuminati (Spring Arbor distributors, 1998) 390. GlobalGrey PDF edition 2013 <http://www.globalgrey.co.uk/Pages/Books-Conspiracies/Bloodlines-Of-The-Illuminati.html> Web page as of 03/07/13.

in Germany escaped the wrath of Allied bombardment. And the elitists on the boards of these companies were never tried later at Nuremberg.

Enter Wall Street

Anthony Sutton in his definitive work *Wall Street and the rise of Hitler*[779] sheds light on how the German I.G. Farben, the largest chemical conglomerate in history, was created. This conglomerate was created through the exhaustive support of Wall Street capital. To quote Sutton

> On the eve of World War II the German chemical complex of I.G. Farben was the largest chemical manufacturing enterprise in the world, with extraordinary political and economic power and influence within the Hitlerian Nazi state. I. G. has been aptly described as "a state within a state.

Rothschild affiliated J.P Morgan and Co. came up with the Dawes plan through American banker Charles Dawes, which involved loaning capital to Nazi Germany and setting up I.G Farben. Three Wall Street banking houses, Dillon, Read & Co., Harris, Forbes & Co., and National City handled three-quarters of the loans used to create I.G Farben.[780] The operative who coordinated this funding was Max Warburg. Warburg is seen as being affiliated to Rothschild interests. Hitler would meet with Max Warburg and apparently had no qualms over the latter's Jewishness. Max Warburg directed I.G. Farben's German division. During World War I, he was head of the German Secret Police and helped Lenin and Trotsky into Russia. He was also head of the Frankfurt branch of the Warburg bank (affiliated with Rothschilds). He then became director of I.G Farben Germany while his brother Paul Warburg became the head of the American Warburg bank, head of I.G Farben America and the first chairman of the privately owned Federal Reserve Bank of the United States.

In essence, the Nazi war machine was like a dummy corporation being erected by Wall Street capital. Hitler would later have the German branch of the Warburg bank shut down to hide their association to the Nazi war machine. Even John Foster Dulles of the CIA was involved in the secret

---

[779] Anthony C. Sutton, Wall Street and the rise of Hitler (GSG and Associates, 1976). Ebook edition. <http://www.reformed-theology.org/html/books/wall_street/index.html> Web page as of 16/03/04

[780] Michael Haupt, "What Really caused world war 2," ThreeWorldWars.com <http://www.threeworldwars.com/world-war-2/ww2.htm> Web page as of 11/07/2004

rearmament of Germany.[781] While the Germans are an industrious people, establishment historians make us believe that they possessed some superhuman regenerative capabilities, and Hitler was able to circumvent the Versailles restrictions all on his own. Another diversion is that the Rockefellers and the Rothschilds were competing against each other for securing Nazi contracts. In reality, rebuilding Germany required large amounts of capital to be sunk in, and was not exactly as lucrative as it sounded. It is obvious that Roosevelt was fully aware of this activity. For example, William Dodd, American ambassador to Germany before World War II, wrote to President Roosevelt:

> Much as I believe in peace as our best policy, I cannot avoid the fears which Wilson emphasized more than once in conversations with me, August 15, 1915 and later: the breakdown of democracy in all Europe will be a disaster to the people. But what can you do? At the present moment more than a hundred American corporations have subsidiaries here or cooperative understandings. The Du Ponts have three allies in Germany that are aiding in the armament business. Their chief ally is the I. G .Farben Company, a part of the Government which gives 200,000 marks a year to one propaganda organization operating on American opinion. Standard 0il Company (New York sub-company) sent $2,000,000 here in December 1933 and has made $500,000 a year helping Germans make Ersatz gas for war purposes; but Standard 0il cannot take any of its earnings out of the country except in goods. They do little of this, report their earnings at home, but do not explain the facts. The International Harvester Company president told me their business here rose 33% a year(arms manufacture, I believe), but they could take nothing out. Even our airplanes people have secret arrangement with Krupps. General Motor Company and Ford do enormous businesses here through their subsidiaries and take no profits out. I mention these facts because they complicate things and add to war dangers. If you wish proof of this story, talk with our Commercial Attaché here, Douglas Miller, in the United States till early December.
>
> *Full quote can be viewed at the FDR library.*[782]

Anthony Sutton and Fritz Springmeier reveal further information on the American rearmament of Nazi Germany. To quote Springmeier,

---

[781]Fritz Springmeier, Bloodlines of the Illuminati (Spring Arbor distributors, 1998) 131-132. GlobalGrey PDF edition 2013 <http://www.globalgrey.co.uk/Pages/Books-Conspiracies/Bloodlines-Of-The-Illuminati.html> Web page as of 03/07/13.

[782] William Dodd, FDR Library: Dodd 11/09/36 <http://www.fdrlibrary.marist.edu/andyc/fdr/psf/box32/a300l07.html> Accessed 25/10/06.

During the 1920s, the W. Averill Harriman, Prescott Bush, Fritz Thyssen and Friedrich Flick created several entitles to help finance Hitler and to produce the weapons Hitler would need to fight W.W. II. One of these companies was the German Steel Trust (*Vereinigte Stahlwerke*). This company produced 35% of Nazi Germany's explosives, 50.8% of Germany's pig iron, 38.5% of Nazi Germany's galvanized steel, 36% of Germany's heavy plate, 22.1 % of Germany's wire, and many other things essential for Hitler. If it had not been Harriman' and Bush's money helping Thyssen who was Hitler's major backer, Hitler would never had been able to have launched W.W. II. Thyssen even wrote a book in the 1930. I paid Hitler (now rare) telling about how he financed Hitler and the Nazis beginning in Oct. 1923.[783]

On the German side, all prominent German industrialists lent their support to the rearmament of Germany. Sutton quotes the U.S. Kilgore Committee Records:

Hugo Stinnes was an early contributor to the Nazi Party. By 1924 other prominent industrialists and financiers, among them Fritz Thyssen, Albert Voegler, Adolph [sic] Kirdorf, and Kurt von Schroeder, were secretly giving substantial sums to the Nazis. In 1931 members of the coal owners' association which Kirdorf headed pledged themselves to pay 50 pennings for each ton of coal sold, the money to go to the organization, which Hitler was building.[784]

Among the figures in American government, industry and banks supporting Hitler, Sutton notes that:

Albert Voegler mentioned in the Kilgore Committee list of early Hitler supporters were the German representatives on the Dawes Plan Commission. Owen Young of General Electric was a U.S. representative for the Dawes Plan and formulated its successor, the Young Plan.[785]

According to Anthony Sutton, Hitler created inner circles in the Nazi party, populated by bankers and industrialists who supported him. One of the most important of these circles was known first as the Keppler

---

783 Fritz Springmeier, Bloodlines of the Illuminati (Spring Arbor distributors, 1998) 47. GlobalGrey PDF edition 2013 <http://www.globalgrey.co.uk/Pages/Books-Conspiracies/Bloodlines-Of-The-Illuminati.html> Web page as of 03/07/13.

784 Elimination of German Resources 648. Quoted in Anthony C. Sutton, Wall Street and the rise of Hitler (GSG and Associates, 1976). Ebook edition. <http://reformed-theology.org/html/books/wall_street/chapter_07.htm#31> Web page as of 16/03/04

785 Elimination of German Resources 648. Quoted in Sutton, Rise of Hitler

Circle.[786] This clique originated as a group of German businessmen, such as Hitler's friend Wilhelm Keppler, who supported Hitler's rise to power during 1933. In the mid-1930s the Keppler Circle came under the influence and protection of SS Chief Heinrich Himmler and under the organizational control of the Cologne banker and prominent Nazi businessman, Kurt von Schroeder. Schroeder was head of the J.H. Stein Bank in Germany and associated with the L. Henry Schroeder Banking Corporation of New York. It is within this innermost of such inner circles, the very core of the Nazi war machine, that we find big movers and shakers of Wall Street.[787] For example, one member of the Keppler circle, Emil Helfrich, was the chairman of Dapag, which in turn was owned by Standard Oil. Other members of the Keppler circle can be found on the boards of American corporations such as A. E. G. and I. T. T.

I.G. Farben

To quote Anthony Sutton,

> The Farben cartel dated from 1925, when organizing genius Hermann Schmitz (with Wall Street financial assistance) created the super-giant chemical enterprise out of six already giant German chemical companies — Badische Aniline, Bayer, Agfa, Hoechst, Weiler-ter-Meer, and Griesheim-Elektron. These companies were merged to become Internationale Gesellschaft Farbenindustrie A.G. — or I.G. Farben for short. Twenty years later the same Hermann Schmitz was put on trial at Nuremberg for war crimes committed by the I. G. cartel. Other I. G. Farben directors were placed on trial but the American affiliates of I. G. Farben and the American directors of I. G. itself were quietly forgotten; the truth was buried in the archives.[788]

Sutton further states that:

---

[786] Anthony C. Sutton, Wall Street and the rise of Hitler (GSG and Associates, 1976). Ebook edition. <http://reformed-theology.org/html/books/wall_street/chapter_09.htm#7> Web page as of 16/03/04.

[787] Anthony C. Sutton, Rise of Hitler (GSG and Associates, 1976). Ebook edition. <http://reformed-theology.org/html/books/wall_street/chapter_09.htm> Web page as of 16/03/04.

[788] Anthony C. Sutton, Wall Street and the rise of Hitler (GSG and Associates, 1976). Ebook edition. <http://reformed-theology.org/html/books/wall_street/chapter_02.htm> Web page as of 16/03/04.

[…] I.G. Farben contributed 400,000 RM to Hitler's political "slush fund." It was this secret fund, which financed the Nazi seizure of control in March 1933. Many years earlier Farben had obtained Wall Street funds for the 1925 cartelisation and expansion in Germany and $30 million for American I. G. in 1929.[789]

Qualified observers have argued that Germany could not have gone to war in 1939 without I. G. Farben. Between 1927 and the beginning of World War II, I.G. Farben doubled in size, an expansion made possible in great part by American technical assistance and by American bond issues, such as the one for $30 million offered by National City Bank. By 1939 I. G. acquired a participation and managerial influence in some 380 other German firms and over 500 foreign firms. The Farben Empire owned its own coalmines, its own electric power plants, iron and steel units, banks, research units, and numerous commercial enterprises. There were over 2,000 cartel agreements between I. G. and foreign firms — including Standard Oil of New Jersey, Dupont, Alcoa, Dow Chemical, and others in the United States.[790]

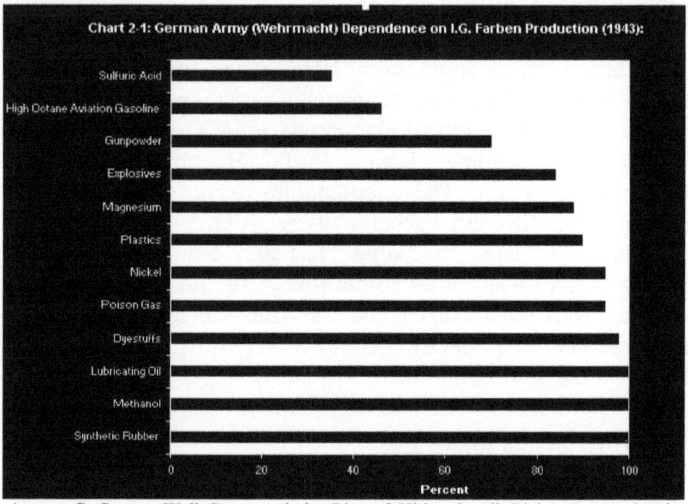

Source: Antony C. Sutton, Wall Street and the Rise of Hitler © All Rights Reserved. Altered and Minimalized Reproduction Under Fair Dealing.

---

789 Anthony C. Sutton, Wall Street and the rise of Hitler (GSG and Associates, 1976). Ebook edition. <http://reformed-theology.org/html/books/wall_street/chapter_02.htm> Web page as of 16/03/04.

790 Anthony C. Sutton, Wall Street and the rise of Hitler (GSG and Associates, 1976). Ebook edition. <http://reformed-theology.org/html/books/wall_street/chapter_02.htm> Web page as of 16/03/04.

According to Fritz Springmeier, the Duponts are allegedly a privileged bloodline. DOW chemical, another American corporation mentioned by Sutton would later become infamous for one of the worst industrial accidents in history, the Bhopal Gas Tragedy.

To further quote Sutton,

> "There were numerous Farben arrangements with American firms, including cartel marketing arrangements, patent agreements, and technical exchanges as exemplified in the Standard Oil-Ethyl technology transfers."[791]

I.G. Farben's subsidiaries in more than a 100 countries.

I.G. Farben's Headquarters in Frankfurt later survived Allied bombardment.

Employees in an I.G. factory, 1938.

I.G. Farben monthly, June-July 1943. Note war graphics.

Pictures sourced from Dr. Rath Health Foundation. copyright © 2005 All Rights Reserved. For more images in high resolution, please visit http://www4.dr-rath-foundation.org/open_letters/omgus/omgus10.htm Copyright status of some images is unknown. Minimized Reproduction Under Fair Dealing

The largest I.G. Farben Factory in Auschwitz, which was supported by labourers from concentration camps.

The Rockefellers were the founders of Standard Oil that became best known for its infamous monopoly tactics. The name was later changed to S.O and Esso may have been derived from these initials. I.G. Farben, with its huge contractual relationship with North America, was able to double up as an espionage base for the Nazis. To quote Sutton,

---

791 Anthony C. Sutton, Wall Street and the rise of Hitler (GSG and Associates, 1976). Ebook edition. <http://reformed-theology.org/html/books/wall_street/chapter_02.htm> Web page as of 16/03/04.

> The Berlin N.W. 7 office of I.G. Farben was the key Nazi overseas espionage centre. The unit operated under Farben director Max Ilgner, nephew of I.G. Farben president Hermann Schmitz. Max Ilgner and Hermann Schmitz were on the board of American I.G., with fellow directors Henry Ford of Ford Motor Company, Paul Warburg of Bank of Manhattan, and Charles E. Mitchell of the Federal Reserve Bank of New York.[792]

I.G. Farben was Nazi Germany's largest earner of foreign exchange.[793] Despite a complete blackout by the press, some of this information would trickle down. And that's when PR firms were hired for I.G. Farben. To quote Sutton,

> The most notable public relations firm in the late 1920s and 1930s was Ivy Lee & T.J. Ross of New York. Ivy Lee had previously undertaken a public relations campaign for the Rockefellers, to spruce up the Rockerfeller name among the American public. The firm had also produced a sycophantic book entitled USSR, undertaking the same clean-up task for the Soviet Union — even while Soviet labor camps were in full blast in the late 20s and early 30s. From 1929 onwards Ivy Lee became public relations counsel for I. G. Farben in the United States.[794]

The Rockefellers sold Hitler oil via Spain to keep the war going on, through their Standard Oil refinery at Aruba. Allied submarines never sank these tankers. Spain stayed neutral during the war to serve as a conduit of Allied supplies to the Nazis. Similarly, either side did not attack Switzerland since keeping it neutral was important to the Powers that Be. At the close of the war, German and Allied Globalists would conduct meetings in Switzerland to plan the future dividing of I.G Farben assets.

---

[792] Anthony C. Sutton, Wall Street and the rise of Hitler (GSG and Associates, 1976). Ebook edition. <http://reformed-theology.org/html/books/wall_street/chapter_02.htm> Web page as of 16/03/04.

[793] Anthony C. Sutton, Wall Street and the rise of Hitler (GSG and Associates, 1976). Ebook edition. <http://reformed-theology.org/html/books/wall_street/chapter_02.htm> Web page as of 16/03/04.

[794] Anthony C. Sutton, Wall Street and the rise of Hitler (GSG and Associates, 1976). Ebook edition. <http://reformed-theology.org/html/books/wall_street/chapter_02.htm> Web page as of 16/03/04.

Henry Ford merged his German assets with I.G. Farben in 1928. Ford was a renowned anti-Semite but the Jewish Rothschilds and Rockefellers had no qualms teaming up with him to back Nazi Germany. A U.S. Air Force bombing intelligence report written in 1943 noted "Principal wartime activities [of the Ford plant] are probably manufacture of light trucks and of spare parts for all the Ford trucks and cars in service in Axis Europe."[795] Pictured on the right is a 1944 German ad for Ford trucks. Henry Ford (who was probably not an elitist[796]) was awarded "the Grand Cross of the German Eagle, a Nazi decoration for distinguished foreigners. The New York Times reported that it was the first time the Grand Cross had been awarded in the United States.[797] The idea was to make Henry Ford the centrepiece of Nazi-American industrial collaboration, which would help distract from the major banking and oil magnates behind I.G. Farben. One should consider why Hitler did not award any Grand Crosses to the Rothschilds and Rockefellers, who played a far more important role in the rearmament of Germany. For example, the Rockefeller owned Standard Oil facilitated the technological means for the Nazis to overcome their fuel shortages.

I.G Farben discovered the hydrogenation process (turning coal into gasoline). The Germans were able to overcome their fuel shortage and were able to fight World War II through the use of synthetic fuels. Hydrogenation technology would not have been fully developed by World War II, but I.G. Farben made a deal with Rockerfeller Standard Oil, who was able to complete the research, facilitating the war.

---

795 Josiah E. Dubois, Jr., Generals in Grey Suits (London: The Bodley Head, 1958) 251. Quoted in Anthony C. Sutton, Wall Street and the rise of Hitler (GSG and Associates, 1976). Ebook edition. <http://reformed-theology.org/html/books/wall_street/chapter_06.htm> Web page as of 16/03/04.

796 Though the author cannot say the same of his successors.

797 New York Times, August l, 1938. Quoted in Anthony C. Sutton, Wall Street and the rise of Hitler (GSG and Associates, 1976). Ebook edition. <http://reformed-theology.org/html/books/wall_street/index.htm> Web page as of 16/03/04.

Germany would produce 75 per cent of its fuel synthetically by the end of the war.[798] Standard Oil would later "loan" $20 million of high-grade aviation fuel to Germany after Hitler invaded Poland and Austria.[799] In 1938, I.G Farben would "borrow" 500 tonnes of Tetra Ethyl lead (a gas additive) from Standard Oil.[800]

To quote Springmeier,

> One of the largest tank manufacturers for Germany was Opel, which was controlled by the J.P. Morgan Group. Another company connected to the J.P. Morgan Group was Bendix Aviation, 'which supplied data [to Germany] on automatic pilots, aircraft Instruments and aircraft and diesel engine starters.[801]

ITT (International telephone and Telegraph) was a leading telephone equipment company that was indirectly owned by banking interests. To quote Anthony Sampson,

> Thus while I.T.T. Focke-Wolfe planes were bombing Allied ships, and I. T. T. lines were passing information to German submarines, I.T.T. direction finders were saving other ships from torpedoes.[802]

The parent board of I.T.T. reflected J.P. Morgan interests, with Morgan partners Arthur M. Anderson and Russell Leffingwell.

The Rockefeller Standard Oil helped channel Rumanian oil to the Nazis. To quote,

---

[798] Michael Haupt, "What Really caused world war 2," ThreeWorldWars.com <http://www.threeworldwars.com/world-war-2/ww2.htm> Web page as of 11/07/2004

[799] Michael Haupt, "What Really caused world war 2," ThreeWorldWars.com <http://www.threeworldwars.com/world-war-2/ww2.htm> Web page as of 11/07/2004

[800] Anthony C. Sutton, Wall Street and the rise of Hitler (GSG and Associates, 1976). Ebook edition. < http://reformed-theology.org/html/books/wall_street/chapter_02.htm> Web page as of 16/03/04

[801] Fritz Springmeier, Bloodlines of the Illuminati (Spring Arbor distributors, 1998) 212. GlobalGrey PDF edition 2013 <http://www.globalgrey.co.uk/Pages/Books-Conspiracies/Bloodlines-Of-The-Illuminati.html> Web page as of 03/07/13.

[802] Anthony Sampson, The Sovereign State of I.T.T. (New York: Stein & Day, 1973) 40. Quoted in Anthony C. Sutton, Wall Street and the rise of Hitler (GSG and Associates, 1976). Ebook edition. <http://reformed-theology.org/html/books/wall_street/chapter_05.htm> Web page as of 16/03/04

Before Rumania was invaded by the Germans, it was selling oil to Germany. Life magazine of February 19, 1940, has a picture of Rumanian oil being loaded into oil tank cars. The picture has a caption under it which reads, in part: "Oil for Germany moves in these tank cars of American Essolube and British Shell out of Creditui Minier yards near Ploesti (Rumania.) Notice that cars are marked for German-American Oil Co. and German Railways, consigned to Hamburg and Wuppertal in Germany. They were sent from Germany to speed up Rumanian oil shipments." This picture was taken after Germany had invaded Austria and Poland, yet American and British oil companies are transporting oil for the German government, (the tank cars in the picture are clearly marked "Essolube," and "Shell").[803]

While the Allies were advancing through France, The Powers that Be conducted meetings between the I.G Farben German and American directors in Switzerland, to protect their assets from Allied attacks, and to negotiate on the future of these assets.

The I.G. Farben HQ survived Allied bombing raids.

It is said that General Eisenhower gave specific instructions to avoid Allied bombing of the I. G. Farben Headquarters in Frankfurt. By the end of the war the refineries owned by overseas interests had experienced minimal damage.

After the end of the war, the tribunals that investigated Nazi war criminals censored "any materials recording Western assistance to

---

[803] Michael Haupt, "What Really caused world war 2," ThreeWorldWars.com <http://www.threeworldwars.com/world-war-2/ww2.htm> Web page as of 11/07/2004

Hitler" according to historian Anthony C. Sutton.[804] The American directors were never held accountable at Nuremberg. Three Germans on the Board of Governors for I.G. Farben were convicted as war criminals after the war, but major American figures were not. As for those convicted, it is hard to tell whether they served the full sentence or got away like Alfred Krupp.

The Directors of American I.G. at 1930:

American I. G. Director	**Citizenship**	**Other Major Associations**
Carl BOSCH	German	FORD MOTOR CO. A-G **Trial not held or acquitted**
Edsel B. FORD	U.S.	FORD MOTOR CO. DETROIT **Trial not held or acquitted**
Max ILGNER	German	Directed I.G. FARBEN N.W.7 (INTELLIGENCE) office. Guilty at Nuremberg War Crimes Trials.
F. Ter MEER	German	Guilty at Nuremberg War Crimes Trials
H.A. METZ	U.S.	Director of I.G. Farben Germany and BANK OF MANHATTAN (U.S.) **Trial not held or acquitted**
C.E. MITCHELL	U.S.	Director of FEDERAL RESERVE BANK OF N.Y. and NATIONAL CITY BANK **Trial not held or acquitted**
Herman SCHMITZ	German	On boards of I.G. Farben (President) (Germany) Deutsche Bank (Germany) and BANK FOR INTERNATIONAL SETTLEMENTS. Guilty at Nuremberg War Crimes Trials.
Walter TEAGLE	U.S.	Director FEDERAL RESERVE BANK OF NEW YORK and STANDARD OIL OF NEW JERSEY **Trial not held or acquitted**
W.H. yon RATH	Naturalized	Director of GERMAN GENERAL U.S. ELECTRIC (A.E.G.) **Trial not held or acquitted**
Paul M. WARBURG	U.S.	First member of the FEDERAL RESERVE BANK OF NEW YORK and BANK OF MANHATTAN **Trial not held or acquitted**
W.E. WEISS	U.S.	Sterling Products **Trial not held or acquitted**

Source: Moody's Manual of Investments; 1930, p. 2149.

Note: Walter DUISBERG (U.S.), W. GRIEF (U.S.), and Adolf KUTTROFF (U.S.) were also Directors of American I.G. Farben at this period.

Source: Anthony Sutton-Wall street and the rise of Hitler, Chapter One. © Antony Sutton, All Rights Reserved. Modified and Minimized Reproduction Under Fair Dealing.

***Bold text has been added and was not present in the original table of Sutton.**

[804] Fritz Springmeier, Bloodlines of the Illuminati (Spring Arbor distributors, 1998) 212. GlobalGrey PDF edition 2013 <http://www.globalgrey.co.uk/Pages/Books-Conspiracies/Bloodlines-Of-The-Illuminati.html> Web page as of 03/07/13.

The Onassis Connection

The Onassis family kept the war going by selling material to both sides, such as oil, guns and ITT telephones, which were used in German submarines.[805] Neither the Germans nor the Allies would touch the ships of Aristotle Onassis, though they sailed through war zones. Aristotle did not suffer any losses. His large fleet did not lose a single ship, even the ones that were in Scandinavia when the Germans invaded.[806]

Hjalmar Horace Greeley Schacht, president of Hitler's Reichbank, was hired by Onassis after the war.[807] Schacht helped Onassis' shipyards in Germany build tankers after the war. CIA operative Clay Shaw, who was charged by New Orleans District attorney Jim Garrison for the murder of President Kennedy, was a close friend of Schacht.[808] Schacht was also related to Italian Prince Spadofora, President of Swiss based Permindex, which had a subsidiary Centro Mondiale Commerciale, associated with Clay Shaw.[809] After the Kennedy assassination, a member of the Onassis family married Kennedy's widow to presumably placate her. Schacht was also the father in law of Otto Skorzeny, another Nazi who escaped.

Schacht with Hitler in 1934, laying the foundation of the New Reichbank building. <http://www.reformation.org/roosevelt-and-hitler.html> Accessed 25/10/06. Copyright information is not available.

Antony Sutton compiled some more information on the interesting connections of William Schacht, the father of Hjalmar Horace Greeley Schacht. To quote,

> In 1916 the cashier of the Berlin Equitable Life office was William Schacht, the father of Hjalmar Horace Greeley Schacht — later to become Hitler's banker, and financial genie. William Schacht was an American citizen, worked thirty years for Equitable in Germany, and owned a Berlin house known as "Equitable Villa." Before joining Hitler, young Hjalmar Schacht

[805] Springmeier, Bloodlines 132.
[806] Springmeier, Bloodlines 133.
[807] Springmeier, Bloodlines 131.
[808] Mae Brussells, "The Nazi Connection to the Dallas JFK murder," The Rebel January 1984: ?? An archived copy is available at: <http://www.maebrussell.com/Mae Brussell Articles/Nazi Connection to JFK Assass.html> Web page as of 16/03/04
[809] Brussells, "The Nazi Connection."

served as a member of the Workers and Soldiers Council (a soviet) of Zehlendoff; this he left in 1918 to join the board of the Nationalbank fur Deutschland. His codirector at DONAT was Emil Wittenberg, who, with Max May of Guaranty Trust Company of New York, was a director of the first Soviet international bank, Ruskombank.[810]

Putzi Hanfstaengl

Putzi (Ernst) Hanfstaengl was an American at the very heart of the Nazi inner circles from the early 1920s to the late 1930s. He may have played a role for the Powers that Be as an intermediary between Hitler and Roosevelt. Anthony Sutton[811] formed the following conclusions about Putzi:

Hitler and Putzi.

< http://www.reformation.org/roosevelt-and-hitler.html> Accessed 25/10/06. Copyright information is not available.

- Putzi was connected to Roosevelt and the American ruling elite.
- Putzi composed the Nazi Storm trooper marching songs.[812] To quote Sutton, "Putzi averred that the genesis of the Nazi chant 'Sieg Heil, Sieg Heil,' used in the Nazi mass rallies, was none other than 'Harvard, Harvard, Harvard, rah, rah, rah.'"
- Putzi helped finance the first Nazi daily press, the *Volkische Beobachter* started by the Thule society.
- Putzi financed the publication of Mein Kampf.
- When Roosevelt came to power in March 1933, a private "emissary" was sent from Roosevelt in Washington, D.C. to Putzi in Berlin, with a message to the effect that Hitler would soon achieve power in Germany.
- Putzi had close ties to Heinrich Himmler.

---

[810] Antony C Sutton, Wall Street and the Bolshevik Revolution (Buccaneer Books, 1993). Chapter Three of Online edition. <http://reformed-theology.org/html/books/bolshevik_revolution/chapter_08.htm> Accessed 25/10/06.
[811] Anthony C. Sutton, Wall Street and the rise of Hitler (GSG and Associates, 1976). Ebook edition. <http://reformed-theology.org/html/books/wall_street/chapter_08.htm#7> Web page as of 16/03/04
[812] Ernst Hanfstaengl, Unheard Witness (New York: J.B. Lippincott, 1957) 122. Quoted in Sutton, Rise of Hitler <http://reformed-theology.org/html/books/wall_street/chapter_08.htm#7> Web page as of 16/03/04.

- “Putzi — by his own admission — was in the Palace room at the other end of the tunnel leading to the Reichstag. And according to *The Reichstag Fire Trial,* Putzi Hanfstaengl was actually in the Palace itself during the fire.”[813]
- His friend and protector, President Franklin D. Roosevelt, bailed Putzi out of a Canadian prisoner of war camp towards the end of the war.

The FDR - 120 Broadway-Standard Oil - General Electric Connection

Anthony Sutton has uncovered that the New York address of 120 Broadway (which was connected to the buildup of both the Soviet Union and Nazi Germany) was then host to the following entities[814]:

American International Corp 120 Broadway
National City Bank 55 Wall Street
Bankers Trust Co Bldg 14 Wall Street
New York Stock Exchange 13 Wall Street/12 Broad
Morgan Building corner Wall & Broad
Federal Reserve Bank of NY 120 Broadway
Equitable Building 120 Broadway
Bankers Club 120 Broadway
Simpson, Thatcher & Bartlett 62 Cedar St
William Boyce Thompson 14 Wall Street
Hazen, Whipple & Fuller 42nd Street Building
Chase National Bank 57 Broadway
McCann Co 61 Broadway
Stetson, Jennings & Russell 15 Broad Street
Guggenheim Exploration 120 Broadway
Weinberg & Posner 120 Broadway
Soviet Bureau 110 West 40th Street
John MacGregor Grant Co 120 Broadway
Stone & Webster 120 Broadway
General Electric Co 120 Broadway
Morris Plan of NY 120 Broadway
Sinclair Gulf Corp 120 Broadway
Guaranty Securities 120 Broadway
Guaranty Trust 140 Broadway

---

[813] George Dimitrov, The Reichstag Fire Trial (London: The Bodley Head, 1934) 309. As quoted by Suttton, Rise of Hitler.
[814] Antony C Sutton, Wall Street and the Bolshevik Revolution (Buccaneer Books, 1993). Chapter Three of Online edition. <http://reformed-theology.org/html/books/bolshevik_revolution/chapter_08.htm > Accessed 25/10/06.

But having a common address does not necessarily imply association. Until we consider the following:

> When Franklin Delano Roosevelt was working in Wall Street, his address was also 120 Broadway. In fact, Georgia Warm Springs Foundation, the FDR Foundation, was located at 120 Broadway. The prominent financial backer of an early Roosevelt Wall Street venture from 120 Broadway was Gerard Swope of General Electric. And it was "Swope's Plan" that became Roosevelt's New Deal — the fascist plan that Herbert Hoover was unwilling to foist on the United States. In brief, both Hitler's New Order and Roosevelt's New Deal were backed by the same industrialists and in content were quite similar — *i.e.,* they were both plans for a corporate state. There were then both corporate and individual bridges between FDR's America and Hitler's Germany. The first bridge was the American I.G. Farben, [...] The second bridge was between International General Electric, a wholly owned subsidiary of General Electric Company and its partly owned affiliate in Germany, A.E.G. Gerard Swope, who formulated FDR's New Deal, was chairman of I.G.E. and on the board of A.E.G. The third "bridge" was between Standard Oil of New Jersey and Vacuum Oil and its wholly owned German subsidiary, Deutsche-Amerikanisehe Gesellschaft. The chairman of Standard Oil of New Jersey was Walter Teagle, of the Federal Reserve Bank of New York. He was a trustee of Franklin Delano Roosevelt's Georgia Warm Springs Foundation and appointed by FDR to a key administrative post in the National Recovery Administration."[815]

Research by Fritz Springmeier indicates that the Delano family of Roosevelt traces its origins to Black Venetian Nobility, which played a major role in European politics for centuries. In addition, Springmeier has discovered that the lives of these families also intertwine with the Astors, prominent old world elites. For example, Franklin Hughes Delano, heir to a massive whale oil fortune, married Lavia Astor, daughter of the famous William Backhouse Astor. James Roosevelt married Helen Astor, daughter of William Backhouse, Jr. The Illuminati fraternity Skulls and Bones was founded by Samuel Russell. One of Russell and Company Chief of Operations in Canton (China) was

---

[815] Anthony C. Sutton, Wall Street and the rise of Hitler (GSG and Associates, 1976). Ebook edition. <http://reformed-theology.org/html/books/wall_street/chapter_08.htm#7> Web page as of 16/03/04.

Warren Delano, Jr., grandfather of Franklin Roosevelt.[816] The Russells were involved in the Chinese opium trade.

Tyler Gatewood Kent, an officer in the U.S. Consular service in Britain, worked in the top-secret code room where he had access to transmissions between heads of states. He was appalled to witness that Roosevelt was involved activity that was embroiling America into the war. Kent secretly took 1,500 pages of secret documents from the American embassy,[817] which he was going to show to the public to expose the conspiracy. Instead, his diplomatic immunity was revoked and he stood a staged trial in Britain rather than the US!

The Krupps

The German Krupp family has been extensively studied in Bloodlines of the Illuminati. The following is condensed from the same source. Springmeier largely bases his assertions from William Manchester's masterpiece, *The Arms of Krupp 1587-1968*.[818]

The German Krupp family started playing a role among the Global Elite around 1839. The Krupps were the owners of Germany's largest steel firms. They also produced agricultural equipment (later for Russia on behalf of Lenin), locomotives and tanks. Many of the armaments they produced for the Nazis were arranged to fall into the hands of the Soviets in mint condition. They indirectly owned a major Dutch shipyard. The Krupps lived in Essen, Germany, in a huge palace called Villa Huegel, whose small wing has 60 rooms. They also had other castles and villas. They still own a castle in the Austrian Alps named Bluehnbach.[819]

Kaiser Wilhelm was a friend of the Krupp family. The police commissioner would run damage control for the activities of Friedrich Alfred Krupp who was a pedophile.[820] His wife was thrown into a mental asylum when she notified the authorities.[821] Even though pictures of him

---

[816] Kris Millegan, "The Order of the Skull and Bones-Everything you wanted to know but were afraid to ask," July 1997 CTRL.org An archived copy is available at <http://www.mega.nu:8080/ampp/skull.html> Web page as of 11/07/2004

[817] Fritz Springmeier, Bloodlines of the Illuminati (Spring Arbor distributors, 1998) 104. GlobalGrey PDF edition 2013 <http://www.globalgrey.co.uk/Pages/Books-Conspiracies/Bloodlines-Of-The-Illuminati.html> Web page as of 03/07/13.

[818] William Manchester, The Arms of Krupp 1587-1968 (New York: Bantam Books, 1970).

[819] Springmeier, Bloodlines 215.

[820] Springmeier, Bloodlines 386.

[821] Springmeier, Bloodlines 387.

engaged in pedophilia were released, the entire media participated in a cover-up. Those who had gained knowledge were intimidated and even assassinated.[822] The Kaiser attended the funeral of Friedrich Krupp.

Gustav Krupp was one of the leaders of a secret group of 12 powerful German industrialists called the Ruhrlade,[823] which secretly made industrial decisions during German rearmament. The secret governing body of the Ruhrlade conducted their meetings on the pretext of having hunting expeditions.[824]

After World War I had ended, the head of the Krupp family, Gustav Krupp von Bohlen und Halbach, began secretly planning to rebuild Germany's military through the Ruhrlade. Gustav Krupp bought coalmines after the war for future weapons production. When the Allied Control Commission departed Germany in 1928, Krupp factories began secretly turning out a few tanks.[825] The Christian Science Monitor sent reporters to Krupp's factories during the 1920s to report that the Germans were complying satisfactorily with the Versailles Treaty arms limitations.[826]

It is clear that Gustav Krupp was informed of I.G. Farben's secret research into synthetic nitrates prior to W.W.II, because Gustav told the renowned German chemist Emil Fischer not to worry about the guncotton problem caused by low nitrate supplies.[827]

During World War II, high-grade animal fat was required for holding the cotton in place for explosives. Was the fat of people killed in concentration camps used for this?[828] Prisoners were tortured in the basement of the Krupp executive office building in Essen, all within earshot of Alfred Krupp's office.[829] Many of these slave laborers were Jews. A concentration camp was made at Buschmannhof for the babies of Krupp prisoners. These children would barely survive the revolting

---

[822] Springmeier, Bloodlines 387.
[823] Springmeier, Bloodlines 215.
[824] Springmeier, Bloodlines 215.
[825] Springmeier, Bloodlines 214.
[826] Springmeier, Bloodlines 214.
[827] Springmeier, Bloodlines 382.
[828] Springmeier, Bloodlines 382.
[829] Springmeier, Bloodlines 385.

and inhuman conditions.[830] In other words, the slaves of Krupp did not even have the rights of slaves; they were more like "sandpaper."[831]

Alfred Krupp was the most powerful and richest man in the common market of Europe during the 1960s.[832] However, after his death, an appropriate Krupp heir could not be found. Arndt Krupp, Alfred's son opted for a life of leisure and bought an estate in Brazil. This estate covered 43 square miles, with dwellings for 180 servants (back in the 1960's) and had a park modeled after Versailles, as well as the largest horse stables in Brazil.[833] His private jet carried his custom-built Rolls Royce.[834]

Hitler's most important advisors were Rudolf Hess, Martin Bormann, Gustav Krupp and Alfred Krupp. After Hess fled or disappeared, Gustav became more influential on Hitler.[835] He saved the Nazi party from bankruptcy in 1932 by throwing in 100,000,000 German marks.[836] By 1919 Krupp was already giving financial aid to one of the reactionary political groups, which sowed the seed of future Nazi ideology.[837] Gustav Krupp may have been the most powerful German industrialist ever. He was the sole owner and the sole proprietor of all his companies. There were no shareholders. When Hitler came to power, Gustav Krupp billed the Nazi government RM 300 Million for having secretly built up the German war machine during the 1920s,[838] and the Nazi's paid without delay. When the war ended, Gustav was at his Bluehnbach Castle in the Austrian Alps. The American officer who captured the castle was Chip Bohlen's brother-in-law Col. Charles W. Thayer,[839] who made sure the American troops did not loot the castle. Chip Bohlen was a distant relative of the Krupps.

At the Nuremberg trials, Gustav was declared unfit health wise for trial, and Alfred was let go on a lenient sentence. Other Nazis put on trial were

---

830 Springmeier, Bloodlines 388.
831 Springmeier, Bloodlines 385.
832 Springmeier, Bloodlines 382.
833 Springmeier, Bloodlines 390.
834 Springmeier, Bloodlines 390.
835 Springmeier, Bloodlines 383.
836 Springmeier, Bloodlines 383.
837 Elimination of German Resources 648 Quoted by Anthony C. Sutton, Wall Street and the rise of Hitler (GSG and Associates, 1976). Ebook edition. <http://reformed-theology.org/html/books/wall_street/chapter_07.htm#3> Web page as of 16/03/04
838 Springmeier, Bloodlines 384.
839 Springmeier, Bloodlines 384.

tried and sentenced to death with far less evidence and far less crimes than Alfred. The trial of Alfred Krupp spawned five years, and yielded 330,000 pages of court transcripts.[840] Most of trial documents of the Krupps were never printed in Germany.[841] John J. McCloy, head of the Council of Foreign Relations, was made High Commissioner of Occupied Germany. He had Alfred Krupp exonerated.[842] There is reason to believe that witnesses in the trial may have been intimidated or even worse.[843] McCloy later became President of the World Bank.

According to the analysis of Mae Brussells, [844] a certain John J. McCloy shared the box with Hitler at the 1936 Berlin Olympics. McCloy became legal counsel to I.G Farben. Then he would become assistant secretary to the U.S. War Department. This was the same War Department, which refused the entry of Jewish refugees into the United States. He would return to become President of the Chase Manhattan bank and legal counsel to several American oil firms, apart from supervising the construction of the Pentagon. One of his clients would be Nobel Oil firm, which is connected to White Russian George de Mohrenschildt (who was smuggled into the US by Reinhardt Gehlen). This firm was founded by the Russian Nobel brothers, who entered the oil business in 1873, and dominated all oil supply in Russia. They may have collaborated with the Rothschilds on Baku oil in World War I. George de Mohrenschildt befriended Lee Harvey Oswald in Dallas, and later produced evidence, implicating Oswald in the Kennedy assasination. He had links to Tsarist Russian nobility and the White Russians. After the assassination of Kennedy, McCloy would serve for Johnson on the Warren Commission.

Charles E. Bohlen, "Distinguished American Diplomat." © 2005 USPS. Used with permission. All rights reserved.

Another distant relative of the Krupps was Charles E. Bohlen. His grandfather and Alfred Krupp's great grandfather were brothers.[845] He was

---

[840] Springmeier, Bloodlines 385.
[841] Springmeier, Bloodlines 385.
[842] Springmeier, Bloodlines 385.
[843] Springmeier, Bloodlines 385.
[844] Mae Brussells, "The Nazi Connection to the Dallas JFK murder," The Rebel January 1984: ?? An archived copy is available at: <http://www.maebrussell.com/Mae Brussell Articles/Nazi Connection to JFK Assass.html> Web page as of 16/03/04
[845] Springmeier, Bloodlines 382.

also known as Chip Bohlen. Chip was relatively scandal free and kept a very low profile. He rose to become one of the most powerful political figures of the United States and served as the U.S. ambassador to the USSR for many years. Senator McCarthy who was investigating "Soviet conspiracy" tried to block Chip's appointment as the American "Ambassador extraordinary and plenipotentiary to the U.S.S.R.,"[846] but failed. But McCarthy managed to expose Chip's brother in law who subsequently quitted. Chip also served as an advisor to three secretaries of state. Charles Bohlen was advising Roosevelt on how to give the Soviets Eastern Europe at Yalta in 1943 while his relatives Gustav and Alfred Krupp were directing the manufacture of Hitler's best armaments. The U.S. State Department trained Chip to speak Russian several years before the America had diplomatic ties with the Soviet Union.[847] When the U.S. established an embassy in Moscow in 1934, Chip played a role in the coordination of its activities.[848] Chip was present at the Yalta conference and later at the Tehran Conference. Chip was also present at the Potsdam conference between Truman and Stalin. He also participated in the San Francisco conference, where the UN was born. Chip also contributed to the creation of Marshall Plan, which allowed America to turn NATO allies into its surrogates.

Hausofer' s mysticism works for the Soviets

From its very inception by Baron Von Sebottendorf, the Thule society worked towards the ultimate goal of German conquest by the Soviet Union. This is evident when the Thule Society organized the Freikorps (later to become National Socialist German Workers Party) to overthrow a socialist government installed by a Jewish intellectual named Kurt Eisner. Localized Socialism and localized Communism were seen as competitors to Nazism (and Nazism was meant to pave the way for the triumph of Soviet-Communsim in Germany). Therefore uprooting localized Socialism/Communism would be prominent in Nazi agenda. But the Thule Society was not the only organization working for the rise of Hitler. Even the German Comintern (the KPD) never allied with the socialist SPD to thwart Hitler, and instead called the SPD another wing of Fascism. It is more logical that the KPD was in league with the Powers that Be, and was contributing indirectly to the rise of Hitler. Trotsky contributed to this end, churning rhetoric that the SPD was a wing of

---

[846] Springmeier, Bloodlines 389.
[847] Springmeier, Bloodlines 389.
[848] Springmeier, Bloodlines 389.

Fascism.[849] Stalin's Comintern also never allied with the SPD and instead worked to destroy it, thus helping the Nazis make the most of the infighting.

Another Thulist Karl Hausofer shaped Nazi ideology such that a provocative attack on Russia followed by a suicidal advance eastwards would always be part of Nazi agenda:

> Hausofer disguised racial mysticism in a veil of geography and science, providing Germans with a powerful reason to return to those areas in the hinterland of Asia where the Aryan race supposedly originated. His appeal for Lebensraum for the German people and his plans to achieve it were no more than a justification for international pillage on a grand scale, virtually a blueprint to world conquest.[850]

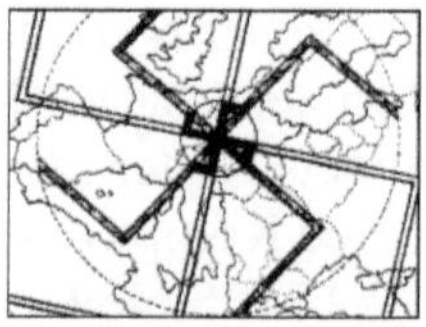

The Nazi war machine was at the mercy of Hausofer's vodooism such as this plan for conquest, which is based on a spiraling swastika.

In other words, the Nazis were to suicide en mass after being marched into the arms of the Soviets, with Hitler playing the role of a Pied Piper.

While one would assume that the Nazis based their military expeditions on plans drafted by professional military experts, we instead find huge reliance on the occult. While this can be dismissed as fatal stupidity resulting from mixing the occult and the empiric, it is more plausible that such diversions were clearly intended to bring catastrophe upon them. The blame would always point towards the occult, which would obfuscate the role of the Powers that Be.

For example, we find Blavatsky and numerous other esotericists such as Houston Stewart Chamberlain reiterating the fact that Aryan-Nordic roots were in the east. When Hitler came to power, the SS Ahnenerbe conducted archaeological expeditions digging up sites in Eastern Europe, trying to find evidence of a once existing Aryan culture. This would be used as political fodder for Germans to continue supporting Hitler's suicidal march eastwards, even though it was in their best interests to maintain a defensive position. Rosenberg would reinstate the need to advance towards the south-east and Himmler would point out in his

---

[849] Leon Trotsky, "Germany, the key to the international situation," The Struggle Against Fascism in Germany Ed. George Brietman and Merry Maisel. (NY. Pathfinder press inc. 1971) 125.

[850] Peter Levenda, Unholy Alliance (Avon Books, 1995) ??

speech how Germans needed to secure a perimeter in the Urals against "Asians." However, it was Nazi party philosopher and Blavatsky disciple Karl Hausofer who would give this concept a concrete basis in Nazism. His geopolitical theories also found their way into the *Mein Kampf*. Such as the aforementioned quest for supposed Aryan origins in the East. It was this concept of Hausofer, which became known as lebensraum (living space) that Hitler would adopt.

> Hausofer advised Hitler to enlarge the living space of the Third Reich by moving out from a powerful territorial hub and by accomplishing this conquest progressively, step by step, following the accelerating movement of a growing spiraling sinistroverse swastika [See figure].[851]

Hausofer also had close contact with British members of the Golden Dawn Society and would later direct Rudolf Hess's secret meetings with them.

Since the Powers that Be had also earmarked Japan for destruction along with Germany, Hausofer would forge the alliance between Germany and Japan. Hausofer would claim that he based the alliance on astrological predictions.[852] As per the Tripartite Pact with Japan, Germany was not obliged to declare war with enemies of Japan. Yet Hitler made the fatal decision to do so. And this worked to the advantage of the biggest enemy of Germany; the Soviets. The Soviet Union on the other hand had secured a Treaty of non-aggression with Japan in advance, to avoid losing any territory to Japan when they would be at war with Germany.

As the Nazi conquest advanced, Hausofer applied his theories and overruled the military leadership in directing troop movements.

Nazi ideologues denied the existence of objective reality leading to their rejection of valid astronomy and physics in favor of occult-based pseudo-science, such as the "doctrine of eternal cosmic ice," concocted by Hans Hoerbiger, a mechanical engineer.[853] Thule mythology insisted on new ages birthed from ice.[854] Hoerbiger declared war on "objective science," which he labeled as "a pernicious invention," and instead

---

[851] Servando González, Origins of the Swastika: The Hausofer Connection. Note # 4. <http://www.intelinet.org/swastika/swasti02.htm> Web page as of 11/07/2004

[852] Dusty Sklar, The Nazis and the Occult (1989) 69.

[853] Hannah Newman, The Rainbow Swastika- A Report to the Jewish People About New Age Anti-Semitism; Nazism and the new age <http://philologos.org/__eb-trs/naF.htm> Web page as of 11/07/2004.

[854] Newman, Rainbow Swastika; Nazism and the New Age.

advocated substituting the "uselessness" of mathematics with a mystical "knowing" of the universe. He targeted Albert Einstein as an archenemy.[855] Hoerbiger's cause was taken up by the Hitler Youth, and later, the SS Ahnenerbe. And the Storm Troopers became fanatic supporters of Hoerbiger, disrupting meetings of conventional astronomers with shouts and threats.[856] There may be a reason why the Powers that Be wanted to disrupt scientific astronomy; Hoerbigerian weather forecasting was used to fix 1941 as a mild winter, convincing the Nazis to leave behind heavy winter gear for the invasion of the Soviet Union. In actuality, they were sent into record-breaking cold, and their retreat marked a turning point in the war.[857] Even after the disaster, Hoerbiger's theories were never repudiated and Hitler instead blamed the German people.

Regardless of the commitment and scientific expertise of Nazi troops, they were doomed when their most crucial decisions were based on the "occult." Were the Nazi top brass such diehard fans of the occult that voodooist ideas took priority over conventional wisdom and commonsense? Did these ideas attributed to the "occult" really originate in occult teachings or were they cold and calculated doom formulae created by the Powers that Be? If the Nazis were being sabotaged from within, the best way for the conspirators to disguise their motives would be claims of relying on "occult guidance."

The Tibet Connection

In order to keep feeding Germans with historical reasons to continue supporting Hitler's suicidal advance towards the southeast, Himmler spent vast sums of money on esoteric research projects such as an expedition to Tibet "to look for traces of a pure Germanic race which might have been able to keep intact the ancient Nordic mysteries."[858] Helena Blavatsky and other Theosophists considered the Tibetan Himalayas the home of the Spiritual Hierarchy itself.[859] According to some, Hitler sent SS officers to the Himalayas not only to seek out the source of the Aryan race, but to make contact with "Asgard" and consult directly with the "ascended masters." The Ahnenerbe also organized

---

[855] Jean-Michel Angebert, The Occult and the Third Reich (Macmillan, 1974) 183. Quoted in Newman, Rainbow Swastika; Nazism and the New Age.

[856] Dusty Sklar, The Nazis and the Occult (1989) 75-77. Quoted in Newman, Rainbow Swastika; Nazism and the New Age.

[857] Newman, Rainbow Swastika; Nazism and the New Age.

[858] Dusty Sklar, The Nazis and the Occult (1989) 102.

[859] Newman, Rainbow Swastika; Nazism and the New Age.

several expeditions to Tibet. Their purpose was to locate the origins of the "Nordic" race, which was, according to the Nazi theoreticians, of Indo-Germanic stock. They also wanted to get in touch with a supposed spiritual "power-plant" which produced "Vril," another fantastic creation of the contemporaries of Blavatsky. A colony of Tibetan Buddhists flourished in Berlin.[860] It is plausible that Buddhism with its strict discipline standards was being used to train some sections of the SS so that they could carry out orders with numbness, compliance and impunity. Russian troops entering Berlin in May 1945 found "the corpses of a thousand men of Himalayan origin, in German uniform, but carrying no papers or identification."[861] By far, the Tibet connection is considered to be an important esoteric link between the Nazis and contemporaries of Blavatsky. Recently, a U.N. leader imported Tibetan monks into the Bakaa Valley Colorado for indoctrinating New Agers.[862]

The Nazi plan for Mass Suicide

Nazi war strategies are riddled with inconsistencies, usually resulting from decisions made in higher echelons. These strategies were bound to doom regardless of the expertise German soldiers or their commitment. The following are some of the major preplanned errors which sabotaged Nazi strategy:

A. Paul Weber, illustration for the book *Hitler: Germany's Ruin,* by Ernst Niekisch (1933). Minimized Reproduction Under Fair Dealing.

The Allies "Escape" at Dunkirk

In May 1940, erroneous Allied military maneuvers resulted in 330,000 (mostly British) Allied troops being stranded on the beaches of Dunkirk. Their capture would have been a big scoring point for the Nazis, putting them in a position to throttle Britain. Yet Hitler halted his Generals for three days, allowing almost all of the Allies to escape. The Allied evacuation at Dunkirk is considered to be one of the biggest in history. The Powers that Be have spread disinformation that the troops at Dunkirk were heroically rescued through an extraordinary evacuation

---

860 Jean-Michel Angebert, The Occult and the Third Reich (Macmillan, 1974) 215

861 Jean-Michel Angebert, The Occult and the Third Reich (Macmillan, 1974) 281-282, Note by Lewis Sumberg, translator.

862 Fritz Springmeier, The Illuminati formula used to create an undetectable total mind controlled slave (Web edition) 410

just ahead of the Nazis. Another myth is that Hitler's avoidance to capture them was a "peace gesture." There is no doubt that Hitler would have had better chances at peace if he had captured the Allied soldiers and used them to bargain for peace. To quote Hitler on the occasion, "Our two people belong together racially and traditionally."[863] Hitler's sudden bonding for the non-Aryan British is suspect since the same courtesy was not extended to Slavs. The obvious answer to this treachery is that defeat of the Allies was never part of the agenda.

Nazis avoid invading Britain

In 1940, Hitler prepared for an invasion of Britain (Operation Sea Lion). Instead of focusing on subduing this key opponent, the invasion plan was abandoned after aerial combat, which became known as the Battle of Britain. These German attacks on civilian population were used to suffocate antiwar sentiment in Britain and generate an atmosphere of fear and hate. Hitler would then abandon Britain unsubdued, to engage the Soviet Union, and later America.

Repeating Napoleon's Blunder

The goal of the Nazi military suicide on the Eastern front is discernable without any requirement for expertise on military history. Such an exercise had been previously conducted to destroy Napoleon, who had stolen the French Revolution from the Illuminati. But Napoleon was lured into the trap, whereas Hitler participated in the entrapment of his forces.

It is apparent that those directing the Nazi war machine on the Eastern front were deliberately sabotaging the Germans, whenever they successfully gained ground. The purpose was the suicidal exhaustion of the Nazis and their resources. Hoerbigerian (occult) weather forecasting was used to fix 1941 as a mild winter, convincing the Nazis to leave behind heavy winter gear for the invasion of Russia, and they were sent into a record-breaking cold front that marked a turning point in the war.[864] The advance on Moscow, which was going smoothly and which would have incapacitated Soviet morale, was left aside in favor of Leningrad, even though the Nazis had arrived within a few kilometres of Moscow. Then, Nazi forces were directed towards the Caucasian oil fields, which in turn were abandoned for Stalingrad. The Nazis left the

---

[863] Louis Kilzer, Churchill's Deception (Simon & Schuster, 1994) 213. Quoted by Henry Makow, "Hitler didn't want world war," Savethemales.ca <http://www.savethemales.ca/000369.html> Web page as of 11/07/2004

[864] Newman, Rainbow Swastika; Nazism and the New Age.

Caucasian oil fields[865] undamaged without blowing them up or destroying them, and these resources were crucial to later Soviet success. At Stalingrad, the German Sixth Army was trapped by the Soviets and was in desperate conditions. Yet, Hitler refused requests for a break out. The Germans were eventually forced to surrender. The next offensive would then focus on Moscow. It was on this second move on Moscow that the cream of German military youth would be decimated. By then, The Nazi war machine had been significantly crippled. It is questionable whether it was in the best interests of the Nazis to advance eastwards into the cold, vast and resource-starved area rather than establish a defensive perimeter where they were. When the Nazis would conduct their operations without interference of Hitler, they obtained huge successes, such as Manstein's brilliant post Stalingrad recovery. Nazi leadership however, would reverse such successes.

Hitler used the defeats inflicted on Germany in the Soviet Union as an excuse for taking away the power of career generals. And instead centralized the command so that he could engineer Nazi defeat without interruption. After 1941, Hitler began recalling, arresting and ordering the deaths of his most capable generals. Such as Field Marshal von Brauchitsch, the Commander and Chief of the Army, and General Guderian, the genius of the Panzer Corps.[866] Only three generals survived the war without removal.[867]

Nazis Avoid Allying with Enemies of the Soviets

Though Nazis superficially allied with enemies of the Soviets, the purpose of such alliances was merely to create reactionary dialectical opposition groups to the Soviets, who were bound to be highly unpopular among their fellow countrymen, and who could be used to execute Nazi policies. For example, the Nazis allied with the Croats, traditional enemies of the pro-Russian Serbs. But instead of using them against the Soviets, they were given roles in the persecution of Jews. Sociopaths like Erich Koch were assigned to Ukraine, where he operated death squads instead of creating a popular resistance against the Soviets. A similar conduct can be observed towards the Poles. When Germans discovered the bodies of 4000 Polish army officers killed by the Soviets, they kept a tight lid on the story rather than turn it into a propaganda coup, even

[865] Prior to the Soviets, these oil fields represented Rothschild interests.

[866] Rhawn Joseph, The Mind and God of Adolf Hitler Part I <http://brainmind.com/Hitler.html> Accessed 13/12/06.

[867] Rhawn Joseph, The Mind and God of Adolf Hitler Part I <http://brainmind.com/Hitler.html> Accessed 13/12/06.

after the alliance with the Soviets fell apart. In the case of the Slavs, entire villages were wiped out during Operation Barbarossa. Similarly, Nazi support of some Catholic Irish groups against the British was ridden with inconsistency.

In August 1944, Poles were cajoled by the Soviets into conducting an uprising against the Germans. The destruction of Poles, in particular, their army, was crucial to later Soviet hegemony in the region. Hitler took the opportunity of destroying up to 85 per cent of Warsaw for the Soviets. The Soviet army, which was across the river, watched on and did not assist the Polish uprising.

Similarly, Soviets and Nazis would battle over Budapest, which destroyed most of the city and its inhabitants, leaving the Soviets with the advantage of occupying an empty shell city, which could be rebuilt on their own terms. In the battle of Budapest, Soviets became notorious for mass rapes. Up to 50,000 women may have been raped.[868]

The Germans could have greatly unburdened themselves on the Eastern front by forming armies consisting of Russians. White Russians and many groups were highly supportive of such a venture. Instead, the Gestapo would persecute Russians like General Malishkin and General Vlasov, who were prominent in the anti-Soviet Russian Liberation movement. Such moves were designed to frustrate any such effort from the Russians. In addition, members of the powerful Russian anti-communist organization (NTS) were arrested by the Gestapo and were sent to the Dachau concentration camp for operating independent of the Axis! Using a failed assassination attempt as a pretext, Hitler had many Germans sympathetic to the idea of supporting the Russian Liberation Movement arrested and executed. Hitler claimed that such movements would promote Russian nationalism! And he continued to make such excuses even after the Stalingrad disaster.

Betraying loyalists

William Joyce was an American living abroad in Britain. In 1939, he fled to Germany and began his psychological warfare career by making his first propaganda broadcast for the Nazis, and would become known as Lord Hawhaw. He would call upon Britons to not fight for "Jews." His propaganda broadcasts across Britain became extremely popular, and

---

[868] James Mark, "Remembering Rape: Divided Social Memory and the Red Army in Hungary 1944–1945," Past and Present 188 (August 2005) 133.

Britons began questioning the war effort. At about that time, two British secret agents kidnapped Joyce and took him back to Britain. He was hanged in 1946 though he never was a British subject. However, the greater mystery is possible Nazi complicity in his kidnapping on the Danish border. Why was a chief Nazi propagandist left alone and unguarded on the Danish border?

We got your Codes!

One of the biggest secret of World War II was that the largest onus of Allied and Soviet victory was their ability to intercept and decipher the German Ultra code. This was the absolute intelligence coup, allowing the Allies (in particular the Soviets) exact details on all forthcoming operations, from date, place and time to unit strength. These intercepts were instrumental in the reversal of Nazi fortunes on the Soviet front and North Africa. The question is, how did the Allies acquire this top-secret code? Such top secret documents could not have been obtained without insider betrayal. And why was this kept secret even after the war?

Nazis grow Soviet Ears in Tokyo

The German embassy in Tokyo had a Soviet spy, Richard Sorge. He relayed information that Japan did not intend to capitalize on Operation Barbarossa and advance against the Soviets. This allowed 200,000 Soviet soldiers to be diverted to the Eastern front with no fear of Japanese aggression.

Hitler cuts Rearmament

To quote, "Having barely begun in 1935, Hitler cut armament plans by 30% after Munich. He cut them again drastically after the defeat of France [1940] and was reducing them even after the invasion of Russia [June 1941]. Indeed large scale rearmament began only in the summer of 1943."[869] In other words, German forces would face insufficient resources when dealing with the Soviet invasion.

The Cicero Betrayal

A Turkish valet of the British ambassador in Turkey (codenamed Cicero) started selling British top-secret papers to the German embassy. The Nazi high command never used the information, and instead paid Cicero in counterfeit, presumably to get him caught by police. Ludwig Moyzisch, the German handler of Cicero was so appalled by the Nazi handling of the situation that at the end of his book, he refers to the Nazis

---

[869] A. J. P. Taylor, "War Origins Again," Past and Present 30 (April 1965) 110.

as counterfeit patriots.[870] Moyzisch later learnt that he too was to be charged for treason when he would return to Germany. This is indicative of top-level Nazi and Allied Intelligence collaborating to engineer the defeat of Germany, which would be instrumental to the future of the Soviet Union. Even though Hitler was able to read all diplomatic traffic of British embassies in Central Europe, the information was never put to use. On the day of the Allied D-day operation, Erwin Romell, in charge of the Nazi Western front, was in Berlin. We are supposed to believe he was there for his wife's birthday!

The Jewish Holocaust

Why did the Nazi regime divert wartime resources towards the persecution of Jews when the entire future of the German people was at stake? This topic attempts to provide a brief overview of little known information concerning the Jewish Holocaust.

The advancement of eugenics was another accomplishment of the Powers that Be. Eugenics did not start in Nazi Germany; it started in USA. To quote

> In War Against the Weak,[871] Black lays bare the veins of collaboration between American eugenicists and Nazi scientists. There was financial support of genetic research and travel by Nazi doctors from the Rockefeller Foundation, the Carnegie Institution of Washington, and Cold Spring Harbor Laboratory, a leading genetics research institute. There was research collaboration and reports on the Nazi efforts in respected journals like the Journal of the American Medical Association (JAMA).[872]

The Rockefeller Foundation continuously directed the German Kaiser Wilhelm Institute for Psychiatry and the Kaiser Wilhelm Institute for Anthropology, Eugenics and Human Heredity.[873] The Rockefeller appointed chief executive of these institutions was a Fascist Swiss psychiatrist named Ernst Rudin. When Hitler took over Germany, Rudin

---

[870] Ludwig C. Moyzisch, Operation Cicero (Allan-Wingate-Baker 1969) 187.
[871] Edwin Black, War Against the Weak: Eugenics and America's Campaign to Create a Master Race (Four Walls Eight Windows, 2004)
[872] Dan Vergano, "Book explores Eugenics' origins," USA TODAY 14th October 2003, <http://www.usatoday.com/news/health/2003-09-14-book-usat_x.htm> Accessed 13/12/06.
[873] Matt C. Abbott, "Here We Go Again," Michigan News November 15th 2003. An archived copy is available at < http://www.freemasonrywatch.org/rockefeller_foundation.html> Accessed 13/12/06.

became head of the Racial Hygiene Society.[874] Rudin was also part of the task force of Heredity Experts chaired by SS chief Heinrich Himmler.[875]

The Powers that Be would like us to believe that Hitler managed to create the sophisticated gas chambers and all contrivances used in the Holocaust on his own. But a recent book by Edwin Black[876] has elucidated the role of IBM in providing a punch card collating system for the Nazis to organize the detention and gassing of Jews on such a gargantuan scale. But bigger than this revelation is Anthony Sutton's tracing of the origins of the Zyklon B gas used in the Jewish Holocaust. This gas was invented, produced and distributed by I.G Farben. To quote Anthony Sutton in Wall Street and the Rise of Hitler,

> Zyklon B was pure Prussic acid, a lethal poison produced by I.G. Farben Leverkusen and sold from the Bayer sales office through Degesch, an independent license holder. Sales of Zyklon B amounted to almost three-quarters of Degesch business; enough gas to kill 200 million humans was produced and sold by I.G. Farben. The Kilgore Committee report of 1942 makes it clear that the I.G. Farben directors had precise knowledge of the Nazi concentration camps and the use of I.G. chemicals.[877]

Sutton further quotes the 1945 interrogation[878] of I.G. Farben director Von Schnitzler that reads as:

> Q. What did you do when they told you that I.G. chemicals was [sic] being used to kill, to murder people held in concentration camps?
> A. I was horrified.
> Q. Did you do anything about it?
> A. I kept it for me [to myself] because it was too terrible.... I asked Muller-Cunradi is it known to you and Ambros and other directors in Auschwitz that the gases and chemicals are being used to murder people.

---

874 Abbott, "Here We Go Again."
875 Abbott, "Here We Go Again."
876 Edwin Black, IBM and the Holocaust: The Strategic Alliance Between Nazi Germany and America's Most Powerful Corporation (Three Rivers Press, 2002).
877 Anthony C. Sutton, Wall Street and the rise of Hitler (GSG and Associates, 1976). Ebook edition. <http://reformed-theology.org/html/books/wall_street/chapter_02.htm> Web page as of 16/03/04
878 Anthony C. Sutton, Wall Street and the rise of Hitler (GSG and Associates, 1976). Ebook edition. <http://reformed-theology.org/html/books/wall_street/chapter_02.htm> Web page as of 16/03/04

Q. What did he say?
A. Yes: it is known to all I.G. directors in Auschwitz.

With the Holocaust underway, the American administration not only prohibited Jewish refugees from coming to America to escape the Holocaust, but also prevented American and British bombers from bombing the railroads leading to the concentration camps. Such a move could have diminished scale of the Holocaust casualties.

The only door left open for some Jews to escape was that of Zionism. Though this conduit was certainly not large enough to save all Jews, it was the only door left open in some cases. The Nazis would institute the Havara program.[879] This program allowed German Jews to exchange their money for its value in German products in Palestine. The German Jews were also provided with safe transit to Palestine via a Nazi steamer, which sometimes even flew the swastika. As a result, the fledgling Jewish colony received about 70,000 highly educated German Jews and RM 140 million worth of German industrial equipment. This laid the foundation of Israel's infrastructure.[880] The program can be considered odd when we consider that the Nazis were in a position to confiscate all Jewish wealth without providing either an escape route or goods in exchange. In his book, *The Holocaust Victims Accuse*, Rabbi Moshe Shonfeld claims that Zionist led Jewish Councils (Judenrats) collaborated with the Nazis and deceived non Zionist Jews into migrating to Israel.[881] Roosevelt would close American doors to Jewish immigrants fleeing persecution. To quote Newman "the U.S. government which turned away Jewish refugees even though immigration quotas left room for over one million between 1933 and 1943."[882] The Holocaust refugee ship St. Louise was not allowed to dock by Roosevelt.

---

[879] Quoting Klaus Polkehn, The Secret contacts. Quoted by Henry Makow, "Zionism: A Conspiracy Against Jews," Savethemales.ca <http://www.savethemales.ca/000482.html> Web page as of 27/06/2004. Also see Edwin Black's The Transfer Agreement – The Dramatic Story of the Pact Between the Third Reich and Jewish Palestine. (Carroll and Graf Publishers, 2001).
[880] Henry Makow, "Zionism: A Conspiracy Against Jews," Savethemales.ca <http://www.savethemales.ca/000482.html> Web page as of 27/06/2004.
[881] Henry Makow, "Zionism: A Conspiracy Against Jews," Savethemales.ca <http://www.savethemales.ca/000482.html> Web page as of 27/06/2004.
[882] Hannah Newman, The Rainbow Swastika- A Report to the Jewish People About New Age Anti-Semitism; Nazism and the new age <http://philologos.org/__eb-trs/naF.htm> Web page as of 11/07/2004.

Holocaust Denial

Holocaust Denial continues to be one of the biggest distractions for serious historians investigating Nazism. While there always will be an educated debate on the numbers of the Holocaust, we can reasonably assume that the holocaust was big enough to alter Jewish demographics in Europe and secondly, made Jews realize the necessity of Zionism and an Israeli homeland.

Nevertheless, whenever some inquirer stumbles upon discrepancies in the figures, the establishment moves in to persecute and even imprison those involved. This gives the impression of intrigue and cover-up. Truth seekers assume that the Holocaust and Hitler's anti-Semitism are "Jewish" exaggerations and all that is needed is a little bit of prodding to liberate Hitler and place him alongside Gandhi and Buddha.

It is true that Zionists misuse the memory of the Holocaust, and some Florida retirees claim to be Holocaust survivors when they are not. But that set aside, the Holocaust and nitpicking investigations into its dimensions significantly distract from issues more central to World War II. Like, how did Germany fall to the Soviets and end up with half of its territory on the Soviet side? Even if Holocaust deniers are trying to clean Hitler from wrongful slander, they usually do not subject Hitler to a balanced critique (if any critique). In my personal opinion, some random Panzer commander may have made a better strategist than Hitler. Yet Nazi fetishists insist that his command was brilliant. Some involved in Holocaust denial merely play favorites without the slightest effort at critical thinking.

Some crypto-elites have now moved into the arena of Holocaust denial (the ones that never go to jail). Their writings are usually characterized by the complete denial of Globalist-Banker connections to the Nazi State, as well as denial of the occult nature of Nazism.

Eagles, Phoenixes, Ashes…. the esotericism of the Jewish Holocaust

The Coat of arms of the city of Auschwitz.

A large Nazi eagle atop the Mauthausen concentration camp. The eagle was later pulled down.

Right: Three phoenixes atop a memorial to the liberation of Majdanek concentration camp. The phoenixes are atop an urn containing actual ashes from the crematorium

Nazism: Mission Accomplished?

This photograph was taken by Evgenii Khaldei, a TASS correspondent. It pretty much epitomizes the role of Nazism in accomplishing the unthinkable. The Nazis succeeded in bringing half of Germany and

Eastern Europe under direct Soviet control, a feat unprecedented in contemporary history.

This photograph was originally captioned "Reichstag flag 1945," but Soviet authorities released another retouched version, "Red army soldiers raising the Soviet flag on the roof of the Reichstag Berlin Germany." The retouched version removed the multiple stolen watches on the hands of one soldier, and made the smoke appear more recent, giving the impression that the flag was raised immediately after the battle, whereas it may have been raised some days later. The information on the retouching comes from a book by Khaldei.[883]

Among those "liberated" by the Soviets were millions of German, Hungarian and Romanian women. The scale of the rape of German women is still to be ascertained. The extent of rape can be gauged by the fact that two million women had illegal abortions during the years 1945-1948, and in the winter of 1946-47, the Soviet authorities imposed serious penalties on members of its armed forces fraternising with the conquered enemy due to the spread of venereal disease.[884]

Such rapes have even been "justified" as revenge for German atrocites. But historian Antony Beevor[885] has found archive documents detailing Soviet rapes of Russian and Polish women liberated from Nazi concentration camps as well![886]

Such claims have been met with denial and criticism from even present day Russian authorities. They are very particular about not being mistaken for "savage barbaric Asian hordes," and insist on being regarded as civilized people. Nevertheless, all is considered forgiven, since the Red Army saved the world from Nazism.

---

[883] Evgenii Khaldei, Von Moskau nach Berlin: Bilder des russischen Fotografen Jewgeni Chaldej (Parthas, 1999 ISBN 3932529677).

[884] Daniel Johnson, "Russians Angry at war Rape Claims," Telegraph.co.uk 25/02/02 <http://www.telegraph.co.uk/news/main.jhtml?xml=/news/2002/01/25/wruss25.xml> Accessed 30/12/06

[885] Antony Beevor, Berlin: The Downfall 1945 (Viking Books, 2002).

[886] Daniel Johnson, "Red Army troops raped even Russian women as they freed them from camps," Telegraph.co.uk 24/01/02 <http://www.telegraph.co.uk/news/main.jhtml?xml=/news/2002/01/24/wbeev24.xml> Accessed 30/12/06.

Apart from rapes, two million Germans were murdered, and 15 million were violently expelled.[887]

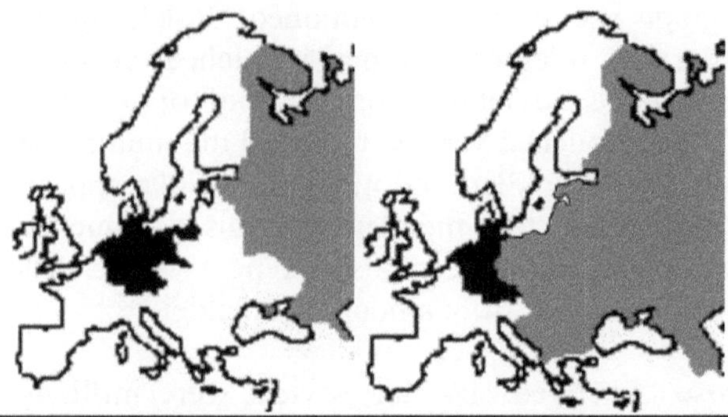

Left: Soviet borders after the signing of the March 1918 Brest-Litovsk Treaty between the Soviet Union and Germany. Many Soviet losses were recuperated following Germany's defeat on the Western front. The Allies made Germany repudiate the treaty as a condition for armistice. Right: The extended borders of Soviet influence after World War II. Cartographic details are not to scale. © Hamad Subani; Licensing: same as book; see introductory section on Licensing.

Italy

The intended role of Fascism in Italy and Spain was providing a dialectical opposition for the Soviets, similar to the Nazis, so that Soviets could advance into the Mediterranean and Africa. This has been discussed in Chapter Two on the First World War. Despite Gallipoli being secured by a pro-Bolshevik Kemalist Turkey after World War I, this objective never bore fruition due to a number of factors. The mistrust between the Globalists and Stalin, and the pathetic state of Soviet forces, which were dependent on huge handouts of Allied aid, were key factors. When Pike referred to putting Communism at par with the forces of Christendom, he probably meant Soviet influence over Italy and Spain.

A component of Italian Fascism was Futurism. The Futurist manifesto made references to all the typical elements of "revolution," long before the Bolshevik Revolution was even a probability. We find the same themes and content being recycled for different dialectical predecessors of Soviet Communism, including Nazism.

To quote John J. Ray,

---

[887] Eric Margolis, "The 20th Century's Worst Crime Goes Unpunished," The Toronto Sun November 16th 2003. Also published on ericmargolis.com <http://www.ericmargolis.com/archives/2003/11/the_20th_centur.php> Accessed 13/12/06

> Hitler was not however original in being both a socialist and a nationalist. The Italian nationalist leader, Mussolini, came to power much before Hitler but was in fact even more Leftist than Hitler. Although generally regarded as the founder of Fascism, in his early years Mussolini was one of Italy's leading Marxist theoreticians. He was even an intimate of Lenin. He first received his well-known appellation of Il Duce ("the leader") while he was still a member of Italy's "Socialist" (Marxist) party and, although he had long been involved in democratic politics, he gained power by essentially revolutionary means (the march on Rome). Even after he had gained power, railing against "plutocrats" remained one of his favorite rhetorical ploys. He was, however, an instinctive Italian patriot and very early on added a nationalistic appeal to his message, thus being the first major figure to add the attraction of nationalism to the attraction of socialism. He was the first 20th century far Leftist to learn the lesson that Hitler and Stalin after him used to such "good" effect.[888]

At the same time, prominent American elites like Time magazine's Henry Luce[889] and theoreticians like Strassmeier were vigorously pedaling Fascism (These ideologues are currently being recycled to promote American unilateralism).

Antony Sutton discovered that the same interests at 120 Broadway, who were supporting the Bolshevik Revolution, also supported the emergence of Fascist Italy. To quote,

> John P. Diggins, in *Mussolini and Fascism: The View from America,*[890] has noted in regard to Thomas Lamont of Guaranty Trust that of all American business leaders, the one who most vigorously patronized the cause of Fascism was Thomas W. Lamont. Head of the powerful J.P. Morgan banking network, Lamont served as something of a business consultant for the government of Fascist Italy. Lamont

---

888 John J. Ray, "Hitler was a Socialist," October 2006 <http://jonjayray.tripod.com/hitler.html> Accessed 05/11/06.

889 Steven P. Meyer and Jeffrey Steinberg, "Henry Luce's Empire of Fascism," Executive Intelligence Review June 25th, 2004. < http://www.larouchepub.com/other/2004/site_packages/3125ccf_luce.html > Accessed 05/11/06.

890 John P. Diggins, Mussolini and Fascism: The View from America (N.J.: Princeton University Press, 1972).

secured a $100 million loan for Mussolini in 1926 at a particularly crucial time for the Italian dictator.

> We also have observed that Basil Miles, in charge of the Russian desk at the State Department and a former associate of William Franklin Sands, was decidedly helpful to the businessmen promoting Bolshevik causes; but in 1923 the same Miles authored a pro-fascist article, "Italy's Black Shirts and Business."[891] "Success of the Fascists is an expression of Italy's youth," wrote Miles while glorifying the fascist movement and applauding its esteem for American business.[892]

In 1943, after occupying North Africa and Sicily, the Allies continued their war in the Mediterranean theatre by invading Italy. Why not push further into Farnce and Germany? Was the Italian campaign being used as a diversion so that the Soviets could make gains in the East?

Britain

Appeasement

According to establishment historians, everyone failed to notice German rearmament until it was too late. And British Prime Minister Chamberlain was appeasing Germany for the sake of peace. To the contrary, Neville Chamberlain may have knowingly extended a window for Nazi rearmament. He was related to Houston Stewart Chamberlain, who was the occultist mentor of Nazi party philosopher Alfred Rosenberg.

Douglas Reed, a Berlin correspondents for the London Times witnessed his newspaper suppress reports of Hitler's rearmament in the 1930s.[893] It appears that powerful elitist figures like press baron William Randolph Hearst were also suppressing news on Nazi rearmament until it was time to go to war. To quote, "Hearst had his chief European correspondent William Bayard Hale met with Hitler early in the 1920s at Hale's lavish

[891] Quoting Nation's Business, February 1923, pp. 22-23.
[892] Sutton, Antony C., Wall Street and the Bolshevik Revolution. Online edition. <http://reformed-theology.org/html/books/bolshevik_revolution/chapter_11.htm > Accessed 25/10/06.
[893] Douglas Reed Controversy of Zion. Quoted by Henry Makow in "Hitler didn't want world war," Savethemales.ca <http://www.savethemales.ca/000369.html> Web page as of 11/07/2004

suite at the Hotel Bayrisher Hoff."[894] Appeasement was also extended towards Fascist Italy and Fascist Spain. The following two sections on appeasement are based on sources from the excellent book by Richard Cockett, *Twilight of Truth; Chamberlain, Appeasement and Manipulation of the Press*, unless indicated otherwise.

Selling Appeasement

When Chamberlain assumed premiership, he addressed a special group of protégé reporters known as "The Lobby." His personal advisor Sir Joseph Ball emerged as his unofficial press lieutenant. Ball, with his Intelligence background, created an anonymous weekly publication known as *Truth*, with the sole purpose of disseminating appeasement views and attacking opposing ones. The Public National Publicity Bureau was used to fund *Truth* for the cause of Chamberlain and his party. Ball arranged this such that even members of the Bureau were unaware.[895] Ball would later champion the cause of British Fascists, though it was later uncovered that Ball was drafted in a secret committee created in 1940 to imprison such subversive Fascist sympathisers![896] When Ball finally exited this covert post, he destroyed all records and communiqués, giving a more ominous cloak and dagger tone to his activities. George Steward, the Press Relations Officer on the other hand, went to the extent of clarifying the source of British news items to an attaché at the German embassy in the interests of Chamberlain's policy of maintaining good relations with Germany. Crockett considers this activity as treason if Steward was acting on his own.[897] Steward's cordial relationship with the German press attaché ended when an M15 source within the German embassy alerted the Foreign Office. It is inferred that Steward was acting on behalf of Ball (and therefore Chamberlain). Even after the episode, Steward continued being at good terms with Chamberlain and retained his Downing Street post.

Apart from Steward and Ball, Lord Halifax (later foreign secretary) had an extraordinarily close relationship with Geoffrey Dawson of the Astor's *Times*. Another Astor publication, *The Observer* edited by J.L

---

[894] Fritz Springmeier, Bloodlines of the Illuminati (Spring Arbor distributors, 1998) 215. GlobalGrey PDF edition 2013 <http://www.globalgrey.co.uk/Pages/Books-Conspiracies/Bloodlines-Of-The-Illuminati.html> Web page as of 03/07/13.
[895] Richard Cockett, Twilight of Truth; Chamberlain, Appeasement and Manipulation of the Press (Palgrave Macmillan, 1989) 11.
[896] Cockett, Twilight of Truth 184.
[897] Cockett, Twilight of Truth 15.

Garvin also jumped into the Appeasement bandwagon. The *Times* became read as an unofficial conduit of government foreign policy both at home and abroad. The Astors were admirers of Chamberlain as was Lord Kemsley, proprietor of *Sunday Times*. The Astor countryseat at Cliveden became synonymous with appeasement. This peculiar arrangement of press ownership by elitist royals make British press a unique case study in disinformation. Crockett points out British Press's comparatively unusual character during the 1936 Abdication crisis. They maintained a collective silence, finally breaking it on 3rd December while the scandal had assumed epidemic proportions in the rest of the world. Lord Beaverbrook, who owned several major newspapers including the *Daily Express*, was also a friend of Chamberlain, as was Lord Rothermere, proprietor of *Daily Mail*. *News Chronicle*, owned by the Cadbury brothers of the chocolate empire were more than willing to let their editor Walter Layton "help" the government. Except for a few papers such as the *Daily Mirror* and *Reynolds News*, all major British papers became part of the "appeasement syndicate." Other agencies such as the BBC followed suit because of their government funding. Chamberlain engineered the removal BBC's first Director General in 1938. When Harold Nicholson sought to do a radio talk on the Czechoslovak crisis of 1938, the talk was subjected to censorship and the technician was told to fade out Nicholson's voice if he strayed into controversial areas. Needless to say, there were stronger grounds for this arrangement apart from commercial interest.[898] Crockett refers to "[...] those informal contacts that are such a hallmark of English way of life [...]"[899] in his introduction.

During the invasion of Austria, *Times*' Rupert Ward wrote how Nazis were being welcomed but he also cut out negative feedback which had been sent by the same correspondent. When German designs on Czechoslovakia became more than apparent, Ward Price of Rothermere's *Daily Mail* accused Czechoslovakia of being obstinate on the Sudetenland issue! Beaverbrook's papers adopted a similar line and the largely circulating *Manchester Guardian* followed suit. *Times* even proposed a plebiscite in favor of Sudeten Germans. Cockett again attributes this to a Lobby briefing of Chamberlain. The Foreign Office leaked news about a secret visit of Hitler's friend to Britain where he met

---

[898] The Royal commission later conducted an enquiry and advertising revenue was blamed, which Crockett refers as an 'easy scapegoat'.Most of the press barons did not survive appeasement with their reputation and circulation figures intact; with the exception of Lord Beaverbrook.

[899] Cockett Twilight of Truth 2.

Lord Halifax (1939). Chamberlain ordered the Foreign Office to 'to say nothing whatever at any cost,"[900] thereby gagging the Foreign Office.

Hitler invaded Czechoslovakia in March 1939, yet the appeasement editors never lashed out against Chamberlain. When Poland faced the Nazi threat, Chamberlain reworded his concerns by claiming support for Polish "Independence" rather than the territorial integrity of Poland. Oliver Harvey of the *Times* wrote that the disputed Polish city of Danzig was not worth Britain's involvement in war. Chamberlain even exercised his ancient legal power of censoring plays! The Charlie Chaplin film on Hitler *The Great Dictator* was blocked for a year. A BBC News editor referred to this phenomenon as a "conspiracy of silence."[901] Chamberlain's inner circle was still digging for reasons to appease even as late as September 1938. Horace Wilson talked about an internal revolution in Germany and Samuel Hoare proposed that economic weaknesses would stall Germany. Ball's *Truth* newsletter featured an article on Hitler's watercolor sensitivities, in order to persuade the British subject population into buying appeasement.

Appeasement Recycled

Interestingly, Cockett notes the methodology of appeasement being recycled by the *Times* and the *Observer* (which were then owned by the Astors) to later promote appeasement of the Soviets. Assistant editor E.H Carr not only promoted the welfare state, but also advocated accepting Soviet occupation of east Europe at the end of the war.

Canadian Nickel

Canadian nickel supply in the Allied war effort in World War I has been covered in Chapter Two. The same J.P. Morgan interests that operated the Sudbury copper mines were back in action. In World War II, Sudbury supplied 75% of the Allied demand of nickel, extracting more nickel during the war than in the first 55

---

[900] Cockett, Twilight of Truth 66.
[901] Cockett, Twilight of Truth 111.

years of their history![902] Although Canadian nickel was secretly diverted to the Axis in World War I, it remains to be investigated whether or not Canadian nickel also found its way into Hitler's war machine through intermediate countries.

The Dieppe Raid Disaster

As a strong supporter of the British Empire, Canada was to have its resources diverted towards any major venture the British would undertake.

In late 1942, pressure was building up within the subject populations of the Allies, such as those in Canada, to launch a counterattack against Hitler on the West European mainland. However, a successful move on behalf of the Allies would give them a head start in the conquest of Germany. And the Soviet Union would have a hard time catching up and making territorial gains.

To give these eager Allies a shot, Lord Mountbatten organized the Dieppe Raid. This undertaking involved the deaths of more than 3300 mostly Canadian soldiers, who accounted for around 2/3rds of the original invasion force. This event would discourage further Allied undertakings on the West European mainland, until the Soviets made further advances. This would be instrumental in securing Soviet post war geopolitical hegemony. Reports of the Dieppe raid would only be released 30 years later, and would be thoroughly censored.

Though unskilled as a commander, Mountbatten would be appointed to preside over the independence of the Indian subcontinent, which was a long-term plan to transfer the entire subcontinent to the Soviets. He was also appointed commander of South East Asia in 1943; where he displayed inordinate sympathy for Chiang Kai-Shek. His mentor was Peter Murphy, a self avowed Marxist. Some writers have drawn direct connections between Mountbatten and the Soviets, but further investigation is required.[903]

---

[902] The Hole Story, prod. Richard Desjardins and Robert Monderie, National Film Board of Canada, 2011.

[903] See Richard Deacon, The Greatest Treason: The bizarre story of Hollis, Liddell and Mountbatten (London: Century, 1990). Also see Lynn Picknett, Clive Prince and Stephen Prior, War of the Windsors: A Century of Unconstitutional Monarchy (Mainstream Publishing, 2002).

Left: A D-Day commemorative stamp issued by the Canadian Government. © Canada Post. All Rights Reserved. Right: George Bush making a hand gesture. Copyright: Unknown. D-Day was also known as V-Day. It happened to be on 6-6-44. The V symbol made by the hands is used by secret societies. Note how the centerpiece of the above stamp illustration coincidentally bears resemblance to the same.

America

Commencement of anti-Nazi propaganda

To quote a gaming website,[904]

> "In the late 1930s, the first issues of Captain America comics hit the stands. The cover is a brave and striking image: Captain America, the Sentinel of Liberty, leaping through the air to deliver a devastating right cross to Der Fuhrer's face. That comic, drawn by Jack Kirby, was controversial because it predated the U.S. entering WWII."[905]

Conclusion on American involvement

The entire American World War II effort was bankrolled on inflation, creating major future losses for the American economy. The Americans would coordinate their offensive such that the Soviets would be able to make huge gains without much merit or effort of their own. In addition, the Americans would eliminate the Empire of Japan, which would have otherwise been the greatest threat to postwar Soviet prospects in the Far East.

The Powers that Be went to great lengths to ensnare Japan against America. Hitler would take this occasion to enable American entry into

---

904 In a preview of Freedom Force made by developer Irrational Games.

905 Yahoo Games Domain, "Preview of 'Freedom Force' by Irrational Games," <http://gamesdomain.yahoo.com/pc/freedom_force_vs_the_third_reich/preview/60113 > Accessed 27/01/05.

the European theatre, which was necessary for the gainful success later made by the Soviets. These efforts directed against Japan will be detailed in chapter seven.

As for American involvement in the European theatre, it is clear that America did not involve itself out of concern for Nazi tyranny. If that were the case, American leaders would have prevented the rearmament of Germany through American enterprises. In this late stage, they were still in a position to cut off Nazi oil supply, but they didn't. American leaders were neither committed to liberating the Jews under Nazi occupation. They could have made the Holocaust less deleterious by bombing the railroads connecting the concentration camps, and opening their own borders to Jewish refugees. It is ludicrous to believe that Allied intelligence was completely unaware of the Holocaust and only stumbled upon it while liberating Europe.

The Nazis as Clearing House for the Powers that Be

Since the Nazis had been earmarked for destruction long before their rise to power, there are many activities Hitler and the Nazis engaged in which were intended to help the Illuminati, and which could have never been accomplished without the smokescreen of World War II.

Secret Research

The SS Ahnenerbe conducted heavy research into ancient Illuminati Cathar treasures and relics. This research would disappear (See section on Ahnenerbe and Hitler's peculiar brand of Christianity in Chapter Three). The devotion of public resources towards such arcane subjects on a national level would otherwise be impossible. There was also secret research into weapons technology and UFO-like craft, which was later continued by the United States.

Haj Amin al Husseini

The Nazis would be conspicuous in extending friendship and asylum to Haj Amin al Husseini, Mufti of Jerusalem and archenemy of the Zionists. This was mainly for photo-ops, and was intended to discredit the Mufti. In reality, siding with Hitler would bring the downfall of Husseini and the forces he had mustered in the Balkans for the struggle against the Zionists. The Nazi leadership was actively engaged in thwarting his cause. In one instance, a Palestinian bomb-maker named Fauzi Kutbi entered Germany for advanced training and support. But was detained in a concentration camp after the Nazis incited him into an argument. The Mufti had to arrange for his release.

Eugenics

The Nazis contributed to furthering Eugenics, which was originally intended for trimming subject populations to more manageable sizes. The Nazi regime allowed its implementation on a scale that couldn't have been possible in other circumstances, making Germany a viable testing ground for Eugenics. They closely followed the writings of Madison Grant, an associate of the director of the American Birth Control League, Lothrop Stoddard. The Nazis publicly thanked both Grant and Stoddard. The American Birth Control League likewise took a great interest in ongoing Nazi developments, and published an article in May 1933 entitled *Eugenic Sterilization, an Urgent Need* by Ernst Rudin, founder of the Nazi Society for Racial Hygiene. A group of American eugenicists sat as guest judges in the German eugenic courts and returned with praises of the German system. To quote, "The [Nazi] sterilization law is weeding out the worst strains in the Germanic stock in a scientific and truly humanitarian way."[906] To quote Newman, "Margaret Sanger had no quarrel with the Nazis' compulsory sterilization program. Another Birth Control League member, Harry Laughlin, received an honorary MD degree from the University of Heidelberg, in appreciation of his 'contributions to the Third Reich.'"[907] In return, a number of American eugenicists urged the Eugenics Record Office (associated with the Birth Control League) to make Adolf Hitler an honorary member.[908] Although this was not done, Nazi articles were printed and Nazi sterilization policies were praised in the *Birth Control*

---

[906] Lothrop Stoddard, 1940, after spending 4 months in Germany. For excellent source material, see Professor Stefan Kuhl, The Nazi Connection: Eugenics, American Racism, & German National Socialism (Oxford 2002).

[907] Richard Hertz, Chance and Symbol: A study in Aesthetic and Ethical Consistency (University of Chicago Press, 1948) 107 Quoted in Hannah Newman, The Rainbow Swastika- A Report to the Jewish People About New Age Anti-Semitism; Human history according to the new age <http://philologos.org/__eb-trs/naB.htm> Web page as of 11/07/2004.

[908] Robert Proctor, Racial Hygiene; Medicine Under the Nazis (Harvard University Press, 2006) 103. Quoted in Hannah Newman, The Rainbow Swastika- A Report to the Jewish People About New Age Anti-Semitism; Human history according to the new age <http://philologos.org/__eb-trs/naB.htm> Web page as of 11/07/2004.

Review, even after American eugenicists were invited to witness their coercive and often brutal methods."[909]

Research into Mind Control and Torture

To quote Springmeier, "The Germans and Italians under the Nazi and Fascist governments began to do serious scientific research into trauma-based mind control. Under the auspices of the Kaiser Wilhelm Medical Institute in Berlin, Joseph Mengele conducted mind-control research on thousands of twins, and thousands of other hapless victims."[910] Later, the Allies would confiscate this research. According to Springmeier, it is currently being housed in the Suitland Annex (Washington) and only elitists are given clearance to access it. The only reason to preserve this research rather than destroy it is that it is currently being used. It is obvious that this barbaric research was conducted through the Nazis since the wartime conditions allowed unlimited German national resources to be dedicated to it. As of now, Springmeier estimates that there are over two million Americans who have been subjected to mind control, and though the CIA publicly admitted to undertaking mind control projects in 1970, the subject populations of Western countries are usually oblivious.[911]

To further quote Springmeier,

> […] insiders say that programmed DID (MPD) was developed in the Nazi concentration camps. The worldwide Illuminati planned the camps with the goal to determine what programs would work on children, and used the cover story of Nazi racial hatred to hide the real purpose of the camps--mind-control experiments that used large numbers of children traumatized by their separation from their parents.[912]

While writing his book, Springmeier came into contact with hundreds of mind control survivors. According to one of them, "[...] the genetic model wonder children born in Nazi Germany are still around. According to one source, the Nazi's produced numerous offspring of

---

909 Quoted in Hannah Newman, The Rainbow Swastika- A Report to the Jewish People About New Age Anti-Semitism; Human history according to the new age <http://philologos.org/__eb-trs/naB.htm> Web page as of 11/07/2004.

910 Fritz Springmeier, Deeper Insights into the Illuminati Formula (Web edition) 3

911 Fritz Springmeier, The Illuminati formula used to create an undetectable total mind controlled slave (Web Edition) 413.

912 Springmeier, Deeper Insights 10.

Hitler which were secretly taken to many countries [...]"[913] Elsewhere he is quoted as "[...] the authors [Springmeier and Wheeler] are aware of Hitler's descendants being in Oregon, and Washington as well as Pennsylvania. One of them in Portland, Oregon works for the Federal Government."[914]

To further quote,

> One of the Illuminati's research projects was to discover the psi gene--the genetic gene that would permit them to breed a master race with psychic abilities. One of the groups that the Illuminati has controlled which did research in this area was Nazi Germany. Mengele, in fact, was interested in the co-relation of blood types to psychic abilities.[915]

Mengele also contributed to sophisticating programming of multiple personalities. Mengele was trying to discover for the Nazi's how to change eye colour, and blinded several "test-subjects" in the process.

The Nazis were pursuing some research on the human skull, which may be related to mind control. Springmeier comments in Nazi "skull research," "We see only glimpses of this research in such things as the SS skeleton collection, written about in SS letters used as Nuremberg Trial Doc. No.s 87, 88, 91. Prof. Hirt at the Strassburg Anatomical Institute received 150 Jewish skeletons for research according to a secret SS document, marked Exhibit no. 086."[916]

The Nazis further expanded existing torture techniques. This research was later confiscated by the U.S. Navy and may be in use in Guantanamo Bay, Iraq, Uzbekistan and Turkey. To quote Springmeier, "Charts were made showing how much torture a given body weight at a given age can handle without death."[917] The Nazis "[...] did not research using parrots--they used live but expendable people. The Nazis were not above injecting drugs that induce respiratory paralysis or other responses and testing how the person's body would respond to drowning. I [Springmeier] would suggest that they analyzed oxygen contents in the human guinea pigs with mass spectrometers."[918]

---

[913] Springmeier, Deeper Insights 16.
[914] Springmeier, The Illuminati formula 176.
[915] Springmeier, Deeper Insights 134.
[916] Springmeier, Deeper Insights 168.
[917] Springmeier, The Illuminati formula 23.
[918] Springmeier, The Illuminati formula 290.

Transfer of gold and treasures

The Nazi invasion of surrounding Europe offered the Powers That Be a never before chance to confiscate priceless wealth and treasures which would otherwise be confined to churches, museums, private properties and institutions. As the Nazis would retreat towards Berlin, the same would be accomplished throughout Germany. In the confusion, which would ensue after the fall of Germany, the greatest robberies of all time took place. The legend of Nazi gold[919] has a real basis. Nazi elites like Himmler were noted for their tendencies to stash their palaces with select loot from conquered territories. This loot in terms of gold, silver, glassware, china, rugs, paintings, jewelry and currency is still to be estimated. Even among what was accidentally recovered by the Allies, 2.76 billion RM in boxes were found. When Germany fell, the Berlin Reichbank vaults were emptied. The presence of organized plunder on this scale can only point towards the Illuminati, whose foreknowledge of events would be used to their advantage (Recall the organized theft from the Baghdad museum immediately after the fall of Saddam).

There are indications of that certain Swiss Banks may have participated in ferreting away such wealth to South America. The more ugly fact is that a large portion of this wealth belonged to Jews who perished in the Holocaust, and even consisted of gold tooth filings recovered from crematoriums. The existence of this wealth broke out as a scandal, which was later hushed up. P.W Botha, President of South Africa in the 1980s revealed that the Rothschilds approached him when he was President, requesting to move the massive wealth belonging to German Jews who perished in the Holocaust, from the Swiss banks to South Africa![920] Hitler's personal gold, cash and diamonds may have been ferreted out of Germany through his agent, Otto Skorzeny in Spain.

Where did the Nazi Elite go?

We are expected to believe that Nazis were hunted down and prosecuted at Nuremberg. While others such as Eichman, were captured and brought

---

[919] The crew at Rotten.com has some interesting data in this regard. Rotten.com: Nazi Gold <http://www.rotten.com/library/history/nazi/nazi-gold/> Web page as of 11/07/2004

[920] In a conversation with David Icke. Note that this author is critical of Icke, who has brought incredulity to Fritz Springmeier's bloodline theory by inserting "Reptilians" into it. Icke has also displayed New Age tendencies. David Icke, "Was Hitler a Rothschild?," Davidicke.com <http://www.davidicke.com/icke/articles/hitler.html> Web page as of 11/07/2004

to justice later. And the remainder lived as fugitives in South America. The truth is that the Illuminati leadership of the Nazis were transferred through a pre-arranged relocation, to low profile places such as Chile and Argentina. They were ignored at Nuremberg. And even when sentenced to death, there is no way of telling whether the sentence was actually delivered. For example, it has now been revealed that Allied Intelligence faked the death of some Nazi operatives such as Horst Kopkow, in order to successfully rehabilitate them elsewhere.[921] Many others, such as scientists who would be useful for Illuminati projects elsewhere, were rescued by the Intelligence Agencies of the Allies. To quote,

> The Biographical Directory of Fellows and Members of the American Psychiatric Association reveals that in 1957 there were 7,104 American members in the American Psychiatric Association. Of those 7,104, a total of 1,253 had moved to America from Germany and Eastern Europe. This helps us understand the enormous influence Operation Paperclip had on America. Operation Paperclip was the CIA's project to smuggle Nazi criminals into our nation, some of which have now made Penn's campus infamous. No wonder the False Memory Syndrome got started at Pennsylvania University.[922]

The American Joint Chief of Staff approved Operation Overcast (later known as Operation Paperclip) on 6th July 1945. Allen Dulles had also conceived a parallel exercise, known as Operation Sunrise, which was to facilitate the escape and recruitment of Nazis by the CIA. His negotiator on the German side was SS commander Karl Wolfe, who had dispatched 300,000 Jews to Treblinka.[923] Towards the end of the war, the battle of the Bulge was coordinated by both the Nazi and Allied leadership, such that a large number of the Nazi elite would fall safely into Allied hands, to later undergo pre-arranged escapes. Nearly 10,000 Nazi elite and scientists were smuggled into America.[924] In order to make these individuals more palatable to the Intelligence Community, they were given a facelift as Anti-communist crusaders. They, along with other former Fascists from Italy and Spain formed the WACL (World Anti-

---

[921] Sarah Helm, "MI6 protected Nazi who killed 100 British agents," The Times May 14th 2005 <http://www.timesonline.co.uk/article/0,,2-1611185,00.html> Accessed 13/12/06.

[922] Fritz Springmeier, Deeper Insights into the Illuminati Formula (Web edition) 239.

[923] Mae Brussells, "The Nazi Connection to the Dallas JFK murder," The Rebel January 1984: ?? An archived copy is available at: <http://www.maebrussell.com/Mae Brussell Articles/Nazi Connection to JFK Assass.html> Web page as of 16/03/04

[924] Fritz Springmeier, The Illuminati formula used to create an undetectable total mind controlled slave (Web edition) 410.

Communist League).[925] If the United States leadership was really intent on fighting Communism, they would have not destroyed Germany and Japan in World War II.

Adolf Hitler

One would expect the death of the biggest figure of World War II would be subject to intense scrutiny. After all, if we are to believe in the myth of Hitler as a lone madman, Hitler was expected to die in vindication of his stance. However, the death of Adolf Hitler is an enigma, the analysis of which is beyond the scope of this book. It is obvious that such an important operative would be relocated after successful completion of his assignment. The US administration bent over its back to accommodate thousands of Nazi leadership figures and operatives. Wouldn't Hitler be shown some consideration? Chuck Anesi[926] raises some interesting points.

- According to the official story, Hitler and Eva Braun committed suicide by swallowing cyanide.[927] Hitler and Eva Braun's corpses were allegedly cremated in the garden after being doused with gasoline. It was only Hitler's teeth found in the ashes, which were used to identify Hitler.[928] Accounts of Hitler's associates regarding his last hour are inconsistent with each other.
- Most of the research and analysis into the death and purported remains of Hitler was done by the Soviets. As most may understand, the Soviet Union was a place where there were no fair investigative procedures, and everything is subject to doctoring and tampering. Again, the Soviet Union offered contradictory conclusions. At Potsdam, Stalin blurted out that Hitler had escaped. Then the Soviet Government released photos of what was purported to be Hitler's corpse, which was apparently in good condition and showed full facial features. Even though the official story states that the Russians found charred remains.[929] It is still not known how the Soviet's

[925] Springmeier, The Illuminati formula 412.
[926] Chuck Anesi, "The World was Lied to About Hitler's Death," Blackraiser.com < http://www.blackraiser.com/nredoubt/identity.htm > Accessed 04/11/06.
[927] Robert G. L. Waite in Walter C. Langer, The Mind of Hitler – The Secret Wartime Report (NY & London: Basic books Inc., 1972) 238.
[928] Also confirmed by Robert G. L. Waite in Walter C. Langer, The Mind of Hitler – The Secret Wartime Report (NY & London: Basic books Inc., 1972) 238.
[929] Robert G. L. Waite in Walter C. Langer, The Mind of Hitler – The Secret Wartime Report (NY & London: Basic books Inc., 1972) 238.

acquired the photos, whom these photos represented and when they were actually taken. Again, the photos exhibit inconsistencies.

- Hitler and many of his associates had doubles. They also had access to plastic surgery.
- A hundred-year ban was imposed on some data concerning the so-called deaths of some Nazi leaders.
- According to Ada Petrova and Peter Watson,[930] "the US Office of Censorship intercepted a letter in July 1945 written from someone in Washington. Addressed to a Chicago newspaper, the letter claimed that Hitler was living in a German-owned hacienda 450 miles from Buenos Aires!" Though the US Government followed it up and debunked the report, one can draw different conclusions considering the covert role of United States Intelligence in rehabilitating prominent Nazis.

Ron T. Hansig has written a thorough and scholarly book on the subject.[931] According to him, there was absolutely no trace of the corpse of Hitler's mistress, Eva Braun. The Gestapo chief Heinrich Mueller told his US interrogators in 1948 that he had arranged Hitler's escape to Spain.

Fritz Kraemer

> There is one name and two persons, and I think it's one name and one person. That's why it's important to pursue this particular problem.
>
> *-Mae Brussels, Broadcast # 787, January 5th 1987*

This section attempts to illustrate the controversy surrounding Fritz Kraemer. The author has tried his best to present a neutral viewpoint and has avoided taking sides. The purpose of including this section in the book is to provide a balanced account of the controversy surrounding Fritz Kraemer.

To illustrate the controversy of Fritz Kraemer and his namesake in the highest echelons of U.S. administration, the table below has been created. It is based on key facts culled from relevant sources. When the American Fritz G.A. Kraemer passed away, the details that emerged

---

930 Ada Petrova and Peter Watson, " The Death of Hitler – The Full Story with New Evidence from Secret Russian Archives," Washingtonpost.com <http://www.washingtonpost.com/wp-srv/style/longterm/books/chap1/deathofhitler.htm > Accessed 04/11/06.

931 Ron T. Hansig, Hitler's Escape (Athena Press Publishers, 2005)

following his death were probably the most comprehensive ever, on an individual who was otherwise very elusive and kept a low profile.

The following tabulates the differences between the German General Fritz Kraemer and the American Fritz Gustav Anton Kraemer. Mae Brussell's key claims are included as well. The late Mae Brussells was the most popular conspiracy historian of our time. Many of her analyses on the murder of President Kennedy were later incorporated into almost all relevant conspiracy literature and film. Therefore, her claims should not be dismissed at first hand. Brussells was fully confident of her claims about Fritz Kraemer. She announced them over public radio and wrote to President Reagan to launch an inquiry. But the authorities snubbed her. Throughout her lifetime, no one, including Fritz G. A. Kraemer came forward to rebut her claim.

There are several different possibilities. I leave it to the reader to judge. The following are some possibilities I have come up with:

1. Mae Brussells got her analysis wrong. Fritz G.A. Kraemer and General Fritz Kraemer are two separate entities
2. Fritz G.A. Kraemer and General Fritz Kraemer are two separate entities, but General Fritz Kraemer was secretly ferreted to the United States, where he worked for the U.S. government. And would be mistaken by Mae for the namesake, Fritz G.A. Kraemer.
3. Fritz G.A. Kraemer and General Fritz Kraemer are two separate entities, but Fritz G.A. Kraemer may have had a controversial past, and was forced to keep a low profile until his death.
4. Mae Brussells got her analysis right.
5. General Fritz Kraemer didn't exist (improbable).

The sources used are as follows:

1. F.V. DeLaglio, "SS Brigadefuhrer Fritz Kraemer," 12. SS-Panzerdivision "Hitlerjugend" An essential rundown on Hitler's General, Fritz Kraemer. Compiled from German Literature. <http://home.att.net/~SSPzHJ/FritzKraemer.html> Accessed 04/11/06.
2. World Security Network, Fritz Kramer on Excellence. <http://www.worldsecuritynetwork.com/fritzkraemer/index.cfm> Accessed 05/11/06.
3. Michael T. Kaufman, "Fritz Kraemer, 95, Tutor to U.S. Generals and Kissinger, Dies," New York Times 19/11/03. Accessed 04/11/06.

<http://www.nytimes.com/2003/11/19/national/19KRAE.html> Accessed 04/11/06.

4. Telegraph.co.uk, Fritz Kraemer. 10/11/03. <http://www.telegraph.co.uk/news/main.jhtml?xml=/news/2003/11/10/db1001.xml&sSheet=/portal/2003/11/10/ixportal.html > Accessed 04/11/06.
5. Nick Thimmesch, "The iron mentor of the Pentagon – Why even Henry Kissinger needs Dr. Fritz Kraemer," Washington Post March 2nd 1975.
6. Mae Brussells, Transcription of World Watchers International Broadcast # 787, January 5th 1987. A copy is available at <http://www.maebrussell.com/Transcriptions/787.html> Accessed 04/11/06.
7. Mae Brussells, Transcription of World Watchers International. Broadcast # 560, August 30th 1982. A copy is available at <http://www.newsmakingnews.com/MBtape560,8,30,82.htm> Accessed 04/11/06.

<table>
<tr>
<th>Fritz Kraemer (Nazi General)</th>
<th>Fritz Kramer according to Mae Brussells</th>
<th>Fritz Gustav Anton Kraemer (Pentagon official)</th>
</tr>
<tr>
<td>
Copyright © 1999 F.V.DeLaglio
F.V.DeLaglio, SS Brigadefuhrer Fritz Kraemer, <http://home.att.net/~SSPzHJ/FritzKraemer.html> Accessed 04/11/06. Original Copyright: unknown

DeLaglio cites his information from Waffen-SS Commanders Vol.1 - Mark C. Yerger Pgs. 326-327 and Die Eichenlaubträger 1940-45 Band 1 - Franz Thomas Pg. 399</td>
<td>"Hitler's Fritz Kraemer disappeared from all Nazi history books after he was released from Dachau prison. There's only one picture of him as a prisoner, and nothing before, whereas all the others have a history before or after or since. A group of almost 70, I believe, were arrested. The only one who has no face in any history books is Hitler's Fritz Kraemer (Mae 787)."</td>
<td>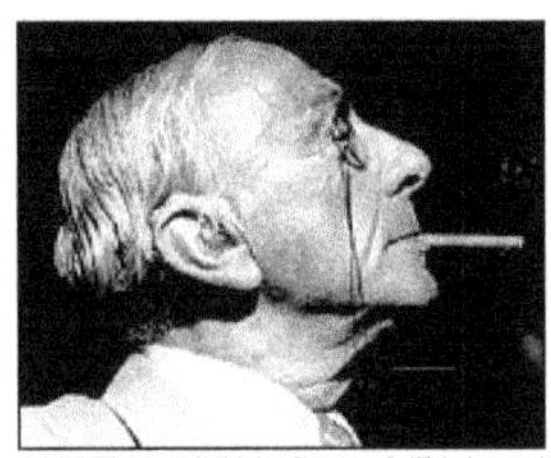
© NY Times. All Rights Reserved. This image is a thumbnail; Access the full picture at the source website. Kaufman, Michael T., Fritz Kraemer, 95, Tutor to U.S. Generals and Kissinger, Dies. New York Times 19/11/03. Accessed 04/11/06. Minimized Reproduction Under Fair Dealing.

Original Caption: Fritz Kraemer struck up a friendship with Henry Kissinger when the two, fellow German refugees, were privates in the United States Army.</td>
</tr>
<tr>
<td>Born: 12th December 1900 (DeLaglio)</td>
<td></td>
<td>Born: July 3rd 1908 (Telegraph)</td>
</tr>
<tr>
<td>Location of birth: Stettin, Germany</td>
<td></td>
<td>Location of birth: Essen, Germany (NYT). He was the only adult male of the small village in Essen, who survived the war (Telegraph).</td>
</tr>
</table>

Prussian nobility.	Brussells hints at I.G. Farben. (Mae 787).	Son of a prosecutor and a heiress (NYT). Mother was daughter of a Ruhr industrialist. (Telegraph). Prussian aristocracy. 19?? Parents divorced. Mother ran a children's home on the family estate near Weisbaden. (WP75)
Joined Wehrmacht at age of 18 (DeLaglio)		Wore a monocle and carried a riding crop (Telegraph)
Joined Prussian Police at age 22 (DeLaglio)		Was supporting the Hohenzollern monarchy against Communists and Nazis in street battles in 1930. In 1933, left Germany to work as advisor the League of Nations and wrote eight books on International Law. (NYT) Married his Swedish wife Britta Bjorkander in 1933.
Became Oberlieutenant on October 1st 1934 (DeLaglio)	Brussells hints at connections to Mussolini.	Studied at Berlin's Arndt Gymnasium, the LSE, and Geneva and the universities of Berlin and Frankfurt. Also studied in the London school of Economics and obtained a doctorate in Political Science from the University of Rome in 1934 (WSN).
	Mae Brussells claims that L. Fletcher Prouty, author of *The Secret Team — The CIA, It's Allies, and Control of the World* (Ballantine, 1970),' disclosed to her that Sven Kraemer was working with Frank Carlucci, the National Security Advisor. Carlucci would later become infamous for his association with the Carlyle group. (Mae 787).	19?? Had a son called Sven, who is currently a Pentagon official. To quote, "enjoyed a distinguished career on the National Security Council staffs of four presidents and 10 national security advisers - a 16-year unbeaten record (Telegraph)." Also had a daughter, Madeleine Bryant. (NYT)

<table>
<tr>
<td>Graduated from the Berlin War Academy in May 1935. (DeLaglio)

Appointed commander of 5.Kompanie / Infanterieregiment 55 in 1936. (DeLaglio)

In March 1936, he was assigned Ib of the 13. Motorized Infanterie Division

On 6th October 1939, Won Iron Cross Second Class for actions in Poland. (DeLaglio)

On 26th May 1940, won Iron Cross First Class for actions in France. (DeLaglio)

On 11th October 1940, he was promoted to Ia of the 13. Infanterie Division. On that very day, that infantry was reorganized into the 13. Panzerdivision (DeLaglio). I suppose timing works when you have a bloodline.

As 1a of the 13. Panzerdivision, he served in Russia, winning German Gold Cross on February 26th 1942. (DeLaglio)

Won Knights Cross on 17th December 1942. (DeLaglio)

In January 1943,General Josef 'Sepp' Dietrich selected him as senior administrative officer (1a) of the I.SS Panzer Corp. (DeLaglio)

Made SS-Oberführer on 1st September 1943. (DeLaglio)</td>
<td>Mae quotes the following information obtained on the American Fritz G. A. Kraemer: "8/18/82, National Records Center, 9700 Page Blvd. St. Louis, Miss.63132 "Served U.S. Army April 19, 1945 to Feb 25, 1948","Honorably Relief" (sic) "Prior service SN 33741993, May 28, 1943 to April 18, 1945." Earlier letter, Defense Investigate Service, Wash. D.C. "Kraemer inducted Ft. Meyer, Va 21 May 1943". SN0-201-2160. Two Army</td>
<td>Fled to the United States in 1939. (NYT) leaving behind wife and infant son (Telegraph). Though wife had Swedish citizenship and the infant was born in Britain, the Nazis denied them exit. (WP75).

19??: Worked as a woodcutter in New Hampshire (WP75)

19??: Worked at the Library of Congress for $50 per month. (WP75)

19??: Worked as a proctor in the dorm of an American University. (WP75)

19?? Graduated from the US National War College (WSN).

Drafted into the US Army in 1943 (Telegraph). His commanding officer was Maj-Gen Alexander Bolling of the 84th "Railsplitter" Division (Telegraph).

</td>
</tr>
</table>

	Serial Numbers, two enlistments, two discharges (Mae 560)."	*Original Caption: Henry Kissinger (left), the talent, with his scout and mentor Dr. Fritz Kraemer, in 1945, as soldiers in the 84th US Infantry division in Germany again, their Heimat until 1938.*
Officially admitted into the SS as SS-Brigadeführer on 1st August 1944. (DeLaglio) Acted as deputy for Dietrich during the Allied invasion of Normandy. (DeLaglio) Succeeded Hubert Mayer as commander of the 12.SS-Panzerdivision "Hitlerjugend" on 24 October, 1944. (DeLaglio) On 13th November 1944, he was transferred to the Reserve, and Hugo Kraas now commanded Hitlerjugend. (DeLaglio) Served as Dietrich's Ia with the 6.Panzerarmee (DeLaglio) Surrendered to Allies along with Dietrich (DeLaglio) and Skorzeny ((Mae 787).		1944: Was a private in the United States Louisiana Army Camp in World War II. Met Henry Kissinger and Donald Rumsfield. Kissinger would later write "Fritz Kraemer was the greatest single influence in my formative years." (NYT). Kissinger was also a German-Jewish refugee. Though trained as riflemen, both Kissinger and Kraemer were assigned to intelligence units (WP75). They interrogated captured Nazis (WP75).
Branded war criminal for the Malmedy Massacre in the **battle of the Bulge** (1944-1945). (DeLaglio). This massacre of Americans might have been an attempt to eliminate soldiers who had witnessed covert collaboration between the Americans and the Germans. What was the role of Fritz Kraemer?	"When the Battle of the Bulge was over and America won the war, by May of 1945, all three of these men important to Hitler, were taken prisoner together: Kraemer, Dietrich, and Skorzeny. All three were in charge of the Battle of the Bulge for Hitler after the war. And all three were stationed in the exact locations of Henry Kissinger and Fritz Kraemer, who were German, who wore American military uniforms, and were located in the same location as Hitler's agents (Mae 787)."	Fought in the Battle of the Bulge and in the Battles of the Ruhr and the Rhineland (WSN). Captured in the Battle of the Bulge by Germans, precisely, the defenders of Geilenkirchen (Telegraph). "Persuaded" them to surrender themselves and the town to him, and was awarded a Bronze Star and a battlefield commission. (NYT). 1945: Reunited with wife and son (WSN).

 Kraemer on trial at Dachau in May 1946. The number 33 has esoteric significance. Copyright: Unknown	Brussells quotes that the book *The Last Days of Patton* by Ladislas Farago, (McGraw Hill, 1981) claims that the American Fritz Kraemer was with Patton, and that he was a U.S. Army General (as opposed to Lieutenant, Mae 787). Skorzeny was an expert in training Germans to impersonate Americans (Mae 787).	
Tried in Dachau in 1946. Sentenced to 10 years. (DeLaglio)	Oberammergau was the place where Hitler's Fritz Kraemer was held prisoner (Mae 787). There are underground Nazi installations in this region.	Assigned to Counter Intelligence Corps (C.I.C.) School at Oberammergau in Bavaria, along with Kissinger (WSN) 19??: Assigned to Fort Riley in Kansas (WP75). 1948: Left Active Duty (WSN)
Released in 1948 by intervention of John J. McCloy, a mentor of Kissinger, who also terminated the sentences of the Krupps. (Mae 787). After his release, lived in Hoxter, Germany. (DeLaglio)	Commenting on an article in the Houston Post dated December 24th 1986, Brussells claims "He isn't appointed by the Congress; he isn't approved by the Congress. He is hand-picked by Jeanne Kirkpatrick who comes out of that Centre for Strategic and International Studies." She further claimed that Brzezinski and Kissinger were both loyal to Kraemer. (Mae 787). She also suggests that Fritz Kraemer was a Plans Officer for the	1951: Gained employment in the Pentagon. To quote, "became chief civilian adviser to successive US Army Chiefs of Staff and Secretaries of the Army; for much of the Cold War he wielded an influence out of all proportion to the formal position that he held (Telegraph)." He was a master of geopolitics, though his mastery may have not saved the Americans at Vietnam. Served as Senior Advisor to the US Army Chief of Staff (WSN). Plans Officer for the Chief of Staff, U.S. Army (WP75) Began working for the Pentagon in 1951. He is said to have occupied an office

	Pentagon for up to 30 years (Mae 560).	connected with strategic developments in South East Asia. Considered to be a Tutor to U.S. Generals 1963: Retired from the Army Reserve as a Lt. Colonel (1963). "He approved Kissinger's hard-line agreement on the use of U. S. troops in the Cambodian invasion, 1970, and the mining and bombing of Haiphong in the spring of 1972 (WP75)" Retired from the Pentagon in 1978. Died in Washington on September 8th 2003 at the age of 95. Buried at Arlington National Cemetery (WSN). Posthumously rehabilitated as an intellectual; despite the US debacle in Vietnam.

Reinhardt Gehlen

The head of Hitler's intelligence, Reinhardt Gehlen, later worked for the CIA to transfer Nazi elite to America. Gehlen would later form what was known as the Gehlen Organisation, a CIA front dedicated to recruiting and rescuing former Nazis. The Gehlen organisation would become the basis for West Germany's foreign intelligence service, the Bundesnachrichtendienst (BND).[932] Newly revealed CIA documents have shown that the CIA recruited five of Adolf Eichmann's associates,[933] presumably through the Gehlen organization. Gehlen would later retire to a chalet in the Illuminati homeland of Bavaria. The chalet was a gift from Allen Dulles.[934] Gehlen would also receive the Sovereign Military Order of Malta award from the Knights of Malta. Gehlen's agent in the United States was Otto Albrecht von Bolschwing,

---

932 Yossi Melman, "CIA Recruited Five Of Adolph Eichmann's Associates," Haaretz.com 2-5-05 The article is no longer available on the Haaretz Website.
933 Yossi Melman, "CIA Recruited Five Of Adolph Eichmann's Associates," Haaretz.com 2-5-05 The article is no longer available on the Haaretz Website.
934 Mae Brussells, "The Nazi Connection to the Dallas JFK murder," The Rebel January 1984: ?? An archived copy is available at: <http://www.maebrussell.com/Mae Brussell Articles/Nazi Connection to JFK Assass.html> Web page as of 16/03/04

a captain of Himmler's notorious SS. The Powers that Be would let Bolschwing freely enter the United States where he would be associated with the elitists in Nixon's political campaign and with Reagan's appointment secretary.[935] Another member of Bolschwing's Gestapo network, Nicolae Malaxa moved to United States in 1952 with $200 million. Chase Manhattan bank financially assisted him and Nixon introduced a private bill to let him gain residence.[936]

Rudolf Hess

We are told that Hess flew to England on a peace mission and was arrested and imprisoned for life. Hess landed in England on the Estate of the Duke of Hamilton, a Scottish member of the Golden Dawn. The Duke of Hamilton had also met Hess at the Berlin Olympics before. Hess is said to have taken this action on advice of Karl Hausofer, the Nazi party philosopher who maintained close contact with British members of the Golden Dawn.[937] According to Fritz Springmeier,

> Rudolf Hess was hidden by the Illuminati during World war II. There is a book out which shows the military medical records of the real Rudolf Hess who was wounded in World war I, and the medical records of the fake 'Hess' who was imprisoned in Spandau prison after World war II. This is why the Nazi's on trial at Nuremberg laughed when they saw 'Hess' for the first time in custody, they laughed because they knew he wasn't the real Hess.[938]

Hess is said to have died/committed suicide/murdered or was secretly whisked away from Spandau prison in 1987. The controversy surrounding the strange circumstances has resulted in the release of Hess's files to the public in 1992, in advance of the 2017 schedule. Yet the findings are inconclusive. A convincing book[939] places him on the plane that crashed in Scotland, killing the Duke of Kent, George Edward Alexander Edmund. This may explain the necessity to prosecute and imprison a duplicate Hess.

---

[935] Brussells, "The Nazi Connection."
[936] Brussells, "The Nazi Connection."
[937] Servando González, Origins of the Swastika: The Hausofer Connection. <http://www.intelinet.org/swastika/swasti02.htm> Web page as of 11/07/2004
[938] Fritz Springmeier, Bloodlines of the Illuminati (Spring Arbor distributors, 1998) 383. GlobalGrey PDF edition 2013 <http://www.globalgrey.co.uk/Pages/Books-Conspiracies/Bloodlines-Of-The-Illuminati.html> Web page as of 03/07/13.
[939] Lynn Picknet, Clive Prince and Stephen Prior, Double Standards – The Rudolf Hess Coverup (Time Warner Paperbacks, 2002)

Joseph Mengele

Josef Mengele

Source: <http://www.gesch.med.uni-erlangen.de/gewissen/ausstell/zwill/text_03.htm> Accessed 30/11/06 © Photographie, 1943, Gedenkstätte und Museum Auschwitz-Birkenau, Neg.-Nr. 21383/12 Minimized Reproduction Under Fair Dealing.

Mengele in 1971, photo for a fake ID.
Copyright: Unknown

Joseph Mengele hailed from a Bavarian family, and was the most notorious of Nazi scientists. He used the Holocaust as an opportunity to experiment in the areas the Illuminati sought to further research, such as mind control and genetics. The Holocaust presented a window of opportunity which was never before to be witnessed in history. A large number of people from different categories of gender, age, race and physical attributes were available to Mengele for experimenting on. Mengele was also said to be a practitioner of Kabala (Babylonian black magic).[940] Mengele is most infamous for the comfort with which he executed his job at Auschwitz. According to an Auschwitz eyewitness, "Some like Werner Rhode who hated his work, and Hans Koenig who was deeply disgusted by the job, had to get drunk before they appeared on the ramp [to separate newcomers to Auschwitz for immediate extermination or further 'experiments']. Only two doctors performed the selections without any stimulants of any kind: Dr. Josef Mengele and Dr. Fritz Klein. Dr. Mengele was particularly cold and cynical."[941] Mengele also introduced the use of trained German shepherds on concentration camp inmates.[942] Dr. Mengele used 3,000 twins during the time of 1943-1944 for research. Most of these twins died.[943] The Powers that Be arranged for Mengele to escape to Argentina, which was being ruled by the

---

[940] Fritz Springmeier, The Illuminati formula used to create an undetectable total mind controlled slave (Web edition) 248.

[941] Douglas Lynott, "Killers from history-Josef Mengele," Crime Library <http://www.crimelibrary.com/serial_killers/history/mengele/aus_4.html?sect=6> Web page as of 16/03/04

[942] Fritz Springmeier, The Illuminati formula used to create an undetectable total mind controlled slave (Web edition) 23.

[943] Springmeier, The Illuminati formula 412.

Freemason Juan Peron, who actively aided Nazis relocating in Argentina. While pop history portrays Mengele as a fugitive on the run, he was still engaged in research for the Intelligence Agencies of the Allies, and was being pampered throughout this time. According to Springmeier, an authority on mind control, Mengele had a large circular red bed in a private castle in Death Valley, California, which he stocked with his little girl slaves, who already had sexual alters.[944] Springmeier reveals the following information,

> Actually Mengele spent a great deal of time travelling worldwide especially to places like Tavistock and China Lake's Naval Intelligence base where Monarch slaves were created from innocent children. [...]In 1956, as part of the ongoing deception [and a testament to the audacity of the elitists] Joseph Mengele applied and got an Argentinean foreign resident permit under his own name. He even travelled to Europe to various countries in 1956 using his own name.[945]

Springmeier met a mind control victim of Mengele who claimed that Mengele continued to program him in Canada.[946] Springmeier arranged the rescue hundreds of survivors of mind control trauma through his books and personal intervention. In one book for mind control survivors, he writes that "Mengele is well-known by his Monarch victims for his daisy game programming. He would pull off a daisy and say 'I love you.' Then he would pull of one and say, 'I love you not.' When the last daisy petal came out 'I love you not,' he would then kill a small child in front of the child he was programming."[947] When word spread that Mengele was still alive and traveling among elitist circles, Mengele's death was staged as a drowning accident in Brazil. Later, the bones would be dug up to "confirm" to the world that he had been dead. However, his family never claimed his bones.

Dr. D. Ewen Cameron

According to Springmeier, Dr. Cameron worked with Mengele and became a programmer codenamed Dr. White.[948] Though Cameron was

---

[944] Fritz Springmeier, Deeper Insights into the Illuminati Formula (Web edition) 229.
[945] Springmeier, Deeper Insights 429.
[946] Fritz Springmeier, The Illuminati formula used to create an undetectable total mind controlled slave (Web edition) 410.
[947] Springmeier, The Illuminati formula 429.
[948] Fritz Springmeier, The Illuminati formula used to create an undetectable total mind controlled slave (Web edition) 413.

not a Nazi, his association with the likes of Mengele makes his career worth investigating. Elsewhere, Springmeier writes,

> Cameron was president of the powerful American Psychiatric Association, and later the president of the Canadian Psychiatric Association, and then later the first president of the World Association of Psychiatrists. He was chairman of the Canadian Scientific Planning Committee. Dr. D. Ewen Cameron, of Montreal, Canada was Dr. White when carrying out Monarch programming. Cameron tried to continue some of Mengele's eye colour research in Canada. Mengele was trying to discover for the Nazi's how to make brown eyes blue. Cameron received funding from the Illuminati. Cameron also got funding from the CIA. The Rockefeller Foundation gave him $40,000 in 1943 to create the Allen Memorial Institute for psychiatry, an Illuminati front.[949]

According to another source "A secret laboratory was established and funded by CIA director Allen Dulles in Montreal, Canada at McGill University in the Allen Memorial Institute headed by psychiatrist Dr. Ewen Cameron."[950] If the likes of Cameron were on the Nuremberg tribunal hearing cases against Nazi doctors, one can only assume how many other associates of Mengele were rescued. Dr. Cameron and his associates researched virtual reality, electro shock, sleep deprivation, memory implantation, memory erasure, sensory modification, psychoactive drug experiments etc. Though we are expected to believe this was done for the cold war (a cover for many questionable activities), this perverted research has no use except for the Illuminati. It is important to note Springmeier's observation that in huge countries like India, there are almost no cases of multiple personality disorders whereas in countries where the Illuminati has pervasive influence, all these disorders abound.

The Interpol

The Interpol originally consisted of members of the Berlin based Nazi International Secret Police. After the war, it was moved to Paris and Herbert Hoover was made vice-president. The Interpol was noted for its

---

[949] Springmeier, The Illuminati formula 413.

[950] Illuminati Conspiracy Archive: Operation Paperclip Case file <http://www.conspiracyarchive.com/NWO/project_paperclip.htm> Web page as of 16/03/04

refusal to hunt escaped Nazi elites. According to Mae Brussells, A former SS officer, Paul Dickopf was later made its President.[951]

The Knights of Malta

One of the many forerunners of the Templar Knights, the Knights of Malta[952] have independent sovereign status under international law and even have a permanent observer status at the UN.[953] Were Knight of Malta passports issued to aid escaping members of the Third Reich?[954] This escape scheme became known as the Rat Run. Reinhardt Gehlen played a major role in coordinating the Rat Run. Gehlen was evacuated by the CIA dressed as an American General. He immediately went for work with the CIA.

Richard Von Weizsacker and the Vatican

The Vatican may have participated in the Rat Run, considering the fact that Pope Eugenio Pacelli hailed from bloodlined nobility. The Vatican has still not been forthcoming in this affair. The Nazi Baron Von Weizsacker worked as a liaison between Adolf Hitler and Pope Pius XII during the battle of the Bulge (such as to affect Nazi defeat but at the same time, leaving a window of escape for prominent Nazis to the Vatican). Baron Weizsacker was convicted at Nuremberg for deporting French Jews to Auschwitz. His son, Richard Von Weizsacker became the President of Germany.[955] Another curious character connecting the Vatican, the Soviet Union, the Nazis, the Gehlen organisation, Freemasonry, George Bush, South America and the big banks is Licio Gelli. Gelli supplied Vatican passports to Nazis in the Rat Run. Gelli

---

[951] Mae Brussells, "The Nazi Connection to the Dallas JFK murder," The Rebel January 1984: ?? An archived copy is available at: <http://www.maebrussell.com/Mae Brussell Articles/Nazi Connection to JFK Assass.html> Web page as of 16/03/04

[952] The name was adopted after the Templars fled Jerusalem for Malta, from the Muslims.

[953] Anonymous, New World Order- The Movie: Knights of Malta <http://www.geocities.com/newworldorder_themovie/knightsofmalta.html> Web page as of 16/03/04

[954] Anonymous, New World Order- The Movie: Knights of Malta <http://www.geocities.com/newworldorder_themovie/knightsofmalta.html> Web page as of 16/03/04

[955] Mae Brussells, World Watchers International, Broadcast # 650, 5/21/84. Some information on Weizsacker is also revealed by Brussells in a letter to President Reagan. Brussells interpreted the presence of ex-Nazis as Fascist resurgence, a conclusion I find erroneous. Rather, Fascists were being rehabilitated after their role in the emergence of the Soviet Union.

also founded the P2 Masonic lodge, which was used to buy out the Italian parliament by special interests. Gelli has also been fingered in the murder of people who went rogue against the Illuminati, such as Pope John Paul I and banker Roberto Calvi.[956]

The Roman Catholic Archbishop of Poland, Archbishop Stanislaw Wielgus, who took office on 5th January 2007, was forced to resign a day later, amid revelations that he cooperated with the Communist era secret police.[957] Was the Vatican also involved in preparing the ground for expanding Soviet influence following the World Wars?

Klaus Barbie

Klaus Barbie, head of the French Gestapo and became known as the Butcher of Lyons for his role in the death of more than 4000 people under Nazi occupation. He was recruited by the CIA and offered safe passage to South America. Though later caught and tried, he only served four years of his conviction after which he "died." Barbie and other Nazi elite were hidden with the 370th Counter Intelligence Corps at Obergamergau, along with Hitler's General Fritz Kraemer. One of their keepers was Private Henry Kissinger, who would emerge as a protégé of McCloy, another character who helped shield many prominent Nazis.[958] Barbie was involved in violent coups in South America.

Goering and Hausofer

Herman Goering (actually a Bavarian born as Rosenheim), the founder of the Gestapo and advocate of the Final Solution, committed "suicide" after being captured. Himmler and Hausofer also committed "suicide" after being caught. This could have been a staged exit strategy to discard their public personas and start with new identities.

---

[956] Illuminati Conspiracy Archive: Operation Paperclip Case file < http://www.conspiracyarchive.com/NWO/project_paperclip.htm> Web page as of 16/03/04

[957] Associated Press, "Warsaw Archbishop quits amid spying scandal," AP January 7th 2007 <http://www.msnbc.msn.com/id/16508126/> Accessed 7/01/07.

[958] Mae Brussells, "The Nazi Connection to the Dallas JFK murder," The Rebel January 1984: ?? An archived copy is available at: <http://www.maebrussell.com/Mae Brussell Articles/Nazi Connection to JFK Assass.html> Web page as of 16/03/04

Otto Skorzeny

Otto Skorzeny lived in Franco's Spain after the War and died there in 1975. During his years with the Nazis, he participated in the hunting of Merovingian relics in France and rescued Mussolini on one occasion. Skorzeny also founded the secret organisation called Odessa, which facilitated the escape of Nazi top brass to South America. Skorzeny played a role in a number of violent coups in South America.

Otto Olendorf

SS General Otto Olendorf participated in the Holocaust but wasn't considered important enough to be prosecuted.

Martin Bormann

Martin Bormann, Hitler's former Riechsleiter was present at Hitler's "suicide," but managed to "escape" through the burning half-conquered city of Berlin. He escaped[959] to South America protected by the network coordinating the Rat Run. He was later reported as dead. To quote Springmeier, "Bormann came from a generational occult family. He was noted for his harshness, brutality and dominating personality."[960] Bormann is said to have used the funds of the Perons (Nazi sympathizers in Argentina) to fund the clandestine activities of the Gehlen organization and Odessa.[961] To further quote Brussells,

> In *A Study of a Master Spy*, published in London in 1961, Bob Edwards, a Member of Parliament and Kenneth Dunne, presented documentary evidence that Allen Dulles of the CIA carried on secret conferences with representatives of Hitler's SS Security Office in February and March 1943. They learned that Official Washington knew Martin Bormann, Deputy Fuhrer of Hitler's Germany, masterminded the international 'Die Spinne' (Spider) underground organization [...].[962]

---

[959] A book worth reading in this regard is Ladislas Farago, Aftermath: Martin Bormann and the Forth Reich (Avon, 1975) This book was the chief inspiration for Peter Levenda.

[960] Fritz Springmeier, Bloodlines of the Illuminati (Spring Arbor distributors, 1998). <http://www.thewatcherfiles.com/bloodlines/index.htm> Web page as of 16/03/04

[961] Mae Brussells, "The Nazi Connection to the Dallas JFK murder," The Rebel January 1984: ?? An archived copy is available at: <http://www.maebrussell.com/Mae Brussell Articles/Nazi Connection to JFK Assass.html> Web page as of 16/03/04

[962] Brussells, "The Nazi Connection."

Walter Dornberger

General Walter Dornberger was to be hanged at Nuremberg for war crimes.[963] But instead landed a cozy job as Director of Research and Development at Bell Aircraft. Dornberger was the boss of Michael Paine,[964] in whose home Lee Oswald spent some time. The Paines would later provide "evidence" against Oswald. The Paines are descendants of the elitist Cabot family.[965]

Heinrich Rupp

Heinrich Rupp would go to work for the CIA and was involved in torpedoing Jimmy Carter's re-election, by delaying the freeing of American hostages in Iran.[966]

Helmet Streikher

Helmet Streikher was an SS officer under Reinhardt Gehlen. The CIA immediately accepted him and from then onwards, he lead the life of a regular CIA operative. He helped plan the Bay of Pigs operation,[967] which could have been an engineered failure aimed at discrediting Kennedy.

Kurt-George Kiesinger

Kurt-George Kiesinger directed the Nazi radio propaganda division of Von Ribbentrop with 195 specialists under his supervision during World War II. He also acted as a liaison between his department and propaganda minister Joseph Goebbels. Kurt-George Kiesinger became Chancellor of West Germany.[968]

The Scientists

It is important to note that not all Nazis who left Germany were Illuminati operatives. There were thousands of scientists whom the

---

963 Brussells, "The Nazi Connection."
964 Brussells, "The Nazi Connection."
965 Brussells, "The Nazi Connection."
966 Illuminati Conspiracy Archive: Operation Paperclip Case file <http://www.conspiracyarchive.com/NWO/project_paperclip.htm> Web page as of 16/03/04
967 Brussells, "The Nazi Connection."
968 Brussells, "The Nazi Connection."

Illuminati brought into America and the Soviet Union to work for new projects. They held a circumstantial affiliation with the Nazis. However, even among these scientists, many had their charges of human rights violations hoodwinked to let them into America. The following are some point cases, courtesy the Illuminati Conspiracy Archive.

- Arthur Rudolph was the operations director of the infamous Mittelwerk factory at the Dora-Nordhausen concentration camps, where 20,000 workers died from abuse. Rudolph was naturalised as a US citizen and later designed the Saturn 5 rocket used in the Apollo moon landings.[969] Though his controversial past was well known to the American officials who had granted him entry into the United States in the first place, the American administration had him expelled back to Germany after Rudolph's past became known.
- Wernher von Braun was the technical director of the Peenemunde rocket research center, where the GermanV-2 rocket was researched and developed. Von Braun worked on guided missiles for the U.S. Army and later became a director at NASA.[970] He later did serious damage to the Illuminati by leaking their plans for future wars involving UFOs and pseudo-aliens. He also publicly doubted the moon landings.
- Kurt Blome was tried at Nuremberg in 1947 on charges of practicing euthanasia and experimenting on humans. Though acquitted, he was hired by the U.S. Army Chemical Corps and subsequently worked on chemical warfare.[971]
- "The US military tribunal at Nuremberg heard evidence that "Major General Walter Schreiber assigned doctors to experiment on Nazi concentration camp prisoners and was in charge of financially coordinating such research. On May 22, 1952, he was flown to Buenos Aires after his Nazi past was publicized.[972]
- "Hermann Becker-Freysing was convicted and sentenced to 20 years in prison for conducting experiments on Dachau inmates,

---

[969] Illuminati Conspiracy Archive: Operation Paperclip Case file <http://www.conspiracyarchive.com/NWO/project_paperclip.htm> Web page as of 16/03/04

[970] Illuminati Conspiracy Archive: Operation Paperclip Case file

[971] Illuminati Conspiracy Archive: Operation Paperclip Case file

[972] Illuminati Conspiracy Archive: Operation Paperclip Case file < http://www.conspiracyarchive.com/NWO/project_paperclip.htm> Web page as of 16/03/04

such as starving them, then force-feeding them sea water that had been chemically altered to make it drinkable. SiegfriedRuff was acquitted on charges that he had killed as many as 80 Dachau inmates in a low-pressure chamber designed to simulate altitudes in excess of 60,000 feet. Freysing and Ruff were later paid by the U.S. Army and the U.S. Air Force to write reports about their grotesque experiments."[973]

I.G. Farben may have been involved in secret research, such as the enigmatic saucer shaped aircrafts Nazis were observed in. And special weapons based on electromagnetic and nuclear technology. Nazi scientists were goaded into completing such weapons under the hope that they could turn the tide of the war. But once these scientists achieved success, the research programs would be halted and all related paperwork would be consolidated by Nazi top brass. In some cases, the underground research centers where such scientists worked were sealed from the outside by the Nazis, leaving the scientists to die. And all technology was secretly transferred to the Allies upon Nazi defeat, for use in future Illuminati projects. Indeed, Nazi Germany would have presented the best opportunity to pursue such ventures.

Kurt Waldheim

Kurt Waldheim is a prominent Austrian who became Secretary General of the UN. According to Timothy Noah,

> [...Waldheim] had been an intelligence officer in Germany's Army Group E when it committed mass murder in the Kozara region of Western Bosnia. (Waldheim's name appears on the *Wehrmacht*'s "honor list" of those responsible for the atrocity.) In 1944, Waldheim had reviewed and approved a packet of anti-Semitic propaganda leaflets to be dropped behind Russian lines, one of which ended, "enough of the Jewish war, kill the Jews, come over." After the war, Waldheim was wanted for war crimes by the War Crimes Commission of the United Nations, the very organization he would later head.[974]

Robert Muller, a prominent New Age figure served as Assistant UN Secretary General to Waldheim. Waldheim is also a close friend of

---

[973] Illuminati Conspiracy Archive: Operation Paperclip Case file < http://www.conspiracyarchive.com/NWO/project_paperclip.htm> Web page as of 16/03/04

[974] Timothy Noah, "Arnold's Nazi problem; Why wont he repudiate Waldheim?," MSN Slate: August 7th 2003 <http://slate.msn.com/id/2086742> Web page as of 16/03/04

Arnold Schwarzenneger, who has refused to repudiate Waldheim. Arnold is married into the Kennedy Clan. Arnold's father, Gustav Schwarzenneger was a volunteer Nazi storm trooper and Arnold has expressed admiration for Hitler. It is interesting to note how most Jewish vigilante groups have chosen to ignore Arnold's anti-Semitic affiliations.

The U-Boat off Cape Cod

Recently, an operation was held to raise a Nazi U-boat off Cape Cod. The vessel was a special type of U-boat only rumored to be in existence. It departed the port of Danzig on the afternoon of 20th July 1944. And would be sunk by the American Navy on 20th August 1944, off Cape Cod. It is known that the U-boat was sending messages to the Allies in a special diplomatic signal, which the White House received and never released.[975] It is also known that the Dutch Royal family had arrived in Chatham (Cape Cod) for some rendezvous with the U-boat. They left immediately after it was sunk.[976] Recovering vessels from the ocean floor is a very expensive operation. It can only be speculated what the U-Boat might have contained.

---

[975] Subsearecovery.com, "Efforts to Raise Super Secret Nazi U-boat off Cape Cod," 8/7/04. An archived copy is available at <http://www.rense.com/general56/supsec.htm> Accessed 05/11/06.

[976] Subsearecovery.com, "Efforts to Raise Super Secret Nazi U-boat off Cape Cod," 8/7/04. An archived copy is available at <http://www.rense.com/general56/supsec.htm> Accessed 05/11/06.

Chapter Six
The Far East

ジャングルの突破

> If the European Powers would apply to the Far East even a tenth of the flexibility of attitude which they display in dealing with the problems of their own continent, the attainment of stability in this part of the world would be very simple indeed.[977]
>
> *-Japanese Premier Prince Fumimaro Konoe, January 1938*

[977] Bradford A. Lee, Britain and the Sino Japanese war 1937-39 - A study in the dilemmas of British decline (California: Stanford University Press, 1973) 205.

Background

The Illuminati in the Far East

In his book, Bloodlines of the Illuminati,[978] Fritz Springmeier informed his readers of the presence of an Illuminati bloodline, the Li bloodline, in the Far East. Though Li is a common surname, Springmeier was referring to an ancient underworld cabal. It is difficult to judge whether this clique is an extension of Western Illuminati or are merely collaborators whom the Western Illuminati[979] came into contact with, during European colonization of the region. The massive Chinese opium trade could not have been conducted without local collaboration. In addition, Springmeier pointed out that the Li's were very influential in the power politics of the Far East, and held considerable power in China, Singapore and Taiwan. In fact, the latter two were probably created as personal protectorates for the Li's. Not surprisingly, Chiang Kai-Shek would eventually retreat into Taiwan. Another faction of the Kuomintang would retreat into Burma and Thailand, controlling what would become known as the Golden Triangle, an area that produces a majority of the global opium trade. This opium is usually shipped to Taiwan, from where it reaches Western markets.

The Emergence of Westernized China - Dr. Sun Yat Sen

China's lack of interest in international trade resulted in a war with Britain in 1842, forcing her to open her ports for the opium trade. This war ended with the Treaty of Nanking, giving Europeans Concessions to build buildings, houses and residences in select zones. An Open Door Policy was established in 1899 by the United States, to prevent Japan from single-handedly dominating trade in China. All these measures culminated Chinese discontent in the Boxer Rebellion. The Boxer Rebellion was probably the last concerted effort by the Chinese people to take back their country. A more Westernized China emerged with the revolution of 1911 under Sun Yat Sen, who was succeeded by Chiang

---

[978] Fritz Springmeier, Bloodlines of the Illuminati (Spring Arbor distributors, 1998) GlobalGrey PDF edition 2013 <http://www.globalgrey.co.uk/Pages/Books-Conspiracies/Bloodlines-Of-The-Illuminati.html> Web page as of 03/07/13.

[979] It is important to note that many Western Illuminati operatives entered the area pretending to be missionaries. And therefore the later backlash against them. Similar "missionaries" created the crisis of separation in the oil rich region of East Timor and the Nigerian Delta.

Kai Shek. Here is what Antony Sutton has to say about Sun Yat Sen, whose Revolution was a predecessor to Mao's Revolution:

> The best-documented example of Wall Street intervention in revolution is the operation of a New York syndicate in the Chinese revolution of 1912, which was led by Sun Yat-sen. Although the final gains of the syndicate remain unclear, the intention and role of the New York financing group are fully documented down to amounts of money, information on affiliated Chinese secret societies, and shipping lists of armaments to be purchased.
>
> The work of the 1910 Hill syndicate in China is recorded in the Laurence Boothe Papers at the Hoover Institution.[980] These papers contain over 110 related items, including letters of Sun Yat-sen to and from his American backers. In return for financial support, Sun Yat-sen promised the Hill syndicate railroad, banking, and commercial concessions in the new revolutionary China.[981]

Chiang Kai Shek

Chiang Kai Shek was more controversial than Dr. Sun. Despite his rise as a revolutionary leader, Shek had a background that consisted of underworld figures and secret societies.[982] He was related by marriage to Sun Yat Sen. With his brother in law being the influential T.V Soong, the chairman of the Bank of China, Shek represented the new Westernized ruling elite of China. These new elites were well connected with European banking elites. Kai Shek's leadership qualities are still disputed. The Soviet Comintern organized his Kuomintang party.[983] Yet in 1927, Shek started purging members of the Communist party allied to the Kuomintang, resulting in a civil war. The internecine civil war would occupy priority even after the Japanese invasion, and it was only after 1935 and intense internal opposition that Shek would divert his activities against Japan. Despite fighting Communists, Shek continued to receive active Soviet support, which indicates that the dialectical war against the Communists was in accordance with a larger plan.

---

980 Stanford, Calif. See also the Los Angeles Times, October 13, 1966 (Reference by Sutton).

981 Antony C Sutton, Wall Street and the Bolshevik Revolution (Buccaneer Books, 1993). Chapter Three of Online edition. <http://reformed-theology.org/html/books/bolshevik_revolution/chapter_03.htm> Accessed 25/10/06.

982 Chiang Kai-Shek was affiliated with secret societies such as the Green Gang of Tu Yueh-sheng, among many others.

983 Bradford A. Lee, Britain and the Sino Japanese war,1937-39. A study in the dilemmas of British decline (California: Stanford University Press, 1973) 3.

During the years 1911-1941, Shek would also be the generous recipient of German assistance. This assistance was organized by the Illuminati to further bolster Shek in his consolidation of China. Taiwan's later industrialization can be traced to these plans.

Sino German Cooperation; Note the Masonic handshake.

Shek was originally being prepared for a dialectical war with Japan on behalf of the Soviets. But since the Japanese proved to be far more powerful in Sino-Japanese wars, Japan was earmarked for destruction by America. And Shek was set aside to play a nominal role in the war against Japan. But was intended to play a major role in Maoist (Soviet-Communist) consolidation of China, by acting as a dialectical adversary to Communism.

In other words, Shek was meant to play a role of a Fascist, similar to Mussolini and Franco. He was to provide dialectical opposition for the Soviet advance into China, which would be accomplished by Soviet backed and Soviet controlled Communists. This explains Shek's sudden antipathy for the Communists. One may claim that the same could be accomplished without the creation of the Kuomintang, since Japan could be used as a bogeyman for rallying Soviet backed communists in China. But both the Soviets and Chinese Communists, as well as Shek were completely incapable of dealing with Japan (which is why America had to enter the war). In addition, Japanese influence was mainly along the coast. Whereas the staged war against the Kuomintang would deliver all of China to Soviet backed Communists. In addition, the Koumintang-Communist civil wars would reduce the population of China by creating millions of casualties. The Powers that Be prefer to keep subject populations at manageable levels. In accordance, Mao would later enforce a limit on the number of children Chinese people could have. The Kuomintang-Communist civil war also helped subduing numerous independent powers in the region, which were derisively labeled as warlords. These wars were essential for the creation of a totalitarian power structure out of scratch. Neither the Communists nor the Kuomintang were hardly representative of China or Chinese interests. And even after the Japanese surrendered, they continued to be a serious detriment for the Chinese people. British ambassador to Tokyo, Robert Craigie, would express his dismay at British support for Shek as follows:

I have never believed that 'cooperation' need necessarily involve a complete surrender to the wishes of the Japanese extremists or the abandonment of the cause of China - quite the contrary. It would however definitely mean the abandonment of any further scheme to support, or give material assistance to, the regime of General Chiang Kai Shek. It would be recognition of the actual fact of Japan's military and economic predominance in China today, and an effort to win back ultimate Chinese independence through cooperation, both with China and Japan, in establishing that assured market and that source of raw material which represent Japan's primary needs in the economic field.[984]

Since Shek represented the interests of Powers that Be, it is not surprising that even the Soviets would support him long after he deserted Communism, while at the same time, the Soviets would also be supporting the Kuomintang against him. With the conclusion of a 1937 non-aggression pact, the Soviet Union was providing the most active assistance to Chiang Kai Shek, which also included a credit of US $100 million in 1938, along with aircraft, personnel, pilots, armaments and munitions. Mao's Communists were also assisted by the Soviet Union, but Shek initially received more assistance because he was to play the role of a dialectical adversary to the Soviet backed Communists, delivering all of China to them. This conclusion is supported by a 1920 conversation[985] between Stalin and Mao Zhedong. Stalin tells Zhedong that it is in his best interests to negotiate with Shek! Stalin pursues the same idea as late as 1949[986] and refuses to station Soviet troops at Mao's assistance.

America also provided much needed monetary assistance, which saved Chiang Kai-Shek from imminent collapse. Even before America declared war on Japan, it was violating its neutrality by providing armed assistance to Shek. Roosevelt intimate Thomas G. Corcoran organized the First American Volunteer Group, also known as the Flying Tigers. These were American military pilots employed by an American defense contractor. They were to act as the airforce of Shek and counter Japanese offensives against Shek. They helped protect the Burma Road from the Japanese, which was the most important Allied supply line to Shek.

---

[984] Roger Louise, British Strategy in the Far East 1919-39 (Oxford: Clarendon, 1971) 255.

[985] Ronald Grigor Suny, The structure of Soviet History - essays and documents (Oxford University Press, 2003) 315.

[986] Suny, Soviet History 315.

Apart from Shek, Appeasers of the Japanese were also present on the Chinese political scene.[987] These pragmatists then offered a much better alternative to the Chinese people especially at a time when Sino-Japanese relations were not characterized by mutual hatred. But since the Japanese Empire had been earmarked for destruction by the Illuminati, such idealogues were violently opposed in China by the Powers That Be.

How Chamberlain and Roosevelt baited Japan

British breed anti-Japanese insurgency

Britain had an alliance with Japan in 1902 and renewed it in 1905 and 1911, which gave Japan a free hand against Russia and allowed her to establish influence in Korea and China. At that time, the Powers that Be wanted to use Japan to pave way for the Bolshevik Revolution by inflicting humiliating defeats on the Imperial Russian forces. This arrangement allowed Japan to secure a treaty allowing her to station troops in Southern Manchuria (Northern Manchuria being a Soviet zone). The Japanese supplanted the last emperor of the overthrown Manchu dynasty in China as the head of Southern Manchuria.

On May 15th 1925, a striking Chinese textile worker was shot dead outside his Japanese factory in a British concession zone. The British concession police opened fire on protestors. The Communist cause against the Japanese suddenly gained momentum. The incident aided the Communists in establishing an urban presence. The European Concession Zones would start being used by the Powers that Be to breed anti-Japanese insurgency.

[987] Han-sheng Lin in his article A New Look at Chinese Nationalist "Appeasers" suggests that the largely ignored appeaser Wang Ching-Wei was closer to the Sino-Japanese cooperation advocated by Sun Yat Sen and his early appeasement contained the Japanese in the North, resulting in stability, prosperity and in the build up of the Kuomintang. Lin extends his argument as far as to say that the likes of Wang could have prevented Sino-Japanese conflict in the Second World War. Wang took retirement after an attempted assassination. For the complete article, see Alvin D. Cook and Hillary Conroy ed. China and Japan-Search for Balance since World war 1(Oxford: ABC-Clio Inc,1978).

Kuomintang and the British provoke the Japanese

In 1931, the Japanese staged a railway explosion as a pretext to annex Manchuria. Typical of intricate events leading to large-scale conflict, this event is disputed. According to one version, the Japanese had to stage the incident after its spies in the Chinese zone were killed, most likely by the Kuomintang. The killing of Japanese operatives alone would not have been sufficient grounds for annexation, let alone aggression.

It is clear from many other occasions as well, that the Kuomintang was trying to provoke the Japanese into pursuing a reactionary policy against the Chinese. The Japanese annexation of Manchuria was not well received by the then isolationist America. In the surprising "Stimson Note" of January 7th 1932, Secretary of State Henry Stimson refused the American recognition of Japanese occupied Manchuria. This was a complete break from the isolationist tradition of America. The roots of this gesture can be traced to the years 1931-1937, during which the Illuminati began grooming America for war with Japan. When the Soviets invaded and annexed North Manchuria, they would receive no such "Stimson notes," of course. The Soviets had foreknowledge of Americans being used to bring down the Japanese. With this foreknowledge, the Soviet Union would postpone its usual expansionist activities in the Far East, and even sell its interest in the strategic Chinese Eastern railway to the Japanese puppet government in Manchuria in 1935. All of these territories and assets would later be recovered by the Soviets, along with much more, after the Japanese Empire was destroyed.

Though the original Anglo-Japanese Alliance of World War I made the Japanese initially look forward to permanent good relations with Britain, British statesmen had devolved the Alliance into the formal Nine Power Treaty, in which Britain had no guarantees against a Japanese attack on her territories in the Far East. In 1933, Britain further provoked Japan by imposing a quota on Japanese imports into British colonies such as India.[988] . Japanese goods had started surpassing British goods in quality. And colonies such as India had been converted from once productive

[988] Bradford A. Lee, Britain and the Sino Japanese war 1937-39. A study in the dilemmas of British decline (California: Stanford University Press, 1973) 7.

nations into large scale importers of British goods. The Powers that Be had no intention of sharing profits with the Japanese.

Marco Polo Bridge incident

In July 1937, Japanese forces moved South after an altercation at the Marco Polo Bridge (in the vicinity of Peking). A Japanese search party looking for a missing Japanese soldier was denied access to the Chinese zone. Reacting to the Kuomintang's provocation, the Japanese proceeded to occupy Peking (establishing a provisional government), Tientsin and later Shanghai and Canton.

More Kuomintang provocation

A demilitarized zone was established around Shanghai in 1932. But in June 1937, the Chinese corps mandated to patrol the zone began building a military presence. Japan, being a Treaty Power, had naval landing rights and on 11th August 1937, landed 1000 troops to protect its interests and citizens who numbered around 20,000.[989] According to James Dodds (charge of affairs in Tokyo for British PM Eden), Japan was willing to withdraw if the Chinese backed out of the demilitarized zone.[990]

But before any mediation could take place, ill trained Chinese pilots dropped bombs into the crowded streets of Shanghai on August 14th 1937. Over 2000 civilians were killed in what became known as Bloody Saturday. A larger Japanese army was dispatched to Shanghai. It was later discovered that the Chinese had begun offensive military preparations in Shanghai long before hostilities broke out, and according to Ronald B. Nigel (an observer for the British Foreign Office Far Eastern department), the Chinese had staged the attack to damage Western interests, bringing Western Powers on their side against Japan.[991] Predictably, the British solely blamed Japan and sought peace through mediation and a return to the earlier status quo. Peace could not be achieved because of Chiang Kai Shek's insistence on a complete removal of Japanese troops from Shanghai, which the Japanese would never agree to because of the endangerment of their citizens.[992] On

---

[989] Lee. Britain and the Sino Japanese war 35.
[990] Dodds to FO, August 13th 1937,FO F5167/9/10. See also Diary August 13th 1937, Grew Papers. Quoted by Lee, 36.
[991] Minute by Ronald on memo. By Pratt, Dec. 13th 1937, FO F10934/9/10. Quoted by Lee, 40.
[992] Dodds to FO, August 19th 1937, FOF5428/9/10. Quoted by Lee 38.

August 23rd 1937, the Japanese launched an offensive against Kuomintang forces in Shanghai and drove them out.

The British Ambassador on Shek' s route

On August 26th 1937, the British Ambassador to China, Knatchbull-Hugessen, suffered injuries from the firing of Japanese planes while he was traveling in a flagged diplomatic car. British Prime Minister Anthony Eden pressed for an apology and got it, even though the Japanese insisted that Chiang Kai Shek was supposed to be on that road at that time and the Ambassador should have notified military authorities before journeying.[993] It is not clear how the British Ambassador ended up on that road or what he was doing there.

Around the same time, the Japanese instituted searching of ships on the Chinese coastline suspected of supplying munitions to Shek. Both Chamberlain and Roosevelt sheepishly raised no objections. Maybe they were privy to the role of the British as crypto-belligerents, secretly arming the Kuomintang.

Roosevelt calls for "Quarantine"

Roosevelt surprised everyone with his October 1937 speech, of imposing quarantine on certain rogue nations. With the issue of sanctions brought up, the Powers decided to meet at Brussels in early November. The British ambassador to Tokyo, Sir Robert Craigie held an optimistic hope that mediation with Japan would result in the moderates gaining control of its military and this would prevent the Soviets from manipulating tensions to their own advantage.[994]

Roosevelt's quarantine speech in Chicago on October 5th 1937.
Image courtesy FDRL.

One of the fundamental demands of the Japanese to the Chinese was to put an end to the spread of Communism in China. Chiang Kai Shek once

---

[993] Dodds to FO, August 31, 1937, FO F5926/5727/10. Quoted by Lee 41.
[994] Robert L. Craigie, Behind the Japanese mask (London: Hutchinson, 1946) 49-51. Craigie to FO, Sept. 25th and 27 and Oct. 29,1937,FO F6972/9/10, F7020/6799/10, and F8754/44/23. Quoted by Lee, 56.

again torpedoed the negotiation by insisting on complete control over North China. Japan then refused to attend the conference. The British Foreign Office prepared a report that sanctions by several nations on both Japanese imports and exports could cripple Japan within six months. During the last days of the Brussells' Conference, the Chinese appealed the British for armaments and a loan. The Foreign Office guided the Chinese for armaments procurement but the loan was avoided in order to prevent heightening tensions with Japan. The idea of a naval show of force against Japan was also considered, but avoided since it would compromise British interests in the Mediterranean. This was while the British were still pretending to be neutral, as opposed to being crypto-belligerent supporters of the enemies of Japan.

American escort to Kuomintang supply ships comes under fire

On December 12th 1937, Japanese artillery accidentally shelled ships moving up the Yangtze, resulting in damage and loss of life on two British ships. This was followed by the aerial bombing of three Standard Oil tankers, as well as their escort,[995] the USS Panay, which ended up sinking.[996] The US Secretary of state, Cordell Hull avoided any mention[997] of the Panay escorting tankers supplying Chiang Kai Shek. British newspapers, which were otherwise synonymous with German appeasement such as *The Times* that would later accuse the Czechs of being "stiff" on the Sudeten issue, carried surprisingly strong denunciations of Japan.[998] The Roosevelt administration put forth many ideas, such as a naval blockade of Japan, a visit to Singapore by American cruisers and an exchange control against the Japanese.[999] For

---

[995] Harold S. Quigley, Far Eastern War, 1937-41 (Boston: World Peace Foundation, 1942) 213.

[996]Admiralty to FO, December 12 1937, FO F10816/10816/10; War Office Intelligence Summary, December 16th 1937, FO11331/9/10. For details of these attacks, see Manny T. Koginos, The Panay Incident: prelude to War (Lafayette, Ind.: Purdue University Studies,1967), pp26-30; and Masatake Okumiya, "How the Panay was sunk," United States Naval institute Proceedings, 79 (June 1953):587-96. The complete newsreel of the bombing of the USS Panay was filmed under fire for News of the Day by Eric Mayell who was on board the US gunboat as it was sinking! This video is available in the 'Prelude to War video library' produced by the UCLA Film and television library.

[997] Harold S. Quigley, Far Eastern War, 1937-41 (Boston: World Peace Foundation, 1942) 213

[998] Bradford A. Lee, Britain and the Sino Japanese war 1937-39. A study in the dilemmas of British decline (California: Stanford University Press, 1973) 89.

[999] Bradford A. Lee, Britain and the Sino Japanese war 1937-39. A study in the dilemmas of British decline (California: Stanford University Press, 1973) 93.

the first time, a contingency plan for an Anglo-American naval blockade against Japan was made.[1000] But the affair was settled when the Japanese apologized and agreed to pay indemnity. Even at this point, the American administration, like the British, was pretending to be neutral to the political situation in China, as opposed to being crypto-belligerent supporters of the Kuomintang.

Japan to Britain: Please stop assisting our enemies

Premier Konoe of Japan made Kazushige Ugaki his foreign minister near the end of 1938. Ugaki wanted to establish friendly terms with Britain. When dialogue resumed with Craigie, remarks of action against Japan in the British parliament infuriated the Japanese and Ugaki as well.[1001] Ugaki remained adamant on having the British stop supporting Chiang Kai Shek and having the British stop the operations of Chinese Communist terrorists based in their Concessions. As Lee notes, "Britain's refusal to conciliate the Japanese was in complete contrast to her desperate attempts to appease Germany."[1002] Compared to Chamberlain's vaunted plane trips to Germany, it was more of a reverse of "appeasement" for Japan. It should be recalled that appeasement of Germany was conducted by the Illuminati to facilitate the rearmament of Germany by American interests. Japan, on the other hand, was not meant to be appeased, since it could not be internally controlled for dialectical wars the way Germany could. Ugaki's failure led to his resignation and replacement by hardliners. At the same time, the United States expressed disapproval for any concessions to Japan.

Say no to Japanese New Order and say hello to Our New World Order

On January 22 1938, Japanese foreign minister Koki Hirota announced the Japanese pursuit of a "New Order" in Asia. Premier Konoe proposed revised terms to Shek. But Chiang Kai Shek also rebuffed Konoe's revised terms, even though the prospect of China joining the "New

---

[1000] Markham (Admiralty) to Harvey, Jan. 17th 1938,FO F716/84/10; Pratt, "Naval Conversations," 760-63;Mark S Watson, Chief of Staff, Prewar Plans and Preparations (Washington DC: Historical Divisions, Department of Army, 1950)92-93, in the series United States Army in World war 2:The War department. Quoted by Lee, 93.

[1001] Bradford A. Lee, Britain and the Sino Japanese war 1937-39. A study in the dilemmas of British decline (California: Stanford University Press, 1973) 143-144.

[1002] Bradford A. Lee, Britain and the Sino Japanese war 1937-39. A study in the dilemmas of British decline (California: Stanford University Press, 1973) 146.

Order" was becoming realistic. The Japanese backed Peking Provisional Government sought to control the silver used to back currency by having it deposited in their bank rather than Settlement banks in the European Concessions. Soon, all revenue from occupied ports was to be placed in Japanese banks. This had given the Japanese an advantage in pursuing their "New Order" in China. This new bloc presented a danger to both Australia and British Indo-China. In order to prevent the scheme from being an attractive alternative for the Chinese, Britain began to seriously debate the idea of issuing a loan to the Chinese for stabilizing Chinese currency. In mid December, America took the lead by issuing $25 million in credits, a first sign of active American intervention in the Far East.

On March 8th 1939, Chamberlain arranged for a loan of £5 million to Chiang Kai Shek as an alternative to the British not pursuing sanctions against Japan. This was the first time significant monetary assistance had been given to the Chinese by the British. Despite this, Premier Konoe was opposed to any undertaking, which would involve Japan in a war with Britain and the America.[1003] Lee brings to our attention a brazen attempt by Premier Hiranuma to avert war by sending a secret message to Roosevelt, expressing willingness to participate in a joint effort to establish peace in Europe and the resolution of the Chinese issue in a world conference![1004] Despite bringing absolute proof of their Non-Axis leaning, the Japanese were rebuffed by Washington.

More Allied Provocations from the Settlements

In 1939, the European Settlements at Shanghai, Amoy and Tientsin became a bone of contention among Western powers and Japan. The Settlements ultimately infringed on Japan's "New Order." Lee quotes one Chief of Staff in Japan's army stationed in China emphasizing the need to overcome the issue of the Settlements "[...] to make third powers abandon their pro-Chiang policy and so awaken China and the Chinese

---

[1003] F.C Jones, Japan's New Order in East Asia; Its Rise and Fall, 1937-45 (London: Oxford University Press, 1954) 102,107-9; Ernst L. Presseien, Germany and Japan: A study in totalitarian diplomacy, 1933-41 (The Hague: Martinus Nijhoff, 1958) 193, 197-200; Frank W. Ikle, German Japanese Relations, 1936-1940 (New York: Bookman Associates, 1956), 78-80,84-89. Quoted Lee, 175.

[1004]Craigie to FO, may 26th 1939, DBFP, 9.116 and 118: 107-9 [F5037,5038/1236/23]; Craigie to FO, June 2 1939, FO F5299/1236/23. Hiranuma's message can be found in FRUS/Japan, 2:I. See also Jones, Japan's New Order, 122-23 and Waldo H. Heinrichs, Jr., American Ambassador: Joseph C. Grew and the Development of the United States Diplomatic Tradition (Boston: Little Brown,1966)285-86 Quoted by Lee,178-79.

people from their ominous dream of 'dependence upon Europe and America.'"[1005] In early 1939, Shanghai was hit by a wave of terrorism and assassination against the Japanese directed from the European Settlements. Japan was put at loggerheads with Britain when it insisted in being allowed to take "necessary measures" in the Settlements. On May 11th, the pro-Japanese chairman of the local Chamber of Commerce was murdered in the international Settlement of Kulangsu, an island off Amoy. Japanese marines landed to conduct a search. In response, Britain, France and America landed their own sailors for provoking the Japanese. However, all previous crises in the history of Anglo-Japanese alienation were dwarfed by the events of Tientsin in the summer of 1939.

Tientsin Crisis

Tientsin is the nearest seaport to Peking and is one of the largest ports in China. It is situated on the banks of a massive navigable waterway called the Grand Canal. In 1939, Tientsin also had a large British Settlement, which attracted Japanese contention. The Japanese wanted the cessation of all guerrilla activities against them by Chinese Communists based in the Settlement. In addition, they wanted to impose Japanese currency and the deposit of silver reserves in Japanese banks, mainly because the silver was being shipped out of Tientsin.[1006] In other words, the Settlements were being used to drain Chinese silver reserves into overseas European banks. Despite producing evidence of the Settlements being used to stage terrorist activity, the British ambassador to China, Sir Archibald Clark Kerr refused to hand over Chinese suspects in Tientsin wanted by Japan. This resulted in the Japanese erecting barriers around the Concessions and regulating entry and exit. Major General Piggott who was influential in Japanese circles arrived in Tientsin on 3rd April at the behest of Craigie.

Gordon Hall was the seat of the British administration in Tientsin.

> He warned Ambassador Clark Kerr and the Foreign Office that the situation was very serious, explaining that there was in fact anti-Japanese organizations operating in the Concession and that the

[1005] "Situation Estimate of central China Expeditionary Army," July 24th 1939, in IMTFE, Document 605. Quoted by Lee, 179.

[1006] Bradford A. Lee, Britain and the Sino Japanese war 1937-39. A study in the dilemmas of British decline (California: Stanford University Press, 1973) 181-182.

Japanese were bewildered and resentful at not receiving British cooperation.[1007]

One of the individuals arrested, Ssu Ching-wu was the head of the North China anti-Japanese Army and according to Craigie, he had admitted to the British Consul General of being the head of a 25,000 band of guerrillas who were blowing up railroads, cutting telegraph wires etc.[1008] Piggott's warnings were greeted with hostility by Brenan and the foreign office. And only six days later, an official of the Japanese backed Peking puppet regime was assassinated by Chinese, in the British Concession! Despite a Japanese deadline, the British refused to hand over the suspects. Frustrated, the Japanese blockaded the British Settlement and expressed a new demand along with the delivery of the suspects; that Britain cease supporting Chiang Kai-Shek and participate in the building of their "New Order."[1009] Not surprisingly, Madame Shek was pressing Clark Kerr against the delivery of the suspects,[1010] who were most likely operatives of the Kuomintang. The Times, which always heralded German appeasement, expressed deep bitterness for Japan.[1011] With Britain not in a position to divert capital ships from the Mediterranean, Chamberlain expressed that Britain would make "[...] every endeavor to reach an early settlement of the dispute at Tientsin."[1012] It is remarks like these, which made Tientsin to be considered as British "appeasement," in the Far East by establishment historians. To the contrary, there are hints that a British fleet may have been dispatched if Americans supported the venture.[1013] And again, key officials from Clark Kerr, Ronald Lindsay (Ambassador to Washington), Robert Vansittart

---

1007 Lee, Britain and the Sino Japanese war 183.

1008 Roger Louise, British Strategy in the Far East 1919-39 (Oxford: Clarendon, 1971) 262,263. Craigie's information is dated October 4th 1938.

1009 Clark Kerr to FO, June 14th 1939, DBFP,9.196:169 [F5784/1/10];Craigie to FO, June 21 1939, DBFP,9.242:211-12[F6130/1/10]. Arita shared the military's view that issues other than the case of four suspects would have to be settled. He also told Craigie that the Japanese army in China had a free hand on "defence questions". See Craigie to FO, June 14,1939,DBFP,9.198:170-71[F5790/1/10] Comments by Bradford. Quoted by Lee, 185.

1010 Jamieson to FO, May 13th 1939, DBFP,9.64:66-67 [F4531/1/10];Craigie to FO, May 19th and 26th 1939,DBFP,9.89 and 114:85,106 [F4781,5039/1/10]; Clark Kerr to FO, may 19th 1939,DBFP, 9.86:82-84 [F4808/1/10]. Quoted by Lee, 184.

1011 Bradford A. Lee, Britain and the Sino Japanese war 1937-39. A study in the dilemmas of British decline (California: Stanford University Press, 1973) 186.

1012 Bradford A. Lee, Britain and the Sino Japanese war 1937-39. A study in the dilemmas of British decline (California: Stanford University Press, 1973) 189.

1013 See, for example, letter from Runciman to Chamberlain, June 19th, 1939, premier I/316; Cabinet Conclusions, June 21,1939, CAB 23/100; and reports by Chiefs of Staff, June 18, 1939, F.P. (36) 96, CAB 27/627. Comments by Lee. Quoted by Lee, 191.

(Permanent Undersecretary) and Lord Halifax (Foreign Minister) to Foreign Office heavyweights like Ronald Nigel and Alexander Cadogan (head of the F.O) were all seeing Japan as the ultimate enemy. Washington refused to take part in the British negotiated settlement. British ambassador to Tokyo, Sir Robert Craigie finally arrived at an agreement with Japan, which went as follows:

> His majesty's Government has no intention of countenancing any act or measures prejudicial to the attainment of the above mentioned objects by Japanese forces and they will take this opportunity to confirm their policy in this respect by making it plain to British authorities and British nationals in China that they should refrain from such acts and measures.[1014]

Note the reference to "British authorities and British nationals" who were supposedly acting against Japanese interests. Far from being appeasement, this Craigie-Arita formula only symbolized Britain's observance of status quo by formalizing its return to the position of a non-belligerent rather than an open supporter of Chiang Kai Shek; a group engaged in active wartime hostilities against Japan. Even this formality was quickly dispelled by Chamberlain, who while announcing the agreement to parliament on July 24th made it clear that it did not impact British policy towards the Chinese. On July 26th 1939, Roosevelt gave Japan notice of its intention to terminate the American-Japanese Commercial treaty of 1911, which was nothing but a prelude to a blockade all trade with the United States. From then onwards, Japanese-Western relations would spiral downwards, culminating in the attack on Pearl Harbor.

Lifelines for Chiang Kai Shek

The famous 21 curves of the Burma Road at Anan, China.

Image courtesy US department of Army and signal Corps. Compiled by Carl Warren Weidenburner © 2005. Minimized Reproduction Under Fair Dealing.

The Burma Road

The Burma Road is an engineering wonder that links Kunming in China to Lashio in the then British Burma snaking across mountains and gorges (it

---

1014 Lee, Britain and the Sino Japanese war 194.

was later extended even further into Burma). The Burma Road had become a lifeline for Chiang Kai Shek, who was supplied arms and ammunition through it. As early as August 1937, the Japanese had started searching foreign vessels suspected of supplying arms to Chiang Kai Shek. With their domination of the coastline, Hong Kong became a focal point of British munitions supply to Shek. From July 1937 to November 1938, approximately 60,000 tonnes of munitions reached Shek through Hong Kong every month[1015]. Britain never made any expression of neutrality towards Japan nor did she ever deny the express facilitation of Chinese rearmament, and this became a serious contention with the Japanese. During the Settlement crisis, the Japanese had even informed Major-General Piggott that closure of British Hong Kong to sea-bound munitions destined for China would result in reciprocal positive gestures by the Japanese towards British interests.[1016] With no show of interest by the British in this regard, the Japanese proceeded to capture Canton in October 1938, to isolate Hong Kong and its sea-bound munitions supply to Shek. The Burma Road, which was completed in December 1938, thus became the alternate lifeline for Shek. The Japanese surrounded Hong Kong (a trade blockade the British did not resist,[1017] since the Japanese had a firm case of British belligerence). Chamberlain sneakily approved the construction of a Burma-China railway in November 1938 to further supplement the Burma Road as an alternative to

A map of the Far East with a close up of the Burma Road.

[1015] F.F. Liu, A Military History of Modern China 1924-49 (N.J: Princeton University Press, 1956) 156. Quoted by Lee, 60.
[1016] Craigie to FO, March 30 and April 26, 1938, FO F3468,4462/71/23. Quoted Lee, 126.
[1017] Harold S. Quigley, Far Eastern War 1937-41 (Boston: World Peace Foundation, 1942) 240.

the sea-based route through Hong Kong. During 1939 to 1940, approximately £7 million worth of arms and ammunition landed in Rangoon (British Burma) for re-export to China, with the United States and the Soviet Union being the chief suppliers.[1018] The British gave anti-aircraft armament to the Chinese for the defense of bridges on the Burma Road from the Japanese.[1019] The extent of British support to Shek can be best symbolized by the fact that credit was extended to Shek to purchase trucks for use on the Burma Road.[1020] With the Burma Road being the last and only link of the Kuomintang to the outside world, Britain had saved the forces of Chiang Kai Shek from eventual collapse by constructing and maintaining the road. Even Americans played an outstanding role in the supply of munitions to Shek, and licensed shipments of arms from American companies totaled to around $35.5 million up till 1941.[1021] In the summer of 1941, the American Government conducted a reorganization scheme of the Burma Road, which was implemented by Shek, and American technicians were dispatched to repair the trucks.[1022] However, the real intention behind the creation of the Burma Road went well beyond supplying Shek. The Allies were seeking a protracted war with Japan. And the Burma Road would later prove invaluable in shuttling supplies from British India. When the Japanese would partially close the Burma Road, a massive airlift was organized over the Himalayas, to provide American assistance from British India to Chiang Kai-Shek. Later the Ledo road was constructed to further link British India with Burma.

The Closure of the Burma Road

With the German blitzkrieg victory of May 1940 and the fall of France in June, the Japanese began dispatching troops to Indochina and finally

---

[1018] Peter Lowe, Ed. Ian Nish Britain and the Opening of the War in Asia, 1937-41: Anglo-Japanese Alienation 1919-52 (London: Cambridge University Press) 108.
[1019] Paul Haggie, Britannia At Bay- The Defence of the Empire Against Japan 1931-41 (Oxford: Clarendon Press, 1981) 161.
[1020] Cabinet Conclusions, Nov. 30 and Dec. 7 and 21, 1938, CAB 23/96; memo. by W.B Brown, Dec.1 1938, CAB 21/679; memo by Stanley, Dec. 5, 1938, C.P 277(38), CAB 24/281; FO to Clark Kerr, Dec 19, 1938, DBFP, 8.355;336-37 [F13505/78/10]; Nixon (Export Credits Guarantee Department) to Howe, Jan 5, 1939, FO F203/203/10. Quoted Lee, 162.
[1021] Figures from the Second and Third Annual reports and the later monthly reports of the National Munitions Control Board; the latter are printed in the *Press Releases* and *Bulletins* of the Department of State; data not published after those for May 1941. Note by Quigley. Quoted in Quigley, 271.
[1022] Harold S. Quigley, Far Eastern War, 1937-41 (Boston: World Peace Foundation, 1942) 271.

signed the Tripartite Pact with the Axis on 27th September 1940. In the absence of an expected German amphibious attack on the British Isles, the Japanese did not consider turning their attention to Hong Kong and Malaya.[1023] In June 1940, the Japanese War Ministry informed Craigie and the British military attaché that the Burma Road must be closed at once, or war would ensue.[1024] The closure was to include not only arms and ammunition but also fuel, fuel oil, trucks and railway material.[1025] Craigie devised a scheme by which the Burma Road would be closed for 3 months during which Japanese and Chinese were to strive for a peaceful settlement. And Craigie and Arita agreed on 17th July to the same with little objection from America. However, Britain never pursued the Sino-Japanese settlement, presumably because it would free up Japanese forces and resources in China, giving Japanese the opportunity to turn against the Soviets. On 18th July 1940, Churchill told parliament that Britain in the interests of its own survival could not pay attention to China or Burma anymore and finally shut down the Burma Road the same month. The Burma Road was reopened in October on grounds that no Sino-Japanese settlement was reached. The acquiescence of the British to Japanese demands can be explained by the fact that the Japanese had a firm case of belligerency against the British. And the Illuminati did not seek to engage Britian with Japan until firm American commitment could be obtained following Pearl Harbor. Britain on its own, did not stand a chance against the Empire of Japan.

American trucks on the Burma Road after America's entry into the war. *Image courtesy US department of Army and signal Corps.. Compiled by Carl Warren Weidenburner © 2005.* Minimized Reproduction Under Fair Dealing.

Anticipation of War

In May 1940, Churchill displaced Chamberlain. By August 1940, Britain announced withdrawal of all its forces from Peking, Shanghai and Tientsin within a month. They were followed by the Americans who relocated their small guard from the Tientsin Concession to the Philippines in November 1941. It is clear that the Allies were

---

1023 Hosaya Chihiro, Ed. Ian Nish, Britain and the US in Japan's view, 1937-41: Anglo-Japanese Alienation 1919-52 (London: Cambridge University Press) 65.

1024 FRUS (1940), vol.IV, 26-27. Quoted by Lowe in Anglo-Japanese Alienation 1919-52 108.

1025 Craigie to FO, 24th June 1940, F3479/43/10, FO 371/24666. Quoted by Peter Lowe, Great Britain and the origins of the Pacific War. A study of British Policy in East Asia 1937-41 (Oxford: Clarendon Press, 1977) 140.

looking forward to war with Japan, long before Pearl Harbor was even on the horizon.

The Final Provocation of Japan

In October 1940, the Far Eastern Committee was established and chaired by R.A Butler to identify and restrict resources crucial to Japan from being exported from the European colonies. By November 1940, the Japanese began encouraging Thailand to recover lost territory from French Indochina with the objective of establishing bases in Southern Indochina. According to Hosoya Chihiro, the "Far Eastern Crisis" being drummed up by British newspapers was largely propaganda created to pressure the United States into supporting Britain; and Japan was still intent on keeping diplomatic channels open.[1026] When the Japanese began advancing into Southern Indochina after Vichy France capitulated, the United States invoked a total embargo on oil, steel, scrap, iron and equipment exports to Japan on August 1st 1940, followed by a freezing of Japanese assets. It was this move, which was later replicated by the European Allies; which in the opinion of Captain Malcolm Kennedy, made the Japanese set a limited timeframe for negotiations.[1027] Churchill and Roosevelt then unveiled the Atlantic Charter on August 14th 1940, which threatened that any advance of Japan Southward would be considered as grounds for war. With its oil supply cut, Japanese military and industrial activities would come to a halt within six months[1028], unless the oil resources of the Dutch East Indies were obtained. To aggravate things further, Roosevelt even proposed to forcefully cordon off all Japanese access to nitrates in South America (used in explosives). To quote,

> In October 1940, Secretary of the Navy Frank Knox sent for Admiral J.O. Richardson, Commander-in-Chief of the American fleet in the Pacific. Knox advised him that the President wanted him to establish a patrol of the Pacific—a wall of American naval vessels stretched across the western Pacific in such a way as to make it impossible for Japan to reach any of her sources of supply; a blockade of Japan to

[1026] Hosaya Chihiro, Ed. Ian Nish, Britain and the US in Japan's view, 1937-41: Anglo-Japanese Alienation 1919-52 (London: Cambridge University Press) 70.
[1027] Malcolm D Kennedy, The Estrangement of Great Britain and Japan 1917-35 (Berkeley: Univ. of California Press, 1969) 344.
[1028] Hosaya Chihiro, Ed. Ian Nish, Britain and the US in Japan's view, 1937-41: Anglo-Japanese Alienation 1919-52 (London: Cambridge University Press) 72.

> prevent by force her use of any part of the Pacific Ocean. Richardson protested vigorously. He said that would be an act of war [...]"[1029]

The Illuminati within the Japanese (see next chapter) arranged a Neutrality Pact with their traditional adversary, the Soviet Union in April 1941, even though the Soviet Union did not stand a chance against the Empire of Japan. Between January and March 1941 Anglo-American talks were held on the issue of conflict with Japan. It was agreed that Singapore was to be defended at all costs. In March 1941, Roosevelt approved the Lend-Lease Act which allowed funding, selling, equipment exchange and technology transfer to all non-Axis countries. A total of $50 billion (unadjusted for present-day inflation) was allocated and China got around $1 billion, which was enough to save the Kuomintang from collapse. In June 1941, The German attack on the Soviet Union allowed for the British Navy to be finally diverted back to the Far East. Churchill arranged for two capital ships to be dispatched for Singapore (which were later sunk by the Japanese when war was declared). Clearly, Britain was now preparing for war and negotiations were out of question. Roosevelt getting more irritated by the idea of peace advised Admiral Nomura to completely reverse Japanese policies, but the decision for war had been ratified by the Japanese Imperial conference on 1st December 1941 and on the 7th, the Japanese attacked Pearl Harbor.

During the course of the war, the Japanese would conduct horrendous atrocities against the Chinese and other people they conquered. This would discredit their Imperial goals and their "New Order." But things might have been different had the war not unfolded as planned by the Powers That Be.

1029 Michael Haupt, "What Really caused world war 2," ThreeWorldWars.com <http://www.threeworldwars.com/world-war-2/ww2.htm> Web page as of 11/07/2004.

Chapter Seven
Why the Bomb was dropped

```
This dispatch is top secret.
This order is effective at 1730 on 2 December:
(***** Combined Fleet Serial) #10.
Climb NIITAKAYAMA 1208, repeat 1208![1030]
```

-Admiral Yamamoto to Japanese Attack Fleet, 2nd December 1941. This plaintext message was intercepted by the Americans, and has been declassified from NSA Archives. NIITAKAYAMA is the highest mountain in Japan. '1208' refers to the date of the Pearl Harbor Attack, Japanese time.

[1030] Mark Emerson Willey, Pearl Harbor: the Mother of all Conspiracies < http://www.geocities.com/Pentagon/6315/pearl.html> Accessed 12/11/06

Background

The Illuminati in Japan

The earliest attempts of the Illuminati to conquer Japan date to the Mongol invasion of the Islamic World in the thirteenth century. The Mongol leadership had been infiltrated by members of the European Byzantine royal family, and the purpose of the Mongol invasion of the Islamic World was to put an end to the Islamic threat to Byzantine and Europe. But there were secondary objectives as well, such as the conquest of China and Japan. To conquer Japan, a large Mongol fleet was assembled in Korea two times. But on both of these occassions, the entire Mongol fleet sank before it reached Japan. The Japanese had ardently prayed for deliverance from the Mongol threat. And they credited this gratefully received deliverance to *kamikaze*, or "divine wind." The same term would be used for Japanese suicide bombers in World War II.

Japanese culture was noted for its insularity and opposition to foreigners. Eventually, foreign influence crept in, and was able to take down the Tokugawa Shogunate. The so called Meiji Restoration, which coincides with the Majalli Reforms in the Ottoman Empire, were designed to destroy the traditional structure of the Japanese State and create robotic Western style armies. Commodore Matthew Perry would sail into Yokohama at the head of a large American fleet in 1853. The idea was to use diplomacy to force open Japan's closed doors. Perry was the father in law of August Belmont. According to Clifford Shack, Belmont was related to the European banking elite.[1031] European traders established Freemasonry in Japan in 1864. And there is the possibility that a Japanese Emperor was assassinated to make room for the Illuminati in Japan. Despite these far-reaching intrigues, foreign influence faced heavy opposition from traditional conservative elements. At one point, the Samurai even started attacking foreigners. Nevertheless, a gradual acquiescence to foreign capital and foreign power took place. In addition, pre-existing Japanese crime syndicates such as the Yakuza were readily absorbed by the Illuminati.

[1031] Clifford Shack, "The Rothschilds Take Japan," Cliff Shack < http://www.geocities.com/cliff_shack/rothschilds_japan.html > Accessed 04/11/06.

The Russo-Japanese War (1904-1905)

The Russo-Japanese war (1904-1905) of the new Japanese empire resulted in a devastating blow to Imperial Russia, the reverberations of which were crucial to the Illuminati Bolshevik Revolution of 1917. During the Russo Japanese war, Britain was allied with Japan to give it a free hand in this operation. The Japanese were able to catch the Russians off guard and sink an entire Russian fleet, which hints at possible collusion of the Imperial Russian Illuminati. This humiliating defeat of Imperial Russia was essential for the later Bolshevik Revolution. Some Russian prisoners in Japanese POW camps were brought to America[1032] and trained as fighters to participate in the Revolution of 1917 in Petrograd.

Securing the Far East for the Soviet Union following 1917

In the confusion surrounding the Bolshevik Revolution in 1917, Imperial Russian forces were withdrawn from all frontier areas. All of Siberia was vulnerable to Japanese expansion. Those behind the creation of the Soviet Union sought all means to diffuse this threat.

Around April 1918, Thomas D. Thacher, a Wall Street lawyer and a member of the American Red Cross Mission to Russia, suggested to the British director of propaganda (Lord Northcliffe) that "First of all [...] the Allies should discourage Japanese intervention in Siberia."[1033] This was clearly meant to be priority number one for the Powers That Be. On September 1 1918, an "American Expeditionary Force" landed in Vladivostok under General William S. Graves. While the official objective was to protect the supplies and powers of their Tsarist Allies, Graves avoided supporting the pro-Tsarist White Russian Government of Kolchak. Secondly, Graves, managed to secure the operation of the

---

[1032] The questioning of the accused Christian Georgievitch Rakovsky by Gavriil Gavriilovitch Kus'min on the 26th January, 1938. An archive of the interrogation can be found online < https://archive.org/details/RedSymphony> Web page as of 22/01/14

[1033] A note by Sutton reads as "Letter reproduced in full in Appendix 3. It should be noted that we have identified Thomas Lamont, Dwight Morrow, and H. P. Davison as being closely involved in developing policy towards the Bolsheviks. All were partners in the J.P. Morgan firm. Thacher was with the law firm Simpson, Thacher & Bartlett and was a close friend of Felix Frankfurter." Antony C Sutton, Wall Street and the Bolshevik Revolution (Buccaneer Books, 1993). Chapter Five of Online edition. <http://reformed-theology.org/html/books/bolshevik_revolution/chapter_05.htm > Accessed 25/10/06.

Trans-Siberian railroad, which was important for the evacuation of Czech POWs via Vladivostok. These POWs had escaped following the Revolution, and had managed to take back their confiscated arms. The Czechs were seeking to return to their native country by moving westwards. And along the way, they were successfully engaging the Bolsheviks. Their anti-Bolshevik rampage had begun to assume a populist character, and had thus become a threat to Bolshevik authority. In order to provide a safe conduit for the soldiers of the Czech legion who had already made it to East Europe, the Allies secured Archangel and Murmansk from the Bolsheviks (North Russian Campaign, May 1918). This also prevented Allied war material stockpiled at these ports from falling into non-Bolshevik hands. Lastly, and most important of all, General Graves was able to prevent the Japanese from taking advantage of the turbulence in Russia, by making them a part of this mission to "restore order."

World War II

There has been speculation about the presence of a Japanese "I.G. Farben" behind the rise of the Empire of Japan. Writing on Chip Bohlen, an influential American diplomat associated with the Krupp family, Springmeier writes that:

> "Chip stayed in Communist USSR until 1940, when the U.S. government moved him to Tokyo to help in Japan. According to Chip (in his book[1034]), he and others were not surprised that Pearl Harbor took place because there were strong indications that it was going to happen. After the attack on Pearl Harbor, Chip was placed under arrest by the Japanese. Then on June 20, 1942, Chip, Keith Meyers head of Standard Oil in Tokyo, and some other Americans were put on board the Asama Maru and returned to the United States via Portuguese East Africa."[1035]

Readers will be well aware of the role of Standard Oil in Germany. But the full role of Standard Oil in Japan has yet to be ascertained. Rakovsky[1036] was aware of the Illuminati backing Hitler and the Japanese for the Second World War, which would ultimately serve the

---

1034 Charles E. Bohlen, Witness To History (WW Norton, 1973) 110-112.

1035 Fritz Springmeier, Bloodlines of the Illuminati (Spring Arbor distributors, 1998) 389. GlobalGrey PDF edition 2013 <http://www.globalgrey.co.uk/Pages/Books-Conspiracies/Bloodlines-Of-The-Illuminati.html> Web page as of 03/07/13.

1036 The questioning of the accused Christian Georgievitch Rakovsky by Gavriil Gavriilovitch Kus'min on the 26th January, 1938. An archive of the interrogation can be found online < https://archive.org/details/RedSymphony> Web page as of 22/01/14 interests of the Soviets, and also allow the Illuminati to further infiltrate the Japanese war machine. However, his interrogator had some doubts as to how the Illuminati would engineer the defeat of Japan in the end. Unlike Germany, the Japanese high command was not completely infiltrated by the Illuminati or under their direct control. Rakovsky figured that China would be enough for Japan and Japanese had suicidal tendencies. As events would unfold, Rakovsky would prove to be wrong. The Chinese weren't enough to bring down Japan, even with enormous Allied backing. The entry of America had to be engineered and nuclear weapons had to be developed to bring down Japan.

Japanese entry into World War II

Prominent Nazi and Thule Society member, Karl Hausofer, forged Hitler's alliance with Japan forming a Tripartite agreement between the two and Italy, which would ensure that America would automatically go to war with Germany when a war between America and Japan took place. Hausofer would credit this fatal treaty to astrologic predictions,[1037] since commonsense did not seem to figure in the treaty. Nevertheless, Japan maintained that it had no obligation to take part in World War II and the Japanese did not trust Hitler. They signed the treaty for future division of the British Empire, and it was agreed with Germany that America was not to be engaged. All this would change when the Japanese were baited into attacking Pearl Harbor. Hausofer is also credited with engineering other concepts fatal to the Nazis, such as lebensraum, in which Germans had to preemptively attack the Soviet Union to return to their Nordic roots in the Himalayas! This would destroy the German Army and justify Soviet retaliation and future annexation of Germany, which was the ultimate goal of the Powers that Be.

While in Japan, Hausofer was active in the ultra-secret Green Dragon Society.[1038] Very little is known about this Society except that the term "dragon" is frequently used in Illuminati circles. For example, The Imperial and Royal Dragon Court & Royal Dragon Order was one of several secret societies created by the Illuminati aristocracies of Europe, following the formation of the Catholic Priory of Sion and the Knights Templar in the 12th Century.[1039] They comprised of princes and

---

[1037] Dusty Sklar, The Nazis and the Occult (1989) 69.

[1038] Servando González, Origins of the Swastika: The Hausofer Connection. <http://www.intelinet.org/swastika/swasti02.htm> Web page as of 11/07/2004

[1039] New world Order-The Movie: Dragon Court <http://www.geocities.com/newworldorder_themovie/dragoncourt.html> Web page as of 11/07/2004 aristocrats of Merovingian descent, such as the Hapsburgs. Outrageous conspiracy theorist David Icke has turned the study of this dragon phenomenon into a career.

For those who believe that the Japanese leadership had become compromised, there are a few indications in this regard as well. The militant Tojo clique that brought Japan into war with America came to power after a series of political assassinations. The date chosen for the Pearl Harbor attack seems to have occult timing. And the attack took place when the prized American aircraft carriers were not in the vicinity. What the Japanese ended up destroying was junk from World War I, such as the USS Arizona, built in 1913. The fuel supply, electrical grid and dry-docks of Pearl Harbor were left intact.[1040] Despite having the capability, a second wave of aerial attack was not organized by the Japanese. Later in the war with America, it is not clear why the super-secret Japanese Navy ship Yamato, the most advanced and largest battleship of its time, was ordered to sail unprotected directly into the 1500 ship American fleet advancing towards Japan. It was swarmed by up to 400 American fighter planes. A massive explosion occurred on board concurrently. Its 3000 crewmen were killed in one of the worst naval disasters in history. Another mystery relates to two of the Japanese "Sen-Toku" class submarines (the I-400 and the I-401). These were the largest pre-nuclear submarines ever built, and could travel one and a half times around the world without refueling. They also held three folding wing bombers that could be launched within minutes of surfacing. These two submarines were on a mission to attack the Panama Canal and render it inoperable, which would have been a huge disadvantage to the American fleet. It is unclear how American forces managed to find the precise locations of these submarines and scuttle them before they damaged the Panama Canal. They may have received some insider help.

The Countdown to Pearl Harbor

A small sacrifice for a bigger sacrifice

Pearl Harbor was a small sacrifice of the American subject population, conducted to induce them into making bigger sacrifices for the goals of the Powers that Be. A detailed study of how the ruling elite of America

[1040] Robert Stinnet, Author of Day of Deceit - The Truth About FDR and Pearl Harbor Interview with Mike McCormick/TalkingStickTV, Mind Over Matters Series. Date unknown. Recording available at <http://www.radio4all.net/proginfo.php?id=5123> Accessed 11/11/06.

allowed its subject population to be sacrificed in an act of war is necessary, for understanding the extent of control they hold over North America. Thousands can be murdered by a conspiracy coordinated in broad daylight. Yet the ones whose reputations were knifed were not those who allowed the tragedy to happen, but the Kimmels and Shorts who tried their best to prevent it. Investigation after investigation somehow always protects the Criminal Elite from scrutiny. An anatomy of this conspiracy suggests the extent to which American institutions and services are hopelessly compromised.

The Antiwar Movement

The most vocal opponent of American involvement in World War II was the American First Committee, which was formed in September 1940. It not only opposed the war but also questioned Roosevelt's support of Britain. The famous aviator, Charles Lindbergh[1041] had become one of its most vocal speakers. However, Lindbergh was trapped into sympathizing the Nazis. Nevertheless, support for American non-intervention was still vocal, even after Pearl Harbor. And the AFC suggested that America fight Japan alone. This was when Hitler would intervene to change this scenario, by declaring war on America. To quote Andrew McClusky (a WWII Veteran),

> If you read the book... *The New Deal* is won by Fleming, he covers this and he says that in October of 1941, the polls showed that 80% of the American public were actually absolutely opposed to going to war in Europe. And I remember my father saying to my mother, he [Roosevelt] can't get us into...and he can't even explain WWI yet. How is he going to get us into another war?[1042]

[1041] The kidnapping of Charles Lindbergh's infant child in March 1932, by alleged extortionists and the subsequent murder of the child after the ransom was paid, was likely to have been related to Lindbergh's ambition to enter politics. His father was a Congressman who had fought the Enactment of the Federal Reserve Act of 1913. And he also demanded an investigation of the sinking of the Lusitania in 1917. Therefore, the famous aviator's political ambitions may have upset many interests. All sides of law enforcement worked to frame Bruno Hauptman, a carpenter. The strongest evidence against Hauptman was possession of some of the ransom money. Hauptman claimed Isidore Fisch, a former business associate, gave this money to him. A witness at the trial, Peter Sommer testified he had seen a nurse of the Lindbergh household (Violet Sharpe, who would later commit "suicide") with Fisch. Fisch departed for Germany in December 1933, possibly with the ransom money. According to the official story, he died in Germany in 1934.

[1042] Andrew McClusky (WWII Veteran), Interview with Mike McCormick/TalkingStickTV, Mind Over Matters Series. Date unknown. Recording available at <http://www.radio4all.net/proginfo.php?id=5123> Accessed 11/11/06.

Eight Provocations

Robert Stinnett came across secret memo in the archives in 1995, in which President Roosevelt called for eight provocations against Japan, which commenced in the fall of 1940. All of these provocations were eventually carried out. President Roosevelt signed orders for most of the provocations. The memo was withheld from both the 1945 and 1995 Congressional investigations into Pearl Harbor.[1043]

Lieutenant Commander Arthur McCallum may have been the original author of this memo. He was the head of Far East Intelligence and had direct contact with Roosevelt. He was born in Japan to Baptist minister parents. And he was very close to the Japanese crown, making him knowledgeable about what would provoke the Japanese and get their military hardliners into power.[1044]
On October 16, 1941, the Prince's cabinet of Japan would resign, to be replaced by the military administration of General Tojo and his cabinet.[1045] Washington would overlook this war measure. On the same day, Henry Stimson (Skull and Bones member), Roosevelt's Secretary of War, wrote in his diary how Japan had to be lured into making an overt move against America.[1046]

Later, Stimson openly suggested that Roosevelt allowed the attack to happen. According to Stimson,

> The President brought up the event that we were likely to be attacked perhaps [as soon as] next Monday, for the Japanese are notorious for making an attack without warning. In spite of the risk involved, however, in letting the Japanese fire the first shot, we realized that in order to have the full support of the American people, it was desirable to make sure that the Japanese be the ones to do this so that there should remain no doubt in anyone's mind as to who were the aggressors.[1047]

[1043] Robert Stinnet, Author of Day of Deceit - The Truth About FDR and Pearl Harbor Interview with Mike McCormick/TalkingStickTV, Mind Over Matters Series. Date unknown. Recording available at <http://www.radio4all.net/proginfo.php?id=5123> Accessed 11/11/06.
[1044] Stinnet, Mind Over Matters.
[1045] Michael Haupt, "What Really caused world war 2," ThreeWorldWars.com <http://www.threeworldwars.com/world-war-2/ww2.htm> Web page as of 11/07/2004
[1046] Haupt, "What Really caused world war 2."
[1047] Haupt, "What Really caused world war 2."

Betrayal at Pearl Harbor

The American Fleet at Pearl Harbor

A large American fleet had begun to be based in Pearl Harbor in 1939, and Washington was well aware of the dangers.[1048] Admiral J.O. Richardson, Commander-in-Chief of the American fleet in the Pacific, requested twice during 1940, that the American Fleet be withdrawn from Pearl Harbor since the location was exposed and defenses were not adequate.[1049] His suggestions were not acted upon and he was relieved of command in 1941. Admiral Husband E. Kimmel was chosen in January 1941 as commander of the fleet. There is reason to believe that he had been chosen as a scapegoat for the upcoming attack. Unlike other major commanders, Kimmel was not backed by political connections. He had succeeded by his professional service, and was not a bloodlined elitist.

General Walter Short, who was responsible for air patrols and coastal batteries, commanded defense of Pearl Harbor. He felt Pearl Harbor could be well defended if advance warnings were provided, but he was worried about the shortage of reconnaissance aircraft.[1050] Short had only a handful of aircraft suitable for reconnaissance.

When General Short was finally informed that diplomatic relations had been terminated and hostile action was expected, no specifics were given. Washington was informed that Short took their message against a threat of ground-based sabotage and had the planes bunched together. But the War Department did not correct him.[1051] The arrangement of the planes bunched together, prevented them from taking off and engaging the Japanese on short notice. Short was also prevented from taking defensive measures even when Japanese planes were detected heading for Pearl Harbor. To quote, "On the morning of Dec 7th, our radar operators located the Japanese aircraft, once they took off from the carriers and were proceeding towards Pearl Harbor."[1052] This information was not relayed to General Short.

1048 Sacrifice at Pearl Harbor, prod. Roy Davies, BBC, 1989.
1049 Haupt, "What Really caused world war 2."
1050 Sacrifice at Pearl Harbor, prod. Roy Davies.
1051 Sacrifice at Pearl Harbor, prod. Roy Davies.
1052 Stinnet, Mind Over Matters.

Admiral Kimmel and General Walter C. Short, the commander of the armed forces at Pearl Harbor, would later request a court martial to clear their reputations, but their wish was never granted.[1053] A court martial would exonerate them and open a can of worms, implicating individuals in the higher echelons of power.

British Intelligence

British Naval operations in the Far East brought British Intelligence into frequent possession of Japanese Naval intercepts. Reception points such as Singapore and Hong Kong provided almost complete coverage of Japanese activities. According to Eric Nave who worked for the British on Japanese codes, the British had been reading Yamamoto's secret codes up to two years[1054] before the August 1941 USS Augusta meeting, attended by Churchill and Roosevelt. As the decision was made to divert more American ships to the Atlantic for a possible war with Germany, Churchill did have more information on the Japanese fleet and its intentions.

Eric Nave claims that the British decoded intercepts from Yamamoto's fleet when it was slipping into Saiki Bay on the island of Kyushu.[1055] Carriers, battleships, cruisers, submarines and a fleet of tankers were all named. They were assembling to move out into the Pacific.

When war with the United States became inevitable, Japanese diplomats were told to lookout for the Japanese translation of the words "East Wind Rain" in weather reports. This code would indicate a break with America. The British also intercepted instructions on the usage of this code. On November 20th 1941, a code breaker working for Eric Nave picked up the ominous phrase in a Japanese weather report.[1056] Nave also intercepted and decoded Japanese orders to consulates, to destroy all secret codes.[1057] On November 22nd, the Japanese strike force was given its sailing orders.

Eric Nave claimed that Washington had been made well aware of the significance of the "East Wind Rain" phrase, and were scouring radio broadcasts for it as well. To quote Emerson,

---

[1053] Haupt, "What Really caused world war 2."
[1054] Sacrifice at Pearl Harbor, prod. Roy Davies.
[1055] Sacrifice at Pearl Harbor, prod. Roy Davies.
[1056] Sacrifice at Pearl Harbor, prod. Roy Davies.
[1057] Sacrifice at Pearl Harbor, prod. Roy Davies.

> This message was deleted from the files. One of the main cover-ups of Pearl Harbor was to make this message disappear, Japanese Dispatch # 7001. In response to the Winds Execute, the Office of US Naval IQ had all Far Eastern stations (Hawaii not informed) destroy their codes and classified documents including the Tokyo Embassy.[1058]

Kimmel and Short were never warned though, and later, reception of the message was denied. Captain Laurance Safford of the Office of Naval Intelligence and Colonel Otis Sadtler of the Signal Corps would both later testify at having seen the "East Wind Rain" message.

In Singapore, one message intercepted by the British caused great interest in London. To quote, "It was a prearranged signal for attack. Deciphered, it ordered the Battle force to strike on December 8th Tokyo Time."[1059] Pearl Harbor was only five days away.

To quote Roy Davies,

> For nearly 50 years, one question has been repeatedly asked, did Roosevelt allow Pearl Harbor to happen so that the surprise attack would give him the excuse to take America into the Second World War? The new evidence that has come to light strongly suggests that he did. It is now clear that Roosevelt and his advisors new far more than was openly admitted in any of the nine separate inquiries into the attacks. William Casey, a former director of the CIA was in a position to testify where some of that information came from. In his book [The Secret War Against Hitler] Casey says quite openly that the British told the Americans that a Japanese fleet was heading East across the Pacific towards Hawaii. It is now known that Churchill used this intelligence to give British commanders in the Far East early warnings of the imminence of a Japanese attack. But no similar warnings were ever sent by Roosevelt to the American commanders in the Pacific. This fact alone suggests a degree of culpability alone on the part of the President. That cannot have been so strongly argued before now.[1060]

It is said that it was in response to this British intelligence that Roosevelt ordered both US aircraft carriers out of Pearl Harbor and had almost half of the planes removed from the vicinity. However, no effort was made to warn those left behind, as these sacrificial lambs would help create a storm of indignation that would bring America into World War II.

[1058] Mark Emerson Willey, Pearl Harbor: the Mother of all Conspiracies < http://www.geocities.com/Pentagon/6315/pearl.html> Accessed 12/11/06
[1059] Sacrifice at Pearl Harbor, prod. Roy Davies.
[1060] Sacrifice at Pearl Harbor, prod. Roy Davies.

Wiretaps

To keep abreast of political undercurrents in the Japanese expatriate community, the U.S. Naval intelligence operated several wiretap stations (against the law[1061]) near places frequented by the Japanese. One major station was in San Francisco, and specialized in the bugging of hotels of the Chinatown by planting microphones.[1062] To quote Robert Danford Ogg, who conducted the surveillance, "We wiretapped every known Japanese espionage location [...] in the 12th Naval district.[1063]"[1064]

All along the West coast, radio operators were told to look for unfamiliar signals.[1065] Their intercepts were all brought to 717 Market Street, San Francisco. And Ogg plotted them on a chart. Ogg was thus able to get a good fix on the location of the Japanese fleet.[1066] Captain Richard McCullough, chief of twelfth Naval district, went through Ogg's plotting of the Japanese Fleet.[1067] He had direct links to Roosevelt. As the Japanese Fleet edged towards Pearl Harbor, Ogg was able to place it within 400 miles of Pearl Harbor.[1068]

The Purple Code

The Purple Code was a secret communication code used by the Japanese for diplomatic messages. The Army Signal Intelligence cracked this code as early as 1940. To quote,

> The result was that the Americans knew every move the Japanese foreign ministry made from then to the end of the war. Only a handful of Roosevelt's staff and top Naval and Army commanders knew of this cryptographic success. For a nation on the brink of war, the information flowing from it was priceless.[1069]

To quote, "In Honolulu, the Japanese [consulate] were also being asked for details of the defense of Pearl Harbor. These requests were received and dispatched to and from the embassy through an American cable

---

1061 Sacrifice at Pearl Harbor, prod. Roy Davies.
1062 Sacrifice at Pearl Harbor, prod. Roy Davies.
1063 California north of Pt. Arguello, Nevada, Utah and Colorado.
1064 Sacrifice at Pearl Harbor, prod. Roy Davies.
1065 Sacrifice at Pearl Harbor, prod. Roy Davies.
1066 Sacrifice at Pearl Harbor, prod. Roy Davies.
1067 Sacrifice at Pearl Harbor, prod. Roy Davies.
1068 Sacrifice at Pearl Harbor, prod. Roy Davies.
1069 Sacrifice at Pearl Harbor, prod. Roy Davies.

company."[1070] All the messages that passed between Tokyo and its consulates in America are kept in the National Archives. The designation given to decoded Japanese diplomatic traffic was "Magic."

A Japanese Naval officer was sent to Pearl Harbor and made Chancellor of the Japanese consulate under a false name. The FBI discovered that his name did not show up in Japanese ministry list, and started spying on him.[1071] He was intercepted sending messages to the Japanese Navy. In August 1941, he started preparing data for the upcoming Japanese bombing run.[1072] He was dividing Pearl Harbor into grids so that aircraft could have more clarity when bombing. These intercepts were sent to Washington and shown to President Roosevelt, but no action was taken.[1073]

Emerson cites an incident on November 29th:

> The FBI embassy tap made an intercept of an un-coded plain-text Japanese telephone conversation in which an Embassy functionary (Kurusu) asked 'Tell me, what zero hour is. Otherwise, I won't be able to carry on diplomacy. The voice from Tokyo (K. Yamamoto) said softly, 'Well then, I will tell you. Zero hour is December 8th (Tokyo time, i.e. December 7th US time) at Pearl Harbor. (US Navy translation 29 Nov)[1074]

As the date for attack on Pearl Harbor closed, one of the staff from the Japanese consulate began undertaking strange activities. To quote,

> On Thursday evening, on a beach across the island from Pearl Harbor, one of the staff from the Japanese Consulate prepared to show lights out to sea from a deserted beach house. The timing of the lights would tell watching Japanese submarines, which ships were in the harbor. If that failed, a bonfire would be lit.[1075]

This consulate later reported to its Foreign Office about establishing bonfires and lights in windows. A translator at the Office of Naval Intelligence, Dorothy Edgers, found it suspicious that the consulate would report to the Foreign Office on such seemingly trivial

---

[1070] Sacrifice at Pearl Harbor, prod. Roy Davies.
[1071] Stinnet, Mind Over Matters.
[1072] Stinnet, Mind Over Matters.
[1073] Stinnet, Mind Over Matters.
[1074] Willey, Mother of all Conspiracies
[1075] Sacrifice at Pearl Harbor, prod. Roy Davies.

occurrences.[1076] Her superior, Lt. Commander Kraemer, didn't take her inquisition seriously.

Recently, the discovery of some of these Japanese midget submarines, which were sunk in the vicinity prior to the aerial attack indicate that war was not declared even when enemy submarines were being detected and sunk. The American leadership intended to inform the gullible subject population of a declaration of war *after* the dramatic Japanese aerial bombings.

MS5

MS5 was the designation of a secret monitoring station set up by Washington (Army Signal Corps) on Pearl Harbor.[1077] Its purpose was to intercept all diplomatic messages coming to and being sent by the Japanese consulate in Honolulu.

Admiral Kimmel did not have access to any of these intercepts. He had to rely on Washington for all intercept information. In fact, no machine to break the Purple Code was dispatched to MS5. These intercepts would be sent without deciphering[1078] to the Office of Naval Intelligence in Washington, where the appropriate machines would decipher the Purple Code.

Admiral Kimmel was not even aware of the existence of MS5, and neither was General Short. Even though MS5 had been set up a few yards from his home.[1079]

On September 24th, a message was intercepted for the Japanese Consulate in Honolulu. It demanded information consistent with an aerial bombing plan.[1080] Five days later, another signal was picked up at MS5. Chief of Naval Intelligence in Washington, Captain Allan G. Kirk, recognized the messages and tried to contact Kimmel and warn him.[1081] But he was assigned to other duties. Kimmel had no way of knowing that Captain Kirk had been repeatedly refused permission to warn him. Kimmel thought the Japanese fleet was at its homeport.

[1076] Sacrifice at Pearl Harbor, prod. Roy Davies.
[1077] Sacrifice at Pearl Harbor, prod. Roy Davies.
[1078] Sacrifice at Pearl Harbor, prod. Roy Davies.
[1079] Sacrifice at Pearl Harbor, prod. Roy Davies.
[1080] Sacrifice at Pearl Harbor, prod. Roy Davies.
[1081] Sacrifice at Pearl Harbor, prod. Roy Davies.

Station Hypo

Station Hypo was another intercepting station on Pearl Harbor, operated by the Office of Naval Intelligence. Its duties did not include intercepting diplomatic traffic. And instead focused on obtaining intercepts of JN25 (see next section). Station Hypo was operated by Joseph Rochefort. Though Kimmel's staff intelligence officer Edmund Layton was authorized to go through all of Rochefort's summaries, it seems he was either misinformed or evasive with Kimmel. To quote,

> Kimmel: "What, you don't know where the carriers are?"
> Layton: "No sir."[1082]

It is possible to ascertain the location of a ship once radio silence is broken. Rochefort's transmitters swept across the Pacific for information on Japanese fleet. But his daily summaries contained no indication of an immediate threat. On November 26th 1941, Rochefort's daily summary mentioned an intercept.[1083] Two days later, another intercept was obtained, but the position was not able to be determined.[1084]

Kimmel, on the other hand, began having his own suspicions. Two weeks before the Pearl Harbor attacks, Kimmel recalled 200 warships[1085] on West Coast and sent them North of Oahu. This would be the exact location where the Japanese would later launch the attacks. The exercise was supposed to last until Nov 25th but was called off on Nov 24th when Washington learnt about it.[1086]

The SS Lurline, a passenger ship en route to Honolulu was able to pick up Japanese radio transmissions around the final week of the attack. Leslie E. Grogan, the liner company's most experienced radio operator began to log the unfamiliar signals. As they neared Honolulu, he began to make out the letters of JCS Yokahama.[1087] He informed his captain that the signals were coming from Northwest Honolulu.[1088] Grogen gave his intercepts to the Office of Naval Intelligence in the Alexander Young

---

1082 Sacrifice at Pearl Harbor, prod. Roy Davies.
1083 Sacrifice at Pearl Harbor, prod. Roy Davies.
1084 Sacrifice at Pearl Harbor, prod. Roy Davies.
1085 Stinnet, Mind Over Matters.
1086 Stinnet, Mind Over Matters.
1087 Sacrifice at Pearl Harbor, prod. Roy Davies.
1088 Sacrifice at Pearl Harbor, prod. Roy Davies.

Building in Honolulu.[1089] Kimmel was never informed of the signals Grogan had picked up. The logbook has vanished from naval archives.

On 2nd December, the commander of the Combined Japanese Imperial Fleet sent a radio message to the attack fleet in un-coded plaintext Japanese "Climb NIITAKAYAMA 1208, repeat 1208!"[1090] Mount Niitaka was the highest mountain in Japan and 1208 referred to December 8th Japanese time, or December 7th, American time. This message was intercepted and has been finally released from the archives. This was the most specific warning of the upcoming Japanese attack. Yet this warning was not passed to Kimmel and Short.

A constantly updated myth is that the Japanese fleet maintained absolute radio silence, and they thus afforded the element of surprise. To quote Emerson, "Serial numbers prove that the Striking Force sent over 663 radio messages between November 16th and December 7th, or about 1 per hour."[1091] Stinnet found over a 100 messages from the Japanese fleet.[1092]

JN25

The JN25 was the top secret Japanese Naval Code, used to coordinate the attack on Pearl Harbor. The Japanese had started using it in June 1939. There is ample reason to believe that it had been cracked prior to Pearl Harbor. In fall 1941, the seventh edition of the code was broken and all messages were being read by Nov 16th, and Admiral Hart in the Philippines notified Washington that they had been intercepting and decoding JN25 traffic.[1093] General George Marshall called select members of the US media, summoning them to secrecy, and told them that codes had been broken and trouble was expected first week of December.[1094] These were the bureau chiefs of important American media outlets. On the other hand, Hawaiian commanders were not told. It would be later in 1995 when the breaking of JN25 would be made public.[1095]

1089 Sacrifice at Pearl Harbor, prod. Roy Davies.
1090 Willey, Mother of all Conspiracies
1091 Willey, Mother of all Conspiracies
1092 Stinnet, Mind Over Matters.
1093 Stinnet, Mind Over Matters.
1094 Stinnet, Mind Over Matters.
1095 Stinnet, Mind Over Matters.

Dusko Popov and the FBI

Three months before Pearl Harbor, the Nazi Secret Service sent Dusko Popov, a Yugoslavian businessman, on a spy mission to America. Dusko Popov was also working for the British, and was codenamed by them as "tricycle."[1096] The Germans asked him to look into American airplane production and report on sensitive locations inside Pearl Harbor, for "objects for immediate bombing".[1097] He was also to make notes of the locations of torpedo nets. This information was to be stored in a microdot on a fake telegram. The FBI identified Popov. J. Edgar Hoover refused to allow him to operate in America. But Hoover now had evidence that Pearl Harbor was a target.[1098] Yet nothing was done.

Roy Davies came across a letter[1099] in the National Archives, which further suggested Hoover's culpability:

> Pittsburgh January 1980,
> Dear Sir,
>
> Early in 1942, only months after Pearl Harbor, I was invited by Congressman George Bender to Ohio, to attend a special meeting of select Congressmen and government officials at the Army and Navy Club in Washington. This was an informal group, which met bi-weekly, to dine and talk freely on matters otherwise held confidential and play poker. One of the group's members was the head of the FBI, J. Edgar Hoover, who said that from early fall 1941 until a few days before the Japanese attacked, they had had warnings that it was coming. Much more important, President Roosevelt had had warnings during all of that time from a number of sources, but he was very assured that they were not passed on to General Marshall, nor General Short, nor Admiral Kimmel, the commanders in the Pacific. Hoover said the President told him not to mention to anyone any of this information, but leave it to be handled in his own judgment.
>
> Yours faithfully,
> Carleton G. Ketchum
> US Army-Airforce retired.

[1096] Sacrifice at Pearl Harbor, prod. Roy Davies, BBC, 1989.
[1097] Sacrifice at Pearl Harbor, prod. Roy Davies, BBC, 1989.
[1098] Sacrifice at Pearl Harbor, prod. Roy Davies, BBC, 1989.
[1099] Sacrifice at Pearl Harbor, prod. Roy Davies, BBC, 1989.

Richard Sorge

Information was flowing from the Soviets to America. Roosevelt was on exceptionally good terms with the Soviets, as he would later demonstrate during the Yalta conference. This relationship also allowed Soviet intelligence regarding Pearl Harbor to be diverted to the United States. To quote Emerson,

> Soviet top spy Richard Sorge, the greatest spy in history, informed Kremlin that Pearl Harbor would be attacked within 60 days. Moscow informed him that this was passed to the US. Interestingly, all references to Pearl Harbor in the War Department's copy of Sorge's 32,000-word confession to the Japanese were deleted (NY Daily News, 17 May 1951).[1100]

Sorge got arrested on October 18th 1941, and Stalin denied he was a Soviet spy. The Japanese hanged him on November 7th 1941. Sorge could have been outed by the Powers that Be to prevent any further release of such information.

What did Cordell Hull know?

Cordell Hull was negotiating with the Japanese over the oil embargo when relations broke down. To quote, "On the Morning of Nov. 26th, the waiting Japanese ambassadors were presented with an impossible ultimatum that stemmed from an angry Roosevelt."[1101] The ultimatum demanded that Japan withdraw from Indochina and all of China! Hull told a colleague "You cannot give an ultimatum to a powerful and proud people, and not expect them to react violently."[1102]

On 29th November 1941, journalist Joe Leib interviewed Cordell Hull, who had invited him. Hull told him that Pearl Harbor would be attacked on Dec 7th.[1103] Leib says he had helped Hull previously as a friend, and Hull may have been expecting Leib to protect him if in case Hull were to be blamed. Leib further claims that Hull pulled out of his pocket a transcript, which stated that Pearl Harbor would be attacked on December 7th.[1104]

[1100] Willey, Mother of all Conspiracies
[1101] Sacrifice at Pearl Harbor, prod. Roy Davies, BBC, 1989.
[1102] Sacrifice at Pearl Harbor, prod. Roy Davies, BBC, 1989.
[1103] Sacrifice at Pearl Harbor, prod. Roy Davies, BBC, 1989.
[1104] Sacrifice at Pearl Harbor, prod. Roy Davies, BBC, 1989.

Douglas Macarthur

Around 4th December, Intelligence based in Hawaii reported that the Japanese aircraft carriers were at sea and in the North (based on traffic analysis). General Douglas Macarthur, who was in the Philippines, responded that the carrier fleet was in fact in the South China Sea.[1105] According to Emerson, Duane Whitlock, who is still alive in Iowa, sent the messages on behalf of Macarthur. Was this a case of blunder, misinformation or disinformation?

When news came of the attack on 7th December, Macarthur issued conflicting orders, which resulted in the destruction of the American Heavy Bomber fleet on the ground in Phillippines.[1106] The fleet was expected to attack Japanese Taiwan. And General Brereton insisted that the fleet could have been saved. In addition, Macarthur may have planned an escape in advance, by preparing emergency escape routes for B-17s.[1107] When he reached South Australia, he made his famous speech, in which he said, "I came out of Bataan and I shall return."

Dutch Intelligence

The Dutch East Indies was a vantage point for eavesdropping on Japanese communications. Dutch intelligence was aware of the Japanese fleet moving towards the Kurile Islands.[1108] A Dutch submarine was involved in visually tracking the Japanese Fleet to this location.[1109] General Hein Ter Poorten, commander of the Netherlands East Indies Army, revealed to the American liaison, Brigadier General Elliott Thorpe, that Pearl Harbor was one of four possible targets of the Japanese. This information was relayed by the Dutch to General George Marshall, chief of the US Army.[1110] On behalf of himself, Thorpe sent three more dispatches. But got back a cable saying, "don't send this anymore, we are not interested."[1111]

Captain Johann Ranneft, the Dutch naval attache visited the Navy Department at Washington on December 3rd. To quote, "He was

---

1105 Willey, Mother of all Conspiracies

1106 Willey also quotes Gordon Prange, At Dawn We Slept, hinting at Macarthur's culpability. Willey, Mother of all Conspiracies

1107 Stinnet, Mind Over Matters.

1108 Sacrifice at Pearl Harbor, prod. Roy Davies.

1109 According to Mark Emerson Willey, the intercepts the Dutch gave are still classified in RG 38, Box 792. Willey, Mother of all Conspiracies

1110 Sacrifice at Pearl Harbor, prod. Roy Davies.

1111 Sacrifice at Pearl Harbor, prod. Roy Davies.

intrigued on the amount of secret information he was allowed to see. Symbols on a chart showed that two carriers had left Japan on an Easterly course across the Pacific."[1112] He wrote in his diary "No one among us mentions the possibility of an attack on Pearl Harbor."[1113]

Washington's Reaction

The Japanese sent the last message to Roosevelt, saying they could not reach an agreement. Roosevelt said this meant war, but dictated no warnings to anyone under his command.[1114] General George Marshall, the man who could have acted was nowhere to be found.[1115]

Colonel Rufus Bratten was in charge of keeping Marshall supplied with such vital information. Colonel William Heimlich (a fellow officer) heard directly of Bratten's frustration. To quote Edward Hanify (McKinley's lawyer),

> On the morning of Dec 7th 1941, Col Bratten called Compton at his home and asked him to come immediately to Bratten's office. As he came into the office at about 6 'o' clock, he found a relaxed Bratten seated at his desk with his feet up on it. And he said, Jimmy come in. They are going to lower the boom on us and I need a witness. Colonel Compton seated himself and Bratten made his first call to the Chief of Staff. His aim of course, was to tell the Chief of Staff, that in his opinion, the intercepts and the information he had available, showed clearly that the Japanese were about to attack. He continued to call for the next several hours. Each time, the person taking the call reported to Bratton that General Marshall, the Chief of Staff was out riding. Each time, out riding. And finally in disgust, Bratton turned to Compton and said Jimmy, I am going to make this the most famous horseback ride since Paul Riviera.[1116]

General George Marshall arrived to learn that Secretary of State Cordell Hull was to be given the note at 1 pm.[1117] The Japanese strike force was now less than 200 miles from Pearl Harbor.[1118] Marshall finally sent a warning to General Short in Pearl Harbor, but it would never reach him on time.

1112 Sacrifice at Pearl Harbor, prod. Roy Davies.
1113 Sacrifice at Pearl Harbor, prod. Roy Davies.
1114 Sacrifice at Pearl Harbor, prod. Roy Davies.
1115 Sacrifice at Pearl Harbor, prod. Roy Davies.
1116 Sacrifice at Pearl Harbor, prod. Roy Davies.
1117 Sacrifice at Pearl Harbor, prod. Roy Davies.
1118 Sacrifice at Pearl Harbor, prod. Roy Davies.

Further Reading

- Robert Stinnett, Day Of Deceit: The Truth About FDR and Pearl Harbor (Free Press; Touchstone edition, 2001).
- Mark Emerson Willey, Pearl Harbor - Mother of All Conspiracies (Xlibris Corporation, 2000).
- Gordon W. Prange, Donald M. Goldstein, At Dawn We Slept (Penguin Reprint edition 1982).
- John Toland, Infamy: Pearl Harbor and its Aftermath (Berkley, 1986)

Advantage Soviet Union

A graphic made by Mark Willey, author of Pearl Harbor – Mother of all Conspiracies.

<http://www.geocities.com/Pentagon/6315/pearl.html>Accessed 12/11/06. Minimized Reproduction Under Fair Dealing.

It was only two days after the 6th August 1945 atomic bombing of Hiroshima (followed by Nagasaki on 9th) that the Soviets would shamelessly violate their treaty of non-aggression with Japan by declaring war on Japan. They would proceed to occupy Manchuria, Japanese Sakhalin and the strategic Kurile islands. In Manchuria, the Soviets dismantled all major Japanese industries and shipped them to Eastern Soviet Union. They not only raped Japanese, but Chinese women as well.

However, major Soviet gains would manifest later during the cold war period. The emergence of a Soviet backed Communist China and a successful Soviet insurgency in Cambodia, Vietnam and Korea was unthinkable without the destruction of the Empire of Japan.

The Atomic Bombings

Were the Atomic Bombings Necessary?

A common theory for the development and deployment of the atomic bomb is that the Japanese had proved to be more indomitable than anticipated. And from early on, huge American loss of life in the capture of islands on the mere periphery of Japan resulted in the deployment of the atom bomb to bring a quick end to the war. However, General Curtis LeMay, chief of Air Force is quoted as saying:

> LeMay: The war would have been over in two weeks without the Russians entering and without the atomic bomb.
>
> PRESS INQUIRY: You mean that, sir? Without the Russians and without the atomic bomb?
>
> LeMay: The atomic bomb had nothing to do with the end of the war at all.[1119]

According to the US Strategic bombing report prepared a month prior to the atomic bombing, Japan would have surrendered by December 1, 1945.[1120] Brigadier General Carter Clark is quoted in an interview as,

> We brought them down to an abject surrender through the accelerated sinking of their merchant marine and hunger alone, and when we didn't need to do it, and knew we didn't need to do it, we used them as an experiment for two atomic bombs.[1121]

Macarthur himself is quoted as

> [...] a dovish coalition was forming in the Japanese capital, and it was headed by Hirohito himself, who had concluded in the spring of 1945 that a negotiated peace was the only way to end his nation's agony. Beginning in early May, a six-man council of Japanese diplomats

---

[1119] Statement made September 29, 1945. Quoted in Gar Alperowitz The Decision To Use The Atomic Bomb (NY: Knopf, 1995) 334. Taken from Eustace C. Mullins, The Secret History of the Atomic Bomb; Did the Atomic Bomb win the war against Japan? (Web edition)
< http://www.whale.to/b/mullins8.html> Web page as of 11/07/2004

[1120] Quoted from Hiroshima's Shadow, ed. Kai Bird (Pamphleteer Press, 1998). Taken from Eustace C. Mullins, The Secret History of the Atomic Bomb; American military Authorities say atomic bomb unnecessary. Web edition. <
http://www.whale.to/b/mullins8.html> Web page as of 11/07/2004

[1121] Statement made September 29, 1945. Quoted in Gar Alperowitz, The Decision To Use The Atomic Bomb (NY: Knopf, 1995) 359. Taken from Eustace C. Mullins, The Secret History of the Atomic Bomb; The Horror of Hiroshima (Web edition)
< http://www.whale.to/b/mullins8.html> Web page as of 11/07/2004

explored ways to accommodate the Allies. The delegates informed top military officials "our resistance is finished."[1122]

Admiral William Leahy is quoted as

> It is my opinion that the use of this barbarous weapon at Hiroshima and Nagasaki was of no material assistance in our war against Japan. The Japanese were already defeated and ready to surrender because of the effective sea blockade and the successful bombing with conventional weapons.[1123]

A myth would later be concocted that one million Americans would have to be sacrificed to conquer Japan. To the contrary, the Joint Chief of Staffs did prepare serious plans for the ground invasion of Japan but never authorized it.[1124] Japan was subjected to barbaric firebombing by B-25s, the news of which was censored to the American public by Truman. Eustace Mullins comments on the condition of Japan as

> Of Japan's 66 biggest cities, 59 had been mostly destroyed. 178 square miles of urban dwellings had been burned, 500,000 died in the fires, and now twenty million Japanese were homeless. Only four cities had not been destroyed; Hiroshima, Kokura, Niigata, and Nagasaki.[1125]

Hiroshima and Nagasaki were not even of military importance to the Japanese and the casualties of the atomic bombing of them would be 95% civilian. The only option given to the Japanese to pull out of the war was acquiescence to the American demand for "unconditional surrender," which was against Japanese cultural values and which degraded their demigod, the Emperor. In May 1945 Illuminati figures gathered at the San Francisco Palace Hotel to write the charter of the UN. This event was attended by Soviet spy Alger Hiss, John Foster Dulles, Soviet plenipotentiary extraordinaire Averill Harriman (who had spent the last two years in Moscow to coordinate with the Soviets on postwar

---

[1122] Douglas Macarthur quoted by William Manchester, American Caesar (Little Brown, 1978) 437. Taken from Mullins, The Secret History of the Atomic Bomb; The Horror of Hiroshima.

[1123] Ellsworth Torrey Carrington, "Reflections of a Hiroshima Pilot," quoting Admiral Leahy I Was There (McGraw Hill) 245. Taken from Mullins, The Secret History of the Atomic Bomb ;A pilot's history.

[1124] Ellsworth Torrey Carrington, "Reflections of a Hiroshima Pilot," quoting Admiral Leahy I Was There (McGraw Hill) 245. Taken from Mullins, The Secret History of the Atomic Bomb ;A pilot's history.

[1125] Mullins, The Secret History of the Atomic Bomb; Will Japan Surrender before the bomb is dropped.

gains) and Secretary of State Edward Stettinius Jr. Stettinius is credited with the idea of unconditional surrender, which the Japanese wouldn't accept; and which would help the war go on long enough for America to test the atom bomb on the Japanese.[1126] To quote Mullins on Stettinus,

> Edward Stettinius Jr. was the son of a J.P. Morgan partner who had been the world's largest munitions dealer in the First World War. He had been named by J.P. Morgan to oversee all purchases of munitions by both France and England in the United States throughout the war.[1127]

We are told that the atom bombs were detonated at around 2000 feet above their targets to minimize the catastrophe. Eustace Mullins has investigated and pointed out that this undertaking is exactly what causes massive casualties![1128] Over 210,000 people were killed in the atomic bombing of Hiroshima and Nagasaki; and the cities were reduced to radioactive rubble.

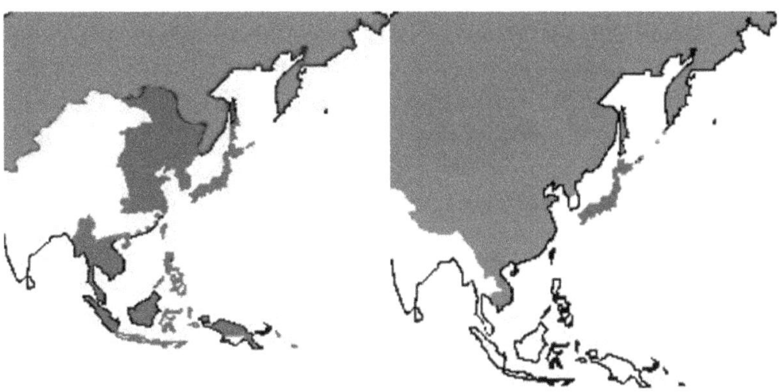

Above: The Japanese Empire at its peak in 1942. Note that Mongolia had been divided into Soviet and Japanese sectors of influence. Right: Soviet influence in the Far East following World War II and other developments, such as the Korean and Vietnam wars. Note that the present Indonesian regime also came to power with Soviet support. Singapore and Taiwan are also under the control of the Powers that Be. Cartographic details are not to scale. © Hamad Subani; Licensing: same as book; see introductory section on Licensing.

Another less common theory is that while the atomic bombing was unnecessary, it was done so to instill fear of the Americans among the Soviets in the upcoming Cold war. If the Soviet threat was so immense,

---

[1126] Mullins, The Secret History of the Atomic Bomb; A. United Nations Project.
[1127] Mullins, The Secret History of the Atomic Bomb; A. United Nations Project.
[1128] Mullins, The Secret History of the Atomic Bomb; Mass Murder.

America could have concluded peace with the Japanese and let the Japanese balance Soviet influence, even letting them batter the Soviet Union at will (as in World War I). The atomic bombing instead guaranteed that there would not be a resurgence of a Japanese Empire for a long time to come. It is important to note that even today, thousands of American troops are placed in Japan and Japanese officials are careful not to take any stand on the atomic bombings.

Beyond Soviet Hegemony

As with the creation of Nazism, the Powers that Be had long-term goals in the creation and deployment of the atomic bomb, other than the immediate goal of the destruction of the Japanese Empire for the Soviets. These objectives came to light in the work of renowned New World Order researcher Eustace Mullins, in his book, *The Secret History of the Atomic Bomb.*

If Japan bowed out, the Powers That Be would lose their only chance to test the atom bomb on a civilian population. This is exactly the conclusion they reached when they gathered at the San Francisco Palace Hotel to write the charter of the UN in May 1945.[1129] Hiroshima and Nagasaki had been spared from B-25 carpet-bombing from the very beginning because these cities were meant to be "sacrificed" to atom bombs.

Apart from securing the Soviet Union, the subtraction of Japan from the power blocs would leave the world with only two power blocs, USA and the Soviet Union which were/are both under firm control of the Illuminati. These blocs would engage in pretend rivalry to make all other countries proxy states of either of them. The threat of nuclear annihilation would be used to make free countries become members of these blocs.

The first successful test of the atomic bomb occurred at the Trinity site, two hundred miles south of Los Alamos at 5:29:45 a.m. on July 16, 1945. Oppenheimer shrieked, "I am become Death, the Destroyer of worlds." The prospect of destruction of the world would be played and replayed throughout the cold war so that both NATO and Soviet governments could pursue their policies as well as develop advanced weapons, which

---

[1129] Mullins, The Secret History of the Atomic Bomb; A. United Nations Project.

would be indispensable for future conflicts of the Powers That Be. By fomenting cold war fears, Americans were made to fight several wars, which ironically, were dialectically engineered to further Soviet goals. To quote Mullins:

> It also forecast the entire strategy of the Cold War, which lasted forty-three years, cost American taxpayers five trillion dollars, and accomplished exactly nothing, as it was intended to do. Thus we see that the New World Order has based its entire strategy on the agony of the hundreds of thousands of civilians burned alive at Hiroshima and Nagasaki, including many thousands of children sitting in their schoolrooms. These leaders had learned from their master, Josef Stalin that no one can rule without mass terrorism, which in turn required mass murder. As Senator Vandenberg, leader of the Republican loyal opposition, was to say (as quoted in American Heritage magazine, August 1977), "We have got to scare the hell out of 'em.'[1130]

And elsewhere,

> In the United States, the schools held daily bomb drills, with the children hiding under their desks. No one told them that thousands of schools children in Hiroshima had been incinerated in their classrooms; the desks offered no protection against nuclear weapons. The moral effect on the children was devastating. If they were to be vaporized in the next ten seconds, there seemed little reason to study, marry and have children, or prepare for a steady job. This demoralization through the nuclear weapons program is the undisclosed reason for the decline in public morality. In 1987, Phyllis Lafarge published *The Strangelove Legacy, The Impact Of The Nuclear Threat On Children*, chronicling through extended research the moral devastation wreaked on the children by the daily threat of annihilation.[1131]

The controlled, domesticated and conditioned populations of the Western world are always kept on edge by the Powers that Be. For example, the hype about climate change commenced immediately after the Berlin wall came down. Fear works as an effective controlling agent.

Atomic bombs were also used to maintain the integrity of the Soviet Union from the prospect of any supposed foreign threats. As the Nazi invasion had shown, many people within the Soviet Union loathed the

---

[1130] Mullins, The Secret History of the Atomic Bomb; A. United Nations Project.
[1131] Mullins, The Secret History of the Atomic Bomb; A. United Nations Project.

Soviets, and would desert in the event of a foreign invasion. But no one sought to provoke the Soviet Union anymore.

The People behind the Atom Bomb

A glance at the people who gifted humanity with the atom bomb reveals prominent Cabal operatives. This section discusses some revelations, which have come light in Eustace Mullin's *The Secret History of The Atom Bomb.*

Around 1930, there were no scientists in America working on nuclear fission. But that was not the case in Nazi Germany, where research on fission had started. The Powers that Be were aware that the research did not have much future in Nazi Germany, which was meant to have a limited lifespan. The Soviets didn't have much expertise, facilities or finance (the first test bomb would cost $2 billion to research) to develop the atomic bomb either. And Stalin was not trusted enough to be allowed to possess such a working weapon. Therefore, the only choice was America.

Albert Einstein

Establishment historians portray Einstein as a peace-lover whose commitment to develop the atom bomb was only for the love of physics, and that he wanted the Japanese to witness a test explosion of the atom bomb rather than use it on them. If these legends were true, the question arises why Einstein didn't do humanity a favor with a swipe of the blackboard duster and dissociate himself from the horrendous invention? At a time when those engaged in the war were seeking bigger and better ways to kill their enemies, the use of such massive energy would certainly not be directed towards producing residential electricity. According to his wife, Einstein "regarded human beings with detestation."[1132] Einstein would arrive in America in 1933. To quote Mullins on Einstein's later activities in America,

> Albert Einstein, presided over the Institute for Advanced Study, a think tank for refugee "geniuses", financed by the Rothschilds through one of their many secret foundations.[1133]

[1132] Mullins, The Secret History of the Atomic Bomb; Criminals on Display
[1133] Mullins, The Secret History of the Atomic Bomb; The New Atomic Age

One of the trustees of this think tank was Robert Oppenheimer, who was directly involved in the development of the atom bomb and in subsequently passing the technology to the Soviets. However, Einstein's biggest role in developing the atom bomb was the August 2nd 1939 letter, in which he and the German immigrant-scientist Leo Szilard, along with his long time friends and fellow Hungarian physicists, Eugene Wigner and Edward Teller[1134] requested the help of Franklin Roosevelt in pursuing the development of the atom bomb in America.

December 31, 1999 Vol. 154 No. 27 © Time Warner. All Rights Reserved. See time.com for additional copyright and usage information

Alexander Sachs delivered Einstein's letter personally to Roosevelt on October 11th 1939. It appears that the atom bomb program could not have been launched without the necessary approval by the Banking Elite. Sachs was more than a messenger. To quote Mullins,

> Sachs was an advisor to Eugene Meyer of the Lazard Freres International Banking House, and also with Lehman Brothers, another well-known banker. Sachs' delivery of the Einstein letter to the White House let Roosevelt know that the Rothschilds approved of the project and wished him to go full speed ahead.[1135]

Secretary of War Henry L. Stimson (Of the Skull and Bones Secret Society) disclosed to the later President Eisenhower the existence of the atomic bomb. Eisenhower became a key opponent of it and he would later make a cryptic speech about the pervasive influences of the "military industrial complex."[1136] In reality, the military industrial complex is nothing but the Illuminati, which Eisenhower would never openly refer to.

President Truman, the one to agree on the deployment of the atom bomb "[...] had only had one job in his career, as a Masonic organizer for the State of Missouri [...]".[1137] "Truman didn't know his own Secretary of

---

[1134] Mullins, The Secret History of the Atomic Bomb; A New Mission
[1135] Mullins, The Secret History of the Atomic Bomb; Atomic Terrorism
[1136] Mullins, The Secret History of the Atomic Bomb; Atomic terrorism
[1137] Mullins, The Secret History of the Atomic Bomb; Criminals on Display

State, Stettinius. He had no background in foreign policy, no expert advisors of his own."[1138] To quote Mullins,

> He was advised by a prestigious group, The National Defense Research Committee, consisting of George L. Harrison, president of the Federal Reserve Bank of New York; Dr. James B. Conant, president of Harvard, who had spent the First World War developing more effective poison gases, and who in 1942 had been commissioned by Winston Churchill to develop an Anthrax bomb. Also on the committee were Dr. Karl Compton, and James F. Byrnes, acting Secretary of State. For thirty years, Byrnes had been known as Bernard Baruch's man in Washington.[1139] "Byrnes spoke with the authority of—personally represented—the president of the United States [Truman] on all bomb-related matters in the Interim Committee's deliberations."[1140]

Bernard Baruch

To quote Mullins,

> The atomic bomb was developed at the Los Alamos Laboratories in New Mexico. The top secret project was called the Manhattan Project, because its secret director, Bernard Baruch, lived in Manhattan, as did many of the other principals.[1141]

Bernard Baruch, courtesy © Smithsonian Institution. Minimized Reproduction Under Fair Dealing.

Bernard Baruch had made enormous profits on Wall Street and was probably the wealthiest man in South Carolina. He was a Presidential Advisor during World War II.

The Bohemian Grove

The Manhattan project was said to have been launched in the Illuminati Bohemian Grove.[1142] To quote,

---

1138 David McCullough, in his laudatory biography of Truman. Quoted in Mullins, The Secret History of the Atomic Bomb; The Horror of Hiroshima.

1139 Mullins, The Secret History of the Atomic Bomb; The Buck Passes to Truman

1140 Quoted in Quoted in Gar Alperowitz The Decision To Use The Atomic Bomb (NY: Knopf, 1995) 196. Mullins, The Secret History of the Atomic Bomb; The Horror of Hiroshima.

1141 The Secret History of the Atomic Bomb by Eustace C. Mullins ; The Jewish Hell Bomb < http://www.whale.to/b/mullins8.html> Web page as of 11/07/2004

1142 The Bohemian Grove is a redwood forest in Sonoma county California where many Illuminati including American Presidents have been sighted. Conspiracy researcher Alex Jones managed to infiltrate the Bohemian Grove and photographed bizarre rituals taking

Chapter Five [of the 'History of the Lawrence Berkeley Laboratory[1143]] contains a 1950 photo of physicist Ernest Lawrence meeting at the Bohemian Grove with former President Herbert Hoover and future President Dwight Eisenhower. The Grove photo in this chapter is dated in July 23, 1950, which means it was made during the club's annual summer encampment. Lawrence played a key role in the development of nuclear weapons, and chapters in this publication mention two planning meetings that were held at the Bohemian Grove during the 1940's regarding development of the atomic bomb and the functioning of the Atomic Energy Commission.[1144]

The original caption reads: "Lawrence lunching with future president Eisenhower and past president Hoover at Bohemian Grove, July 23, 1950."

Robert Oppenheimer

The scientific director at Los Alamos was J. Robert Oppenheimer, scion of a prosperous family of clothing merchants. He became director of research at the newly formed U.S. Atomic Energy Commission, with his mentor, Bernard Baruch, serving as chairman. Oppenheimer continued

place before a huge stone owl. Alex Jones, "Dark Secrets Inside the Bohemian Grove" Infowars.com <http://www.infowars.com/bg1.html> Accessed 07/11/06.

[1143] J. L. Heilbron, Robert W. Seidel, Bruce R. Wheaton, Ed. Judith Goldhaber, Lawrence and His Laboratory (1981 Newsmagazine Publication; 1996 Web Publication). <http://www.lbl.gov/Science-Articles/Research-Review/Magazine/1981/index.html> Accessed 07/11/06.

[1144] Kerry Richardson, Index of Bohemian Grove Reportage <http://www.sonic.net/~kerry/bohemian/photolinks.html> Accessed 07/11/06.

his many Communist Party Associations; his wife was Kitty Peuning, widow of Joe Dallet, an American Communist who had been killed defending Communism with the notorious Lincoln Brigade in Spain. Because Oppenheimer was under Party discipline, the Party then ordered him to marry Kitty Peuning and make a home for her. [1145]

Oppenheimer was later caught spying for the Soviet Union. A hearing was held from April 5 to May 6, 1954.

> After reviewing the results, the Atomic Energy Commission voted to strip Oppenheimer of his security clearance, ruling that he "possessed substantial defects of character and imprudent dangerous associations with known subversives".[1146]

Robert Oppenheimer,
Courtesy US Dept. of Energy.

Einstein was greatly dismayed by the persecution of Oppenheimer.[1147] Among Einstein's half-a-dozen girlfriends was one lady suspected of being a Russian spy.[1148]

Background on the Oppenheimers

When Mayer Amschel Rothschild was yet to make his fortune and left school at the age of 13, he went to Hanover to be an apprentice for the Oppenheimer bank, where he worked for 7 years.[1149] To quote Springmeier on the Oppenheimers,

> Two Jewish families that appear to be prominent are the Oppenheims and the Oppenheimers.... The Oppenheimers were early members of the Bavarian Illuminati. The Bund der Gerechten (League of the Just) was an Illuminati..... This Bund financed in part by the Rothschilds paid the Satanist and Mason Karl Marx to write the Communist

[1145] Mullins, The Secret History of the Atomic Bomb; The New atomic Age
[1146] Mullins, The Secret History of the Atomic Bomb; The New atomic Age
[1147] Diary of Einstein's last girlfriend, Johanna Fantova. The Associated Press 26/04/04. "Diary sheds light on Einstein's final years." AP <http://www.msnbc.msn.com/id/4829521/> Accessed 01/12/06.
[1148] Letters released by the Hebrew University in Jerusalem. Associated Press 10/07/06. "New letters shed light on Einstein's love life," AP <http://www.msnbc.msn.com/id/13804030/> Accessed 01/12/06.
[1149] Fritz Springmeier, Bloodlines of the Illuminati (Spring Arbor distributors, 1998) 176. GlobalGrey PDF edition 2013 <http://www.globalgrey.co.uk/Pages/Books-Conspiracies/Bloodlines-Of-The-Illuminati.html> Web page as of 03/07/13.

Manifesto. The Jew Gumpel Oppenheim was in the inner circle of the Bund. His relative Heinrich Oppenheim masterminded the communist revolution of 1848 in Germany. The Communist Party's official histories even accept the Bund as the predecessor of Communism. The Oppenheimers apparently are close to the Rothschilds. J. Robert Oppenheimer of the CFR was exposed as a communist. Harry Oppenheimer, an international banker, is chairman of the Jewish De Beers worldwide diamond monopoly, and chairman of the Anglo-American Corp. Oppenheimers can be found in important financial positions in the U.S. They help run around 10 large foundations[1150]

William Laurence/Lipmann Sew

To quote Mullins,

> Despite the fact that the Manhattan Project was the most closely guarded secret of World War II, one man, and one many only, was allowed to observe everything and to know everything about the project. He was Lipman Siew, a Lithuanian Jew who had come to the United States as a political refugee at the age of seventeen. He lived in Boston on Lawrence St., and decided to take the name of William L. Laurence. At Harvard, he became a close friend of James B. Conant and was tutored by him. When Laurence went to New York, he was hired by Herbert Bayard Swope, editor of the New York World, who was known as Bernard Baruch's personal publicity agent. Baruch owned the World. In 1930, Laurence accepted an offer from the New York Times to become its science editor. He states in Who's Who that he "was selected by the heads of the atomic bomb project as sole writer and public relations." How one could be a public relations writer for a top-secret project was not explained. Laurence was the only civilian present at the historic explosion of the test bomb on July 16, 1945. Less than a month later, he sat in the co-pilots seat of the B-29 on the fateful Nagasaki bombing run. [1151]

Remains of the Urakami Church in Nagasaki.

During the Nagasaki bombing, a Catholic Church was used as the epicenter of the explosion. A few walls of this Church have managed to

---

[1150] Springmeier, Bloodlines 159.

[1151] Mullins, The Secret History of the Atomic Bomb; Lipman Siew stand till this day.[1152] The decision to make the Urakami Church the epicenter symbolizes the centuries long struggle between the Illuminati and the Church.

Japanese Surrender

After the Japanese surrender, the International Tribunal for the Far East would proceed to prosecute and even execute six Japanese generals including Tojo for war crimes. On the other hand, Charles Willoughby (A German Fascist who was Macarthur's chief of intelligence for the Pacific) arranged to have Japanese scientists responsible for germ warfare experiments on humans (in which more than 3000 died, including an undetermined number of American POWs) to be granted immunity in return for their laboratory records.[1153]

[1152] Also known as the Urakami Catholic Church. William Craig, The Fall Of Japan, (NY: Dial, 1967) 93. Quoted in Mullins, The Secret History of the Atomic Bomb; The Nagasaki bomb

[1153] Mae Brussells, "The Nazi Connection to the Dallas JFK murder," The Rebel January 1984: ?? An archived copy is available at: <http://www.maebrussell.com/Mae Brussell Articles/Nazi Connection to JFK Assass.html> Web page as of 16/03/04

Chapter Eight
Reaping the Harvests of the World Wars: Post War Soviet Activity

Soviet Cold War Poster. The text reads, "We are invincible. 35 years of the Pact of Warsaw."

The following are events, which cannot be separated from the context of the two World Wars and the rise of the Soviet Union.

Panama Revolution of 1903

This revolution severed the Isthmus of Panama from Columbia and made the country an American dependency. According to Sutton (quoting a Congressional investigation), this Revolution too, was the work of the very same backers of the Bolshevik Revolution located at 120 Broadway.[1154]

Mexican Revolution of 1915-1916

According to Antony Sutton, this Mexican Revolution was backed by the same American interests, which backed the Bolshevik Revolution in Russia. The Carranza government was the first in the world to have a Soviet constitution.[1155] To quote,

> The Carranza revolution probably could not have succeeded without American munitions and Carranza would not have remained in power as long as he did without American help.[1156]

Indonesia

The Powers that Be gained control of the resource rich Indonesian islands through the Communist Party, which initially pretended to be Islamist. Its foundations were laid by the Dutch before they departed. President Sukarno would later consolidate power. In 1962, he would receive the Order of Lenin. His oppressive regime is supported by oil and banking interests based in Calgary, Canada. Canada even allowed the mass murderer an official a visit and imprisoned Canadians who protested.

[1154] United States, House, Committee on Foreign Affairs, The Story of Panama, Hearings on the Rainey Resolution, 1913. p. 53. Antony C Sutton, Wall Street and the Bolshevik Revolution (Buccaneer Books, 1993). Chapter Four of Online edition. <http://reformed-theology.org/html/books/bolshevik_revolution/chapter_04.htm > Accessed 25/10/06.

[1155] Sutton, Bolshevik Revolution Chapter Four of Online edition.

[1156] U.S., Senate, Committee on Foreign Relations, Investigation of Mexican Affairs, 1920, pts. 2, 18, pp. 795-96. Sutton, Bolshevik Revolution Chapter Four of Online edition.

Korean War

Korea was divided between America and the Soviet Union, and two separate governments were created in 1948. A Soviet backed attempt to expand the North Korean frontier proved to be premature and a confrontation took place with American forces. The Chinese had to be brought in to restore the status quo of North Korea. During the course of the war, General Douglas Macarthur got too excited about pushing back North Korea (which wasn't part of the plan) and had to be dismissed.

Consolidation of the Soviet Union

Once the Soviet Union was consolidated under Illuminati control after the death of Stalin (1953), its "shareholders" ruled over this large mass of territory from their centers in the Western World. Calgary, Geneva, New York, London, to name a few. The Soviet Union was a modern day colony of undocumented private interests based in the West, and the Soviet Empire was a dramatic renewal of European colonial empires. These links were not conspicuous, and the Western Criminal Elite never undertook direct administration of the Soviet Union. The Illuminati had the role of helmsmen, and this was accomplished through informal contacts.

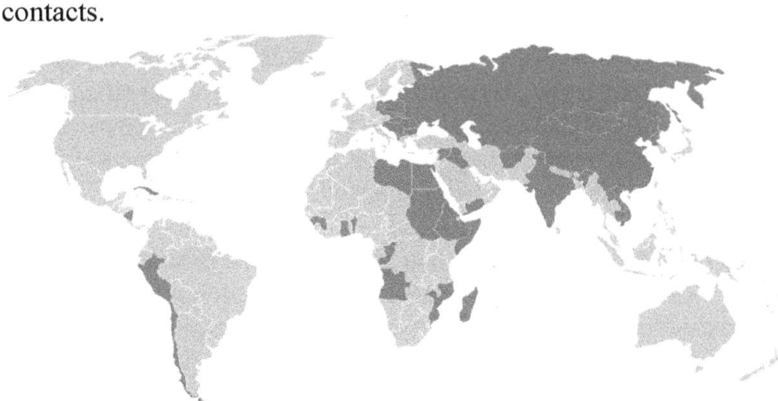

The Soviet Empire was managed from centers in the Western world

All the main wars "capitalist" countries fought henceforth worked mainly to the advantage of the Soviet Union. In addition, academic, technological and scientific research accomplished in North America and Europe would be diverted to the Soviet Union. This activity was detailed in Antony Sutton's *The Best Enemy Money Can Buy*.[1157] The support channeled to the Soviet Union after the war dwarfs Lend-Lease

[1157] Antony C. Sutton, The Best Enemy Money Can Buy (Liberty House 1986).

and I.G. Farben. As the Mitrokhin archive would later reveal, covert activity for Soviet gain was on a much bigger scale than Senator McCarthy could imagine. Operatives from the Soviet bloc were allowed to immigrate to America, where they would not only work towards Soviet espionage, but also serve as the eyes and ears of the local Criminal Elite.

The Soviet Union and the Middle East

A discussion of Soviet policy towards the Middle East is not warranted, but it would suffice to say that while Israel used the cold war pretext to arm itself to the hilt, pro-Soviet Arab countries did no receive much help from the Soviet bloc. For example, during the First Gulf War, the Soviet Union conspicuously abandoned Iraq to the Americans, because the Powers that Be had agreed as such.

Gamal Abdel Nasser was an Arab nationalist leader of Egypt, who executed and tortured his own people. Apart from his oratory skills, his leadership was far from exceptional. Nevertheless, he sought to combat Israel. And sequentially, the Soviet Union befriended him and offered him aid. The Soviet advisors who poured in were rightly suspected of spying by Nasser's successor. The Soviets backed the construction of the Aswan mega-dam. But it was only after its creation that the Egyptians realised that the dam was a security risk to several Egyptian cities. Prior to Aswan, the Soviets instructed Nasser to divert his troops to aid Communist Yemen, where they became involved in atrocities. And Israel attacked once the troops were diverted.

Through Nasser's Egypt, the Soviets were able to infiltrate and create their own Palestinian resistance organizations, and monopolize the anti-Zionist resistance. This would make the Palestinian resistance compromised, and would allow it to be used for future dialectical wars.

Nasser's Egypt also served as a conduit for establishing control over neighbouring areas. It is not surprising that many other leaderships in the Middle East identified with socialism.

The Algerian War of Independence

As we have read in Chapter Five, Fascism was established in the Mediterranean, and the Nazis entered North Africa, exclusively to provide a dialectical opposition for the Soviet advance and the establishment of Soviet hegemony in this region. This plan failed due to Soviet logistical issues.

However, the quest for Soviet hegemony in North Africa and the surrounding Middle East continued after World War II. In the Algerian War of Independence, the French Colonists were to act as a dialectical opposition to a Soviet backed FLN. The FLN was backed by the Soviets through Nasser's Egypt.[1158] The French were used to drive the subject population into the arms of the FLN. The FLN, on the other hand, was used to destroy rival groups such as genuine Islamists, and to also destroy groups who weren't supportive of the FLN. Ahmed Ben Bella has been referred to as a Kremlin operative.[1159] In addition, another Algerian Independence figure, Si Mustapha was not even an Arab, but an East German Communist named Winfried Muller.[1160] To make Algeria more suitable for future Soviet autocracy, the French Army was used to depopulate the Algerian countryside. More than two million Algerians were forcibly resettled to more controlled areas. This worked to the advantage of the FLN.

But things went awry when the non-elitist General Charles de Gaulle ascended power in France. De Gaulle was initially for a French Algeria, but realising how the French had hopelessly discredited themselves in Algeria, he granted Algeria Independence.

The Illuminati responded by trying to prevent French withdrawal, since the French were intended to play a dialectical role until final FLN victory. Premature French withdrawal would allow rival factions coming to power. There was even as assassination attempt on De Gaulle (one of the several) in which a British operative was involved. This was the subject of Frederick Forsythe's novel, *The Day of the Jackal*.

1158 William F. Jasper, "Terrorism's True Roots," 2001-12-03 John Birch Society. <http://www.jbs.org/node/843> Accessed 23/11/06.

1159 William F. Jasper, "Terrorism's True Roots," 2001-12-03 John Birch Society. <http://www.jbs.org/node/843> Accessed 23/11/06.

1160 The John Birch Society forced Newsweek Magazine to issue a redaction to an October 1959 article that portrayed Si Mustapha as a romantic Arab patriot. William F.Jasper, "Forty Years of freedom," The New American. Vol. 14, No. 25, (December 7th 1998).
< http://www.thenewamerican.com/tna/1998/vo14no25/vo14no25_jbs.htm> Accessed 23/11/06.

Cuban Revolution

The revolution of 1959 was a sincere attempt by Cubans opposed to the corrupt Batista government. However, the complete seizure of power by Fidel Castro was unprecedented, and many of the revolutionaries, such as Major Pedro Diaz Lanz (Castro's chief of airforce) saw this consolidation of power as a conspiracy. Castro originally became a millionaire working for the Rockefeller United Fruit Company[1161] (never mind the Proletariat beard). And his socialist system allows his interests to maintain a stranglehold over the Cuban economy.

Castro is often portrayed as living in the crosshairs of American plots. However, it is unlikely that he could have even succeeded in consolidating the Revolution without Washington's covert acquiescence. During the Kennedy Presidency, the CIA conducted the disastrous Bay of Pigs invasion, which might have been a ploy to discredit President Kennedy. Similarly, members of the Joint Chief of Staff would recommend several kooky plots to overthrow Castro. Inherently, each of these plots would have caused great discredit to Kennedy if they were carried out. It is highly unlikely that the United States or its Intelligence is sincere about removing Castro.

When President Kennedy fell apart with the Powers that Be, the Cuban missile crisis was created to force him to resign. Regardless of whether Soviet missiles existed on Cuban soil or on the photographs, both the US, Cuban and Soviet administration were complicit in this plot against Kennedy. But he stood his ground and turned the crisis into a personal victory. Since the American subject population believes everything they see on television, throughout the crisis they ran around like headless chicken.

Dialectical Wars: An Overview

Before we proceed, it is necessary to understand how dialectical wars were engineered. And how America intervened to create Soviet-Maoist domination. A generic dialectical war will be presented below as a series of steps.

1. Assign two zones in a region, one Soviet-Maoist-Warsaw Pact, and the other American-Western-NATO.
2. Have the Soviets establish a loose foothold in their region under the guise of ideology.

[1161] Juri Lina, Architects of Deception (Stockholm, Juri Lina, 2004) 321.

3. Establish a government in the NATO region, which is likely to be viewed with discontent by most of its subjects. (For example, Apartheid South Africa, corrupt South Vietnam).
4. Make the NATO region wage an atrocious war against the other region, even in the absence of a threat of the latter.
5. Keep the war turned on full blast until the people and the leaders of the Warsaw Pact region realize that their only deliverance from NATO barbarity will be in the inviting of unconditional Soviet hegemony in the region. After all, who else is going to save them? (Definitely, not the UN). Since NATO forces don't have any serious issues with barbarism, send in the B-52s. The war can be waged until each and every one on the other side gets the point.
6. As the newly supported Soviet region strikes back, have the NATO region engage in retreats, while conducting more atrocious warfare to herd more civilians into joining the Soviet forces.
7. Have the NATO forces abandon all of its region and its citizens to the Soviet forces. At this time, antiwar voices back home are finally publicized.
8. Rinse and repeat somewhere else. The suckers never get it.

Credit goes to German philosophers such as Hegel, who pioneered dialectics, Karl Hausofer, whose dialectics destroyed the German war machine and delivered Germany and East Europe to the Soviets, and of course, the next generation of German born Hausofer protégés, who inhabited the US Joint Chief of Staff. Note that with the dissolution of the Soviet Union, there are more complicated variants of the original two-party dialectical war in progress across the globe.

The Vietnam War

The Allies created the Vietnam crisis by dividing Vietnam into two regions, the North and the South, as per the Yalta conference. The North was to be under the Soviet sphere of influence. During the Presidency of Kennedy, the CIA conspired to have the President of South Vietnam, Ngoh Dinh Diem and his brother to be removed and executed. The regime, which replaced them was infamous for its corruption. It appears Kennedy was not fully aware of the details of this conspiracy until later. Kennedy did not want to proceed with a war in Vietnam, and it is not surprising that he was assassinated three weeks after the coup in Vietnam. He was succeeded by Lyndon Johnson, who used the peculiar incident at the Gulf of Tonkin to embroil America into a war with

Vietnam. This plot resulted in the Americanization of South Vietnam, at a time when such a move was completely unnecessary, and only worked to the advantage of the Communist North. On 2nd March 1965, American troops based in South Vietnam were faced with another sudden provocation. In response, the American airforce launched Operation Rolling Thunder, during which more than a million flight missions were undertaken, dropping up to 3/4th of a million tonnes of explosives.[1162] This carpet-bombing would last till November 1968. However, major North Vietnamese targets in Vietnam, Laos and Cambodia would be spared. The aim of this operation was to herd the people of those areas into joining the North Vietnamese cause. General William Westmoreland advocated a "search and destroy" modus operandi, in which Americans were to subject villages to their barbarism. This further made entire villages join the cause of the North Vietnamese.

When faced with the full brunt of the American military industrial complex, the North Vietnamese leadership was driven completely into the arms of the Soviets and the Soviet backed Chinese. Without the role of American savagery, such a momentous Illuminati accomplishment would have never been achieved.

Since America was only meant to provide dialectical opposition to force the North Vietnamese into the arms of the Soviets, American soldiers never held the ground they captured. They did not fight in large formations, and instead, small sized units were deployed to engage in savagery while retreating. The very fact that American soldiers could be made party to this venture and would continue this horrendous activity without questioning its strategic benefits paints a disturbing picture of the American psyche. The Americans were then suddenly taken aback by the Tet offensive. The brutality of Americans had now driven ample number of Vietnamese villagers into the Communist camp. Despite this massive failure, General Westmoreland was promoted to the Army Chief of Staff.

When the time came for a Soviet backed takeover of the entire Vietnam, the antiwar movement in America was finally given voice, massacres were finally publicized and the complicity of the US government was finally leaked.

[1162] Earl L. Tilford, Setup: What the Air Force did in Vietnam and Why (Maxwell Air Force Base AL: Air University Press, 1991) 89.

In 1969, the Nixon administration launched massive B-52 strikes against North Vietnamese supply lines in Cambodia. This attack was coordinated with an American and South Vietnamese incursion into Cambodia. The North Vietnamese fighters were pushed deeper into Cambodia, destabilizing the country. And the Soviet backed Khmer Rouge came to power in Cambodia. A similar attempt was made at Laos.

Apart from the establishment of Soviet-Maoist-Illuminati hegemony in Indochina, there were other motives as well. The Indochina region is a locus of drug production destined for international markets. Seizing control of this area would be concurrent with historic Illuminati activity, such as the opium trade. There are stories that during the war, coffins of American soldiers were used to smuggle drugs into America. In addition, American soldiers were exposed to the drug culture of the area, and brought home the malaise.

There were also claims of the North Vietnamese using sophisticated American weaponry relating to surveillance and early warning. There are persistent claims of prearranged kidnappings of American technicians and equipment specialists, who were later transferred to the Soviet Union, where they would eventually die in prison camps. There is nothing more pitiable than the plight of the arrogant ignorant. And this topic cannot be left without mentioning that the grand geo-politician Henry Kissinger won the Nobel Prize, and his best friend, Fritz Kraemer also presided over the "geopolitics" of the Vietnam War.

The Ethiopian Famine

Derg party badge, 1979

The Soviet backed military junta, the Derg, came to power in 1974, after deposing Emperor Haile Selassie. Its reign is remembered as the Ethiopian Red Terror, during which tens of thousands of people were executed, in an effort to topple all rival groups. With Soviet assistance, Derg Ethiopia became one of the most well armed nations in Africa. The Derg also introduced forced collectivization of farms and the nationalization of industry and property. This resulted in a famine, in which up to seven million Ethiopians died. Theoretically, the United Nations was expected to intervene by any means possible. But this would destabilize the Soviet backed regime.

The Live Aid concert was organized on July 13th 1985. And similar concerts and music records helped raise money to save Ethiopians from the famine. This prevented embroilment of the UN in the affair. The aid was conveyed to Ethiopia through the Derg, which raised some eyebrows.

The UN: Missing in Action

The UN was conspicuously non-committal when it came to Soviet aggression or Soviet backed aggression. The UN was also silent on the deportations, resettlements, atrocities and genocides taking place in the Soviet Union. At the end of World War II, there were 5.5 million prisoners in Stalin's gulags.[1163] Yet no UN "fact-finding missions" were organized. The same UN would later authorize an American invasion over Saddam not allowing UN inspection of its nuclear facilities.

The Creation of India and Pakistan

Background

This topic will be discussed in some detail, because India and Pakistan were meant to be part of a dialectical cold war conflict that would make Vietnam look like picnic, a conflict that was meant to deliver the entire subcontinent to direct Soviet control. Although I do not intend to attribute all the maladies of the Indian subcontinent to outsiders, there is

---

1163 Eric Margolis, "The 20th Century's Worst Crime Goes Unpunished," The Toronto Sun November 16th 2003. Also published on ericmargolis.com <http://www.ericmargolis.com/archives/2003/11/the_20th_centur.php> Accessed 13/12/06 little doubt that European arrival in the Indian subcontinent was the most disastrous blow to the political and economic achievements of the people of the subcontinent..

The Illuminati and Ancient India

The Illuminati links to ancient India are not exactly of relevance to this book, since these links were long extinct, though their legacies remain. For a detailed discussion of these links, see the section "In the Footsteps of the Aryans" in Chapter Three. These ancient riddles are completely irrelevant to the modern day Indian subcontinent. But since sacred literature pertaining to this period has been remarkably well preserved by the Hindu people, it makes for insightful reading.

The Mughal Empire

With the rise of Islam, the Illuminati of Sassanid Persia and the Illuminati of other regions that fell to Islam quickly switched horses, camouflaging themselves as Muslims and seeking the spoils of Islamic conquests. With the extension of the Islamic world into India, The Illuminati connection to India was revived. When the Mughal Empire would be established, the Illuminati Safavid royalty of Iran systematically infiltrated the Mughal royal household and the Mughal nobility.[1164] Historian Dr. Beni Prasad first drew attention towards the presence of this "Iranian" cabal (also known as Khorasanis and Ardabilis), engaged in a perpetual and violent struggle of power against legitimate Mughal royalty. Despite concerted efforts to take over the Mughal Empire, they repeatedly failed. Far more competent heirs produced from marriages to local Rajputs would thwart the Illuminati heirs produced from Safavid intermarriage. And the Mughals produced the most prosperous and bustling economies of all time. The prosperity the Mughals attracted attention from all over the world. Desperate attempts were made by the Western Illuminati in trying to find sea routes to Mughal India, since the Ottomans had blocked land routes. In fact, the mission of Christopher Columbus which discovered the Americas was originally intended to find a sea route to India.

[1164] The Illuminati Safavids ruled Persia in medieval times and subjected the religion of Islam to shameful manipulations and permutations. They originated in Armenia. Prior to morphing into the descendants of the Prophet of Islam, the early Safavids counted ancestors among the Christian Byzantine royals based in Trebizond! V. Minorsky, The Poetry of Shah Isma'il I. Bulletin of the School of Oriental and African Studies. University of London Volume 10, No.4. (1942), page 1053a.

The Illuminati managed to finally take over the Mughal Empire after the death of Aurangzeb. But it wasn't the Safavids who gained control. It was another group, the mysterious Saiyid Brothers, who initially gained a foothold in Mughal nobility through the assistance of the Safavid conspirators. This group had obscure origins, but outwardly professed phony religious credentials. Emperor Aurangzeb, whose letters hint at his highly perceptive abilities, was unaware of the presence of organized conspiracy. But he did make note of something suspicious and ugly about the Safavid nobility/royalty in his household, as well as the Saiyid Brothers.

Takeover of the Mughal Empire

Prime Minister Asad Khan, and later, his son Zulfiqar Khan[1165] represented the Safavid conspirators in the Mughal nobility of Aurangzeb. They would frequently arouse the anger of Aurangzeb by their incompetence and insubordination. In addition, the conspirators had Aurangzeb take a Safavid as a wife. The heirs from this woman were infamous for their revolts and insubordination.

Unfortunately, Aurangzeb mistook the Saiyid Brothers for being genuine descendants of the Prophet (as they claimed) and allowed them access to the echelons of power. In a letter, Aurangzeb wrote:

> To relax the reigns of the Syeds of Barha is to bring on final ruin...because these people boast on getting the least prosperity and promotion, boast 'There is none like me,' stray from the path of right conduct, cherish high views and cause impediment.[1166]

One would expect Aurangzeb's last will for his sons to contain detailed instructions on dealing with external foes such as the Marathas. Instead, we find the ninth item of his will outlining precautions to be taken against the Saiyid Brothers. To quote,

> Ninth- You should treat the Syeds of Barha, who are worthy of blessings, according to the Quranic verse 'Give unto the near relations of the Prophet, their dues,' and never grow slack in honoring and favoring them. In as much as according to the blessed verse, 'I say I do not ask of you any recompense for it except love to [my] kinsmen,' love for this family is the wages of Prophetship, you should never be wanting [in respect for them], and it will bear fruits in this world and

[1165] Also known as Nusrat Jang.

[1166] Hamid al-Din Khan Bahadur; Sir Jadunath Sarkar, Anecdotes of Aurangzeb: English translation of Ahkam-i-Alamgiri.3rd ed.(Calcutta, M.C. Sarkar, 1949) 89.

> the next. But you should be extremely cautious in dealing with the Syeds of Barha. Be not wanting of love of them in the heart, but externally do not increase their rank, because a strong partner in government soon wants to seize the kingship for himself. If you let them take the reins ever so little, the result will be your won disgrace.[1167]

As soon as Aurangzeb died, the Saiyid Brothers took over the Mughal Empire. They placed a puppet prince on the throne. The princes who were uncooperative were killed or disabled by having their eyes blinded with needles. In order to finance their power struggle, the Saiyid brothers proceeded to auction off the agricultural crown lands to revenue farming thugs, who destroyed the very engines of Mughal prosperity. However, a power struggle erupted from within. As one can expect, what was at stake was control over the Mughal Empire, the richest economy in the world. The "Iranian cabal" believed it deserved more than the Saiyid brothers whom they helped supplant, since they were the ones conspiring from the last three centuries. Infighting erupted, and the Saiyid Brothers were killed. And finally, the Iranian cabal ascended. Only to find themselves faced with a resurgent authentic Mughal royalty. The "Iranian cabal" would continue well into British India, through princely states such as the Nawabs of Oudh. And the first Indians to be admitted into the newly formed British Freemasonry in India were descendants of the Safavids, who had played a major role in the destruction of the Mughal Empire. The Illuminati thus inflicted from within, more serious damage upon the Mughal Empire than all its external enemies combined together.

Western Illuminati reach India

However, the Indian subcontinent was still safe from direct intervention of Western Illuminati. That was until a Portuguese Knight Templar, Vasco de Gama, managed to discover a sea route to India. Following his path, the British landed. And using their cunning rather than bravery or industry, proceeded to tear everything apart with their characteristic phillistinism.

Since no viable substitute for the waning Mughal power emerged, the entire Indian subcontinent stood defenseless and exposed.

[1167] Hamid al-Din Khan Bahadur; Sir Jadunath Sarkar, Anecdotes of Aurangzeb: English translation of Ahkam-i-Alamgiri.3rd ed. (Calcutta, M.C. Sarkar, 1949) 54.

As soon as Western powers arrived, the Illuminati within the Muslim kingdoms and nobility joined hands to destroy all remnants of Mughal authority in India. They also took out kingdoms and groups, which would be an obstacle to the British. For example, when Tipu Sultan began serious opposition to the British in the South, he was approached by a strange Shiite Muslim named Mir Sadiq. Sadiq managed to infiltrate Tipu Sultan's household by having his sister married to Tipu Sultan. When the British would launch a concerted assault against Tipu, the treachery of Sadiq would be instrumental to their victory. Lord Cornwallis was also involved in the downfall of Tipu. He went on to play a major role in Illuminati operations in other parts of the British Empire. Similarly, when the Rohillas sought to ally with the Marathas against the British, some Illuminati nobles among the Muslim rulers mobilized to thwart them.

Colonialism: The Pirate phase

The "Pirate phase" was the initial phase of colonialism when the British first landed in Bengal. Why choose Bengal? Because Bengal was the richest province of the Mughal Empire. And the Powers that Be were seeking to lay hands on the jugular vein of Mughal Revenue. The British were not the coastal traders of Adam Smith's free market economy, as often depicted. They used all forms of trickery and deceit to gain control of the entire province of Bengal and even snatched revenue collection rights from the Mughals. British "revenue collection" was so rapacious that it resulted in a famine in Bengal. Though Bengal recovered later, the Mughal military-agricultural complex had been destroyed. And since then to the present day, Bengal is associated with blight and poverty. Centuries later when Mother Teresa would seek to help the poorest of the poor in India, she chose Calcutta, the capital of Bengal. The feats involved in the British subjugation of Bengal were so dark that even the official chronicler of the British venture in India, Robert Orme, never extended his formal history of the early British Empire beyond 1762.[1168] To quote,

> Why should I be doomed to commemorate the ignominy of my countrymen, and without giving the money story that has accompanied every event since the 1st of April 1757?[1169]

[1168] Nicholas B.Dirks, The Scandal of Empire- India and the Creation of Imperial Britain (Cambridge: The Belknap Press of the Harvard University Press, 2006) 246.
[1169] Dirks, The Scandal of Empire 246.

The East India Company had become the largest creditor to the British Crown, second only to the Bank of England.[1170] The fortunes of the East India Company were inextricably tied with its Illuminati investors and directors based in Britain. To quote Conspiracy historian David Allen Rivera,

> The British East India Company was a British commercial and political organization established in India in the late 1600s, which was known as the Governor and Company of the merchants of London. A forerunner of this group was the London Mercers Company, and earlier than that, the London Staplers. The organization traced their lineage back to the ancient commercial groups involved in trading between the Mediterranean and India. They were closely related to the Levant Company, and the Anglo-Muscovy Company, and spawned the London Company, which was chartered in 1606 to establish the Virginia Plantation on a communistic basis, and the Plymouth Colony in 1621.[1171]

Rivera also quotes the Jewish Encyclopedia that one of Amschel Rothschild's son held a significant gold investment in the East India Company.[1172] At the same time, non-elite individuals such as Lord Clive and later, Warren Hastings were taking advantage of what remained of India's level playing field, and they advanced their personal prospects. They would return back to Britain with newfound wealth, and start influencing local British politics. This raised alarm bells among Britain's Illuminati, who were in no mood to dilute their power. On their behalf, the trial of Warren Hastings was brought about to put an end to privateering in India. And instead, only the "British government" and the shadowy interests behind it would be allowed to maraud in an India now rendered defenseless by the fall of Mughal power. All British subjects who were enterprising on their own were now discouraged from doing so.

The Indian subcontinent possessed a "Wild West" type of promise and attraction. But this attribute seemed to evaporate with the onset of the British, and has since then disappeared for good. There were many factors involved, but the most important one was the inflating of Indian silver, which was used as a medium of exchange. This was done by the

---

[1170] Dirks, The Scandal of Empire 146.
[1171] David Allen Rivera, Final Warning: A History of the New World Order (Online Ebook edition)
[1172] David Allen Rivera, Final Warning: A History of the New World Order (Online Ebook edition)

British using silver from newly discovered mines in the New World in exchange for the loyalties and services of Indian sepoys. Somewhere between the 18th and 19th centuries, the allure of the riches Mughal India disappeared for good. Even the European and American pirates who had started hovering around the Indian coastline in the 17th century packed up and left. The British remained in India though, as the Indian people needed to be fully subjugated. The most notorious British Governor General in this regard was Lord Dalhousie, who descended from a German-Illuminati pirate lineage.

India, Opium and the American Revolution

This flag of the British East India Company (1707) has thirteen stripes to symbolize the thirteen Illuminati families. George Washington chose a similar flag for America because he had connections to the Illuminati families involved in the British East India Company's opium trade. One such family, the Russells, went on to form the Skulls and Bones Society in America. The Skull and Bones Society is located on Yale University campus, which is named after Elihu Yale, who served the East India Company as Governor of Fort St. George, Madras. Money from the opium trade may have been used in the American Revolution. With growing discontent with British rule in North America, the American Revolution was able to harness all such discontent for bringing power back into the hands of the Illuminati. It had to be undertaken to prevent genuine non-Illuminati revolutions from taking place, and to prevent non-elites from taking power. America was created as a future super state destined to exclusively serve the Illuminati and perish in the process of doing so (Manifest Destiny).

1882 Engraving of the British Opium warehouse in Patna

Courtesy Takao Club <takaoclub.com> Copyright:Unknown

During their tenure, the Mughals would never subdue non-threatening states and dependencies, out of respect for regional claimants. For example, when the Rajput Chief Jaswant Singh died and a succession crisis ensued, Aurangzeb consolidated Jaswant Singh's territory to arrange its transfer to a claimant from the clan of Jaswant Singh. As opposed to turning the principality into a Mughal province.

On the other hand, Lord Dalhousie introduced the Doctrine of Lapse, according to which any Indian kingdom that had a succession issue would become territory of the British Empire. The career of Lord Dalhousie in India is considered the most rapacious. Since none of the British officers or their subordinates were expected to stay in India permanently as other conquerors of India did, their relationship with India became very predatory. Irfan Habib calculated that the drain from the economies of Bengal and Bihar to England was up to 9 per cent of the GNP, "[...] a crippling drain for any economy."[1173] In addition, only opium and indigo were encouraged for cultivation. Both had a deleterious effect on soil. And the opium grown in India would destroy an entire generation of Chinese. Those involved in the opium trade were none other than the Illuminati Russell family, who are also founders of the Yale Skull and Bones secret society.

The Mughal Empire had been reduced to a city state surrounding Delhi. Despite this, the Mughal King held considerable legitimacy over the Indian people. He was the only person seen as the righteous ruler of India. And the system left behind by the Mughals was the only workable system known to people of the Indian subcontinent. Up to this point, the British and the Europeans were seen for what they were; pirateering predatory interests who had no legitimacy whatsoever. Therefore, the Powers that Be devised means to consolidate their Power even further, by staging the 1857 War of Independence.

Colonialism: The Barbarian Phase

> The beating heart of Indo-Islamic civilization had been ripped out, and could not be replaced.
>
> *-William Dalrymple*[1174]

The 1857 War of Independence was staged by the British with the aim of completely knocking down and burying the Indo-Islamic civilization of India, and rebuilding the Indian Subcontinent, and the identity of the Indian people on terms more amenable to the Illuminati. Since the Mughal King was too weak for a war with the British, the Powers that Be forcibly supplied him troops by creating disaffection within the British Army in India. One of the commonsense facts about India is that cows are sacred to Hindus. The British, who conducted sociological studies back then, were fully aware of this. Yet, they deliberately forced

---

[1173] Irfan Habib, Essays in Indian History; Towards a Marxist Perception (New Delhi: Tulika Publishers, 1995) 304.
[1174] William Dalrymple, The Last Mughal (London: Penguin Books, 2007) 464.

their Bengal regiments, consisting of up to 65 per cent high caste Hindus,[1175] to use cartridges greased with cow fat (The cartridges had to be removed from their casing with teeth). Agent provocateurs were placed among these regiments to create further disaffection. Once the revolt within these regiments gained momentum, well placed British spies among the mutineers like Gauri Shankar Sukul[1176] directed the revolt and marched the disaffected troops to Delhi. In total, the revolting troops represented a small fraction of British-Indian troops in India. At Delhi, they insisted the Mughal King, a senile man with no apetite for war, to lead them against the British. In Mughal culture, betraying one's previous master was considered as a serious personality defect, and the Mughal King was doubtful of the rebels.[1177] But the Mughal King, seeing that the rebels were giving him no option, reluctantly agreed. By then the revolt had attracted hundreds of thousands of people, in particular, the Muslim ruling elite, who had converted the revolt into a full-scale jihad. Even some independent kingdoms joined the revolt. But the British were well prepared to finish off the revolt once it had succeeded in creating an atmosphere of revenge and racial hatred among their British subjects in India. For this purpose, minor massacres of British women and children were organized by Illuminati operatives close to the Mughal King, such as Hakim Ahsanullah Khan. The British had loyal Sikh forces in the Punjab region.[1178] And these were kept as a reserve to brutally crush the revolt once it gained momentum.

The Illuminati Safavid elements were able to hamper the coordination of the Muslim rulers. For example, the most powerful kingdom of the Nizam sided with the British because the Safavids had compromised their royalty through intermarriage.

[1175] Dalrymple, Last Mugha135.

[1176] Dalrymple, Last Mughal 329.

[1177] Dalrymple, Last Mughal 301.

[1178] The decision to employ Sikhs proved to be immensely profitable. In 1857, the Sikhs enthusiastically participated in the destruction of the remnants of Mughal India. The Punjab, with 8% of the population provided for half of the British army in 1911. Sikhs, being 1% of the Indian population formed 20% of Indians in military service, while Punjabi Muslims and Gurkhas accounted for 16% and 12% respectively. Bernard S. Cohn, Colonialism and its Forms of Knowledge (Delhi: Oxford University Press, 1996) 110. When crushing the revolt of 1857, all British troops in Punjab were directed to Delhi, yet there was no anti-British uprising in Punjab, despite the power vacuum. William Dalrymple, The Last Mughal (London: Penguin Books, 2007) 304. British ordnance factories in the Punjab continued to supply the British throughout the uprising. Dalrymple, Last Mughal 334.

The British were able to use the pretext of this revolt to crush all powers that could become potential opposition to their planned New World Order in the Indian Subcontinent. The scale of attrition pursued by the British is without parallels in Indian history. The last King of the Mughal Empire was exiled in a prison in Burma, where he would be later buried in an unmarked grave. The remainder of important courtiers were deported to a specially constructed gulag in the Andaman Island of the Indian Ocean. What remains of the seat of Mughal royalty, the Red Fort, is only a cluster of walls. Their actual palace, said to be rivaling the Taj Mahal, was razed to the ground.[1179] There was an actual plan to raze the entire city of Delhi,[1180] and this was averted by the pleas of a Mughal sympathetic British officer. Orders were given to shoot everyone in Delhi.[1181] All people associated with the powerful Indo-Islamic civilization of Delhi, both Hindus and Muslims were destroyed. Their institutions were physically demolished. In addition, the British amassed loot. Wherever the British could lay hands on solid gold, they ensured that it would be transferred to East India Company interests. Even the golden spires of the Taj Mahal were removed and replaced with brass ones. Among the loot were famous artifacts of Mughal royalty, such as the largest diamond in the world, the Kohinoor, which ended up in the British crown jewels. Another invaluable artifact, the Peacock Throne of the Mughal emperor, was secretly transferred to the banking elite for private use.[1182]

Colonialism: The Enlightened Phase

It was decided that India be turned into a captive consumer market for British industrial goods. This would be accomplished by the liquidation of the giant indigenous textile industry of India, and the gearing up of British industry to cater to the same demand. Fostered by Mughal prosperity and security, Indian weavers had made India the most preferred destination for the trade of cloth. It was the primary import of the East India Company into Britain.[1183] The liquidation of the Indian textile industry lead to the development of industrial capitalism in Britain, in an attempt to give the small number of British entrepreneurs

---

[1179] Dalrymple, Last Mughal 5.
[1180] Dalrymple, Last Mughal xxiv.
[1181] Dalrymple, Last Mughal 4.
[1182] There are two common fables of disinformation with regards to the Peacock Throne. The first claims that the ship carrying it to Britain sank off Madagascar. The second claims that the throne never fell in British hands and had been earlier taken by the invader Nadir shah to Persia. This Persian throne is not the Peacock Throne.
[1183] Bernard S. Cohn, Colonialism and its Forms of Knowledge (Delhi: Oxford University Press, 1996) 77.

the technological means to cater to the huge demand of textiles in the Indian subcontinent.[1184] Thereafter, imports of Indian textiles were curtailed and Indians were forced to buy British cloth. The so-called Industrial Revolution that started in Manchester was driven by the demands of the then bustling Indian economy, and ironically, the same Industrial Revolution was being used to smother this very bustling economy.

After 1857, the British established a more civil role in India. One of their first maneuvers was the establishment of legal codes for all religions, which were to be administered under the auspices of British courts. The motive was to take away the power of local arbitrators, religious authorities and legal experts, who enjoyed an autonomous position in Indo-Islamic Civilisation. They would no longer be a hindrance for the British, who wanted speedy "settlement" of all land disputes, for the extraction of revenue.

After 1857, the British also developed administrative structures to make large sectors of the population participative. Not unlike a pyramid scheme, multitudes were offered a share of the spoils of colonialism, in exchange for legitimising it. These huge participatory bureaucracies were not as much about efficiency as they were about placating a large section of the population. These systems are certainly not practiced in Western countries, including Britain. The result was unbridled corruption in exchange for a stable administrative base for the British. Even after the British left, the structure of these bureaucracies remained unchanged. And they continue to be the root cause of corruption in the Indian subcontinent, Egypt and Nigeria. On the other hand, the Mughals managed a far more productive economy using a small but highly capable group of loyal officers (*mansabdars*).

Silver coins and silver were a popular medium of exchange in India. One of the key elements of British success in India was the inflation of Indian silver by dumping silver from newly discovered mines in the New World. This inflated silver was used to buy the loyalties and services of sepoys. When a huge silver deposit was discovered in Cobalt (Canada), 40 silver mines popped up around it. The European labour force worked in slavery like conditions, with 25 people sharing the same toilet and the average life expectancy of the miners being 40 years.[1185] An estimate of

[1184] Cohn, Colonialism 77.

[1185] The Hole Story, prod. Richard Desjardins and Robert Monderie, National Film Board of Canada, 2011.

the amount of silver flooding India can be gathered from the fact that as late as 1906, Cobalt exported $2 billion dollars worth of silver bars to the British Empire in India.[1186] None of this was used for the development of Canada. In other words, the European miner-serfs at Cobalt, while being complete strangers to the idea of living as free people and never producing much of a bustling economy of their own, were busy helping their overlords destroy and enslave free people and productive economies in other parts of the world.

The Groundwork for Soviet takeover - Linguistic tampering

Colonialism had a limited lifespan. Cognizant of this, the Powers That Be had begun working towards Soviet Communism, which was meant to succeed colonial rule. The Indian Subcontinent was now being groomed for the creation of nation states. In the previous chapters, we had read how the groundwork for Nazism had begun to be laid in the 19th century itself. Similarly, the Illuminati, looking forward to exchange the British Empire for the future Soviet Empire, now sought to create two nation states out of the Hindu and Muslim populations. Nation states were to be used for dialectically advancing Soviet influence over the entire subcontinent.

In 1837, Governor General Lord William Bentink introduced a Language Act giving powers to substitute "vernacular" languages in place of Persian for communication. Getting rid of Persian, the official language of Mughal communication throughout India was necessary in order to severe the former ruling class from their past. The Orientalist John Gilchrist established the "Hindustani" language as a substitute to Persian.[1187]

Gilchrist then proceeded to lay the groundwork for future creation of India and Pakistan. According to Frank E. Keav[1188], Gilchrist and his team at Fort William College (Calcutta) isolated and excised words of Persian-Arabic origin in Hindustani, and added to what remained, more words from Sanskrit and dialects of Hindustani spoken by Hindus. This new Hindustani was termed Hindi, the language of the Hindus. It was given a non-Arabic Devnagiri script. The old Hindustani (with words

---

[1186] The Hole Story, prod. Desjardins and Monderie.

[1187] The origins of the "Hindustani" language are controversial. There is no space to discuss the same.

[1188] M. Beg., Sociolinguistic Perspective of Hindi and Urdu in India (New Delhi: Bahri Publications, 1960) 44.

from Sanskrit and Hindu dialects excised, while retaining its Arabic script) was termed Urdu, the language of the Muslims. Despite both Urdu and Hindu being mutually intelligible when spoken, association with Urdu politicised the former Muslim elite as a group of foreign origin, engaged in opposition, antagonism and competition with the Hindus.

The Groundwork for Soviet takeover - Tampering with History

A tampered history of India was created for the subject population. The very origin of "Oriental Studies" is related to distorting the history of the conquered subjects. Within a generation of British education, the people of the Indian Subcontinent became disenchanted with their past. Lord Macaulay, the creator of the new (Westernized) Indian intelligentsia had ensured British education would portray Indian history prior to the British as shamefully unacceptable.[1189]

In addition, the British had to cover up their act. The British were portrayed as a postive force whose conquest was inevitable following the "decay" of the Mughal Empire. It is important to note that establishment historians have access to original documents and historical manuscripts, which they sometimes tamper with. And the Orientalists would accomplish the same, by portraying Mughal rule in India as a hegemony of the Muslim community over the Hindu community. This would further antagonize both communities, leading to the creation of separate identities and separate nation states. The Orientalists even churned out doctored manuscripts to support their claims. One such doctored manuscript was *Storia Do Mogor*, by Niccolao Manucci,[1190] as well as

---

[1189] Mansoor Moaddel, Islamic Modernism, Nationalism, and Fundamentalism: Episode and Discourse (Chicago: The University of Chicago Press, 2005) 55.

[1190] Niccolao Manucci was a Venetian who arrived at Surat in 1656. It appears that his account was a mishmash of facts culled from other original sources available to the Orientalists, interspersed with narrative, which portrayed the Mughals as indolent and intolerant buffoons. Spending almost his entire life in India, he sent home his manuscript which was lent to French historian Catrou in 1707, who wrote his own abridged version of it as 'Historic Generale de l'Empire du Mogol' in 1715. A number of Western and Indian historians incorporated his work as a primary source. The original manuscript 'Storia do Mogor' resurfaced in a Berlin library around 1915 and was written in French, Portuguese and Italian. It was translated and published in a four part series and has been highly regarded as a primary source. Though it is equally possible that the very document, including the original in possession of Catrou, was nothing more than a forgery. Among those who have doubted the document's authenticity are Stanley Lane-Poole, who referred to Manucci as a disappointed backstairs underling. Stanley Lane-Poole, Aurangzeb and the Decay of the Mughal Empire (Delhi: S. Chand & Co., 1964) Note on Authorities. Ali Sadiq has pointed several major contradictions in the document some other accounts of pre-British India by European "travellers."[1191] On the other hand, locals who had written first-hand accurate accounts of Mughal India were ignored.[1192]

Rudyard Kipling would portray British colonialism as a favor upon the world, by penning racist epithets like *White Man's burden*. Kipling also wrote *The Jungle Book*, which portrayed socialist themes of man living in harmony with nature and animals, with no contact with actual human society. The main character in this story is Mowgli, a kid raised in the Indian forest by animals. With Mowgli being a play on Mughal, the choice of the name is reflective of Kipling's prejudice for the previous rulers in India. Orientalists revived the very word "Mughal," since it gave the impression of barbarian Mongols. The "Mughals" never referred to themselves by this label. Another early novelist, Wilkie Collins in his novel *The Moonstone*, portrayed all Muslim rulers in India as pathological temple smashers. These narratives were adopted as fact by the subject population, which had little resources for an investigative inquiry.

Scanned image of the swastika logo from a Rudyard Kipling book - a 1911 edition of *Puck of Pook's Hill.*

The Emergence of India and Pakistan

The Theosophical Society and the Independence of India

Helena Petrova Blavatsky founded the Theosophical Society. Its first headquarters would be in Adyar, India. The Theosophical Society has been covered in great depth in Chapter Three.

Sadiq Ali, A vindication of Aurangzeb in two parts (Calcutta: New Age Press. 1918). In the manuscript, Manucci and his editors go to unusually great lengths to prove his authenticity.

1191 Some of these writings are replete with sketches of topless Mughal Queens. It is highly unlikely that female residents of the secluded Mughal harem would pose semi-naked in front of strange travelers.

1192 For example, Khafi Khan, a Mughal noble, wrote an unflattering account of the British and their actual pirate operations in the high seas near Bombay. Khafi Khan would be later portrayed as unreliable. A new document was suddenly found, authored by a certain Abul Fazl Mamuri, which contained tracts from Khafi Khan. It was to be assumed that Khafi was thus a plagiarizer. Even though it was equally possible to cook up the Mamuri document using Khafi Khan's text. This controversy took place after Indian independence, and illustrates the stranglehold over scholarly study in this subject.

The Theosophical Society played a pivotal role in the formation of the Indian National Congress. In an 1890 letter, Blavatsky addresses her Indian initiates pointing out "Would your political Congress itself have even been a possibility, without the Theosophical Society?"[1193] One of the earliest initiates into HPB's theosophy was Allen O. Hume. Mr. Hume and Mr. Wederburn played a key role in the early years of the Indian National Congress. Indian historians have not overlooked the role of the Theosophical Society in this respect. They have attributed the role of the Theosophical Society as a pro-colonial organization that was preventing the Congress from mutating into a powerful rebellion. However, it was unlikely that another mass rebellion was possible in post-1857 India.

H.P. Blavatsky's brooch

Another close initiate (said to be HPB's lover[1194]) was Annie Besant, who was associated with population control advocacy, feminism and socialist activity in Britain. She moved to India and would eventually become the Theosophical Society's President in 1907. In 1916, Annie Besant launched the Home Rule League in India. She coordinated the activities of the Home Rule League, ranging from rallies to active agitation. This was before the Congress had become an effective mobilizing force for Indian Independence. She and her supporters demanded Home Rule for India. Besant was arrested on June 1917 and detained at a British hill station. She was released later in September, and

[1193] H.P. Blavatsky, letter by HPB to brothers of Aryavarta, April 1890, "Why I do not return to India," This letter was published in the Theosophist of January 1922. Blavatsky.net

[1194] "Mrs. Besant's extraordinary transformations from Anglican minister's wife through birth control propagandist and labour leader to Theosophist…are…well known… Arthur Nethercot, her biographer, suggests an element of the lesbian in the rapid domination of Mrs. Besant by H. P. Blavatsky. James Webb, The Occult Underground (LaSalle Illinois: Open Court Publishing Co. 1974) 94. "She addressed Annie in suspiciously fulsome and endearing terms," writes Nethercot, "'Dearest,' 'My Dearest,' 'Dearly Beloved One,' and signing herself 'Very adoring.'" Nethercot also reports that "she dispatched missives to Annie...and addressed them to 'My Darling Penelope' from 'Your...female Ulysses'" Arthur H. Nethercot, The First Five Lives of Annie Besant (Chicago: University of Chicago Press, 1960) 306. Both these quotes are from Scott Lively and Kevin Abrams, The Pink Swastika-Homosexuality in the Nazi Party 4th ed. (Sacramento: Veritas Aeterna Press, 2002) 106.

her demand for moving towards Home Rule was recognized. Following her release she was awarded the Presidency of the Congress for a year.

The British authorities were unusually lenient towards Theosophical Society operatives involved in the Independence movement. On the other hand, political leaders and intellectuals not associated with the Theosophical Society would end up getting long sentences in British prisons. For example, another leader of the Congress Party, Maulana Abul Kalam Azad, served up to five years in jail following the outbreak of World War I. He and other Congress leaders were later jailed for another four years in 1942, during the Quit India movement.

Once the freedom movement gained momentum, several dedicated and sincere leaders joined the Congress Party of India. Preventing them from acquiring positions of control became a key Illuminati priority.

The Muslim League

As a twin of the Congress, the Muslim League was created for the genesis of a Muslim nation state. Agha Khan III, Sir Sultan Muhammad Shah was one of the main founders of the Muslim League. The followers of the Agha Khan (Ismailis) were historically estranged from mainstream Muslims. Cardinal Rodriguez comments on the original founder of the Ismaili sect (Abdullah Iba Maymun) as "[...] seems to have served as a model for Weishaupt, the founder of the Illuminati."[1195] The Ismailis were associated with the Fatimids of Egypt in medieval times, whom mainstream Muslims considered to be heretics. The Fatimids would plot against Saladin who was fighting the crusaders. As a result, Saladin put an end to the Fatimids. Many settled in Iran. Around the 1840s, the Agha Khan launched a revolt against the ruling Qajars of Iran.[1196] When this revolt failed, he and his followers were forced to flee to India. In India, the Ismailis flourished as an active business community, though they were still estranged from mainstream Muslims.[1197] The British were very considerate towards them. When Agha Khan III became involved with the Muslim League, many eyebrows were raised. But it was assumed that

---

[1195] Jose Maria Cardinal Caro Y. Rodriguez, The Mystery of Freemasonry Unveiled – With a reprint of Pope Leo XIIIth Encyclical Humanum Genus 2nd edition (Imprimatur, Jose Maria Cardinal Caro Y. Rodriguez, Cardinal Archbishop of Santiago, Chile, 1920s). 201.

[1196] Nikki R. Keddie, Modern Iran- Roots and Results of Revolution (New Haven: Yale University Press, 2003) 45.

[1197] This estrangement exists to the present day. For example, controversial lesbian Muslim "reformer" Irshad Manji is a follower of the Agha Khan. The same has been said about Salman Rushdie.

involvement of a rich and internationally influential person would be advantageous to the cause. As with the Congress, the Muslim League too, became deluged with sincere and committed leaders, which had to be disposed by the Powers that Be after the creation of Pakistan.

Lord Mountbatten

A key elitist player during this scenario was Lord Mountbatten, the last Governor General of India.[1198] Mountbatten has been accused for creating the border disputes between India and Pakistan, which are a perpetual source of conflict. Some even saw Mountbatten as being responsible for the partition riots.

The Elimination of Leaders

The Assassination of Mahatma Gandhi

Sincere leaders had deluged both the Indian National Congress and the Muslim League. The Powers That Be tolerated them only to the extent of ending British rule in India. They were not meant to play any role whatsoever in the future direction of these independent nation states. Therefore, many such leaders were later done away with once these nation states were created.

Gandhi had emerged as the single most influential leader of the Indian independence. But Gandhi also had very radical ideas for post-independence India. For example he saw the establishment of huge national armies as instruments of coercion (as sadly demonstrated in post-independence Pakistan). Instead, his idea of defense was every village being "[...] self sustained and capable of managing its affairs to the extent of defending itself against the whole world."[1199] In addition, Gandhi was completely opposed to large-scale industrialization. To quote,

> Industrialization on a mass scale will necessarily lead to passive or active exploitation of the villagers as the problems of competition and

---

[1198] For a critical account of Lord Mountbatten, see the book, Lynn Picknett, Clive Prince and Stephen Prior, War of the Windsors: A Century of Unconstitutional Monarchy (Mainstream Publishing, 2002).

[1199] M. K. Gandhi, The Completed Works of Mahatma Gandhi; Independence (Delhi: Publications Division 1958) Vol. 85 page 32. Quoted in Partha Chatterjee, Nationalist Thought and the Colonial World - A Derivative Discourse (Minneapolis: University of Minnesota Press, 2004) 121.

> marketing come in. Therefore, we have to concentrate on the village being self-contained, manufacturing mainly for use.[1200]

As far-fetched as Gandhi's ideas appeared, Gandhi possessed the zeal and stubbornness characteristic of visionaries. He would die trying to obtain his goals even if he couldn't reach them. As one can imagine, his ideas for post-independence India were completely at odds with the Illuminati plans for a completely Sovietized India. His assassination cleared a major obstacle for the Illuminati.

Though some Hindu extremists were gleeful about the assassination, this is only part of a psychology that characterizes reactionary groups. Gandhi was not an Islamist and there was little he could do to stop the partition. In fact he was the lone voice opposing partition. But once partition took place, he saw no necessity of war and attrition with Pakistan. The logic of the assassins that Gandhi had become too Islamist never made sense.

There were five unsuccessful attempts on Gandhi by the same group of stalkers who finally assassinated him. In all these attempts, the would-be assassins were neither arrested nor subjected to long-term detention.

Those involved in the plot were connected to the city of Pune, home to one of the largest British military bases in India. This city was the hub of British Intelligence in India. Some of the conspirators even worked in the British Army in Intelligence related activities such as wireless operators.

I have come across an account from people who lived through those times that initial reports claimed that a Muslim had assassinated Gandhi. It appears that Godse had grown a beard and was trying to pass off as a Muslim. But an onlooker recognized him during his arrest. He subsequently reverted back to the Hindu Godse. If Godse was indeed seeking to impersonate some other group and escape doing so as well, he could not have been alone. The connections to Savarkar and other individuals were probably never intended to come to light. The police and authorities were still at this point taking informal directives from the British Raj. And therefore it was possible to arrange a false official story

---

[1200] M. K. Gandhi, The Completed Works of Mahatma Gandhi; Discussion with Maurice Frydman (Delhi: Publications Division 1958) Vol. 63 page 241. Partha Chatterjee, Nationalist Thought and the Colonial World - A Derivative Discourse (Minneapolis: University of Minnesota Press, 2004) 88.

of the assassination, and a non-publicized escape for the assassin. Those who have read through this book will note that the Powers that Be have means staging executions as exit strategies for retiring operatives to a comfortable second life in faraway places. It is obvious that the plot also involved some dupes as well, who were not privy to the real motives and getaway plan(s) of the conspirator(s).

Madan Lal Dhingra

Britons like Nesta Webster identified with British colonialism out of a mistaken sense that common Britons like them were also beneficiaries of such an enterprise. Such British common folk also assumed that those who colonized India were their brethren, whereas British colonialism was an exclusively Illuminati enterprise, and the same powers were now overturning colonial rule. The likes of Webster watched in horror as they saw the British government in India retreat from its colonial mandate, to cave in to the demands of agitators. The British Empire, whose map was held with pride, was being forsaken for the future Soviet Empire right before their eyes.

Nesta Webster in her study of secret societies involved in revolution may have stumbled across evidence of the existence of such groups in India. She claims that proceedings of the Commission on the Indian Army, presided by Field Marshall Lord Nicholson uncovered the existence of a conspiracy in 1912, "[...] organized with extraordinary ingenuity by some center which could not be discovered [...]."[1201] This may have been a group connected to the Powers that Be, which sought to hijack the independence movement on the subcontinent for its own ends.

On July 1st 1909, Colonel Sir W. Curzon Wyllie, aide to Lord John Morley (the secretary of state for India) was assassinated by an Indian. Wyllie was attending the annual day celebration of the Indian National Association at London. The assassin, Madan Lal Dhingra, shot Wyllie at close range, killing both him and his wife. He made no attempt to escape. Dhingra was sentenced to death and hanged on August 17th 1909. Dhingra's judgment in targeting Wyllie made little sense. Wyllie was one among the many important British officials. The elimination of this functionary neither damaged British interests nor furthered the interests of Indians seeking independence. Both the British and the Indians

---

[1201] Nesta H. Webster, The Cause of World Unrest – With an Introduction by the Editor of The Morning Post (London: Grant Richards Ltd., 1920) 193.

admired Wyllie and his Indian wife.[1202] Gandhi was aghast as Dhingra's actions. To quote,

> It is being said in defense of Sir Curzon Wyllie's assassination that...just as the British would kill every German if Germany invaded Britain, so too it is the right of any Indian to kill any Englishman.... The analogy...is fallacious. If the Germans were to invade Britain, the British would kill only the invaders. They would not kill every German whom they met.... They would not kill an unsuspecting German, or Germans who are guests.
>
> Even should the British leave in consequence of such murderous acts, who will rule in their place? Is the Englishman bad because he is an Englishman? Is it that everyone with an Indian skin is good? If that is so, there should be [no] angry protest against oppression by Indian princes. India can gain nothing from the rule of murderers—no matter whether they are black or white. Under such a rule, India will be utterly ruined and laid waste.[1203]

Was Dhingra eliminating an internal opponent of the Powers that Be, as Nesta Webster pointed out?[1204]

Dhingra came from a rich pro-British family. During his studies in Europe, he was in contact with a "group" based in Paris, which appeared to be operating against British colonial interests without arousing the suspicion of French authorities.[1205] There were many Europeans associated with this group, including Germans. Even British intelligence operatives such as Dr. Briess of the Pro-India Committee in Geneva were associated with this group, either for espionage or for infiltration on behalf of the Powers that Be.[1206] Dhingra's body was denied the Hindu rites of cremation and was not returned to India until 1976. Was his execution real?

Vinayak Damodar Savarkar

1202 Webster, World Unrest 198.

1203 Indian Opinion (in Gujarati), August 14, 1909, Collected Works of Mahatma Gandhi (New Delhi: Publications Division) vol. 9, p. 302. Quoted in Rajmohan Gandhi, "Mohandas Gandhi, Abdul Ghaffar Khan, and the Middle East Today," World Policy Journal Vol. XXII Spring (2005): 92. An archived copy is available at <http://www.worldpolicy.org/journal/articles/wpj05-sp/gandhi.pdf> Accessed 21/12/06.

1204 Webster, World Unrest 200.

1205 Webster, World Unrest 198-199.

1206 Interestingly, Dr. Breiss spent a lot of time with Shyamji Krishnavarma, an associate of Vinayak Savarkar.

One of Dhingra's mentors, Vinayak Damodar Savarkar, was later alleged to have been involved in the assassination of Mahatma Gandhi. Savarkar too, hailed from a rich family of estate owners. He represented the Chitpavani Brahmins, who had become so powerful under the Marathas that they carved their own princely states under the Maratha banner. The origins of the Chitpavanis are obscure, and one theory traces them to a large group of Jews who shipwrecked on the West Indian coast (This could explain why Godse, another Chitpavani, dined in a non-vegetarian restaurant and was found to be circumcised). Savarkar had contact with the aforementioned "Paris group." He also had contact with a veteran of the Russian revolution, who taught Savarkar's group about bomb making. While being deported from France, Savarkar attempted a daring escape with the assistance of collaborators in France, but failed. He was deported to the special British cellular jail on the Andaman and Nicobar islands, where he negotiated with the British for clemency. Surprisingly, he was freed on January 6th 1924, even though the cellular jail was known as a place of no return. During his period in jail Savarkar started increasingly associating with Hindu revivalism, though he had originally dabbled with atheism in his earlier years. In one of his most controversial moves, Savarkar criticized the Quit India Rebellion carried out by the Congress Party in 1942. Savarkar instead advocated his followers to actively join the British effort in World War II. This was exactly what the Powers that Be sought. Why would Savarkar support the British war effort, which was clearly counter to his own stated political convictions, at a time when other freedom fighters such as Subhash Chandra Bose advocated supporting the enemies of the British in World War II?

Savarkar's exact connections to the assassination of Mahatma Gandhi are a matter of controversy. Witness Digambar Ramchandra Badge insisted that Savarkar was directly involved. His connections with Nathuram Godse, the assassin of Mahatma Gandhi are documented.

The death of Jinnah

Jinnah died on September 11th 1948, an auspicious date to the Powers That Be. There are some controversies related to his death, which won't be detailed here. Questions remain about Jinnah's motivations in his quest for Pakistan. Did he personally believe in the idea of Pakistan or was he following the directive of the Ismaili Imam Agha Khan III?

The Disappearance of Netaji Subhash Chandra Bose

Netaji Subhash Chandra Bose was probably the most powerful opponent of British power in India. This is evidenced by the fact that British

Intelligence gave a top-secret order to assassinate Bose after his escape from British India.[1207] Bose came up with a plan to form the Indian National Army from volunteers and Indian British soldiers who had been captured by the Empire of Japan. The Indian National Army may have played a major role in the liberation of India, if the Empire of Japan had not made the fatal decision to attack Pearl Harbor. Nevertheless, Bose still awaited a hero's welcome in India.

But the Powers that Be did not desire the role of such independent minded nationalists in post-independence India, who would have opposed efforts to Sovietize India. Bose was lured into the Soviet Union, which at that time was pretending to be sympathetic to anti-colonial activity.[1208] According to Politburo member Babajan Gouffrav, Bose crossed into the Soviet Union somewhere across the Manchurian border.[1209] Some units of the INA went with Bose up to the Manchurian border. When the Soviets would pour into Manchuria after the atomic bombing of Japan, they stumbled into these INA units.

A conversation allegedly took place between Stalin and Molotov 1946 on whether Bose should remain in the Soviet Union or not, a year after Bose was reportedly dead. Gouffrav also claimed that India's ambassador to the Soviet Union, Dr. Radhakrishnan was allowed a sneak a peek at Netaji being held in captivity.[1210]

The Assassination of Prime Minister Liaqat Ali Khan

Prime Minister Liaqat Ali Khan of Pakistan was assassinated by an Afghan. The motives of the assassin are unclear because he was killed in the ensuing confusion. During his tenure, Liaqat Ali was faced with an attempted coup to overthrow him (The Rawalpindi conspiracy case of February 1951). Among those involved were Faiz Ahmed Faiz, an Urdu

---

1207 Reviewing a book by Eunan O'Halpin. Subir Bhaumik, "British 'attempted to kill Bose.'" BBC News 15/08/05<http://news.bbc.co.uk/2/hi/south_asia/4152320.stm> Accessed 18/11/06.

1208 See the section on Enver Pasha and Djemal Pasha in Chapter Two. Both these former Ottoman ministers were lured into the Soviet Union for the purpose of fighting the British Empire in India, and ended up being murdered. Also see the section on Congressman Lawrence Patton Macdonald in this chapter. Macdonald had his commercial flight diverted to the Soviet Union where he and all the passengers disappeared.

1209 Rai Singh, "Politburo member said Netaji was in USSR," MissionNetaji.org <http://www.missionnetaji.org/newsite/page/babajan_gouffrav.html> Accessed 18/11/06.

1210 Rai Singh, "Politburo member said Netaji was in USSR," MissionNetaji.org <http://www.missionnetaji.org/newsite/page/babajan_gouffrav.html> Accessed 18/11/06.

poet who wrote bombastic socialist poetry. Faiz would later be awarded the Lenin Peace Prize, the Soviet equivalent to the Nobel Prize. One of the chief accused, General Akbar Khan, was educated in Britain, and appointed to a key position in the British Army (later Pakistani Army) despite his well known socialist sympathies. Some people involved in the plot trace their origins to the Safavids. Liaqat Ali Khan traced his ancestry to the pre-Islamic Sassanids of Iran, and he was credited with initiating the unnecessary Americanization of Pakistan. Why then, did the Powers That be dispose him?

The murder of Fatima Jinnah - The Americanization of Pakistan

Jinnah's influential sister entered politics in 1965 against General Ayub Khan, who was the first Pakistani military leader to seize power through a coup. Ayub Khan implemented the Americanization of Pakistan, turning Pakistan into an American proxy. This had been planned for Pakistan's dialectical role in furthering Soviet hegemony, long before the very creation of Pakistan. Fatima Jinnah lost an election but continued to play an active role in politics. She died from poisoning in 1967.[1211]

The murder of Indian Prime Minister Lal Bahadur Shastri

Prime Minister Shastri had to sign the Tashkent declaration to conclude a war with Pakistan. At Tashkent, Shastri died a mysterious death, which has been attributed to his Soviet hosts.[1212] It is clear that the Soviet Union was seeking intense Sovietization of India to turn the Indian-Pakistani conflict into a proxy war. And those who opposed such measures were to be eliminated at all costs.

The 'Vietnamization' of the Indian Subcontinent

Consistent with the original goal of an Americanized Pakistan and a Sovietized India, the Powers That Be began arranging for both of these nation states to fall under the shadow of their respective sponsoring superpowers.

The Sovietization of India

During the years 1954-1965, Soviet economic aid to India topped the list among all Soviet economic aid to less developed countries. It stood at a

[1211] In 2003, a nephew of Jinnah, Akbar Pirbhai, claimed Fatima Jinnah was assassinated.
[1212] There was no medical report by the Soviets.

whopping US$1022 million.[1213] This aid was not a no-strings-attached affair. It helped create conditions of dependency and made the Indian Government reciprocate, by allowing more Soviet involvement in internal affairs. For example, with trade restrictions lifted, a number of KGB officials moved in, under the cover of promoting trade, as the Mitrokhin archive would later reveal. To quote,

> A number of senior KGB officers have testified that, under Indira Gandhi, India was one of their priority targets. [...] India became "a model of KGB infiltration of a Third World government"[...] The KGB "residency" in Delhi was one of the largest in the world outside the Soviet bloc, and was awarded the rare honor by the Center (KGB HQ in Moscow) of being promoted to "main residency".[1214]

By 1973, ten Indian newspapers and a press agency were on KGB payroll.[1215] By 1975, the KGB had planted 5510 articles in the Indian media.[1216] Indian military hardware was sourced from the Soviet Union. In the event of a war with Pakistan, India would become dependent on the Soviet Union for parts.

It is important to note that local Communist/ Marxist/ Socialist organizations in India were not directly involved with the Soviet Union, or any ongoing Soviet plots in India. The Soviets were instead seeking to use traditional players. Local Communists were completely unaware of the political intentions and internal conditions of the Soviet Union. Apart from ideological commonality, they held no special favoring for the Soviets. And local Communist/ Marxist/ Socialist organizations in India have on the whole, played a positive role in Indian politics, as opposed to other parties.

The Americanization of Pakistan

The following are a compilation of clippings related to Pakistan, declassified from the U.S. National Archives, courtesy researcher Paul

---

[1213] Arthur Stein, India and the Soviet Union, the Nehru Era (Chicago: University of Chicago Press, 1969) 185-186.
[1214] Michael Binyon, "KGB Records show how spies penetrated the Heart of India," The Times September 17th 2005. <http://www.timesonline.co.uk/newspaper/0,,175-1783946,00.html> Accessed 18/11/06.
[1215] Binyon, "KGB Records."
[1216] Binyon, "KGB Records."

Wolfe.[1217] The comments below the quotes are mine. They document the extent of American interference in Pakistan from 1947.

Note: GOP refers to Government of Pakistan

> Then came our meeting in Washington in October '54. On it we were told that America would be prepared to complete 1 1/2 Division of our Armour and four Divisions of Infantry, and as we were spending the maximum we could on Armed Forces, apart from weapons etc required our additional internal expense would also be covered for these Formations. The program was to take three years to complete. Thereafter our dealings began with the USMAAG.
>
> *Letter from Pakistani General Mohammad Ayub Khan to Admiral Arthur Radford, Chairman Joint Chiefs of Staff (Classified Top Secret) Sept. 27, 1955*

> [...] Specifically, Gupta alleges that: despite the US Government's embargo on arms shipments, the US Air Force sent to Karachi on November 29, 1971, a C-147 loaded with spares; US and other foreign aircraft were spotted unloading military supplies at Karachi airport during the December 10-11 cessation of air activity agreed to by India to permit third countries to evacuate their nationals from Karachi; President Nixon "authorized" Jordan and Saudi Arabia to transfer to Pakistan US-supplied jet aircraft; the Pakistani cargo ship "Padma" unloaded $1.3 million worth of US arms during the December war [...].
>
> *A letter from the U.S. Consulate (New Delhi) to the U.S. Department of State, sending a review of Vinod Gupta's book Anderson Papers: A Study of Nixon's Blackmail of India, released June 30, 1972. The book covers US "Support" for Pakistan in the 1971 Subcontinent Crisis. The very fact that US officials in India would discuss Gupta's little known book indicates that Gupta had ruffled a few feathers.*

> Lahore American School, and Four Non-Official Americans (three from Ford) in Lahore have received telephone threats over past few days. Unidentified caller to school said building would be blown today. Individuals were told to leave country within five days or "be slaughtered."
>
> *Letter from American Consulate (Lahore) to American Embassy (Islamabad). The reference made to "Ford" maybe schools operating under the auspices of the Ford Foundation,*

[1217] Paul Wolfe, "Pakistan: Partition and Military Succession: Documents from the US National Archives," <http://www.icdc.com/~paulwolf/archivesindex.htm> Accessed 18/11/06.

which allegedly has links to American Intelligence. March 25, 1971

PPP Urdu daily *Musawat* reported that Dr. Abdus Salam Khurshid, Chairman of the Punjab University Department of Journalism, was participating in a CIA-sponsored, mobile seminar. *Musawat* claimed the American "Agency for International Mass Media" was behind a seminar for Asian professors of journalism that is holding sessions in Hong Kong, Bangkok, Singapore, Taipei and Djakarta. Information developed during the seminars would then be used to pursue CIA objectives. On September 22 *Musawat* followed up with a report that Dr. Khurshid had been investigated by the Pakistani CIA in 1966 after it was learned that he had been offered a large payment from USIS for translations to be used against Pakistan's interests. The Pakistani CIA allegedly discovered 60 people translating material for USIS and a firm called Franklin Publications and that their position was that of agents of America. As a result, the GOP ordered no foreign sponsored research without its approval. *Musawat* claimed the report later vanished from the then West Pakistan Governor's office before action could be taken but now another investigation of Dr. Khurshid had been completed. ... There was a USIS book translation program in 1966 and anti-American elements were highly critical of USIS-sponsored public opinion surveys and of Franklin Publications. There were also representatives from the GOP on the surveys.

From the American Consulate (Lahore) to the US Department of State, Sept. 24, 1971

[...] For the last will the Division of Biographic Information inform Lahore what category index breakdown is being used for Pakistan. Biographic data reports of about 250 Pakistan and Indian national are now in the post files arranged alphabetically but not in separate folders [...].

Letter from the American Consulate (Lahore) to the U.S. State Department, Biographic Information Program, March 26, 1952

Embassy has received request from GOP Defense Ministry for Information concerning an airplane which overflew East Pakistan on November 14, 1963 apparently without proper clearance. Airplane reportedly identified itself via radio as American craft belonging to Air America, Inc. enroute from Calcutta to Bankok. Gave U.S. registry N2002F and claimed GOP clearance telex 023/22/1/1625. GOP Defense Ministry has no record of such clearance. Embassy unable to identify Air America Inc.

Telegram from Karachi Embassy to American Secretary of State, Feb. 17, 1964. Air America was later revealed to be a

CIA front airline, which specialized in covertly shuttling weapons to specified groups. The role of America in the East Pakistan crisis is beyond the scope of this book. In reply, the U.S. government flimflammed, that Air America was a legitimate airline and was indeed at the sighted location at the specific time, and was conducting legitimate business, but may have went off course.

"Recently Ambassador Farland finalized a plan, with the help of some experts, to murder Maulana Kausar Niazi. He made a special trip (accompanied by his experts in four big cars) to Mianwali on July 22. An Ambassador of another country was also with him. These people arrived at 10 a.m. at the house of a Nawab of Mianwali who is known for keeping a force of "trained Goondas." According to SHAHAB sources, this Nawab has been entrusted with the job of killing Maluana Kausar Niazi. The murder plan was made with the help of CIA representatives in Lahore. (Probably a reference to Congen staff at Lahore.) The people (at Lahore) have been collecting information about Kausar Niazi for the last month. ... Earlier Ambassador Farland had gone to Hunza to finalize a conspiracy to murder Maulana Hazarvi (of Jammiat-ul-Ulema-Islam). According to the (CIA) plan all these leaders will be killed by the people of their native areas to avoid any political connection."

American Embassy (Rawalpindi) to the U.S. Department of State, Reporting allegations of a local newspaper SHAHAB against the American Ambassador, Aug. 14, 1970. The U.S. State Department denied these allegations.

The 1979 Revolution in Iran

The 1979 "Islamic" Revolution in Iran is an anomaly, because it never fit into the then dialectics of propping up Soviet and NATO proxies. Was this a genuine attempt to free Iran of foreign influence, both American and Soviet? Or was the ground being prepared for the emergence of a future reactionary Muslim power that would spearhead the "Clash of Civilizations" dialectic that is to play an important role in World War III?

Even before World War I, we observe the strange phenomenon of the British and the Russians cooperating together to play a "developmental" role in Iran (as opposed to the usual game of predatory conquest). On September 4th 1907, Sir Cecil Spring Rice, the British Minister at Teheran, sent a memo to the Persian Minister for Foreign Affairs, explaining the nature of the Anglo-Russian Convention. To quote,

> The object of the two Powers in making this agreement is not in any way to attack, but rather to assure for ever, the independence of Persia. Not only do they not wish to have at hand any excuse for intervention, but their object in these friendly negotiations was not to allow one another to intervene on the pretext of safeguarding their interests. The two Powers hope that in the future Persia will be for ever delivered from the fear of foreign intervention, and will thus be perfectly free to manage her own affairs in her own way.[1218]

In Chapter Two, we discussed at length the Secret Treaty between Britain and Imperial Russia, where such nurturing of Iran by both the powers was further affirmed. Was Iran saved from the usual predation of Western Powers because they foresaw a bigger role for a future "Islamic" Iran?

We find both America and the Soviet Union secretly facilitating the revolution, and the Soviet Union was definitely more overt in this regard. The influential Soviet backed Tudeh Party of Iranian Communists seems to have quietly acquiesced to Khomeini, and some of their leaders even switched to Khomeini's side. Soviet backed forces could have easily invaded Iran in the ensuing confusion, but instead they invaded Afghanistan. While most of the Islamic World was supportive of Afghan resistance to the Soviets, the new Islamic Republic of Iran was surprisingly noncommital. Following the revolution, Soviet-backed socialist regimes popped up in Iraq and Syria, as if they were meant to provide a dialectical false opposition to Iran, ultimately delivering these areas to Iran. While this did not happen due to a number of reasons, the Soviet Union and Communist China were prominent in backing Iran's war with Iraq.

The Soviet Invasion of Afghanistan (1979-1989)

> The Soviet Union has a number of objectives deleterious to U.S. interests and has given its relations with Afghanistan a high priority -- over a billion dollars in economic and military aid. The Soviets have had the immediate aims of limiting U.S. influence and any sort of Western alignment. In the longer run, the USSR probably aspires to control the area, either directly or indirectly through a sympathetic leftist regime, in pursuance of its historic aim of a direct land link with the sub-continent and access to the Indian Ocean. It is likely the Soviet

---

[1218] Frederick Seymour Cocks, The Secret Treaties and Understandings: Text of the Available Documents (London: Union of Democratic Control, 1918) 24: Note#7.

> Union expects to achieve this central objective without the use of force. Rather, it probably hopes that current efforts to establish clandestine intelligence and political action resources, its strong position within the Afghan military forces, the cautious encouragement of a socialist bias in the nation's economic life, its favorable position in Afghan trade, the careful dissemination of propaganda, and the opportunities offered by training hundreds of Afghans will pave the way for Soviet success.
>
> *An American policy review towards Afghanistan, October 24th 1968, declassified from the National Archives, courtesy Paul Wolfe.*[1219]

The Soviet invasion of Afghanistan commenced on December 27th 1979. As per the Illuminati plan, the Soviets were to overrun the entire Afghanistan, under the excuse of fighting American backed insurgents based in Pakistan. Similarly, Pakistan would surrender its sovereignty to American advisors in the face of Soviet threat (Kissinger et all); if they didn't, coups would be arranged. Once Pakistan would fall into American hands, it would be used for launching aggression against India. The Indian leadership would then become dependent on the Soviets to counter the threat. And as a result, the Soviets would start backing Indian activity against Pakistan. This new Indian front against Pakistan would help deflect Soviet loss of personel in Afghanistan. America would use Pakistan to undertake Vietnam style bombing raids against "Soviet backed insurgents" in India, until all of the Indian leadership agreed to Soviet demands for future hegemony in the region, as well as the installment of Soviet puppets in the Indian administration.

Then, the Soviet backed forces would close in on Pakistan, pincer style, from Afghanistan and India. The Americans would shamelessly abandon Karachi as they abandoned Saigon. In effect, the entire Indian subcontinent would be delivered on a plate to the Soviet Union.

India and Pakistan may have been created on religious lines. But they were to play a role similar to North Vietnam and South Vietnam. In the case of Vietnam, the Soviets came to inherit both Vietnams. Similarly, the Soviets were to ultimately inherit both India and Pakistan (the entire Indian subcontinent).

The Mujahideen

[1219] Paul Wolfe, "Afghanistan: Experiment in Democracy. Documents from the US National Archives."
< http://www.icdc.com/~paulwolf/pakistan/afghanistan.htm> Accessed 18/11/06.

It is important to note that the CIA did not back the mujahideen. They instead backed certain "friendly" elements that were able to rally Afghan anti-Soviet resistance. Among such individuals were Gulbuddin Hekmatyar and Ahmed Shah Masood, who received millions from the CIA through Pakistan. Were Hekmatyar and Masood really committed mujahideen,[1220] or had they grown beards for playing their part in the dialectical struggle? Were they tied to the Powers that Be by bloodline?

The CIA did not start actively backing the mujahideen when the Soviet invasion commenced. Instead, Brzezinski believed that it was better to wait till the Soviets entered Afghanistan. This appears to be consistent with the Illuminati strategy discussed earlier. The mujahideen were meant to be a reactionary force, giving the Soviets due cause for moving east. But that's where things went wrong. The mujahideen spiraled out of control. Their leadership and operations could no longer be centralized and controlled. And enthusiastic new recruits flocked to the cause from all over the Islamic world.

The war between the mujahideen and the Russians was an ultimate clash of values. On one side were residents of Orwell's animal farm, who had completely acquiesced to the worst forms of control and conquest. And who only engaged in violence as mercenaries of the state. On the other side were people who had never completely acquiesced to human control or conquest, whether it be direct (as the early British attempts) or through social institutions. They historically carried their own weapons and fought their own wars on their own desired time. Given the importance the Illuminati attached to this venture, the Soviets would be herded in, marching as per the most unreasonable directives, like toy soldiers. In the beginning, they were lush with euphoria; after all, even the mighty German war machine could not stop them. But in the end, even the worst Soviet barbarism couldn't scare the mujahideen. The catastrophe faced by the Soviets in Afghanistan put an end to the Soviet Empire.

The Assassination of General Zia

> There are 120,000 Soviet occupation forces. They're using Special Forces much more than they have. We've seen increased bombing there

---

[1220] During the battle for Kabul, both Hekmatyar and Masood engaged in atrocities, inimical to the mujahideen. Masood's significance is often hyped. It appears the Soviets arranged for a few victories for him in the last phase. In effect, certain "preferred" Mujahideen were being groomed for installation when Soviet evacuation had to be undertaken. They would later resurface as American-backed drug lords. It would be many more civil wars before these so-called Mujahideen were finally dislodged.

> [in the] past year -- carpet bombing of villages, napalming of civilians -- and this continuation of genocide directed against the Afghan people.... more than one third of the Afghan people are refugees, either refugees in their own country or in neighboring countries. The Soviets, for example, use mines, which are disguised as toys, which children pick up, doing great damage to the children and great harm to the people. It is in every sense of the word genocide.
>
> *American ambassador to Pakistan, Arnold Raphael, on the MacNeil/Lehrer NewsHour -- December 27, 1985*[1221]

When President Zia-ul-Haq came to power, it was expected that he would restore democracy to Pakistan. But he consolidated power for himself. He was killed when his C-130 Hercules crashed on August 17th 1988. General Zia had grown too enthusiastic about supporting the mujahideen. For example, he ordered visas to be given to all foreigners who sought to fight the Russians. This resulted in an influx of Arab combatants who played a key role in turning the tide against the Soviets. According to the analysis done by Edward J. Epstein, a small container containing some lethal gas may have been dropped into the air vents of the C-130, and exploded upon takeoff. The Soviets were in possession of such gas. To quote Epstein,

> According to the State Department's special report 78 on "Chemical Warfare in Southeast Asia and Afghanistan," which he sent me, corpses of rebel Mujahideen guerrillas were found still holding their rifles in firing positions after being gassed. This showed that they had been the victims of "an extremely rapid acting lethal chemical that is not detectable by normal senses and that causes no outward physiological responses before death." This gas manufactured by the Soviet would have done the trick.[1222]

Recall the events of the Russian siege of Beslan, during which a top-secret gas was deployed. However, Epstein is of the opinion that American "VX Nerve gas" could have accomplished the same results as well.[1223]

[1221] Arnold Raphael, "Afghanistan: War Without End? ," The MacNeil/Lehrer NewsHour -- December 27, 1985. <http://www.pbs.org/newshour/bb/asia/afghanistan/afghan_12-27-85.html> Accessed 19/11/06.

[1222] Edward Jay Epstein, "Who killed Zia?," Vanity Fair September 1989. An archived copy is available at < http://www.edwardjayepstein.com/archived/zia3.htm> Accessed 19/11/06.

[1223] Epstein, "Who killed Zia?"

Epstein quotes an American chemical warfare expert that such a gas was likely to leave behind phosphorus as residue. There were traces of phosphorus in the cockpit of the C-130.[1224] A policeman at the airstrip was found murdered before the plane took off.[1225] Secretary of State George P. Schultz recommended to the FBI to keep out of the investigation,[1226] even though the American ambassador to Pakistan, Arnold Raphael had died in the crash as well. Raphael had developed views sympathetic to the mujahideen. The Soviets had declared publicly, a week before the crash, that Zia's "obstructionist policy cannot be tolerated."[1227] The Soviet foreign ministry told the American ambassador in Moscow Jack Matlock, that they intended to teach Zia a lesson.[1228] The Soviets were using Afghan intelligence to conduct bombings inside Pakistan at that time.

Pakistan's autocratic dictatorial culture provides many advantages for the Powers that Be to bring down opponents and move in more sympathetic operatives. The closeness of some Pakistani officials to the American administration has even baffled 911 conspiracy theorists. For example, the man who is considered by the FBI to be the "money man" behind the alleged 9/11 hijackers is none other than the head of Pakistani Millitary Intelligence, General Mahmoud Ahmed.[1229] He is said to have authorized a $100,000 wire transfer to Mohammed Atta. From the 4th to the 13th of September 2011, General Ahmed was on an official visit to Washington, meeting Colin Powell, Richard Armitage and his counterpart George Tenet![1230]

The Assassination of Rajiv Gandhi

The biography of Rajiv Gandhi reads like Macbeth. He wanted to stay clear of politics, and therefore became a licensed pilot and married an Italian. But the murder of his mother forced him into politics. Once in politics, the corrupt advisors of his mother soon surrounded him.

Upon stepping into office, Rajiv Gandhi refused playing the Great Game in the subcontinent. He distanced India from the Soviet Union, and ended

---

1224 Epstein, "Who killed Zia?"
1225 Epstein, "Who killed Zia?"
1226 Epstein, "Who killed Zia?"
1227 Epstein, "Who killed Zia?"
1228 Epstein, "Who killed Zia?"
1229 Michel Chossudovsky, interviewed in Aftermath – Unanswered Questions from 911. dir. Stephen Marshall, prod. Ian Inaba & Kyle Hence, nar. Paris. Oct. 22 2004. GNN TV. <http://www.gnn.tv/videos/video.php?id=22>
1230 Chossudovsky, Aftermath.

up throwing a wrench in the plans for the Vietnamization of India. In other words, Rajiv Gandhi had unknowingly prevented Illuminati efforts dating back to the creation of India and beyond, as well as the subsequent Sovietization of India, from achieving their objectives. He thus became their prime target.

One such attempt to bring down Rajiv Gandhi was the Bofors scandal. Some individuals had received kickbacks from Bofors AB for securing a very large contract of supplying 155mm Howitzer field guns to the Indian Army. Those allegedly involved were members of the Congress party. Rajiv Gandhi was defeated in the subsequent 1989 General Elections. While there may have indeed been corruption and wrongdoing on part of the government of Rajiv Gandhi and maybe Rajiv Gandhi himself, it is important to note that the case came to light after a Swedish radio broadcast originally broke the story in 1987. This was a smear campaign against Rajiv Gandhi directed from International circles.

Though he would not become Prime Minister again, he had unknowingly done insurmountable damage to the Vietnamization plot. The Soviets had withdrawn from Afghanistan. But Rajiv Gandhi's non-cooperation in this grand plot was not to be forgiven. On May 21st 1991, an LTTE suicide bomber assassinated Rajiv Gandhi. Although there is more than sufficient proof that the LTTE was responsible, their motives cannot be precisely explained. After the assassination, the LTTE was embroiled in a two front war against India and Sri Lanka. The assassination was strategically a huge mistake. It is more plausible that the leadership of the LTTE had been compromised by overseas interests. When Yasir Arafat would visit India after the assassination, he claimed in a press conference that he was aware of an international plot against Rajiv Gandhi, and claimed that he had personally warned Indian Intelligence two times.

Lawrence Patton McDonald - The Congressman who ended up in the Gulag?

Lawrence Patton McDonald was a Congressman noted for his anti-Soviet views. He was President of the John Birch Society, a right-wing anti-Communist organization. On September 1st 1983, McDonald took Korean Airlines Flight 007 to Seoul, South Korea. He intended to establish a South Korean branch of his Western Goals Foundation,[1231] which was a private intelligence network, intended to gather intelligence on not just Soviet activity but Western collusion with the Soviets.

McDonald's flight never made it to Seoul. What took place on September 1st 1983 may never be known. There is indication that the plane was diverted to Soviet Sakhalin, and the passengers, including Congressman McDonald were taken prisoner. In 1993, Avraham Shifrin, an expert in Soviet era gulag systems reported the existence of Soviet eyewitnesses who had seen the Congressman as a captive.[1232] In 1987, former NSA agent Jerry Mooney testified before Congress that skilled American POWs with technical knowledge were brought to a prison in Karaganda (Kazakhstan). In order to keep McDonald's presence there a secret, he was moved to another small prison in Kazakhstan (Temir-Tau). The wardens of this prison identified him from a computer-aged photograph.[1233] The United States wrapped up its investigation only after ten weeks, as opposed to the investigations into TWA-800 and Lockerbie bombing, which would continue for years.[1234]

South Africa

Apartheid was instituted by the Illuminati in South Africa. The massive farms, as well as gold and diamond mines were owned by the Globalists, and required the use of large labor gangs. Since most of the local Europeans in South Africa did not seem to have any issue with encroachment upon the lives and property of African people, apartheid

---

[1231] Todd Brendan Fahey, "Who Killed Congressman Lawrence Patton McDonald? The State Department Cover-Up Of KAL Flight 007," Rense.com 29th August 2003 <http://www.rense.com/general40/007.htm> Accessed 13/12/06.

[1232] Fahey, "Who Killed Congressman Lawrence Patton McDonald?"

[1233] Bert Schlossberg, Ben Torrey, "Frequently Asked Questions Concerning the Downing of KAL Flight 007 and Attendant Matters," The International Committee for the Rescue of KAL 007 Survivors <http://www.rescue007.org/faq.htm> Accessed 13/12/06

[1234] Fahey, "Who Killed Congressman Lawrence Patton McDonald?"

was successfully implemented. Once the gold and diamond mines surpassed their peak levels of output, the Powers that Be found another use for the apartheid state; South Africa would be groomed by Western powers for a dialectical war with Soviet backed Angola, until Angolans overran them. The war in Angola was meant to be a test phase for this future war. But the plot was shelved in the aftermath of the Soviet debacle in Afghanistan.

Chapter Nine
A Concluding Note on World War III

> The Third World War must be fomented by taking advantage of the differences caused by the "agentur" of the "Illuminati" between the political Zionists and the leaders of Islamic World. The war must be conducted in such a way that Islam (the Moslem Arabic World) and political Zionism (the State of Israel) mutually destroy each other. Meanwhile the other nations, once more divided on this issue will be constrained to fight to the point of complete physical, moral, spiritual and economical exhaustion...We shall unleash the Nihilists and the atheists, and we shall provoke a formidable social cataclysm which in all its horror will show clearly to the nations the effect of absolute atheism, origin of savagery and of the most bloody turmoil. Then everywhere, the citizens, obliged to defend themselves against the world minority of revolutionaries, will exterminate those destroyers of civilization, and the multitude, disillusioned with Christianity, whose deistic spirits will from that moment be without compass or direction, anxious for an ideal, but without knowing where to render its adoration, will receive the true light through the universal manifestation of the pure doctrine of Lucifer, brought finally out in the public view. This manifestation will result from the general reactionary movement, which will follow the destruction of Christianity and atheism, both conquered and exterminated at the same time.

-A quote attributed to Albert Pike, August 15th 1871[1235]

[1235] For a detailed discussion on this quote, see the introductory section 'A note on the World War Quotes attributed to Albert Pike.'

The Sykes Picot Agreement of 1916

The groundwork for World War III was already laid in the aftermath of World War I. With the creation of a Zionist state geared towards perpetual expansion, and the creation of several Arab states. These Arab states are firmly under control of the Powers that Be, either as clients or by rule through bloodlined elite. They were placed in power following the collapse of the Ottoman Empire. The proof of this is that they have not used their oil resources to solve their issues, and instead have completely diverted these resources to outsiders.

Clash of Civilizations

World War III will be fought among civilization blocs, comprised of religious, ethnic and racial blocs. All Muslim countries are expected to fight the Western-Zionist combine.

China trailed off the Soviet Union after World War II and instead began to be groomed by the West. It appears that China will play a leading role as well, likely as an ally of the Muslim world. Which is ironic considering the state of Muslims in China.

The Soviet Union broke apart after the debacle in Afghanistan. But in Russia, the parasitical Soviet social structure is as strong as ever and what happened in 1990 was more of a facelift. The same Criminal Elite are in charge, as they were for centuries. The re-engineering of the Soviet Union into numerous countries had been planned long in advance. It was coordinated by Gorbachev, and was executed by interests in the city of Calgary (Canada), who were the informal shareholders of the Soviet Empire. Since World War III will be fought on civilization blocs as opposed to ideological blocs, it was necessary to create new nations organized on civilizational-cultural-religious-racial differences. All of the countries that emerged from the former Soviet Union are free only in an extremely superficial sense. These new nations, along with Russia will align to their assigned "civilizational blocs," both Christian and Muslim, when preparations for World War III are finalized.

The Indian-Pakistani conflict never saw fruition on terms of establishment of Soviet hegemony. But it is clear that these tensions will once again be recycled.

American Empire + Zionism

> Architect: You are here because Zion is about to be destroyed - its every living inhabitant terminated, its entire existence eradicated.
> Neo: Bulls***!.
> TV Neos: Bulls***!
> Architect: Denial is the most predictable of all human responses, but rest assured, this will be the sixth time we have destroyed it, and we have become exceedingly efficient at it.
> *-Scene in The Matrix Reloaded, 2003*

The plan of World War III is to have the main religious-civilizational blocs (Islam-Judaism-Christianity) cancel each other out. Apart from being destroyed, they will lose their moral credibility when they hurl weapons of mass destruction against each other in the name of religion.

It is important to note that World War III will not result in American-Zionist hegemony, as some naively conclude. American Empire and Zionism are nothing more than rallying points, for some other end. For example, Zionism could have been a constructive development for the entire Middle East. Instead we see Israeli leaders embroiling their population in hate and attrition. Though the sacred city of Jerusalem will be used as a ploy to involve all three religions, there is no indication that Jerusalem is intended to be the seat of World Government. The Powers that Be have little regard for the spiritual importance of Jerusalem, and instead see it as a tool for embroiling all the three major religions in conflict. American intervention could have been positive in some cases. Instead we see Americans pursuing unseen objectives that go well beyond the acquisition of oil. For example, American involvement in Iraq seems to be working to the advantage of Iran, a reactionary power that is wholeheartedly pursuing the "Clash of Civilizations" doctrine.

What is the grand ultimate end? Someone analyzing the political scene in 1914 could not have predicted the future emergence of Soviet Union; neither could one have envisioned what the Soviet Union would be like. Similarly, our understanding of the upcoming "New World Order" is limited to educated guesses.

Terrorism

The subject populations of Western countries are conditioned with fear, from nuclear winters and Martian invasions to climate change and terrorism. As in the previous World Wars, it is possible to divert their efforts, their lives and their entire economies[1236] towards concealed objectives, while conjuring up some mythical threat to their existence and well-being. Popular belief that fighting two transatlantic World Wars has saved their "freedom" and "way of life" is indicative of this symptom.[1237]

The Powers that Be understand that making their subject populations overcome their sensibilities is only a matter of giving them the required dosage of fear and danger. The Powers that Be are in control of several Muslim countries. They are in control of several Muslim reactionary groups. They are also the creators and controllers of the technology of mass destruction. As we have seen in the two World Wars, sacrifices were made to establish a "New World Order." Roosevelt provoked the Empire of Japan and duped the people of the United States into annihilating it. When it comes to dealing with nameless, faceless terrorists with no return address, the possibilities for war are endless. No longer do nations have to make a formal declaration of war to be considered as hostile. Acts of terrorism can easily be attributed to any undesirable nation.

September 11th 2001

On October 28th, 1993, there was a small-scale terrorist attack on the World Trade Center by alleged Muslim militants. Those who were jailed were the blind Egyptian cleric Shaikh Omar Abdul Rahman, Ramzi Yousef, and Eyad Ismail. This alleged "terrorist cell" also included Ali Mohammed, who graduated from the U.S. Army Special Forces School in Fort Bragg.[1238] During the trial of the alleged bombers, federal prosecutors avoided bringing in critical evidence, such as wiretap information between the Sudanese mission to the UN and Khartoum. Those responsible for suppressing the evidence were none other than the main prosecutors, Patrick J. Fitzgerald and Michael Chertoff.[1239] Chertoff would later become United States Secretary of Homeland Security. According to Alex Jones,

---

[1236] During World War II, all major participating countries reorganized their domestic sector to produce armaments, munitions and soldiers. 40-60 percent of the GDP was directed towards the war effort. Women were drafted in Britain and the Soviet Union.

[1237] In the movie Pearl Harbor which was released in 2001, just four months before the September 11th attacks, the American audience is told that a Japanese land invasion could reach up to Chicago before it was engaged.

[1238] WayneMadsenReport.com, August 27th 2006.

[1239] WayneMadsenReport.com, August 27th 2006.

> [...] New York Times and Dec 15th Chicago Tribune, Federal agents were caught on tape by the government ordering them to let the bombing go forward, to cook the bomb, to give the terrorists the detonators [...] FBI hired a retired 43 year old Egyptian army officer Amad Salam and paid him one million dollars and gave him real explosives and a detonator, and told him to build a bomb and give it to the foolish people he was controlling to allow them to attack the World trade Center [...] Salam got concerned as to why he was being given real explosives if this was a sting operation. But they told him to go ahead and let the attack go forward [...] He secretly recorded the head of the FBI in NY ordering him to let the bombing take place [...] the drivers of the truck didn't park it up the main support column as they had been ordered to do by Mr. Salam. They parked it a dozen feet away [...].[1240]

The question is not how such a conspiracy could have taken place. The question to be considered is why the World Trade Center was targeted for a small-scale terrorist attack? Was this some kind of psychological conditioning for the upcoming 9-11 attacks?

If that is the case, are the 9-11 attacks psychological conditioning for a grand attack that will kick-start America's entry into World War III? Consider the way the establishment media played and replayed the 9-11 attacks, until they were embedded into the memories of television viewers.

Nowadays, if a building falls in New York City, people are not content until terrorism is ruled out. And New Yorkers are too "busy" to verify facts for themselves. Similar to their dependence on processed fast food, the subject populations of the Western world require news to be fed in prepackaged morsels. The packaging and content selection for both fast food and news happens to be an exclusive preserve of the Powers that Be.

North America - Manifest Destiny

> He stepped to the window and pointed at the skyscrapers of the city. He said that we had to extinguish the lights of the world, and when we would see the lights of New York go out, we would know that our job was done.
>
> *-Francisco d'Anconia on John Galt, characters in Ayn Rand's prophetic novel, Atlas Shrugged.*

[1240] 911-The Road to Tyranny. prod. And dir. Alex Jones, Alex Jones Films, 2001.

Plans are afoot to integrate the entire North American countries into a single economic bloc. This will allow all their economies to be collectively harnessed for war. This is part of a centuries old process, the most notable phase of which was the forceful and violent union of the various states into what now comprises USA. A command structure for all these areas was created, under the flag of thirteen stripes, one stripe each for the thirteen bloodlines of the Illuminati.[1241]

It is assumed that North America will only be used for exporting war, and as such, will avoid the more deleterious effects of war, as before. And it is assumed that since the Powers That Be operate from financial centers in North America, they will not bring the war home.

Or maybe they will. The creation of future concentration camps, the leveling of civil liberties for future tyrants and the creation of a bogus terrorist threat for the sake of using portable warfare on American soil, are indicative of major plans for the future. As a plan of doom, American embroilment in the Middle East is not unlike the Nazi march into the Russian wasteland. It may be the best and only opportunity to destroy the existing order in North America. It is very likely that Iran is being groomed as a dialectical enemy that will embroil the entire West in a deadly conflict with the Middle East.

The Powers that Be are no fans of American hegemony. They have repeatedly hinted throughout American history that America has a "Manifest Destiny," and is to play a particular role in the creation of a New World Order. The question is, what happens to America after it fulfills that role?

We know what became of Germany, the homeland of the Illuminati.

[1241] They will tell you it is for the original 13 colonies. Why only 13 colonies? The confederate flag also had 13 stars. Presently, the United States is grouped into 4 regions with 13 states in each. When American soldiers get killed, a peculiar Masonic flag folding ritual takes place, which emphasizes the number 13.

Bibliography

Books[1242]

Abd-Allah, Umar F. A Muslim in Victorian America: The Life of Alexander Russell Webb (Oxford University Press, 2006).

Baigent, Michael, Richard Leigh and Henry Lincoln. The Holy Blood and the Holy Grail (London: Arrow Books, 1996).

Beg, M. Sociolinguistic Perspective of Hindi and Urdu in India (New Delhi: Bahri Publications, 1960).

Blavatsky, H.P. The Secret Doctrine Vol.2 (Theosophical University Press Online Edition).

Brinkley, Alan. The Unfinished Nation – A Concise History of the American People Volume II: From 1865. 4th ed. (New York: McGraw Hill 2004).

Carr, Joseph J. The Twisted Cross (Vital Issues Press, 1985).

Chatterjee, Partha. Nationalist Thought and the Colonial World - A Derivative Discourse (Minneapolis: University of Minnesota Press, 2004).

Cockett, Richard. Twilight of Truth: Chamberlain, Appeasement and Manipulation of the Press (Palgrave Macmillan, 1989).

Cocks, Frederick Seymour. The Secret Treaties and Understandings: Text of the Available Documents (London: Union of Democratic Control, 1918).

Cohn, Bernard S. Colonialism and its Forms of Knowledge (Delhi: Oxford University Press, 1996).

Carr, William Guy. Satan, Prince of This World (Omni Publications, 1997)

Cracraft, James. Ed. Major Problems in the History of Imperial Russia (D.C Heath and Co, 1994).

Dadrian, Vahakn N. German Responsibility in the Armenian Genocide: A Review of the Historical Evidence of German Complicity (Watertown MA: Blue Crane Books, 1996)

Dalrymple, William. The Last Mughal (London: Penguin Books, 2007)

Deresky, Helen. International Management –Managing Across Borders and Cultures 5th ed. (New Jersey: Pearson-Prentice Hall, 2004).

[1242] Includes Published books available online. Does not include books quoted indirectly from other books.

Dirks, Nicholas B. The Scandal of Empire- India and the Creation of Imperial Britain (Cambridge: The Belknap Press of the Harvard University Press, 2006).

Durham, Mary E. The Sarajevo Crime (London: George Allyn and Unwinn, Ltd, 1925)

Fisk, Robert. The Great War for Civilisation: the Conquest of the Middle East (London: Fourth Estate, 2005).

Habib, Irfan. Essays in Indian History; Towards a Marxist Perception (New Delhi: Tulika Publishers, 1995).

Hogan, Michael J. ed., The Ambiguous Legacy - U.S. Foreign Relations in the "American Century." (Cambridge: Cambridge University Press, 1999).

Jordan, George Racey and Richard L. Stokes, From Major Jordan's Diaries (NY: Harcourt, Brace and Company, 1952).

Kapur, Harish. Soviet Russia and Asia 1917-1927 (NY: The Humanities Press, 1967).

Kennedy, Malcolm D. The Estrangement of Great Britain and Japan 1917-35 (Berkeley: Univ. of California Press, 1969).

Langer, Walter C. The Mind of Hitler – The Secret Wartime Report (NY & London: Basic books Inc., 1972).

Lee, Bradford A. Britain and the Sino Japanese war 1937-39 - A study in the dilemmas of British decline (California: Stanford University Press, 1973).

Levenda, Peter. Unholy Alliance (Avon Books, 1995).

Lina, Juri. Architects of Deception (Stockholm: Referent Publications, 2004).

Lively, Scott and Kevin Abrams, The Pink Swastika-Homosexuality in the Nazi Party 4th ed. (Sacramento: Veritas Aeterna Press, 2002).

Lockman, Zachary. Contending Visions of the Middle East – The History and Politics of Orientalism (Cambridge: Cambridge University Press 2004).

Louise, Roger. British Strategy in the Far East 1919-39 (Oxford: Clarendon, 1971).

Levy, Avigdor. The Jews of the Ottoman Empire (Princeton, 1994).

Moaddel, Mansoor. Islamic Modernism, Nationalism, and Fundamentalism: Episode and Discourse (Chicago: The University of Chicago Press, 2005).

Moyzisch, Ludwig C. Operation Cicero (Allan-Wingate-Baker 1969).

Mullins, Eustace C. The Secret History of the Atomic Bomb (Staunton: Web edition, 1998).

Nish, Ian ed. Britain and the Opening of the War in Asia, 1937-41 (London: Cambridge University Press).

Orga, Irfan & Margarete Orga, Ataturk (London: Michael Joseph, 1962).

Perry, Roland. Introduction. The Fifth Man (London: Pan Books, 1994) xx.

Pidcock, David M. Satanic Voices – Ancient and Modern Internet edition (Oldbrook, Milton Keynes: Mustaqim, 2002).

Pierce, Leslie P. The Imperial Harem – Women and Sovereignty in the Ottoman Empire (NY: Oxford University Press, 1993).

Richard Pipes, Russia under the old regime (New York: Scribner, 1974).

Prinz, Joachim. The Secret Jews (Random House, 1973).

Quigley, Harold S. Far Eastern War, 1937-41 (Boston: World Peace Foundation, 1942)

Raeff, Marc. The Decembrist Movement (Prentice Hall Inc.-New Jersey, 1966).

Riasanovsky, Nicholas V. A History of Russia (Oxford University Press, 1963).

Rivera, David Allen. Final Warning: A History of the New World Order (Conspiracy, 2004).

Rodriguez, Jose Maria Cardinal Caro Y. The Mystery of Freemasonry Unveiled – With a reprint of Pope Leo XIIIth Encyclical Humanum Genus 2nd edition (Imprimatur, Jose Maria Cardinal Caro Y. Rodriguez, Cardinal Archbishop of Santiago, Chile, 1920s).

Royle, Trevor. Crimea: The Great Crimean War, 1854-1856 (Palgrave Macmillan, 2000).

Sklar, Dusty. The Nazis and the Occult (1989).

Springmeier, Fritz. Bloodlines of the Illuminati (Spring Arbor distributors, 1998).

---, The Illuminati formula used to create an undetectable total mind controlled slave (Private Edition date NA).

---, Deeper Insights into the Illuminati Formula (Private edition, date NA)

Stein, Arthur. India and the Soviet Union, the Nehru Era (Chicago: University of Chicago Press, 1969).

Suny, Ronald Grigor. The structure of Soviet History - essays and documents (Oxford University Press, 2003).

Sutton, Antony C. Wall Street and the Bolshevik Revolution (Buccaneer Books, 1993).

---, Wall Street and the Rise of Hitler (GSG & Associates, 1976).

Tilford, Earl L. Setup: What the Air Force did in Vietnam and Why (Maxwell Air Force Base AL: Air University Press, 1991).

Trotsky, Leon. "Germany, the key to the international situation," The Struggle Against Fascism in Germany Ed. George Brietman and Merry Maisel. (NY: Pathfinder Press Inc. 1971).

Vokogonov, Dmitri. Stalin, Triumph and Tragedy Ed. and trans. by Harold Shuckman. (Weidenfield and Nicholson, 1991).

Webster, Nesta. The Cause of World Unrest (London: Richards Limited, 1920).

Zallum, Abdul Qadeem. How the Khilafah was Destroyed (Gloucester: Al-Khilafah Publications, 2000).

Journals

Ayubi , Shaheen. "Uzbekistan's Long Road to Democracy and Political Stability." Journal of South Asian and Middle Eastern Studies 18.3 (1995) 1-20.

Bamshad, Michael. and Toomas Kivisild,W. Scott Watkins, Mary E. Dixon, Chris E. Ricker, Baskara B. Rao, J. Mastan Naidu, B.V. Ravi Prasad, P. Govinda Reddy, Arani Rasanayagam, Surinder S. Papiha, Richard Villems, Alan J. Redd, Michael F. Hammer, Son V. Nguyen, Marion L. Carroll, Mark A. Batzer and Lynn B. Jorde, "Genetic Evidence on the Origins of Indian Caste Population," Genome Research 11 (2001).

Blavatsky, H.P. Letter by HPB to brothers of Aryavarta, April 1890, "Why I do not return to India," The Theosophist, January 1922.

Gandhi, Rajmohan. "Mohandas Gandhi, Abdul Ghaffar Khan, and the Middle East Today," World Policy Journal Vol. XXII Spring (2005): 89-94.

Haggie, Paul. Britannia At Bay- The Defence of the Empire Against Japan 1931-41 (Oxford: Clarendon Press, 1981).

Hantman, Joseph. "The Turkish Israeli Connection and its Jewish Roots," Kulanu quarterly newsletter summer 1999, Volume 6 Number 2, page 3, 12.

Heine-Geldern, Robert. "The Coming of the Aryans and the end of the Harappa Civilization," Man 56 (Oct. 1956) 139.

Hess, Andrew C. "The Battle of Lepanto and its Place in Mediterranean History," Past and Present (57) Nov. 1972, 53-73.

Jones, Dr. Steven E. "Why Indeed did the WTC Buildings Completely Collapsed," Journal of 911 Studies September 2006 Vol. 3. [page numbers NA].

Knight, A., L.A Zhivotovsky, ,D.H. Kass, D.E. Litwin, L.D. Green, P.S. White, J.L Mountain, "Molecular, forensic and haplotypic inconsistencies regarding the Ekaterinburg remains," Annals of Human Biology 31.2 (2004) 129-138.

Mark, James. "Remembering Rape: Divided Social Memory and the Red Army in Hungary 1944–1945," Past and Present 188 (August 2005) 133-161.

Metzer, Ralf. "In the Eye of a Hurricane: German Freemasonry in the Weimar Republic and the Third Reich," Totalitarian Movements & Political Religions 4.2 (2003) [page numbers NA].

Minorsky, V. "The Poetry of Shah Isma'il I," Bulletin of the School of Oriental and African Studies University of London 10.4 (1942), 1006a-1053a.

Paksoy, H. B. "Basmachi Movement from within: Account of Zeki Velidi Togan," Nationalities Papers 23.2, June 1995, 373-399.

Taylor, A. J. P. "War Origins Again," Past and Present 30 (April 1965).

Williams, Brian Glyn. "The Crimean Tatar Exile in Central Asia: A Case Study in Group Destruction and Survival," Central Asian Survey 17.2 (1998).

Wolfe, Bertram D. "Nationalism and Internationalism in Marx and Engels," American Slavic and East European Review 17.4 (1958) 403-417.

Newspapers and Magazines

Bernbeim, Alain. "German Freemasonry and Its Attitudes Toward The Nazi Regime," The Philaltethes Magazine February 1997.

General Lieutenant Bronsart von Schellendorf, "A Witness for Talaat Pasha," Deutsche Allgemeine Zeitung July 24, 1921.

Brussells, Mae. "The Nazi Connection to the Dallas JFK murder," The Rebel January 1984.

Epstein, Edward Jay. "Who killed Zia?," Vanity Fair September 1989.

Halkin, Hillel. "When Kemal Ataturk Recited Shema Yisrael - "It's My Secret Prayer, Too," He Confessed," Forward January 28th 1994.

Jasper, William F. "Forty Years of freedom," The New American. Vol. 14, No. 25, (December 7th 1998).

Margolis, Eric. "The 20th Century's Worst Crime Goes Unpunished," The Toronto Sun November 16th 2003.

Meyer, Steven P. and Jeffrey Steinberg, "Henry Luce's Empire of Fascism," Executive Intelligence Review. June 25th, 2004.

Nick Thimmesch, "The iron mentor of the Pentagon – Why even Henry Kissinger needs Dr. Fritz Kraemer," Washington Post March 2nd 1975.

UPI, "US Aided Rescue of Czar Nicholas, British hint," The Chicago Tribune December 14th 1970.

Wines, Michael. "New Study supports idea Stalin was poisoned," New York Times March 5th 2003. Late ed.: A3.

Speeches and Interviews

Fetzer, James. Speech on the political assaults taking place against academics studying the events of 9/11. University of Wisconsin (Madison). 1 Nov. 2006. Archived video at <http://www.youtube.com/watch?v=_967jIpFVfo>

McClusky, Andrew, Interview with Mike McCormick/TalkingStickTV, Mind Over Matters Series. Date NA. Archived audio recording available at <http://www.radio4all.net/proginfo.php?id=5123>

Rakovsky, Christian G. The questioning of the accused Christian Georgievitch Rakovsky by Gavriil Gavriilovitch Kus'min on the 26th January 1938. Archived transcript at <https://archive.org/details/RedSymphony>

Stinnet, Robert. Author of Day of Deceit - The Truth About FDR and Pearl Harbor Interview with Mike McCormick/TalkingStickTV, Mind Over Matters Series. Date NA. Archived audio recording available at <http://www.radio4all.net/proginfo.php?id=5123>

Videos, TV Shows and Radio Broadcasts

911-The Road to Tyranny. prod. And dir. Alex Jones, Alex Jones Films, 2001.

Aftermath – Unanswered Questions from 911. dir. Stephen Marshall, prod. Ian Inaba & Kyle Hence, nar. Paris. Oct. 22 2004. GNN TV. <http://www.gnn.tv/videos/video.php?id=22>

Brussells, Mae. World Watchers International, Broadcast # 650, 21st May 1984.

---, World Watchers International. Broadcast # 560, August 30th 1982.

---, World Watchers International. Broadcast # 560, August 30th 1982.

History Channel, "Organized Crime-Russia," Aired Oct. 20th 2006.

"Nazis: The Occult Conspiracy," BMG Distribution, narr. Malcolm McDowell, dir. Tracy Atkinson and Joan Barron, Discovery Channel, 22nd February 1998.

Raphael, Arnold. "Afghanistan: War Without End?" The MacNeil/Lehrer NewsHour -- December 27, 1985.

"Russian Mysteries." Interviews by Sherman Skolnick. Broadsides. Chicago Public Access Cable TV on Channel 21. [Airing date NA].

Sacrifice at Pearl Harbor, prod. Roy Davies, BBC, 1989.

The Hole Story, prod. Richard Desjardins and Robert Monderie, National Film Board of Canada, 2011.

Internet SourcesS

Abbott, Matt C. "Here We Go Again," Michigan News November 15th 2003. <http://www.freemasonrywatch.org/rockefeller_foundation.html> [archived copy].

Anesi, Chuck. "The World was Lied to About Hitler's Death," Blackraiser.com <http://www.blackraiser.com/nredoubt/identity.htm>

Atli, Altay. "Cemal Pasa," turkeyswar.com <http://www.turkeyswar.com/whoswho/cemal/who-talat.htm>

---, "Enver Pasa," Turkeyswar.com <http://turkeyswar.com/whoswho/enver/who-enver.htm>

---, "Gallipoli:Part II," turkeyswar.com <http://www.turkeyswar.com/campaigns/gallipoli_cont.htm>

Aravosis, John. "AMERICAblog just bought General Wesley Clark's cell phone records for $89.95," AMERICAblog 1 Dec. 2006 <http://americablog.blogspot.com/2006/01/americablog-just-bought-general-wesley.html>

Armenian Youth Federation, Greece. "Declaration: The Punishment – of those responsible for the Armenian Genocide," AYF Greece <http://www.hyeetch.nareg.com.au/genocide/punish_p1.html>

Armeniapedia, "Armenian Genocide Quotes." 16/12/06 Armeniapedia

Associated Press, "Diary sheds light on Einstein's final years." AP 26th April 2004 .<http://www.msnbc.msn.com/id/4829521/>

---, "New letters shed light on Einstein's love life," AP 10th August 2007 <http://www.msnbc.msn.com/id/13804030/>

---, "Warsaw Archbishop quits amid spying scandal," AP January 7th 2007 <http://www.msnbc.msn.com/id/16508126/>

BBC News, "Ataturk Diaries to remain secret," BBC.com Published 4th Feb. 2005. <http://news.bbc.co.uk/2/hi/europe/4235691.stm>

Bernheim, Alain. "The Blue Forget-me-not,' Another Side of the Story," Masonic Papers
<http://www.freemasons-freemasonry.com/bernheim3.html>

Bhaumik, Subir. "British 'attempted to kill Bose.'" BBC News 15/08/05<http://news.bbc.co.uk/2/hi/south_asia/4152320.stm>

Binyon, Michael. "KGB Records show how spies penetrated the Heart of India," The Times September 17th 2005. <http://www.timesonline.co.uk/newspaper/0,,175-1783946,00.html>

Blavatsky.net <http://www.blavatsky.net/blavatsky/madame-blavatsky.htm>

Blavatsky, H.P. Letter to Prof. H. Corson, date not available. "Some Unpublished letters of H. P. Blavatsky, compiled by E.R. Corson. Theosophical University Press Online Edition <http://www.theosociety.org/pasadena/corson/cors-lt1.htm>

Bloy, Marjie. "The Crimean War: Immediate Causes," The Victorian Web <http://www.victorianweb.org/history/crimea/immcauses.html>

British Embassy Helsinki, "News: Special Feature: The Baltic Campaign of the Crimean War: Introduction," British Embassy Helsinki <http://www.britishembassy.gov.uk/servlet/Front?pagename=OpenMarket/Xcelerate/ShowPage&c=Page&cid=1065719062885>

Carreon, Hector. "FBI closes in on Anthrax suspect," Aztlan.net 26 Feb. 2002. <http://www.aztlan.net/zack.htm>

Chabad Online, "The Parsha in a nutshell- Bamidar Numbers 1:1-4:20," Chabad Online Media Center, Bamidbar magazine, #5761, May 25th 2001. <http://www.chabad.org/parshah/article.asp?AID=2121>

Chamish, Barry. "Kerry, Gaza and the New Sabbatean Holocaust," barrychamish.com Published 09/02/04. An archived copy is available at: <http://www.redmoonrising.com/chamish/Feb04.htm#February%209>

Channel4.com, "The First World War," Channel 4 < http://www.channel4.com/history/microsites/F/firstworldwar/cont_jihad_1.html>

Crosette, Barbara. "Russia and China Called Top Business Bribers," New York Times on the Web May 17th 2002.

Crystal, Ellie. "Helena Petrovna Blavatsky," Crystalinks <http://www.crystalinks.com/blavatsky.html>

Davidson, Michael and Michael Ruppert, "A Career in microbiology can be harmful to your health," Fromthewildreness.com <http://www.fromthewilderness.com/free/ww3/02_14_02_microbio.html>

DeLaglio, F.V. "SS Brigadefuhrer Fritz Kraemer," 12. SS-Panzerdivision "Hitlerjugend" An essential rundown on Hitler's General, Fritz Kraemer. Compiled from German Literature. <http://home.att.net/~SSPzHJ/FritzKraemer.html>

Dodd, William. FDR Library: Dodd 11/09/36

<http://www.fdrlibrary.marist.edu/andyc/fdr/psf/box32/a300l07.html>

Fahey, Todd Brendan. "Who Killed Congressman Lawrence Patton McDonald? The State Department Cover-Up Of KAL Flight 007," Rense.com 29th August 2003. <http://www.rense.com/general40/007.htm>

Free Press International 24/01/05, "Author Theorizes Forty biologists killed before unleashing ultimate epidemic," Free Press International <http://freepress2005.blogspot.com/2005/01/author-theorizes-40-microbiologists.html>

Freemasonrywatch, "The Dukes of Kent," Freemasonrywatch <http://www.freemasonrywatch.org/P2.html>

---, "Quotations written by high level Masons praising Lucifer," Freemasonrywatch <http://freemasonrywatch.org/luciferquotes.html>

Gonzalez, Servando. The Swastika and the Nazis (1998) <http://www.intelinet.org/swastika>

Guardian.co.uk, "A monumental dance of death," Guardian Online 1/03/00 <http://www.guardian.co.uk/irving/article/0,,191821,00.html> Accessed 11/12/06

Haupt, Michael. "What Really caused world war 2," ThreeWorldWars.com <http://www.threeworldwars.com/world-war-2/ww2.htm>

Heilbron, J. L. Robert W. Seidel, Bruce R. Wheaton, Ed. Judith Goldhaber, Lawrence and His Laboratory (1981 Newsmagazine Publication; 1996 Web Publication). <http://www.lbl.gov/Science-Articles/Research-Review/Magazine/1981/index.html>

Helm, Sarah. "MI6 protected Nazi who killed 100 British agents," The Times May 14th 2005 <http://www.timesonline.co.uk/article/0,,2-1611185,00.html>

Henley, John. "In a Secret Paris Cavern, the Real Underground Cinema," The Guardian September 8th 2004. <http://film.guardian.co.uk/News_Story/Guardian/0,,1299449,00.html>

Hopsicker, Daniel. "FBI Terror Alert in South Pacific," Mad Cow Morning News <http://www.madcowprod.com/11162006.html>

Hughes, Donna M. "Nyet to Trafficking- Russians show political will to fight prostitution," June 18th 2003 National Review Online <http://www.nationalreview.com/comment/comment-hughes061803.asp>

Hyde, Henry J. "A Brief History of Russian Spying," Spybusters.com <http://www.spybusters.com/Great_Seal_Bug.html>

Icke, David. "Was Hitler a Rothschild?," Davidicke.com <http://www.davidicke.com/icke/articles/hitler.html>

Illuminati Conspiracy Archive: Operation Paperclip Case file <http://www.conspiracyarchive.com/NWO/project_paperclip.htm>

Infowars.com, "Foreign Troops Operating Secret Detention Centres." Infowars July 14th 2000 <http://www.infowars.com/detcamp.html>

Irbe, George. "The Roots of evil," <http://www.interlog.com/~girbe/roots.html>

Jasper, William F. "Terrorism's True Roots," 2001-12-03 John Birch Society. <http://www.jbs.org/node/843>

Johnson, Daniel. "Red Army troops raped even Russian women as they freed them from camps," Telegraph.co.uk 24th Feb. 2002. <http://www.telegraph.co.uk/news/main.jhtml?xml=/news/2002/01/24/wbeev24.xml>

---, "Russians Angry at war Rape Claims," Telegraph.co.uk 25th Feb. 2002 <http://www.telegraph.co.uk/news/main.jhtml?xml=/news/2002/01/25/wruss25.xml>

Jones, Alex. "Dark Secrets Inside the Bohemian Grove," Infowars.com <http://www.infowars.com/bg1.html>

Joseph, Rhawn. The Mind and God of Adolf Hitler Part I <http://brainmind.com/Hitler.html>

Michael T. Kaufman, "Fritz Kraemer, 95, Tutor to U.S. Generals and Kissinger, Dies," New York Times 19/11/03. Accessed 04/11/06. <http://www.nytimes.com/2003/11/19/national/19KRAE.html>

Keddie, Nikki R. Modern Iran- Roots and Results of Revolution (New Haven: Yale University Press, 2003)

Khan Bahadur, Hamid al-Din. Sir Jadunath Sarkar ed. Anecdotes of Aurangzeb; English translation of Ahkam-i-Alamgiri.3rd ed. (Calcutta, M.C. Sarkar, 1949).

Klomegah, Kester Kenn, "Poverty Drives Russian Women into Prostitution Abroad," The Dawn Internet edition August 31st 2005 <http://www.dawn.com/2005/08/31/int10.htm>

Krushelnycky, Leonida. "The mystery of Stalin's death," BBC News World Edition 24/02/03. <http://newswww.bbc.net.uk/2/hi/europe/2793501.stm>

Lemons, Stephen. Hitler's Clairvoyant Salon.com <http://www.salon.com/people/feature/2002/02/27/hanussen/>

Louter, Michiel. "Disreputable forces at work among the sect researchers at CESNUR," August 13th 1997, De Groene Amsterdammer. An archived copy is available at <http://www.rickross.com/reference/apologist/apologist16.html>

Luscombe, Stephen. "The Crimean War: Charge of the Light Brigade," 25th October 1854. Britishempire.co.uk

<http://www.britishempire.co.uk/forces/armycampaigns/europeancampaigns/crimeanwar/crimeanwar.htm>

Lynott, Douglas. "Killers from history-Josef Mengele," Crime Library

<http://www.crimelibrary.com/serial_killers/history/mengele/aus_4.html?sect=6>

Makow, Henry. "Hitler didn't want world war," Savethemales.ca 21st March 2004 <http://www.savethemales.ca/000369.html>

---, "Rothschilds conduct Red symphony," Savethemales.ca 9th Nov. 2003. <http://www.savethemales.ca/000275.html>

---, "Zionism: A Conspiracy Against Jews," Savethemales.ca June 27th 2004 <http://www.savethemales.ca/000482.html>

Marrs, Texe. "Unmasking the sexual perversions of the Illuminati: Two on a saddle Part 1," Power of the Prophecy January 2002 <http://www.texemarrs.com/012002/two_on_a_saddle.htm>

McShane, Larry. "Book Paints Escape Artist Houdini as Spy," Saturday October 28th 2006. Associated Press <http://sfgate.com/cgi-bin/article.cgi?f=/n/a/2006/10/28/entertainment/e100630D77.DTL>

Melman, Yossi. "CIA Recruited Five Of Adolph Eichmann's Associates," Haaretz.com 2nd May 2005. [The article is no longer available on the Haaretz Website].

Millegan, Kris. "The Order of the Skull and Bones-Everything you wanted to know but were afraid to ask," July 1997 CTRL.org An archived copy is available at <http://www.mega.nu:8080/ampp/skull.html>

New World Order: The Movie "Nazis and Aryans," <http://www.geocities.com/newworldorder_themovie/nazisandaryans.html>

---, "Knights of Malta," <http://www.geocities.com/newworldorder_themovie/knightsofmalta.html>

---, "Dragon Court," <http://www.geocities.com/newworldorder_themovie/dragoncourt.html>

Newman, Hannah. The Rainbow Swastika- A Report to the Jewish People About New Age Anti-Semitism: Nazism and the New age <http://philologos.org/__eb-trs/default.htm#toc>

Noah, Timothy. "Arnold's Nazi problem; Why wont he repudiate Waldheim?," MSN Slate: August 7th 2003 <http://slate.msn.com/id/2086742>

George Orwell, "Arthur Koestler," 1946. <http://www.george-orwell.org/Arthur_Koestler/0.html>

"Otto Rahn and the Quest for the Holy Grail," <http://www.geocities.com/CapitolHill/6824/otto.htm>

Petrova, Ada and Peter Watson, " The Death of Hitler – The Full Story with New Evidence from Secret Russian Archives," Washingtonpost.com <http://www.washingtonpost.com/wp-srv/style/longterm/books/chap1/deathofhitler.htm >

Pravda.ru, "Three Centuries of Russian Prostitution," Pravda 30th April 2002 <http://english.pravda.ru/fun/2002/04/30/28157.html>

Ray, John J. "Hitler was a Socialist," October 2006 <http://jonjayray.tripod.com/hitler.html>

Rice, Boyd. "The Sumerian Origins of the Iconography of the Templars, Masons & Merovingians," Dagoberts Revenge <http://web.archive.org/web/20040607071402/http://dagobertsrevenge.com/articles/rlc/icon.shtml>

Richardson, Kerry. Index of Bohemian Grove Reportage <http://www.sonic.net/~kerry/bohemian/photolinks.html>

Ross, A.C. Fascist Treachery <http://www.bigelowconsulting.com/CRAweb/essay13.htm> An archived version is available at <http://web.archive.org/web/20041205024342/http://www.bigelowconsulting.com/CRAweb/essay13.htm>

Sabeheddin, Mehmet. "The Secret of Eurasia – The key to Hidden History and World Events," New Dawn No. 68 (September-October 2001), <http://www.newdawnmagazine.com>

Schlossberg, Bert and Ben Torrey, "Frequently Asked Questions Concerning the Downing of KAL Flight 007 and Attendant Matters," The International Committee for the Rescue of KAL 007 Survivors <http://www.rescue007.org/faq.htm>

Shack, Clifford. "Was Stalin a Rothschild?" Cliff Shack <http://www.geocities.com/cliff_shack/stalinrothschild.html>

---, "Oil and the Holocaust," Cliff Shack <http://www.geocities.com/cliff_shack/oil_chrono.html>

Sichos in English, Volume 28 <http://www.sichosinenglish.org/books/sichos-in-english/28/12.htm>

Singh, Rai. "Politburo member said Netaji was in USSR," MissionNetaji.org <http://www.missionnetaji.org/newsite/page/babajan_gouffrav.html>

Sisson, Maria Cissor. "Helena Blavatsky and the Enigma of John King," Blavatsky Archives Online <http://www.blavatskyarchives.com/sisson1.htm>

Skolnick, Sherman H. The Overthrow of the American Republic Part 54. Archived copy. <http://www.rense.com/general52/over54.htm>

Skolnick, Sherman H. Great Secrets of the 20th Century Part 1. <http://www.skolnicksreport.com/great_secrets.html>

Spielvogel, Jackson and David Redles, "Hitler's Racial Ideology: Content and Occult Sources," Simon Wiesenthal Center – Museum of Tolerance Online > Multimedia Learning Center > Annual 3. 1997 < http://motlc.wiesenthal.com/site/pp.asp?c=gvKVLcMVIuG&b=395043>

Stefanovics, G. Enver Pasha and his Times <http://www.geocities.com/enver1908/>

Subsearecovery.com, "Efforts to Raise Super Secret Nazi U-boat off Cape Cod," 8/7/04. An archived copy is available at <http://www.rense.com/general56/supsec.htm>

Sutton, Willy. "Adolf Hitler's Socialism," 20th March 2004 Counterblast <http://willysutton.blogspot.com/2004/03/ssalistinn-adolf-hitler.html>

Telegraph.co.uk, Fritz Kraemer. 10/11/03. <http://www.telegraph.co.uk/news/main.jhtml?xml=/news/2003/11/10/db1001.xml&sSheet=/portal/2003/11/10/ixportal.html >

Twyman, Tracy. "The Real Tomb of God: The Grail, The Ark, the Emerald Tablet, and the Forgotten Father of Mankind," 21st Century Radio <http://www.21stcenturyradio.com/realtomb-twyman.htm>

Van den Bosch, Lourens Peter. "Theosophy or Pantheism? Friedrich Max Muller's Gifford Lectures on Natural Religion." Here-Now4U Online Magazine < http://www.here-now4u.de/eng/theosophy_or_pantheism__friedr.htm>

Vergano, Dan. "Book explores Eugenics' origins," USA TODAY 14th October 2003, <http://www.usatoday.com/news/health/2003-09-14-book-usat_x.htm>

WayneMadsenReport.com, August 27th 2006.

Willey, Mark Emerson. Pearl Harbor: the Mother of all Conspiracies < http://www.geocities.com/Pentagon/6315/pearl.html>

Paul Wolfe, "Afghanistan: Experiment in Democracy. Documents from the US National Archives." < http://www.icdc.com/~paulwolf/pakistan/afghanistan.htm>

---, "Pakistan: Partition and Military Succession: Documents from the US National Archives," <http://www.icdc.com/~paulwolf/archivesindex.htm>

World Security Network, Fritz Kramer on Excellence. <http://www.worldsecuritynetwork.com/fritzkraemer/index.cfm>

Yahoo Games Domain, "Preview of 'Freedom Force' by Irrational Games,"

<http://gamesdomain.yahoo.com/pc/freedom_force_vs_the_third_reich/preview/60113>

Lightning Source UK Ltd.
Milton Keynes UK
UKHW011855160620
365110UK00001B/45